Making Commercial La[w]

Making Commercial Law Through Practice 1830–1970 adds a new dimension to the history of Britain's commerce, trade, manufacturing and financial services, by showing how they have operated in law over a crucial period of one hundred and forty years. In the main law and lawyers were not the driving force; state regulation was largely absent; and judges tended to accommodate commercial needs. That left market actors to shape the law through their practices. Using legal and historical scholarship, the author draws on archival sources previously unexploited for the study of commercial practice and the law's role in it. This book will stimulate parallel research in other subject areas of law. Modern commercial lawyers will learn a great deal about the current law from the story of its evolution, and economic and business historians will see how the world of commerce and trade operated in a legal context.

Ross Cranston is a Professor of Law at the London School of Economics and Political Science. His previous books in the Law and Context series are *Consumers and the Law* and *Legal Foundations of the Welfare State*.

The Law in Context Series

Editors:

William Twining (University College London),
Maksymilian Del Mar (Queen Mary, University of London) and
Bronwen Morgan (University of New South Wales).

Since 1970 the Law in Context series has been at the forefront of the movement to broaden the study of law. It has been a vehicle for the publication of innovative scholarly books that treat law and legal phenomena critically in their social, political and economic contexts from a variety of perspectives. The series particularly aims to publish scholarly legal writing that brings fresh perspectives to bear on new and existing areas of law taught in universities. A contextual approach involves treating legal subjects broadly, using materials from other social sciences, and from any other discipline that helps to explain the operation in practice of the subject under discussion. It is hoped that this orientation is at once more stimulating and more realistic than the bare exposition of legal rules. The series includes original books that have a different emphasis from traditional legal textbooks, while maintaining the same high standards of scholarship. They are written primarily for undergraduate and graduate students of law and of other disciplines, but will also appeal to a wider readership. In the past, most books in the series have focused on English law, but recent publications include books on European law, globalisation, transnational legal processes, and comparative law.

International Journal of Law in Context: A Global Forum for Interdisciplinary Legal Studies

The *International Journal of Law in Context* is the companion journal to the Law in Context book series and provides a forum for interdisciplinary legal studies and offers intellectual space for groundbreaking critical research. It publishes contextual work about law and its relationship with other disciplines including but not limited to science, literature, humanities, philosophy, sociology, psychology, ethics, history and geography. More information about the journal and how to submit an article can be found at http://journals.cambridge.org/ijc

Books in the Series
Acosta: *The National versus the Foreigner in South America: 200 Years of Migration and Citizenship Law*
Ali: *Modern Challenges to Islamic Law*
Alyagon Darr: *Plausible Crime Stories: The Legal History of Sexual Offences in Mandate Palestine*
Anderson, Schum & Twining: *Analysis of Evidence, 2nd Edition*
Ashworth: *Sentencing and Criminal Justice, 6th Edition*
Barton & Douglas: *Law and Parenthood*
Baxi, McCrudden & Paliwala: *Law's Ethical, Global and Theoretical Contexts: Essays in Honour of William Twining*

Beecher-Monas: *Evaluating Scientific Evidence: An Interdisciplinary Framework for Intellectual Due Process*
Bell: *French Legal Cultures*
Bercusson: *European Labour Law, 2nd Edition*
Birkinshaw: *European Public Law*
Birkinshaw: *Freedom of Information: The Law, the Practice and the Ideal, 4th Edition*
Broderick & Ferri: *International and European Disability Law and Policy: Text, Cases and Materials*
Brownsword & Goodwin: *Law and the Technologies of the Twenty-First Century: Text and Materials*
Cane & Goudkamp: *Atiyah's Accidents, Compensation and the Law, 9th Edition*
Clarke: *Principles of Property Law*
Clarke & Kohler: *Property Law: Commentary and Materials*
Collins: *The Law of Contract, 4th Edition*
Collins, Ewing & McColgan: *Labour Law, 2nd Edition*
Cowan: *Housing Law and Policy*
Cranston: *Making Commercial Law through Practice, 1830–1970*
Cranston: *Legal Foundations of the Welfare State*
Darian-Smith: *Laws and Societies in Global Contexts: Contemporary Approaches*
Dauvergne: *Making People Illegal: What Globalisation Means for Immigration and Law*
David: *Kinship, Law and Politics: An Anatomy of Belonging*
Davies: *Perspectives on Labour Law, 2nd Edition*
Dembour: *Who Believes in Human Rights?: Reflections on the European Convention*
de Sousa Santos: *Toward a New Legal Common Sense: Law, Globalization, and Emancipation*
Diduck: *Law's Families*
Estella: *Legal Foundations of EU Economic Governance*
Fortin: *Children's Rights and the Developing Law, 3rd Edition*
Garnsey: *The Justice of Visual Art: Creative State-Building in Times of Political Transition*
Garton, Probert & Bean: *Moffat's Trusts Law: Text and Materials, 7th Edition*
Ghai & Woodman: *Practising Self-Government: A Comparative Study of Autonomous Regions*
Glover-Thomas: *Reconstructing Mental Health Law and Policy*
Gobert & Punch: *Rethinking Corporate Crime*
Goldman: *Globalisation and the Western Legal Tradition: Recurring Patterns of Law and Authority*
Haack: *Evidence Matters: Science, Proof, and Truth in the Law*
Harlow & Rawlings: *Law and Administration, 3rd Edition*
Harris: *An Introduction to Law, 8th Edition*
Harris, Campbell & Halson: *Remedies in Contract and Tort, 2nd Edition*
Harvey: *Seeking Asylum in the UK: Problems and Prospects*
Herring: *Law and the Relational Self*
Hervey & McHale: *European Union Health Law: Themes and Implications*
Hervey & McHale: *Health Law and the European Union*
Holder & Lee: *Environmental Protection, Law and Policy: Text and Materials, 2nd Edition*

Jackson & Summers: *The Internationalisation of Criminal Evidence: Beyond the Common Law and Civil Law Traditions*
Kostakopoulou: *The Future Governance of Citizenship*
Kreiczer-Levy: *Destabilized Property: Property Law in the Sharing Economy*
Kubal: *Immigration and Refugee Law in Russia: Socio-Legal Perspectives*
Lewis: *Choice and the Legal Order: Rising above Politics*
Likosky: *Law, Infrastructure and Human Rights*
Likosky: *Transnational Legal Processes: Globalisation and Power Disparities*
Lixinski: *Legalized Identities*
Loughnan: *Self, Others and the State: Relations of Criminal Responsibility*
Lunney: *A History of Australian Tort Law 1901–1945: England's Obedient Servant?*
Maughan & Webb: *Lawyering Skills and the Legal Process, 2nd Edition*
McGlynn: *Families and the European Union: Law, Politics and Pluralism*
Mertens: *A Philosophical Introduction to Human Rights*
Moffat: *Trusts Law: Text and Materials*
Monti: *EC Competition Law*
Morgan: *Contract Law Minimalism: A Formalist Restatement of Commercial Contract Law*
Morgan & Yeung: *An Introduction to Law and Regulation: Text and Materials*
Nicola & Davies: *EU Law Stories: Contextual and Critical Histories of European Jurisprudence*
Norrie: *Crime, Reason and History: A Critical Introduction to Criminal Law, 3rd Edition*
O'Dair: *Legal Ethics: Text and Materials*
Oliver: *Common Values and the Public–Private Divide*
Oliver & Drewry: *The Law and Parliament*
Palmer & Roberts: *Dispute Processes: ADR and the Primary Forms of Decision-Making, 1st Edition*
Palmer & Roberts: *Dispute Processes: ADR and the Primary Forms of Decision-Making, 3rd Edition*
Picciotto: *International Business Taxation*
Probert: *The Changing Legal Regulation of Cohabitation, 1600–2010: From Fornicators to Family, 1600–2010*
Radi: *Rules and Practices of International Investment Law and Arbitration*
Reed: *Internet Law: Text and Materials*
Richardson: *Law, Process and Custody*
Roberts & Palmer: *Dispute Processes: ADR and the Primary Forms of Decision-Making, 2nd Edition*
Rowbottom: *Democracy Distorted: Wealth, Influence and Democratic Politics*
Sauter: *Public Services in EU Law*
Scott & Black: *Cranston's Consumers and the Law*
Seneviratne: *Ombudsmen: Public Services and Administrative Justice*
Seppänen: *Ideological Conflict and the Rule of Law in Contemporary China: Useful Paradoxes*
Siems: *Comparative Law, 2nd Edition*
Stapleton: *Product Liability*
Stewart: *Gender, Law and Justice in a Global Market*
Tamanaha: *Law as a Means to an End: Threat to the Rule of Law*

Turpin & Tomkins: *British Government and the Constitution: Text and Materials*, 7th Edition
Twining: *General Jurisprudence: Understanding Law from a Global Perspective*
Twining: *Globalisation and Legal Theory*
Twining: *Human Rights, Southern Voices: Francis Deng, Abdullahi An-Na'im, Yash Ghai and Upendra Baxi*
Twining: *Jurist in Context: A Memoir*
Twining: *Karl Llewellyn and the Realist Movement*, 2nd Edition
Twining: *Rethinking Evidence: Exploratory Essays*, 2nd Edition
Twining & Miers: *How to Do Things with Rules*, 5th Edition
Ward: *A Critical Introduction to European Law*, 3rd Edition
Ward: *Law, Text, Terror*
Ward: *Shakespeare and Legal Imagination*
Wells & Quick: *Lacey, Wells and Quick: Reconstructing Criminal Law: Text and Materials*, 4th Edition
Zander: *Cases and Materials on the English Legal System*, 10th Edition
Zander: *The Law-Making Process*, 6th Edition

Making Commercial Law Through Practice, 1830–1970

ROSS CRANSTON
London School of Economics and Political Science

CAMBRIDGE
UNIVERSITY PRESS

CAMBRIDGE
UNIVERSITY PRESS

University Printing House, Cambridge CB2 8BS, United Kingdom

One Liberty Plaza, 20th Floor, New York, NY 10006, USA

477 Williamstown Road, Port Melbourne, VIC 3207, Australia

314-321, 3rd Floor, Plot 3, Splendor Forum, Jasola District Centre, New Delhi - 110025, India

103 Penang Road, #05-06/07, Visioncrest Commercial, Singapore 238467

Cambridge University Press is part of the University of Cambridge.

It furthers the University's mission by disseminating knowledge in the pursuit of education, learning and research at the highest international levels of excellence.

www.cambridge.org
Information on this title: www.cambridge.org/9781316648377
DOI: 10.1017/9781108182836

© Ross Cranston 2021

This publication is in copyright. Subject to statutory exception and to the provisions of relevant collective licensing agreements, no reproduction of any part may take place without the written permission of Cambridge University Press.

First published 2021
First paperback edition 2022

A catalogue record for this publication is available from the British Library

ISBN 978-1-107-19889-0 Hardback
ISBN 978-1-316-64837-7 Paperback

Cambridge University Press has no responsibility for the persistence or accuracy of URLs for external or third-party internet websites referred to in this publication, and does not guarantee that any content on such websites is, or will remain, accurate or appropriate.

For Hazel

Contents

List of Figures	*page*	xiii
Preface		xv
Note on Terms and Archives		xix
Table of Cases		xx
Table of Legislation		xl

1 Commercial and Legal Contexts — 1
　1.1 Introduction — 1
　1.2 Commercial Context: Markets, Organisations and Players — 3
　1.3 Legal Context: Principles, Practices and Realities — 30
　1.4 Conclusion — 57

2 The Commodity Markets of London and Liverpool — 61
　2.1 Introduction — 61
　2.2 Organisation and Membership — 63
　2.3 Brokers, Rules and Third Parties — 71
　2.4 Emergence of Futures Markets — 80
　2.5 Clearing and Settlement — 89
　2.6 Maintaining Market Integrity — 107
　2.7 Conclusion — 123

3 Agents, 'Agents' and Agency — 127
　3.1 Introduction — 127
　3.2 Agents and Agency Law — 130
　3.3 Law Facilitating Agency — 142
　3.4 Agents as Principals — 153
　3.5 Varieties of Agent — 165
　3.6 Managing Agents — 178
　3.7 Conclusion — 196

4 Sale, Hire and the Distribution of Manufactured Goods — 200
　4.1 Introduction — 200
　4.2 Sales Law in Outline: Quality — 203

4.3　Heavy Manufactured Goods: Plant and Machinery, Chemicals,
　　　　　Locomotives　　　　　　　　　　　　　　　　　　　　　　　　219
　　　4.4　Hire, Hire Purchase and Asset Finance　　　　　　　　　　242
　　　4.5　Distribution: Controlling the Market　　　　　　　　　　　264
　　　4.6　Conclusion　　　　　　　　　　　　　　　　　　　　　　　289

5　International Commodity Sales　　　　　　　　　　　　　　　294
　　　5.1　Introduction　　　　　　　　　　　　　　　　　　　　　　294
　　　5.2　Origins: Bought and Sold Notes　　　　　　　　　　　　　 296
　　　5.3　Trade Associations and Standard Form Contracts　　　　　 299
　　　5.4　Commodity Auctions　　　　　　　　　　　　　　　　　　 317
　　　5.5　Private Law-Making: The Processes of the Trade Associations　330
　　　5.6　The Legal Framework: Contract-Making and the Courts　　 344
　　　5.7　Disputes and Arbitration　　　　　　　　　　　　　　　　 361
　　　5.8　Conclusion　　　　　　　　　　　　　　　　　　　　　　　373

6　Bank Finance for Trade and Industry　　　　　　　　　　　　 376
　　　6.1　Introduction　　　　　　　　　　　　　　　　　　　　　　376
　　　6.2　Trade Finance　　　　　　　　　　　　　　　　　　　　　381
　　　6.3　Financing Business　　　　　　　　　　　　　　　　　　　409
　　　6.4　Institutional Underpinning　　　　　　　　　　　　　　　442
　　　6.5　Conclusion　　　　　　　　　　　　　　　　　　　　　　　459

Index　　　　　　　　　　　　　　　　　　　　　　　　　　　　　463

Figures

1.1 Landing goods in Calcutta (Kolkata), India, 1860s
((c)The British Library Board) *page* 15
1.2 Mackenzie Chalmers (President and Fellows of Trinity College, Oxford) 35
1.3 Lord Atkin on the jetty at Aberdovey, Wales (Treasurer and Masters of the Bench, Gray's Inn) 44
2.1 The Baltic Exchange, St Mary Axe, London (The Baltic Exchange) 67
2.2 Futures dealing in cotton, Liverpool, 1909 (Dr Nigel Hall, liverpoolcotton.com) 85
3.1 Agents, brokers, auctioneers: Dalgety & Co., Australia, c. 1930 (Dalgety plc) 166
3.2 Managing and general agents: Jardine Matheson & Co. Ltd, Hong Kong, 1953 (Hugh Farmer and the Industrial History of Hong Kong Group) 180
4.1 Locomotives for export: Robert Stephenson & Hawthorns Ltd engines bound for India (National Railway Museum and Alstom) 230
4.2 Asset finance: the beginnings with North Central Wagon Co. (Grace's Guide to British Industrial History) 254
5.1 Auctioning colonial wool, Wool Exchange, London, 1889 (Alamy Ltd) 318
5.2 Arbitration by members of Liverpool Cotton Association, 1930s (A. Garside, Cotton goes to Market, 1935) 363
6.1 Bill of exchange drawn by The Bank of the United States to pay £750 to Stephen Whitney, accepted by Baring Brothers in London (The Syndics of Cambridge University Library, Jardine Matheson Archive) 387
6.2 Overend Gurney trial, December 1869 (Alamy Ltd) 448

Preface

Just north of King's Cross railway station in London is a large and innovative development on previously derelict land with open spaces, shops, offices, flats, galleries, bars, restaurants, schools, as well as the world-renowned arts and design college Central Saint Martins. The development was initially centred on the old goods warehouses of the Great Northern Railway, the main building called the Granary. The development now extends well beyond that, on either side of Regent's Canal. During our period, both the railway and the canal linked London with the industrial areas of the north, transporting goods to and from the capital. The railway became a vital link to Scotland and the cause of engineering achievements.

Coal was in huge demand in London for fuel, and this was reflected in one area of the development named the 'Coal Drops', populated (at least until the Covid-19 virus arrived) by high-end shops and restaurants. It opened in the 1850s to receive coal from the collieries of the Midlands, Yorkshire and the north. Coal wagons arrived at one level, the coal being tipped into hoppers at another, bagged at yet another and then despatched by road and canal. The empty railway wagons were moved sideways on a traverser for return on a separate viaduct. But when the history of the Coal Drops was investigated in the early 1990s, its operations were something of a mystery. As with many industrial buildings it had been taken for granted, and during its lifetime it had never occurred to anyone to record the full details.[1]

This book explores the functioning of commercial law within the context of commercial practice over the 140-year period from around 1830 until 1970, with an emphasis on the international dimensions. The focus is transactional rather than institutional – commodity markets, agency, the trade in manufactured goods and 'soft' commodities (grain, cotton, tea, etc.), and the financing of trade and industry. As a study in law in context it is not a doctrinal history, although there is a considerable amount of doctrine to digest. A key feature of the relevant doctrinal law is that it furnished a broad framework in which

---

[1] R. Thorne, 'The Great Northern Railway and the London Coal Trade', in M. Hunter & R. Thorne (eds.), *Change at King's Cross: From 1800 to the Present*, London, Historical Publications, 1990, 114–115. See also P. Darley, *The King's Cross Story*, Stroud, The History Press, 2018, 83–93.

commercial parties could make their own rules and regulations and design their own institutions. The upshot was that in this broad sense commercial practice was the source of commercial law.

Understanding this creative process parallels, in a way, the task of interpreting the King's Cross Coal Drops: aspects of nineteenth- and early twentieth-century commercial practice and the role of law in it are not fully recorded and, in some cases, forgotten. The international commodity markets and auctions in London and Liverpool have disappeared, as have the working docks and warehouses of the period, most of the British-based trading (agent) houses in Asia and elsewhere, and the discount houses of the London money market. Moreover, the history of legacy institutions and practices – the London clearing arrangements for settling accounts in international financial and commodity derivatives, the standard form contracts for the international trade in grain and cotton, and the arrangements for international commodity arbitration – is not, on the whole, appreciated.

That does not mean starting with a blank sheet. First, the law reports of our period throw light on how commercial transactions were effected, although, as every lawyer knows, the litigation process funnels facts to meet procedural, evidential, doctrinal and forensic requirements. It is a surprise that historians have not exploited the law reports more when writing about some of the events covered in the book, especially when litigation was part of the story, the reports throwing more, and in some cases a different, light on it. Secondly, there is the dazzling array of studies by economic and business historians which bear on the topics covered in the book. Given their scholarly interests, accounts of commercial law and practice are harder to come by, but their findings have proved an invaluable foundation for the book.

Thirdly, there are the contemporary accounts of commercial practice, or at least what it should aspire to. Banking was especially favoured. To mitigate the risks facing nineteenth-century banks, by the 1850s there were several accounts of good banking practice and the canons governing it. Imitations were spawned with the founding in the 1870s of Institutes of Bankers in both Edinburgh and London and the subsequent need for intending bankers to obtain their qualifications. There was no comparable professional body in international trade until the Institute of Export was established in 1935. Those in commodities trading, marketing and sales learnt on the job and the knowledge not generally written down for general distribution. In the interwar period, however, Isaac Pitman & Sons and other publishers adopted a policy of actively producing primers aimed at those engaged in these and related activities.

To complement these sources the book draws, fourthly, on a number of business and bank archives to understand more fully the commercial practices of the period and law's role as it relates to them. By good fortune, archives relating to the commodity markets and commodity trading in both London and Liverpool have been preserved. There is also a rich seam of bank archives. Scattered around the country are the archives of trading houses, as well as those of manufacturers of plant and machinery, railway wagons and motor vehicles. To a limited extent gaps in the British archives have been plugged abroad. As might be expected, the various archives have been utilised by economic and business historians, but their interest has not generally extended to the legal facets of an organisation's operations. Where business and bank archives are available they must be treated with some care. Only parts of these archives have been preserved, and, by themselves, they may paint a fragmented picture. When combined with other sources, however, it is possible to learn a great deal about commercial practice during our period and the role of law (and lawyers) in shaping and being shaped by it.

A few words about what this book is not. During our period the functioning of commodity markets, international trade, manufacturing and sales had a dark underbelly, exploitative and racist. It was a world for the most part of men. Law sometimes reinforced these tendencies; occasionally it was ameliorative. This is not a book about these issues, although there is no getting away from circumstances like slavery and the Liverpool cotton trade in its early days, the Chinese opium trade and Opium wars, and the shameless treatment of labour in the textile mills and industry of Britain and its estates and factories abroad. Nor is it a book about the historians' concerns with matters such as 'gentlemanly capitalism', Empire, or the relationship between manufacturing and finance in Britain's story. And it is not the place for a further instalment in the debate going back to Max Weber, whether law has contributed to, or impeded, economic development, not least because others have tackled the issue so expertly.[2]

What can be said, in brief, as regards the law–economy nexus is that during our period the hand of state law was largely benign in the field of commercial transactions, absent fraud and egregious market abuse. Regulation was virtually non-existent, and the common law was predominantly facilitative, containing default rules which commercial parties could largely vary at will. State law offered a capacious and flexible framework within which commercial practices could operate and evolve, and the tools for this to occur, notably a pliable contract law, instruments such as bills of exchange and easily workable rules like those for lending short-term and taking security (collateral) as backing. A familiar pattern when matters occasionally reached court was of the common law incorporating a commercial practice as a rule, reshaping existing rules in its shadow, or at the very least conferring its blessing on how things were being done.

---

[2] e.g., W. Cornish, S. Banks, C. Mitchell, P. Mitchell & R. Probert, *Law and Society in England 1750–1950*, 2nd ed., Oxford, Hart, 2019, 6–10; *Oxford History of the Laws of England*, Oxford, Oxford University Press, 2010, vol. XI, pt. 1, Ch. 6; vol. XII, pt. 2, Ch. 1 (M. Lobban); J. Getzler, *A History of Water Rights at Common Law*, Oxford, Oxford University Press, 2006; R. Harris, *Industrializing English Law*, Cambridge, Cambridge University Press, 2000, 3–9, 288–293; J. Getzler, 'Theories of Property and Economic Development' (1996) 26 *J Interdisciplinary Hist* 639; R. Kostal, *Law and English Railway Capitalism, 1825–1875*, Oxford, Clarendon, 1994, 5–6, 358–372.

Commercial parties could thus engage in private law-making, drawing their own rules and settling the disputes which arose themselves. The formal legal system furnished the assurance that the private law commercial parties formulated would be enforced by state power if the threat of more immediate, informal sanctions failed to have their salutary effect, sanctions such as exclusion from a market, a refusal to deal with an offending party in the future, trade association 'fines' or calling in a loan and enforcing security. None of this meant that commercial parties did not face the occasional legal wrinkle or snag. But on the whole they could pursue profit unbridled by the common law. Indeed, in some cases, as we will see, the common law moulded or developed doctrine to facilitate commercial practice. If economic growth was impeded, as with restrictive trade practices, that was a result of commercial action, not the common law; the law fell in behind commercial practice when the very rare challenge reached the courts. If on occasion the courts were not accommodating to commercial practice, the relevant market, trade association or institution could generally reshape their rules and institutions to accord with the law and proceed unimpeded.

Work for this book began many years ago, its gestation interrupted by an errant career. Over time I have built up many debts to those who have generously assisted me in one way or another: Sonali Abeyratne, Bill Blair, Michael Bridge, Hugh Collins, Joshua Getzler, David Goldblatt, Roy Goode, Michael Lobban, Catharine MacMillan, Charles Mitchell, Pennie Pemberton, Francis Reynolds, James J. Rogers, Mildred Schofield, David Sugarman, William Twining, Philip R. Wood, Lucien Wong and Sarah Worthington. Over several Southern Hemisphere summers Neil and Jenny Cranston generously provided their garden, with its wonderful view over the Derwent estuary, for work on the manuscript.

Acknowledgments are also owing to three institutions: the Centre for Commercial Law Studies at Queen Mary University of London, where I learnt a great deal of commercial law and which funded some of the early research; the Law Department at the London School of Economics, where most of the manuscript was written, for furnishing a supportive and interdisciplinary environment; and the Stockholm Centre for Commercial Law at Stockholms universitet, where Jan Kleineman and Lars Gorton allowed me to test my ideas by generously inviting me for a number of visits. Special thanks are due to the help provided by those at the archives I visited and to those ever-helpful librarians, Stephanie Curran, Sam Bryan, Nicholas Stock and Philip Rowbottom at the Royal Courts of Justice and Maria Bell and Wendy Lynwood at the London School of Economics. I am also indebted to Finola O'Sullivan, Marianne Nield, Becky Jackaman and Allan Alphonse who for Cambridge University Press guided a proposal to its final publication.

Note on Terms and Archives

The term 'during our period' refers to the years c. 1830–1970, the period covered by the book. The 'interwar period' refers to the years between the First World War (1914–1918) and the Second World War (1939–1945). Original place names are used, with the modern name in brackets. The colony of the Straits Settlements included places like Malacca and Penang, now part of Malaysia, but as indicated in the text the focus is on what was its capital, Singapore.

The following abbreviations are used for the archives from which material has been drawn:

BA&C	Birmingham Archives and Collections, Birmingham Library
CUL	Cambridge University Library (Jardine Matheson Archive)
GRO	Gloucestershire Archives, Gloucester
LI	Lincoln's Inn Library (Printed cases, judgments and appeal documents, House of Lords/Privy Council)
LMA	London Metropolitan Archives, City of London
LRO	Liverpool Record Office, Liverpool Central Library
MLD	Museum of London Docklands, Port and River Archive
MMM	Merseyside Maritime Museum, National Museums Liverpool
MSI	Museum of Science and Industry Archives, Manchester
NA	National Archives, Kew
NBAC	Noel Butlin Archives Centre, Australian National University
RBS	Royal Bank of Scotland Archives, Edinburgh[*]
SCA	Sheffield City Archives, Sheffield
SRO	Staffordshire Record Office, Stafford
TA	Tasmanian Archives, Hobart, Tasmania
WMRC	Modern Records Centre, University of Warwick, Coventry

[*] As a result of corporate rebranding the RBS Archives became the NatWest Group Archives in 2020.

Table of Cases

Aberdeen Railway Co v. Blaikie, 132
Agra & Masterman's Bank, In re, 448
Agra Bank ex parte Tondeur, Re, 392
Alec Lobb (Garages) Ltd v. Total Oil (Great Britain) Ltd, 278, 281
Alexander v. Vanderzee, 55
Alexiadi v. Robinson, 48
Alicia Hosiery v. Brown Shipley & Co, 442
Allchin, Linnell & Co. Ltd, Re, 243
A. L. Underwood, Ltd v. Bank of Liverpool & Martins, 435
Anchor Line (Henderson Bros) Ltd, Re, 243
Andrews Brothers (Bournemouth) Ltd v. Singer & Co Ltd, 271
Anglo African Shipping Co of New York Inc v. J. Mortner Ltd, 157, 163
Anglo Auto Finance Co Ltd v. James, 261
Anglo-Italian Bank v. Wells, 386
Anglo Overseas Transport Ltd v. Titan Industrial Corp Ltd, 50
Anglo-Persian Oil Co Ltd v. Dale (Inspector of Taxes), 189
The Annefield, 53
Arab Bank v. Ross, 53
Arcos v. Ronaasen, 42, 132, 208, 215
Armagas Ltd v. Mundogas SA, 145
Armstrong v. Stokes, 147, 148, 154, 155, 156, 167
Aronson v. Mologa Holzindustrie AG, 371
Arunachalam Chettiar v. Kasi Nevenda Pillai, 157
A/S Awilco of Oslo v. Fulvia S.P.A. Di Navigazione of Cagliari, 42
Associated Distributors, Ltd v. Hall, 261
Associated Enterprises Ltd v. Brunner Mond & Co Ltd, 239, 240
Atlantic Shipping & Trading Co v. Louis Dreyfus & Co, 53
Attorney-General v. Forsikringsaktieselskabet National, 54
Attorney General v. Great Eastern Railway Co, 230
Attorney General of Australia v. Adelaide Steamship, 36
Auchteroni & Co v. Midland Bank Ltd, 455
Aune v. Cauwenberghe & Fils, 8, 312

Austin Motor Co Ltd's Agreements, Re, 274, 275
Automatic Bottle Makers Ltd, In re, 409, 435

Bacmeister v. Fenton, Levy & Co, 73
Baillie & Harrison, In re, 440
Baillie & Harrison ex parte Harrison, Re, 437
Baldry v. Marshall, 211
Bank Line Ltd v. Arthur Capel & Co, 31
Bank Negara Indonesia 1946 v. Taylor, 161
Bank of Baroda Ltd v. Punjab National Bank, 459
Bank of Bengal v. Macleod, 428
Bank of England v. Vagliano Bros, 54
Bank Polski v. K. J. Mulder & Co, 385
Barber v. Meyerstein, 382
Barber & Co ex parte Agra Bank, Re, 392
Barclays Bank v. Bank of England, 459
Barclays Bank v. Tom, 437
Baring v. Corrie, 131, 167
Barned's Banking Co, Re, 393
Barned's Banking Co ex parte Stephens, Re, 437
Barnett, In re, 243
Barnett; R v., 329
Barnett v. Sanker, 122
Barrow's Case. *See* Overend Gurney & Co, Re
Barry v. Croskey, 114, 120
Bateman, National Discount Co (Ltd), Overend, Gurney, & Co (Ltd) v. Mid-Wales Railway Co, 446
Bayliffe v. Butterworth, 78
B. Davis Ltd v. Tooth & Co Ltd, 281, 283, 284, 285
Beckhuson & Gibbs v. Hamblet, 103
Beck & Co v Szymanowski & Co. *See* Szymanowski & Co v. Beck & Co.
Behnke v. Bede Shipping Co Ltd, 317
Bell v. Lever Brothers Ltd, 59
Bentinck v. London Joint Stock Bank, 430
Berry, Barclay & Co v. Louis Dreyfus & Co, 310
Bexwell v. Christie, 327
Bigge v. Parkinson, 210
Biggin & Co Ltd v. Peemanite Ltd, 41
Bird v. Boulter, 323
Bishirgian; R v., 117
Blanshard ex parte Hattersley, In re, 50, 257
Blyth Shipbuilding & Dry Docks 1925 Co Ltd, Re, 216, 217

Board of Trade v. Christie Grain & Stock Co, 122
Boddington v. Schlencker, 454
Boden v. French, 150
Bolam v. Regent Oil Co Ltd, 277
Bolton v. Salmon, 426
Bolus & Co Ltd v. Inglis Bros Ltd, 157, 269
Bombay Burmah Trading Corporation, Re, 192
Bombay Burmah Trading Corporation Ltd v. Dorabji Cursetji Shroff, 183, 192
Borrowman, Phillips & Co v. Free & Hollis, 88
Bostock v. Jardine, 78
Bostock & Co Ltd v. Nicholson & Sons Ltd, 208
Boulton & Watt v. Bull, 220
Bourgeois v. Wilson Holgate & Co Ltd, 351
Bowes v. Shand, 49, 208, 303, 354, 356, 363, 364
Boyd v. Siffkin, 83
Bradford Banking Co Ltd v. Henry Briggs Son & Co, 431
Bradford Old Bank Ltd v. Sutcliffe, 418, 428
Bramwell v. Spiller, 159
Bridge v. Campbell Discount Co Ltd, 261
Brighty v. Norton, 421
Bristol Tramways etc Carriage Co Ltd v. Fiat Motors, 211
Bristow v. Waddington, 87
British Bank of the Middle East v. Sun Life Assurance Co of Canada (UK), 145
British Imex Industries Ltd v. Midland Bank Ltd, 395, 396
British Movietonews Ltd v. London & District Cinemas Ltd, 42
British Waggon Co & the Parkgate Waggon Co v. Lea & Co, 252
Brookman v. Rothschild, 168
Brown v. Edgington, 209
Brown Jenkinson & Co Ltd v. Percy Dalton (London) Ltd, 237
Brown Shipley & Co Ltd v. Alicia Hosiery Ltd, 55, 386, 442
Brown Shipley & Co Ltd v. Kough, 390
Bryan v. Lewis, 118, 119
Buckerfields Ltd v. Smith, 357
Buckingham & Co v. London & Midland Bank Ltd, 422
Bulmer, In the Matter of, 437
Bunge SA v. Nidera BV, 295
Burnett v. Bouch, 177
Burrell & Sons v. F. Green & Co, 55
Burton v. Slattery, 421

Calcutta Jute Mills Co Ltd v. Nicholson, 187
Calder v. Dobell, 75
Caliot v. Walker, 421

Cammell Laird & Co Ltd v. Manganese Bronze & Brass Co Ltd, 212, 213, 216, 217, 219, 223, 224
Canada Atlantic Grain Export Co (Inc) v. Eilers, 213, 347
Cannon Manufacturing Co v. Cudahy Packing Co, 289
Carlill v. Carbolic Smoke Ball Co, 118, 267
Carlos v. Fancourt, 42
Carter v. Wake, 430
Cassaboglou v. Gibb, 129, 155
Cassel v. Inglis, 70
Cassel; R v., 70
C. E. B. Draper & Son Ltd v. Edward Turner & Son Ltd, 347, 375
Cebora SNC v. SIP (Industrial Products), 59
Cederberg v. Borries, Craig & Co, 357
Cefn Cilcen Mining Co, In re, 416
C. Groom Ltd v. Barber, 54, 334
Chamberlain's Wharf Ltd v. Smith, 69, 93
Champsey Bhara & Co v. Jivraj Balloo Spinning & Weaving Co Ltd, 370
Chandris v. Isbrandtsen-Moller Co Inc, 56, 358
Chanter v. Hopkins, 209
Charterhouse Credit Co v. Tolly, 264
Chicago Board of Trade v. Christie, 96
The Chikuma. See A/S Awilco of Oslo v. Fulvia S.P.A. Di Navigazione of Cagliari
Christoforides v. Terry, 76, 88
Churchill v. Siggers, 437
Churchill & Sim v. Goddard, 160
Cia de Comercio Limitada Van Waveren v. Spillers Ltd, 354, 359
City Discount Co Ltd v. McLean, 438
City Equitable Fire Insurance Co Ltd, Re, 116
Clark v. Gray, 217
Clay v. Yates, 217
Cleveland Petroleum Co Ltd v. Dartstone Ltd (No 1), 278
Clews v. Jamieson, 79
Coates, Son & Co v. Pacey, 113
Cole v. North Western Bank, 152
Collie, In re, 440
Collie, ex parte Manchester & County Bank, In re, 440
Colonial Bank v. Whinney, 424, 431
Commercial Banking Co of Sydney Ltd v. Jalsard Pty Ltd, 150, 396
Commissioner of Income-tax v. Ashok Leyland Ltd, 189
Committee of London Clearing Bankers v. Inland Revenue Commissioners, 457
Compagnie Continentale d'Importation v. Union der Sozialistischen Sovjet Republiken, Handelsvertretung in Deutschland, 360

Conflans Stone Quarry Co Ltd v. Parker, Public Officer of the National Bank, 391
Connolly Brothers Ltd, In re, 434
Contract Corporation v. Claim of Ebbw Vale Co, In re, 446
Cooke & Sons v. Eshelby, 57, 75, 76, 126, 148
Cooper v. Neal, 120
Cooper v. Wandsworth Board of Works, 364
Cooper (Inspector of Taxes) v. Stubbs, 96, 122, 123
Couturier v. Hastie, 158, 159
Cox, McEuen & Co v. J J Cunningham Ltd, 355
Cramer v. Giles, 263
Cropper v. Cook, 78, 167
Crouch v. Credit Foncier of England Ltd, 50
Crowder v. Austin, 328
Cumming v. Shand, Registered Public Officer of the Royal Bank of Liverpool, 415, 416
Cunliffe Brooks & Co v. Blackburn & District Benefit Building Society, 416
Cunliffe-Owen v. Teather & Greenwood, 78
Cunningham & Co Ltd, In re, 187
Cuthbert v. Robarts Lubbock & Co, 415
Czarnikow v. Roth Schmidt & Co, 31, 371

David Allester Ltd, In re, 54
David Sassoon Sons & Co v. Wang Gan-Ying, 141
Dawson v. Collis, 214
De Berenger; R v., 109
Deeley v. Lloyds Bank Ltd, 434
De Monchy v. Phoenix Insurance Co of Hartford, 57
Denbigh, Cowan & Co v. R Atcherley & Co, 355
Derry v. Peek, 449
Diamond Alkali Export Corp v. Fl Bourgeois, 52, 57
Dickson v. Zizinia, 205
Die Elbinger Actien-Gesellschaft v. Claye, 156
Dingle v. Hare, 205
Dodwell & Co Ltd v. John, 139
Donoghue v. Stevenson, 267
Doolubdass Pettamberdass v. Ramloll Thackoorseydass, 329
Downie Bros v. Henry Oakley L Sons, 157
Dramburg v. Pollitzer, 136, 156
Drury v. Victor Buckland Ltd, 264
Dublin City Distillery (Great Brunswick Street, Dublin) Ltd v. Doherty, 352, 353
Dudgeon v. E. Pembroke, 56
Dukinfield Mill Co Ltd v. Shorrock, 160
Dunlop Pneumatic Tyre Co Ltd v. New Garage & Motor Co Ltd, 272, 276

Table of Cases

Dunlop Pneumatic Tyre Co Ltd v. Selfridge & Co Ltd, 275, 276
Dunster v. Glengall, 429
Dyster, Ex parte, 77

E. & S. Ruben Ltd v. Faire Brothers & Co Ltd, 216
Earl of Sheffield v. London & Joint Stock Bank, 46
E. Bailey & Co Ltd v. Balholm Securities Ltd, 76, 95, 100
Edmunds v. Bushell, 144
EE & Brian Smith (1928) Ltd v. Wheatsheaf Mills Ltd, 356
Ellerman Lines Ltd v. Read, 47
Elsey & Co Ltd v. Hyde, 261
Embiricos v. Sydney Reid & Co, 31
English Hop Growers v. Dering, 40
English Scottish & Australian Bank Ltd v. Bank of South Africa, 395
Equitable Trust Co of New York v. Dawson Partners Ltd, 393, 395
Esso Petroleum Co Ltd v. Harper's Garage (Stourport) Ltd, 279, 280
Esso Petroleum Co Ltd v. Mardon, 281, 293
European Asian Bank AG v. Punjab & Sind Bank (No.2), 150
European Assurance Society, Re, 98
European Bank, In re, 418

Fairlie v. Fenton, 75, 300, 362
Faizulla v. Ramkamal Mitter, 142
Farina v. Home, 352, 405
Farmeloe v. Bain, 407
Farquharson Brothers & Co v. C. King & Co, 32, 145
F.E. Hookway & Co Ltd v. Alfred Isaacs & Sons, 96, 347
Fergus Motors Inc. v. Standard-Triumph Motor Co Inc, 287, 289
Ferguson v. Fyffe, 421
Firth, In re, 439
Flatau Dick & Co v. Keeping, 167, 356
Fleet v. Murton, 167
Fleming v. Bank of New Zealand, 416
Foley v. Classique Coaches, 57
Folkes v. King, 151, 153
Ford Motor Co (England) Ltd v. Armstrong, 134, 272
Foss v. Harbottle, 191
Foster v. Smith, 205–206
Fothergill, In re, 439
Fothergill ex parte Turquand, Re, 439
Fox, Walker, & Co, Re, 439, 440, 445, 450
Fred Drughorn Ltd v. Rederiaktiebolaget Transatlantic, 146
Freeman v. Banker, 206
Freeman v. East India Co, 174

Freeman & Lockyer v. Buckhurst Park Properties (Mangal) Ltd, 145
Fuentes v. Montis, 152, 406
FW Green & Co Ltd v. Brown & Gracie Ltd, 153

Gadd v. Houghton, 167
Galton v. Emuss, 328
Gannow Engineering Co Ltd v. Richardson, 269
Gardiner v. Gray, 211, 214, 299, 346
Garnett v. M'Kewan, 418
Geddling v. Marsh, 210
General Credit & Discount Co v. Glegg, 421
George Inglefield Ltd, In re, 262
Gerald McDonald & Co v. Nash & Co, 441
G. H. Myers & Co v. Brent Cross Service Co, 223
G H Renton & Co v. Palmyra Trading Corp of Panama, 359
Gibson v. Small, 49
Gilliat v. Gilliat, 328
Gillman v. Robinson, 143
Gloucester Railway Carriage & Wagon Co Ltd v. Commissioners of Inland Revenue, 249
Glover v. Langford, 157
Glyn Mills Currie & Co v. East & West India Dock Co, 382
Glynn v. Margetson & Co, 55, 56, 355
Goddard v. Raahe O/Y Osakeyhtio, 160
Gokal Chand-Jagan Nath v. Nand Ram das-Atma Ram, 143
Golden Strait Corp v. Nippon Yusen Kubishika Kaisha, 42
Goldsbrough Mort & Co Ltd v. Maurice, 165
Goodwin v. Robarts, 50, 51, 407
Gordhandas Nathalal v. Gorio Ltd, 133–134
Gorrisen v. Perrin, 83
Governor & Company of the Bank of England v. Anderson, 29
Gowerr v. Von Dedalzen, 212
Graham v. Ackroyd, 159
Graham v. Dyster, 150
Graham v. Johnson, 437
Grange v. Taylor, 50
Grant v. Australian Knitting Mills Ltd, 211, 212
Grant v. Fletcher, 83
Grant Smith & Co v. Juggobundhoo Shaw, 142
Graves v. Legg, 49
Gray v. Dalgety & Co Ltd, 165
Great Cobar Ltd, In re, 166
Great Western Food Distributors v. Benson, 117
Greaves v. Legg, 73, 78

Table of Cases

Green v. Low, 250
Greenhalgh & Sons v. Union Bank of Manchester, 390
Greer v. Downs Supply Co, 46
Gregory v. Commissioner of Police of the Metropolis, 326
Gregson v. Ruck, 168
Grieve, Re, 121
Griffiths v. Peter Conway Ltd, 211
Grizewood v. Blane, 120
Guaranty Trust Co of New York v. Hannay & Co, 387, 390
Gunn v. Bolckow Vaughan & Co, 407
Gurney v. Behrend, 54
Gurney & Others; Queen v., 448

Hadley v. Baxendale, 360
Halliday Re Hall & Jones, Ex parte, 84
Hamilton v. Mendes, 42
Hammond & Co v. Bussey, 41
Hamzeh Malas & Sons v. British Imex Industries Ltd, 398
Hannay v. Muir, 191, 192
Hardy & Co v. Hillerns & Fowler, 216
Hare v. Henty, 49, 78
Harris v. Nickerson, 324
Hasonbhoy Visram v. Clapham, 133
Hatfield v. Phillips Court, 152
Hawes v. Humble, 83
Hawes v. Watsons Wharf, 404
Heap v. Motorists' Advisory Agency Ltd, 153
Heilbut, Symons & Co v. Buckleton, 206, 320
Heilbut, Symons & Co v. Harvey, Christie-Miller & Co, 352
Helby v. Matthews, 257, 259, 261, 262,
  291, 292
Henderson & Co v. Williams, 32
Henry Kendall & Sons v. William Lillico & Sons Ltd, 123, 210, 347
Herbert v. Salisbury & Yeovil Railway Co, 421
Heyman v. Darwins Ltd, 20
Heyn, Ex parte, 110
Hibblewhite v. M'Morine, 88, 119, 120
Hill v. Regent Oil Co, 279
Hillas & Co Ltd v. Arcos Ltd, 55, 56, 57
Hinde v. Whitehouse, 319
Hip Foong Hong v. H. Neotia & Co, 141
Hoare v. Dresser, 159
HO Brandt & Co v. HN Morris & Co, 157
Hobson v. Gorringe, 256

Hollins v. Fowler, 137, 167, 300
Hollis Bros Co Ltd v. White Sea Timber Trust Ltd, 357
Holme v. Brunskill, 426
Holmes Wilson & Co Ltd v. Bata Kristo, 133
Holt & Moseley (London) v. Sir Charles Cunningham & Partners, 157
Homburg Houtimport BV v. Agrosin Private Ltd, 42
Hong Kong & Shanghai Bank v. Glover & Co, 425
Hong Kong Milling Co Ltd v. Arnold Karberg & Co, 179
Hope Prudhomme & Co v. Hamel & Horley Ltd, 134
Hopkins v. Hitchcock, 205
Hopkins v. Tanqueray, 205–206
Hornblower & Maberly v. Boulton & Watt, 220
Horsfall v. Thomas, 206
Hudson v. Ede, 49
Hughes & Kimber Ltd, Re Thackrah, Ex parte, 243
Humble v. Hunter, 74, 146
Humfrey v. Dale, 298, 373
Hutton v. Bulloch, 154, 156
Hutton v. Warren, 49
Hynds v. Singer Sewing Machine Co Ltd, 263

Illingworth v. Houldsworth, 431
Imperial Bank v. London & St Katharine Docks Co, 73
Imperial Japanese Government v. Peninsular & Oriental Steam Navigation Co, 141
Imperial Marine Insurance Co v. Fire Insurance Corp Ltd, 49
Importers Co Ltd v. Westminster Bank Ltd, 444
Independent Automatic Sales Ltd v. Knowles & Foster, 244
Indo-China Steam Navigation Co, In re, 184
Indo-China Steam Navigation Co v. Jasjit Singh, 185
Inland Revenue Commissioners v. Rowntree & Co Ltd, 441
Inman v. Clare, 73
International Harvester Co of Australia Pty Ltd v. Carrigan's Hazeldene Pastoral Co, 135
International Life Assurance Society & Hercules Insurance Co ex parte Blood, Re, 98
International Paper v. Spicer, 144
Introductions Ltd, In re, 436
Ireland v. Livingston, 131, 149, 150, 154, 155, 209
Ironmonger & Co v. Dyne, 123
Irvine v. Union Bank of Australia, 434
Irvine & Co v. Watson & Sons, 147, 148, 167
Irwin v. Williar, 79

Table of Cases

Isaac Cooke & Sons v. Eshelby, 146
Ivanoff Oberin & Co v. Jardine Matheson, 177

Jackson v. Rotax Motor & Cycle Co, 213, 215
Jacobs v. Morris, 137, 144
Jager v. Tolme & Runge & the London Produce Clearing House Ltd, 99, 101, 103
James Drummond & Sons v. E H Van Ingen & Co, 214
James Finlay & Co Ltd v. N. V. Kwik Hoo Tong Handel Maatschappij, 57
James Lamont & Co Ltd v. Hyland Ltd, 386
James Shaffer v. Findlay Durham & Brodie, 162
Jardine Matheson & Co v. Burke, 177
Jardine Matheson & Co v. Jones, 177
Jardine Matheson & Co v. Kin Cheu Quai, Kah Yan Koau, Wei Tsung Yuan, 177
J Aron & Co v. Comptoir Wegimont Societe Anonyme, 348
Jeffryes [Royal Bank of Liverpool] v. Agra & Masterman's Bank, 389
Jewell v. Parr, 437
JF Adair & Co Ltd (in Liquidation) v. Birnbaum, 351
J. H. Rayner & Co Ltd v. Hambro's Bank Ltd, 395
Jindal Iron & Steel Co Ltd v. Islamic Solidarity Shipping Co Jordan Inc, 42
J. M. Wotherspoon & Co Ltd v. Henry Agency House, 162, 163
John v. Dodwell & Co Ltd, 139
Johnson v. Credit Lyonnais Co, 152, 405
Johnson v. Raylton Dixon & Co, 49
Johnston v. Kershaw, 149
Johnston v. Usborne, 73, 74
John Towle & Co v. White, 136
Jones v. Bright, 209
Jones v. Gordon, 437
Jones v. Just, 33, 210, 212, 298, 361
Jones v. Padgett, 211, 213
Joseph Crosfield & Sons Ltd, In re, 239
Joseph Crosfield & Sons Ltd v. Techno-Chemical Laboratories Ltd, 239
Josling v. Kingsford, 208
J. S. Robertson (Aust.) Pty. Ltd v. Martin, 163
Jumma Dass v. Eckford, 187
Jungheim, Hopkins & Co v. Foukelmann, 366
Jurgenson v. F.E. Hookway & Co Ltd, 8

Kain v. Old, 206
Kaltenbach, Fischer & Co v. Lewis & Peat, 74–75, 171
Karberg & Co v. Blythe, Green, Jourdain & Co Ltd, 313–314

Keene v. Biscoe, 422
Keighley, Maxsted & Co v. Durant (t/a Bryan Durant & Co), 146
Keighley, Maxsted & Co & Bryan Durant & Co, In re Arbitration between, 146
Kemble v. Farren, 420
Kennedy v. De Trafford, 196
Kenworthy v. Schofield, 323
Kepitigalla Rubber Estates Ltd v. National Bank of India Ltd, 32
Kingsford v. Merry, 406
Kreditbank Cassel GmbH v. Schenkers Ltd, 384
The Kronprinsessan Margareta, 394
Kum v. Wah Tat Bank Ltd, 51
Kursell v. Timber Operators & Contractors Ltd, 370
Kylsant; R v., 116
Kymer v. Suwercropp, 74, 146

Labouchere v. Earl of Wharncliffe, 69
The Laconia. *See* Mardorf Peach & Co Ltd v. Attica Sea Carriers Corporation of Liberia
Laing v. Fidgeon, 211
Lambert v. Lewis, 267
Laming v. Cooke, 168
Lancashire Waggon Co (Ltd) v. Fitzhugh, 252
Lancaster v. J.F. Turner & Co Ltd, 350
Land Credit Co of Ireland ex parte Overend Gurney & Co, Re, 448
Lang v. Crude Rubber Washing Co Ltd, 350
Latham v. Chartered Bank of India, 389
Leaf v. International Galleries, 206
Lee v. Butler, 259–260
Lee v. Griffin, 216
Leonard v. Wilson, 54
Lever Bros v. Associated Newspapers, 238
Lever Bros v. Brunner Mond & Co Ltd, 240
Lever Bros v. The 'Daily Record' Glasgow Ltd, 238
Levi v. Levi, 328
Levitt v. Hamblet, 78
Lewis v. Great Western Railway Co, 52
Lewis & Peat Ltd & Catz American Co (Inc) (No 1), Re Arbitration between, 172, 370
Lewis & Peat Ltd & Catz American Co (Inc) (No 2), Re, 172, 371
Lewis Merthyr Consolidated Collieries Ltd, In re, 435
Libyan Arab Foreign Bank v. Bankers Trust Co, 459
Lickbarrow v. Mason, 32, 351, 382
Linck Moeller & Co v. Jameson & Co, 167
Lincoln Waggon & Engine Co v. Mumford, 247

Liverpool Corn Trade Association Ltd v. Monks (HM Inspector of Taxes), 65
Livingstone v. Whiting, 96
Lloyd (Pauper) v. Grace, Smith & Co, 131, 137
Loders & Nucoline Ltd v. Bank of New Zealand, 343
Lombard Banking Ltd v. Central Garage & Engineering Co Ltd, 442
London & Midland Bank v. Mitchell, 431
London Chartered Bank of Australia v. White, 421
London, Chatham & Dover Railway Co v. South Eastern Railway Co, 420
London Investment Trust Ltd v. Russian Petroleum & Liquid Fuel Co Ltd, 432
London Joint Stock Bank Ltd v. Macmillan, 32
London Joint Stock Bank Ltd v. Simmons, 46
Lorymer v. Smith, 119, 214
Louis Dreyfus & Co v. Produce Brokers' New Co (1924) Ltd, 357
Lovatt v. Hamilton, 83
Lowe v. Lombank Ltd, 264
L Schuler AG v. Wickman Machine Tool Sales Ltd, 134
L Sutro & Co & Heilbut, Symons & Co, In re Arbitration between, 56, 355
Lucas v. Dorrien, 403
Lyall v. Jardine Matheson & Co, 177
Lyons v. Tramways Syndicate Ltd, 457

Mackay v. Dick, 221, 222
Mackenzie & Lindsay v. Scott, 158
Mackinnon Mackenzie & Co v. Lang Moir & Co, 133
Maclaine v. Gatty, 42
MacPherson v. Buick Motor Co, 267
Mahomdally Ebrahim Pirkhan v. Schiller, Dosogne & Co, 133–134
Mair v. Himalaya Tea Co, 189
Maitland v. Chartered Mercantile Bank of India, London & China, 392
Manchester & Oldham Bank Ltd v. W A Cook & Co, 420
Manchester Liners Ltd v. Rea Ltd, 224
Manchester, Sheffield, & Lincolnshire Railway Co v. Brown, 31
Manchester, Sheffield, & Lincolnshire Railway Co v. North Central Wagon Co, 251, 254, 291
Manchester Trust v. Furness, 45, 145
Mardorf Peach & Co Ltd v. Attica Sea Carriers Corporation of Liberia, 42
Maritime Stores v. HP Marshall & Co, 157
Martin v. Boure, 391
Mason v. Hunt, 391
Matthiessen v. London & County Bank, 455
May v. Butcher, 33, 57
McEntire v. Crossley Brothers Ltd, 243, 252, 259, 291

McEwan v. Smith, 352
McGowan & Co v. Dyer, 131
Medway Oil & Storage Co v. Silica Gel Corporation, 33, 219, 224, 225
Mehmet Dogan Bey v. G. G. Abdeni & Co Ltd, 168
Merchant Banking Co of London v. Phoenix Bessemer Steel Co, 353, 407
Merrifield, Ziegler & Co v. Liverpool Cotton Association Ltd, 69
Mesnard v. Aldridge, 323
Michelin Tyre Co Ltd v. Macfarlane (Glasgow) Ltd, 136
Midland Bank Ltd v. Seymour, 150, 396
Mildred, Goyeneche & Co v. Maspons Y Hermano, 153
Miles v. Haslehurst, 150
Millar's Machinery Co Ltd v. David Way & Son, 221
Miller v. Race, 54
Miller, Gibb & Co v. Smith & Tyrer Ltd, 155, 157, 160
Miller's Case. *See* European Assurance Society, Re
Misa v. Raikes Currie, G. Grenfell Glyn, 451
Mitsui v. Mumford, 168
Mondel v. Steel, 205, 217
Montague L Meyer Ltd v. Kivisto, 215
Montague L Meyer Ltd v. Osakeyhtio Carelia Timber Co Ltd, 349, 371
Moore v. Campbell, 353
Moore v. Shelley, 421
Moore & Co Ltd & Landauer & Co, Re Arbitration between, 43
Morgan v. Gath, 85
Morgan v. Lariviére, 393
Mortimer v. Bell, 328
Moss, Ex parte, 430
Munn v. Illinois, 307
Mutton v. Peat, 418

Naoroji v. Chartered Bank of India, 388
National Bank of Egypt v. Hannevig's Bank Ltd, 396
National Provincial & Union Bank of England v. Charnley, 435
National Provincial Bank of England Ltd v. United Electric Theatres Ltd, 436
Navulshaw v. Brownrigg, 33
Neill v. Whitworth, 84, 300
Nelson Line (Liverpool), Ltd v. James Nelson & Sons Ltd, 56
Nevill. *See* White Re Nevill, Ex parte
Newall v. Tomlinson, 75
New Zealand & Australian Land Co v. Watson, 159, 197
Nichol v. Godts, 207, 208
Nickoll & Knight v. Ashton Edridge & Co, 362
Nielson v. James, 113
Niger Co Ltd v. Yorkshire Insurance Co Ltd (No 2), 54

Nitedals Taendstikfabrik v. Bruster, 132
The Njegos, 52, 53
Norrington v. Wright, 348
North Central Wagon Finance Co Ltd v. Brailsford, 28
North Central Wagon Finance Co Ltd v. Graham, 28
North Western Salt Co Ltd v. Electrolytic Alkali Co Ltd, 37
Nova Scotia Steel Co v. Sutherland Steam Shipping Co, 43
N. Roy & Co v. Surana, Dalai & Co, 133–134
Nusserwanji Merwanji Panday v. Gordon, 183
NV Arnold Otto Meyer v. Andre Aune, 356

Oakes v. Turquand, 445, 447
The Ocean Frost. *See* Armagas Ltd v. Mundogas SA
Official Assignee of Madras v. Mercantile Bank of India Ltd, 400
Oil Products Trading Co Ltd v. Societe Anonyme, Societe de Gestion D'Entreprises Coloniales, 370
The Okehampton, 55
Oldershaw v. Knowles, 99
Olds Discount Co v. John Playfair Ltd, 262
Olympia Oil & Cake Co & MacAndrew, Moreland & Co, Re, 371
Olympia Oil & Cake Co & the Produce Brokers Co Ltd, Re Arbitration between, 371
Oriental Bank Corporation v. Baree Tea Co, Ltd, 187
Oriental Commercial Bank, In re, 439
Oriental Financial Corporation v. Overend, Gurney, & Co, 438, 445
Overend Gurney & Co, Re, 447
Overend Gurney & Co v. Gibb, 449
Overend Gurney & Co Ltd (Liquidators) v. Oriental Financial Corp Ltd (Liquidators), 448

Page v. Newman, 420
Pahang Consolidated Co Ltd v. State of Pahang, 186–187
Pallyram v. W.R. Paterson & Co, 142
Parker, In re, 50, 243
Parker v. Palmer, 214
Parker v. South Eastern Railway Co, 217
Parkinson v. Lee, 214
Parr's Bank Ltd v. Thomas Ashby & Co, 455, 458
Paterson v. Tash, 150
Paul Beier v. Chhotalal Javerdas, 133–134
Pavia & Co S.P.A. v. Thurmann-Nielsen, 394
Payne v. Wilson, 261
Pearson v. Rose & Young Ltd, 153
Peek v. Directors, etc. of the North Staffordshire Railway Co, 217

Peek v. Gurney, 445, 449
Perez v. John Mercer, 371
Perishables Transport Co v. Spyropoulos (N) (London) Ltd, 154
Perry v. Barnett, 113
Peruvian Railways Co, In re, 438
Petrocochino v. Bott, 50
Petrofina (Great Britain) Ltd v. Martin, 279, 280
Phelps, Stokes & Co v. Comber, 390
Phillips v. Huth, 152, 399
Photo Production Ltd v. Securicor Transport Ltd, 264
Picker v. London & County Banking Co Ltd, 50
Pickering v. Busk, 145
Pike Sons & Co v. Ongley & Thornton, 73, 75
Pillans v. Van Mierop, 391
Pinnock Brothers v. Lewis & Peat Ltd, 172, 208
Pinto Leite & Nephews, In re, 441
Podar Trading Co Ltd Bombay v. Francois Tagher, Barcelona, 354, 358
Pollard v. Bank of England, 454
Ponsolle v. Webber, 78
Port Line Ltd v. Ben Line Steamers Ltd, 46
Postlethwaite v. Freeland, 48
Powell Duffryn Steam Coal Co v. Taff Vale Railway Co, 245
Prager v. Blatspiel Stamp & Heacock Ltd, 54
Prehn v. Royal Bank of Liverpool, 392
Premier Industrial Bank, Ltd v. Carlton Manufacturing Co Ltd, 441
Priest v. Last, 211
Protector Endowment Loan & Annuity Co v. Grice, 422
PST Energy 7 Shipping v. OW Bunker Malta, 42
Pye v. British Automobile Commercial Syndicate Ltd, 134
Pyrene Co Ltd v. Scindia Navigation Co Ltd, 148

Raffles v. Wichelhaus, 33
Randall v. Newson, 210
R & H Hall Ltd v. W H Pim Jnr & Co Ltd, 360
Rawlings v. General Trading Co, 36, 329
Regent Oil Co Ltd v. Aldon Motors Ltd, 279
Regent Oil Co Ltd v. J T Leavesley (Lichfield) Ltd, 280
Regent Oil Co Ltd v. Strick (Inspector of Taxes), 278
Reigate v. Union Manufacturing Co (Ramsbottom) Ltd, 281
Reinhold & Co & Hansloh, In re Abitration between, 371
The Res Cogitans. *See* PST Energy 7 Shipping v. OW Bunker Malta
Reuter, Hufeland & Co v. Sala & Co, 43, 363
Reynolds v. Chettle, 454

Rice, People ex rel v. Board of Trade of Chicago, 64
Ritter v. Jardine Matheson & Co, 178
Robarts v. Tucker, 454
Robert A. Munro & Co v. Meyer, 349
Robertson, In re, 291
Robert Stewart, Ex parte, 430
Robinson v. Graves, 217
Robinson v. Mollett, 49, 57, 78, 79, 126, 155
Robson v. Bennett, 454
Rogers, Ex parte, 80
Root v. French, 32
Roper v. Castell & Brown Ltd, 434
Rose & Frank Co v. J. R. Crompton & Brothers Ltd, 268
Rouse v. Bradford Banking Co Ltd, 416, 426
Rowe v. Young, 439
R. Simon & Co Ltd v. Peder P. Hedegaard A/S, 358
Rusby; R v., 108
Rusholme & Bolton & Roberts Hadfield Ltd v. S. G. Read & Co (London) Ltd, 164
Russel v. Langstaffe, 391
Russell v. Nicolopulo, 214
Russian & English Bank v. Baring Bros & Co Ltd, 43
Russian Commercial & Industrial Bank v. Comptoir d'Escompte de Mulhouse, 428
Russian Steam-Navigation Trading Co v. Silva, 49, 223
Russo-Asiatic Bank, In re, 441
Russo Chinese Bank v. Li Yau Sam, 141

Saint Line Ltd v. Richardsons, Westgarth & Co Ltd, 222
Salaman v. Warner, 114
Salomon v. Salomon & Co Ltd, 423
Salomons v. Pender, 131
Salt v. Marquess of Northampton, 43
Sampson v. Shaw, 114
Samuel Hammond, Ex parte, 440
Sanders Brothers v. Maclean & Co, 137
Saxby v. Gloucester Waggon Co, 246
Scandinavian Trading Tanker Co AB v. Flota Petrolera Ecuatoriana, 31
The Scaptrade. *See* Scandinavian Trading Tanker Co AB v. Flota Petrolera Ecuatoriana
Scarf v. Jardine, 98
Schiller v. Finlay, 133
Schloss Brothers v. Stevens, 56

Scott v. Bourdillion, 295
Scott v. Brown Doering McNab & Co, 110
Scott v. Geoghegan & Sons Pty Ltd, 162
Scriven Brothers & Co v. Hindley & Co, 325
Seddon v. North Eastern Salt Co Ltd, 206
Seton v. Slade, 420
Shalagram Jhajharia v. National Co Ltd, 196
Shamrock Steamship Co v. Storey & Co, 52
Shanklin Pier Ltd v. Detel Products Ltd, 267
Shanti Prasad Jain v. Director of Enforcement, 181
Shearson Lehman Hutton Inc v. Maclaine Watson & Co Ltd, 78
Shell UK Ltd v. Lostock Garage Ltd, 281
Shepherd v. Kain, 217
Shepherd v. Pybus, 210
Shipton, Anderson & Co (1927) Ltd (In liquidation) v. Micks, Lambert & Co, 350, 358
Simmonds v. Millar & Co, 350
Simond v. Braddon, 298, 361
Sinason-Teicher Inter-American Grain Corporation v. Oilcakes & Oilseeds Trading Co Ltd, 394
Sinclair v. Brougham, 45
Singer Manufacturing Co v. Clark, 257
Singer Manufacturing Co v. Galloway & Beasley, 257
Singer Manufacturing Co v. J. Wright (Irvine's Trustee), 257
Singer Manufacturing Co v. The London & South Western Railway Co, 257
Slingsby v. District Bank Ltd, 53
Small v. National Provincial Bank of England, 434
Smethurst v. Taylor, 144
Smith v. M'Guire, 144
Smith, Coney & Barrett v. Becker, Gray & Co, 101
Sobell Industries Ltd v. Cory Bros & Co Ltd, 154, 164
Sobhagmal Gianmal v. Mukundchand Balia, 142
Société Générale de Paris v. Walker, 429, 431
Solloway v. McLaughlin, 47
Solomons, In re, 437
Soopromonian Setty v. Heilgers, 133
Sorrell v. Smith, 272
Southwell v. Bowditch, 74–75, 167
Spears v. Travers, 403
Spencer Trading Co Ltd v. Devon, 211
Speyer; R v., 70
Staffs Motor Guarantee Ltd v. British Wagon Co Ltd, 28, 153
Stainton ex parte Board of Trade, Re, 110
The Starsin. *See* Homburg Houtimport BV v. Agrosin Private Ltd

Steels & Busks Ltd v. Bleeker Bik & Co Ltd, 347
Stephens, Paul & Co v. Goodlake & Nutter, 357
Stevens v. Biller, 131
Stewart & Co v. Merchants Marine Insurance Co Ltd, 55
Strathlorne Steamship Co Ltd v. Hugh Baird & Sons Ltd, 48
Street v. Blay, 205–206
Stucley v. Baily, 205–206
Stunzi Sons Ltd v. House of Youth Pty Ltd, 163
Sutton v. Tatham, 78
Sven Hylander & Co v. Blake, Dobbs & Co, 349, 355
Swire v. Francis, 137
Swire v. Redman & Holt, 16
Szymanowski & Co v. Beck & Co, 215, 218, 348

Tahiti Co, In re, 430
Tamvaco v. Lucas, 159
Tankexpress A/S v. Compagnie Financiere Belge des Petroles SA, 43
Tata Hydro-Electric Agencies Ltd Bombay v. Commissioner of Income Tax, 181
Tate & Lyle Refineries Ltd v. International Commodities Clearing House Ltd, 105
Taylor v. Bullen, 206
T.D. Bailey, Son & Co v. Ross T Smyth & Co Ltd, 345, 353, 356, 357
Teheran-Europe Co Ltd v. S T Belton (Tractors) Ltd, 146, 157, 224
Tellrite Ltd v. London Confirmers Ltd, 163
Tetley v. Shand, 346
Thacker v. Hardy, 120, 121, 125
Thackrah. *See* Hughes & Kimber Ltd Re Thackrah, Ex parte
Thalmann Frères & Co v. Texas Star Flour Mills, 313–314
Thanawala v. Jyoti Ltd, 195
Thomas Gabriel & Sons v. Churchill & Sim, 131, 160
Thomas George White, Ex parte, 439
Thomas William Brook, F. & A. Delcomyn & F. & J. Badart, Freres, In the Matter of an Arbitration between, 364
Thorburn v. Barnes, 84, 300, 362
Thorne v. Motor Trade Association, 40, 272
Thornett & Fehr v. Beers & Son, 212
Thornton v. Fehr, 51
Thornton v. Union Discount Co of London, 429
Transport & General Credit Corporation Ltd v. Morgan, 28, 256, 292
Tregaskis ex parte Tregaskis, Re, 110
Tregelles v. Sewell, 208
Trueman v. Loder, 50, 181

Tutika Basavaraju v. Parry & Co, 157, 187
Tye v. Fynmore, 299

Union Bank of Manchester Ltd v. Beech, 426
United Dominions Trust Ltd v. Kirkwood, 28, 55
United Kingdom Mutual Steamship Assurance Association Ltd v. Nevill, 74
United States v. Patten, 114
Universal Stock Exchange Ltd v. Strachan, 121
Urquhart Lindsay & Co Ltd v. Eastern Bank Ltd, 394

Vagliano v. The Bank of England, 57
Vallejo v. Wheeler, 41
Valletort Sanitary Steam Laundry Co Ltd, In re, 46
Venice Steam Navigation Co Ltd v. Ispahani, 165
Vernede v. Weber, 298, 361
Victoria Laundry (Windsor) v. Newman Industries, 222
Vigers Bros v. Sanderson Bros, 349
Von Dreitche v. Hong Kong & Shanghai Bank, 425
V.R. Mohanakrishnan v. Chimanlal Desai & Co, 157

Wackerbarth v. Masson, 218, 297
Waddington v. Bristow, 87
Wait, Re, 43, 45
Walker v. Hicks, 384
Walkers, Winser & Hamm & Shaw, Son & Co, Re Arbitration between, 51
Wallingford v. Mutual Society, 420, 422
Wallis v. Hirsch, 302
Wallis v. Pratt, 208, 218
Ward v. National Bank of New Zealand Ltd, 426
Ware & de Freville Ltd v. Motor Trade Association, 272
Waring v. Favenck, 74, 146
Warwick v. Rogers, 452, 454, 455
Waterlow v. Sharp, 417
Watteau v. Fenwick, 144, 145
Watts v. Porter, 429
Weigall & Co v. Runciman & Co, 150
Weiler v. Schilizzi, 207
Weinberger v. Inglis, 70, 80
Weis & Co v. Produce Brokers' Co, 56, 310
Wells v. Porter, 119
Wells (Merstham) Ltd v. Buckland Sand & Silica Co, 237, 267
W.E. Marshall & Co v. Lewis & Peat (Rubber), 172, 371
Wheeler & Wilson Manufacturing Co v. Shakespear, 136
White v. Munro, 178

Table of Cases

White Re Nevill, Ex parte, 158
White Sea Timber Ltd v. W W North Ltd, 349
Wickham Holdings Ltd v. Brooke House Motors Ltd, 264
Wilks v. Atkinson, 88
Willers Engel & Co v. E. Nathan & Co Ltd, 8
Williams v. Reynolds, 84, 85, 86
Wills v. Jimah Rubber Estates Ltd, 180
Wilson v. Darling Island Stevedoring & Lighterage Co Ltd, 135
Wilson v. Lloyd, 98
Wilson v. Rickett Cockerell & Co, 211
Wilson IIolgate v. Belgian Grain & Produce Co, 52
Winterbottom ex parte Winterbottom, Re, 420
Wolcott v. Reeme, 99
Wood v. Lectrick Ltd, 267
Wood v. Smith, 205–206
Wood v. Wood, 69
Woodhouse AC Israel Cocoa Ltd SA v. Nigerian Produce Marketing Co Ltd, 149
Woodward v. Wolfe, 122
Wookey v. Pole, 428
W. P. Greenhalgh & Sons v. Union Bank of Manchester, 56, 418
W. T. Lamb & Sons v. Goring Brick Co Ltd, 135, 264

Yeoman Credit Ltd v. Odgers, 264
Yorkshire Banking Co v. Beatson & Mycock, 437
Yorkshire Railway Wagon Co v. Maclure, 253
Young v. Bank of Bengal, 418, 428
Young v. Ladies' Imperial Club, 70
Young v. United States, 440

The Zamora. *See* Cia de Comercio Limitada Van Waveren v. Spillers Ltd
Zwinger v. Samuda, 403, 404

Table of Legislation

An Act for Abolishing the Offences of forestalling, regrating and engrossing etc 1844, 108
Arbitration Act 1889, 367, 370
Arbitration Act 1934, 367, 370
Arbitration (Foreign Awards) Act 1930, 369
Assurance Companies Act 1909, 54
Auctioneers Act 1845, 323
Auctions (Bidding Agreements) Act 1927, 329, 330

Bank Charter Act 1833, 26
Bank Charter Act 1844, 26, 27, 29, 446
Banking Companies' (Shares) Act 1867, 112
Banking Companies' (Shares) Act 1967, 112, 113
Banking Co-partnership Act 1826, 26
Bank Notes Act 1833, 27
Bankruptcy Act 1861, 110
Bankruptcy Act 1869, 429
Bankruptcy Act 1883, 110, 253
Bankruptcy Act 1890, 110
Bankruptcy Act 1914, 261
Bankrupt Law Consolidation Act 1849, 110, 388
Barnard's Act, 113
Bills of Exchange Act 1855, 384
Bills of Exchange Act 1882, 33, 35, 53, 203, 384, 385, 440, 458, 459
Bills of Sale Acts, 37, 254, 256, 259
Bills of Sale Act 1882, 255

Common Law Procedure Act 1854, 370
Companies Acts, 126, 181
Companies Act 1862, 89, 445
Companies Act 1867, 429
Companies Act 1900, 432, 435
Companies Act 1907, 435

Companies Act 1929, 262, 436
Companies (Consolidation) Act 1908, 262
Consumer Credit Act 1974, 264
Crossed Cheques Act 1876, 458

Electricity (Supply) Act 1926, 226
Export Guarantees Act 1937, 161
Export Guarantees Act 1939, 161
Export Guarantees Act 1945, 161

Factors Acts, 36, 143, 151, 152, 197, 198, 400, 405, 406
Factors Act 1823, 151
Factors Act 1825, 405
Factors Act 1842, 151, 152, 172
Factors Act 1877, 152
Factors Act 1889, 152, 259, 260, 351
Fertilisers and Feeding Stuffs Act 1926, 347
Finance Act 1949, 323
Financial Services Act 1986, 108, 118

Gaming Act 1845, 118, 119, 120, 121, 122, 124, 125

Hire Purchase Acts, 264
Hire Purchase Act 1938, 263, 292

Joint Stock Companies Act 1856, 66, 185, 430
Judicature Acts, 252
Judicature Act 1873, 43, 252, 384, 385

Larceny Act 1861, 36, 108, 116, 447
Law of Distress Amendment Act 1908, 261
Law of Property Act 1925, 424
Leeman's Act. *See* Banking Companies (Shares) Act 1867
Limited Liability Act 1855, 185, 246
London and St. Katharine Docks Act 1864, 407
London Brokers' Relief Act 1870, 77

Marine Insurance Act 1906, 154, 203
Mercantile Law Amendment Act 1856, 426
Merchandise Marks Act 1862, 36, 292
Merchandise Marks Act 1887, 36, 292
Merchant Shipping Act 1894, 408
Mersey Dock Acts Consolidation Act 1858, 407
Misrepresentation Act 1967, 206
Moneylenders Acts, 257

Moneylenders Act 1900, 28
Monopolies and Restrictive Practices (Inquiry and Control) Act 1948, 37, 273

Overseas Trade (Credits and Insurance) Act 1920, 161
Overseas Trade Guarantee Act 1939, 161

Partnership Act 1890, 426
Port of London (Consolidation) Act 1920, 407
Prevention of Fraud (Investments) Act 1938, 108

Railway Clauses Consolidation Act 1845, 245, 255
Railway Clearing Act 1850, 456
Railway Companies Act 1867, 252
Railway Rates and Changes Order Confirmation Acts 1891& 1892, 245
Railway Regulation Act 1844, 253
Railway Rolling Stock Protection Act 1872, 252
Resale Prices Act 1964, 37, 274
Restrictive Trade Practices Act 1956, 37, 273, 274, 276

Sale of Food (Weights and Measures) Act 1926, 36
Sale of Goods Act 1893, 33, 35, 43, 134, 152, 158, 201, 203, 204, 207, 208, 210, 211, 212, 214, 215, 216, 217, 218, 219, 222, 223, 225, 259, 264, 271, 290, 324, 328, 346, 347, 351, 352, 374
Sale of Land by Auction Act 1867, 328
Statute of Frauds Act 1677, 106, 159, 216, 298, 323
Statute of Frauds Amendment Act 1828, 426

Trade Facilities Act 1921, 161
Treasury Bills Act 1877, 450

Unfair Contract Terms Act 1977, 264
Canada
  Grain Act 1912, 308
  Manitoba Grain Act 1900, 308
India
  Companies Act 1882, 183
  Companies Act 1913, 182, 194
  Companies Act 1956, 195, 196
  Companies (Amendment) Act 1960, 195, 196
  Contract Act 1872, 133, 157, 187
  Insurance Act 1938, 194
  Joint-stock Companies Act 1857, 183

United States
  Commodity Exchange Act 1936, 64, 114, 117
  Grain Futures Act 1922, 64, 114
  Grain Standards Act 1916, 307
  Harter Act, 346

1

Commercial and Legal Contexts

1.1 Introduction

Those seeking to understand the role of commercial law in a society will not get far without an appreciation (at least in broad outline) of the relevant legal doctrines. These contain the categories which the law has invented, and which provide the framework in which commercial practices and institutions can operate. Law in context must begin with the law and a knowledge of doctrine. Focusing on the doctrine alone, however, tells only part of the story of how commercial law has worked in practice and the ends pursued within its remit. A case-centred approach neglects, for instance, the types of commercial transaction which have been rarely litigated. The common-law system depends on parties bringing cases to court. Commercial parties characteristically seek to avoid entanglement in the law, decidedly so among some well-organised commercial groups able to sustain their own dispute resolution mechanisms.

Even if matters have arisen in legal proceedings, a focus on doctrine misses out on the impact of legal decisions (and legislation), which has often been mitigated by commercial parties redrafting contracts and market rules, by deals being restructured and by the modification of existing institutions or the creation of new ones. An overabundant concern with doctrine also neglects the reality that commercial parties have never been devoted to its purity or rational development when pursuing profit. Nor have their lawyers at the expense of winning a case. For both commercial parties and their lawyers, law has generally been a framework and malleable resource to be used instrumentally to achieve commercial ends.

This book is about English commercial law over the period of about 140 years, from about 1830 to 1970, with an emphasis on its international reach. As a study of commercial law the focus, in the main, is on commercial transactions, in particular those involving the sale and supply of goods and related financial services.[1] So it is not primarily concerned with business organisations

---

[1] C. Twigg-Flesner & G. Villalta Puig, 'Introduction: Boundaries of Commercial Law', in C. Twigg-Flesner & G. Villalta Puig (eds.), *Boundaries of Commercial and Trade Law*, Munich, Sellier European Law Publishers, 2011, 1. cf. the wider approach in R. Goode, *Commercial Law in the Next Millennium*, London, Sweet & Maxwell, 1998, 8–9, and Lord Wright's institutional

such as companies; utilities such as the railways; or the constitution, operation and insolvency of either.[2] Nor is it about transport (the carriage of goods) or insurance. Further, as a study of commercial law, it is primarily about transactions between commercial parties, not those between commercial parties and consumers.[3] Consequently, the emphasis is on raw materials and commercial not consumer goods, and attention in the distribution of goods is given to the channels between producers and retailers, not between retailers and consumers.

With the focus on commercial transactions, the chapters deal with where and how they occurred during our period – the commodities markets, where parties entered spot, forward and futures transactions for sale, purchase and speculation (Chapter 2); intermediaries, such as agents, brokers, distributors and financial institutions, whose prime function was to facilitate the transactions of others – to market their products and services or, in the case of banks, to marshal finance for this (Chapters 3 and 6); sale and related techniques such as hire and hire purchase, employed for the marketing and distribution of manufactured goods (Chapter 4); the international trade in products and commodities (Chapters 4 and 5); and the backing of banks through trade finance and advances to manufacturers for products to be supplied both at home and abroad (Chapter 6).

As an account of commercial law in context, the book cannot be a full legal history.[4] As indicated, however, the substantive law is often a key, since understanding how particular aspects of trade and commerce worked demands a knowledge of the legal framework within which they were conducted. So there are accounts of doctrine in the following chapters. However, the legal parts of the book are far from comprehensive and in the main cover only the bare bones necessary to understand law's relationship with commercial practice. There are other reasons for referring to legal decisions. One is to determine the extent to which the courts moulded legal doctrine, if at all, to accommodate commercial need. Another is to mine from the case reports the factual findings about how commercial transactions during our period were conducted. As well as the case law, reference is made to the work of economic and business historians, which is essential to understanding the broader context in which commercial law operated.

approach, 'Some Developments of Commercial Law in the Present Century', Presidential Address, Holdsworth Club, Faculty of Law, University of Birmingham, 17 May 1935, 1 (the law dealt with in the Commercial Court).

[2] e.g., R. Kostal, *Law and English Railway Capitalism 1825–1875*, Oxford, Clarendon, 1994; R. Harris, *Industrializing English Law: Entrepreneurship and Business Organization 1720–1844*, Cambridge, Cambridge University Press, 2000.

[3] cf. C. Scott & J. Black (eds.), *Cranston's Consumers and the Law*, Law in Context series, Cambridge, Cambridge University Press, 2000.

[4] cf. W. Cornish, J. Anderson, R. Cocks, M. Lobban, P. Polden & K. Smith, *Oxford History of the Laws of England*, Oxford, Oxford University Press, 2010, vol. XI–XIII (hereafter, *Oxford History of the Laws of England*).

The book also draws on business and bank archives to understand, in a more complete way than can be derived from these other sources, how commercial parties perceived and used the law during our period. This is the counterpart to modern-day empirical studies of the law in action. Despite the ravages of time, there is a plethora of business and bank archives relevant to the topic. Those referred to are roughly representative of the different aspects of commercial law covered (trade associations/markets, agents, merchants, manufacturers, financiers and banks), although I have only scratched the surface of what is available. The petering out of these archives by the 1960s is one reason that the story is drawn to a close in 1970. Another is that by 1970 London and Liverpool as world centres for trade had faded, as had Britain's role as a leader in manufacturing – activities which, during our period, were central to the story of commercial law as the law of transactions.

This introductory chapter provides an overview of both the commercial and legal context of the book. Part 1.2 paints a picture in outline of the markets, techniques and institutions of the industrial age associated with trading commodities, distributing manufacturing products and financing both. This context is revisited in different ways in the course of the book. Then in part 1.3, the chapter turns to the legal context. Relevant bodies of commercial law appear in later chapters. At this point the aim is to explore the general principles which framed the body of transactional law later examined. It was within this framework that commercial parties constructed through private law-making the markets, techniques and institutions which appear in the narrative.

1.2 Commercial Context: Markets, Organisations and Players

> There were only a dozen passengers all told, for this was primarily a cargo boat. One of these fellow travellers caught Mr Golspie's eye, nodded, and then came nearer ... 'This port of London's a bit of an eye-opener to me,' Mr Golspie remarked.
>
> [Mr Sugden] Ever been all round it? Tremendous – oh tremendous! There's the West India Docks further up here, and then Surrey Commercial on the other side. You never saw such a place. It's a hard day's work looking round the Surrey Commercial. ...
>
> And where do you live when you're at home?
>
> St. Helens. That's where my firm is, and that's where I live. (J. B. Priestley, *Angel Pavement*, 1930)[5]

The setting for Priestley's 1930 novel is the City of London and its commercial dealings, but in the closing pages, as the fraudulent timber agent, Golspie, leaves by ship for South America, the author draws on other aspects of Britain's

---

[5] London, William Heinemann, 1930.

commercial life at the time – the port of London through which the vessel initially passes, and the industrial Midlands and north of England, represented by Mr Sugden, whose firm is based in St Helens, Lancashire. This was part of the context in which commercial law worked and developed during our period. As the first industrial nation, Britain's dominance in manufacturing was gradually forfeited in the years prior to the First World War with the growth of Germany and the United States, and in relative decline after that.[6]

The other side of the coin was Britain as a great trading nation, and the size of its ports like London, as Golspie and Sugden observed. These handled the manufactured goods for export, but also the huge imports – raw materials for manufacturing, food for the new middle classes and workers in the factories and service industries, and timber for building. Domestic production of grain, wool and timber was inadequate, and these needed to be obtained from abroad. Raw materials like cotton, jute and rubber were only available from more conducive climes. Rising prosperity and changing tastes meant a greater demand for commodities such as tea, coffee, sugar, rice and spices.[7]

Against this backdrop of imports, it should not be surprising that commodity markets emerged. Nor should it be surprising that these markets should occasion trade associations with a mission of bringing order – through establishing standards for goods, laying down rules and regulations for dealings, and drafting standard form contracts to govern individual transactions. Associated with Britain as the leading trading nation, and these markets, were London's banks and sterling as the world's reserve currency, the advanced state for the time of its communications network with the rest of the world, and the country's shipping and marine and general insurance business. By the end of the nineteenth century Britain was the world leader in all these, with the added advantage that clustered in the City of London they were greater as a whole than as individual institutions.[8] Not to be forgotten in all this was British

---

[6] K. Harley, 'The Legacy of the Early Start'; M. Kitson & J. Michie, 'The De-Industrial Revolution: The Rise and Fall of UK Manufacturing, 1870–2010', in R. Floud, J. Humphries & P. Johnson (eds.), *The Cambridge History of Modern Britain Growth and Decline 1870 to the Present*, vol. II, 2nd ed., Cambridge, Cambridge University Press, 2014; J. Tomlinson, 'De-industrialization Not Decline: A New Meta-narrative for Post-war British History' (2016) 27 *Twentieth Century British Hist* 76; N. Broadberry, *The Productivity Race: British Manufacturing in International Perspective, 1850–1990*, Cambridge, Cambridge University Press, 1997; B. Elbaum & W. Lazonick (eds.), *The Decline of the British Economy*, Oxford, Oxford University Press, 1986 (chapters by Lazonick, Lewchuk); P. Mathias, *The First Industrial Nation*, London, Methuen, 1969, 340–341, 380.

[7] M. Turner, 'Agriculture, 1860–1914', in R. Floud & P. Johnson (eds.), *The Cambridge Economic History of Modern Britain, Economic Maturity 1860–1939*, Cambridge, Cambridge University Press, 2004, vol. II, 150–151; C. Harley, 'Trading 1870–1914', in ibid., 166–167.

[8] S. Mollan & R. Michie, 'The City of London as an International Commercial and Financial Centre since 1900' (2012) 13 *Enterprise & Society*, 538, 543–544, 576. Among contemporary accounts, see F. Jackson, *Lectures on British Commerce Including Finance, Insurance, Business and Industry*, London, Pitman, 1912 (chapters by Owen and Bisgood).

military, especially naval, power, its large merchant marine fleet and its Empire, with the economic resources which that afforded.[9]

Although by the First World War Britain had been overtaken by the United States in industrial production, it remained the largest trading nation. Trade was still a matter of exporting manufactured goods and importing food and raw materials. Britain had been an important entrepôt, but as that declined it had become a centre for organising trade elsewhere.[10] Until the middle of the nineteenth century textiles had been the dominant export, but after that machinery and other capital goods became a significant component of total exports.[11] Trade demanded a network of agency and other arrangements both in Britain and abroad to facilitate transactions, as well as sound financial backing. This was furnished by a sophisticated system of trade finance arranged by the merchant (and later the joint stock) banks in the City of London. There has been a long debate whether this was matched by an equally effective system for financing British industry.[12]

1 Markets, Trade Associations and Standard Form Contracts

Organised markets in commodities like grain, cotton, sugar, tea and rubber were established in London and Liverpool in the nineteenth and early part of the twentieth centuries. They were a product of the rising volume of international trade as Britain became the first industrial nation, a major importer of these commodities for the needs of its factories and population, and a centre for arranging their distribution elsewhere. Added stimulus to trade was provided in the second half of the nineteenth century with the improvements in communications and infrastructure. The telegraph meant parties could more easily garner information about, and order, commodities, and the railways, the steamship lines, and the ports and docks meant improved productivity, more efficient flows and cheaper prices.[13] World prices were struck as a result of the numerous transactions by brokers on the London and Liverpool commodities markets.[14]

---

[9] K. O'Rourke, 'From Empire to Europe: Britain in the World Economy', in R. Floud, J. Humphries & P. Johnson (eds.), *The Cambridge History of Modern Britain Growth and Decline 1870 to the Present*, 2nd ed., Cambridge, Cambridge University Press, 2014, 70–72.

[10] R. Michie. 'The City and International Trade', in D. Platt, A. Latham & R. Michie (eds.), *Decline and Recovery in Britain's Overseas Trade 1873-1914*, London, Macmillan, 1993.

[11] S. Chapman, *Merchant Enterprise in Britain: From the Industrial Revolution to World War I*, Cambridge, Cambridge University Press, 1992, 3–4, 7.

[12] 376–377 below.

[13] E. Williams, 'Thirty Years in the Grain Trade' (July 1895) 161 *North American Review* 25.

[14] e.g., S. Topic & A. Wells, *Global Markets Transformed 1870–1945*, Cambridge, MA, Harvard University Press, 2012, 48–50, 62–64, 84–92; K. O'Rourke, 'The European Grain Invasion, 1870–1913' (1997) 57 *J Econ Hist* 775; S. Mercier, 'The Evolution of World Grain Trade' (1999) 21 *Review Agricultural Econ* 225; C. Harley, 'Transportation, the World Wheat Trade, and the Kuznets Cycle 1850–1913' (1980) 17 *Explorations Econ Hist* 218; W. Malenbaum, *The World Wheat Economy 1885–1939*, Cambridge, MA, Harvard University Press, 1953.

Chapters 2 and 5 pursue in greater detail these international commodity markets, the brokers dealing on them, the trade associations and their work in formulating standards, rules and standard form contracts – and the role of law as the framework for all three activities. What follows is a background sketch. The key commodity markets are outlined, along with the brokers who worked there and the role of auctions in the process of commodity dealings (although that role was limited in time and scope). There is then an account of the trade associations, which played a pivotal role in designing the standards, rules and standard form contracts for commodity trading and of the institutional underpinning.

(i) Commodity Markets, Brokers and Auctions

The London and Liverpool commodities markets started life as informal meetings of merchants interested in foreign commodities trading based at the London coffee houses, the Royal Exchange and the docks.[15] The Baltic Exchange traces its origins to 1744, when the Virginia and Maryland coffee house changed its name to the Virginia and Baltick, to reflect the fact that the merchants and shipowners who gathered there had business in both North America and the Baltic Sea region. The formalisation of the Baltic Exchange in 1823, by the adoption of rules for membership, was a reaction against the extreme speculation in tallow on the Baltic Walk of the Royal Exchange.[16] Initially, commodity dealings on the Baltic Exchange took place in tallow, linseed, flax and hemp.[17]

The sharp increase in grain imports in Britain after the repeal of the Corn Laws established a world market.[18] Wheat came initially from the Black Sea region of Russia and from the Continent, then from the 1860s from the United States and India. In the 1890s there were new entrants such as Canada, Argentina and Australia.[19] From the middle of the nineteenth century large-scale transactions in grain cargoes from abroad took place between brokers on the Baltic Exchange, which continued to be a major venue for grain trading into the twentieth century.[20] In the late 1920s the Baltic was said to be the most

---

[15] B. Lillywhite, *London Coffee Houses*, London, Allen & Unwin, 1963. See also B. Cowan, *The Social Life of Coffee: The Emergence of the British Coffeehouse*, New Haven, Yale University Press, 2005, 134, 165.

[16] H. Barty-King, *The Baltic Exchange*, London, Hutchinson Benham, 1977, 58–60, 70.

[17] Tallow was an important lubricant in the early nineteenth century and a source of light in the form of candles until the arrival of the kerosene oil lamp and gas. Linseed oil was used for finishing surfaces (varnish; paint). Hemp was used for making rope, bags and cloth.

[18] Note that corn was the English expression for grain; it was not confined to maize or American corn.

[19] M. Ejrnæs, K. Gunnar Persson & S. Rich, 'Feeding the British: Convergence and Market Efficiency in the Nineteenth-Century Grain Trade' (2008) 61 *Econ Hist Rev* 140, 146; M. Atkin, *International Grain Trade*, Cambridge, Woodhead Publishing, 1992, 18; P. Herlihy, *Odessa: A History 1794–1914*, Cambridge, MA, Harvard Ukrainian Research Institute, 1986, 105, 204–206.

[20] D. Kynaston, *The City of London. The Golden Years 1890–1914*, London, Pimlico, 1995, 19, 23, 258–263; *The City of London. Illusions of Gold 1914–1945*, London, Pimlico, 1999, 252–255; R.

important European market for grain, with transactions in a single day sometimes amounting to over £2,500,000.[21]

Brokers in the grain trade in the 1930s did a considerable business for customers in continental Europe. Customary brokerage in that trade was 1½ pence per quarter,[22] but more was charged when cable and telephone expenses were high, or as a premium to cover del credere risk.[23] Over time, the concentration of millers and their vertical integration with the large bakers, coupled with government encouragement of home cereal production, led to changes in the structure of the grain trade and the role of intermediaries.[24] There was not the same level of activity for them after the Second World War, although grain was still being traded on the Baltic in the 1960s. At the end of our period the transnational grain traders like Cargill, Bunge, Garnac, Continental and Louis Dreyfus – names known though important cases in the law reports – were acting as principals.[25] The Baltic continued as a leading shipping market, where shipowners and charterers could charter and buy and sell vessels.

The Baltic Exchange was for grain; the venue for trading other commodities was elsewhere. Early on there were printed conditions for the sale of commodities by public auction at places like Garraway's Coffee House and, after their opening in Mincing Lane in 1811, the London Commercial Sale Rooms.[26] By the middle of the nineteenth century brokers were buying and selling sugar, coffee, tea, spices and other 'foreign and colonial' produce in Mincing Lane.[27] Mincing Lane continued to provide the venue for the markets for these and other commodities like rubber, which arrived later in the century. By the early twentieth century there could be sixty commodity auctions a day at the Commercial Sale Rooms – tea, sugar, coffee, cocoa and spices, as well as other produce such as jute, shellac, tortoiseshell and mother-of-pearl.[28] No samples of the commodities being sold were permitted at the Commercial Sale Rooms, and they had to be inspected at the warehouses, wharfs and docks where they were stored, at brokers' offices or, after trade associations were

---

Michie, *The City of London: Continuity and Change 1850–1990*, Basingstoke, Macmillan, 1992, Ch. 2.

[21] S. Dowling, *The Exchanges of London*, London, Butterworth & Co, 1929, 180–181, 155.

[22] A quarter in imperial measurement is 28 lbs.

[23] A. Hooker, *The International Grain Trade*, 2nd ed., London, Pitman, 1939, 38. On del credere commission, 157–161 below.

[24] *Report on the Marketing of Wheat, Barley and Oats in England and Wales*, London, Ministry of Agriculture and Fisheries Economic Series, No. 18, 1928, 130; G. Rees, R. Craig & D. Jones, *Britain's Commodity Markets*, London, Paul Elek Books, 1972, 161, 168.

[25] D. Morgan, *Merchants of Grain*, London, Weidenfeld and Nicolson, 1979; W. Broehl, *Cargill Trading the World's Grain*, Hanover, NH, University Press of New England, 1992.

[26] Garraway's closed in the middle of the nineteenth century.

[27] Anon, *The City; or, the Physiology of London Business*, London, Groombridge, 1852, 157.

[28] G. Rees, *The History of the London Commodity Market*, London, Commodity Analysis Ltd, 1978, 15.

formed, where they kept them.[29] Plantation House in Mincing Lane became the location of rubber and tea auctions.

Ubiquitous in the commodity markets until the First World War were the brokers, acting as agents for others or in some cases as principals for themselves. Brokers from the beginning of our period traded with each other and issued bought and sold notes containing the basic terms of a sale.[30] They also conducted auctions, and over time the management of these became a sophisticated business.[31] Brokers organising and participating in commodity dealings formed themselves into associations. The terms established by the London General Produce Brokers' Association, which dated from 1878, covered trading in a number of commodities.[32]

As well as the London General Produce Brokers' Association, there were associations of brokers for specific commodities, such as the Tea Brokers' Association of London (for selling brokers, who auctioned the tea, and guaranteed payment to their principal) and the Tea Buying Brokers' Association (as the name suggests, for buying brokers).[33] While Britons were not great coffee drinkers, London was an important centre for coffee dealing from the nineteenth century because of the banking, insurance and shipping services located there.[34] The rules of the Coffee Trade Association of London governed some sales in Mincing Lane.[35]

Separate from dealings in other commodities were the auction sales for wool from Australia, New Zealand and South America. These were conducted in London from the first part of the nineteenth century, after 1875 at the Wool Exchange in Coleman Street in the City of London. Prior to the First World War European and American buyers took around half the quantity sold there.[36] As with other commodity auctions, catalogues were prepared for each sale, briefly describing the lots to be auctioned and stating the dock or warehouse where they could be inspected. From the late nineteenth century auctions conducted in wool-producing countries like Australia and New Zealand assumed greater importance. It was the same story with tea – auctions

---

[29] Ibid., 61–62. [30] 296–299 below.
[31] See Port of London Authority, Dock & Traffic Manager's Office, *Tenth Report of Research Committee*, 1934, 85–98, Appendix 9.
[32] US Department of Commerce, Bureau of Foreign and Domestic Commerce, *Market Methods and Custom and usages in London*, Special Consular Reports No. 86, Washington, 1923, 66. Willers Engel & Co v. E. Nathan & Co Ltd (1928) 30 Ll L Rep 208 turned on the association's invoicing back terms. For the counterpart association in Liverpool: Aune v. Cauwenberghe & Fils (1938) 60 Ll L Rep 389.
[33] Monopolies and Restrictive Practices Commission, *Report on the Supply of Tea*, London, HMSO, 1956, 10–11.
[34] S. Topik, *The World Coffee Market in the Eighteenth and Nineteenth Centuries, from Colonial to National Regimes*, Department of History, University of California, Irvine, Working Paper No. 04/04, 2004, 26.
[35] cf. Jurgenson v. F.E. Hookway & Co Ltd [1951] 2 Lloyds Rep 129.
[36] J. Clapham, *The Woollen and Worsted Industries*, London, Methuen, 1907, 97.

being held in producer countries like Ceylon (Sri Lanka) and India – although important auctions continued to be held in London. In the twentieth century faster transport and communications, the development of grading and standards for commodities, and the growth of larger, integrated businesses all led to the decline of the London commodity auctions. After 1945 London's place as a world centre for trading physical commodities was past.[37]

(ii) Trade Associations, Standard Form Contracts and Market 'Plumbing'

None of the Baltic Exchange, the London Commercial Sale Rooms, Plantation House or the other London commodity exchanges set the rules for trading in commodities. They provided the venue and, in the case of the Baltic, regulated membership. It was the trade associations, formed from the last quarter of the nineteenth century, which developed (or indorsed) standards, drew up rules and regulations and drafted the standard form contracts to govern commodity trading. In addition, traders, trade associations and others like the banks were responsible for institutional developments such as the establishment of clearing systems, which are the essential 'plumbing' for any sophisticated market. Of prime importance was the London Produce Clearing House (LPCH), which initially cleared futures dealings in coffee and sugar, later wheat, maize, pepper, rubber, raw silk, silver and indigo. After several metamorphoses it is, today, the LCH Group, which is an international multi-asset clearing house covering financial products and commodities.[38] The counterpart for clearing payments was the London Bankers' Clearing House (Chapter 6, 6.4).

The London Corn Trade Association (LCTA) was formed in 1878, and by the early twentieth century most international dealings in grain were on the standard form contracts which it drew up and according to the standards which it collected or endorsed for reference purposes in the case of disputes.[39] LCTA's membership was drawn from the wide range of parties concerned with the international grain trade – brokers, importers, shippers and millers. In its work it was in close contact with other interests, shipping, insurance and banking, but government rarely.[40] By the early twentieth century LCTA also had standard form contracts for dealing in grain futures, although the internationally significant grain futures market of the interwar period was in Liverpool.[41]

Following LCTA there was a profusion of trade associations, including the London Cattle Food Trade Association (1906), the London Oil and Tallow

---

[37] R. Hartley, *No Mean City*, London, Queen Anne Press, 1967, 101.   [38] 89 below.
[39] 302–308, 312–313 below.
[40] J. Sgard, 'The Simplest Model of Global Governance Ever Seen? The London Corn Market (1885–1914)', in E. Brousseau, J-M. Glachant & J. Sgard (eds.), *The Oxford Handbook of Institutions of International Economic Governance and Market Regulation*, Oxford, Oxford University Press, 2019. Sgard notes the membership of Dreyfus Freres, the leading French grain dealer of the day. But see the role of the National Federation of Corn Trade Associations: 302n below.
[41] 81–82 below.

Trades Association (1910), the London Copra Association (1913) and the Rubber Trade Association (1913).[42] The Rubber Trade Association had standard form contracts, a certification process (before rubber could be considered good tender on a contract, its standard had to be certified) and rules for the settlement of forward dealings.[43] There were four trade associations for sugar, reflecting its different origins (beet, cane sugar) and condition (raw, refined sugar). All four comprised buyers and sellers. For raw sugar the Beetroot Sugar Association and the Sugar Association of London were established in 1882; they later amalgamated.[44] All associations had their own rules and regulations. Along with rules for beetroot sugar contracts were those for storage, clearing and futures dealings in the commodity. The Refined Sugar Association followed in 1891.

By contrast with London, the two leading trade associations in Liverpool, for cotton and grain, did not rely on other organisations to house their trading activities. Eventually, they had their own venues: the Liverpool Cotton Exchange in Exchange Flags and the Liverpool Corn Exchange in Brunswick Street.[45] A special market for cotton developed relatively early and was the main exemplar for the development of international commodity markets in Britain.[46] Liverpool had become the most important cotton port in Britain, with the major cotton (textile/spinning) mills within sixty or eighty miles in Manchester and Lancashire connected to it by canals, rivers and later rail. Its pre-eminence as a port of entry was guaranteed once the United States became the major supplier to Britain of raw cotton. The industry comprised mainly small manufacturers who faced prices for cotton which fluctuated considerably with commercial circumstances, movements in fashion, rumour and war.

The Cotton Brokers' Association, formed in Liverpool in 1841, gradually functioned to regulate cotton trading. Until 1863 the association had no written rules and the thriving market was based on accepted practice, what lawyers would characterise as custom and usage. The massive speculation in cotton accompanying the American Civil War promoted the adoption of the first edition of 'The Constitution, Law, and Usages of the Liverpool Cotton Brokers Association'. A further version followed in 1869, and by 1878 there were printed contracts, with rules on the back, for American cotton.[47] The Cotton Brokers' Association merged with a rival Liverpool Cotton Exchange to

---

[42] H. Barty-King, Food for Man and Beast, op cit, 39–43; A. Coates, Commerce in Rubber, Singapore, Oxford University Press, 1987, 186. The Timber Trade Federation was already in existence: for its standard form contracts drawn up around this time: B. Latham, History of the Timber Trade Federation of the United Kingdom, London, Benn, 1965, 37, 54. See 304n below.

[43] US Department of Commerce, op cit, 63–64.

[44] Beetroot Sugar Association, Rules and Regulations, 4th ed., London, 1892, Constitution, II. (Kindly provided by D. G. Moon, Sugar Association of London.) The objects were 'to provide for the proper conduct [of the beetroot sugar trade], and particularly to provide rules for sampling, weighing, analysing, and for the supervision of these operations; and for the settlement of all differences that may arise in carrying out of Contracts'.

[45] 11, 363 below.   [46] S. Chapman, Merchant Enterprises in Britain, op cit, 76.

[47] 301 below.

become the Liverpool Cotton Association Ltd in 1882.[48] In the early 1920s the Liverpool cotton market was said to provide the central world market for raw cotton.[49] By 1939, however, the British cotton industry had collapsed, with exports a fifth of 1913 levels.[50]

After the American Civil War Liverpool became an important centre for imported grain as well as for cotton, for a period becoming the largest grain port in Europe. What became the Liverpool Corn Trade Association was formed in 1853 and in 1886 amalgamated with the Liverpool Corn Exchange.[51] It drew up standard form contracts and rules. More important in the interwar period were its future contracts. At its height in the 1930s, Liverpool had the leading international market in wheat futures. Trading was carried on in the association's newsroom. Although much smaller than the futures exchanges for grain in the United States, the Liverpool wheat market was acknowledged in American circles as having an international character compared with the largely domestic reach of their own markets.[52]

In addition to these markets for so-called soft commodities, the London Metal Exchange offered an organised market for trading in some of the 'hard' commodities, by then in great demand as a result of the Industrial Revolution in Europe and North America. Metal trading had occurred at the Royal Exchange in previous centuries, although in domestically produced copper and tin. The increasing volume of international trade during the nineteenth century was associated with the emergence of new metal broking firms. As in other markets forward dealings developed. In 1869 a specialised exchange for metals was agreed, which grew out of the regular meetings of metal dealers. The London Metal Exchange, as it became known, had its first meeting in 1877. It issued formal rules in July 1881, concerned largely with the constitution and conditions of membership. These were elaborated in the pre–First World War years.[53] With fluctuating success in the twentieth century, the London Metal Exchange is now said to be the largest futures exchange in metals in the world.[54]

The London and Liverpool markets facilitated the distribution of commodities not only through space with spot transactions for prompt delivery but also through time with forward and futures contracts. The telegraph in the second half of the nineteenth century, and the telephone from the early twentieth

---

[48] 'The Exchange', *Liverpool Review*, June 11, 1887, 10.
[49] J. Smith, *Organised Produce Markets*, London, Longmans Green & Co, 1922, 31.
[50] A. Kidd, *Manchester*, 3rd ed., Edinburgh, Edinburgh University Press, 2002, 187.
[51] *Liverpool Corn Trade Association 1853–1953*, Liverpool, Liverpool Corn Trade Association, 1953, 9, 11. See also G. Broomhall & J. Hubback, *Corn Trade Memories*. Liverpool, Northern Publishing, 1930, 1–19.
[52] 81 below.
[53] Economist Intelligence Unit, *A History of the London Metal Exchange*, EIU, London, 1958, 16, 31–36; R. Gibson-Jarvie, *The London Metal Exchange*, 2nd ed., Cambridge, Woodhead-Faulkner 1983, 9–13.
[54] J. Park & B. Lim, 'Testing Efficiency of the London Metal Exchange: New Evidence' (2018) 6 *Int'l J Fin Stud* 32, 32.

century, allowed international sales and the shipping to transport commodities to be organised from London and Liverpool offices.[55] Hedging on the markets enabled the producers of commodities in various parts of the world, and the manufacturers using them in Britain and further afield, to secure protection from risk. Although open to abuse, speculation in futures worked to level out the prices of commodities on and between markets.[56]

The international physical markets in London and Liverpool, and the brokers working there, tailed off after the Second World War with the changed pattern of international trade.[57] However, they left a legacy – infrastructure (at least in London) for the international futures and derivatives markets in commodities, as well as financial products, and the machinery for standard setting and dispute resolution in the international trade in grain, animal feed and cotton.[58] The contracts of LCTA's successor, the Grain and Feed Trade Association (Gafta), still govern international trading which is not conducted on private or in-house terms.[59] Despite the cotton industry's decline, the Liverpool Cotton Association also remains an international standard setter for trading through its Bylaws & Rules, but under the nomenclature adopted in 2004, the International Cotton Association.[60]

2 Agents, Trading Houses and Supplying Goods and Services

[T]ransactions so extensive between persons removed at great distances from each other could not be managed either so conveniently or so beneficially without the intervention of some third party between the principals in the contract. To conclude bargains with advantage, it is necessary to be always on the spot, to catch the favourable turns in the market; whilst on the other hand the superintendence of a large establishment forbids the frequent absence of the proprietor. Again, in foreign trade it is desirable, if not indispensably requisite, to have agents resident abroad, to receive consignments of goods exported, to dispose of them advantageously for the owner, to purchase and ship off such foreign commodities as he may want in return, and to make and receive the necessary payments and remittances. It may readily be supposed, therefore, that mercantile agents have long constituted a separate and important class. (*Law Magazine*, 1829)[61]

---

[55] R. Michie, 'The International Trade in Food and the City of London since 1850' (1996) 25 J *European Econ Hist* 369, 382. See also B. Lew & B. Cater, 'The Telegraph, Co-Ordination of Tramp Shipping, and Growth in World Trade 1870–1910' (2006) 10 *European Rev Econ Hist* 147.
[56] 87 below.
[57] D. Hill, 'The Impact of Trade Usage on Commercial Agency at Common Law', in *New Directions in International Trade Law*, Dobbs Ferry, New York, Oceana, 1977, vol. II, 530–531.
[58] 295 below.   [59] 317 below.
[60] A. Quark, *Global Rivalries: Standards Wars and the Transnational Cotton Trade*, Chicago, University of Chicago Press, 2013, 193–200.
[61] (1829) 1 *Law Magazine*, at 261–262.

Around the middle of the nineteenth century the consignment pattern for sales of imported commodities and exported textiles, mentioned in this extract, began to disappear.[62] No longer were trading houses simply consigned parcels of goods to sell on commission, at least to the same degree as previously. Rather, they were more involved in the sale and purchase of specific orders, acting to a greater extent on their own account, as well as performing additional functions such as conducting shipping, insurance and banking agencies, and managing as agents estates, mines and factories. In broad terms the changes coincided with the spread of new technology (communications, railways, steamships), institutional transformation (the growth of some overseas agents into larger trading houses) and the advent of new methods of financing trade, in particular the documentary credit.

Agency law was of almost equal importance to contract law as a legal device facilitating commercial activity during our period.[63] Occupying a range of different roles, agents were central to the functioning of commercial life and agency relationships were ubiquitous. What agents did and the functioning of agency law are explored at greater length in Chapter 3; what follows is an outline of the commercial picture.

(i) From Sale on Consignment to the Agency House and Beyond

In the first part of the nineteenth century agency came to the fore as a form of business organisation. Trading in raw cotton and cotton textiles is illustrative. Liverpool merchants obtained cotton from the United States either from those who forwarded it to them for sale on commission or through having agents purchase it on their behalf, perhaps on joint account. Commission-based imports to Liverpool declined from the 1860s with the improvements in communication brought about by the Atlantic cable. Instead of cotton being consigned for sale on commission, firm offers could be cabled to Liverpool merchants by their American branches or agents, or by independent sellers.[64] There was no longer the same need for expert advice from agents on prices, since the information was now more widely distributed by cable and business publications. In the cotton-growing areas of the southern United States, 'growers sold their cotton directly to merchants or mill agents,

---

[62] N. Miller, 'Bills of Lading and Factors in Nineteenth Century English Overseas Trade' (1957) 24 *U Chi LR* 256, 265–266.
[63] W. Müller-Freienfels, 'Law of Agency' (1957) 6 *Amer J Comp L* 165, 165.
[64] S. Beckert, *Empire of Cotton*, London, Penguin, 2015, 231; N. Hall, 'Liverpool's Cotton Importers c.1700–1914' (2017) 54 *Northern Hist* 79, 87–89; S. Chapman, *Merchant Enterprise in Britain*, op cit, 104–106, 151; S. Marriner, *Rathbones of Liverpool, 1845–73*, Liverpool, Liverpool University Press, 1961, 61–62, 110–112; A. Ellis, *Heir of Adventure: The Story of Brown, Shipley & Co., Merchant Bankers, 1810–1960*, London, Brown, Shipley 1960, 54–55; N. Buck, *The Development of the Organisation of Anglo-American Trade, 1800–1850*, New Haven, Yale University Press, 1925, 37–39, 41.

or even to foreign buyers, instead of entrusting it for sale to a factor in a distant port'.[65]

As the global trade in cotton was increasingly dominated by the large cotton exchanges in places like Liverpool, New York and New Orleans, the role for the old-fashioned importer, broker and factor diminished.[66] Accounts in the first part of the twentieth century identified three broad categories of intermediaries for getting the raw cotton to the textile mills of Lancashire: agents acting between the Southern exporters and the Liverpool importers; the Liverpool houses selling to the mills as principals or through brokers; and the brokers engaged by the spinning mills on commission to obtain suitable samples from which purchases could be made.[67] That picture was muddied in various ways: for example, cotton could also pass through Manchester brokers on its way to the mills, and some of the larger cotton mills bought directly from importing merchants or from US exporters through Liverpool brokers.

The other side of the coin from importing the raw cotton was the export of the manufactured cloth and shirtings (cloth for making shirts). In the first part of the nineteenth century the textile mills often marketed their products by sending consignments to various parts of the globe for sale through agents acting on commission. The methods in the 1840s of the Calcutta (Kolkata) firm Mackinnon Mackenzie & Co. offer an example. It had consignments of cotton and textiles – along with pig iron, iron rails and iron plates – forwarded to it by its associate firms, Wm Mackinnon & Co. in Glasgow and Mackinnon Frew & Co. in Liverpool. The goods were sent on a commission basis, but also on the firm's own account or on joint account with others.[68] A sideline to our story, but a crucial part of the subcontinent's history, was the devastating impact which the importation of machine-made cotton goods had on the livelihoods of the traditional Indian weavers.

By the middle of the nineteenth century, British exporters moved away from supplying textiles on consignment to places like India. Trading houses in those markets purchased on their own account as principals for onward sale, becoming independent intermediaries in the chain of distribution.[69] Better communications also transformed the dynamics of importing commodities to Britain from abroad. The head of a large Manchester firm, with a network of branches

---

[65] S. Beckert, Ibid., 318.   [66] Ibid., 320.
[67] M. Copeland, *The Cotton Manufacturing Industry of the United States*, Cambridge, MA, Harvard University Press, 1912, 354–355; A. Garside, *Cotton Goes to Market*, New York, Frederick A. Stokes, 1935, 116.
[68] J. Munro, *Maritime Enterprise and Empire. Sir William Mackinnon and his Business Network 1823–93*, Woodbridge, Suffolk, Boydell Press, 2003, 21, 24–26, 29–32. The firm also arranged for produce such as jute to be exported, some in vessels it owned, on the return voyage. This would be sold on commission by Mackinnon Frew & Co. in Liverpool or other firms such as Scott Bell & Co. in London. See also C. Jones, *International Business in The Nineteenth Century: The Rise and Fall of a Cosmopolitan Bourgeoisie*, Brighton, Wheatsheaf, 1987, 61–62.
[69] S. Chapman, Merchant Enterprise in Britain, *op cit*, 69–67, 85, 88–89, 98–99, 109–110, 136–138, 165, 298; S. Cunyngham-Brown, *The Traders*, London, Newham-Neame, 1971, 37–38;

Figure 1.1 Landing goods in Calcutta (Kolkata), India, 1860s ((c) The British Library Board).

in India, told a Royal Commission in 1887 that as a result of the telegram there were very few 'Manchester' (cotton) goods shipped to India for sale on consignment. He explained:

> We look from day to day at the price we can get for the produce in the currency of the country in which we sell it. We have everyday fluctuations in the rupee price, the rate of exchange and the rate of freight, and as the whole thing is worked by telegram, of course we practically stop operations if the margin is against us, until one of the three things gives way.[70]

Agency was not, however, eliminated. It still had a role in the sale and distribution of textile products in the early twentieth century, albeit to a decreasing degree. In one contemporary account a cloth agent selling the entire product of a spinning mill received 1 per cent commission, but 1½ or 2 per cent if it guaranteed the account. If it had only a partial agency, the agent received 2 per cent without a guarantee and 4 per cent with a guarantee.[71]

As with cotton, the arrangements for importing other commodities could also involve agency. Liverpool importers of wheat from California – for a time a key source for British millers – appointed agents, with a preference for exclusive agents, although in the case of firms like Balfour, Guthrie & Co. Ltd a branch was also opened in the state.[72] At one point coffee had been sent to London and Liverpool for sale by agents on consignment, but from the second half of the

---

[70] *First Report of the Royal Commission to Inquire into the Recent Changes in the Relative Values of the Precious Metals*, London, HMSO, 1887, 114, quoted in R. Ray, 'Asian Capital in the Age of European Domination: The Rise of the Bazaar 1800–1914' (1995) *Modern Asian Stud* 449, 478.

[71] M. Copeland, The Cotton Manufacturing Industry of the United States, *op cit*, 364–365.

[72] R. Paul, 'The Wheat Trade between California and the United Kingdom' (1958) 45 *Mississippi Valley Hist R* 391, 406–407.

nineteenth century importers had increased market power and appointed agents abroad who were able to control the market and set the prices where it was produced.[73] In London, commodity brokers acted as agents for foreign producers, and importers might appoint their own agents abroad, having authority to buy up to a certain limit and to supervise the shipping arrangements.[74]

(ii) The Trading Firm ('Agency' House) and Managing Agent

The term 'agency house' was used in some parts of the world to reflect how trading firms (trading houses) bought and sold goods on commission, as well as providing other agency services such as shipping, insurance and banking. '[T]he Agency House ... though primarily a trading house, also acted as bankers, bill-broker, ship-owner, freighter, insurance agent, purveyor etc.'[75] As well as acting as agent, these trading firms acted on their own account. In 1863 most of the Calcutta (Kolkata) trading firms had agency arrangements with London merchants. Twenty-six were also directly linked to business outside London through agencies in Liverpool, Manchester and Glasgow.[76]

Advances on sales might be made to manufacturers by a trading firm abroad or its British agent accepting bills of exchange drawn on them for payment. Once accepted, the bills could be discounted in the market with the proceeds used to pay the manufacturer's invoice.[77] Advances were relatively safe since the trading firm or its agent would have control of the goods through possession of the shipping documents, notably the bill of lading, which was the document of title representing the goods.[78] By the early twentieth century the larger trading houses would have departments for goods (perhaps styled 'Imports' for European manufactured goods; 'Produce' for exports). There would then be separate departments for agency business in shipping, insurance and banking.[79]

---

[73] S. Topik, *The World Coffee Market in The Eighteenth and Nineteenth Centuries, From Colonial to National Regimes*, Department of Economic History, London School of Economics and Political Science, Working Paper No. 04/04, 2004, 27.
[74] S. Dowling, The Exchanges of London, *op cit*, 156.
[75] M. Greenberg, *British Trade and the Opening of China 1800–42*, Cambridge, Cambridge University Press, 1951, 144. On shipping agents, e.g., S. Jones, *Two Centuries of Overseas Trading: The Origins and Growth of the Inchcape Group*, London, Macmillan, 1986, 45–46, 243–244; S. Ville, 'James Kirton, Shipping Agent' (1981) 67 *Mariners Mirror* 149; P. Davies, *Henry Tyrer : A Liverpool Shipping Agent and his Enterprise, 1879-1979*, London, Croom Helm, 1979; F. Hyde & J. Harris, *Blue Funnel : A History of Alfred Holt and Company of Liverpool from 1865 to 1914*, Liverpool, University Press, 1956.
[76] *Thacker's Bengal Directory 1863*, Calcutta, 1863, Part IX, Commercial, cited in J. Munro, Maritime Enterprise and Empire. Sir William Mackinnon and His Business Network 1823–1893, *op cit*, 16.
[77] e.g., *Swire v. Redman & Holt* (1876) 1 QBD 536. See Chapter 6.2, 1.
[78] R. Steffen and F. Danziger, 'The Rebirth of the Commercial Factor' (1936) 36 *Colum LR* 745, 769.
[79] e.g., Gray Mackenzie & Co, merchants and agents in the Persian Gulf: see 'Administrative History', LMA, CLC/B/123-31, Gray, Mackenzie and Company Ltd.

On the eve of the First World War a writer for the *British Export Gazette* explained that buying agents (sometimes called 'home commission agents'), working on commission, were frequently employed by trading firms abroad to obtain manufactured goods from Britain and elsewhere in Europe. The orders (indents) either specified the name of the manufacturer (say) from whom the goods were to be purchased or were open orders for specified goods, to be obtained from the best source.[80] In the interwar years London commission (or indent) houses still acted for foreign buyers in placing orders with British manufacturers.[81] In the late 1950s trading houses in Malaya (Malaysia) and Singapore still described themselves as 'general merchants and agents'. The merchant side comprised the import of construction and building materials, consumer items, estate supplies, engineering and electrical goods; the agency side included shipping, airlines, insurance, estates, mines and export sales.[82]

Another reason that the term 'agency house' survived was because British trading firms took on the role of managing businesses as agents. The managing agent system was a crucial, if now a largely forgotten, aspect of British services and investment funds being supplied abroad.[83] Managing agents had begun early on, as British merchants in India began investing in plantations of indigo, an important source of cotton dye, retaining tight control of the business even when there were other investors in the company being managed.[84] Later, estates growing tea, cotton and rubber; mines; cotton mills and factories; and utilities – all featured in the managing agent's repertoire.[85] The managing agent system became the prevalent feature of British mercantile enterprise in India, with a network of diversified businesses orbiting around the original trading firm.[86] The system was emulated in Hong Kong, Malaya (Malaysia), Singapore, South Africa, Persia (Iran) and elsewhere. The trading firm (agency house) was appointed as agent to manage members of the group, often after floating them on the stock exchanges in London or locally. Managing agents were the face of British economic power and direct investment in many colonial societies.

A distinctive feature of this form of business group was that control was retained through the appointment of the trading firm as the manager of the businesses in the investment group.[87] Those controlling it benefited from the management fees for the businesses being managed, from the

---

[80] F. Dudeney, *The Exporter's Handbook and Glossary*, London, Pitman & Sons, 1916, 36–44.
[81] *An Export Handbook*, London, Institute of Export, 1939, 34.
[82] J. Drabble and P. Drake, 'The British Agency Houses in Malaysia: Survival in a Changing World' (1981) 12 *J. Southeast Asian Stud.* 297, 304–306, 314.
[83] T. Roy & A. Swamy, *Law and the Economy in Colonial India*, Chicago, University of Chicago Press, 2016, 152–156; S. Metcalfe, 'The Structure and Evolution of an Operational Network: The Borneo Company Ltd, 1850–1919' (2000) 7 *Asia Pacific Bus Rev* 17, 33.
[84] T. Roy, 'Indigo and Law in Colonial India' (2011) 64 *Econ Hist Rev* 60, 62: P. Kumar, *Indigo Plantations and Science in Colonial India*, New York, Cambridge University Press, 2012, 83–84.
[85] G. Jones, *Merchants to Multinationals*, Oxford, Oxford University Press, 2000, 29–30, 52–53.
[86] Ibid., 30.   [87] Ibid., 51.

commissions earned on agency business in selling their goods and getting them to market, and from the dividends flowing from the shares held in them.[88] Agency and company law combined to facilitate managing the businesses in the interests of the controllers. For most of their history there was no special legislation for managing agents. However, since they represented foreign control, curbing their role became a platform of the independence movement in India, and to a lesser extent elsewhere. It did not assist the cause of managing agents that they had an advocacy role behind the scenes in matters of political economy.

3 Manufactured Goods, Distribution Methods and Infrastructure

Up to thirty years ago the engineering and machinery businesses of this country were to a great extent dependant for their overseas trade on the large merchant shipping houses which had their own branches in various parts of the world and bought and sold on commission … As a result the shipping houses got choked up with agencies … banking, shipping, exchange, insurance, and their own export business in raw materials … Accordingly an entirely new policy was adopted … [We established] overseas branches wherever the existing or prospective trade justified the expense. (Sir John Wormald, manufacturer, 1919)[89]

Distributing manufactured goods in the industrial age occurred in myriad ways; only a few are explored in Chapter 4. As we have just seen, the agent was a key player early on in distribution, then the independent intermediary who bought manufactured goods for their onward marketing as principal. As reflected in this quoted passage from a leading British industrialist of the early part of the twentieth century, a further stage was the British manufacturer utilising more direct methods by itself distributing products abroad. To some judicial annoyance, distributors did not always accommodate to the categories of the law. For marketing reasons some wore the mantle of 'agent', although they were not agents in the legal sense.

Sale, as we will see, was not the exclusive avenue for marketing the products of the industrial age. From the second half of the nineteenth century hire and hire purchase took on a significant role in this (Chapter 4.4). A further strand to distribution were the methods manufacturers and producers used to bind those distributing and marketing their products, including the price at which they could sell to others down the distribution chain (Chapter 4.5)

Before developing these points, a short digression on infrastructure is appropriate, since it was crucial to the efficient distribution of commodities and manufactured goods. It is not pursued in any detail in this book, which is concerned with transactions. However, there is frequent mention of one

---

[88] Ibid., 160.
[89] J. Wormald, 'The Export Trade of our Engineering & Machinery Business' (1919) 1 *Ways & Means* 237, 237. Wormald was managing director of Mather & Platt, Ltd, mechanical, electrical, and hydraulic engineers, Manchester.

important aspect of the infrastructure for trade, the ports. Goods moved across oceans by ship, first sail, but by the end of the nineteenth century that was largely supplanted by steam. Often the vessels were members of a shipping line, and the move to steam power meant that they could run to a timetable. The efficient loading and unloading of goods for export and of imported goods became an important issue in public policy. This led, in London, to an extensive building programme of docks in the early nineteenth century, and later their reorganisation and nationalisation, in effect, in the early twentieth century.[90] Docks were also constructed in other places like Liverpool.[91] Associated with the docks were large-scale wharves and warehouses, and railway and road connections. As well as warehousing goods, the docks performed extensive work necessary for the marketing and sale of goods, including through auctions.[92] By the end of our period containerisation, for one, had put paid to all of this.[93]

(i) Manufacturers and Distribution of their Products

Over time, larger British manufacturers reduced their reliance on trading firms abroad to distribute their products. From the end of the nineteenth century they were opening branches in foreign countries, sometimes with the dual role of both selling products and purchasing local raw materials for transmission to their factories at home.[94] The twentieth-century norm for larger businesses became forward integration and centralised control.[95] The corporate amalgamations of the interwar years led to a significant increase in the size of some British manufacturers, typified by Unilever and Imperial Chemical Industries.[96] Selling was undertaken by specialised sales departments within manufacturing firms, reducing their reliance on wholesalers and other intermediaries.[97] Given advances in communications, they might deal directly with customers abroad. They might even establish a direct presence abroad, cutting out the number of intermediaries needed to market their products.

---

[90] P. Stone, *The History of the Port of London*, Barnsley, Pen & Sword, 2017, 163–171; R. Cranston, 'Commercial Law and Commercial Lore', in J. Lowry & L. Mistelis (ed.), *Commercial Law: Perspectives and Practice*, London, Butterworths, 2006, 76–80.

[91] See T. Hunt, *Ten Cities that made an Empire*, London, Allen Lane, 2014, 389–391; S. Palmer, 'Ports', in M. Daunton (ed.), *The Cambridge Urban History of Britain*, Cambridge, Cambridge University Press, 2001, 140–146.

[92] On dock warrants covering warehoused goods: Chapter 6.2, 3.

[93] M. Levinson, *The Box: How the Shipping Container Made the World Smaller and the World Economy Bigger*, Princeton, Princeton University Press, 2016.

[94] P. Davies, *The Trade Makers. Elder Dempster in West Africa 1852–1972*, London, George Allen & Unwin, 1973, 30.

[95] C. Jones, International Business in The Nineteenth Century: The Rise and Fall of a Cosmopolitan Bourgeois, *op cit*, 184–185.

[96] 220 below.

[97] M. Thomas, 'The Service Sector', R. Floud & P. Johnson (ed.), *The Cambridge Economic History of Modern Britain Economic Maturity 1860–1939*, Cambridge, Cambridge University Press, 2004, 115.

British-based multinational companies also established manufacturing subsidiaries overseas, as well as sales and distribution networks. Courtauld was early in the field. In the first part of the twentieth century Samuel Courtauld & Co. appointed agents both at home and abroad to sell rayon, its new synthetic fibre. In 1908 it appointed an English merchant in New York as the exclusive agent, on a 1 per cent commission of net sterling receipts from US customers. Sixteen years later he became the president of the company's American subsidiary, American Viscose Corporation, which had factories in a number of states making rayon and other artificial fibres.[98] Other British companies followed suit. To find markets for their motor vehicles, processed foods and pharmaceuticals, as well as for intermediate goods such as chemicals, industrial gases and engineering products, they established factories abroad.[99]

None of this meant the complete demise of British manufacturers selling abroad through wholesalers or agents.[100] Many manufacturers were small and could not afford an employed salesforce for overseas markets. They continued to depend on agents, merchant importers and direct dealings.[101] In some cases, the continued use of agents reflected a failure to move with the times and to take marketing seriously. As well as complacency, the fate of the Sheffield cutlery industry after the Second World War has been attributed, in part, to its continued use of agents, who secured orders on commission but did not carry stocks or order on their own account. When competition arrived from foreign manufacturers like the Japanese, the industry therefore lacked the marketing tools to match it.[102]

---

[98] D. Coleman, *Courtaulds: An Economic and Social History, Rayon*, Oxford, Clarendon Press, 1969, vol. II, 67–68.

[99] see G. Jones, *Multinationals and Global Capitalism: From the Nineteenth to the Twenty First Century*, Oxford, Oxford University Press, 2004, 21–24, 173, 194–195, 232; B. Tomlinson, *The Economy of Modern India: From 1860 to the Twenty-First Century*, 2nd ed., Cambridge, Cambridge University Press, 2013, 122; E. Jones, *A History of GKN The Growth of a Business 1918-1945*, Basingstoke, Macmillan, 1990, 34–35; M. Wilkins, 'European and North American Multinationals, 1870–1914: Comparisons And Contrasts' (1988) 30 *Bus Hist* 8, 15–16; S. Nicholas, 'Agency Contracts, Institutional Modes, and the Transition to Foreign Direct Investment by British Manufacturing Multinationals before 1939' (1983) 43 *Journal of Economic History* 675; W. Reader, *Imperial Chemical Industries: A History*, London, Oxford University Press, 1975, 33–36; C. Wilson, *The History of Unilever*, London, Cassell & Co, 1954, vol. I, 102–103.

[100] e.g., *Heyman v. Darwins Ltd* [1942] AC 356 (Sheffield manufacturer used New York agent to sell its tool steels – for making into tools – under a 1938 agreement).

[101] P. Payne, *British Entrepreneurship in the Nineteenth Century*, 2nd ed., Basingstoke, Macmillan Education, 1988, 41, 51.

[102] G. Tweedale, *The Sheffield Knife Book*, Sheffield, Hallamshire Press, 1996, 135. cf. S-A. Taylor, *Tradition and Change: The Sheffield Cutlery Trades 1870-1914*, PhD thesis, University of Sheffield, 1988, 101–102. See also G. Tweedale, 'English versus American Hardware: British Marketing Techniques and Business Performance in the USA in the Nineteenth and Early-Twentieth Centuries', in R. Davenport-Hines (ed.), *Markets and Bagmen: Studies in the History of Marketing and British Industrial Performance 1830-1939*, Aldershot, Gower, 1986, 73–74.

(ii) Sale, Hire and Distribution Networks

With manufactured goods the distributor might be labelled as the manufacturer's 'agent', with the marketing advantages of a reputation and brand – and possibly also an access to spare parts and the authorised provision of after-sales services – which this conferred. In legal terms the 'agent' was in fact an independent intermediary who obtained the goods from the manufacturer and then dealt with its own customers as principal. In other words there were at least two contracts, a sale (say) between the manufacturer and the 'agent', and a sale or hiring between the 'agent' and its customers. The motor-vehicle dealer, labelled as the manufacturer's 'agent', was an example. It was also with products like motor vehicles that new techniques for financing their distribution emerged. For the dealer, the manufacturer might arrange inventory finance, provided by means of various types of stocking plan; for the ultimate customer, credit might be provided by means of hire or hire purchase. Chapter 4 covers hire and hire purchase as important legal devices in the narrative about the distribution of manufactured goods to commercial parties as well as consumers.

Another part of this narrative is how manufacturers and producers used their market power to control those in the distribution chain. At the international level they might allocate geographic areas, giving distributors the exclusive right to sell there. At a time of European empires, an allocated area might encompass the territory of both the metropolitan power and its colonies.[103] A range of factors would determine the prices at which distributors obtained the goods from the manufacturer or producer. Discounts could turn, for example, on whether a distributor arranged for payment against shipping documents, perhaps under a documentary credit. Under their contract distributors might be contractually obliged to 'push' the manufacturer's products (or use reasonable or best efforts in marketing them) and have their endeavours monitored. The ultimate sanction against bad performance was termination of the distributorship.

Control over those in the distribution chain was heightened at the domestic level. As well as distributors being confined to an allocated area, they might have to sell a manufacturer's products at set prices and their marketing efforts might have to proceed along strict lines. Controls over marketing might descend into the details of how the product was to be displayed, whether the products of other manufacturers could be marketed alongside, servicing obligations and the availability of spare parts, and a distributor's opening hours.[104] Resale price maintenance – a common tool in the British manufacturer's distribution toolbox – was virulent in the first part of the twentieth century and only gradually began to wither at the end of our period under the force of legislation.[105]

---

[103] 270 below. [104] 272, 274, 278 below.
[105] B. Yamey, *Resale Price Maintenance*, London, Weidenfeld & Nicolson, 1966. See 273–274 below.

4 Banks, Banking and the Finance of Trade and Industry

With the emergence of the joint-stock banking in 1830s, historians observe that the physical image of banking and its symbolical capital changed ... London and Westminster [Bank]'s headquarters, built in 1838, embodied symbols of power and authority in London's city space. Ambitious building of bank headquarters continued into the twentieth century. Midland [Bank] commissioned new head offices (built between 1924 and 1939) for what was, at the time, the world's largest clearing bank, ensuring that the design of the building reflected the bank's status. (Victoria Barnes and Lucy Newton, 2019)[106]

Reflecting the advanced state of its economy and the position of the City of London as the world's leading financial centre, by the end of the nineteenth century Britain's banking system was large and diversified.[107] Capital was accumulated and allocated for use around the globe. Merchant banks like the Rothschilds and the Barings were already engaged at the beginning of our period in organising the funding of governments and, by mid-century, in mobilising capital for American railways and similar infrastructure projects there and around the world.[108] Critical to our story was that the merchant banks throughout our period also financed international trade by accepting bills of exchange, thereby assuming primary liability for paying on them when they matured (the acceptance business). As a result, exporters could be paid as soon as goods were shipped, and importers obtained credit until closer in time to when they in turn were paid by those to whom they marketed the goods.

By the beginning of the twentieth century, joint stock banks like the London and Westminster Bank, the Midland Bank and the National Provincial Bank had grown enormously from their beginnings in the 1820s and 1830s. They had overtaken the private banks and made symbolic statements about their achievements (as Victoria Barnes and Lucy Newton describe in the passage quoted) in the size and elaborate architecture of their head offices in the City of London. At the same time they began to have a significant international reach. Partly it was through what they did as bankers, moving in on the merchant banks' acceptance business to finance international trade. Partly it was also through establishing an international presence, initially by the agency and correspondent relationships they forged around the world to service customers. By 1914, for example, the London City and Midland Bank (which became

---

[106] V. Barnes & L. Newton, 'Symbolism in Bank Marketing and Architecture: The Headquarters of National Provincial Bank of England' (2019) 14 *Management & Org Hist* 213–244, 214, 221 (notes omitted). See also I. Black, 'Rebuilding "The Heart of the Empire": Bank Headquarters in the City of London 1919–1939' (1999) 22 *Art History* 593; V. Barnes & L. Newton, 'Visualizing Organizational Identity: The History of a Capitalist Enterprise' (2018) 13 *Management & Org Hist* 24.

[107] R. Michie, *British Banking: Continuity and Change from 1694 to the Present*, Oxford, Oxford University Press, 2016, 92.

[108] 376, 438 below. See also R. Cranston, 'Globalization: Its Historical Context', in S. Worthington (ed.), *Commercial Law and Commercial Practice*, Hart Publishing, Oxford, 2003.

part of Hongkong and Shanghai Banking Corporation (HSBC)) had forty-five correspondent banks in the United States alone.[109] After 1914 the joint stock banks began to have a direct presence abroad through establishing branches, taking shareholdings in foreign banks and making other service arrangements with them.[110]

In keeping with the transactional focus of the book, the discussion in Chapter 6 is about how the banking system as a whole, rather than individual parts of it, went about financing international trade and British industry. An appreciation of the institutional background, however, throws some light on the transactional side. What follows, therefore, sketches a little more of the background to the important banking institutions of our period, the merchant banks and the joint stock banks. There is also brief mention of the finance houses, responsible for the hire purchase boom of the twentieth century, with their history in the nineteenth. In addition to the merchant banks, joint stock banks and the finance houses, there were a variety of other institutions which had a bearing on the financing of trade and industry. In Chapter 6 we examine just two, the money market and the clearing system for bank payments, to illustrate the wider financial architecture of which these banking and financial institutions were part.

(i) The Merchant Banks

As their name suggests, the merchant banks began life as merchants as well as bankers. Thus, the Barings and the Rothschilds traded commodities internationally, both on their own account and through agents.[111] The Barings dealt in a wide range of goods, making advances to induce overseas merchants to send consignments through the firm.[112] For example, in the 1830s the Second Bank of the United States authorised agents to purchase cotton and to ship it to Barings Brothers & Co. in Liverpool.[113] N. M. Rothschild & Sons was choosier than Barings, attempting to dominate in particular commodities such as cotton, tobacco and sugar from the Americas, and copper from Russia. Rothschild tended to deal through partners and salaried agents in key markets such as New Orleans, Havana and St Petersburg.[114] As well as finance, George Peabody & Co. (whose business became J.P. Morgan & Co. after Peabody's

---

[109] R. Cameron & V. Bovykin, *International Banking 1870–1914*, New York, Oxford University Press, 1991, 245.
[110] G. Jones, *British Multinational Banking 1830–1990*, Oxford, Oxford University Press, 1995, 78–79, 138–156.
[111] S. Chapman, *The Rise of Merchant Banking*, London, Allen & Unwin, 1984, 18–19, 32, 34, 38.
[112] P. Ziegler, *The Sixth Great Power Barings 1762–1929*, London, Collins, 1998, 131; J. Orbell, *Baring Brothers & Co, Limited. A History to 1939*, London, Baring Brothers & Co Ltd, 1985, 30–33; J. Hidy, *The House of Baring in American Trade and Finance*, Cambridge, Mass, Harvard University Press, 1949, 102–106, 189–190, 360–361.
[113] W. Buckingham Smith, *Economic Aspects of the Second Bank of the United States*, Cambridge, Mass, Harvard University Press, 1953, 196.
[114] N. Ferguson, *The World's Banker: The History of the House of Rothschild*, London, Weidenfeld & Nicolson, 1998, 293, 297.

retirement) had been dealing in American grain and the China trade. In 1849 it began to engage directly in the export trade from Britain of iron rails for American railways. Peabody's rationale was that the profits on exporting the rails exceeded what he could make in financing the transactions.[115] Early on J. Henry Schroder & Co. specialised in the Baltic trade, for example receiving tallow on consignment from St Petersburg.[116] A number of other merchant banks such as Kleinwort Sons & Co. and Antony Gibbs & Sons continued to have trading arms throughout the nineteenth century.[117]

From the perspective of the merchant banks, banking and trading were intertwined. To others the merchant banks offered trade credit by lending their names to bills of exchange drawn by exporters which would pay for their goods. Given their reputation, if a merchant bank accepted a bill of exchange (by writing this on its face), that meant the bill could be readily sold (discounted) in the money market either in London or abroad. The bills might be issued under letters of credit. This financing of trade through bills of exchange was the so-called acceptance business, which from the mid-1820s began with British trade with Europe and the United States.[118] What became known as the Bill on London – a bill of exchange accepted by one of the first-class London banks, payable in London in pounds sterling – became the benchmark for financing international trade. When Britain was under the gold standard the pound sterling became the reserve currency of the world, literally convertible into gold.[119] Closely related to the acceptance business was the exchange business – in other words, dealing in bills of exchange to take account of the differences in currencies between London and elsewhere. For example, a bill of exchange might be drawn in pounds sterling, but the exporter might want payment in the local currency, say the Indian rupee. Until the 1870s, the leading merchant bankers gathered twice weekly at the Royal Exchange to settle the rates of exchange for bills and currencies. When the Rothschilds and the Barings decided that there were more profitable outlets for their activities, other merchant banks such as Samuel Montagu & Co. became foreign exchange and arbitrage specialists.[120]

As well as the acceptance business, the merchant banks assisted in securities issues. Hence, they were sometimes called 'issue houses'.[121] Early in the

---

[115] K. Burk, *Morgan Grenfell 1838–1988: The Biography of a Merchant Bank*, Oxford, Oxford University Press, 1989, 14.

[116] R. Roberts, *Schroders*, Basingstoke, Macmillan, 1992, 36, 38.

[117] S. Diaper, *The History of Kleinwort Sons & Co in Merchant Banking 1855–1961*, PhD thesis, University of Nottingham, 1983, 254–256; G. Jones, *Merchants to Multinationals*, Oxford, Oxford University Press, 2000, 53,

[118] Y. Cassis & P. Cottrell, *Private Banking in Europe: Rise, Retreat, and Resurgence*, Oxford, Oxford University Press, 2015, 122.

[119] C. Schenk, 'Sterling and Monetary Policy 1870–2010' in R. Floud, J. Humphries & P. Johnson (eds.), *The Cambridge History of Modern Britain Growth and Decline 1870 to the Present*, 2nd ed., Cambridge, Cambridge University Press, 2014, 450–451.

[120] S. Chapman, The Rise of Merchant Banking, op cit, 47. See T. Moxon, *English Practical Banking*, 15th ed., Manchester, John Heywood, 1910, 39, 43–44.

[121] R. Roberts, 'What's in a Name? Merchants, Merchant Bankers, Accepting Houses, Issuing Houses, Industrial Bankers and Investment Bankers' (1993) 35 *Business Hist* 22.

nineteenth century, those like the Rothschilds and the Barings had been appointed by foreign states for the issue of government bonds.[122] Other merchant banks followed, along with a few mavericks like Parr's Bank Ltd, an expanding joint stock bank, which assisted with Japanese government issues in the early twentieth century.[123] As well as government bonds, the merchant banks became involved in the issue, underwriting and marketing of corporate shares and bonds. In the nineteenth century this was mainly for companies operating abroad, such as American railways, although in the early twentieth century the Barings organised some domestic issues and took investments (both for itself and customers) in developments like the London tramways and underground railway, and the Liverpool docks.[124] After the First World War the merchant banks turned to domestic issues as international business dried up. The company amalgamations and rationalisations of the 1920s and 1930s were a source of opportunities.[125] It was at this point that their role in proffering corporate advice became an important avenue of activity. Morgan Grenfell was a leader in this with its role in the acquisition of Vauxhall Motors by General Motors in 1925.[126] Following the Second World War exchange controls remained in place and there was a decline in the acceptance business. The advent of the hostile takeover in the late 1950s filled the gap.[127] From the 1960s there was further expansion for the merchant banks with unit and investment trusts, insurances broking, asset finance, venture capital and, of major significance, a resurgence of international issues and international lending with the arrival of the Euromarkets.

(ii) The Joint Stock Banks and the Finance Houses

Merchant banking was well established when the joint stock banks arrived on the scene. Unlike the merchant banks their focus, at least initially, was domestic banking as rivals to the private banks, which predated them. The joint stock banks were a creation, it seems almost accidental, of nineteenth-

---

[122] M. Flandreau & J. Flores, 'Bonds and Brands: Foundations of Sovereign Debt Markets, 1820–1830' (2009) 69 *J Econ Hist* 646, 656–675; F. Dawson, *The First Latin American Debt Crisis; The City of London and the 1822–25 Loan Bubble*, Princeton, Princeton University Press, 1990.

[123] RBS, Parr's Bank Ltd, PAB/135, 4% loan agreement to Japanese government, 1899.

[124] e.g., V. Carosso & R. Carosso, *The Morgans: Private International Bankers 1854–1913*, Cambridge, Mass, Harvard University Press, 1987, 222–223, 488; P. Ziegler, *The Sixth Great Power Barings 1762–1929*, London, Collins, 1988, 287–288.

[125] J. Grady & M. Weale, *British Banking 1960–85*, Basingstoke, Macmillan, 1986, 97. See also S. Diaper, 'Merchant Banking in the Inter-War Period: The Case of Kleinwort, Sons & Co' (1986) 28 *Business Hist* 55, 56–60.

[126] K. Burk, *Morgan Grenfell 1838–1988: The Biography of a Merchant Bank*, Oxford, Oxford University Press, 1989, 92–93. See D. Ross, 'Industrial and Commercial Finance in the Interwar Years', in R. Floud & P. Johnson (eds.), *The Cambridge Economic History of Modern Britain Economic Maturity, 1860–1939*, Cambridge, Cambridge University Press, 2004, 424.

[127] e.g., N. Ferguson, *High Financier: The Lives and Time of Siegmund Warburg*, London, Allen Lane, 2010; R. Cranston, 'The Rise and Rise of the Hostile Takeover', in K. Hopt & E. Wymeersch (eds.), *European Takeovers: Law and Practice*, London, Butterwort, 1992.

century statute.[128] At least for a time, there was intense rivalry with the private banks. An Act of 1826 enabled unlimited liability joint stock banks outside a sixty-five miles radius of London.[129] The Bank Charter Act 1833 allowed such joint stock banks also to be established in London.[130] Large numbers of joint stock banks were formed, and thus the possibility of a system of national banking. An attempt to restrict them, through curtailing their right to issue bank notes, was contained in the Bank Charter Act 1844.[131] Further legislation in 1858 and 1862 allowed them to assume the mantle of limited liability.[132]

It was outside London that the Industrial Revolution had its base, and it was there that an extensive network of private and joint stock banks existed, so-called country banking. These were sometimes established by local industrialists intent on making money, providing payment services and financing their businesses.[133] They linked to London banks and others through agency arrangements. There was no love lost between the private and joint stock banks. For a while the private banks excluded the joint stock banks from the London Bankers' Clearing House. But the deposits of the joint stock banks grew, and in the final decades of the nineteenth century the private banks transformed into joint stock banks or loitered for a while as smaller rivals to them.[134] In part as a reaction to the 1844 restrictions, the joint stock banks had continued to establish branches. By the end of the century these had become relatively large national networks, constituting the core of their banking business.[135] Bank amalgamations which began in the 1880s culminated in 1918 in a domestic banking market dominated by five of the joint stock banks – Lloyds, Barclays, Midland, National Provincial and Westminster – all with extensive branch networks.[136] This combination of growth and amalgamation had transformed them into powerful financial institutions, which they remained for the rest of our period.

---

[128] V. Barnes & L. Newton, *The Introduction of the Joint-Stock Company in English Banking and Monetary Policy*, Discussion Paper, Henley Business School, September 2016.

[129] Banking Co-partnership Act 1826, 7 Geo. IV c. 46. The term 'joint stock' was because a number of individuals ('joint') held shares (stock) in the bank's capital. At this point there was no limited liability.

[130] 3 & 4 Wm IV, c. 98. [131] 7 & 8 Vic, c. 113, ss.10–12.

[132] M. Collins, *Money and Banking in the UK: A History*, London, Croom Helm, 1988, 51–56; B. Anderson & P. Cottrell, *Money and Banking in England: The Development of the Banking System 1694–1914*, Newton Abbot, David and Charles, 1974, 241–250.

[133] L. Pressnell, *Country Banking in the Industrial Revolution*, Oxford, Clarendon Press, 1956, 13–36; S. Jones, 'The Cotton Industry and Joint-Stock Banking in Manchester 1825–1850' (1978) 20 *Business Hist* 165.

[134] R. Michie, British Banking: Continuity and Change from 1694 to the Present, Oxford, *op cit*, 38–39; Y. Cassis & P. Cottrell, *Private Banking in Europe: Rise, Retreat and Resurgence*, Oxford, Oxford University Press, 2015, 167–170. By 1909 there were only two private banks remaining in the City of London: Y. Cassis, *City Bankers 1890–1914*, Cambridge, Cambridge University Press, 1994, 15n.

[135] V. Barnes & L. Newton, 'How Far Does the Apple Fall From The Tree? The Size of English Bank Branch Networks in the Nineteenth Century' (2018) 60 *Business Hist* 447, 459, 466.

[136] M. Billings, S. Mollan & P. Garnett, 'Debating Banking in Britain: The Colwyn committee 1918', Business History, DOI: 10.1080/00076791.2019.1593374.

In the nineteenth century, the main functions of the joint stock banks were to facilitate their customers' payments, to make short-term advances and, later, to take and keep safe their deposits. An efficient payments system was especially important. Inland bills of exchange and the banks' own bank notes facilitated payments in the first part of the nineteenth century. But the system still fell short. In the mid-nineteenth century, for example, obligations between members on the Liverpool Cotton Exchange were being directly settled in cash and gold.[137] The use of inland bills declined, and, as we have seen, the 1844 Act limited the banks in issuing their own notes. Cheques and Bank of England notes, which had become legal tender in 1833 for sums above five pounds, began to dominate.[138] In the second half of the nineteenth century and until the end of our period the cheque became the commonly used instrument for commercial payment domestically.[139]

As for bank advances, these were primarily for short-term, not long-term, capital purposes. Most British industries in the nineteenth century were modest in size; the services of the merchant banks for securities issues were simply not appropriate, although by the end of our period the picture was different. For working capital, however, industry could turn to a bank, or at least its branch at the local level, which might provide an overdraft facility, or perhaps a loan. Before the amalgamation movement in banking took hold at the end of the nineteenth century, the acceptance business was not regarded as the work of the joint stock banks, although Liverpool banks like the Liverpool Union Bank began accepting bills in the 1880s.[140] Then in the early twentieth century the larger joint stock banks, at least in London, became rivals to the merchant banks in offering their customers trade finance and foreign exchange services.[141] The issuing business remained with the merchant banks. For example, in the interwar period Barclays occasionally underwrote issues for first-class borrowers, but it was usually content to refer customers wanting to raise capital through shares or debenture issues to a merchant bank.[142]

Standing apart from the banks were the finance houses. These took various forms, but one type in the twentieth century provided what today is called 'asset finance', in other words credit secured on the asset being financed. Asset

---

[137] A. Ellis, *Heir of Adventure The Story of Brown, Shipley & Co Merchant Bankers 1810–1960*, London, Brown, Shipley & Co, 1960, 60. A former partner of that firm recalled: 'I have seen a long row of boys from brokers' offices, with bags of gold on their shoulders and Bank of England notes in their pocket-books, waiting to make their settlements with our cashier.' Cash payment through the post was by cutting notes in half and sending the halves by different post: ibid., 112.

[138] Bank Notes Act 1833, s.6.   [139] 389 below.

[140] A. Wilson, *Banking Reform*, London, Longmans, Green & Co, 1879, 168; S. Chapman, Merchant Enterprise in Britain: From the Industrial Revolution to World War I, *op cit*, 212; T. Gregory, *The Westminster Bank through a Century*, London, Oxford University Press, 1936, vol. I, 263.

[141] P. Cottrell, 'Domestic Finance, 1860–1914', in R. Floud & P. Johnson (eds.), *The Cambridge Economic History of Modern Britain* Economic Maturity, 1860–1939, op cit, 275; D. Kynaston, *The City of London The Golden Years 1890–1914*, London, Pimlico, 1995, 293; C. Goodhart, *The Business of Banking 1891–1914*, London, Weidenfeld and Nicolson, 1972, 136.

[142] M. Ackrill & L. Hannah, *Barclays: The Business of Banking 1690–1996*, Cambridge, Cambridge University Press, 2000, 97–98.

finance began in the nineteenth century as hire and deferred (hire) purchase. Some of these finance houses had their origin in the railway wagon companies, which from the late 1850s built and repaired wagons for use on the railways and provided them to customers on hire and hire purchase. The British Wagon Company provided hire purchase for motor vehicles and lorries in the interwar years, as did the Birmingham Wagon Company.[143] Perhaps the best example is the North Central Wagon Company, which began business in 1861, incorporated in 1894 and, in the twentieth century as the North Central Wagon and Finance Company Ltd, became an important provider of hire purchase and leasing (hire) facilities for motor vehicles and lorries.[144] In time, it became Lombard North Central (after amalgamating with Lombard Bank) and part of National Westminster Bank.[145] It was not the only finance house to be acquired by a bank.[146] At the end of our period Lombard North Central was a provider of asset finance, leasing items such as aircraft, ships and petrochemical works.

In addition to the wagon companies, new finance houses appeared on the scene.[147] One of the most important, United Dominions Trust (UDT), began in 1919 as a branch of Continental Guaranty Corporation of New York. It was acquired by British interests in 1923.[148] It concluded agreements in the 1920s with Austin Motor Company and Morris Motors to finance their vehicles on hire purchase, and agreements with other motor vehicle manufacturers followed. The UDT credit facility with Morris was partly financed by the company itself, which had a veto over who was to be given hire purchase contracts.[149] Most hire purchase for motor vehicles was accounted for by UDT and the other finance houses, but in London some of the large car dealers operated their own hire purchase schemes.[150] In the post–Second World War

---

[143] see *Staffs Motor Guarantee Ltd* v. *British Wagon Company Ltd* [1934] 2 KB 305; J. Hypher, C. Wheeler & S. Wheeler, *Birmingham Railway Carriage & Wagon Company*, Cheltenham, Runpast Publishing, 1995, 5–8.

[144] e.g., *North [Central] Wagon & Finance Co Ltd* v. *Graham* [1950] 2 KB 7 (the company is incorrectly named in the official report); *North Central Wagon Finance Co Ltd* v. *Brailsford* [1962] 1 WLR 1288.

[145] R. Reed, *National Westminster Bank: A Short History*, London, National Westminster Bank, 1983. In the post–Second World War period Lombard Bank had offered credit facilities for household, leisure and other consumer goods.

[146] *Report of the Committee on the Working of the Monetary System*, Cmnd 827,1959, 74 (the Radcliffe Report).

[147] R. Harris, *Hire Purchase in a Free Society*, 3rd ed., London, Hutchinson, 1961, 24.

[148] *United Dominions Trust Ltd* v. *Kirkwood* [1966] 1 QB 783, 790–791 (on appeal [1966] 2 QB 431, upholding the finding that it was carrying on a banking business within section 6(d) of the Moneylenders Act 1900 and so need not be registered under that Act as a moneylender: see 55 below).

[149] P. Scott, *The Market Makers: Creating Mass Markets for Consumer Durables in Inter-war Britain*, Oxford, Oxford University Press, 2017, 279.

[150] Ibid., 280–281. See also *Transport and General Credit Corporation Ltd* v. *Morgan* [1939] Ch 531 (subsidiary of company selling radios formed to offer hire purchase to customers).

period controls over lending by the finance houses were used by the government as an instrument of monetary control. Industrial output of consumer durables was adversely affected when the tap was turned down.[151]

(iii) Financial Architecture

The merchant banks, joint stock banks and finance houses were important parts of Britain's financial architecture during our period. Other parts of that architecture, ensuring before the First World War London's role as the world's leading financial and commercial centre, included Lloyds of London (the insurance market), the Baltic Exchange (as a shipping market) and the London Stock Exchange. At the centre, and an essential part of Britain's wider history, was the Bank of England.

The Bank of England was a private institution until 1946, and as such it had private customers and occasionally rubbed up against other financial interests in competition with it. The Bank was especially troubled in the first part of the nineteenth century by the competitive threat from the newly founded joint stock banks. In 1837, for example, it resorted to law and obtained an injunction against the London and Westminster Bank accepting demand bills and bills with maturities of less than six months, which it regarded as its privilege to handle in London. The injunction lasted until the 1844 Act.[152] Despite public criticism, the Bank also refused to open an account for the new bank or to discount bills payable there. However, in the second half of the nineteenth century there was a general expectation that the Bank of England would act in the national, not in its private, interest. In 1890 it averted any wider financial crisis when leading the rescue of Barings, which as a result of the failure of its Argentinian interests had thought itself unable to carry on business.[153] The Bank's special status derived from its position as the government's bank, the monopoly provider of banknotes[154] and the backstop in providing accommodation in times of financial stress.[155] By the time of the First World War the Bank's function as the lender of last resort was confirmed.[156]

---

[151] P. Scott & J. Walker, 'The Impact of 'Stop-Go' Demand Management Policy on Britain's Consumer Durables Industries 1952–65' (2017) 70 *Econ Hist Rev* 1321.

[152] *Governor and Company of the Bank of England v. Anderson* (1837) 2 Keen 328, 48 ER 655. See D. Kynaston, *Till Time's Last Sand: A History of the Bank of England 1694–2013*, London, Bloomsbury, 2017, 130; T. Gregory, *The Westminster Bank*, London, Oxford University Press, 1936, vol. I, 150; J. Slinn, *A History of Freshfields*, London, Freshfields, 1984, 83. (Freshfields acted as the Bank's solicitors.)

[153] Among accounts of the crisis: D. Kynaston, Till Time's Last Sand: A History of the Bank of England 1694–2013, op cit, 226–232; R. Vasudevan, 'Quantitative Easing through the Prism of the Barings Crisis in 1890' (2014) *J Post Keynesian Econ* 91. On its causes e.g., P. Vedoveli, 'Information Brokers and the Making of the Baring Crisis, 1857–1890' (2018) 25 *Financial Hist Rev* 357.

[154] Eventually, the banks still issuing bank notes under the Bank Charter Act 1844 forfeited their right altogether.

[155] see S. Battilossi, 'Money Markets', in Y. Cassis, R. Grossman & C. Schenk (eds.), *The Oxford Handbook of Banking and Financial History*, Oxford, Oxford University Press, 2016, 224–229.

[156] 443, 449 below.

In the money market the Bank of England acted primarily through the discount houses, which bought and sold acceptances (bills of exchange accepted by a first-class London bank) and took surplus funds from the banks on a short-term (often overnight) basis.[157] From 1864 the Bank became a member of the Bankers' Clearing House. The clearing house functioned to short-circuit the payment process for the banks. They no longer needed to pay individually each cheque or other payment order but could set off with other banks all the payment orders received in a day. Members of the clearing house held accounts with the Bank of England so that, at end of the day, they were able to settle across the Bank's books the net amounts they owed the others. These accounts with the Bank provided the banking sector with a source of liquidity.

1.3 Legal Context: Principles, Practices and Realities

> ... the late Vice-Chancellor, Sir William Page Wood, afterwards Lord Chancellor Hatherley, made the order to take the Agra and Masterman's Bank out of liquidation nearly six months after its stoppage. I remember on that occasion a charming old solicitor, a neighbour of ours in Old Jewry, before the case came on, using every argument he could ... to induce me to abandon what he considered the absolutely hopeless attempt, he being instructed on behalf of some of the Indian banks ... but the evidence we brought forward was so overwhelming as to the view and wishes of both creditors and shareholders that the Vice-Chancellor was persuaded into make the order. I afterwards called upon my solicitor friend and neighbour and consoled with him ... [H]e said to me: 'Oh Morris, I see now how you did it – the law was dead against you but you went to the poor man's heart!' (John Morris, solicitor, Ashurst Morris Crisp & Co., 1903)[158]

There were a number of principles animating English commercial law during our period. The basal principle was freedom of contract. One dimension to this was that commercial parties (and others) should be held to their bargains. As the *Law Times* expressed the principle in 1870, absent fraud or misrepresentation 'an adamantine degree of hardness in a contract is no ground for relief'.[159] Just because the turn of events bore heavily on a party, or circumstances significantly changed to a party's detriment, was no

---

[157] R. Michie, British Banking: Continuity and Change from 1694 to the Present, *op cit*, 111–112.
[158] LMA/4537/F/10/005, Ashurst Morris Crisp and Company, Report of proceedings at John Morris's 80th birthday celebration, 11–12. Morris was a leading City of London solicitor in the second half of the nineteenth century: J. Slinn, *Ashurst Morris Crisp: A Radical Firm*, Cambridge, Granta, 1997, 55; I. Doolittle, *Ashurst Morris Crisp*, London, Ashurst Morris Crisp, n.d., 8–9; C. Jones, *International Business in the Nineteenth Century: The Rise and Fall of a Cosmopolitan Bourgeoisie*, Brighton, Wheatsheaf, 1987, 173, 239–240.
[159] e.g., 'Unconscionable Bargains' (1870) 49 *LT* 223, 223. This is one of many such statements: see e.g., 'Unreasonable Contracts' (1884) 48 *JP* 401. See also C. Macmillan, 'Contract Terms between Unequal Parties in Victorian England', in L. Gullifer & S. Vogenauer (eds.), *English and European Perspectives on Contract and Commercial Law: Essays in Honour of Hugh Beale*, Oxford, Hart Publishing, 2014.

justification to intervene.[160] As important for commercial law was another dimension to freedom of contract, party autonomy. As a result of party autonomy, commercial parties could design, in a largely unfettered manner, the arrangements they desired for their individual transactions, the standards and standard form contracts for their regular dealings, and the rules for the organised markets, institutions and dispute resolution procedures behind them. It was private law-making writ large, within a benign framework of state law.[161] But it was not law without the state. English law took the view – as expressed by one of the leading commercial judges – that there could be 'no Alsatia in England where the King's writ does not run'.[162]

The second principle was certainty.[163] To put it another way, commercial law should comprise bright-line rules which traders, merchants, brokers and bankers could readily understand and apply in commercial practice. This ensured that parties could not only plan for their future relationship but also, as Lord Sumner put it on one occasion, 'gather their fate then and there' if things went wrong.[164] If a rule did not meet commercial needs, the principle also meant that there could be a clear expression of what otherwise was required. This ready ability to correct matters was also a corollary of party autonomy. Both principles meant that if legal doctrine proved an obstacle to commercial or financial dealings, commercial parties were able to draft around it with clear-cut modifications in the terms of their contracts, the rules of their markets or the design of their institutions.

A third principle was that the law should be flexible enough to accommodate commercial expectations, needs and developments. As Scrutton LJ put it on one occasion, commercial parties 'must be entitled to act on reasonable commercial probabilities'.[165] If legal doctrine rubbed up against commercial practice – for example, its implications for certain transactions were unanticipated or the results unacceptable – the two should be capable of being reconciled. In some cases this principle meant that the courts went as far as giving normative force to commercial practice by adopting commercial custom and trade usage as the foundation for decision-making. In others commercial practices, even if they did not have normative force, could feed into the application of legal doctrine to help achieve a compatible result.

---

[160] e.g., *Manchester Sheffield and Lincolnshire Railway Co v. Brown* (1883) 8 App Cas 703, at 712–713, 716, 718–719, 722. See also 114 below.

[161] On private law-making, see, e.g., D. Snydner, 'Private Lawmaking' (2003) 64 *Ohio State LJ* 371; L. Bernstein, 'Opting out of the Legal System: Extralegal Contractual Relations in the Diamond Industry' (1992) 21 *J Leg Stud* 115; R. Ellickson, *Order Without Law: How Neighbors Settle Disputes*, Cambridge, Mass, Harvard University Press, 1991.

[162] *Czarnikow* v. *Roth Schmidt & Company* [1922] 2 KB 478, 488, per Scrutton LJ. See 371 below.

[163] Modern statements include R. Goode, 'The Codification of Commercial Law' (1988) 14 *Monash ULR* 135, 150; Lord Irvine, 'The Law: An Engine for Trade' (2001) 64 *MLR* 333, 339, 348–349; *Scandinavian Trading Tanker Co AB* v. *Flota Petrolera Ecuatoriana (The Scaptrade)* [1983] QB 529, 540–541, per Robert Goff LJ.

[164] *Bank Line Ltd* v. *Arthur Capel & Co* [1919] AC 435, 454.

[165] *Embiricos* v. *Sydney Reid & Co* [1914] 3 KB 45, 54. (At this point as Scrutton J.)

Although courts made occasional reference to these principles, they were not at the forefront expressly of judicial (or parliamentary) decision-making.[166] English conventions of judgment writing meant that there were few references to general principles or legal policy. There were exceptions, one factor being the personality of the judge. In his judgments Scrutton LJ made frequent references to the expectations of the business community and his knowledge of commercial practice as a basis for his specific conclusions.[167] His pupil Lord Atkin, another strong personality, was also forthright in the legal principles he thought should govern judgments.[168] For most judges, however, the watchword of the craft was careful reasoning, dressed up in blandness.

The absence of these principles from judgments should give pause to assertions that they were always, or even mainly, in play. On the occasions when legal principle or policy was articulated, it was typically to resolve first-order issues, such as the common problem in commercial disputes of where the loss should fall between two innocent parties because of the fraud or insolvency of a third party. In that context, one approach was to identify which side, in the circumstances, was at greater fault; as Ashurst J. put it in the leading case of *Lickbarrow* v. *Mason*,[169] 'who has enabled such third person to occasion the loss must sustain it'.[170] Another approach was to place the loss on the party better able to bear it, as Bray J did in a contest between a bank and a company whose secretary had forged its cheques. 'The truth is', he said, 'that the number of cases where bankers sustain losses of this kind are infinitesimal in comparison with the large business they do, and the profits of banking are sufficient to compensate them for this very small risk'.[171]

Moreover, a heavy dose of realism is necessary about litigation, illustrated in the story John Morris (quoted at the outset) told during his eightieth birthday celebrations. While the outcome of commercial litigation might ostensibly turn on the application of doctrine and possibly also high principle, it was regularly unpredictable and might depend on the money thrown at it. As every lawyer knew, the immediate outcome of a case could be the product, in practice, of a range of additional factors: the persuasiveness of the advocate and personality of the judge

---

[166] In as much as English law favoured creditors over debtors, this was never expressed as a principle or policy and is better conceptualised as an outcome: see P. Wood, *Maps of World Financial Law*, 6th ed., London, Sweet & Maxwell, 2008.

[167] D. Foxton, *The Life of Thomas E. Scrutton*, Cambridge, Cambridge University Press, 2013, 268–269.

[168] G. Lewis, *Lord Atkin*, London, Butterworths, 1983, 68–93.

[169] (1787) 2 Term Rep 63, 100 ER 35. On the case, 351, 382 below.

[170] at 70, 39 respectively. See also *Henderson & Co.* v. *Williams* [1895] 1 Q.B. 521 (sale of sugar in Liverpool warehouse; Lord Halsbury at 529 cited the American case, *Root v. French*, 13 Wend 570, where Savage CJ adopted Ashurst J's formulation). cf. *Farquharson Brothers & Co* v. *King & Co* [1902] AC 325, 332, 342 (sale of timber stored at Surrey Commercial Docks).

[171] *Kepitigalla Rubber Estates Ltd* v. *National Bank of India Ltd* [1909] 2 KB 1010, 1025–1026. The company had estates in Ceylon (Sri Lanka). Bray J's analysis was approved in *London Joint Stock Bank Ltd* v. *Macmillan* [1918] AC 777, although this passage was not mentioned.

(as in the example John Morris gave); in the early nineteenth century, the impact of the stylised rules of common-law pleading; how the evidence emerged at trial; the answers juries gave to questions the judges posed (at least until the decline in jury trials in commercial causes); and a judge's sense of the merits of the specific dispute before the court and how they should be met.[172]

Further, the application of common law doctrine (or of the occasional statutory provision) was not necessarily straightforward. One aspect was the existence of a compendium of doctrine into which a specific case could be fitted. That was important in dictating how a dispute was best conceptualised and in which web of rules it fell. In the first part of the nineteenth century bills of exchange law had a reasonably well-developed set of rules, although during the nineteenth century these became disordered and codifying legislation in the form of the Bills of Exchange Act 1882 won wide support.[173] With areas such as contract and sales law, a coherent body of doctrine came later. In contract law this was brought to fruition, it seems, in the treatises published in the second part of the nineteenth century.[174] In sales law, there was the occasional distillation of doctrine by the courts,[175] and Judah Benjamin's treatise of 1868 assembled it in a more orderly fashion.[176] Later, the Sale of Goods Act 1893 gathered it into a simplified, authoritative whole.

Apart from overall bodies of doctrine, a further difficulty was to know which rule governed in the circumstances of a specific case. A 'leading case' might be unreported or unexpectedly conjured out of the air later in the day to govern the situation now before the court.[177] Conversely, what a court thought significant at the time of a decision might fade from the picture relatively quickly.[178] As every

---

[172] J. Getzler, 'Interpretation, Evidence, and the Discovery of Contractual Interpretation', in S. Degeling, J. Edelman & J. Goudkamp (eds.), *Contract in Commercial Law*, Sydney, Thompson Reuters, 2016, 122–123. See *Oxford History of the Laws of England*, Oxford, Oxford University Press, 2010, vol. XI, 590 (P. Polden) on the reforms in the Common Law Procedure Act 1852. On civil juries, see 55 below.

[173] 35, 384 below.

[174] For contract, see e.g., *Oxford History of the Laws of England*, Oxford, Oxford University Press, 2010, vol. XII, 308, 312–313 (M. Lobban); W. Swain. *The Law of Contract 1670–1870*, Cambridge, Cambridge University Press, 2015, 228; C. Macmillan, *Mistakes in Contract Law*, Oxford, Hart 2010, 112; J. Gordley, *The Philosophical Origins of Modern Contract Doctrine*, Oxford, Clarendon Press, 1991, 216.

[175] e.g., Mellor J on the implied terms about quality in *Jones v. Just* (1868) LR 3 QB 197.

[176] J. Benjamin, *Sale of Personal Property*, London, Henry Sweet, 1868. See 210 below. For agency, see 72 below on Story's influential contribution. See also 'Liability of Agent to Repay Money Received on behalf of Principal' (1877) 62 *LT* 383, 384 for five principles 'deductible from the cases'.

[177] e.g., 57 (*May v. Butcher* [1934] 2 KB 17) and 224 (*Medway Oil and Storage Co v. Silica Gel Corporation* (1928) 33 Comm Cas 195) below. The resuscitation of *Raffles v. Wichelhaus* (1864) 2 Hurl & C 906, 159 ER 375 is also instructive: B. Simpson, 'Contracts for Cotton to Arrive: The Case of the Two Ships *Peerless*' (1989) 11 *Cardozo LR* 287; C. Macmillan, Mistakes in Contract Law, *op cit*, 117. See also E. Lim, 'Of 'Landmark'; or 'Leading' Cases: Salomon's Challenge' (2014) 41 *JLS* 523.

[178] 'This is a case of very great importance to the mercantile world', said the Lord Chancellor in *Navulshaw v. Brownrigg* (1852) 2 De G M & G 441, 42 ER 943, although the case was soon eclipsed by others. See 152 below.

lawyer knew, even if doctrine was available it was, as the *Law Times* put it on one occasion, 'difficult to say, with the certainty the man in the street generally expects a lawyer to speak, whether the facts of a particular case bring it within the principles'.[179] On countless occasions judges disagreed about doctrine or its bearing as a case ascended the judicial hierarchy, and about whether it applied on subsequent occasions, was to be distinguished, or required variation or radical surgery. Unsurprisingly in these circumstances, commercial parties could be mightily unimpressed with the law, their lawyers and the courts.

1 Party Autonomy, Legislation and Private Law-making Party

> I do not see why businessmen should require the Court and Barristers to interpret what they mean. (Letter, W. H. Lever [Lord Leverhulme] to F. W. Brock, 25 May 1915)[180]

Freedom of contract as an underlying principle of English law is a familiar theme. It was well understood by trade and industry, although as Lever's letter illustrates some businesspeople were so frustrated with the law and lawyers that they thought party autonomy should go further to exclude the courts from the picture altogether. During our period there was a transformation in contract law doctrine. Notions of fairness and equality of exchange, coupled with liability based on reliance and the receipt of benefit, were substituted by a contract law based more on the expressed will of the parties and liability grounded on promises. Whether this transformation was as stark as sometimes portrayed, nineteenth-century contract law was related, in a way, to the ideas of the day.[181] In broad terms the emphasis on abstraction and formalism in nineteenth-century contract law fitted with the market economy of the industrial age.[182] It should not be surprising that the judges brought to their daily tasks the dominant ideas of the society in which they lived and worked. Just how these were reflected in their judgments is a complex matter. Judgment writing eschewed a discussion of policy issues or high principle, different judges inevitably placed a different weight on such matters, and in any event those ideas jostled with legal doctrine and other factors as specific fact patterns were litigated. It does not seem in the least controversial to assert that, during our period, the law gave support to the market economy, stood behind market

---

[179] 'Wrongs independent of a Contract' (1896) 101 *LT* 295.
[180] Unilever Archives, Brunner Mond & Co, LBC/93, File 632. Lever was replying to his solicitor's suggestion that the court be asked about the meaning of a Lever Bros-Brunner Mond & Co agreement: see 237–242 below. I am grateful to Jacob Corbin, Archivist at Unilever.
[181] See, e.g., P. Atiyah, *The Rise and Fall of Freedom of Contract*, Oxford, Oxford University Press, 1979, 389. cf. *Oxford History of the Laws of England*, Oxford, Oxford University Press, 2010, vol. XII, 297–298 (M. Lobban); B. Simpson, 'Innovations in Nineteenth Century Contract Law' (1975) 91 *LQR* 247, 277–278.
[182] L. Friedman, *Contract Law in America*, Madison, University of Wisconsin Press 1965, 84–85.

Figure 1.2 Mackenzie Chalmers (President and Fellows of Trinity College, Oxford)

transactions and enforced them in accordance with rules which generalised economic behaviour.

(i) The Legislative Framework

Legislation intruded little, if at all, on commercial transactions. The design of one body of legislation was explicitly to facilitate commerce, not curb it. The codifications pertinent to our story of transactions, the Sale of Goods Act 1893 and the Bills of Exchange Act 1882, fell into that category.[183] Their facilitative aim was made explicit on various occasions by Mackenzie Chalmers, who drafted them. As he put it in the first edition of his book on the 1893 Act, it 'does not seek to prevent the parties from making any bargain they please. Its object is to lay down clear rules for the cases where they had either formed no intention, or failed to express it.'[184] Legislative intention had some impact on implementation, not least this indication that his codified sales law comprised default rules, at work if parties did not choose otherwise, but freely modified or avoided if they so wished.

---

[183] See also 407 below (legislation making dock warrants documents of title).
[184] *The Sale of Goods 1893*, London, William Clowers & Sons, 1894. v-vi.

Similarly, the Factors Acts were facilitative of commerce. They were aimed at protecting against claims by owners those third parties who were caught out by the wrongful actions of the owner's agent – for example, the merchant purchasing goods in an ordinary commercial dealing not knowing that they were not the agent's, or the bank making an advance to an agent, wrongly believing that the documents of title to goods proffered as collateral were his, not the principal's. We see in Chapter 3 there was an affection for owners leading courts to undermine the legislative intent in the Factors Acts to protect third parties entering market transactions. Over time, that led to Parliament throughout the nineteenth century periodically rewriting the legislation to maintain the goal of protecting third parties in their market dealings.[185]

In addition to facilitative legislation like this, there was a body of statutes which were regulatory in character, although in practice commercial and financial dealings were largely untouched. At one extreme was the Larceny Act 1861, which on rare occasion was wheeled out to address fraud and egregious market abuse.[186] Short of the full weight of the criminal law there was, as regards sales, statutory control to ensure reliable weighing and measuring equipment, relevant to some spot sales. Prohibiting short weight and measure did not really arrive until the Sale of Food (Weights and Measures) Act 1926, which, as its title suggests, had a limited ambit.[187]

Next, there was some control on the claims circulated when selling goods. The Merchandise Marks Act 1862 criminalised applying false marks in the sale of goods with intent to defraud. The legislation was, though, a dead letter.[188] Its successor, the Merchandise Marks Act 1887, prohibited the false application to goods of the marks and names of others, false trade descriptions of goods and false indications that goods were made in Britain.[189] But again it fell short of the mark: the offences were unclear, had limited scope, were rarely enforced and applied only where the offending occurred within the jurisdiction. In commercial circles it was regarded as a dead duck.[190]

Further, there was the regulation of anticompetitive practices in sales. The common-law doctrine of restraint of trade had taken a benign view of such practices. The judicial justification for this echoed the conventional wisdom and public policy of the time: first, the courts said, commercial parties had freedom to enter the contracts they wished, even those restricting competition in marketing;[191] and, second, there were benefits from such practices in

---

[185] 151–152 below.   [186] 116, 447 below.
[187] See R. Cranston, *Consumers and the Law*, London, Weidenfeld & Nicolson, 1978, 262–263. For control on food quality: ibid., 256–257.
[188] H. Payn, *Merchandise Marks Act 1887*, London, Stevens & Sons, 1888, 1–2.
[189] ss. 2, 16. Trade descriptions applied by sellers were deemed to be warranted as true: s. 17.
[190] D. Higgins & A. Velkar, '"Spinning a Yarn": Institutions, Law, and Standards c.1880–1914' (2017) 18 *Enterprise and Society* 591, 605, 607–611; R. Cranston, Consumers and the Law, *op cit*, 235.
[191] *Attorney General of Australia v. Adelaide Steamship* [1913] AC 781, 795. See also *Rawlings v. General Trading Company* [1921] 1 KB 635, 650, per Atkin LJ. See 279–280, 292 below.

steadying prices and preventing ruinous competition.[192] Towards the end of our period attitudes and public policy advanced, and the anticompetitive practices of manufactures and producers in marketing and distributing their goods started to face regulatory challenge.[193]

As for banking services, apart from the restraints of company law (such as they were) banks as institutions were largely unregulated until after our period.[194] Banks were limited in issuing banknotes, but as long as they complied with bills of exchange law they were free in the payment services they offered customers. Once the usury laws were repealed in 1854, there were no statutory restrictions relevant to the overdrafts and loans they furnished. The Bills of Sale Acts required the registration of chattel mortgages, but this was not the type of collateral banks took when they wanted security to back an advance to a commercial customer.[195] Nor, after judicial clarification, were the Bills of Sale Acts relevant to those providing asset finance through hire and hire purchase facilities.[196]

(ii) Private Law-Making – Markets and Institutions

In this almost regulation-free environment, party autonomy gave free rein to the private law-making of commercial parties. One aspect was the founding of organised markets and of the institutions to underpin them. Firstly, there were the rules and regulations governing the membership of venues where dealings were conducted; and, secondly, there were the standards, rules and regulations for trading on these markets and for the settlement of the disputes which arose. In the London and Liverpool commodity markets the standards, rules and regulations were contained, in part, in the standard form contracts drawn up by the trade associations to govern individual sales, in separate rules establishing standards, and in the terms and conditions for the auctioning of imported commodities where this occurred.[197] Private law-making on financial markets tended to be less extensive and dealings less formulaic. For example, the London money market embraced a relatively small, close-knit group of banks and discount houses, with the Bank of England casting its shadow from the background. Verbal agreements were common for individual dealings, without being reduced to writing in the same detail they were on the commodity markets.[198] Trust and the pressure of informal norms smoothed the edges if problems arose.

---

[192] *North Western Salt Company Ltd* v. *Electrolytic Alkali Company Ltd* [1914] AC 461, 471–472, per Lord Haldane LC.
[193] Monopolies and Restrictive Practices (Inquiry and Control) Act 1948; Restrictive Trade Practices Act 1956; Resale Prices Act of 1964. See 273–274 below.
[194] see 378 below. The Banking Act 1979 provided the first systematic regulation.
[195] W. Cornish, S. Banks, C. Mitchell, P. Mitchell & R. Probert, Law and Society in England 1750–1950, *op cit*, 221, 234.
[196] see 259 below.
[197] see Chapter 6 below. On standards: A. Velkar, *Markets and Measurements in Nineteenth Century Britain*, Cambridge, Cambridge University Press, 2012, 191.
[198] 452 below.

Accompanying the private law-making for the organised markets was the establishment of market-supporting structures. Notable with the commodity markets were the rules and regulations for the clearing and settlement of individual transactions. These were prepared by private bodies such as the London Produce Clearing House (LPCH). Again, contract was central – standard form contracts for individual trades combined with the rules of the clearing house as regards how the mechanism worked. The contractual network framing the work of the LPCH dressed it in the drapery of a law-making body.[199] As to financial markets, the London Bankers' Clearing House was an important market-supportive institution, formed by the banks and enabling them to handle payments between their customers in bulk, so only net differences needed to be paid.[200] The rules of the clearing house were spartan and mechanical, but backed by formal and informal understandings between the banks, with the backing of the Bank of England.

The systems of private law constituted by these rules, regulations and standard form contracts had a number of characteristics. One was standardisation, which reduced transaction costs in contracting since there was no need on each deal to negotiate all the terms anew.[201] Multilateral standardization boosted confidence in a market, in part because commercial parties knew that they were getting terms no worse than others.[202] A second characteristic was that the system of private law created was detailed and sophisticated. It was drawn up by commercial parties, after input from relevant interests. Unlike some state law-making, there was a wealth of experience to draw on regarding the problems likely to be encountered, the different contexts in which they occurred and their incidence at different times. Third, although these systems of private law governing markets and institutions were erected on a foundation of profit-making and competitive interests, their architects worked to certain principles and were attuned to the balance of interests to be accommodated.[203]

Fourth, lawyers had little hand in this private law-making. The drafting of standards, rules and contracts was by commercial parties, knowing what they wanted, with lawyers having an ancillary role of vetting for legal error and occasional advice on drafting. When disputes arose, the involvement of lawyers was discouraged on the basis that commercial parties would be better able to understand the issues and be more motivated to reach a quick and efficient solution.[204] That only changed if legal proceedings ensued. Fifth, almost from the

---

[199] cf. J. Lurie, 'Commodities Exchanges as Self-Regulating Organizations in the late 19th Century: Some Perimeters in the History of American Administrative Law' (1975) 28 *Rutgers LR* 1107, 1116.
[200] 454 below.
[201] H. Collins, *Regulating Contracts*, Oxford, Oxford University Press, 1999, 230.
[202] See J. Hurst, *Law and Markets in United States History*, Madison, University of Wisconsin Press, 1982, 37.
[203] see 335–337 below on drafting standard form contracts.
[204] cf. Y. Dezalay & B. Garth, *Dealing in Virtue: International Commercial Arbitration and the Construction of a Transnational Legal Order*, Chicago, University of Chicago Press, 1996, 133. See 369–373 below.

outset these systems of private law had an international reach. That was attributable to Britain's leading role during our period in trade, banking, shipping and insurance, and the outward looking nature of those involved, many of whom were foreign or whose families originated abroad.[205] Britain's dominant role in private law-making was not uncontested.[206] However, once international merchants and bankers reached a certain size, the reality was that they had to deal through London (and, to a lesser extent, Liverpool) with its banks and reserve currency, its marine insurance and its shipping and commodity markets.

Sixth, and as a corollary, to engage in these activities – finance, ship chartering, marine insurance, international commodity sales and so on – commercial parties, wherever they were, had to comply with the rules of these London and Liverpool institutions and markets. This meant that English law – and these systems of private law it spawned – was at the same time both local and global.[207] Thus the standard form contracts predominantly employed for international commodity sales were drawn in Britain.[208] (First-mover advantage means that their descendants still apply to dealings in a considerable volume of international trading in commodities like grain and cotton.[209]) Crucially, commercial dealings were deemed to be made and performed in England – whatever the reality – and the mandatory dispute resolution mechanism of trade arbitration occurred there.[210] The upshot of arbitration was, on scattered occasions, the subject of supervision by the English High Court.[211]

Seventh, if these systems produced untoward results, the principle of party autonomy was generally there to remedy matters through redrafting the relevant rule or standard form contract, or institutional redesign.[212] Finally, enforcement was largely self-contained and free of state law. Markets and institutions exercised the power to exclude members in cases of serious non-

---

[205] e.g., R. Michie, 'Insiders, Outsiders and the Dynamics of Change in the City of London since 1900' (1998) 33 *J Contemp Hist* 547, 555–557, 558–559; S. Chapman, 'The International Houses: The Continental Contribution to British Commerce, 1800–1860' (1977) 6 *J Eur Econ Hist* 5.

[206] e.g., for commodity sales, see A. Quark, *Global Rivalries: Standards Wars & the Transnational Cotton Trade*, op cit, 47, 54, 65, 104.

[207] G. Mallard &. J. Sgard, 'Contractual Knowledge: One Hundred Years of Legal Experimentation in Global Markets', in G. Mallard &.J. Sgard (eds.), *Contractual Knowledge*, Cambridge, Cambridge University, 2016, 12. cf. T. Röder, *From Industrial to Legal Standardization 1871–1914*, Leiden, Brill, 2011, a case of limited standardization in insurance law.

[208] 313–315 below.   [209] See 295 below.

[210] On commodities arbitration: D. Kirby-Johnson, *International Commodity Arbitration*, London, Lloyd's of London Press, 1991; A. Slabotzky, *Grain Contracts and Arbitration*, London, Lloyd's of London Press, 1984; 361–373 below. On maritime arbitration: B. Harris, 'London Maritime Arbitration' (2011) 77 *Arbitration* 116; P. Tassios, 'Choosing the Appropriate Venue: Maritime Arbitration in London or New York?' (2004) 21 *J Int'l Arb* 355, 355–359; C. Ambrose, K. Maxwell & M. Collett, *London Maritime Arbitration*, 4th ed., London, London, Informa Law, 2017, 2–3.

[211] cf. J. Braithwaite, 'Standard Form Contracts as Transnational Law' (2012) *MLR* 779, where parties choose English law and jurisdiction. See also H. Collins, Regulating Contracts, *op cit*, 329; M. Bridge, *The International Sale of Goods*, 4th ed., Oxford, Oxford University Press, 2017 17–19.

[212] See for example 358–361 below.

compliance with the system of formal norms, although with the maverick or recalcitrant this might fall short in bringing them to heel. The courts adopted a hands-off approach to member discipline.[213] In some contexts informal norms operated within close-knit groups where trust was at a maximum and future interactions, both commercial and perhaps social, were anticipated. This was a characteristic of London and local financial markets.[214] It was less the case with the commodity markets, where size alone meant more rough and tumble. Informal norms, and the big stick of the courts in reserve, buttressed compliance with arbitration awards, albeit that observance abroad was an occasional concern.[215]

(iii) Private Law-Making – Distribution Networks

Party autonomy allowed individual manufacturers and producers to control the marketing of their products down the distribution chain.[216] Distributors in handling goods for onward sale were bound by contract to do this in specified ways, confining their efforts to particular parts of the country or the world, obliging them to 'push' the product or use their 'best endeavours' in marketing it and requiring them to supply goods to their own customers at the prices the manufacturer or producer laid down. These contracts could also contain sanctions for errant distributors. Manufacturers and producers might act individually in such cases, with the possibility of *in terrorem* enforcement through an injunction from the court obliging compliance.

During our period manufactures and producers also acted collectively through trade associations, which had powers conferred under their rules to impose fines and, as an ultimate sanction, stop orders, effectively preventing a distributor handling a product for non-compliance with these strictures.[217] The courts saw nothing wrong in this.[218] When these systems of fines and stop lists were challenged, they upheld them as legitimate practices in furtherance of business interests. Parties, as the court said in a parallel case, were the best judges of what was reasonable among themselves in relation to such practices, and all the courts should do was 'within due bounds to facilitate, not to fetter, trade and industry'.[219] The upshot was, as the Board to Trade put it in 1951, that 'the collective punitive action by which most fixed resale prices are

---

[213] 69–71 below.
[214] P. Thompson, 'The Pyrrhic Victory of Gentlemanly Capitalism: The Financial Elite of the City of London, 1945–90. Part 2' (1997) 32 *J Contemp Hist* 427, 434; R. Michie, 'Outsiders and the Dynamics of Change in the City of London since 1900' (1998) 33 *J Contemp Hist* 547, 563.
[215] 369 below.
[216] N. Isaacs, 'Business Postulates and the Law' (1928) 41 *Harv LR* 1014, 1018–1019.
[217] W. Cornish, S. Banks, C. Mitchell, P. Mitchell & R. Probert, Law and Society in England 1750–1950, *op cit*, 262. In practice trade association powers may have been a damp squib: see J. Turner, 'Servants of Two Masters: British Trade Associations in the First Half of the Twentieth Century', in H. Yamazaki & M. Miyamoto (eds.), *Trade Associations in Business History*, Tokyo, University of Tokyo Press, 1988.
[218] *Thorne v. Motor Trade Association* [1937] AC 797; see 272 below.
[219] *English Hop Growers v. Dering* [1928] 2 KB 174, 187, per Sankey LJ.

enforced amount to a private system of law which in effect is outside the jurisdiction of the Courts'.[220] It was not until the competition legislation of the post–Second World War period that this type of behaviour vis-à-vis distributors came under a cloud. Effective regulation of restrictive trade practice was slow in coming, and when it arrived, towards the end of our period, the relevant law initially lacked bite. When cases reached the courts, enforcement efforts did not always receive a sympathetic audience.[221]

2 Certainty, Predictability and Equitable Rules

> In mercantile matters I imagine that the certainty and definiteness of a rule are of more importance than a very nice and exact adjustment of conflicting interests in each particular case. (Mackenzie Chalmers, 1881)[222]

The need for certainty, or bright-line rules, was another principle of English commercial law, expressed here by the drafter of the Bills of Exchange Act 1882 and the Sale of Goods Act 1893, Mackenzie Chalmers. There was, firstly, its forward-looking aspect. Certainty, it was assumed, assured predictability for commercial parties and allowed them to plan their affairs in the way they thought best. They could anticipate risks by contractual provisions or in some cases through insurance. As well as this advantage in rule design, certainty also meant that, should a dispute arise, commercial parties would in most cases know where they stood. That would facilitate settlement and discourage delay and litigation.[223] As a result of pursuing certainty, the merits of a case could be secondary considerations in decision-making. In as much as equitable doctrines were thought to introduce uncertainty into commercial dealings, commercial (and other) judges took a dim view of their intrusion in this context.

(i) Certainty vs Merits

Certainty as a component of modern English commercial law can be traced to Lord Mansfield, who in a marine insurance case in 1774 said: 'In all mercantile transactions the great object should be certainty: and therefore it is of more consequence that a rule should be certain, than whether the rule is established one way or the other. Because speculators in trade then know what ground to go upon.'[224] That was litigation where Mansfield wanted a clear definition of barratry as it related to a contract of marine insurance, so that in the future underwriters and insurers would feel more confident in entering commercial

---

[220] Board of Trade, *A Statement on Resale Price Maintenance*, Cmd. 8274, 1951, 11.
[221] 275 below.
[222] M. Chalmers, 'On the Codification of Mercantile Law with Especial Reference to the Law of Negotiable Instruments', J Institute of Bankers, vol. II, March 1881, 113, 121–123.
[223] cf. *Hammond & Co v. Bussey* (1887) 20 QBD 79, 94, per Bowen LJ; *Biggin & Co Ltd v. Pemanite Ltd* [1951] 2 KB 314, 321, per Somervell LJ.
[224] *Vallejo v. Wheeler* (1774) 1 Cowp 143, 153, 98 ER 1012, 1017.

contracts. This was not an isolated sentiment.[225] As the touchstone for commercial law, certainty echoed throughout our period.[226]

A corollary of certainty was a strict application of the rules. In 1920 the House of Lords considered the lender's use of a clause imposing default interest, in other words, a higher rate of interest absent punctual payment. Lord Birkenhead LC observed that 'it would be a very singular circumstance if he who had been careful to stipulate that certain payments of interest under an instrument of this kind should be made to him punctually upon a certain specified day, were deprived by a decision of the Law Courts of the right of insisting upon the strict implement of that for which he had so stipulated'.[227] In circumstances like this, the assumption ran, borrowers could bargain with their lenders for the inclusion of provisions such as days of grace or negotiate for relief post-default.[228]

In light of the certainty principle, the merits of individual cases took a back seat to the strict application of legal rules. Adherence to bright-line rules, it was accepted, could result in some commercial parties with unmeritorious claims profiting at the expense of others. Despite this, the assumption ran, bright-line rules meant a greater consistency in the courts' decision-making, and that promoted its own fairness. Further, what was sauce for the goose was sauce for the gander. Markets oscillated, and commercial parties seeking to take advantage of unmeritorious points one day faced the possibility of being victims the next. Lord Atkin in *Arcos* v. *Ronaasen*[229] thought that there was no difference between the views of businesspeople and lawyers on the point: commercial parties should be able to insist on their strict legal rights, regardless of the harsh consequences for the other side.[230] A familiar example was the owner's withdrawal of a vessel for failure of the charterer to pay hire on the due date. The courts sanctioned this, notwithstanding that late payment was neither deliberate nor negligent; that the payment, when made, was only a few days late; or that the owner's motivation was to snatch back the vessel to charter it else-

---

[225] See his earlier comments: *Hamilton* v. *Mendes* (1761) 2 Burr 1198, 1214; 897 ER 787, 795. See also *Carlos* v. *Fancourt* (1794) 5 Term Rep. 482, 486, 101 ER 272, 274.

[226] Indeed, to the present day: e.g. *Mardorf Peach & Co Ltd* v. *Attica Sea Carriers Corporation of Liberia* (The Laconia) [1977] AC 850, 878 per Lord Salmon; *A/S Awilco of Oslo* v. *Fulvia S.P.A. Di Navigazione of Cagliari* (The Chikuma) [1981] 1 W.L.R. 314, 321, 322 per Lord Bridge; *Homburg Houtimport BV* v. *Agrosin Private Ltd* (The Starsin) [2003] UKHL 12; [2004] 1 AC 715, [13], per Lord Bingham; *Jindal Iron and Steel Co Ltd* v. *Islamic Solidarity Shipping Co Jordan Inc* [2004] UKHL 49, [2005] 1 WLR 1363, [16], per Lord Steyn; *Golden Strait Corpn* v. *Nippon Yusen Kubishika Kaisha* (The Golden Victory) [2007] UKHL 12, [2007] 2 AC 353, [1]. cf. *PST Energy 7 Shipping* v. *OW Bunker Malta* (The Res Cogitans) [2016] UKSC 23, [2016] AC 1034. See J. Lian Yap, 'Predictability, Certainty, and Party Autonomy in the Sale and Supply of Goods' (2017) 46 *Common Law W'ld Rev* 269.

[227] *Maclaine* v. *Gatty* [1921] 1 AC 376, 385–386.

[228] Denning LJ's views to the contrary in *British Movietonews Ltd* v. *London and District Cinemas Ltd* [1951] 1 KB 190, 202 do not seem to have survived the appeal: [1952] AC 166, 181–184, 187–188.

[229] [1933] AC 470. See 208–209 below about the case.   [230] at 480.

where on a rising market in chartering rates.[231] A parallel example was the buyer's use of an immaterial breach in a sales contract to refuse delivery, when with a movement in market prices the goods could be obtained more cheaply elsewhere. Again, the courts were unmoved.[232]

(ii) 'Business against Chancery'

> We had an interesting case some time ago winding up a dissolved Russian Bank: business against Chancery. It shocked the purists. (Letter, Lord Atkin to Professor Gutteridge, Spring 1936)[233]

During our period, and particularly after the Judicature Act 1873, some judges expressed trenchant views that equitable doctrines should be kept at arm's length from English commercial law so as not to threaten its bright-line rules.[234] It would be 'dangerous and unreasonable' to apply to mercantile agreements the equitable rules that a contract might be enforced although the time fixed for its completion had passed, said Cotton LJ about a typical commodity sale in *Reuter, Hufeland & Co v. Sala & Co*.[235] In the twentieth century Lord Atkin was the forthright opponent of equitable niceties blurring the bright-line rules of English commercial law. 'Business against Chancery' as he put it in the private correspondence quoted, a regular theme of his work as a law lord.[236] Eschewing equity's influence in sales law was the basis of his well-known judgment in *Re Wait*.[237]

---

[231] *Tankexpress A/s v. Compagnie Financiere Belge des Petroles SA* [1949] AC 76, disapproving *Nova Scotia Steel Co v. Sutherland Steam Shipping Co* (1899) 5 Com Cas106. In *Tankexpress*, Le Quesne QC and Roskill for the owners argued that the charterers' contentions for leniency on payment would introduce uncertainty: 82; and see Lord Wright at 94–95.

[232] 215 below. See also Atkin LJ, along with Bankes and Scrutton LJJ, in *Re An Arbitration between Moore and Company Ltd and Landauer and Co* [1921] 2 KB 519 (buyer could reject when about half the Tasmanian canned fruit stated as being in cases containing 30 tins each arrived in London with 24 tins to a case, although this made no difference in value. The ship's arrival was much delayed by strikes and the buyer likely rejected for this reason).

[233] Quoted in G. Lewis, *Lord Atkin, op cit*, 74. The reference was to *Russian & English Bank v. Baring Bros & Co Ltd (No.4)* [1936] AC 405. Gutteridge had been Cassel professor of commercial law at the London School of Economics and was later professor of comparative law at Cambridge: see R. Cranston, 'Praising the Professors: Commercial Law and the LSE', in R. Rawlings, *Law, Society and Economy*, Oxford, Oxford University Press, 1997, 119–121.

[234] G. Kennedy, 'Equity in Commercial Law', in P. Finn (ed.), *Equity and Commercial Relationships*, Sydney, Law Book Company, 1987, 2. See also *Salt v. Marquess of Northampton* [1892] AC 1, 18–19, per Lord Bramwell. Although Bramwell's views were somewhat nuanced, he was a well-known exponent of laissez-faire: see A. Ramasastry 'The Parameters, Progressions, and Paradoxes of Baron Bramwell' (1994) 38 *Amer J Legal Hist* 322; R. Epstein, 'For A Bramwell Revival' (1994) 38 *Amer J Legal Hist* 246.

[235] (1879) LR 4 CPD 239, 249 (sale in 1876 on a broker's standard form contract of some twenty-five tons of Penang black pepper, October and/or November shipment; only twenty tons declared as compliant, the remainder being shipped under a December bill of lading. Held, entire contract, so buyers not bound to accept anything less than full twenty-five tons – an approach codified in Sale of Goods Act 1893, ss. 30(1) and 31(1)).

[236] G. Lewis, *Lord Atkin, op cit*, 74–75.   [237] [1927] 1 Ch 606.

Figure 1.3 Lord Atkin on the jetty at Aberdovey, Wales (Treasurer and Masters of the Bench, Gray's Inn)

There in another commodity sale Wait bought 1,000 tons of Western White wheat from Balfour Williamson & Co., London, ex *Challenger*, expected to load in December 1925 at Oregon or Washington. It was a CIF contract, dated 20 November 1925, on LCTA's form 22.[238] The following day Wait sold 500 tons to sub-buyers. The wheat was shipped in bulk on 21 December, a bill of lading for the 1,000 tons reaching Wait on 4 January 1926. Payment was due thirty-three days after sight, that is on 6 February. The previous day the sub-buyers gave Wait a cheque, although they had no bill of lading, delivery order or document of title. Wait paid this cheque into his account and pledged the bill of lading to his bank. He became bankrupt before the ship arrived and so never appropriated the 500 tons to the sub-buyers. His trustee in bankruptcy redeemed the bill of lading and the entire 1,000 tons, leaving the sub-buyers to their remedy in damages. It was argued that they had a pro rata equitable

---

[238] 208, 305 below.

interest in the cargo. A Divisional Court in the Chancery Division agreed and gave them specific performance of their contract, an equitable remedy.

The Court of Appeal (Lord Hanworth MR and Atkin LJ) held that the sub-buyers could not obtain specific performance. That remedy required as a precondition that goods be specific or ascertained. That was not the case since Wait had never allocated the 500 tons in relation to the sub-buyers. The court rejected the argument that there had been an equitable assignment, giving the sub-buyers a beneficial interest or lien in the 500 tons. The sub-buyers had taken the well-known risk of insolvency in paying Wait without receiving a bill of lading or other document of title. Atkin LJ was scathing about the role of equitable principles in sales. They had beneficial results in their own sphere, he said, but in this context he felt 'bound to repel the disastrous innovations' which would be introduced into well-settled commercial relations. Trade finance would be adversely affected, he continued, because a financing bank would be affected by notice of the sub-buyer's equitable interest, even though it acquired legal title through the documents of title.[239] It would have to satisfy itself on being paid that those equitable interests were not being defeated, presumably by contacting the sub-buyers. The effect would be, he concluded, 'to throw the business world into confusion, for credit would be seriously restricted'.[240]

Atkin was not the only commercial judge to inveigh against equitable notions (and what might now be the law of unjust enrichment). 'There is now no ground left for suggesting as a recognizable "equity" the right to recover money in personam', said Lord Sumner in *Sinclair v. Brougham*, 'merely because it would be the right and fair thing that it should be refunded to the payer'. But Atkin was the most insistent. In *Re Wait* there was a strong dissent by Sargant LJ ('complete and fundamental' disagreement[241]). In a pointed comment on the majority judgments in the *Law Quarterly Review*, Sir Frederick Pollock observed that the modern equity lawyer felt that he was 'walking in a shadow of archaic superstition'.[242] Nonetheless, as Pollock conceded, the majority judgments represented the law, indeed, continue to do so.

Constructive notice was another equitable doctrine whose recognition in commercial dealings was deprecated. *Manchester Trust v. Furness*[243] was the leading case. There the Court of Appeal held that the bank as the indorsee of bills of lading – it had made an advance – did not have constructive notice that the charterparty contained a special clause that the captain, although appointed and paid for by the owners, was the agent of the charterers. If the bank had had notice it would have had to sue the charterers, not the owners, as the party liable for the captain's failure to deliver the cargo of Merthyr steam coal to Rio de Janeiro. It was 'perfect good sense', said Lindley LJ, that the

---

[239] 381–382 below. [240] at 639–640. [241] at 641.
[242] 'Notes. Re Wait' (1927) 43 *LQR* 293, 295. [243] [1895] 2 QB 539.

courts had resolutely set their face against an extension of the equitable doctrines of constructive notice to commercial transactions. '[I]n commercial transactions possession is everything, and there is no time to investigate title; and if we were to extend the doctrine of constructive notice to commercial transactions we should be doing infinite mischief and paralyzing the trade of the country.'[244]

A few years earlier, in *London Joint Stock Bank* v. *Simmons*, Lord Herschell had said that he would be 'very sorry to see the doctrine of constructive notice introduced into the law of negotiable instruments'.[245] That was a case where brokers, now insolvent, had pledged foreign bonds, which a client left with them, to their bank to support an overdraft. In reversing the Court of Appeal, the House of Lords held that there were no suspicious circumstances to put the bank on inquiry.[246] It therefore took in good faith (and of course because of the overdraft, for value), and so its security was good. In Sir John Paget's view, the case put paid to what he described as the 'pernicious theory' of constructive notice as regards negotiable instruments.[247] The upshot of the case was that a bank was not put on inquiry in such circumstances: simply because it dealt with brokers did not infect it with knowledge that they might be pledging, without authority, the bonds and instruments of their clients as collateral for an advance. As Lord Halsbury LC put it, the deposit of securities as cover in a broker's business was a well-known commercial practice, and it would be a startling proposition that in every case the bank had to inquire whether a broker had the authority of his customer to do so.[248] To put it another way, this was standard commercial practice, and the court should be loath to upset it.

The protection against constructive notice in commercial transactions was further extended. In general, banks were held not to be on constructive notice in conducting standard banking operations.[249] In 1926 Scrutton LJ generalised the position: in commercial transactions, he said, a person could not be taken to know what he had the means of knowing.[250] Summing up the approach of the courts during our period, Diplock J said in 1958: '"Reason and justice" do not seem to me to prescribe the introduction into commercial matters ... of the doctrine of constructive notice.'[251]

---

[244] at 545. Lopes and Rigby LJJ agreed. Before appointment to the bench Lindley had practised at the Chancery bar, which reinforced the point: G. Jones & V. Jones, 'Lindley, Nathaniel, Baron Lindley (1828–1921)', *Oxford Dictionary of National Biography*.

[245] *London Joint Stock Bank* v. *Simmons* [1892] AC 201, 221.

[246] The Court of Appeal applied the earlier House of Lords decision, *Earl of Sheffield* v. *London and Joint Stock Bank* (1888) 13 App Cas 333, which (as in the nature of these things) the House in *London Joint Stock Bank* v. *Simmons* had much grief distinguishing.

[247] J. Paget, *The Law of Banking*, London, Butterworth, 1904, 244. See also W. Willis, *The Law of Negotiable Securities*, London, Stevens, 1896, 4 (House of Lords in the case had rendered great service to the commercial community and restored confidence in banking transactions).

[248] [1892] AC 201, 211–212.

[249] e.g., *In Re Valletort Sanitary Steam Laundry Company Ltd* [1903] 2 Ch 654.

[250] *Greer* v. *Downs Supply Company* [1927] 2 KB 28, 36 per Scrutton LJ.

[251] *Port Line Ltd* v. *Ben Line Steamers Ltd* [1958] 2 QB 146,167.

But while there was a good deal of huffing and puffing about equitable principles not being allowed to pollute commercial transactions, they had, in certain situations, an acceptable, indeed essential, purchase. Agency was the best example, where equitable principles governing the duties of the agent to the principal were brought to bear against the dishonest agent, the agent failing to disclose crucial information to their principal or those agents acting in their own and not their principal's interests. In such cases, even Lord Atkin was disposed to act, albeit not always willing to ascribe the remedy's source to equity.[252] In Chapter 3 we encounter a number of examples of dishonest agents being brought to book as a result of a breach of their fiduciary duties.[253] After our period, the role of equity in commercial law obtained a much firmer, albeit ring-fenced, footing.[254]

3 The Normative Force of Commercial Practice

The influence of commercial details ... has more than once been shown to be a very important factor in the development of English law in modern times. Its effect has naturally been to simplify it, and to bring it more into harmony with common sense by the extinction of useless technicalities. (*The Law Times*, 1885)[255]

As a matter of legal policy, English courts took steps to accommodate the law to commercial practice. This happened in several ways. The first was straightforward and consistent with legal doctrine. That was through the notion that commercial custom and usage could be employed to interpret contracts and supplement them by implying additional terms. As a result, normative force was given to some commercial practices of markets, trades and ports.[256] However, by the 1950s, if not earlier, custom and usage had become a spent force in transposing commercial practices into law. Partly, this was attributable to greater formalism in legal reasoning; partly, to customs and usages being subsumed in standard form contracts; and, partly, to imperial decline and the loss of the markets, ports and trades which engendered them.[257]

---

[252] e.g., *Solloway v. McLaughlin* [1938] AC 247; *Ellerman Lines Ltd v. Read* [1928] 2 KB 144,155.
[253] 132, 136–139 below.
[254] e.g., W. Goodhart & G. Jones, 'The Infiltration of Equitable Doctrine into English Commercial Law' (1980) 43 *MLR* 489; P. Millett (1998) Equity's Place in the Law of Commerce' (1998) 114 *LQR* 214; M. Briggs, 'Equity in Business' (2019) 135 *LQR* 567.
[255] 'The Conflict between Law and Business as to Agreements between Debtors and Creditors' (1885) 78 *LT* 351, 351.
[256] cf. current debates at the international level (e.g., J. Coetzee, 'The Role and Function of Trade Usage in Modern International Sales Law' (2015) 20 *Uniform LR* 243; J. Dalhuisen, 'Custom and its Revival in Transnational Private Law' (2008) 18 *Duke J Comp & Int'l L* 339) and national level (L. Bernstein, 'Custom in the Courts' (2016) 110 *Northwestern ULR* 63).
[257] See J. Basedow, 'The State's Private Law and the Economy: Commercial Law as an Amalgam of Public and Private Rule-Making' (2008) *Amer J Comp L* 703, 709; L. Bernstein, 'The Questionable Empirical Basis of Article 2's Incorporation Strategy: A Preliminary Study' (1999) 66 *U Chi LR* 710, 737, 770, 776, 779; R. Epstein, 'Confusion about Custom:

The second way commercial practices could have normative force was more subtle, indeed mysterious. In many cases it was below the surface, turning on a commercial ethos which many judges deciding commercial cases shared by dint of their background, time at the commercial bar or temperament. Occasionally, however, this disposition to accommodate commercial practices was articulated. In some instances the court expressly adopted a commercial practice as the template for its reasoning, albeit that it fell short of trade usage. In others, commercial practice or opinion was more a prop for the court's reading of a contract or statute, or an added justification for the conclusion it reached through more conventional avenues. There were other more tenuous examples, difficult to pin down with the passage of time. What can be said is that this disposition in English law to accommodate commercial practice had enduring mileage – unlike custom and usage – when London had revived fortunes, after our period, as an international financial, insurance and dispute resolution centre.[258]

(i) Custom and Usage

> [T]he admissibility of evidence of a usage of trade for the purpose of importing terms into commercial contracts ... is a question of paramount importance in an industrial age and a commercial country. (J. Balfour Browne, *The Law of Usages and Customs*, 1875)[259]

The common law accepted that commercial practice could have normative force if it constituted trade usage.[260] Whether it did depended on whether the practice was so widely observed and so well known in a market or locality that it was taken as the basis of contracting. In practice the courts took a flexible approach, although to have normative force a commercial practice had to be proved as a matter of fact. Until the First World War, when civil juries faded, the existence of trade usage might be decided by them.[261] Once the existence of usage was established, the courts used it in two main ways. First, as Lord Cairns LC held in a case of an international commodity sale, while it was for the court

---

Disentangling Informal Customs from Standard Contractual Provisions' (1999) 66 *U Chi LR* 821, 822–823.

[258] e.g., Lord Goff, 'Commercial Contracts and the Commercial Court' [1984] LMCLQ 382, 391 ('we are there to oil the wheels of commerce, not to put a spanner in the works, or even grit in the oil'); Lord Steyn, 'Contract Law: Fulfilling the Reasonable Expectations of Honest Men' (1997) 113 LQR 433 (courts give effect to reasonable expectations of honest businesspeople).

[259] J. Balfour Browne, *The Law of Usages and Customs*, London, Stevens & Haynes, 1875, 43.

[260] Although the terms 'custom' and 'usage' were sometimes used interchangeably, strictly speaking custom applied to practices which had an immemorial existence and if recognised became the law of a place. Usage was more flexible, a settled and established practice of a trade or port, so universally observed to be regarded as binding: *Postlethwaite v. Freeland* (1880) 5 App Cas 599, 616, per Lord Blackburn; *Strathlorne Steamship Co Ltd v. Hugh Baird & Sons Ltd* 1916 SC (HL) 134, 141.

[261] e. g., *Alexiadi v. Robinson* (1861) 2 F & F 679, 175 ER 1237.

to interpret the words of the contract, that was subject to 'any peculiarity of meaning which may be attached by reason of the custom of the trade'.[262] Second, as Parke B put it in another case, usage 'may be used to annex incidents to all written contacts, commercial or agricultural, and others, which do not by their terms, exclude it, upon the presumption that the parties have contracted with reference to such usage'.[263]

Through contractual interpretation and 'annexing incidents' to contractual terms, trade usage introduced flexibility into different areas of commercial law. With organised markets the courts gave welcome effect to commercial practices operating there.[264] *Graves v. Legg*[265] is just one case in point. London merchants employed a Liverpool broker to purchase wool, who bought bales for them deliverable at Odessa, the contract stating that 'the names of the vessels to be declared as soon as the wools were shipped'. Custom and usage in Liverpool was that all a vendor needed to do was to inform the broker of the name of the vessel, not the buyer. Consistently with that practice, the Exchequer Chamber held that the vendor was not in breach of contract in failing to pass on to the buyer the ship's name. '[Having] employed an agent at Liverpool to make a contract there, it must be taken to have been made with all the incidents of a contract entered into at Liverpool', said Cockburn CJ.[266]

The normal rule was that, as agents, brokers on the commodity markets would drop out of the picture and liabilities on the transaction would be between the principal and the third party. That did not accord with the commercial need to make the person on the spot liable. In various decisions the courts invoked trade usage to impose liability directly on brokers when things went wrong.[267] There was even authority that a third party employing a broker to conduct a transaction on a market, in the usual manner, impliedly assented to the market's reasonable usages, whether aware of them or not.[268]

The ports generated various cases. Early on it was held that the usage of a port might bind a party, ignorant of it, if it was well known in the trade.[269] As late as 1959 it was held that it was a usage of the London freight market that forwarding agents should incur personal liability to

---

[262] *Bowes v. Shand* (1877) 2 App Cas 455, 462. See also *Russian Steam-Navigation Trading Company v. Silva* (1863) 13 CBNS 610, 143 ER 242 (meaning of bill of lading). The practice developed earlier: C. Mitchell, 'Mercantile Usage, Construction of Contracts and the Implication of Terms, 1750–1850' in C. Mitchell & S. Watterson (eds.), *The World of Maritime and Commercial Law*, London, Hart, 2020.

[263] *Gibson v. Small* (1853) 4 HLC 353, 397, 10 ER 499, 516–517, citing *Hutton v. Warren* (1836) 1 M&W 446, 150 ER 517.

[264] e.g., *Johnson v. Raylton Dixon & Co* (1881) 7 QBD 438 (iron trade); *Imperial Marine Insurance Co v. Fire Insurance Corp Ltd* (1879) 4 CPD 166 (underwriters).

[265] (1859) 4 Hurl & N 210, 157 ER 88. cf. 'A man who employs a banker is bound by the usage of Bankers': *Hare v. Henty* (1861) 10 CBNS 65, 77, 142 ER 374, 379, per Willes J in argument.

[266] at 213, 89.   [267] 73n below.

[268] *Robinson v. Mollett* (1875) LR 7 HL 802 was a leading case on the requirement that with custom and usage there be knowledge of its existence: see 78–79 below.

[269] *Hudson v. Ede* (1868) LR 3 QB 412.

shipowners.[270] *Petrocochino v. Bott*[271] had entered the books much earlier: where goods were consigned to a particular port, delivery was to be according to the customs and usages prevailing there. In that case the court held that it was the usage in the Victoria Docks in London that, as soon as the goods left the ship's deck, the liability of the vessel owner ended and that this was not affected by any terms of the bill of lading.[272] Accordingly, the shipowner was not liable when one of sixty-nine bales of hides from Calcutta (Kolkata), ex the steamer *Zeno*, went missing between the vessel's discharge in the Victoria Docks and arrival of the bales by lighters at Sun Wharf, further up the Thames, for storage for the consignees. No doubt all this was gratifying to some using the ports, if not to those on the wrong end of it.

Trade usage featured as well with sales transactions, although there was less scope when deals were conducted according to standard form contracts, since it had long been accepted that usage could not be invoked to contradict the terms of a written contract.[273] Hire and deferred (hire) purchase as marketing tools were given a boost in the late nineteenth century by decisions that the hiring of furniture was usage in the hotel trade and that 'the three years' system' for hiring pianos 'was a custom well known to the mercantile world and the public generally'.[274] As regards high finance, Cockburn CJ led the charge in *Goodwin v. Robarts*,[275] invoking usage to extend negotiability to the new types of international bonds flooding the market. It was a question of fact, the courts held, but negotiability could attach by usage to instruments, even of recent origin. This liberal approach did not pass unchallenged, but to no avail.[276] It meant that there was no need for statute to confer the protection (if it was such) of negotiability on the bonds and corporate instruments which could find their way into the investment portfolios of the upper middle classes; the common law undertook the task.

In some quarters there was a concern that the courts might be accepting usage too readily. There was a looseness, the *Law Times* opined in 1878, as

---

[270] *Anglo Overseas Transport Ltd v. Titan Industrial Corp Ltd* [1959] 2 Lloyd's Rep 152.
[271] (1874) LR 9 CP 355.
[272] The docks, as Brett J put it, were 'an intermediate place of delivery'. On the common-law position: T. Scrutton, *Charterparties and Bills of Lading*, 13th ed., edited by S. Porter & W. McNair, London, Sweet & Maxwell, 1931, 345. See also *Grange v. Taylor* (1904) 9 Com Cas 223, another Victoria Docks case. On the usages of the Port of London: R. Cranston, 'Commercial Law and Commercial Lore', *op cit*, 80–81.
[273] *Trueman v. Loder* (1840) 11 Ad & E 589, 113 ER 539 (a transaction in tallow).
[274] *In re Parker* (1885) 14 QBD 636; *In re Blanshard ex parte Hattersley* (1878) 8 Ch D 601, 603. See 256–258 below.
[275] (1875) LR 10 Ex 337; affirmed (1876) 1 App Cas 476. Cockburn was differing from Blackburn J's conservative approach in *Crouch v. Credit Foncier of England Ltd* (1873) LR 8 QB 374. cf. *Picker v. London & County Banking Co Ltd* (1887) 18 QBD 515. See W. Blair, 'Negotiability and Estoppel' (1988) 3 *JIBL* 8.
[276] F. Bosanquet, 'Law Merchant and Transferable Debentures' (1899) 15 *LQR* 130, 143. cf. F. Palmer, 'Negotiability of Debentures to Bearer and the Growth of the Law Merchant' (1899) 15 *LQR* 245, 253–258.

regards the legal tests applied, which had led to an 'enormous amount of litigation', and an 'impression among commercial men that the cloak of usage and custom will cover a multitude of mercantile shortcomings'.[277] There may well have been something in this. Despite the condemnation, however, a steady stream of cases continued in the years prior to the First World War in which, in commercial dealings, custom and usage were recognised as binding. In one extraordinary case it was held that the standard term in LCTA contracts – that generally speaking buyers could not reject poor-quality grain but must cope with an allowance on the price – was the custom and usage of the London market and applied despite the parties contracting on their own terms without using a LCTA contract![278]

In the interwar years there were attempts to rekindle Cockburn CJ's enthusiasm in *Goodwin* v. *Robarts* for the efficacy of custom and usage, invoking his rhetorical question as to why the door should be shut to their further adoption.[279] Commercial parties, said a writer in 1922, would then be assured that their transactions 'will not necessarily be illuminated only by the farthing rushlight of mercantile customs prevalent in the days before the New World was discovered or the steam engine invented'.[280] As late as 1935, Mackinnon J upheld the conclusion of the arbitrators in the case that there was a trade usage in the London oil and tallow trade that brokers acting for an undisclosed principal were liable, along with their principal, on the contract with the third party.[281] By then, however, the ground for trade usage was rather barren. One problem, said Professor Chorley, was that commercial practice had moved on from the usages recognised by the courts in a previous era, yet these could not be overruled under the English system of precedent. That, he added, struck a blow at the whole conception of keeping commercial law developing through incorporating contemporary customs and usages.[282]

By the end of our period the prerequisites to establishing custom and usage had hardened and were almost impossible to satisfy. *Kum* v. *Wah Tat Bank Ltd*[283] serves as an example. There the Privy Council considered in the context of trade between Sarawak (East Malaysia) and Singapore whether mate's receipts could be a document of title as a result of the custom of that trade. It did not rule out the possibility, although in the end it did not have to decide the point. However, the Privy Council emphasised that, if proved, the custom would take effect as part of the common law of Singapore, be applied by any court applying Singaporean law and thus bind anyone anywhere in the world.[284] So stated, this was a high hurdle and assimilated trade usage to custom as a source of law. Lord

---

[277] 'Mercantile Customs' (1878) 64 *LT* 418.
[278] *Re an Arbitration between Walkers, Winser & Hamm and Shaw, Son & Co* [1904] 2 KB 152 (Channell J was much influenced by the findings of the arbitrator, who was LCTA's chair).
[279] (1875) LR 10 Ex 337, 346, 352.
[280] R. Negus, 'Negotiability of Bills of Lading' (1921) 37 *LQR* 442, 444.
[281] *Thornton* v. *Fehr* (1935) 51 Ll L Rep 330.
[282] R. Chorley, 'The Conflict of Law and Commerce' (1932) 48 *LQR* 51, 52, 61.
[283] [1971] 1 Lloyd's Rep 439.   [284] at 444, per Lord Devlin.

Devlin, the author of the Privy Council's opinion, had expressed the view in a lecture at the London School of Economics in 1951 that a successful claim of custom was by then extremely rare and that it 'can no longer be regarded as a revivifying source of commercial law'.[285] That, at the end of our period, was the prevailing view.

(ii) Accommodating Commercial Practice

Here the cases fell along a spectrum as the courts accommodated commercial practice in their decision-making. At one end, a commercial practice could bear heavily on the outcome of the legal issue, even if it did not constitute custom and usage; at the other end, commercial opinion in, for example, the City of London was advanced to bolster a conclusion on other grounds. Either way this diverged from the approach in other branches of law, where the courts would have looked askance at the notion of according any leverage to the practices or views of landlords, motorists or burglars in decision-making in those areas.[286] The explicit harmonising of law with commercial practice not only injected English law with a desirable responsiveness but also enhanced its legitimacy. It was one element in its reputation that in commercial causes it took commercial practice and need seriously.

At one end of the accommodating spectrum was the line of argument in a 1909 book on custom and trade usages by Dr Robert Aske (later Sir Robert Aske QC, MP). Commercial practices, he contended, while not hardened into definite and uniform shape were not devoid of worth as regards the performance of a contract.[287] If adopted by those engaged in trade, a commercial practice would almost invariably possess the merits of fairness and convenience, or at least would not be unsuitable for the purpose of determining performance issues such as the usual manner or time taken.[288] In 1936 Aske had some luck to appear as counsel in *The Njegos*,[289] which went a little way to boosting his textbook speculations. One issue in determining the proper law of the bills of lading in that litigation was whether the arbitration clause in the charterparty was incorporated into them. Aske (and counsel for the shipowners) had to accept that in the absence of a specific contractual provision, the commercial practice in London was that this was never the case. At that

---

[285] P. Devlin, 'The Relation between Commercial Law and Commercial Practice' (1951) 14 *MLR* 249, 264–265 (reproduced in *Samples of Lawmaking*, London, Oxford University Press, 1962). Examples were *Wilson Holgate v. Belgian Grain and Produce Co* [1920] 2 KB 1; *Diamond Alkali Export Corporation v. Fl Bourgeois* [1921] 3 KB 443. See also R. Goode, 'Usage and its Reception in Transnational Commercial Law' (1997) 46 *LQR* 1, 8–9.

[286] C. Schmitthoff, 'Commercial Law in Action' (1957) 101 *Sol J* 10, 11, reprinted in C. Schmitthoff, *Select Essays on International Trade Law*, London, Graham & Trotman, 1988.

[287] R. Aske, *The Law relating to Custom and the Usages of Trade*, London, Stevens, 1909, 199.

[288] Ibid., 199–200. Aske cited cases like *Lewis v. Great Western Railway Company* (1877) 3 QBD 195, 208, per Brett LJ ; *Shamrock Steamship Company v. Storey & Co* (1899) 81 *LT* 1 (interpretation of charterparty with time for loading coal specified as 36 running hours on terms of 'usual colliery guarantee').

[289] [1936] P 90.

point Sir Boyd Merriman P stopped argument; the commercial practice that the arbitration clause was not incorporated in the bill of lading was determinative.[290]

The charterparty in *The Njegos* was on the UK Chamber of Shipping River Plate (Centrocon) form, which had been introduced in 1914. The Centrocon form reappeared in *The Annefield*,[291] another case of the charter of a vessel to carry Argentinian grain to Europe. Rather boldly, counsel for the shipowners contended that *The Njegos* should be overruled on the point of the non-incorporation in the bills of lading of the arbitration clause in the charterparty. The Court of Appeal was having none of it. There was a course of practice from 1914 to 1970, some fifty-six years, and after that lapse of time it would require a very strong case to upset it.[292] There was the additional point weighing in *The Annefield*, that a court had put a construction on a standard form contract and commercial parties would have acted on it. House of Lords authority was that, in commercial cases, it was of the highest importance that legal authority should be certain and that consequently, in circumstances like these, an interpretation of a standard form would only be altered if it was clearly wrong.[293] If the commercial community was not satisfied with the court's judgment, said Lord Denning MR, it should alter the standard form.[294]

Arab Bank v. Ross[295] was another case at the end of the spectrum where Lord Denning, for one, treated commercial practice as determinative. A purchaser of a Lancashire cotton mill gave two promissory notes as payment, which the bank discounted (bought), enabling the vendors to obtain their money earlier than if they had waited for the notes to mature. The vendors were a firm registered in Palestine and as payees of the notes were described as a company. However, when they indorsed the notes to the bank they failed to add the word 'company' to their names. The purchaser when sued on the bills contended that the bank was not a holder in due course of the notes under section 29 of the Bills of Exchange Act 1882 since, at the time it took them, they were not 'complete and regular on the face of it'. The Court of Appeal agreed: there was doubt that the indorsers were the same legal person as the payees. Somervell and Romer LJJ reached their conclusion on an examination of the notes; there was some authority supporting their conclusion.[296] However, Denning LJ thought the question was best determined by banking opinion, which would not accept the indorsements in the case as regular. It was impossible for bankers to inquire whether all indorsements on a bill were genuine, but it was some safeguard against dishonesty that they were regular on their face.

---

[290] at 100. [291] [1971] P 168.
[292] at 183, 185, 186 per Lord Denning MR, Phillimore and Cairns LJJ respectively.
[293] *Atlantic Shipping and Trading Co v. Louis Dreyfus & Co* [1922] 2 AC 250, 257, per Lord Dunedin (a case about the arbitration clause in the Centrocon form).
[294] [1971] P 168, 184.   [295] [1952] 2 Q.B. 216.
[296] *Slingsby v. District Bank Ltd* [1932] 1 KB 544.

'[W]e shall not go far wrong if we follow the custom of bankers of the City of London on this point', he said.[297]

At the other end of the accommodating spectrum were those cases where commercial practice or opinion was offered as support of the court's legal analysis. Lord Mansfield was early in the field in *Miller v. Race*.[298] Trade and commerce 'would be much incommoded by a contrary determination', he said, if bank notes were not negotiable.[299] Referring to the status which a bill of lading had as a document of title, Lord Campbell CJ asserted in an 1854 case that 'it to be of essential importance to commerce that this law should be upheld'.[300] In 1914 Atkin J said that if commercial practice indicated that a contract on CIF terms meant anything different to what it had in the past – he did not believe it did – 'the Courts should be prompt to recognize the altered use if they are satisfied that there is in fact a change'.[301] And in 1924 McCardie J said in a case involving a commodity sale into Europe that the common law's object was 'to solve difficulties and adjust relations in social and commercial life ... An expanding society demands an expanding common law.'[302] These are but a few examples.

In the twentieth century, City of London practice became a source on which courts drew to buttress legal conclusions. In upholding the validity of the trust receipt in *In re David Allester Ltd*,[303] Astbury J said that it was a device enabling the bank to realise the goods over which it already had security 'in the way in which goods in similar cases have for years and years been realised in the City [of London] and elsewhere'.[304] Branson J adduced City practice to aid the construction of the Assurance Companies Act 1909 and held that insurance business encompassed the carrying on of reinsurance. In practice, he said, insurance and reinsurance ran alongside each other, and that, with life assurance, this was 'continually done every day in the City of London'.[305] In 1966 the Court of Appeal held that a party liable on a bill of exchange as acceptor could not resist

---

[297] at 227–228. Denning LJ referred to *Leonard v. Wilson* (1834) 2 Cr & M 589, 149 ER 895 (hence the reference to 120 years) and *Bank of England v. Vagliano Bros* [1891] AC 107, 157, per Lord Macnaghten. Somervell and Romer LJJ did not find banking practice helpful: at 222, 234.

[298] e.g. *Miller v. Race* (1758) 1 Burr 452, 97 ER 398.   [299] at 457, 401 respectively.

[300] *Gurney v. Behrend* (1854) 3 El & Bl 622, 637, 118 ER 1275, 1281.

[301] *C. Groom Ltd v. Barber* [1915] 1 KB 316, 325 (sale by Mincing Lane broker of 100 bales of Hessian cloth; shipment on CIF terms from Calcutta (Kolkata) according to rules and regulations of Jute Goods Association; case coming to court from association's arbitration appeal committee).

[302] *Prager v. Blatspiel Stamp and Heacock Ltd* [1924] 1 KB 566, 570. McCardie J found that in selling the goods the London merchant was dishonest, not an agent of necessity as claimed.

[303] [1922] 2 Ch 211.

[304] at 218. On trust receipts, R. Cranston, 'Doctrine and Practice in Commercial Law', in K. Hawkins (ed.), *The Human Face of Law*, Oxford, Clarendon, 1997, 200–206.

[305] *Attorney-General v. Forsikringsaktieselskabet National* (1923) 16 Ll L Rep 362, 363. Insurance practice was also referred to in *Niger Co Ltd v. Yorkshire Insurance Co Ltd (No 2)* (1919) 1 Ll L Rep 13, 17.

judgment against the holder in due course on the ground that it had a counterclaim on a related trading transaction. Any other result, said Winn LJ, would lead to 'surprise and some disquiet in the City of London'.[306] Earlier that year the majority of the same court had held that the finance company UDT escaped categorisation as an unlicensed moneylender because of its reputation among City bankers as bona fide carrying on banking business.[307] When Parliament had given no guidance on the meaning of that term, said Lord Denning MR, the judges could not do better than look at the reputation of the business among them.[308]

Along the accommodating spectrum were the cases where, for example, the courts stated that their task was to bring business knowledge and sense to the task of interpreting commercial documents. In a case involving construction of a marine insurance policy in 1885 Lord Esher MR stated that 'the proper way is to consider them with the aid of our knowledge of business, and to take it for granted that merchants and insurers have acted in a business like way'.[309] '[B]usiness sense will be given to business documents', said Lord Halsbury in *Glynn* v. *Margetson & Co*, a case turning on the construction of a bill of lading.[310] In *Hillas & Co Ltd* v. *Arcos Ltd*,[311] Lord Wright said that since commercial parties often recorded the most important agreements in crude and summary fashion, it was 'accordingly the duty of the Court to construe such documents fairly and broadly, without being too astute or subtle in finding defects'.[312]

Cases where the courts adopted a commercially sensitive approach in applying the ordinary rules of interpreting contracts are not difficult to find. In *Burrell & Sons* v. *F. Green & Co*,[313] the *ejusdem generis* rule – that words following general words are generally construed as limited to things previously enumerated – was ditched in favour of giving an unrestricted meaning to a charterparty term, 'because charterparties

---

[306] *Brown Shipley & Co Ltd* v. *Alicia Hosiery Ltd* [1966] 1 Lloyd's Rep 668, 669.
[307] *United Dominions Trust* v. *Kirkwood* [1966] 2 QB 431. On UDT and other finance houses, see 28 above.
[308] at 454. See also 473–474, per Diplock LJ.
[309] *Stewart & Co* v. *Merchants Marine Insurance Co Ltd* (1885) 16 QBD 619, 627. Earlier in this passage Lord Esher said that at one time he would have asked a jury for their interpretation. See R. Aske, The Law relating to Custom and the Usages of Trade, *op cit*, 21. In *Alexander* v. *Vanderzee* (1872) LR 7 CP 530, where the jury had been asked whether cargoes of maize were 'June shipments' in the ordinary business sense of the term, Kelly CB and Blackburn J had disapproved the practice. See C. Hanly, 'The Decline of Civil Jury Trial in Nineteenth-century England' (2005) 26 *J Legal Hist* 253; M. Lobban, 'The Strange Life of the English Civil Jury, 1837–1914', in J. Cairns and G. McLeod (eds.), *The Dearest Birthright of the People of England: The Jury in the History of the Common Law*, Oxford, Hart, 2002; R. Jackson, 'The Incidence of Jury Trial during the Past Century' (1937) 1 *MLR* 132, 142.
[310] [1893] AC 351, 358. See also 355–356, per Lord Herschell LC.   [311] (1932) 43 Ll L Rep 359.
[312] at 367. See also 366, per Lord Thankerton. Lord Warrington and Lord Macmillan concurred. See also *The Okehampton* [1913] P 173, 180, per Hamilton LJ (later Lord Sumner).
[313] [1914] 1 KB 293, 303.

often contain many redundant words', an approach adopted by other eminent judges.[314]

Another aspect of a more generous outlook was when the parties had added words to a standard form contract without working through the implications for its other terms. Sometimes this might be nothing more than an application of the general rule that greater effect should be given to what the parties had added over the printed words already there. For example, in *Dudgeon v. E. Pembroke*[315] the court held that although the parties had used a printed form of insurance for a voyage policy, the added terms referring to a voyage from 22 January 1872 to 23 January 1873 meant that it was to be treated as a time policy. Yet Lord Penzance might be thought to have been stating a wider principle of giving effect to any terms the parties added to a standard form when he said: '[T]he practice of mercantile men of writing into their printed forms the particular terms by which they desire ... is too well known, and has been too constantly recognised in Courts of Law.'[316] Other courts reflected a generous approach along these lines as they sought to repair the mangling by commercial parties of standard form documents.[317]

(iii) Hurdles to Commercial Sensitivity

In various ways, then, the courts adopted a commercially sensitive approach, and in some cases went as far as conferring on commercial practices a normative force. But on occasion there were reasons holding them back from doing this. First, to continue with a case of interpreting an amended standard form, the parties may have botched the job so badly that, however magnanimous their outlook, the courts found it impossible to give the result commercial, indeed any, sense. In a decision in the years prior to the First World War, Lord Halsbury recalled Lord Blackburn surmising that the commercial community always wished to write it short and the lawyers to write it long, but that a mixture of the two rendered the whole thing unintelligible.[318] In that case Lord Loreburn LC expressed exasperation: '[I]it is useless to draw the attention of commercial men to the risks they run by using confused and perplexing language in their business documents.'[319] In this regard Lord Atkin was splenetic in a case concerning marine insurance. Commercial parties, he

---

[314] See also *Schloss Brothers v. Stevens* [1906] 2 KB 665, 673, per Walton J; *Chandris v. Isbrandtsen-Moller Co Inc* [1951] 1 KB 240, 245, per Devlin J. There were cautions, however, against taking this too far: e.g., *Hillas & Co Ltd v. Arcos Ltd* (1932) 43 Ll L Rep 359, 363–364, per Lord Tomlin.
[315] (1877) 2 App Cas 284. Lords O'Hagan, Blackburn and Gordon agreed.
[316] at 293. See also *Glynn v. Margetson & Co* [1893] AC 351, 355, 357; *In re an Arbitration between L Sutro & Co and Heilbut, Symons & Co* [1917] 2 KB 348, 361–362, per Scrutton LJ.
[317] e.g., *Weis & Co v. Produce Brokers' Co* (1921) 7 Ll L Rep 211 (CIF sale of China white peas on LCTA form for Chinese and Manchurian Cereals); *W. P. Greenhalgh & Sons v. Union Bank of Manchester* [1924] 2 KB 153 (wrong forms used in depositing bills of exchange with bank in payment for shipment of Egyptian cotton).
[318] *Nelson Line (Liverpool), Ltd v. James Nelson & Sons Ltd* [1908] AC 16, 20.
[319] at 20. Lords Halsbury, Macnaghten and Atkinson agreed. It was a case about the liability of a shipowner under the contract of carriage.

said, habitually ventured large sums of money on contracts which were 'a mere jumble of words', trusting to luck of the opposite party, and 'with the comfortable assurance that any adverse result of litigation may be attributed to the hairsplitting of lawyers and the uncertainty on the law'.[320] Commercial practice, from this perspective, was not something to be encouraged.

Second, there are examples of how a conclusion contrary to what commercial interests thought desirable was driven by legal doctrine or judicial disfavour of the substance of a commercial practice.[321] In some cases, the result was to check the commercial practice; in others, the court's disapproval was surmounted by amending a market rule or the relevant standard form contract.[322] Third, as Scrutton LJ put it in the early 1930s, 'in many commercial matters the English law and the practice of commercial men are getting wider apart'. What Scrutton LJ was suggesting – however inaccurately – was that unlike earlier judges his contemporaries were not as concerned with reconciling commercial practice and commercial law where these were opposed, perhaps did not even think it was their task to do this. The result was, he thought, a flight from the courts, and for commercial disputes to be decided by commercial arbitrators.[323] The immediate background to Scrutton's remarks was his tussles with the House of Lords.[324] However, there was support for Scrutton's view that things were not as right as rain.[325] Commercial practice and commercial law were sometimes out of kilter. Perhaps this is not surprising: on the one hand, there was commerce, ever-changing with new techniques to pursue profit; on the other, a judicature, dependent on commercial parties litigating the right cases so it could bring law up to date, and a Parliament, where law reform was near the bottom of the agenda.[326]

1.4 Conclusion

Vagliano v the Bank of England[327] was, out of the usual course, argued before the six judges of the Court of Appeal and five of those judges were in favour of the

---

[320] *De Monchy* v. *Phoenix Insurance Company of Hartford* (1929) 34 Ll L Rep 201, 209.
[321] See 75, 138, 351, 407 below. See also *James Finlay and Company Ltd* v. *N. V. Kwik Hoo Tong Handel Maatschappij* [1929] 1 K.B. 400, 408 ('lax practice' after the First World War of entering the wrong date on bills of lading) and McCardie J's remarks in *Diamond Alkali Export Corp* v. *Bourgeois* [1921] 3 KB 443, 457. See A. Lentin, *Mr Justice McCardie (1869–1933)*, Cambridge, Scholars Publishing, 2016 on this iconoclastic judge.
[322] See *Robinson* v. *Mollett* (1875) LR 7 HL 802, *Cooke & Sons* v. *Eshelby* (1887) LR 12 App Cas 271 discussed below at 78–79, 75–76 respectively.
[323] *Hillas & Co Ltd* v. *Arcos Ltd* (1931) 40 Ll L Rep 307, 311.
[324] In *May* v. *Butcher*, eventually reported at [1934] 2 KB 17, his view had been rejected. After these remarks in *Hillas & Co Ltd* v. *Arcos Ltd*, when he fell into line with the law lords, his views were again rejected in the House of Lords: (1932) 43 Ll L Rep 359, but see continuation of the tussle in *Foley* v. *Classique Coaches* [1934] 2 KB 1, 9–10. See D. Foxton, The Life of Thomas E. Scrutton, op cit, 282. See also H. Gutteridge, 'Contract and Commercial Law' (1935) 51 *LQR* 91, 113.
[325] R. Chorley, 'The Conflict of Law and Commerce', *op cit*; P. Devlin, 'The Relation between Commercial Law and Commercial Practice', *op cit*.
[326] 397 below.   [327] [1891] AC 107.

plaintiff and agreed with Mr Justice Charles, who tried the case. But in the House of Lords six of the noble Lords were in favour of the defendants and two in favour of the plaintiffs. Thus, in the result, the views of seven judges prevailed over those of eight judges. (John Hollams, *Jottings of an Old Solicitor*, 1906)[328]

Pivotal to the context of commercial law during our period was Britain's dominant role in international trade and finance for a significant part of it, reinforced by its leading position in shipping and insurance. Trade and finance coalesced in the merchant banks. Initially engaged in trade themselves, they also facilitated the trade of others by furnishing credit and payment services through accepting bills of exchange and issuing documentary credits. The joint stock banks later joined in the acceptance business and trade financing, while continuing their traditional services of short-term funding of commerce and industry through overdrafts and on-demand loans.

Trade in commodities occurred through the organised markets in London and Liverpool. Crucially, the trade associations in both cities, which revolved around these markets, engaged in private law-making, drawing up (or indorsing) standards for the many commodities being handled; the rules and regulations channelling the work, including the conduct of the merchants and brokers dealing there; and the standard form contracts recording and governing the transactions entered. Cooperating sometimes with others, the trade associations founded supportive institutions such as clearing houses, which handled more efficiently the accounting side of dealings, in particular the futures transactions which, with time, came to maturity on these markets.

During our period trading firms arranged both the shipping of commodities to Europe and the export of manufactured goods abroad. Trading firms could be agents one minute and principals the next, with a presence in Britain as well as abroad. In some parts of the world trading firms might hold multiple agencies, not only for manufacturers and producers elsewhere, but also for shipping lines, insurance companies and banks. They might also act as managing agents running estates, mines and factories which they had promoted or in which they had invested. Many British manufacturers were small and continued to rely on the trading firms, but a feature in the twentieth century was that the larger sometimes dealt directly abroad or established a presence there, as did some of the banks.

The sale and purchase of heavy manufactured goods could lead to a close association between manufacturers and purchasers as both worked to resolve problems with innovative plant and machinery. Making it could also be accompanied by the close involvement of a buyer in the manufacturing process, and in some cases the engagement of consultant engineers to monitor compliance with

---

[328] J. Hollams, *Jottings of an Old Solicitor*, London, John Murray, 1906, 157. On Hollams, 297 below. Successful counsel for the Bank of England later expressed doubt about the decision: Viscount Alverstone, *Recollections of Bench and Bar*, London, Edward Arnold, 1914, 156–157.

the specifications and drawings for its design. The marketing of other manufactured goods led to innovations in credit financing, the use of hire and hire purchase rather than sale, and the growth of specialist financial institutions to dispense them. Until the state stepped in at the end of our period, the marketing of manufactured goods could be associated with restrictive trade practices as manufacturers and producers – sometimes working collaboratively through trade associations – attempted to control how their goods were distributed and priced.

The law furnished a broad framework in which this commercial and financial activity took place. During our period regulatory law was at a minimum, with no real bearing on the regular operation of commercial markets, marketing transactions or the financing of trade and industry. At most bodies like the Bank of England would indicate desirable courses of action, which were generally followed despite a lack of legal backing. As for the common law, it was animated by broad principles, in theory all facilitative of commercial activity. Party autonomy empowered commercial parties to design the market rules, standard form contracts and institutions they fancied. It also enabled them to keep lawyers and the courts at bay, with the bulk of disputes being dealt with through private dispute settlement in the form of arbitration.[329] Bright-line rules assisted in commercial planning and knowing where parties stood in straightforward cases if a transaction turned sour. That was because, as one judge bluntly put it in a bills of exchange claim just after our period, the strict application of rules was not to be whittled away 'by introducing unnecessary exceptions ... under the influence of sympathy-evoking stories ... [H]ard cases can make bad law.'[330]

Then, if disputes did end in court, the judges could generally be relied on to adopt a commercially sensitive approach, aware of wider public interests, for example, as expressed in the same case, of how the erosion of clear rules in English bills of exchange law would likely 'work to the detriment of this country, which depends on international trade to a degree that needs no emphasis'.[331] This commercially sensitive approach was symbolised in 1895 with the establishment of the Commercial Court, a special list in the Queen's Bench Division of the High Court in London, with judges having a knowledge and experience of commercial practices, and with procedural rules conducive to the expeditious and flexible handling of commercial litigation.[332] At points in its history the court was in the

---

[329] J. Veeder 'Two Arbitral Butterflies: Bramwell and David,' in M. Hunter, A. Marriott and V. Veeder (eds.), *The Internationalisation of International Arbitration*, Leiden, Martinus Nijhoff, 1995. See 361–373 below.

[330] *Cebora SNC* v. *SIP (Industrial Products)* [1976] 1 Lloyd's Rep 271, 279, per Sir Eric Sachs (stay on claim on bill of exchange refused, despite possible counterclaim under a distribution contract). See also *Bell* v. *Lever Brothers Ltd* [1932] AC 161, 226, per Lord Atkin. See other examples at 42–43 above.

[331] at 278. See 54–55 above; 69, 88, 119, 121, 123, 125, 209, 214, 218, 350, 355, 382, 394, 395–396 below.

[332] e.g., J. Veeder, 'Mr Justice Lawrance: the 'true begetter' of the English Commercial Court' (1994) 110 *LQR* 292; *Oxford History of the Laws of England, op cit*, vol. XI, 828–829 (P. Polden); Lord Thomas, 'Keeping Commercial Law up to date', in R. Merkin & J. Devenney (eds.), *Essays in Memory of Professor Jill Poole Coherence, Modernisation and Integration in Contract, Commercial and Corporate Laws*, Abingdon, Informa/Routledge, 2018.

doldrums.[333] However, it emerged strengthened by reforms in the 1960s so that, just after our period, there was a heavy workload, international in character, with the great majority of cases having foreign parties, in many cases on all sides.[334]

The quotation from Sir John Hollams at the head of this conclusion – a leading solicitor of our period – demonstrates that it would be wrong to take too benign a view of the relationship between commercial law and commercial practice. If commercial disputes reached court – and vast numbers did not – the outcome could be a lottery. Further, for good or ill judges did not always take account of commercial practice, and whatever its history or motivation, there could be a disconnect between doctrine and the commercial realties.[335] What can be said is that the formal law for commercial transactions was generally capacious and pliable. It empowered extensive private law-making as markets, merchants and banks moulded transactions through the formulation of rules, the issue of standard form contracts and the establishment of private dispute resolution mechanisms. When difficulties were encountered, these were fairly readily surmounted by contractual or private arrangements. In most cases, lawyers could be kept in the background. Although insolvency and fraud could demand its presence, brushes with the formal trappings of the law could be minimised by mandating arbitration for dispute settlement. Overall, the law cast few shadows over profit making.

---

[333] R. Ferguson, 'The Adjudication of Commercial Disputes and the Legal System in Modern England' (1980) 7 *Brit JL&S* 141, 146.

[334] M. Kerr, 'Modern Trends in Commercial Law and Practice' (1978) 41 *MLR* 1, 4–5.

[335] S. Hedley, 'The "Needs of Commercial Litigants" in Nineteenth and Twentieth Century Contract law' (1997) 18 *J Leg Hist* 85.

2

The Commodity Markets of London and Liverpool

2.1 Introduction

> The heart of the commercial activity of the City of London, as distinct from financial, is *Mincing-lane*. There ... many merchants and brokers engaged in the business of drawing from the sources of supply, often in remote corners of the world, and distributing to the markets at home and abroad ... tea, sugar, coffee, cocoa, rice, tapioca, sago, spices, dried fruit, wine, rubber, hemp, jute ... drugs ... carpets, mica, and canned goods. Auction sales of nearly all the above commodities are held regularly...
>
> The *Baltic Exchange* ... can justly claim to be the finest produce and shipping market in the world ... The membership ... is cosmopolitan in character, most of the countries in the world being represented. Large transactions in wheat, maize, barley, and other produce take place daily, all by word of mouth, the contracts being completed on the return of the members to their offices.[1]

In his study of *Civilisation and Capitalism*, Fernand Braudel writes of the establishment of direct and regular maritime contact between Genoa and Bruges after 1297, and of how this symbolised the transformation of large-scale commerce in the early fourteenth century. 'Merchandise was beginning to travel alone: its movements between Italy and the Netherlands, the two poles of the European economy, were controlled from a distance by written correspondence, and there was no longer any need for merchants to meet and discuss matters half-way.'[2] Subsequently fairs were held, international wholesale markets where goods were sold and accounts extinguished by set-off, 'debts met and cancelled each other out, melting like snow in the sun'.[3] Then followed the Piacenza fair, mainly run by Genoese bankers: without merchandise and little cash, masses of bills of exchange were liquidated, representing 'the entire

---

[1] The Times, *The City of London*, London, Times Publishing Co, 1927, 187–188, 195–196. The centre of activity in Mincing-lane was the Commercial Sale Rooms.
[2] F. Braudel, *The Structure of Everyday Life*, London, Collins, 1984, 419.
[3] F. Braudel, *The Wheels of Commerce*, London, Collins, 1982, 90–91. See also Sir William Holdsworth, *A History of English Law*, London, Methuen, 1924, vol. V, 85–100.

wealth of Europe'.[4] Markets were no longer simply places to trade goods but where contractual claims could be settled and enforced.[5]

This chapter is concerned with the international commodity markets in London and Liverpool in the nineteenth and first part of the twentieth centuries. Now largely forgotten,[6] their major legacy lies in the City of London's derivatives markets (of which commodities derivatives are a part) and the clearing systems, which are a key component of the City's present-day financial infrastructure, settling trades in securities, funds and derivatives. The organised markets in London and Liverpool in commodities like grain, cotton, wool, sugar, tea, coffee and spices were a product of the rising volume of international trade as Britain became the first industrial nation, a major importer of these commodities for its own needs, an entrepôt, especially for Europe, and a centre for organising their distribution elsewhere.

Domestic produce markets such as the corn (grain) exchanges in the major cities and towns of Britain remained but were no longer isolated from international trends.[7] Grain purchased internationally on the Baltic Exchange might be disposed of domestically through the Corn Exchange in Mark Lane, London. Brokers from the Baltic Exchange might sell to the stand-holders and millers based at the latter, the stand-holders in turn on-selling to dealers, millers and others.[8] The London and Liverpool markets facilitated distribution through time with forward dealings.[9] Futures contracts went a step further: they involved obligations to deliver or receive a standardised quality and amount of a commodity at a specified price and time in the future. Actual delivery was not contemplated, and trades were settled by the payment of price differences. Futures trading offered greater protection from risks through the hedging of trades, since sellers (say) knew the price they would receive. Speculation in futures worked to level out prices on markets. Law had little to say about the emergence of this dimension of commodity markets, even its unsavoury and fraudulent aspects.

Following this brief introduction, the chapter then explores the organisation and membership of the international commodity markets in London and

---

[4] F. Braudel, *The Wheels of Commerce*, ibid., 91, 94.

[5] See J. Edwards & S. Ogilivie, 'What Lessons for Economic Development Can We Draw from the Champagne Fairs?' (2012) 49 *Explorations in Econ Hist* 131 on the role of public enforcement.

[6] Professor Ranald Michie has done much to remind us: e.g., R. Michie, *The City of London: Continuity and Change 1850–1999*, London, Macmillan, 1992; S. Mollan & R. Michie,' 'The City of London as an International Commercial and Financial Center since 1900' (2012) 13 *Enterprise & Society* 538.

[7] C. Smith, 'The Wholesale and Retail Markets of London 1660–1840' (2002) 55 *Econ Hist Rev* 31, 40 (London Corn Exchange). See also 'Markets' (1931) 72 *LJ*, 22–23, 38–39; J. Hill, 'Markets and the Common Law' (1985) 5 *Leg Stud* 320.

[8] *Report from the Select Committee on Corn Averages*, Command 312, 1888, 27 (Q413); C. Maughan, *Markets of London*, London, Pitman, 1931, 38–44; The Times, The City of London, *op cit*, 186–187.

[9] see J. Smith, *Organised Produce Markets*, London, Longmans, Green and Co, 1922; S. Hoebner, 'The Functions of Produce Exchanges' (September 1911) 38 *Annals of the Amer Acad of Pol and Soc Sci* 319.

Liverpool in our period and the part played by the trade associations in running them and elaborating systems of private law to do so. Apart from internal organisation and membership (and what this entailed for members' behaviour) (part 2.2), their systems of private law provided for a variety of other matters such as the role of the brokers, dealt with in part 2.3, who bought and sold on these markets. Then in part 2.4 we touch on the emergence of futures dealings, a subject pursued further in part 2.6 (especially section 3(ii)). Part 2.5 addresses a crucial, yet underrated aspect of the commodity markets, clearing and settlement, what is sometimes described as market plumbing. In this respect the City of London's commodity markets left a vital legacy to its standing in modern times as an international financial centre.

Up to this point in the chapter, the focus is on private law-making in the form of the rules and regulations formulated by the markets and the trade associations whose members worked on them. Part 2.6, however, is concerned with state law: the court-imposed and statutory standards offering a semblance of public assurance about market integrity. It was very much light touch. Only the most egregious behaviour, associated with a general financial crisis, or attracting widespread public condemnation and threatening confidence, triggered the intervention of state law.[10]

2.2 Organisation and Membership

> The loss of perhaps the greatest practical statistician of our age deserves more than passing notice from economists ... The case of George Broomhall and the *Corn Trade News* is, however, remarkable, in that he not only built up an extra-ordinarily efficient pioneer institution on a matter of great importance, but has continued to be regarded as the first authority on the matter long after various official and semi-official bodies, including the chief governments of the world ... have taken up the work ... facilitating the orderly and intelligent conduct of the greatest branch of international trade. (John Maynard Keynes, 1938)[11]

Keynes' encomium for George Broomhall in 1938 was notable for several reasons. First, here was the world's most distinguished economist of the day, who had only recently published his *The General Theory of Employment, Interest and Money*,[12] paying effusive tribute to a person some would have regarded as a mere Liverpool-based journeyman. Second, it was a reminder that quite apart from anything else, organised commodity markets were crucial for the collection and dissemination of price and other information. Third, it underlined that, as with Broomhall' invaluable statistics on the international

---

[10] An early version of this chapter appeared in M. Andenæs, et al. (eds.), *Liber amicorum Guido Alpa: Private Law beyond the National Systems*, London, British Institute of International and Comparative Law, 2007.
[11] J. M. K., 'Obituary. George Broomhall 1857–1938' (1938) *48 Econ J* 576, 577–578.
[12] London, Macmillan & Co., 1936.

grain markets, the London and Liverpool commodity markets operated without the intervention of the state, even in areas such as this which were essential to their efficient functioning for the wider society.

During the nineteenth century the London and Liverpool commodity markets had become increasingly sophisticated. More elaborate rules had been needed once they graduated from being produce markets for spot sales to markets where risks could be hedged and speculation engaged in by means of futures contracts. Nonetheless, the London and Liverpool commodity markets never acquired the legal trappings of their counterparts on the Continent or in North America, nor were they ever subject to the legal regulation operating in those jurisdictions. In Germany futures speculation, and certain stock market dealings, led to the German exchange law of 1896, as a result of which exchanges and their rules had to be approved by the state governments and supervised by state commissioners (although the task of supervision was usually performed by chambers of commerce).[13] What became one of the largest wheat markets in North America, the Winnipeg Grain and Produce Exchange, was incorporated in 1891 by a Manitoba statute. United States commodity exchanges like the Chicago Board of Trade and the New York Cotton Exchange were specially chartered by their state legislatures, and the Chicago Board of Trade had conferred on it the right to hire inspectors and measurers, whose decisions were legally binding.[14] In the 1920s and 1930s federal regulation followed in the United States with the Grain Futures Act of 1922 and the Commodity Exchange Act of 1936. Both meant state intrusion into the American commodity markets, which the London and Liverpool markets never experienced.

With the operation of the London and Liverpool commodity markets private law-making was the order of the day during the whole of our period. These markets maintained a club-like character even after they took a more organised form.[15] With international commodities trading there were rules governing the admission to market venues like the Baltic Exchange and to the trade associations formed for the brokers and merchants buying and selling the different commodities. There were also informal conventions as to how members were to behave in their market dealings. With time some of the norms became more explicit and were spelt out as rules. In extreme cases a breach of the informal conventions and the rules could trigger moves for the expulsion of a member of a market or a trade association. But all of this occurred without intervention by the courts or Parliament.

---

[13] E. Loeb, 'The German Exchange Act of 1896' (1897) 11 *Q J Econ* 388; H. Hirschstein, 'Commodity Exchanges in Germany' (May 1931) 155 *Annals of Amer. Acad of Pol & Soc Sci* 208.

[14] But it was still regarded as a voluntary association: *People ex rel Rice* v. *Board of Trade of Chicago*, 80 Ill 134 (1875). See W. Cronon, *Nature's Metropolis*, New York, Norton, 1991, 119.

[15] H. Collins, *Regulating Contracts*, Oxford, Oxford University Press, 2002, 212–221.

1 Organisation of the Markets

While most English commodity exchanges eventually took corporate form, during our period they never matched the American exchanges with their formalised structures and rules governing exchange behaviour. One of the earliest trade associations in the industrial period, the Society of Sugar Refiners of London, was founded in the late eighteenth century. Its rules were simple and concentrated on the criteria for membership. Persons could be expelled, and insolvency meant a person was no longer considered to be a member.[16] The standards expected of members, breach of which could ultimately lead to expulsion, were not articulated in the rules, although at one point there was a move to control jobbing of raw sugar.[17]

As with the sugar merchants, the London and Liverpool commodities markets were started as informal gatherings of merchants interested in specific commodities, who subsequently transformed themselves into formal associations. From the second part of the nineteenth century these provided the organisational framework for trading, as did the bodies spun off such as the London Produce Clearing House. The associations took corporate form from the 1880s. This was both the fashion of the time but also had distinct advantages when the common law of unincorporated associations was underdeveloped. Incorporation offered advantages both internally (e.g., control over membership) and externally (e.g., the ownership of property where trading occurred). Unlike commercial companies, however, where shareholders could come and go, the trading associations and their markets were constituted to ensure a tight rein over the admission (and expulsion) of members.

In organisational terms the Liverpool Corn Trade Association (LvCTA) is illustrative.[18] Although dating back to 1853, it was not until 1897 that it finally incorporated. Its share capital was an impressive £60,000, divided into 400 shares of £150 each. Membership was confined to persons engaged in the grain trade, and every member was required to be a shareholder of the company. Members could not hold more than one share in addition to the one acquired on admission to membership. They might be required to transfer this to a new member who was otherwise unable to acquire a share. Limiting share ownership in this way was self-evidently designed to thwart control by a dominant interest, although a side effect of dispersed ownership was that it could act as a roadblock to change.

---

[16] LMA, CLC/B/204/MS08188/002, Society of Sugar Refiners of London, Minutes and Accounts 1809–1818, 1–2, rr.12–13. For an example of someone blackballed: ibid., 14, 12 December 1809.

[17] LMA, CLC/B/204/MS08189, Society of Sugar Refiners of London, Committee Minutes 1791–1803, 9, 17–18, 17 May, 30 June, 7 July 1791.

[18] See *Liverpool Corn Trade Association Ltd v. Monks (HM Inspector of Taxes)* [1926] 2 KB 110. Rowlatt J held that the association produced taxable profits; for tax purposes it was more a railway company than a golf club. See also R. Forrester, 'Commodity Exchanges in England' (May 1931) 155 *Annals of the Amer Acad of Pol and Soc Sci* 196, 203–204.

Among the objects of the association were promoting the interests of the grain trade, settling disputes between those in the trade, maintaining a market for the grain trade in Liverpool and establishing a clearing house. Under the articles the directors had to approve the transfer of shares, and on the death, bankruptcy or retirement from business of a member could find a purchaser for a member's shares and compel their transfer. With bankruptcy a member ceased to have any rights or privileges except the right of transferring his shares. The articles also provided for subscribers who were not members but who could use the facilities and exchange. Directors were empowered to make by-laws, some of which are examined below. The byelaws set out an organisational structure for the association and thus a framework for the wheat market in Liverpool.

2 Membership: Admission, Expulsion and Codes of Behaviour

Conditions for membership of the markets and the trade associations responsible for organising commodity trading formed an important component of their rules. Illustrative is the Baltic Exchange, which began life in one of the London coffee houses. During our period, it was an international shipping market, as it is today, where ships could be chartered (hired) and sold. During most of our period, however, it was an important venue for international dealings in commodities such as grain, tallow and linseed. The Baltic Exchange's rules related to little other than membership. It remained as an unincorporated association, although a Baltic Company Ltd was incorporated in 1857, under the Joint Stock Companies Act 1856, to buy new premises where dealings could take place.

The rules and regulations drawn up in 1823 for 'The Baltic Coffee-House' limited it to 300 members with no more than six members from the Stock Exchange (associated, it was said, with undue speculation). By 1854 the rules had removed the limitation of 300, and by the 1920s membership of the Baltic Exchange stood at some 2,500. New members were to be admitted on the recommendation of six other members and approval by the committee.[19] They had to be proposed and seconded by members to whom they were personally known, their names had to be publicised to other members and there was then a ballot by the committee.

While typically there was a wide discretion in the rules of the markets and trade associations as to admission, decisions on expulsion were more closely confined. Insolvency became an almost automatic ground for suspension or expulsion. Unable by law to trade in the ordinary way, the insolvent was *ipso facto* unable to be a member of a market. The member who was unable to satisfy creditors, or who came to an arrangement with them to pay part only of

---

[19] Baltic Rules 1823, rr.2–3. See also rr.4–5 (subscriptions), r.7 (visitors), rr.9–10 (meetings). The 1823 rules are set out in J. Findlay, *Baltic Exchange*, London, Witherley & Co., 1927, 14–16.

Figure 2.1 The Baltic Exchange, St Mary Axe, London (The Baltic Exchange)

the debts owing, was in very much the same boat. In 1837 the Baltic Exchange adopted as its thirteenth rule that '[m]embers having the misfortune to fail, or who compound with their creditors, to be by that act excluded from the Society'. In an expression of generosity, the rule contemplated that the member, excluded under this rule, should be eligible for readmission on the same footing as new members, after being discharged from bankruptcy or settling with creditors. In addition, organised markets recognised that they should act preventively in relation to those threatened with bad debts. That was because the market could be disrupted if insolvency should occur and members were unable to settle their accounts with others. Thus, the rules of the Liverpool Cotton Brokers' Association enabled the committee to investigate reports of bad debts of a member. An adverse report could constitute misconduct rendering it undesirable for that person to continue as a member.[20]

Apart from default and insolvency, the grounds for expulsion from markets and trade associations were hazy. Often informal conventions operated. A member's word, it was said on the Baltic Exchange, was his bond. In a narrow sense this meant that, as soon as members made a verbal agreement, they could not resile from it.[21] But it also meant that potentially a member guilty

---

[20] rr.31, 33. See LRO, 380 COT/1/1/1, Liverpool Cotton Brokers' Association Ltd, Constitution Laws and Usages, 1881.

[21] W. Mackenzie, '"The Baltic": Its History and Work' (1900) 12 *The Windsor Magazine*, 559, 562. Extraordinarily, the first code for behaviour was introduced in 1983: *The Baltic Code 2003. Guidance for Brokers in the Baltic Exchange Market*, London, 2003, 4.

of a serious breach of the informal standards governing behaviour could be expelled. It was very much a matter of enforcing the informal standards that could attract widespread support. In 1837 the Baltic Exchange had added its sixteenth rule under which a member could be expelled for conduct both on the Exchange or otherwise, which the committee by two-thirds majority should decide, or twenty-five members should certify, was 'derogatory to his character as a man of business'.[22] The procedures were summary and there was no appeal.

In practice the threat of expulsion could have a salutary effect. In 1863 W. R. Arbuthnot & Co. complained that William Kern had offered them a sample of linseed oil for sale, which could be accepted at 11.20 am at his office at the Commercial Sale Rooms in Mincing Lane. However, he was not there at that time. When located about ten minutes later he refused to sell the linseed on the basis that it was too late. There was a rising market in linseed, and no doubt Kern had been able to obtain a better price elsewhere. At first Kern refused to arbitrate the dispute, until Arbuthnot threatened to refer it to the committee of the Baltic Exchange. When the arbitration went against him, Kern refused to accept the award. Arbuthnot referred the matter to the committee. At that point, with the threat of expulsion on the horizon, Kern agreed to abide by the award.[23]

The Baltic Exchange was a venue for trading. The trade associations were different, formed from those dealing in different commodities. With time they developed rules – rules as to how their standard form contracts were to be used, how transactions were to be effected, the operation of their clearing and settlement systems, and the arbitration of disputes between members.[24] It was natural that the breach of these, at least in extreme cases, should become a basis for expulsion from an association. For example, in its Constitution, Laws and Usages of 1881 the Liverpool Cotton Brokers' Association addressed expulsion under the heading 'Responsibility, Insolvency and Misconduct'. It provided for expulsion if a member was 'persistently guilty of infringement of the Rules or of such misconduct as shall ... render it undesirable that he should continue to be a Member'.[25] Thirty years later the drafting of the Liverpool cotton rules was still open textured – dishonourable or disreputable conduct in a member's dealings – although the range of sanctions had been expanded and the possibility of a reprimand, fine or suspension was added to expulsion. As well as the trade associations there were the clearing houses. Another disciplinary action short of expulsion was that, short of refusing to allow any contracts to be registered, they might restrict a person's trading by limiting the number of contracts it could register.

---

[22] The 1854 rules are reproduced in H. Barty-King, *The Baltic Exchange*, London, Hutchinson, 1977, 99–101.
[23] Ibid., 142–143. See also 137 (expulsion for non-payment in relation to tallow sale).
[24] 89, 299, 361 below.   [25] rr.31–33.

3 Role of the Courts: Hands Off

Prompted by an agreement with the Verein der Bremer Baumwollhändler (the Bremen Cotton Association), in 1909 the Liverpool Cotton Association finally spelt out the meaning of dishonourable or disreputable conduct which justified the expulsion of one of its members. Under the agreement between the two associations each had agreed to expel their own members found by the other association to have acted dishonourably or disreputably. Disciplinary action now included the wilful and intentional non-fulfilment of a contract; the fraudulent and flagrant breach of a contract; a frivolous repudiation of a contract; and a refusal to refer a question in dispute to arbitration or to abide by an arbitration or appeal award, unless arbitration was specifically excluded by the contract.[26] When these arrangements were considered in the Chancery Division in 1911, the judgment reflected the prevailing judicial attitude of non-interference with the actions of trade associations regarding members' behaviour, except in the most extreme circumstances. Eve J upheld these steps of the Liverpool Cotton Association to be able to expel members for their failure to submit to German arbitration in a dispute with a member of the Bremen Cotton Exchange.[27]

Non-interference with the disciplinary decision in that case was based on the ordinary principles of company law, since the association was incorporated. That was the right of a majority of an incorporated association to adopt rules for members.[28] How was the issue couched in the case of an unincorporated association? One example was the expulsion in 1900 of Chamberlain's Wharf from the Tea Clearing House for breach of its price maintenance rule.[29] Members of the association were dock companies and tea warehouses carrying on the business of warehousing tea in bond. Under its rules they agreed to charge set rates for storage and services. Chamberlain's Wharf argued that it had been denied natural justice because it had not been given the opportunity of being heard in its defence against the expulsion.[30] At first instance the judge had agreed. On appeal, the case went off on another point: the association was in law a trade union whose rules the court could not enforce, which it would be doing by adjudicating on the expulsion.[31]

Other than natural justice, and perhaps jurisdictional error, there was little scope in the common law for judicial control of a trade association's decisions. Members would have to prove malice, improper motive or bias on the part of the association if they were to overturn a disciplinary decision, all very high

---

[26] *Merrifield, Ziegler & Co v. Liverpool Cotton Association Ltd* (1911) 105 LT 97.
[27] Eve J referred to Liverpool as the centre of the European cotton trade, hence the need for the German arrangement: at 104.
[28] e.g., F. Palmer and C. Macnaghten, *Company Precedents*, London, Stevens & Sons, 1888, 8–9.
[29] Chamberlain's Wharf still stands on the south side of the Thames, between London and Tower bridges. It is occupied now by the London Bridge Hospital: C. Ellmers & A. Werner, *London's Riverscape*, London, London's Found Riverscape Partnership, 2000, 164.
[30] *Chamberlain's Wharf Ltd v. Smith* [1900] 2 Ch 605.
[31] see also *Wood v. Wood* (1874) LR 9 Ex 190 (mutual insurance society); *Labouchere v. Earl of Wharncliffe* (1879) 13 Ch D 346 (Beefsteak Club). See W. Robson, *Justice and Administrative Law*, London, Macmillan, 1928, 229.

hurdles.[32] The wide berth the courts gave to trade associations became evident in the Stock Exchange cases arising during the First World War. When the Stock Exchange refused to re-elect a naturalised British subject, of German birth, the courts refused to interfere although before the war he had been a member of twenty-two years' good standing. Despite the argument of Francis Gore-Browne KC,[33] that there was no question of his integrity, and that his German birth was irrelevant to his fitness to be a member of the exchange, the House of Lords was caught up in the atmosphere of the time and held that the exchange had not been shown to have acted arbitrarily or capriciously.[34] By modern standards the decision cannot be justified.

In the interwar period of the 1920s and 1930s the standards expected on markets became more formalised. Disciplinary action in the case of some trade associations no longer turned on vague standards like dishonourable or disreputable conduct. The basis for disciplinary action was spelt out. By 1922 the Liverpool Corn Trade Association had a list of causes rendering a member liable to expulsion, suspension or the payment of a fine: neglecting to abide by an arbitration award or other decision under the rules; acting detrimentally to the interests of the association; unbecoming character; other misconduct in relation to the association or its members; dishonourable, disreputable or fraudulent transactions with counterparties, whether members or not; failure to cooperate with an inquiry by the association or to pay a fine; and acting for a firm, with membership of the association, in circumstances which would reasonably lead to the conclusion that the partner instructing him was not acting honourably as regards other members of the partnership.[35]

Perhaps the trend of the law, in particular a tightening of procedural requirements for expulsion, had an influence in this concretisation of the grounds for disciplinary action.[36] Especially in the Liverpool markets, there might also have been some permeation of US legal practice, which was to spell out matters in rules and contracts which in English practice would be left to the discretion of the decision-maker. In the United States the rules for commodity exchanges contained a range of specific prohibitions on behaviour, breach which could lead to expulsion or sanction. These prohibitions included price manipulation, circulating rumours of a sensational character, reckless or

---

[32] D. Lloyd, 'The Disciplinary Powers of Professional Bodies' (1950) 13 *MLR* 281, 292–294; Z. Chafee, 'The Internal Affairs of Associations Not for Profit' (1930) 43 *Harv LR* 993, 1005–1006.

[33] An expert in company law, whose name is still carried by a leading text book on the subject: *Gore-Browne on Companies*, 45th ed., Bristol, Jordans, 2019.

[34] *Weinberger v. Inglis* [1919] AC 606, 616–617, 621, 624–626, 631. See also *Cassel v. Inglis* [1916] 2 Ch 211 (stock exchange). cf. *R v. Speyer; R v. Cassel* [1916] 1 KB 595; [1916] 2 KB 858 (Privy Council). See D. Lloyd, 'The Disciplinary Powers of Professional Bodies' (1950) 13 *MLR* 281, 292–294.

[35] MMM, B/LCTA/43/1, Liverpool Corn Trade Association, Liverpool Corn Trade Association Bye-laws, 1 April 1922 (hereafter LvCTA Bye-laws).

[36] e.g., *Young v. Ladies' Imperial Club* [1920] 2 KB 523. See S. Stoljar, *Groups and Entities*, Canberra, Australian National University Press, 1973, 50.

unbusinesslike dealing, and conduct or proceedings inconsistent with the just and equitable principles of trade.[37]

2.3 Brokers, Rules and Third Parties

> Full many a lot of bales,
> And the question upon every lip
> Is – 'What does he make the sales?'
> I do not know, I really don't,
> But stay – he's coming here;
> My friends, pray let me introduce
> Our Secretary dear.
> The sales, the sales – how many bales?
> How much is done today?
> 'Now, gentlemen, pray – really – don't –
> I can't at present say!'
> 'The sales,' again the brokers shout,
> And press upon him sore –
> What are the sales? – his courage fails –
> 'We'll call them twelve [thousand] – or more'.[38]

1 The Brokers

The emergence of organised commodity markets was accompanied by the growth of a class of specialised brokers. Liverpool's nineteenth-century cotton brokers, the subject of this doggerel, are a case in point. Importing the cotton were the merchants or commission agents (acting for the grower or for an exporter, sometimes a merchant with a base in the United States).[39] For these importers the broker provided an orderly sale of the cargo and a possible source of credit (the cotton acting as security) until they were able to recoup themselves from onward sale; for the spinners (the textile manufacturers) the broker offered a regular and efficient supply of the specialist cottons which he got to know they needed for their mills. When the Cotton Brokers' Association was formed in Liverpool in 1841 there were some 100 members; by 1860 there

---

[37] see G. Hoffman, *Future Trading upon Organized Commodity Markets in the United States*, Philadelphia, University of Pennsylvania Press, 1932, 154–156; J. Lurie, 'Commodities Exchange as Self-Regulating Organisations in the Late 19th Century: Some Perimeters in the History of American Administrative Law' (1975) 28 *Rutgers LR* 1107, 1138–1140; W. Perdue, 'Manipulation of Futures Markets: Refining the Offense' (1987) *Fordham LR* 345, 346, 352–353, 360–362.
[38] F. Dolman, 'Where Merchants Most Do Congregate. The Liverpool Exchange' (1895) 9 *The Ludgate Illustrated Magazine* 599, 604. The 'Secretary' referred to was the secretary of the brokers' association.
[39] see N. Hall, 'Liverpool's Cotton Importers c.1700 to 1914' (2017) 54 *Northern Hist* 79; S. Chapman, *The Cotton Industry in the Industrial Revolution*, London, Macmillan, 1972, 45; 13–15 above.

were 322.[40] Information which the association provided to its broker members on the state of the market – the point of the doggerel – was vital to their buying and selling operations.

It was supposedly the convention of the Liverpool Cotton Exchange – what a participant at the time later described as 'an unwritten, but popularly accepted code' – that brokers should be either buying or selling brokers, not both, and that it was against the etiquette of the market for a buying broker to attempt to deal direct with an importer, rather than a selling broker.[41] In practice throughout the nineteenth century most Liverpool brokers acted for both buyers and sellers and also traded on their own account.[42] Proprietary trading seems to have been accentuated with the great speculation in cotton as a result of the American Civil War.[43] Futures trading further encouraged it. The advent of the telegraphic cable in the 1860s, enabling ready contact with US suppliers, strengthened the practice of some brokers importing cotton themselves.

In this regard, commercial practice was in conflict with contemporary legal theory, which insisted on the rigid distinction between brokers and factors, the broker making contracts between buyers and sellers, the factor entrusted with the possession of the property they dealt with.[44] Another distinction in contemporary legal theory was in the role of the broker, that he was strictly 'a middleman, an intermediate negotiator between other parties' and was not authorised to buy or sell in his own name. This was spelt out in the treatise on the law of agency by the Harvard Law School professor, as well a United States Supreme Court justice, Joseph Story, a book regularly cited in English cases.[45] A modern economic historian has rightly deprecated the 'verbose attempts' of nineteenth-century lawyers to make such firm distinctions about brokers when they seldom existed in commercial practice, and realistically noted the 'entrepreneur's silent determination to pursue profit wherever it beckoned'.[46]

Whatever the default position in legal theory it had to give way, in practice, to the commercial realities. The fundamental reality was profit. For some commodities brokers trading in the markets on their own account, and speculating in futures, was simply more remunerative than relying on the brokerage earned by acting for others.[47] Another reality was the changing character of brokers

---

[40] N. Hall, 'The Business Interests of Liverpool's Cotton Brokers c. 1800–1914' (2004) 41 *Northern Hist* 339, 340.
[41] T. Ellison, *Gleanings and Reminiscences*, Liverpool, Henry Young & Sons, 1905, 243–244; *The Cotton Trade of Great Britain* London, Wilson, 1886, 272–273.
[42] N. Hall, 'The Business Interests of Liverpool's Cotton Brokers c. 1800–1914', op cit, 345–348.
[43] F. Hyde, B. Parkinson, S. Marriner, 'The Cotton Broker and the Rise of the Liverpool Cotton Market' (1955) 8 *Econ Hist R* 75, 78.
[44] e.g., J. Smith, *A Compendium on Mercantile Law*, 6th ed., London, Stevens, 1859, 118.
[45] J. Story, *Commentaries on the Law of Agency as a Branch of Commercial and Maritime Jurisprudence*, Boston, Charles C Little & James Brown, 1839, 24–25.
[46] S. Chapman, *Merchant Enterprises in Britain*, Cambridge, Cambridge University Press, 1992, 77.
[47] C. Woodhouse, *The Woodhouses, Drakes and Careys of Mincing Lane*, self-published, London, 1977, 33.

themselves. By the Second World War, the brokers in London and Liverpool handling internationally traded commodities ranged from small firms, serving mostly a local clientele, through specialists in specific commodities executing orders for others and themselves, to the large brokerage houses, participating in different markets in England and abroad.[48] The rigid distinctions of legal theory could not accommodate all this, as became evident when lawyers and courts had to address specific issues thrown up in the relationship of broker and broker, and broker and third party.

2 Broker and Broker: Surmounting Legal Obstacles

> On this February afternoon Mr. Drem was seated in his private room, on the first floor of the Mincing Lane offices... Downstairs, as the early twilight made the long mahogany desked apartment look dusky and grey, there was profound silence, broken only by a cough or the scratching of a pen. The tea, sugar, coffee, cotton, jute, and other brokers (who are the floats that tell the commercial angler when his bait has taken) had ceased to rush in frantically with bids. (William Black, *The Monarch of Mincing Lane*, 1871)[49]

Law was not irrelevant for brokers, although in the Mincing Lane offices like Drem's they would rarely have given it a thought as they went about the daily activities of buying, selling and recording trades. One aspect of a broker's activities concerned their rights and liabilities vis-à-vis other brokers (and these other brokers' principals). Market practice offered the essential starting point. Until the second part of the nineteenth century, when commodity markets began adopting formal rules, the law relied heavily on trade usage (custom) to define these rights and liabilities. Trade usage was the course of dealing in specific markets which had attained such notoriety that brokers could be said to be bound by it if it was reasonable and not inconsistent with any relevant contractual provision. During our period it was invoked by courts in relation to commodity markets to define a broker's rights and duties.[50]

In the commodity markets the capacity in which brokers were acting was usually evident from the bought or sold notes they gave to clients. 'Sold for AB', 'bought for CD' or 'sold from AB to CD' – all indicated agency. But, as the standard treatises pointed out, the form 'sold to you by me' meant that the

---

[48] A. Hooker, *The International Grain Trade*, 2nd ed., London, Pitman, 1939, 111–114. See also E. Ivamy, *The Growth of the Law Relating to Brokers*, PhD thesis, University of London, 1952, Ch 7.
[49] W. Black, *The Monarch of Mincing Lane*, London, Tinsley Bros, 1871.
[50] e.g., *Johnston v. Usborne* (1841) 11 Ad & E 550, 113 ER 524 (grain trade in London); *Greaves v. Legg* (1856) 11 Ex 642, 146 ER 988 (Liverpool trade, wool from Odessa); *Inman v. Clare* (1858) 5 Jur (NS) 89, 70 ER 629 (Liverpool cotton trade); *Imperial Bank v. London and St Katharine Docks Co* (1877) LR 5 Ch D 195 (London dry goods market); *Bacmeister v. Fenton, Levy & Co* (1883) Cab & E 121 (rice trade); *Pike Sons & Co v. Ongley* (1887) 18 QBD 708 (hop trade). See 48–52 above; 167 below.

broker was assuming the obligation of principal.[51] The courts accepted that a clear expression in a contract or rule would assure privity of contract between the brokers themselves and preclude parol evidence about an undisclosed principal.[52] As well as excluding the doctrine of undisclosed principal, such rules meant that the broker was liable if its principal failed, say, to take delivery or to pay any margin in relation to a futures contract.

Once market rules were formalised these became binding on brokers as members of the trade association which drew them up. We have seen that members of a trade association could be sanctioned for non-compliance with its rules. To reinforce the point the practice of the London Produce Clearing House was to have a broker sign the regulations, 'thereby engaging himself to abide by all these rules'.[53] Signature made unequivocal the commitment of the member to comply with the rules and the authority which the clearing house had over him.[54] Brokerage was an important aspect of the rules, prohibiting brokers from charging less than the official rates and from giving a preference in rates to members over others. When economic times were tough the pressure to enforce minimum rates, and it was thought to protect brokers' livelihoods, increased.

Early on it became the standard practice for brokers on commodity markets to make contracts in their own name. There was evidence of this in the coffee trade in the early nineteenth century,[55] the London grain market of the early 1840s, at least with foreign principals,[56] and Pulling asserted that it was accepted 'in the West India and other trades'.[57] His conclusion was that in the absence of formal rules 'in such cases, the broker is personally answerable for its fulfilment'. That could have only been as a matter of trade usage on those markets, unless a broker made the contract expressly as principal. There was clear authority that a broker would not be personally liable on a contract if he made it as an agent, even when he had not revealed the name of his principal or that he had one.[58]

---

[51] C. Blackburn, *A Treatise on the Effect of the Contract of Sale*, London, W. Benning, 1845, 89. See also J. Benjamin, *Treatise on the Law of Sale of Personal Property*, London, H. Sweet, 1868, 193.

[52] e.g., Humble v. Hunter (1848) 12 QB 310; 116 ER 885; United Kingdom Mutual Steamship Assurance Association Ltd v. Nevill (1887) 19 QBD 110. See S. Stoljar, *The Law of Agency: Its History and Present Principles*, London, Sweet and Maxwell, 1961, 220–222.

[53] e.g., Regulations for Coffee Future Delivery Business, May 1888, Preliminary Regulations for the Admission of Brokers, r.10; Preliminary Regulations for the Admission of Brokers and Agents authorised to deal with the London Produce Clearing House Ltd, in *Sugar Business for Future Delivery*, February 1889, r.12 (LMA, London Produce Clearing House, CLC/B/153/MS03641/001, Minutes of Board Meetings, 118–119, 121).

[54] J. Baer & G. Woodruff, *Commodity Exchanges*, New York, Harper, 1929, 241.

[55] Waring v. Favenck (1807) 1 Camp 85, 170 ER 886; Kymer v. Suwercropp (1807) 1 Camp 109, 180; 170 ER 894, 921.

[56] Johnston v. Usborne (1841) 11 Ad & E 550, 113 ER 524.

[57] A. Pulling, *Laws, Customs, Usages and Regulations of the City and Port of London*, 2nd ed., London, Stevens, 1844, 423n.

[58] Southwell v. Bowditch (1876) LR 1 CPD 374 (a contract made by a colonial broker for export of anthracene, used for dying). See also Kaltenbach, Fischer & Co v. Lewis & Peat (1885) 10 App

Conversely, in *Fairlie* v. *Fenton*[59] a London broker sold as broker on account of a named client 100 bales of cotton to arrive in Liverpool per *Evelyn* from Bombay, 'on the terms of the printed rules of the Cotton Brokers' Association of Liverpool'. He sought to sue the buyers who refused to take the cotton. The four judges of the Exchequer Chamber were clear in rejecting this, Cleasby B citing the passage in *Story on Agency* referred to earlier. If a broker was to sue he had to be made a party to the contract by an express term.[60]

The law to this effect was applied by the House of Lords to the Liverpool cotton market in the leading case, *Cooke & Sons* v. *Eshelby*.[61] That involved the sale by Liversay & Co., brokers, for an undisclosed principal, N. C. Maximos, which was now bankrupt. Eshelby, the trustee in bankruptcy, sued the buyers, Cooke & Sons, who contended that they could set-off against the price of the cotton a debt the brokers owed them. The House of Lords held that was no right of set-off. In an interrogatory Cooke & Sons in effect admitted that they dealt with the brokers knowing that they could be acting as agents or on their own account. The law lords reasoned that given that dual capacity was market practice, a sale by a broker in its own name to a person knowing the practice was no assurance that he was selling on his own account rather than as agent. If a broker desired to deal with another broker as principal, he should make inquiries as to the capacity in which the broker was acting. The House of Lords was unsympathetic to any difficulties posed for brokers by its ruling: 'We must not alter the law to suit the views or the convenience of the Liverpool Cotton Market', said one law lord.[62]

Uncertainty of this nature was far from satisfactory for the functioning of markets. Brokers transacting on a market needed to know at the time of a bargain against whom claims might be levelled. The transaction costs were multiplied if they had to investigate the reliability of those other than their immediate seller or buyer. Certainty was undermined if an undisclosed principal could later emerge as the party to a transaction. It was the point made by one of the witnesses in *Cooke & Sons* v. *Eshelby*, Mr Tobin, whose evidence had been so roughly rejected by the court. He said: 'If I have a number of transactions with a broker I treat that broker as the dealer ... I know nobody else in the transaction. If an undisclosed principal can come forward and claim on a certain portion of the contracts, those that are in his favour, and saddle me with the rest, my position is entirely altered.'[63]

Cas 617 (agent of Singapore merchants for sale for shellac and pepper); *Pike Sons & Co* v. *Ongley & Thornton* (1887) 18 QBD 708 (agent for sale of hops).

[59] (1870) LR 5 Ex 169.
[60] Cleasby B added that the association's rules were of no assistance because they did not treat the broker as a principal in the transaction: at 173.
[61] (1887) LR 12 App Cas 271. See also *Newall* v. *Tomlinson* (1871) LR 6 CP 405 and *Calder* v. *Dobell* (1871) LR 6 CP 486, earlier cases involving Liverpool cotton.
[62] Ibid., 281, per Lord FitzGerald. Fitzgerald was the first Irish judge to be appointed a lord of appeal: J. FitzGerald, revised S. Agnew, 'FitzGerald, John David, Baron FitzGerald of Kilmarnock (1816–1889)', *Oxford Dictionary of National Biography*.
[63] Ibid., 280–281.

Contract offered a solution to the law's technicalities. Bought and sold notes in commodity markets had a clause added that the contract of which they were part was made between the brokers themselves and not with any other person, whether disclosed or otherwise.[64] Trade associations adopted a rule that when dealing either for themselves or for customers members dealt in their own name. C. W. Smith, a broker in Liverpool, recalled how the common law was tamed in his evidence to a Royal Commission:

> [T]here was a celebrated case called *Cooke* v. *Eshelby* ... I brought it before our Association, and I told them that if the thing was going on, no man dare trade under those systems. The consequence was that a committee was formed, and a new contract was made out which makes every man under that contract himself liable, do you see, as his own principal under every contract, so that there was no going behind anybody and therefore, under the settlement system every contract is wrung out compulsorily.[65]

The type of rule to which C. W. Smith referred might provide that brokers dealt on their own behalf, that they were personally liable on any contract and that no rights or liabilities accrued to any principal, except against his own broker.[66] The London Produce Clearing House echoed this approach in its rules, although in some versions conferring a discretion on itself to decide whether to permit a hitherto unidentified person from having its name substituted in a deal and, if so, on what conditions.[67]

3 Broker and Customer: The Law Struggles

The relationship of brokers with their clients fell, in part, within the purview of agency law, although it raised other issues such as the binding quality of market rules on outside parties. Nineteenth-century agency law established that brokers, as agents, were subject to a number of duties: to act within the scope of their authority, to execute market orders with proper care, skill and diligence, and to avoid conflicts of interest and secret profits.[68] Moreover, under the common law brokers had certain rights against their principal, rights to commission and to an indemnity against any costs and liabilities incurred in the course of the agency.[69] In practice there might also be rights and duties

---

[64] H. Bateson, 'Forms of Mercantile Contracts' (1895) 11 *LQR* 266, 268–269 and 271–272. Bateson gives a version of the clause: 'The rights and liabilities of principals not disclosed on the face of this contract are excluded.'
[65] *Royal Commission on Agricultural Depression*, London, C.7400, 1894, 51.
[66] e.g., Beetroot Sugar Association, Rules and Regulations, 8th ed., 1904, rr.44, 215. See a case at the end of our period, concerning the cocoa and sugar futures market in London: *E. Bailey & Co Ltd v. Balholm Securities Ltd* [1973] 2 Lloyd's Rep 404, 408.
[67] e.g., London Produce Clearing House, Coffee Future Delivery Business, May 1888, r.9.
[68] 132 below.
[69] e.g., *Christoforides* v. *Terry* [1924] AC 566. See *Halsbury's Laws of England*, 2nd ed., London, Butterworth & Co, 1931, vol. I, 257–265.

derived from the rules and practices of the relevant commodities market or trade association.

For a period the rights and liabilities in the general law were overlaid for brokers in the City of London by regulations for 'sworn' brokers.[70] The legislation dated from 1697, but the mayor and aldermen of the City remade the rules and regulations in 1817.[71] Under these, brokers had to obtain the permission of the City authorities before acting as such. Admission as a broker meant producing a certificate of competence and knowledge, and then acting in accordance with certain standards.[72] Thus a broker was forbidden from dealing in his own name, had to enter every bargain into a broker's book and could not take or receive double brokerage (e.g., from both buyer and seller). There was uncertainty about the scope of the City's regulations, in particular to what category of broker they applied. The regulations were flouted in practice.[73] On London markets, brokers would act both for customers and on their own account. Criticism that the City's regulations were a restraint of trade, as well as an impediment to business, led to their repeal (in large part) in 1870.[74] A few years after the repeal of the City's regulations the Baltic Exchange introduced a 'Broker's Letter', whereby broker members would undertake not to deal directly or indirectly on the Exchange on their own account but only for customers. By 1931, 192 members had signed the Broker's Letter, including 36 grain brokers and 15 oil brokers.[75] That was a relatively small fraction of the Baltic's membership.

If brokers were bound by the rules and practices of the markets and their associations, to what extent were their customers bound? The law never satisfactorily resolved the issue. On the surface contract law was of no assistance, especially when the doctrine of privity of contract became entrenched. Not being a party to the rules of a market or association, customers were not bound by them, nor were they in a contractual relationship with related institutions like the clearing house. Their contract was with their broker, acting on their behalf. Initially weight was put on agency law to address the problem of the third-party customer.

It was established early in relation to the stock exchange that a customer employing a broker impliedly gave him authority to act in accordance with its rules, and there was some authority that this applied even if the customer

---

[70] e.g., J. Russell, *A Treatise on the Laws relating to Factors and Brokers*, London, H. Sweet, 1844, 344–348; J. Russell, *A Treatise on Mercantile Agency*, 2nd ed., London, H. Sweet, 1873, 607.
[71] E. Ivamy, The Growth of the Law Relating to Brokers, *op cit*, Ch. 12.
[72] 6 Anne, c.16. See also 57 Geo 3, c 60. See 'Rules, Orders and Regulations' in Appendix No. III of J. Russell, *A Treatise on the Law Relating to Factors and Brokers, op cit*, 344–348. See also A. Pulling, Laws, Customs, Usages and Regulations of the City and Port of London, *op cit*, 418–424.
[73] e.g., *Ex p. Dyster* (1816) 1 Mer 155, 169–70, 35 ER 632, 637.
[74] London Brokers Relief Act 1870, 33 & 34 Vict, c.60. See J. Findlay, The Baltic Exchange, *op cit*, 46.
[75] H. Barty-King, The Baltic Exchange, *op cit*, 342. The oil brokers were dealers in vegetable (e.g., palm) oil.

himself was ignorant of them.[76] This use of agency law was subsequently extended beyond market rules to customs and usages. 'A person who deals in a particular market must be taken to deal according to the custom of that market', it was said by the Court of Exchequer in an early stock exchange case.[77] Later stock exchange cases established that customers were bound by the rules relating to the mode of business on the exchange, although the rules could not affect their substantive rights under their contracts.[78]

Commodity markets fell within the scope of this principle, although there were far fewer cases and the matter was not as clear. In one of them the plaintiff, who was speculating on the Liverpool cotton market, instructed the defendant cotton brokers to purchase 50 bales of Surat (Indian) cotton. The brokers, having received orders from other parties, bought 300 bales in their own name, 50 for the plaintiff. The jury found that this was in accordance with market practice. However, the Court of Exchequer held that the plaintiff had no contract with the seller because the brokers had not acted as agents.[79] In another case, however, on the Liverpool wool market, Willes J said that 'by proving that the contract was made in a market when it is usual for the agents to contract in that manner, and the principals knowing of the existence of the custom, or not choosing to inquire about it, must be bound by it'.[80] So by the 1860s the law had reached the stage that a customer could be bound by a commodity market's rules and its usual practices, but within boundaries.

The matter came to a head in a case involving a transaction on the Baltic Exchange in 1869, *Robinson v. Mollett*.[81] Robinson was a Liverpool merchant. As on several previous occasions, he had instructed London brokers Mollett & Co. to buy tallow, in this case in April for June delivery. Tallow was an object of speculation on the Baltic Exchange and subject to significant fluctuations in price. There can be little doubt that Robinson was speculating, a point which Mollett's counsel, J. P. Benjamin QC, made, but to no avail.[82] Robinson was sent bought notes in the usual form, 'We have this day bought of ... for your account.' The practice of the market was that tallow brokers could buy tallow for various persons in their own name, then on settlement day balance orders

---

[76] *Sutton v. Tatham* (1839) 10 Ad & E 27, 113 ER 11. See J. Balfour Browne, *The Law of Usages and Customs*, London, Stevens & Haynes, 1875, 91.

[77] *Bayliffe v. Butterworth* (1847) Exch 425, 429, 154 ER 181, 183, per Anderson B. The idea was applied to banking as well: a 'man who employs a banker is bound by the usage of bankers': *Hare v. Henty* (1861) 10 CBNS 65, 142 ER 374, 379.

[78] *Levitt v. Hamblet* [1901] 2 KB 53; *Ponsolle v. Webber* [1908] 1 Ch 254; *Cunliffe-Owen v. Teather & Greenwood* [1967] 1 WLR 1421. See also a case after our period on the tin market: *Shearson Lehman Hutton Inc v. Maclaine Watson & Co Ltd* [1989] 2 Lloyd's Rep 570, 589.

[79] *Bostock v. Jardine* (1865) 3 H & C 700, 159 ER 707.

[80] *Cropper v. Cook* (1868) LR 3 CP 194, 200. See also another case in the same market: *Greaves v. Legg* (1854) 11 Ex 642, affd. 156 ER 988, 2 H & N 210.

[81] (1875) LR 7 HL 802. John Mollett was a prominent member of the Baltic: H. Barty-King, *The Baltic Exchange, op cit*, 122, 125.

[82] LI, *House of Lords Printed Cases, judgments and appeal documents*, Cases on Appeal to the House of Lords, vol. 302, 1875, 248–253 (52–57), which sets out some of the correspondence.

between themselves, allotting tallow to those who wanted delivery and to speculators paying or claiming price differences.[83]

The price of tallow fell after the transaction and unsurprisingly Robinson wanted to avoid it. He refused to accept delivery or to pay. The brokers laid the matter before the committee of the Baltic, which said that they had acted 'quite straightforwardly in the matter and according to the rules and customs of the trade'.[84] Robinson still refused to take delivery or to pay. On being sued, his lawyer contended that he could not be bound by a market practice of which he was unaware. The lower courts were divided.[85] Those like Bovill CJ and Blackburn J were prepared to countenance the Baltic practice. As Blackburn J put it, it did not upset the fiduciary duties of a broker, nor was it 'against policy, or inconsistent with the fundamental principles of right and wrong'.[86] Brokers in his view would avoid conflicts of interest because of their own sense of propriety or because of fears for their reputation. As to whether the custom and practice was incorporated in the orders given the brokers, he concluded that in this instance that occurred tacitly.[87]

In the House of Lords, formalism won the day. The court opted for a simplistic rule to quarantine conflicts of interest, regardless of market operations and of the fact that, as Blackburn J had pointed out, brokers would still be subject to their fiduciary obligations. The submissions of Judah Benjamin QC for the brokers, which began by referring to the undoubted 'usefulness' of the Baltic's practice, fell on deaf ears.[88] Story's view in *Commentaries on the Law of Agency*, referred to earlier,[89] was cited by counsel for the purchaser: a broker is a mere negotiator between other parties. In a judgment with which other members of the House of Lords agreed, Lord Chelmsford held that what market practice did here was to reverse a broker's character which the customer, who was ignorant of it, could not be taken to have authorised.[90] Neither the bought notes nor other facts of the case gave any indication to third parties of its existence, and it could not be binding on them, even if it could regulate the relationship of the brokers between themselves.[91] Robinson escaped liability because Mollett was employed as a broker but had bought in his own name.

The principle of *Robinson* v. *Mollett* remained; in a leading case about the commodity markets the United States Supreme Court described it as 'incontrovertible'.[92] But it was contrary to commercial practice and later confined to situations where a broker executed his task by selling his own

---

[83] This was also standard practice on the London and New York Stock exchanges: *Clews* v. *Jamieson*, 182 US 461, 487 (1901).
[84] LI, *House of Lords, Printed Cases, judgments and appeal documents*, Cases on Appeal to the House of Lords, V.302, 1875, 268–269 (72–73).
[85] (1870) LR 5 CP 646 (Court of Common Pleas); (1872) LR 7 CP 84 (Court of Exchequer Chamber).
[86] (1875) LR 7 HL 802, 810.
[87] at 811. See his judgment below as well: (1872) LR 7 CP 84, 102–104.
[88] (1875) LR 7 HL 802, 807.   [89] 72 above.   [90] (1875) LR 7 HL 802, 836.
[91] Ibid., 835, 838.   [92] *Irwin* v. *Williar*, 110 US 499, 515 (1884).

goods to a customer.[93] Moreover, when engaging brokers to transact their business on a market, the practice became that customers did so on terms that it would be conducted in accordance with market principles.[94] Contract was used to make that plain. In the commodities markets brokers' bought and sold notes stated the respective liabilities of the parties and added that any contract was made subject to the rules and by-laws of the relevant trade association.[95] Once trade associations began issuing standard form contracts, these also set out key rules for transactions, or incorporated them by reference through one of the terms.[96]

2.4 Emergence of Futures Markets

> ... [I]t is just worthwhile having at the back of one's head that a purchase in terms of settling of commodities having a world price may be in conceivable circumstances a hedge against anything that might happen to sterling. This also applies to the question of buying wheat in Liverpool. On further consideration I think that I overstated the objections to Liverpool as a market. (Letter from John Maynard Keynes, 20 July 1931)[97]

Futures trading took place on standard form contracts, with standardised amounts and types of the commodity being traded without reference to a specific cargo or lot. It had occurred with commodities before the nineteenth century, for example, in grain, herring and tulips in Amsterdam in the seventeenth century, and on the Dojima Rice Exchange in Osaka from the late seventeenth century.[98] The Chicago Board of Trade formalised futures trading in 1865.[99] The Liverpool Cotton Exchange began futures trading in the 1870s. It developed out of a forward market in cotton, where brokers and merchants bought and sold the commodity on 'to arrive' terms before it was available for delivery. The futures market went one step further: it was not expected that physical delivery would occur but that the cotton would be disposed of by

---

[93] e.g., *Ex p Rogers* (1880) 15 Ch 207, 210, 212.
[94] *Weinberger v. Inglis* [1919] AC 606, 619 (stock exchange).
[95] H. Bateson, 'Forms of Mercantile Contracts' (1895) 11 *LQR* 266, 268–269.
[96] see 300, 301, 304, 313, 358 below.
[97] Quoted in T. Foresti & E. Sanfilippo, 'Keynes's Personal Investments in the Wheat Futures Markets, 1925–1935' (2017) 25 *History of Economic Ideas* 63, 79.
[98] A. Goldgar. *Tulipmania Money, Honor, and Knowledge in the Dutch Golden Age*, Chicago, University of Chicago Press, 2007, 217–218, 283; O. Gelderblom & J. Jonker, 'Amsterdam as the Cradle of Modern Futures Trading and Options Trading 1550–1650', in W. Goetzmann & K. Geert Rouwenhorst (eds.), *The Origins of Value: The Financial Innovations That Created Modern Capital Markets*, Oxford, Oxford University Press, 2005; C. Wilson, *Anglo-Dutch Commerce and Finance in the Eighteenth Century*, Cambridge, Cambridge University Press, 1941, 81; M. West, 'Private Ordering at the World's First Futures Exchange' (2000) 98 *Mich LR* 2574.
[99] J. Santos, 'Trading Grain Now and Then: The Relative Performance of Early Grain-Futures Markets' (2011) 45 *Applied Economics* 287, 288–289; J. Markham, *The History of Commodity Futures Trading and its Regulation*, New York, Praeger, 1987, 4.

setting off the different contracts and by the payment of price differences on the deals.[100]

1 Futures Markets in Wheat and Other Commodities

The Liverpool wheat futures market, where John Maynard Keynes traded, had begun when the Liverpool Corn Trade Association drew up its first futures contract in 1883.[101] Although the earliest references to futures prices connect them with No.1 Californian, No.1 Bombay, No.1 Delhi and Kurrachee (Karachi) red wheats, it seems probable that in the first few years buyers and sellers simply agreed on the type of wheat to be delivered. The comparative uniformity of Californian wheat, coupled with the special need for hedging facilities as regards trades in it, led the association to adopt a single futures contract in 1886 based on No.1 Californian. In 1891 the irregularity of Californian supplies and the increasing large amounts of wheat from the American mid-west and Canadian prairies provoked an extension to futures dealings to them. To allow for variations in quality, provision was made for making up standards qualifying for tender.

Liverpool futures were given a boost as a result of the German ban on futures trading in grain in 1896.[102] From 1898 Liverpool futures trading was restricted to wheat for delivery in March, May, July, September and December. Following further attempts at a standard contract in the early 1900s, the 1906 wheat contract established a pattern for all subsequent wheat futures in Liverpool. In 1938 the Food Research Institute at Stanford University ranked the Liverpool wheat futures markets ahead of all others as an index of world prices, even though over the previous decade the volume of trading there had been not a twentieth of that through the Chicago Board of Trade. Liverpool's leading position followed from Britain being a leader in the world wheat trade and the connection of Liverpool futures prices with international influences.[103] As with wheat, so with cotton. At its height the Liverpool Cotton Exchange was

---

[100] B. Simpson, 'The Origins of Futures Trading in the Liverpool Cotton Market', in P. Cane & J. Stapleton (eds.), *Essays for Patrick Atiyah*, Oxford, Clarendon, 1991, 196ff [hereafter 'Futures Trading']; N. Hall, 'The Liverpool Cotton Market: Britain's First Futures Market' (2000) 149 *Transactions of the Historical Society of Lancashire and Cheshire* 99.

[101] Liverpool Corn Trade Association, *Liverpool Corn Trade Association 1853-1953*, Liverpool, 1953, 12-25; H. Working & S. Hoos, 'Wheat Futures Prices and Trading at Liverpool since 1886' (1938) IX (3) *Wheat Studies of the Food Research Institute, Stanford University, California*, 121; G. Broomhall & J. Hubback, *Corn Trade Memories*, Liverpool, Northern Publishing, 1930, 1-13.

[102] S. Lestition, 'Historical Preface to Max Weber, "Stock and Commodity Exchanges"' (2000) 29 *Theory and Society* 289, 298, 300-301; S. Topik & A. Wells, *Global Markets Transformed 1879-1945*, Cambridge, MA, Harvard University Press, 2012, 150.

[103] H. Working & S. Hoos, *op cit*, 129-31. There are descriptions of the Liverpool wheat futures market in R. Smith, *Wheat Fields and Markets of the World*, St Louis, Modern Miller Publishers, 1908, 353-359; *Commodity Markets*, 2nd ed., London, Swiss Bank Corporation, 1935, 32-35.

the leading international futures market, since the other centres for cotton futures, the New York and New Orleans cotton exchanges, concentrated largely on domestic trading.[104]

London was slower than Liverpool in futures trading in commodities. Trading in grain futures began on the Baltic Exchange in 1897 in American wheat and maize, with clearing by the London Produce Clearing House. The futures market was abandoned in the early 1900s with the failure of North American wheat exports through a rust epidemic.[105] The London Corn Trade Association (LCTA) attempted to revive the market in the interwar years. It incorporated the Grain Futures Association in 1929.[106] Initially trading was confined to futures in No.3 Manitoba, with other grades as differentials, the contract being on a CIF basis and the unit being 1,000 quarters of 480 lbs each. Settlement was at the end of September, November, January, March and May. For wheat shipped from an east coast Canadian port, the bill of lading had to be dated within the contract month. Argentinian wheat and maize were subsequently added. Trading in wheat futures occurred around a ring on the Baltic Exchange. Dealers had to be members of both the LCTA and the Baltic Exchange. Clearing was by LCTA's own clearing house, which had been clearing forward sales since 1921. The London wheat futures market was never a match for Liverpool's. After the Second World War there was futures trading in imported barley and maize in London (and Liverpool), but by the mid-1960s trading in futures on the Baltic Exchange became concentrated on home grain.[107]

By the eve of the First World War London had a large futures market in sugar. The disruption to that caused by the 1914–1918 war, coupled with the enormous development of sugar production in Cuba, boosted the New York market so that in the interwar period it surpassed London.[108] With metals, the London Metal Exchange began trading futures at some point between the 1870s and 1880s once standard contract tonnages and grades were adopted. Its leading role on the world stage continued during the interwar period although, unlike other futures markets, it always had significant dealings in the physical product. Its trading was impeded at various points by cartels.[109] After their

---

[104] G. Cifarelli & P. Paesani, 'Speculative Pricing in the Liverpool Cotton Futures Market: A Nonlinear Tale of Noise Traders and Fundamentalists from the 1920s' (2016) 10 *Cliometrica* 31, 35; K. Lipartito, 'The New York Cotton Exchange and the Development of the Cotton Futures Market' (1983) 57 *Bus Hist Rev* 50, 52n; A. Marsh, 'Cotton Exchanges and their Economic Function' (September 1911) 38 (2) *Annals Amer Acad Pol & Soc Sci.* 253, 259.

[105] A. Barker, *The British Corn Trade*, London, Pitman, 1920, 90.

[106] 'London Wheat Futures Market', *The Times*, 6 February 1929, 22.

[107] D. Britton, B. Cracknell & I. Stewart, *Cereals in the United Kingdom*, Oxford, Pergamon, 1969, 339–40.

[108] G. Hodge, *56 Years in the London Sugar Market*, Bristol, privately published, 1960, 34–36; *Report on the Sugar Beet Industry at Home and Abroad*, Ministry of Agriculture and Fisheries, Economic Series, no. 27, London, 1931, 223–225; E. Brunn, 'The New York Coffee and Sugar Exchange' (May 1931) 155 *Annals Amer Acad Pol & Soc Sc* 110, 117.

[109] R. Gibson-Jarvie, *The London Metal Exchange*, Cambridge, Woodhead-Faulkner, 1976, 100–101.

closure during the Second World War the London futures markets in commodities resumed in the 1950s. Following our period they became part of a thriving derivatives market in London in financial and other products.[110]

2 Spot, Arrivals and Future Contracts

At its simplest a futures market in a commodity involves dealings for its sale and purchase where the parties intend to settle otherwise than by its actual delivery.[111] When futures markets had fully developed, by the end of the nineteenth century, the obvious contrast was with the so-called spot, cash or physical market, where sales and purchases were for immediate delivery. There was also a contrast with markets for forward delivery, where sales and purchases were tied to a commodity with a physical existence (sometimes called the arrival markets). These were markets where a commodity was sold either before or after shipment, with delivery to occur at some time later. At a point before it was to be delivered, the relevant cargo was identified.

Futures markets in commodities emerged in Britain out of the forward (or arrivals) dealings which operated in the import trade. From the early nineteenth century the courts were handling disputes about commodities like tallow, hemp and palm oil sold under contracts 'on arrival' or 'to arrive'. In 1834 a London merchant involved in foreign grain sales gave evidence of the sales of grain to be delivered later, and of 'time sales' where grain was deliverable at the end of a month, say, and if not delivered 'whatever the difference of price is in the market of course it must be made good'.[112] Cotton was also sold to arrive.[113]

Arrivals contracts would specify the commodity, its quantity and perhaps quality, as well as the departure date and port (e.g., St Petersburg or Cronstadt (Kronshtadt) in June or July). The ship might be named (e.g., per *Mansfield*) or the contract might provide for the ship's name to be declared later (e.g., 'ship's name declared as soon as known'). Because of the vagaries of sailing times the contract would not specify a date of arrival, although it might provide that it should not exceed a given date.[114] Under the contract buyers might have the option of directing the ships to ports of their choice, including those in continental

---

[110] G. Rees, 'The London Commodity Markets and Commonwealth Trade' (January 1981) 129 *RSA J* 93.
[111] G. Hoffman, Future Trading, *op cit*, 99ff.
[112] *Report from Select Committee on Sale of Corn*, 1834, HC 517, VII, 1, 79–80.
[113] e.g., *Grant v. Fletcher* (1826) 108 ER 163, 5 B & C 436 (Egyptian cotton to arrive).
[114] *Hawes v. Humble* (1809) 2 Camp 327n, 170 ER 1172 (tallow); *Boyd v. Siffkin* (1809) 2 Camp 326, 170 ER 1172 (Riga Rhine hemp); *Lovatt v. Hamilton* (1839) 5 M & W 639, 151 ER 271 (African palm oil to arrive Liverpool *per Mansfield*); *Gorrisen v. Perrin* (1857) 2 CBNS 681, 27 LJCP 29; 140 ER 583 (bales of gambier – used in tanning – from Singapore, 'expected to arrive' in London per two named ships).

Europe.[115] Arrivals contracts meant the buyer knew where the commodity was coming from and what ship was carrying it, if not initially, at least after shipment.

Before the commodity arrived, dealings might occur as the commodity was sold on to others. Thus there was a market in Liverpool cotton contracts 'to arrive'. Trading was especially active in Liverpool during the speculation of 1857.[116] The recommended standard form of contract 'to arrive', settled in the 1860s by the Liverpool Cotton Brokers Association, identified the origins of the cotton as coming from a particular port on a particular ship.[117] In other contracts the ship might not be named until after the contract was made, but it seems to have been a practice, and was certainly later a rule of the association, that a declaration had to be made sometime after the contract.[118]

In the 1860s, reflecting the greater predictability of voyage times, arrivals contracts began to be used which named a one or two month period (e.g., May/June) during which the cotton would arrive. Those contracts ran parallel to the older form of arrivals contract, which only specified a time of shipment and did not attempt to identify a time of performance. More importantly, the form of contract used might not provide for delivery of specific cotton tied to a particular ship, named or to be named, but of cotton of a particular description.[119] This clearly presages the futures contract in cotton, introduced in the following decade.

A second development germane to the emergence of futures markets was the growth of speculation in commodities. There had always been speculation in commodities, for example, purchasing grain and storing it in the expectation of a rise in price. While this type of speculation continued, there was also speculation in the arrivals markets. Speculation in tallow in the first part of the nineteenth century could be in 'delivery' transactions, said by one commentator to be the description of a contract that would allow a rise or fall in price, usually embracing a period of two or three months forward. It was comparable, he argued, to speculation in government securities, and 'thousands and thousands of pounds have passed on these occasions, on the contracts made'.[120]

With cotton, speculation was most likely with spot transactions because the variability in quality meant that there were risks in buying it without the opportunity to inspect. Speculation in relation to arrivals contracts in cotton became common in the 1850s as a result of the improvement in communications. Steamships began carrying the mails, which meant that they could bring word about cargos of cotton afloat, for the cotton itself was transported by the

---

[115] e.g., *Ex p Halliday Re Hall & Jones* (1865) 2 De GJ & S 312; 46 ER 396 (sale of cargo of rice per *Southern Rights*).
[116] S. Dumbell, 'The Origin of Cotton Futures' (1927) 1 *Econ J* 258, 260.
[117] The contract is examined in two articles by Brian Simpson, from which I have learnt much: 'Contracts for Cotton to Arrive: The Case of the Two Ships Peerless' (1989) 11 *Cardozo LR* 287, 306, 312 [hereafter 'Two Ships Peerless']; 'Futures Trading', 185–186. See also the contract in *Neill v. Whitworth* (1865) 18 CB (NS) 433, 144 ER 513.
[118] See rule 2 set out in *Thorburn v. Barnes* (1867) 16 LT (NS) 10, 12.
[119] e.g., *Williams v. Reynolds* (1865) 12 LT (NS) 729, 729.
[120] Anon, *The City; or, the Physiology of London Business*, London, Groombridge, 1852, 138.

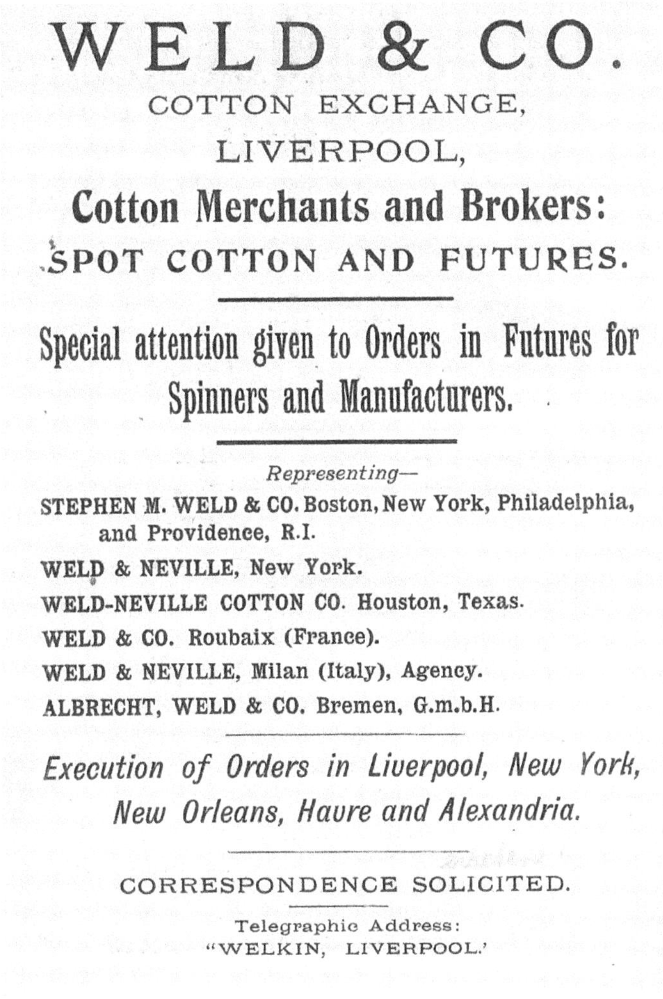

WELD & CO.

COTTON EXCHANGE, LIVERPOOL,

Cotton Merchants and Brokers:

SPOT COTTON AND FUTURES.

Special attention given to Orders in Futures for Spinners and Manufacturers.

Representing—

STEPHEN M. WELD & CO. Boston, New York, Philadelphia, and Providence, R.I.

WELD & NEVILLE, New York.

WELD-NEVILLE COTTON CO. Houston, Texas.

WELD & CO. Roubaix (France).

WELD & NEVILLE, Milan (Italy), Agency.

ALBRECHT, WELD & CO. Bremen, G.m.b.H.

Execution of Orders in Liverpool, New York, New Orleans, Havre and Alexandria.

CORRESPONDENCE SOLICITED.

Telegraphic Address:
"WELKIN, LIVERPOOL."

Figure 2.2 Futures dealing in cotton, Liverpool, 1909 (Dr Nigel Hall, liverpoolcotton.com)

slower sailing vessels.[121] It was the attraction of enormous profits which stimulated speculation in arrivals contracts during the American Civil War. Specified amounts of particular types of cotton were re-sold, sometimes many times so that, on settlement, documents and payment had to pass along a chain of buyers and sellers.[122] Many of those engaged in buying and selling cotton had no interest in taking delivery and simply hoped to profit on reselling it. Short-selling was also in evidence.[123]

---

[121] J. Todd, The Marketing of Cotton, *op cit*, 66.
[122] B. Simpson, Futures Trading, *op cit*, 190–194, 202 writes of the assignment of contracts but this overlooks cases such as *Williams* v. *Reynolds* (1865) 12 LT (NS) 728.
[123] e.g., *Morgan* v. *Gath* (1865) 13 LT (NS) 96.

On the back of arrivals contracts and speculation emerged futures, where trading in cotton occurred without reference to identifiable shipments of a commodity but by description and according to grade. There is a period in the 1860s and 1870s when it was occurring informally, by use of forms of arrivals contracts drawn up by individual traders, with a month or months specified within which the commodity would arrive. This was the form of contract in *Williams* v. *Reynolds*.[124] As Blackburn J noted in that case, the contract 'was not for the delivery of specific cotton, but of cotton of a particular description'.[125] This became the hallmark of the futures contract. In 1873 the Liverpool Cotton Brokers' Association introduced the clear distinction between contracts for specific cargoes of cotton to arrive, and contracts for cargoes of a standard quality ('middling American') for shipment to be made in specific months. A separate contract for cotton futures was adopted in 1873.[126]

Standardised contracts and supervision by a trade association were not essential conditions for futures dealing but certainly facilitated it. Importantly, the Liverpool Corn Trade Association laid down standard grades for grain as well as the time and method of delivery (if delivery was necessary).[127] Identical terms in these contracts, coupled with standardised commodities, meant that the only variable which needed negotiation was price. Fungibility enabled those dealing on a market to close out a position without difficulty by entering an offsetting transaction. One example of these futures contracts suffices. The 1903 Liverpool futures contract for wheat incorporated, at the outset, the rules of the Association. ('We have this day Bought from/sold to [name] on the terms of the Printed Rules of.')[128] The price per 100 lbs was to be inserted, as was the quality and month of delivery. Unlike the earlier 'to arrive' contracts, and contemporaneous 'shipment and delivery contracts', the only specification as to the origin of the wheat was in relation to its grade. We return to standard form contracts for commodities sales, including futures trading, in Chapter 5.

In futures markets, as a result of the gaming legislation the contracts contained an obligation to deliver or take delivery of the commodity, but

---

[124] (1865) 12 LT (NS) 729. The report contains the wording of the contract.
[125] Ibid., 730. It was to be of 'fair' quality. Practice in the cotton trade was to classify cotton into various grades such as fair and middling.
[126] C. Cristiano & N. Naldi, 'Keynes's Activity on the Cotton Market and the Theory of the "Normal Backwardation": 1921–1929' (2014) 4 *Eur J Hist Econ Thought* 1039, 1041–1042; N. Hall, 'The Liverpool Cotton Market: Britain's First Futures Market' (2000) 149 *Transactions of the Historical Society of Lancashire and Cheshire* 99, 104–106.
[127] Settlement in grades other than the standard grade might be permitted, with price differences to compensate for the variation.
[128] Set out, along with the 1934 version, in H. Working & S. Hoos, *op cit*, Appendix Notes. cf. shorter United States grain futures contract from the New York Produce Exchange: A. Stevens, 'Futures in the Wheat Market' (1887) 2 *Q J Econ*, 37, 38.

delivery rarely occurred.[129] In practice futures transactions were almost always closed out by a party entering an off-setting transaction. Because contracts and commodities were standardised, parties needed to negotiate only the price and then settle by paying price differences between the price in the original and the off-setting contract. In effect there was a divorce between the physical and futures markets.

Futures transactions were for hedging or speculative purposes. Hedging in the commodities markets was functionally equivalent to insurance.[130] Banks began to insist that commodities given as security for advances be hedged, so boosting the use of futures.[131] For hedging purposes, a business would enter accompanying transactions, one in real commodities, the other in futures. The futures transaction would be an agreement to buy or sell a commodity on any day in a designated month. The merchant would offset any loss through a fall in the market price for a commodity he had sold by a gain on the futures transaction simultaneously entered. By contrast, those speculating on the futures markets were concerned with the movement in prices, and predicting these accurately, not with the reality of how demand and supply had affected the prices in their physical transactions. It was only when futures dealings were settled, at the end of the months specified, that the prices in the physical and futures markets would coincide and differences settled.

3 Law's Role: An Outline

There was no difficulty with arrivals contracts in English sales law. From early in the nineteenth century the courts upheld contracts for the sale of goods to be delivered at some later point. Thus it was held that the sale of a growing crop of hops did not constitute the old offence of forestalling, where to influence price merchants might purchase goods on their way to market, or persuade others not to place their goods on a market.[132] Brewers had used such contracts for future delivery for many years to secure their supplies of malt. The principle applied as well to commodities to be made by processing. In 1815 Gibbs CJ saw the legal validity of such forward contracts

---

[129] On the gaming legislation: 118 below.
[130] See e.g., S. Chapman & D. Knoop, 'Dealings in Futures on the Cotton Market' (1906) 69 *J Royal Statistical Soc* 321, 321–322; A. Garside, *Cotton Goes to Market*, New York, Frederick A. Stokes,1935, 308–310; A. Hooker, The International Grain Trade, *op cit*, 120–130; Topik & A. Wells, Global Markets Transformed 1879–1945, *op cit*, 123–124.
[131] J. Todd, *The Marketing of Cotton*, London, Pitman, 1934, 69. See also W. Hubbard, 'Hedging in the Cotton Market', (May 1931) 155 *Annals Amer Acad Pol & Soc Sc*.
[132] *Bristow* v. *Waddington* (1806) 2 Bos & P (NR) 355, 127 ER 664; *Waddington* v. *Bristow* (1801) 2 Bos & P 451; 126 ER 1379. The plaintiff in these actions had come unstuck shortly before in a criminal prosecution brought by hops factors allied to London brewers. They resented his advancing credit to growers for their future crops, thus breaking their own hold over the growers: D. Hay, 'The State and the Market in 1800: Lord Kenyon and Mr Waddington' *Past and Present*, No.162, February 1999, 117, 123. See 107–108, 124 below.

as plain common sense.[133] So the legality of a contract to sell what was to be delivered in the future was settled law. Subsequently, the courts upheld contracts when the seller did not have the commodity at the time of sale but was to acquire and deliver it after making the contract.[134] Thus the legal issue with contracts for goods to arrive was not one of general principle but what to do in situations such as the ship arriving without the goods, or with goods to arrive on a particular ship but arriving on another. In general, the courts held that, in the absence of a contractual term, a sale of goods 'on arrival' or 'to arrive' was contingent both on the arrival of the ship in the ordinary course, within any time stated, and on the goods being on board.[135]

The common law followed practice with futures transactions and its impact was peripheral. *Christoforides* v. *Terry*[136] is a useful illustration of the courts' hands-off approach. The case involved speculative dealings on the Liverpool and New York cotton markets. A customer had been caught out by a fall in the price of cotton futures. Since he was unable to make good the call for margins, the broker had closed out his contracts and demanded an indemnity for the losses incurred. By the time the case reached the House of Lords the broker's right to close out had been accepted.[137] However, the customer now contended that the broker was not entitled to his indemnity since he had been in breach of his duties to avoid a conflict of interest. On the day the broker closed out two of the customer's contracts, he had simultaneously repurchased the same quantities of cotton from the same brokers at the same price. It was said that this breached his fiduciary duty not to put himself in a position where his interest conflicted with that of the customer.

The House of Lords held that they should not disturb the finding of the trial judge that the closing out transactions were *bona fide* and not a sham, and thus concluded that the broker's purchases could not vitiate them. But it did not seem that all the judges fully understood the workings of futures markets. Although it may have been the result of infelicitous expression, Viscount Finlay seems to have been taken in by the argument that the purchases were a resale to the broker, whereas he was simply entering a transaction to realise differences. Several of the other law lords also appeared to be struggling.[138] That formidable commercial lawyer

---

[133] e.g., *Wilks* v. *Atkinson* (1815) 6 Taunt 10, 11–12; 128 ER 935, 935–936. The case involved rapeseed oil, used in domestic lighting and as a lubricant.
[134] *Hibblewhite* v. *M'Morine* (1839) 5 M&W 462, 151 ER 195; *Borrowman, Phillips & Co* v. *Free & Hollis* (1878) LR 4 QBD 500, 502, per Bramwell LJ.
[135] J. Benjamin, Treatise on the Law of Sale of Personal Property, *op cit*, 432–433.
[136] [1924] AC 566.
[137] This issue was whether the contract allowed this (provided sufficient security was available): see Sankey J's judgment at first instance in LI, *House of Lords, Printed Cases, judgments and appeal documents*, Cases on Appeal to the House of Lords, vol. 702, 1924, 67–68 (80–82).
[138] [1924] AC 566, 573. Finlay's reputation in commercial cases is reasonable: see G. Rubin, 'Finlay, Robert Bannatyne, first Viscount Finlay (1842–1929)', *Oxford Dictionary of National Biography*.

J. A. Hamilton (Lord Sumner) saw the realities of futures markets most clearly, that the contracts were 'for identical qualities and quantities of cotton deliverable at the same date, and that these contracts were expected to be disposed of by setting them off and by payment of differences without actual tender or delivery'.[139]

We return to the law's implications for futures transactions later.[140]

2.5 Clearing and Settlement

> ... Denry was not satisfied. He had a secret woe, due to the fact that he was gradually ceasing to be a card, and that he was not multiplying his capital by two every six months. He did not understand the money market, nor the stock market, nor even the financial article in the *Signal*; but he regarded himself as a financial genius. (Arnold Bennett, *The Card*, 1911)[141]

As with Arnold Bennett's Denry Machin, 'back office' or 'plumbing' functions like clearing and settlement for markets would be even less appreciated or understood than the workings of the transactions themselves. Yet efficient and effective clearing and settlement are an essential part of commodity (and financial) markets. Clearing is the process whereby counterparties' claims and obligations are offset; settlement then occurs of the net amounts owing. From the eighteenth century clearing and settlement were well developed in the Bankers' Clearing House. The aims were to reduce the administrative burden and the amount of cash banks needed to hold to fulfil their customers' orders.[142] Clearing and settlement in the commodities markets went further than bank clearing because not only financial accounts but contracts also needed to be cleared. Clearing houses for commodities became essential when futures transactions began to dominate, not least because the volume of trading increased considerably. If there were equal sales and purchases, the contract terms were standardised, and the description of the commodity and time of delivery were identical, it was only necessary to settle the difference in prices.

1 Commodity Clearing Houses

The London Produce Clearing House ('the LPCH') was founded in 1888, incorporated as a joint stock company under the Companies Act 1862. It changed its name to the International Commodities Clearing House in 1973, and from 1991 was known as the London Clearing House.[143] What was in 1888 the law firm Hollams, Son & Coward (now Clifford Chance) did the legal work

---

[139] at 578. On Sumner's commercial experience: A. Lentin, *The Last Political Law Lord. Lord Sumner (1859–1934)*, Cambridge, Scholars Publishing, 2008, 33–34.
[140] 107 below. [141] London, Methuen, 1911. [142] 452 below. [143] Later LCH Clearnet.

of incorporation. The firm had represented a number of the brokers behind the scheme (Carey & Brown, Rucker & Bencraft), along with some of the banks (William Brandt's Sons & Co., J. Henry Schroder & Co).[144] From time to time it advised the LPCH on difficult problems such as the effect on contracts of events such as the outbreak of the First World War.[145]

Despite English experience in clearing, especially in banking, continental ideas had a strong influence when commodity clearing took organised form. A Caisse de Liquidation was working in Le Havre from 1882. Subsequently, a clearing house operated on the same lines in Hamburg. From the outset the LPCH was influenced by German expertise in the futures markets.[146] That German influence continued in the years before the First World War and, to a lesser extent, in the interwar period. The LPCH's first secretary and its first manager and two staff were recruited from Germany.[147] It is thus highly likely that its rules were derived from those used on the continent. So it may well have inherited via Hamburg methods first devised in sixteenth-century Antwerp, and seventeenth-century Amsterdam, when those cities were the centre of the world's commodities trading.[148] Continental influence was also manifest in the London description of futures markets into the 1970s, as terminal markets.[149] Liverpool, much more closely tied to the United States, always used the American expression, futures markets.

The LPCH was incorporated with the object, as stated in the prospectus, 'to place on a secure basis, by a system of deposits, the dealing in produce for future delivery'. Its initial capital of one million pounds was provided by prominent City financiers such as Arbuthnot Latham, Baring Bros, William Brandt and Sons, Hambros, Kleinwort, Rothschild and Henry Schroder.[150] The first annual report also hinted at the national advantage 'in giving facility of sale with security of contract, and thereby attracting business to London'.[151] Initially the LPCH cleared futures dealings in coffee and sugar.[152] Sugar was

---

[144] J. Slinn, *Clifford Chance*, Cambridge, Granta Editions, 1993, 43. The firm had its offices on the first floor of the Commercial Sales Rooms in Mincing Lane (ibid., 40, 67), no doubt good for business such as drawing up leases and articles of partnership for brokers, later incorporating their sole trader or partnership firms, and advising them on arbitration and litigation.

[145] Ibid., 90, 147. The firm's records were destroyed during World War II so further details are not available.

[146] e.g., on German expertise at the time see A. Engel, 'Buying Time: Futures Trading and Telegraphy in Nineteenth-Century Global Commodity Markets' (2015) 10 *J Global Hist* 284, 284–285, 294, 300.

[147] LMA, CLC/B/153/MS03641/001, LPCH, Board Minutes, vol. 1, 8, 28 March 1888.

[148] See F. Braudel, *The Wheels of Commerce*, London, Collins, 1982, 97–106.

[149] G. Rees & D. Jones, 'The International Commodities Clearing House Ltd' (1975) 26 *J Agricultural Econ* 239, 240.

[150] G. Rees, *The History of the London Commodity Markets*, London, Commodity Analysis Ltd, 1978, 47.

[151] Kindly provided by David Hardy, previously chief executive of LCH Clearnet.

[152] LPCH decided that the first sugar rules should follow the rules for coffee as closely as possible in respect of the registration of contracts, despite the strong objection of one of its leading lights, Caesar Czarnikow: LMA, CLC/B/153/MS03641/001, LPCH, Board Minutes, 32–34,

especially conducive to futures dealings since, unlike other products like tea and wool, it was easily graded. Later the LPCH cleared futures transactions in wheat, maize, pepper, rubber, raw silk, silver, indigo and, for a while at the turn of the twentieth century, tea.

Clearing of grain futures at the LPCH fell by the wayside early in the twentieth century when supplies of the standard grade of wheat were not available.[153] Subsequent clearing of grain contracts in London was effected by a separate clearing house, established by the London Corn Trade Association in 1921. Clearing in pepper was also discontinued, apparently because the pepper dealers did not want the publicity attached to registering their contracts with the clearing house.[154] The First World War and the downturn in world trade in the interwar years adversely affected the range and volume of commodities the LPCH cleared.[155] That was reversed after the Second World War, and from the late 1950s the LPCH began clearing major commodities except metals.

Initially the LPCH published separate rules for each commodity which, with some exceptions, followed a similar pattern.[156] After the Second World War its rules acquired a general character to cover any commodity where the relevant trade association sponsoring a futures market had an arrangement with it. The LPCH followed the model of an independent clearing house, not tied to any commodity association. That was also the banking model. The privilege of registering contracts was limited to authorised brokers. As a corollary they were obliged to channel all London futures business through the clearing house. The admission of brokers was in the 'absolute discretion' of the LPCH's board, which also had the power to suspend and expel them. Brokers could only engage in clearing for principals resident in Britain. For principals with no place of business within a mile of the clearing house (effectively the City of London) the transaction had to be registered in the name of a broker so qualified, who undertook the principal's obligations.

Unlike the LPCH, other clearing houses for commodities were established by specific markets, and in that sense were their captive.[157]

35–36, 39–40, 43, 47, 50; 31 May, 6, 27 June, 11, 18 July, 1 August 1888. On Czarnikow: 168 below.

[153] G. Rees, The History of the London Commodity Markets, op cit, 48. See also J. Smith, *Produce Exchanges*, Modern Business Text, vol. XI, London, Modern Business Institute, 1922, 501.

[154] J. Smith, *Organised Produce Markets*, London, Longmans Green & Co., 1922, 147.

[155] G. Rees & D. Jones, op cit, 244–246.

[156] I have found the following rules: London Produce Clearing House Ltd, *Regulations for Coffee Future Delivery Business*, May 1888, British Library; *Regulations for Future Delivery Business in Rio Coffee*, July 1893, LMA, CLC/B/153/MS03641/002, LPCH, Board Minutes, 124; *Regulations for Future Delivery in Beetroot Sugar 88°*, June 1913, LMA, CLC/B/153/MS03641/005, LPCH, Board Minutes, 40; *Regulations for Future Delivery Business in Cocoa*, April 1928, Institute of Commonwealth Studies, University of London.

[157] The London Metals Exchange had its own arrangements until well after our period: G. Gemmill, *Should the London Metal Exchange Use a Clearing House?* City University Business School Commodity Paper No.1, London, 1979.

Liverpool's clearing house for cotton – it appears to be the first commodity clearing house in Britain[158] – is an example. The clearing houses for the grain trade in both Liverpool and eventually London also followed a 'captive' model. The Liverpool Corn Trade Association formed a clearing house in 1883, which was incorporated in 1887. No doubt it was influenced by the system for clearing cotton transactions. Initially it acted as a clearing house for CIF contracts. Numerous dealings in these produced a string and the aim of clearing was to facilitate direct settlement between the first seller and the last buyer. In the closing years of the nineteenth century the contracts registered with the clearing house in wheat and maize were over 30,000 per annum. After 1893 the clearing house began clearing futures transactions.[159] Margin adjustments, representing futures transactions, were almost a quarter of a million per annum between 1897 and 1899. In the interwar years registrations with the clearing house were substantial once Liverpool had become an important wheat futures market.[160]

Proposals by the London Corn Trade Association (LCTA) to establish a clearing house in London for registration of CIF contracts in grain were considered in the years leading up to the First World War.[161] One factor in the lack of progress was a decidedly unhelpful opinion from Mr Gore-Browne KC. He was consulted as to the chances of the LCTA obtaining the necessary approval of the Board of Trade and the Court to change its articles of association to operate a clearing house. Delivered from Olympian heights, the opinion was unclear and unhelpful: it was very doubtful, it read, whether consent would be obtained; it was a matter of the Board's discretion and it could not be said how it could be exercised; but if the association was practically unanimous in favour of change it might be obtained.[162]

Eventually, the project of the LCTA for its own clearing house was achieved in 1921. As far as London was concerned, futures dealings in grain never prospered, even after they were provided for in 1929. Those transacting grain futures, including John Maynard Keynes, preferred Liverpool. LCTA's clearing house concentrated on clearing documents in string transactions. A clause was inserted in LCTA standard form contracts under which either party could

---

[158] T. Ellison, *The Cotton Trade of Great Britain*, London, E. Wilson, 1886, 286. Ellison was a cotton trader: see D. Farnie, 'Ellison, Thomas (1833-1904)', *Oxford Dictionary of National Biography*. See also 'The Exchange', *Liverpool Review*, 11 June 1887, 10 (also recording establishment of the Cotton Bank); G. Rees, Britain's Commodity Markets, *op cit*, 94–95.

[159] *Liverpool Corn Trade Association 1853–1953*, Liverpool, Liverpool Corn Trade Association, 1953, 11.

[160] 94 passim below. See also Liverpool Corn Trade Association Ltd, *Eighty-Fourth Annual Report*, 1936–1937, 5.

[161] e.g., LMA, CLC/B/103/MS23174/001, Sub Committee re A Clearing House System, 14 November 1905.

[162] LMA, CLC/B/103/MS23174/003, Minutes of sub-committees, 24 February 1913, 11 March 1913.

register a contract at the clearing house.[163] Registration of CIF grain contracts for this purpose fluctuated, probably reflecting the state of international trade. In the 1920s there were some years when it was about 10,000 contracts per annum, in the early 1930s registration was of 8,600 contracts at its highest (in 1932–1933), but from 1935 numbers fell away and the war put an end to the work.[164]

Documentary clearing, as with LCTA's processing of string contracts in grain sales, was the sole focus of the Tea Clearing House. It was formed in 1888 by dock companies and warehouse keepers, with dealers carrying on a wholesale trade in tea as subscribers. Among the aims of the association was to facilitate the rapid and efficient lodgement and transmission from a central office of warrants, delivery orders, carding, cording and other orders to the various docks and warehouses. In particular it was to provide a central clearing house where all such warrants and orders might be lodged 'to avoid the necessity of the personal attendance of the trade clerks and others at the offices of the various docks, warehouses, wharves, &c.'[165]

A sophisticated system developed for documentary clearing for sugar transactions. After the removal in 1874 of a heavy sugar tax it, too, became an object of mass consumption. By 1880 beet sugar was equal to cane sugar in world markets and the main source of sugar in Europe.[166] Formed in 1882 the Beetroot Sugar Association (from 1905 called the Sugar Association of London) devised a system for the use and clearing of filières. Filières represented sugar which had arrived at a port in Britain or on the continent.[167] Tender by filière was of standard amounts, and filières had to contain the relevant mark, number and country of origin of the sugar.[168] Filières passed from hand to hand, successive holders filling in the date, price and time of delivery. A buyer wanting the sugar would not enter the filière in the clearing but would give instructions as to the sugar's delivery or storage.[169] The documents of title to a cargo of sugar would pass to it.[170]

---

[163] e.g., LCTA, London La Plata Maize Contract. Steamer or Power Vessel. Parcels. Rye Terms. 1938. Conditions and Rules, §11.
[164] LMA, CLC/B/103/MS23172/008-009, London Corn Trade Association, Executive Committee Minutes.
[165] *Chamberlain's Wharf Ltd* v. *Smith* [1900] 2 Ch 605, 606. See *Tea Clearing House Centenary 1888–1988*, London, Tea Clearing House, 1988 for a description of its operation.
[166] e.g., N. Deerr, *The History of Sugar*, London, Chapman & Hall, 1950, vol. II, 490.
[167] Futures transactions in sugar were therefore different; they were cleared by the LPCH.
[168] Beetroot Sugar Association, *Rules and Regulations*, 8th ed., London, 1904, Clearing Contract, rr.224–226. British and German sugar associations established a 'General Agency' in Hamburg to supervise the shipping and storage of sugar in the two countries: Principal Regulations ... for the Guidance of the General Agency in Hamburg, ibid. There is a limited description of the filière system in *Encyclopaedia Britannica*, 11th ed., 1911, 'Clearing'.
[169] Ibid., rr.240–242.   [170] r.294.

Clearing was on a daily basis and the manager of the clearing would, on receipt of tenders, endeavour to liquidate contracts by passing a filière from sellers to buyers until the filière arrived at a buyer who could not pass it on (called, in the rules, the 'stopper').[171] The first seller would then pass the bill of lading or dock or warehouse warrant to the stopper, who paid a price based on the sugar's weight and analysis. Alternatively, the first seller or stopper might arrange a circle, repurchase or other liquidation of its obligations outside the clearing. Upon the manager receiving notice that the documents of title had passed, or liquidation had been otherwise effected, price differences were paid through him.[172]

2 Clearing Processes: Registration, Strings and Margins

Clearing and settlement by commodities clearing houses was perceived of as a routine administrative process, which only occasionally gave rise to difficulties. That was to underestimate both the skill involved in the matching of transactions and the theoretical underpinning of the task.[173] The first step in clearing and settlement was the registration of transactions with the clearing house, to record the parties' respective claims and liabilities, and to identify counterparties. The transactions were according to the terms contained in the standard form contracts of the relevant trade association, with the commodities being graded into the categories it adopted.[174] Registration enabled the matching of those who had bought or sold the same commodities for the same delivery dates and allowed intermediate parties to be eliminated.

Take the method for registering transactions in grain in Liverpool. Either party could register a contract, if accompanied by the requisite payment.[175] The clearing house had discretion to refuse registration if in its opinion a transaction was not *bona fide* or had been entered into for the purpose of evading liability, contrary to good faith.[176] Following registration, the clearing house recorded a contract on a 'string sheet'. As either party closed out its side of the contract, further registrations took place. Strings could be extended indefinitely and joined. Those at the end of the string were designated first

---

[171] Beetroot Sugar Association, *Rules and Regulations*, London, 8th ed., 1904, Clearing Contract, r.317.
[172] r.321.
[173] The task was also laborious: it was only in 1960 that the LPCH began to mechanise it with punch cards. To reduce the administrative burden, the need to prepare contracts for submission to the clearing house was also dropped and the original bought and sold slips became the single source of information on dealings.
[174] see Chapter 5 below.
[175] LvCTA Bye-laws, 1 April 1922, Clearing House Regulations, rr.13–14. See A. Hooker, The International Grain Trade, *op cit*, 34–36.
[176] LvCTA Bye-laws, ibid., r.15. For an example: MMM, B/LCTA/7/1, LvCTA, Clearing House Committee Minutes, 61, 1 February 1926.

seller and last buyer. Once intermediate parties had paid the difference in price in favour of their immediate counterparties, their obligations ceased.

Margins were generally a precondition of registration of a contract at a clearing house.[177] In the rules an initial margin was generally a minimum amount and the clearing house could impose a higher amount if necessary.[178] In addition to the initial margin the LPCH, as with other clearing houses, imposed variable margin requirements. It would fix the market price of a commodity daily, and the margin would be the difference (if a loss) between that price and the contract price. Margins were payable in some cases immediately, certainly within the day.[179] In the early years, margins were payable either in cash or by lodging approved collateral (shares, bonds and the like). Later payment requirements could be satisfied by a letter of guarantee from an approved bank. Failure to keep up margin payments entitled the clearing house to close out the party's contracts and to sell any collateral without obtaining prior approval.[180]

3 Bilateral Settlement, Rings and Novation

Settlement occurred in the commodity markets in various ways.[181] Direct settlement was the most straightforward through the bilateral reconciliation of contractual claims and liabilities. Bi-lateral settlement could also occur with off-setting transaction before the settlement day. The price difference payable might be discounted to recognise that one party was getting its profit earlier than the contract provided. Novation, where one party in the clearing system itself was substituted for another, became the hallmark of the most advanced clearing systems.

(i) Bi-lateral and Ring Settlement

Bi-lateral settlement faced no objection at law. If a seller agreed to set off the price of goods supplied against items admitted to be due to the buyer, Lord Campbell explained that both would be paid because it was as if the parties had met 'and one of them actually paid the other in coin, and the

---

[177] cf. Liverpool grain trade rules: LvCTA Bye-laws, April 1922, Section D, Clearing House Regulations, rr.29–30, which gave parties discretion to call an original margin from the other side. A suggestion for original margins, to prevent serious over-trading, led to inquiries of the Winnipeg Grain Exchange – not, note, London – but it was decided that existing rules had stood the test of time: MMM, B/LCTA/7/1, LvCTA, Clearing House Committee Minutes, 23, 30, 31 March 1925; 19 May, 1925.

[178] London Produce Clearing House Ltd, *Regulations for Coffee Future Delivery Business*, May 1888, r.6.

[179] r.11.

[180] r.13. For an example: LMA, CLC/B/103/MS23205/001, London Grain Futures Association, Minute Book No.1, 24 August 1939. See also *E. Bailey & Co Ltd v. Balholm Securities Ltd* [1973] 2 Lloyds Rep 404, 406–407, 415. cf. the Liverpool grain trade rules, r.41.

[181] J. Moser, *Origins of the Modern Exchange Clearinghouse*, Working Papers Series, Issues in Financial Regulation, Research Department, Federal Reserve Bank of Chicago, WP-94-3, April 1994, 7–15.

other handed back the same identical coin in payment of the cross debt'.[182] Once the price was payable under the contracts the set-off was effective as to both delivery and payment obligations. In the rules of the Liverpool Cotton Association there was a provision that where purchases and sales were made between the same members of the Association for the same quantity of cotton for delivery in the same month, the contracts were closed out, and the transaction was concluded by the receipt or payment of differences. Most future delivery contracts were closed in this way. In a leading American futures case Holmes J put it pithily: 'Set-off has all the effect of delivery.'[183] That was the position in English law as well. In one of the few English cases concerning the commodity markets, the judges in the Court of Appeal simply accepted the effectiveness of the provision in the Liverpool cotton rules.[184]

Although effective in law the problem of bi-lateral settlement was that, as the volume of trading increased with hedging and speculation, it became impractical without the intervention of a clearing house. Thomas Ellison worked in the cotton trade in Liverpool from the late 1840s, published his *Handbook of the Cotton Trade* in 1858, and became recognised at home and abroad for his unrivalled knowledge of the trade.[185] Ellison wrote later of the delays inherent in direct settlement before the establishment of the cotton clearing house: delays in passing on the declaration of tender (e.g., 100 bales of cotton, *ex Asia*, from New York); sampling the cotton; the appointment of arbitrators; forwarding of weighing notices; making out of invoices; and passing through payments on account and payments for final settlement.[186] Sometimes impecunious, intermediate parties, unable to pay their price differences, would delay intentionally. Although there might be a legal remedy, Ellison said, 'then came the "law's delays", which were worse even than the delays from which it was sought to escape'.[187] The multiplication of contracts, and the threat to the entire system of 'arrivals', led to the reform movement for a cotton clearing house, described earlier.

How a clearing house could facilitate bilateral settlement was demonstrated by the method used in the LPCH in relation to coffee futures.[188] The settlement

---

[182] Livingstone v. Whiting (1850) 15 QB 722, 723, 117 ER 632, 632. See J. Benjamin, *A Treatise on the Law of Sale of Personal Property*, 7th ed., London, Sweet & Maxwell, 1931, 883–84 for other authorities.

[183] Chicago Board of Trade v. Christie, 198 US 236, 246 (1905). See J. Levy, *Freaks of Fortune. The Emerging World of Capitalism and Risk in America*, Cambridge, MA, Harvard University Press, 2014, 234–235, 254–263.

[184] Cooper (Inspector of Taxes) v. Stubbs [1925] 2 KB 753, 755. See also F.E. Hookway & Co. Ltd v. Alfred Isaacs & Sons [1954] 1 Lloyd's Rep 491, 503, per Devlin J.

[185] *A Hand-Book of the Cotton Trade: or, a glance at the past history, present condition, and future prospects of the cotton commerce of the world*, London, privately published, 1858.

[186] T. Ellison, *The Cotton Trade of Great Britain*, op cit, 283–284. [187] Ibid., 284.

[188] Some clearing rules recognised that direct settlement could occur outside their remit, e.g., Beetroot Sugar Association, Rules and Regulations, 8th ed., 1904, r.320. In the 1930s probably a third of the Liverpool grain futures trades were not registered; nearly all were offset by

process was initiated, as typically for clearing houses, by the registration of contracts after the payment of the required margin.[189] Following this the clearing house issued to each party a non-endorsable 'certificate of guarantee' in which it declared that it was responsible to both buyer and seller for the fulfilment of the contract.[190] Under rule 14 of the rules, settlement occurred by a contracting party handing the clearing house two certificates of guarantee for the same delivery, in one named as buyer, and in the other, as seller. Absent any default, the clearing house was then 'bound ... to make up accounts at once and to pay or place to the credit of the contracting party, any balance due'. That balance was made up of the margins, which needed to be repaid, and brokerage, but with a discount if payment was prior to the delivery date.[191] If a contracting party was unable to enter an off-setting transaction to settle in this way, it needed to accept tender of the coffee (unless it could subsequently re-sell[192]). Settlement then involved passing the dock or warehouse warrants representing the goods.

Ring settlement was another method used in the commodity markets. Its advantage was to increase the number of potential counterparties available to settle. Where A sold to B, B to C and C to A the same amount of a commodity for delivery on the same date, bringing A, B and C together in a ring meant that the different sales would cancel each other out and all that was needed was for the parties to pay the price differences on their transactions. The ring could involve many more parties than three and price differences could be netted so that payments were reduced. Netting of price differences was facilitated by striking a settlement price, representative of all prices. Parties then needed to pay only the difference between that and the price of their trades.

Ring settlement did not need an organised clearing house. In practice traders might meet after a market closed to trace contracts back so as to form rings, and outdoor clerks might then be sent around to different offices to close up a series of trades.[193] The London Metal Exchange used a form of ring settlement, devised in 1909 by a member of its committee. As noted earlier, it did not have a clearing house. *The Economist Intelligence Unit* described the process in the late 1950s. Members made a daily confidential return to the Exchange's secretary showing the warrants owed or due to each other on the prompt date, together with the balance of transactions with the market as a whole. The secretary would fit these returns together, isolating the members who were long in the market, and direct

---

opposite contracts during the day: H. Working & S. Hoos, *op cit*, 141. Although initially with London grain futures members could not marry contracts themselves, this was later permitted if done in the ring at the same price: LMA, CLC/B/103/MS23205/001, London Grain Futures Association, London Grain Futures Minute Book No.1, 2 July 1929, 21–22; 7 December 1933, 114.

[189] London Produce Clearing House Limited, *Regulations for Coffee Future Delivery Business*, May 1888, rr.6–7. The rules of some commodity clearing systems recognised that direct settlement could occur outside the remit of the rules.

[190] rr. 1, 8.   [191] rr. 14, 20.   [192] rr. 16, 18.

[193] J. Baer & G. Woodruff, *Commodity Exchanges*, New York, Harper & Bros, 1929, 50–51.

them as to whom delivery of warrants should be made. Cash differences arising from transactions were paid privately by the members concerned.[194] However, ring settlement was facilitated if there was a clearing house, to organise rings and to net price differences.[195] It was a regular feature of clearing contracts in the London and Liverpool grain markets. Their clearing houses matched up trades to form rings as best they could.[196]

(ii) Settlement through Novation

A further, and in fact the typical method of settlement once the London and Liverpool commodity markets matured, was settlement by novation. At its simplest novation occurred when a party had bought and sold equal amounts of a commodity for delivery in the same period. It dropped out and its buyer and seller were brought together. It paid anything owing on the two transactions. Novation as a legal technique was familiar to lawyers from partnership law.[197] New partners undertook, and retired partners relinquished, contractual obligations with the acknowledgement of third parties dealing with the firm. There were also instances of the assignment of insurance business, with the policy holders assenting to the transfer of their policies from one business to the other.[198] By the time the London and Liverpool clearing houses were being established, novation was being recognised by the highest legal authorities. In *Scarf* v. *Jardine*[199] Lord Selborne LC said that novation, derived from the civil law, meant in his understanding a new contract being substituted for an existing contract, either between the same or different parties, the consideration mutually being the discharge of the old contract.

But could the rules of a clearing house provide for novation in advance so that one party was substituted for another automatically? There were legal doubts. Pollock proffered the view in his *Principles of Contract* that, apart from novation in the proper sense, a creditor might bind himself once and for all in the original contract to accept a substituted liability at the debtor's option.[200] Other writers were not as bold.[201] When United States courts considered the

---

[194] Economist Intelligence Unit, *A History of the London Metal Exchange*, London, Economist, 1958, 63. R. Forrester, 'Commodity Exchanges in England' (May 1931) 155 *Annals Amer Acad Pol & Soc Sc* 196, 205.
[195] H. Loman, 'Commodity Exchange Clearing Systems' (May 1931) 155 *Annals Amer Acad Pol & Soc Sc* 100, 101–102.
[196] e.g., LvCTA Bye-laws, 1 April 1922, r.18 provided: 'The Secretary shall have power to vary the arrangements of the contacts on a string whenever all or any number of them are capable of being formed into a ring.'
[197] e.g., *Wilson* v. *Lloyd* (1873) LR 16 Eq 60.
[198] e.g., *Re International Life Assurance Society & Hercules Insurance Co ex p. Blood* (1870) LR 9 Eq 316; *Re European Assurance Society, Miller's Case* (1876) 3 Ch D 391.
[199] (1882) 7 App Cas 345, 351.
[200] F. Pollock, *Principles of Contract*, 2nd ed. London, Stevens, 1878, 190.
[201] S. Leake, *An Elementary Digest of the Law of Contracts*, London, Stevens, 1878, 791 could have been read as supportive, but Chitty did not acknowledge novation until the 12th edition by J. Lely & N. Greary: J. Chitty, *Law of Contracts*, London, Sweet & Maxwell, 1890, 862.

substitution of parties to settle commodities contracts, they upheld its legality on the basis of market practice in the Chicago Board of Trade, rather than as a result of novation.[202] It was not until 1915 – after it was well established – that an English court approved novation in the context of the commodities markets.[203]

Illustrative of the rules for novation by party substitution were those for the clearing of futures contracts in grain in Liverpool in the interwar period. Any member who had bought and sold grain for future delivery under contracts, which in the opinion of the clearing house were in all material points identical as to the terms, except as to price, could upon registering those contracts instruct it (the clearing house) to arrange them in a string, whereupon it (the clearing house) appeared as an intermediate party. Upon payment of any loss and/or margin due by any party on any contract appearing on the string, the intermediate party was released from liability, and the contracting parties became the first seller and the last buyer, the same course being followed on each succeeding sale or purchase and payment of loss and/or margin.[204] Under the rules, the clearing house was deemed to be agent of each party for receiving and transferring documents. Notices, payments and releases between the first seller and last buyer operated as if they had passed between intermediate parties.[205] The upshot was that procedures were short-circuited as these documents needed only to pass from the first seller to the last buyer.

The Liverpool rules did not mention the term novation, although that was their effect. Novation was expressly mentioned in the LPCH rules, once they replaced bi-lateral settlement. Rule 1 of the 1928 regulations for settling futures transactions in cocoa provided that, in consideration of the registration of a contract, and the guarantee the clearing house gave both buyer and seller, both parties respectively agreed with each other and the clearing house to accept 'by way of novation' other sellers and buyers as the clearing house might appoint for the sale or purchase of the commodity mentioned in the contract.[206] Rule 13 of the regulations then provided that if a party ('the middle party') requested a settlement of contracts in which it was on the one hand a buyer, and on the other a seller, for the same amount of cocoa and for the same month of delivery, it ceased to be under any liability to receive or deliver that commodity and its seller and buyer were deemed to contract with each other. The clearing house could impose parties by novation so as to effect a settlement: where novation took place in this way the seller and buyer were responsible to each other for the fulfilment of the contract at the market price

---

[202] *Oldershaw v. Knowles*, 6 Ill App 325 (1880), aff'd 101 Ill 117 (1881). See also *Wolcott v. Reeme*, 44 Ill App 196 (1892).
[203] *Jager v. Tolme and Runge and the London Produce Clearing House Ltd* [1916] 1 KB 939. See 101 below.
[204] LvCTA Bye-Laws, April 1922, r.17.   [205] rr.22–23.
[206] London Produce Clearing House Ltd, *Regulations for Future Delivery Business in Cocoa*, April 1928. To the same effect see novation in rubber sales in S. Dowling, *The Exchanges of London*, London, Butterworth & Co, 1929, 117–118.

on the day determined. Any difference between that and the contract price was to be settled between the clearing house and each of the contracting parties.

Novation by party substitution in this way raised some difficult issues in its application. One was the extent to which a compromise between substituted parties could bind those no longer contractually involved. The situation arose in the Liverpool grain trade in 1930. Produce Brokers New Co. (1924) Ltd had sold maize to Sheard Stubbs & Co. at 21/9 per quarter, who had sold the same quantity of the same maize on the same terms to Spillers Ltd at 26/3. In fact the maize declared under the contract was defective. The contracts were registered with the clearing house and Sheard Stubbs & Co. should have dropped out of the picture. But it objected when Produce Brokers and Spillers, as first sellers and last buyers, agreed the contract should be closed without any question of default arising, but at a lower price of 19/4½ per quarter for the defective part of the maize.[207] This agreement was blessed by an arbitration award, which under the arbitration clause of the contracts was binding on intermediate parties. That threatened Stubbs' profits on the contract. The association's solicitor advised that in the circumstances the clearing house rules gave it power to override the award, and that in exercising its discretion under the rules it would be justified in allowing Stubbs their profit, but keeping Produce Brokers to the price it agreed with Spillers.[208]

The operation of novation by party substitution was still in the rules of the LPCH at the end of our period.[209] The rules tracked almost exactly rules 1 and 13 of the 1928 rules, except that the clearing house was also empowered to impose a settlement in and for the delivery month of a futures contract, even if no request for settlement had been made. What had fallen by the wayside, although it was to be revived as the norm once the (renamed) LPCH began to clear financial futures in the 1980s, was novation whereby the clearing house itself was substituted for each of the parties (called 'complete clearing' in the United States). Under this arrangement the seller–buyer contract was transformed into two contracts, a seller–clearing house contract, and a clearing house–buyer contract. An advantage of the substitution of the clearing house in this way was that it, not the parties, carried the credit risk. Sellers and buyers were now bound to the clearing house, which had taken the place of their original counterparty. If either party failed, the clearing house would bear the loss directly.

This method of novation, with the clearing house becoming the central counterparty, seems to have been adopted for the clearing of coffee trades in continental Europe, and there is a suggestion it was instituted pre–First World

---

[207] Where goods tendered were defective, the rules provided for arbitrators to invoice back or make a price allowance: LvCTA Bye-Laws, Clearing House Regulations, rr.50–51.
[208] Letter, Park N. Stone to Secretary, 4 November 1930, MMM, B/LCTA/7/1, LvCTA.
[209] London Produce Clearing House Ltd, *General Regulations for Future Delivery Business and Byelaws for Options*, 1972, r.13. See *E. Bailey & Co Ltd v. Balholm Securities Ltd* [1973] 2 Lloyd's Rep 404, 407–408.

War by the clearing house in Hamburg.[210] It was certainly adopted by the Minneapolis Chamber of Commerce as early as 1891, the New York Cotton Exchange in 1915, the Chicago Board of Trade in 1925 and other United States commodity exchanges on various other dates.[211] By contrast it did not sweep the board in British commodity markets until the modern period. One example of its early use was in sugar clearing just prior to the First World War. It may have been the influence of Hamburg, which had a large sugar market in the early 1900s. Whatever the reason, the 1913 version of the LPCH rules for clearing futures business in beetroot sugar provided for the substitution of the clearing house once settlement occurred, by a party handing in buy and sell certificates of guarantee for the same delivery date.

The Court of Appeal averted to the sugar arrangements in 1916, although it did not refer expressly to the clearing house rule.[212] Rather it relied on the Sugar Association of London's contract for sale of beetroot sugar 88°, which was cleared under LPCH rules, and which contained a clause along the same lines. The Court of Appeal accepted that this meant that the position was the same as if the plaintiff had made a contract with the clearing house, and the liability of the original sellers to the plaintiff was at an end. Given the wording of the sugar beet clearing rules, however, there was no privity between the plaintiff and the substituted sellers, the defendants, which was relevant to the issue in the case. That was whether the defendants were parties to a contract with the plaintiffs so as to be entitled to appeal to the council of the Sugar Association in relation to the dispute between them.

4 Settlement Risk

The possibility of a party defaulting was a potential threat. If it was unable to settle when the time arrived, this would have a domino effect because of the network of transactions which that party was likely to have entered. A clearing house needed rules and practices to mitigate the risk if a party was unable to settle at the end of the day. One aspect was what should happen at the point that default occurred. Clearing houses took power to close out and unwind the defaulter's contracts. Further, they adopted various preventative strategies. Finally, some had compensation or insurance schemes to mitigate the losses experienced by counterparties to a defaulter.

---

[210] H. Emery, *Speculation on the Stock and Produce Exchanges of the United States*, New York, Faculty of Political Science, Colombia University, 1896, 71; H. Hirschstein, 'Commodity Exchanges in Germany' (May 1931) 151 *Annals Amer Acad Pol & Soc Sci* 213.

[211] G. Wright, *op cit*, 198–199; J. Baer & G. Woodruff, Commodity Exchanges, *op cit*, 52–55.

[212] *Jager v. Tolme & Runge and the London Produce Clearing House* [1916] 1 KB 939. See also *Smith, Coney & Barrett v. Becker, Gray & Co* [1916] 2 Ch 86.

(i) Closing Out Rules

Should a party be in default – fail to pay a margin or a price difference or be unable to tender under a contract – the rules of the clearing houses empowered them to close out the defaulter's contracts. On this occurring the defaulting party would be excluded from settlement. What then happened is illustrated by the actions of the London Corn Trade Association clearing house on failure of the grain dealer Bovill & Sons in 1925. The clearing house decided on the price, 42/6 for 24 July, the day the firm collapsed. That price was then used for the contracts closed out between Bovill and its immediate sellers and buyers. What of other contracts in the string? The clearing house had only been operating several years and some firms urged that 42/6 should be used for all contracts on Bovill strings. Following standard practice elsewhere, the clearing house rejected this and said that all other contracts on Bovill strings, apart from the immediate sellers and buyers with Bovill, had to be fulfilled at the prices agreed.[213]

If a defaulting party was in profit on its contracts, there would be no loss on default.[214] If not, it was its immediate counterparties who in the first instance were exposed to loss through the defaulter's inability to pay. With the LCTA, novations would be unwound so that it was the original, not the substituted, counterparty who was exposed to loss.[215] The policy behind the approach was that parties were responsible for evaluating the creditworthiness of their immediate counterparties. However, the rules giving effect to this policy differed, and many trade associations attempted to mitigate the exposure to loss of the immediate counterparties to a defaulter. Under the early rules of the Liverpool cotton exchange, although the defaulter bore the loss, the clearing house had a discretion as to how to fix the prices and dates 'with due regard to "set offs" at which all payments shall be made to the insolvent's estate'.[216]

Another approach was that of the Liverpool grain trade, which tried to spread losses: if more than one party's contracts were affected by the defaulting party, the clearing house 'shall apportion the contracts closed by him, and the loss, if any, incurred thereby, among such members'.[217] LPCH's approach tried to spread the loss equitably. It could close out contracts or invoice back on a party's default, and all buyers and sellers with uncovered positions for the

---

[213] LMA, CLC/B/103/MS23189, London Corn Trade Association, Clearing House Board, Minutes, 11 August 1925.

[214] e.g., closing of CIF strings involving Strauss & Co. Ltd. (in liquidation): MMM, B/LCTA/7/2, Liverpool Clearing House Committee, 59–60, 7 February 1935. There was only a small deficiency (£9.1.7) on Strauss' London dealings. See LMA, CLC/B/103/MS23205/001, London Grain Futures Association, Minute Book No.2, 14 February 1935.

[215] e.g., LMA, CLC/B/103/MS23189, London Corn Trade Association, Clearing House Board, Minutes, 5 June 1933.

[216] Constitution, Laws and Usages of the Liverpool Cotton Brokers Association, 1881, Clearing House Rules, rr.17–18. See also Rules Relating to Cotton Sold to Arrive, r.12; LRO, 380 COT 4/77, Liverpool Cotton Brokers Association, Letter from Mr Hobson and Report of the Clearing House Committee, 15 August 1879.

[217] Bye-Laws of the LvCTA, 1922, Clearing House Regulations, r.19. See also r.20.

same delivery had to share the losses *pro tanto* (or to the nearest fraction) and take the place of the counterparty to the defaulter's contracts as closed.[218] None of these rules for commodities went as far as rule 177 of the Stock Exchange, which, at the turn of the century, obliged members to pay price differences in a defaulter's favour into a fund, rather than to the defaulter, for distribution to members with price differences in their favour.[219]

Settlement risk through party default was one thing; systemic risk through widespread market disruption was another. War was the most obvious cause. Eventually clearing systems had rules for the closing out of contracts in that event. Thus in the troubled period prior to the First World War the Sugar Association of London had been prompted by the foresight of Czarnikow, a leading sugar dealer, to insert a rule deeming contracts to be closed out on official notice being given of a state of war involving Germany with either England, France, Russia and/or Austria.[220] Sugar contracts were cleared by LPCH, and the rule stipulated that closing out was to be calculated in terms of its official price quotations.[221] When war came in 1914, it had a disastrous impact on the international sugar trade. Obviously impacted was the physical trade centred in Hamburg and Magdeburg, which was about twice that of London. Sugar broking in London came to a halt when the refineries agreed not to operate on the raw sugar market but to obtain their supplies from the government alone, at a fixed price.[222] Although the application of the closing out rules was not clear cut, their application saved sugar traders like Czarnikow from insolvency.

(ii) Preventive Steps: Membership, Periodic Settlement, and Margins

Settlement risk through party default was guarded against by various preventive steps. Those without financial integrity might not be admitted to the clearing house in the first place. There were also instances where members had their ability to register contracts withdrawn through a failure to pay margins. That would obviously have raised doubts about their trading. Initial margins on the registration of contracts and variable margins afterwards were devices to curb parties from assuming risks beyond their capacity. Periodic settlement, as a check on parties incurring excessive exposure, was a further measure to mitigate risk. It was adopted by about sixty brokers in Liverpool cotton in December 1883, originally as a reaction to attempts to corner the market. The brokers formed themselves into a Settlement Association with its own by-laws

---

[218] London Produce Clearing House, Regulations for Future Delivery Business in Cocoa, April 1928, rr.11, 15.
[219] *Beckhuson & Gibbs* v. *Hamblet* [1900] 2 QB 18, 22, per Kennedy J. On appeal [1901] 2 KB 73.
[220] Sugar Association of London, Rules and Regulations, r.491A, in *Jager* v. *Tolme & Runge and London Produce Clearing House Ltd* [1916] 1 KB 939, 962 (Note (1)); H. Janes & H. Sayers, *The Story of Czarnikow*, London, Harley Publishing Co, 1963, 59. On Czarnikow: 168 below.
[221] rule 491A.
[222] P. Chalmin, *The Making of a Sugar Giant Tate and Lyle 1859-1989*, London, Harwood Academic, 1990, 730. See also J. Slinn, Clifford Chance, *op cit*, 81.

and rules, although eventually the Liverpool Cotton Association incorporated periodic settlement into its rules.[223] By the early 1920s settlement in Liverpool cotton was on a weekly basis, the trading week running from Monday to Saturday, with the following Thursday being settlement day. Purchases and sales to the same amount of cotton for the same months of delivery were deemed closed, and only the balance was carried forward to the next settlement.[224]

With some clearing systems, margins were tapped more directly on default of a counterparty. The Liverpool Corn Trade Association rules provided that all margins payments were held as security for contracts until fulfilled or closed, with the amounts being paid to parties entitled to receive them.[225] Under the insolvency clause, if a party became insolvent or had a receiver appointed, the clearing house had discretion to pay its margin payments to the other party.[226] When one of the leading grain firms, Shipton, Anderson & Company, collapsed in 1937, owing moneys to the clearing house, its liquidator sought to reclaim the margin payments the firm had made so as to be able to pay other creditors. The clearing house persuaded the liquidator to abandon the claim after referring him to its rules, that is, margin payments of a failed member went to that member's creditors in relation to claims under grain contracts.[227]

(iii) Compensation: Funds, Guarantees and Insurance

Preventative measures would not always work. Some clearing houses built up compensation schemes for parties suffering through the default of other market participants. The financial capacity of clearing houses to compensate those incurring loss derived from three sources, although the mix varied. First, there was capital and reserves; secondly, fees and other funds; and thirdly, other sources such as the failed member's collateral and guarantors. In the case of the LPCH the capital and reserves were considerable, although that was not the case with other clearing houses. Fees charged by a clearing house might be pitched to cover running costs, but in some cases they might have contributed to reserves. Money raised from margin payments were also there. In the case of the LPCH these were available funds to back the guarantee it as an institution gave on every transaction. From 1921 it accepted a bank guarantee in approved form as cover for margins.[228] The

---

[223] T. Ellison, *Gleanings and Reminiscences*, Liverpool, H. Young, 1905, 355–356.
[224] See J. Smith, *Organised Produce Markets*, op cit, 57. See also S. Chapman, *The Lancashire Cotton Industry*, Manchester, Manchester University Press, 1904, 131–132.
[225] r.41. [226] r.36.
[227] MMM, B/LCTA/7/2, LvCTA, Clearing House Committee 1933–1941, 9, 11 July, 8 August 1935, 78–79, 81, 84.
[228] LMA, CLC/B/153/MS03641/005, LPCH, Minutes of board meetings, 216, 7 April, 233, 31 October 1921. It was an early form of demand guarantee – 'At the request of [] we undertake to pay you on demand up to £[] ...' – drafted by the LPCH, although submitted to Coward & Co., solicitors, for review.

amount which some members were obliged to provide by way of bank guarantee was considerable.[229]

Apart from capital and reserves and margins, clearing houses used a variety of other techniques to fund compensation in case of default. Under the rules of the Liverpool Corn Trade Association new members had to provide separate security to underpin their obligations and those of their firms.[230] Although the rules said this separate security was to be returned to the member after three years, it appears that standard practice was to make it permanent. Legally this was done by having the member – or whoever was giving an undertaking on the member's behalf – to agree in the documentation creating the security to disapply that part of the rules.[231] In the interwar years each new member had to put up the sum of £1,000 by way of a deposit of cash, the assignment of satisfactory securities, or arranging for comparable undertakings by other members, a bank or an insurance company. Cash was deposited in a bank account in the name of the association and the rules provided that it was held by it as trustee for the purpose of meeting the member's obligations in respect of debts arising out of grain trading.[232] In an insolvency the clearing house could use the sum to compensate those suffering losses and the liquidator of the failed member could not claim the amount to satisfy the member's other debts.[233]

As we have seen clearing houses might pay compensation as a matter of discretion to those adversely affected by the default of a dealer in the commodity markets. Except where the clearing house stood as a central counter-party on contracts – not typical of commodity clearing houses in London and Liverpool – there was no basis for direct legal liability when a party defaulted. In English law it was not as though providing the service of clearing and settlement should give rise to any duty to ensure that parties would honour their contracts by giving or taking delivery of a commodity or paying the price or any price difference. This lack of legal responsibility was made plain in the early rules of the Liverpool Cotton Brokers' Association, which gave power to its clearing house to act for contracting parties in receiving and passing on delivery orders, notices and so on, but added that this was not to affect the liability of members to each other on their contracts.[234]

---

[229] *Tate & Lyle Refineries Ltd* v. *International Commodities Clearing House Ltd* [1975] 1 Lloyds Rep 477, 479. On this case Nigel Fox Bassett's Further Comments on Chapter 14 [of J. Slinn, Clifford Chance, op cit], 9 April 1992, Clifford Chance Archives. I'm grateful to the firm's partners for access to these archives.
[230] LvCTA By-laws, 1 April 1922, B1, rr.1–9.
[231] MMM, B/LCTA/34/15, LvCTA Ltd., Member's Security, Mr Herbert Ashcroft, admitted October 1935, cl.5.
[232] r.8.
[233] The issue arose in the Shipton, Anderson & Co. collapse: MMM, B/LCTA/7/2, Clearing House Committee, 27 January 1938, 170–173.
[234] Constitutions Law and Usages of the Liverpool Cotton Brokers' Association, 1881, Clearing House Rules, r.2.

From its inception in 1888, the LPCH gave a guarantee that parties would meet their contractual obligations.[235] The process by which the clearing house became a guarantor to buyers and sellers, who might not be members, and therefore parties to the rules, was somewhat convoluted. Immediately after a transaction a broker delivered contracts to the contracting parties in which the clearing house was designated as guarantor. The broker had each party sign the counterpart of the contract, acknowledging their agreement to the rules.[236] That was then lodged with the clearing house, together with the appropriate margin payment. Under the early rules all this was to be done by 3 pm on the working day following the day of sale (2 pm on Saturdays). The clearing house then registered the contract, the name of the contracting parties and of the broker, and the quantity, price and time of delivery. Importantly, the clearing house also sent to each contracting party a 'certificate of guarantee', in which it declared it was responsible under the terms of its regulations for fulfilment of the contract. The guarantee said that it was not 'endorsable', in other words, transferable.[237]

The process by which the LPCH guaranteed the performance of contracts continued into the years after the Second World War.[238] An example of its succinct guarantee from the late 1950s read that, subject to its regulations and conditions, LPCH 'guarantees to you the fulfilment by the Seller of the Contract No. [] for the delivery of 50 Tons of . . . Raw Cane Sugar . . . delivered cif London and/or Liverpool . . . In accordance with the Rules, Conditions and Bye-Laws.'[239] There was no question about the enforceability of this kind of guarantee in English law. The certificate itself performed the function of satisfying section 4 of the Statute of Frauds, 1677: it was the written memorandum or note, signed on behalf of the clearing house, setting out the details of the contract being guaranteed.[240] From the early 1960s certificates of guarantee were issued automatically, based on information extracted from the bought and sold slips.[241]

The Liverpool grain trade adopted a different model, insurance. The clearing house paid a proportion of each registration fee for contracts to an insurance fund. That was then capable of being allocated in the case of the default of any member to make payment to counterparties in respect of a registered contract.[242] The insurance fund was operated by a specially constituted organisation, the

---

[235] e.g., London Produce Clearing House Ltd, Regulations for Coffee Future Delivery Business, May 1888, r.1.
[236] r.5.   [237] r.8.
[238] London Produce Clearing House Ltd, Regulations for Future Delivery Business in Cocoa, April 1928, rr.1, 5, 7.
[239] Kindly provided by David Hardy, former chief executive of the London Clearing House. The certificate is undated but seems related to the No.2 (Preferential) raw sugar contract, introduced in 1959: G. Rees & D. Jones, 'The International Commodities Clearing House Ltd', *op cit*, 247.
[240] e.g., S. Rowlatt, *The Law of Principal and Surety*, London, Sweet & Maxwell, 1898, ch.3.
[241] G. Rees, Britain's Commodity Markets, *op cit*, 186.
[242] MMM, B/LCTA/42/31, LvCTA By-Laws, 1 April 1922, r.21. See also Liverpool Grain Contract Insurance Co. Ltd., MMM, B/LCTA/27/1-2, Liverpool Grain Contract Insurance Co Ltd, Minutes (1940–1964).

Liverpool Grain Contract Insurance Company Ltd. The insurance company paid up to a specific limit (e.g., at one point £100 for each separate contract). Having had a party's claim against the defaulter assigned to it, it sought to recover what it could. If it did recover, after recouping its costs, it was obliged to compensate parties for the unpaid balance of their loss.[243] In the Shipton, Anderson & Co. failure, the clearing house refused to allow the insurance company recourse to the security which it held from the firm.[244] Legally, this was justified since it was the clearing house which held the security, not the counterparties to whose claims the insurance company had been subrogated. Relatively few claims seem to have been made on the insurance fund.[245]

2.6 Maintaining Market Integrity

> '[Melmotte] is a great man . . . I would sooner see that man than your Queen, or any of your dukes or lords. They tell me that he holds the world of commerce in his right hand. What power;—what grandeur!'
>
> 'Grand enough,' said Paul, 'if it all came honestly.'
>
> 'Such a man rises above honesty,' said Mrs. Hurtle, 'as a great general rises above humanity when he sacrifices an army to conquer a nation. Such greatness is incompatible with small scruples. A pigmy man is stopped by a little ditch, but a giant stalks over the rivers.'
>
> 'I fear you will find that your idol has feet of clay.' (Anthony Trollope, *The Way We Live Now*, 1875)[246]

The integrity of markets was regularly threatened by those like Trollope's Augustus Melmotte who, in the words of the American Mrs Hurtle to Paul Montague, 'rises above honesty'. That was especially so with the commodity markets of Trollope's 1870s. The rules on market integrity had come a way from those of Adam Smith's time, with its offences of forestalling, regrating and engrossing – buying up goods on the way to the market, buying in a market for the purpose of reselling on the same market, or hoarding goods with a view to speculation.[247] Smith had compared widespread fears of these practices with 'the popular terrors and suspicion of witchcraft'.[248] These statutory offences had been repealed in 1772, and despite some decisions in

---

[243] MMM, B/LCTA/42/31, LvCTA Bye-Laws Relating to Grain Futures. Insurance of Contracts, r.41.
[244] MMM, B/LCTA/7/2, Clearing House Committee 1933–1941, 27 January 1938, 171.
[245] W. Hudson, '"Futures" Markets and Contracts', Liverpool Corn Trade Association Lectures – No.4, c.1948, at MMM, B/LCTA/34/8.
[246] London, Chapman & Hall, 1875. Melmotte made money in company promotions, not commodity speculation.
[247] W. Holdsworth, *A History of English Law*, London, Methuen & Co., 1924, vol. IV, 379. cf. E. Mason, 'Monopoly in Law and Economics' (1937) 47 Yale LJ 34, 38–39.
[248] Adam Smith, *The Wealth of Nations*, 1776, Modern Library ed., New York, 1937, Bk.4, ch.5, 500.

the early 1800s applying them as part of the common law, surviving statutory repeal,[249] benevolent paternalism gave way to a general legal context of laissez-faire for the organised markets, which lasted in England for over 150 years.[250] It was not until the Financial Services Act 1986 that market manipulation was criminalised by statute.[251]

Notwithstanding the new political economy of the nineteenth century there was a view that speculation, if not dishonourable, was certainly unproductive of anything other than a profit or loss to the speculator. Adam Smith's distinction between productive and unproductive labour acquired a hold on popular thinking about political economy, shared by lawyers, even though judges and lawyers were identified by Smith as among the unproductive.[252] Speculation on the stock market was a special cause of public concern. Commodity markets did not escape unscathed, especially those with a connection to the nation's food. As we have seen, speculation in tallow in the early 1820s was the ostensible reason for the formalisation of the Baltic Exchange, although its existence did not put an end to the practice. In his *History of Prices*, the economist Thomas Tooke wrote of speculation in spices in 1825, which consisted of successive purchases on a rising market without intermediate deliveries, although he added that this was a rare occurrence on commodities markets.[253]

Speculation occurred on the Liverpool cotton market as early as the 1820s, and reference has already been made to the excessive speculation in cotton during the American Civil War. During the 1860s speculators in Liverpool cotton came from sections of society normally investing in foreign ventures.[254] At the end of the nineteenth century, Charles W. Smith published pamphlets calling for the regulation and prohibition of what he described as the gigantic abuses on commodity exchanges. Smith had some insight since he had been involved in the Liverpool cotton trade as editor of a trade sheet. Among Smith's targets for legal measures were forward sales, speculative options and futures.[255]

---

[249] *R v. Rusby* (1800) Peake Add Cas 189, 192, 170 ER 241, 242 *per* Lord Kenyon. Rusby was a dealer in the London Corn Exchange. The cases are discussed in D. Hay, *op cit.*; P. Atiyah, *The Rise and Fall of Freedom of Contract*, Oxford, Oxford University Press, 1979, 364–365. The common-law offences were finally repealed in 1844: An Act for Abolishing the Offences of forestalling, regrating and engrossing etc.: 7 & 8 Vic c.24.

[250] Fraudulent statements in the company context were caught by the Larceny Act 1861, 24 & 25 Vict. c.96, s.84 (see 116 below), and later the Prevention of Fraud (Investments) Act 1938, s.13, but there were no offences for markets.

[251] s.47(2).   [252] A. Smith, The Wealth of Nations, *op cit*, Bk.2, ch.3, 315.

[253] T. Tooke, *A History of Prices and of the State of the Circulation in 1838 and 1839*, London, Longman, 1840, 159–60.

[254] See also W. Henderson, *The Lancashire Cotton Famine 1861–1865*, Manchester, University of Manchester Economic History Series, 1934, 22.

[255] C. Smith, *Commercial Gambling*, London, Sampson Low & Co, 1893; C. Smith, *The Press on Commercial Gambling*, London, Low, 1893. See also F. Hammesfahr, *The Corn-Trade and Options Markets*, Antwerp, 1899, 64–71 (the author had interests in London); W. Baer, 'Market Gambling' (1894) 65 *Contemporary Review* 781.

Maintaining market integrity in the light of purely speculative transactions was not regarded as something for state regulation. Speculation in mainstream opinion was, at worst, a necessary evil. If action were to be taken, it was to be through private law-making by the markets themselves. Market rules for regular settlement days, coupled with deposit and margin requirements with their dampening effect on speculation, were examples. State law was a distant backstop and reserved for egregious behaviour bordering on fraud. Fraud might include rigging the market to avoid true prices, or where dealers cheated their principals, employers or each other.[256] Away from the market Britain seemed never to face, on a large scale, what the Americans called bucket shop operations. These were dealers purporting to act as brokers but not placing orders on the market at all, instead taking a position against their clients, manipulating the contract to their advantage and closing it out when their clients were in a loss position.[257]

Rigging the market, by the deliberate use of false transactions or spreading fictitious information to influence prices, was held to be an offence in England early in the nineteenth century. The leading case, involving false rumours to influence the price of government securities, dated from the Napoleonic era.[258] In the grain markets rigging was said to be frequent prior to the repeal of the Corn Laws in 1846. It was undertaken to take advantage of the lower duty payable on imported grain when the market price was high.[259] Offenders avoided prosecution. In 1834 the Comptroller of Corn Returns gave evidence to a parliamentary select committee of fictitious sales raising the price to import foreign rye at the lower duty permitted under the corn laws. A prosecution had been submitted to the Attorney-General and Solicitor-General. Although satisfied of a fraud, they decided against a prosecution because of uncertainty in securing a conviction.[260] No doubt this precedent continued to be a factor in subsequent years in the failure of state authorities to prosecute market manipulation. Early in the twentieth century there were accounts of Liverpool merchants having

---

[256] e.g., LMA, CLC/B/103/MS23189, London Corn Trade Association, Clearing House Board, Minutes, 18 July 1933 (employee trading on account in false name).

[257] A. Fabian, *Card Sharps, Dream Books and Bucket Shops Gambling in Nineteenth-Century America*, Ithaca, Cornell University Press, 1990, 155–158, 188–200; A. Chadwick, 'Gambling on Hunger? The Right to Adequate Food and Commodity Derivatives Trading' (2018) 18 *Human Rights LR* 233, 249–250. For bucket shops in Britain in company shares: C. Loussouarn, 'Spread Betting and the City of London', in R. Cassidy, A. Pisac & C. Loussouarn (eds.), *Qualitative Research in Gambling*, Abingdon, Oxon, Routledge, 2013, 238.

[258] R v. De Berenger (1814), 3 M & S 67, 105 ER 536. See E. Avgouleas, *The Mechanics and Regulation of Market Abuse: A Legal and Economic Analysis*, Oxford, Oxford University Press, 2005, 113, 122.

[259] G. Dodd, *The Food of London*, London, Longman, 1856, 174.

[260] *Report of the Select Committee on the Sale of Corn*, 1834, HC 517, vii, 1, 208.

their Argentinian agents spread false rumours to raise the price of grain.[261]

Attempts to base civil liability on market fraud or conspiracy came up hard against legal doctrine.[262] Fraud was not sufficient in itself, since it was necessary to show that a fraudulent representation, say, was either made to the plaintiff directly or, if given to the market generally, made with the intention that he should act upon it in a manner occasioning loss. Moreover, the courts had little sympathy for those acting upon their own judgment as to the state of the market, even if the market was affected by fraud. With similarly little effect was bankruptcy legislation. Rash and hazardous speculations could lead a court to postpone the discharge of a bankrupt, but there were few reported cases of this being done following commodity speculation.[263] In any event the power operated *ex post facto* and it is difficult to see how it would have had any sort of deterrent effect.

1 Cornering Markets

> Why, don't you see, Lou it's this way. This is what has happened. We have what's called a corner on the bears. They are caught short and we can squeeze them to our hearts' content ... These fellows who sold 26,000 of our shares – they haven't got them to sell and they can't get them. That is the point – they can't get them for love nor money – they must pay me my own price for them, or be ruined men. (Harold Frederic, *The Market-Place*, 1899)[264]

The idea of cornering a market entered popular consciousness as evidenced by this passage from Frederic's 1899 novel. Cornering was the purchase by a syndicate or ring of enough of a commodity (or securities, as in Frederic's example) so as to drive speculative sellers into a corner and compel them to buy at a high price so they could complete the sales they had made. In the 1830s there was Biddle's celebrated attempt to control the cotton market in the United States and Britain, with its adverse consequences for his reputation and that of the Bank of the United States of Pennsylvania.[265] Corners in the United States commodities markets in the nineteenth century were well known. The most

---

[261] J. Scobie, *Revolution on the Pampas: A Social History of Argentine Wheat 1860–1910*, Austin, University of Texas Press, 1964, 106.
[262] e.g., *Scott v. Brown Doering McNab & Co* [1892] 2 QB 724.
[263] Bankruptcy Act 1861, s.159; Bankruptcy Act 1883, s.28; subsequently, Bankruptcy Act 1890, s.8(3)(f). Earlier legislation was confined to stock and shares: Bankrupt Law Consolidation Act 1849, 12 & 13 Vic, c106, s.201. See *Ex p Heyn* (1867) 2 Ch App 650 (cotton to arrive on Liverpool market); *Re Stainton, ex p. Board of Trade* (1887) 4 Morr 242 (speculation in iron); *Re Tregaskis, ex p. Tregaskis* (1890) 7 Morr 193 (futures in corn).
[264] London, Heinemann, 1899.
[265] e.g., W. Smith, *Economic Aspects of the Second Bank of the United States*, Cambridge, MA, Harvard University Press, 1953, 195–202, 258–259.

notable was a grain corner in 1898 promoted by Joseph Leiter, brother in law to George Nathaniel Curzon, later Viceroy of India.[266]

(i) Cornering in the Commodity Markets and Proposals for Reform

The London and Liverpool commodity markets were not immune from attempts to corner the market. There were corners in tallow on the Baltic Exchange in the first part of the nineteenth century.[267] In the late 1880s there was an unsuccessful attempt by Pierre Secretain, manager of a leading firm in the French metal industry, to corner the world supply of copper and tin. The attempt involved dealings on the London Metal Exchange.[268] Corners in the Liverpool cotton market were a matter of considerable comment.[269]

Thus in 1879 Maurice Ranger sold large quantities of cotton over the summer for November delivery to Russia and North Europe.[270] He and his ring covered themselves by purchases of similar amounts of October delivery on the Liverpool arrivals market. The corner was effective because what Ranger had been sold for October delivery was more cotton than was likely to be in Liverpool that month, further purchases on his part to tighten the squeeze, and bad weather during October which unexpectedly delayed the arrival of (sailing) ships bringing their cargoes. Towards the end of the month dealers who had sold short rushed to buy the cotton they had contracted to deliver to Ranger and prices went up violently. The corner was successful and some spinners, unable to obtain supplies at acceptable prices, went out of business. Two years later Ranger and his ring were again successful, although the following year a gigantic bear operation he conducted failed.

One positive outcome of the Ranger corners was the adoption of the rules for periodic settlements on the Liverpool Cotton Exchange. An informal estimate was that losses from the Ranger corners would have been a tenth of what they were had periodic settlement been in operation.[271] An attempted

---

[266] A. Berg, 'The Rise of Commodity Speculation: From Villainous to Venerable', in A. Prakash (ed.), *Safeguarding Food Security in Volatile Global Markets*, UN FAO, Rome, 2011, 261, 263; J. Lurie, *Chicago Board of Trade 1859-1905*, Urbana, University of Illinois Press, 1979, 52-53, 67-68; J. Markham, *History of Commodity Futures Trading and its Regulation*, New York, Praeger, 1987, 5-6; W. Ferris, *The Grain Traders. The Story of the Chicago Board of Trade*, East Lansing, MI, Michigan State University Press, 1988, 33-34, 39-44.

[267] F. Dolman, '"Where Merchants most do Congregate" "The Baltic"', *Ludgate Monthly*, August 1895, 358, 359.

[268] D. Avery, *Not on Queen Victoria's Birthday. The Story of the Rio Tinto Mines*, London, Collins, 1974, 156; Economist Intelligence Unit, *A History of the London Metal Exchange*, London, Economist, 1958, 85-89.

[269] e.g., E. Guthrie, 'The Effects upon Trade of the Operation Called "Cornering" in Relation to Commodities', *Transactions of the Manchester Statistical Society*, Session 1881-82, 30 November 1881, 31-32. Notice that false rumours were said to accompany the cornering operation.

[270] W. Biggs, 'Cotton Corners', *Transactions of the Manchester Statistical Society*, Session 1894-95, 13 March 1895, 123, 127-134; T. Ellison, Gleanings and Reminiscences, *op cit*, 337-342.

[271] T. Ellison, Gleanings and Reminiscences, ibid, 355.

corner in Liverpool by a Galveston operator faltered in 1887, but the next two years one Steenstrand conducted successful cornering operations. That was attributed at the time to his recognising before others that the demand for cotton was exceeding supply with new mills being built and the adoption of ring spindles, which produced output faster. So he bought up cotton, drove prices up and profited greatly. But by the third year he tried it, 1890, spinners had built up their stocks, did not buy, and in the crash that ensued 'Steenstrand made his final exit'.[272] As a result of the corners some textile manufacturers abandoned futures contracts in favour of CIF contracts, which gave them certainty about the price they would pay.[273] Corners also led to worsening relations between Liverpool and Lancashire, where the cotton mills were, and agitation for a Manchester ship canal as a means of ending the industry's dependence on Liverpool.[274]

As a concept cornering the market was easily understood and a popular topic for commentators. Writing in 1881 William Halhed saw it as a siege operation to undermine and blow up an enemy's citadel before it was aware of what was happening.[275] Cornering was highly detrimental to the manufacturing, he argued, contributed to labour unrest, caused market trends for which no intelligible reason could be found by legitimate traders, and sucked the lifeblood of a market. Since the opportunity to corner markets such as for cotton and sugar was greatly enhanced by futures dealings – 'the fatal facility of trading in paper contracts' – legislation was justified to fence off the legitimate trade 'from influences which are morally objectionable, apart from the material damage and disorganisation they cause'.[276] In Halhed's view, the legislation for regulating speculation in bank shares should be emulated in the commodity markets.

That was a reference to Leeman's Act. Under it, all contracts for the sale or transfer of any shares or interest in a joint-stock bank had to set out in writing the distinguishing numbers of the shares on the company's register, or if the shares were unregistered the names of those in whom they then stood in the company's books.[277] Short-selling would be thwarted, it was thought, because a broker would not be able to insert the requisite numbers or name in the contract. The stock exchange simply thumbed its nose at Parliament and its practice was to disregard the statute in dealings between members. Nothing happened because the statute was not backed by criminal sanctions but only

---

[272] W. Biggs, 'Cotton Corners', *op cit*, 128.
[273] J. Robins, 'A Common Brotherhood for Their Mutual Benefit: Sir Charles Macara and Internationalism in the Cotton Industry 1904–1914' (2015) 16 *Enterprise & Society* 847, 870.
[274] D. Farnie, *The English Cotton Industry and the World Market 1815–1896*, Oxford, Clarendon Press, 1979, 175.
[275] W. Halhed, 'On Commercial "Corners"', *Nineteenth Century*, No.56, October 1881, 532, 532. Notice that false rumours were said to accompany the cornering.
[276] Ibid., 537.
[277] Banking Companies' (Shares) Act 1867 (30&31 Vict, c.29), commonly called Leeman's Act.

rendered non-complying contracts invalid.[278] The practice of the stock exchange was to the contrary and its members were bound to comply with its rules. If parties treated contracts as valid, whatever the law said, the courts decided that they could do nothing, although Bowen and Cotton LJJ were unhappy with the stock exchange practice.[279] The furthest the courts went was to hold that a non-member, ignorant of the practice, could not be bound by it.[280]

It was this suggestion of legislating to curb corners which was taken up by Edwin Guthrie, in a paper read to the Manchester Statistical Society.[281] Concerned in broad terms with these flaws in Leeman's Act, and that the earlier attempt to curb speculation on the stock exchange in Barnard's Act had also proved a dead letter,[282] Guthrie argued against stock market legislation as a model and proposed self-regulation instead. The voluntary law of the market he advocated was that the settlement of transactions in futures should always be in cash, although he conceded that with some markets even that might not eliminate cornering altogether.[283] What markets did, as we have seen, was to require margin payments. Around the beginning of the twentieth century they took other limited steps to curb cornering.

(ii) Self-regulation and the Common Law

In the early 1890s the LPCH adopted regulations for a corner clause in contracts for Santos coffee.[284] That was emulated in 1911 for the contracts it cleared in beet sugar. The clause was drafted by members of the clearing house. Given the issue's prominence, counsel's opinion was sought, rather unusually, regarding its effectiveness.[285] The Liverpool wheat market's attempt to prevent corners was through a rule prescribing generous treatment of short sellers who, as victims of a corner, defaulted: no penalty would be imposed for default, and settlement would be ordered around the spot price. For sellers on CIF terms invoicing back was permitted. In both cases the aim was to thwart buyers attempting

---

[278] It was a misdemeanour to insert in a contract a false entry of numbers or names: s.1.
[279] *Perry v. Barnett* (1885) 15 QBD 388, 396, 397; *Neilson v. James* (1882) 9 QBD 546, 550, 554.
[280] *Perry v. Barnett*; *Coates, Son & Co v. Pacey* (1892) 8 TLR 351. The *Law Journal* was critical of even this limitation: 'The Force of Customs of a Market' (1885) 20 *LJ* 332, 334 (commenting on the approach of Grove J, approved in the Court of Appeal).
[281] E. Guthrie, 'The Effects upon Trade of the Operation called Cornering, in relation to Commodities', op cit, 29.
[282] 7 Geo II, c.8, repealed 23 & 24 Vict. c. 28. See P. Johnson, *Making the Market*, Cambridge, Cambridge University Pres, 2010, 213; S. Banner, *Anglo-American Securities Regulation. Cultural and Political Roots 1690–1860*, Cambridge, Cambridge University Press, 1998, 101–110.
[283] cf. R. Friedman, 'Stalking the Squeeze: Understanding Commodities Market Manipulation' (1990) 89 *Mich LR* 30, 32n.
[284] LMA, CLC/B/153/MS03641/002, LPCH, Board Minutes, 12 April 1893, 115.
[285] LMA, CLC/B/153/MS03641/004, LPCH, Board Minutes, 27 November 1911, 345; 29 November 1911, 346; 22 January 1912, 353.

a corner. The London Metal Exchange went further. It adopted a rule, rule H, which provided that if in its opinion a corner was being attempted, it could investigate and 'take whatever action it considers proper to restore equilibrium between supply and demand'.[286] The tougher approach is probably explained by two factors, first, the membership of the London Metal Exchange was relatively small and secondly, most members were also heavily involved in the physicals market so they would suffer adversely if they were on the wrong end of cornering.[287]

The common law had little to say about cornering. 'Corners are legitimate in the absence of fraudulent representations', explained the short entry on the subject in the first edition of *Halsbury's Laws of England* in 1913, adding the rationale, 'for the court will not assist persons to escape the results of having made unwise bargains'.[288] And certainly when English courts were presented with claims for losses arising from cornering on the stock exchange, they were reluctant to assist. Not only had there to be a fraudulent representation or a conspiracy but that also had to be intended to cause, and in fact must have caused, the loss the plaintiff occasioned arising from the premium he had to pay to the cornering ring to fulfil his bargains. When the issue came before Sir William Page Wood, later Lord Hatherley LC, he drew a distinction between moral and legal responsibility.[289] In administering justice, he said, 'the remote consequences, for which morally a man is responsible, cannot be taken as the measure of his responsibility'.[290] That distinction was again evident thirty years later when a ring (the defendants) had cornered the shares of a company manufacturing patent medicines. To the Master of the Rolls, Lord Esher, it might be very shameful, very wrong, what the defendants had done, but it was not a legal wrong to the plaintiff who did not know what was going on, even though he incurred losses as a result of the corner.[291] To the court the notion of upholding bargains was paramount.[292]

2 Prosecuting the 'Great Pepper Corner' in the 1930s

> The pepper trial is over and the reputation of the City is down another notch … There were things done and admitted which are not legal

---

[286] R. Gibson-Jarvie, The London Metal Exchange, op cit, 35–38, 52–53.
[287] S. Pirrong, 'The Self-Regulation of Commodity Exchanges: The Case of Market Manipulation' (1995) 38 *J Law & Econ* 141, 191–192.
[288] Earl of Halsbury, *The Laws of England*, London, Butterworth & Co, 1913, vol. 27, 264 ('Stock Exchange'). cf. the United States where contracts having a corner as their object were not enforced (*Sampson* v. *Shaw*, 101 Mass 145 (1869)) or anti-trust legislation was invoked (*US* v. *Patten*, 226 US 525 (1911), and with the Grain Futures Act of 1922, re-enacted in 1936 as the Commodity Exchange Act., regulatory action was possible: L. Stout, 'Derivatives and the Legal Origin of the 2008 Credit Crisis' (2011) 1 *Harv Bus L R* 1, 11, 17–18.
[289] *Barry* v. *Croskey* (1861) 2 J & H 1, 70 ER 945.   [290] at 22, 954, respectively.
[291] *Salaman* v. *Warner* (1891) 65 LT (NS) 132, at 133–134. See also Fry LJ at 135. See [1891] 1 QB 734 on an associated procedural issue in the case.
[292] at 133, 135.

offences, but which the public regard as wrong. And possibly the very fact that they are not wrong is more injurious to the City's name than even the conviction on legal charges of three of its 'prominent men'. (*Daily Herald*, 22 February 1936)

From the fifteenth century pepper had been a key spice in the expansion of European powers across the world.[293] By the early twentieth century its comparative importance in international trade had declined but its notoriety continued. Mincing Lane in London was an important international trading centre for pepper, and in the interwar period there were upwards of thirty brokers. Transactions in the London market were with dealers in places like Rotterdam, Hamburg, Singapore and the United States.[294] The General Produce Brokers' Association of London issued standard conditions for the sale of pepper, which were used for trading elsewhere such as the United States.[295]

One of the leading characters in the great pepper corner of the 1930s was John Howeson, eminent in the City as chairman of the London Tin Corporation along with other positions. His co-conspirator was Armenian-born Garabed Bishirgian, who could be characterised as a bad apple outsider. In fact he had been naturalised before the First World War and had conducted business in the City of London for many years. Both had attempted to manipulate the market in tin, but extended their ambitions to shellac, used in making gramophone records, and pepper.[296] Initially in furtherance of the corner pepper was acquired from early 1933 by Bishirgian on behalf of William Henry & Co., which he and Howeson controlled. To further the scheme they acquired the commodity brokers James and Shakespeare Ltd, which they took public in August 1934. It acquired Williams Henry & Co. and Bishirgian & Co. Ostensibly the public issue was to raise funds for a general expansion. In fact it was to continue the cornering operation.[297] The corner failed because the ring had underestimated the stocks of pepper they needed to buy, and because of a large, natural influx of pepper to London.

The crisis came to a head in January 1935. James and Shakespeare Ltd was in financial difficulty – the General Produce Brokers' Association declared it to be in default on 8 February – and several other commodity brokers

---

[293] e.g., M. Shaffer, *Pepper: A History of the World's Most Influential Spice*, New York, St. Martin's Press, 2013; F. Braudel, *The Perspective of the World*, London, Collins, 1979, 148–149, 218–219.

[294] P. Breslin & A. Jones, *The Structure of the Pepper Market in the United Kingdom, the Federal Republic of Germany, the Netherlands and France*, London, Foreign and Commonwealth Office, Tropical Products Institute, 1973, 10–11.

[295] US Department of Commerce, Bureau of Foreign and Domestic Commerce, *Market Methods and Trade Usages in London*, Special Consular Reports No.86, Washington, 1923, 66.

[296] H. Cox, 'Business on Trial: The Tobacco Securities Trust and the 1935 Pepper Debacle' (2007) 49 *Business Hist* 823, 830.

[297] 'James and Shakespeare Ltd. Liquidation Meetings', *The Times*, 5 April 1935, 4; 'Liquidation of James and Shakespeare Ltd. Senior Official Receiver's Report', *The Times*, 10 July, 1935, 4.

hovered precariously. Some of the banks were also exposed, in particular the Midland Bank (now part of HSBC), which had advanced something like £1 million to James and Shakespeare. The General Produce Brokers Association, and then an ad hoc committee of commodity brokers, appealed to the clearing banks to accommodate the firms threatened, to avert widespread failures in the market. Under pressure from the Bank of England, the banks agreed.[298] Trading in pepper was suspended for a week to break the jam. A pepper pool, the London Pepper Sales Control Committee, was formed to dispose of the pepper over the following years. A few commodity brokers still went under.[299]

When a criminal prosecution ensued, it was not for any offence of trying to corner the market, for in English law there was none. Nor was it for conspiracy. Rather, the indictment charged Bishirgian under section 84 of the Larceny Act 1861 with knowingly making a false statement in the prospectus which he had caused James and Shakespeare to issue. Howeson was charged with aiding and abetting Bishirgian. Perhaps it is not surprising that the prosecution should look to section 84, rather than conspiracy, since the section had grounded the successful prosecution of Lord Kylsant in the Royal Mail case a few years earlier.[300] In Kylsant's case the prospectus was false because it had omitted to state that over the years the only way Kylsant's company, Royal Mail Steam Packet Company, had been able to pay the past dividends set out there was by the introduction of certain non-recurring items and adjustments to reserves.

With Bishirgian, the allegation was that the prospectus was false in intimating that the additional capital would be used 'in extending ... the company's activities'. In fact William Henry & Co. had forward positions of nearly £1 million in pepper (and nearly £400,000 in shellac) so that if it failed to meet those commitments, or the additional commitments necessary to keep up prices in the market, its shares would be valueless. All this was omitted from the prospectus; indeed, there was no specific mention in the prospectus of

---

[298] D. Kynaston, *Till Time's Last Stand A History of the Bank of England 1694-2013*, London, Bloomsbury, 2017, 361–362; R. Sayers, *The Bank of England 1891-1944*, Cambridge, Cambridge University Press, 1976, 544–545. Kynaston, who tells the story from the view-point of the banks, concludes that for Midland 'the years of assured dominance were drawing to an end, and the pepper fiasco cruelly symbolised the changing order': D. Kynaston, *The City of London*, London, Chatto & Windus, 2000, vol. III, 425–429.

[299] 'City Pepper Crisis', *The Times*, 9 February, 1935, 12; J. F. Adair and Co. Ltd. 'Senior Official Receiver's Report', *The Times*, 16 July 1935, 5.

[300] *R v. Kylsant* [1932] 1 KB 442. See A. Vice, *Financier at Sea: Lord Kylsant and the Royal Mail*, Braunton, Devon, Merlin Books,1985; P. Davies & A. Bourn, 'Lord Kylsant and the Royal Mail' (1972) *Business Hist* 103; C. Brooks, *The Royal Mail Case*, Edinburgh, William Hodge & Co, 1933; P. Hastings, *Cases in Court*, London, Heinemann, 1949, 213; P. Devlin, *Taken at the Flood*, East Harling, Norfolk, Taverner Publications, 1996, 135–137. (Hastings and Devlin were counsel in the case.) Bevan was convicted of fraud in another corporate scandal of the interwar years: see *Re City Equitable Fire Insurance Co Ltd* [1925] Ch 407, 425; P. Manley, 'Gerard Lee Bevan and the City Equitable Companies' (1973) 9 *Abacus* 107, 107–108.

either shellac or pepper. In the Crown's case this was deliberately so, to create a false impression of its business to investors.

The trial at the Old Bailey was a cause celebre with the Attorney-General prosecuting and some of the leading counsel of the day defending.[301] The jury convicted and Bishirgian and Howeson were each sentenced to 12 months' imprisonment. An appeal was unsuccessful.[302] Never one to mince his words, the Lord Chief Justice, Lord Hewart, said that morally and legally the transaction did not differ, other than in dimensions, from 'the office boy who takes a half-crown from the till because he has a good thing for the Grand National'.[303] The purpose for which the money was wanted, and to which it was applied, 'was the bolstering up of a very ambitious scheme – which failed – to control the pepper supply of the world'. Lord Hewart added that to advertise as an ordinary business seeking development when the money was really being asked to feed and supply an ambitious gamble was simple deceit.[304]

One upshot of the great pepper scandal was that a futures market was inaugurated for pepper in 1937, with clearing and settlement through the London Produce Clearing House.[305] The intention was to regularise dealings within an organised market controlled not by law, as the *Daily Herald* would have wanted, but by City self-regulation. Within only a few years the arrangements were discontinued because of the outbreak of the Second World War. There was no attempt to follow the United States' example, where from 1936 cornering or attempting to corner a commodity in interstate commerce was made a criminal violation under federal law.[306] The reputation of the City for orderly commodity markets suffered. In particular, a substantial share of the world's pepper trading moved to the United States when, in 1937, the New York Produce Exchange inaugurated trading in pepper futures.[307]

3 Gaming, Wagering and Futures Contracts

He had gambled deliberately; he wanted money, money, and saw no other way of obtaining it. In the expansive mood of convalescence, Cecil Morphew left no detail of his story unrevealed ... 'I'm convinced', said the young man presently, 'that any one who really gives his mind to it can speculate with

---

[301] See reports in *The Times* 14, 15, 18, February 1936. Counsel included Sir Patrick Hastings KC, Sir William Jowitt KC (a former Attorney-General and future Lord Chancellor) and W.T. Monckton KC (later a Defence Minister and viscount).

[302] *R v. Bishirgian* [1936] 1 All ER 586.

[303] at 594. See R. Jackson, *The Chief. The Biography of Gordon Hewart Lord Chief Justice 1922–1940*, London, George G. Harrap & Co., 1960, 298–300.

[304] at 593–594.

[305] R. Sayers, The Bank of England 1891–1944, op cit, 546; O. Hobson, *How the City Works*, London, 'News Chronicle' Publications, 1938, 124.

[306] Commodity Exchange Act, s.116, 49 Stat at 1501. See *Great Western Food Distributors v. Benson*, 201 F 2d 476 (7th Cir, 1953), cert denied 345 US 997 (1953).

[307] H. Cox, 'Business on Trial: The Tobacco Securities Trust and the 1935 Pepper Debacle', *op cit*, 837.

moderate success. Look at the big men – the brokers and the company promoters, and so on'. (George Gissing, *The Whirlpool*, 1897)[308]

As the passage from George Gissing's *The Whirlpool* illustrates, there was in the public consciousness a close association between gambling and wagering on the one hand, and the speculation which took place in the financial and commodity markets on the other. Wagering was contrary to public policy and unenforceable at common law. Transactions might also fall foul of the Gaming Act. In the commodity markets it was a background threat, a legal hammer to be invoked by a disgruntled individual to avoid a transaction. As late as the Financial Services Act 1986 it was necessary to insert a provision that contracts falling within the legislation would not be void or unenforceable by reason of the provisions of the Gaming Act 1845.[309]

(i) Wagering, the Law and Futures Transactions

Wagering ranged widely and popped up in the most unexpected circumstances. *Carlill v. Carbolic Smoke Ball Company*[310] is one of the best-known cases in contract law. A promise in an advertisement to pay £100 to any person who contracted influenza, despite using the carbolic smoke ball as directed, was held to be an offer, giving rise to a contract when the customer bought one. The quirky facts, and the breakthrough in doctrine that there could be offers to the world, combined to establish the case's reputation. When the case was at first instance one of the arguments advanced by the company's counsel, H. H. Asquith QC – later Prime Minister – was that the contract was void as being by way of wagering under the Gaming Act 1845.[311] Hawkins J, who tried the case with his fox terrier, Jack, on the bench beside him,[312] rejected the argument and it went no further.[313]

For the commodities markets *Bryan v. Lewis*[314] was an inauspicious beginning, just as these markets were emerging. In February 1823 the plaintiff had the defendant broker sell some nutmeg which at the time he did not own. The broker sold the nutmeg for delivery in May, clearly a forward contract. Subsequently in March the plaintiff bought nutmeg. In May warrants for the nutmeg were tendered to the purchaser, who was unable to pay for them, apparently because he was a minor. Counsel for the plaintiff argued that not to enforce the plaintiff–broker contract would upset dealings at the Royal Exchange, at the time where commodities were traded. Nonetheless Abbott CJ (later Lord Tenterden) ruled at *nisi pruis* that it was a wager, and therefore unenforceable at common law.

---

[308] London, Lawrence & Bullen, 1897.   [309] s. 63.   [310] [1893] 1 QB 256.
[311] [1892] 2 QB 484, 486. On Asquith's career at the bar, R. Jenkins, *Asquith*, London, Collins, 1969, 26–37, 91–92.
[312] B. Simpson, 'Quackery and Contract Law: The Case of the Carbolic Smoke Ball' (1985) 14 *J Leg Stud* 345, 362. Unfortunately, Simpson does not discuss the wagering aspect.
[313] [1892] 2 QB 484, 491–492   [314] (1826) Ry & Mood 386, 171 ER 1058.

Bryan v. *Lewis* came at a bad time. The 1820s had experienced a period of intense speculation both in commodities, in particular tallow, and foreign government securities. In 1824 and early 1825 there was a mania in business promotions, many a swindle, extending to mining and other ventures in South America. The bubble eventually burst, leading to a severe depression from the second part of 1825, and involving the collapse of many banks and stagnation in manufacturing.[315] In the boom running up to the crash the City banker Alexander Baring compared the dealings on the Royal Exchange with gambling in the clubs of St James.[316] All this cannot but have influenced judicial attitudes. Indeed, in *Bryan* v. *Lewis* Lord Tenterden specifically mentioned the distress in the community of the last twelve months, which he asserted 'would have been avoided' if his view of the law, rendering wagering contracts unenforceable, had been acted upon.[317]

Within a decade, in a more benign economic climate and with laissez-faire views having greater circulation, the Tenterden view was discredited.[318] It was finally 'quite exploded',[319] as Judah Philip Benjamin put it in his treatise on sales law, referring to *Hibblewhite* v. *M'Morine*.[320] There the Court of Exchequer was clear that the common law did not make forward transactions illegal. To Baron Parke, Lord Tenterden's views were contrary to law and influenced by the 1825 depression. Alderson B was blunt: the Tenterden view would 'put an end to half the contacts made in the course of trade'. As for Maule B, he had often heard the Tenderden approach spoken of with great suspicion by lawyers as against principle and by mercantile men as against commercial convenience.[321]

So at common law forward transactions were in the clear. But futures trading was not yet out of the legal woods. Unless carefully structured there remained a threat well into the twentieth century that it would constitute wagering.[322] Two factors came into play. The first was the enactment of the Gaming Act in 1845.[323] The Act was not directed at commercial activity but at evils like common gaming houses.[324] However, it contained a general prohibition, section 18, which swept

---

[315] 380, 444–445 below.
[316] See D. Kynaston, *The City of London*, London, Chatto & Windus, 1994, vol. I, 49–55, 63–75.
[317] (1826) Ry & Mood 386, 387, 171 ER 1058, 1059. See also his earlier disapproval in *Lorymer* v. *Smith* (1822)1 B & C 1, 3, 107 ER 1, 2.
[318] See *Wells* v. *Porter* (1836) 2 Bing (NC) 722, 132 ER 278, a case involving Spanish and Portuguese banks.
[319] J. Benjamin, *Sale of Personal Property*, London, Henry Sweet, 1868, 60.
[320] (1839) 5 M & W 462, 151 ER 195. The plaintiff ultimately failed on other grounds: (1840) 6 M & W 199, 151 ER 380. Although a case about shares, the headnote and judgments are couched in terms of the sale of goods.
[321] Ibid.
[322] D. Chaikin & B. Mohen, 'Commodity Futures Contracts and the Gaming Act' [1986] *Lloyd's M&CLQ* 390.
[323] 8 & 9 Vict, c109. See H. Stutfield, *The Law Relating to Betting, Time Bargains and Gaming*, London, Waterlow, 1892, 100.
[324] *Report from the Select Committee on Gaming*, 1844, HC No.297, v–vi.

up a number of existing, specific provisions. It was widely drawn so that all contracts or agreements by way of gaming or wagering were null and void, and no legal action could be brought to recover any money or thing allegedly won or staked in relation to any wager. The second factor was that by the mid-nineteenth century speculators were regularly entering contracts on the stock exchange for the payment of differences, according to the rise and fall in the price of shares, without intending that shares would change hands. There was a body of public opinion which regarded this with distaste.[325]

When the issue came before the Court of Common Pleas in 1852, in *Grizewood* v. *Blane*, Serjeant Best cited *Hibblewhite* v. *M'Morine* and argued that the transaction was not within section 18, any more than if it related to wheat or any other article of commerce or manufacture.[326] However, the judges upheld the direction to the jury that it was a wager and void if the parties did not really intend at the time of the transaction to purchase or sell the shares in question. In the light of this it is perhaps not surprising that the jury found that there was gaming, given that as in a number of previous transactions the defendant, Colonel Blane, had contracted through his broker to sell and repurchase shares with the plaintiff stock jobber, with no intention that shares would pass but only price differences paid.

The legal solution to *Grizewood* v. *Blane* seemed to be to cast contracts in such a way that, ostensibly at least, there was always an intention to deliver what was sold, whatever might happen subsequently with an off-setting transaction. This was upheld in 1878 in the leading case of *Thacker* v. *Hardy*.[327] There the plaintiff, a broker on the London Stock Exchange, sued his client (the defendant) for commission and an indemnity in respect of speculative transactions entered on his behalf. So one distinguishing feature from *Grizewood* v. *Blane* was that the contract being sued on was not in itself a speculative transaction; the sales, purchases and the offsetting transactions were between the defendant and jobbers on the exchange. Although these may have been caught by the Gaming Act, it only rendered transactions void, not illegal. (If it had made them illegal then the plaintiff–broker arrangements were arguably also tainted.) This point was adopted by Lindley J at trial.[328] In other words the plaintiff, with authorisation from his client to deal according to the practices of the stock exchange, would not have intended to consummate unlawful transactions.

In the Court of Appeal this became the mainstay of the decision. These transactions the plaintiff effected for the defendant were intended as real transactions, although subsequently another bargain might be entered to relieve his client from liability by buying or selling again. *Grizewood* v. *Blane*

---

[325] see R. Michie, *The London Stock Exchange: A History*, Oxford, Oxford University Press, 2001, 65, 68, 126–127.
[326] *Grizewood* v. *Blane* (1852) 11 CB 526, 539, 138 ER 578, 583. See also *Barry* v. *Croskey* (1861) 2 J & H 1; 70 ER 945.
[327] (1878) 4 QBD 685. See also *Cooper* v. *Neal* (1878) 48 LJ QB 292n (CA).   [328] at 689.

was distinguished, indeed effectively overruled. Bargains where the parties might gain or lose according to the happening of a future event were not in themselves objectionable.[329] Although Brett and Cotton LJJ expressed disapproval of some practices on the stock exchange Bramwell LJ was, as ever, the political economist: market speculation was no disadvantage, since 'it is owing to a market of that kind that we now have so many railways and other useful undertakings'.[330]

Thacker v. *Hardy*[331] was not the end of the line. A considerable number of cases involving company stocks and shares followed where those wishing to avoid liability raised the Gaming Act. Some were successful. In these cases the courts went beyond the face of the documents or the rules of the Stock Exchange to find the 'real' intention of the parties, that only differences would be paid. That was wagering.[332] This conflict between the formal and subjective intent in the stock market cases was never satisfactorily resolved.

(ii) Gaming and the Commodity Markets

On the commodities markets the issue of the Gaming Act remained quiescent. There is no reported case before the First World War where it was raised. At first glance this is a puzzle because even if brokers themselves might not have invoked it to challenge transactions, as with the Stock Exchange there were customers who might wish to use it to avoid a transaction because the market had turned against them. Perhaps one explanation lies in the clarity of the contracts and rules drawn up by the commodity trade associations, under which both parties had the intention to deliver. These being framed in the language of buying and selling a commodity, and an intention to deliver, proof of a contrary intention was difficult, even though in futures transactions delivery rarely occurred.

Another explanation is that by the end of the century hedging in commodities – which did not contemplate physical delivery – was accepted as performing a useful economic function along the lines of insurance.[333] Finally, there was the character of the commodity markets and those dealing on them. The stock market was a well-known avenue for investment, and government securities and shares were held by a number of the wealthy and professional middle classes. The commodity markets were not of their nature places readily thought of as for investment. In the nineteenth century it seems that only exceptionally were outsiders drawn in to speculate, as with cotton on the Liverpool market in the 1860s.[334] Only later, in the interwar period, do the likes of John Maynard Keynes speculate in commodity futures as investment. Contrast this with the United States where, by the early twentieth

---

[329] at 692, 696, per Bramwell, Cotton LJJ.   [330] Ibid., 692–693.   [331] (1878) 4 QBD 685.
[332] e.g., *Universal Stock Exchange Ltd* v. *Strachan* [1896] AC 166; *Re Grieve* [1899] 1 QB 794.
[333] H. Emery, 'Futures in the Grain Market' (1899) 9 *Econ J* 45, 47–48.   [334] 85, 108 above.

century, speculation on the commodity markets for profit was comparatively widespread.[335]

When in the 1920s the English Court of Appeal finally examined the validity of futures dealings on commodities markets, it was not as a result of a direct attack on the practice but in the context of a tax appeal.[336] The taxpayer was employed by a cotton broker in Liverpool. The issue was how profits he made from private futures dealings on the Liverpool, New York and New Orleans cotton exchanges ought to be assessed for tax purposes.[337] The special commissioners for income tax had found as a fact that his dealings were gaming transactions and he had no intention of taking actual delivery of cotton or hedging against risk. Notwithstanding this, Sir Ernest Pollock MR adopted a robust approach: these were real transactions, with real parties, which the dealer or broker could have implemented at any moment, and were gaming only in a loose or colloquial sense.[338] Warrington and Atkin LJJ were more circumspect given the commissioners' findings of fact, but still regarded them as real transactions: whatever the intention of the taxpayer, there was no evidence that his counterparties did not intend to take delivery of the cotton.[339]

A month later, McCardie J adopted an equally robust approach in a case involving a direct attack on futures dealings on the London Metal Exchange.[340] With respect to the gaming issue, McCardie J said that these were framed as commercial contracts containing express obligations to deliver and to take delivery, even if the parties had no intention of doing so when they entered them. There was no reference to *Cooper* v. *Stubbs*. In formulating a test McCardie J erected a very high hurdle for challengers: if the parties intended to enter into a legal contract, which gave legal rights and imposed legal obligations, it was enforceable, despite being of a speculative character. There was no echo of this unorthodox approach when in 1936 Hilbery J upheld speculative transactions on the Liverpool Cotton Exchange in the face of a Gaming Act challenge.[341]

The upshot of all this was that by the Second World War futures dealings on the commodities markets could be made legally safe. The shadow cast by the Gaming Act 1845 could be avoided in the drafting of market rules and the standard form contracts between members and those dealing through them on the markets. There was some uncertainty as to the test the courts would apply

---

[335] e.g., T. Taylor, 'Trading in Commodity Futures – A New Standard of Legality' (1933) 43 *Yale LJ* 63, 63–65. On US law see T. Dewey, *A Treatise on Contracts for Future Delivery and Commercial Wagers*, New York, Baker, Voorhis & Co., 1886. In *Board of Trade* v. *Christie Grain and Stock Co* 198 US 236, 249 (1905) the Supreme Court upheld futures transactions. See E. Patterson, 'Hedging and Wagering on Produce Exchanges' (1931) 40 *Yale LJ* 843, 845–846.
[336] *Cooper (Inspector of Taxes)* v. *Stubbs* [1925] 2 KB 753.
[337] Arbitraging between the three exchanges was no doubt an aspect of his dealings.
[338] at 763. [339] at 768, 770–771.
[340] *Barnett* v. *Sanker* (1925) 41 TLR 660. On McCardie 57 above.
[341] *Woodward* v. *Wolfe* [1936] 3 All ER 529, 533–534.

to identify gaming transactions. The objective test of intention of Pollock MR in *Cooper* v. *Stubbs* gained important support from Scrutton LJ in *Ironmonger and Co* v. *Dyne*,[342] a case involving dealings in foreign exchange. As Scrutton LJ put it, referring to a sale of goods, even a contract in which differences in prices were to be paid would not be a gaming contract unless it could be shown that there was an agreement between the parties that the purchaser had no right to claim delivery of the goods, and the seller had no right to demand their acceptance.[343]

So the English courts offered a safe haven for futures speculation. First, even if they were gaming, they were void, not illegal. Consequently, the contracts a member of a market acting as broker had with a customer escaped the taint of illegality, despite the broker knowing the customer was simply speculating, with no intention of delivering or taking delivery of the commodity. Secondly, the onus was on those challenging a transaction to prove that neither party had the requisite intention to deliver or to take delivery of the commodity. It would take exceptional circumstances to prove that in relation to dealings between brokers, for brokers would be acting according to exchange rules. Even if a customer (or broker) might not intend to deliver, a broker, acting in accordance with market rules, had the intention to effect delivery under the contract because the standard form futures contracts provided for it.

2.7 Conclusion

> On many commodity markets, where business or speculative dealings take place between persons on the market, it would no doubt be true that each buyer relies on his own judgment and it would be wrong to seek to impose on sellers any implied condition based on reliance. To do so would impede the play and working of the market and would be in opposition to commercial reality. (Lord Wilberforce, 1969)[344]

In his 1922 book on *Organised Produce Markets*, J. G. Smith of the Faculty of Commerce at the University of Birmingham set out five prerequisites for organised commodity markets: first, the commodity must be sufficiently durable to be carried for a reasonable length of time if the market was unduly depressed; second, it must be easily weighed or measured, with accuracy obvious to all, and its quality or grade capable of ready testing; third, it must be fungible, so that any part was as good as another and served the purpose of the purchaser equally well; fourth, dealings in it must be sufficiently frequent to attract a large number of buyers and sellers; and fifth, there must be fluctuations in price, so that dealers could make profits from trading. Commodities like grain and cotton satisfied these conditions: they were fungible, could be

---

[342] (1928) 44 TLR 497.
[343] Ibid., at 499. Scrutton LJ offered some robust criticism of currency speculation: 498.
[344] *Henry Kendall & Sons* v. *William Lillico & Sons Ltd* [1969] 2 AC 31, 124–125.

handled in bulk, stored without risk of deterioration for lengthy periods, weighed and graded into standard qualities.[345]

Writers like Smith and those operating the commodity markets of London and Liverpool rarely mentioned law. Perhaps this was because, unlike the commodity markets in Germany and the United Sates, these markets did not have the trappings of statute and state regulation. In England the old market offences of forestalling, regrating and engrossing were a dead letter in the early part of our period and traces repealed mid-century. There was no offence of market manipulation until 1986, and only after that were commodity markets the subject of more detailed regulation.[346] Not only was state law not seen as a precondition to the satisfactory operation of these markets, but it was conceived as a hindrance as with the Gaming Act 1845. Indeed, the lesson of the German regulation of futures markets in the 1890s was probably not lost on policy makers: business had been driven elsewhere, including to Britain. Regulation of the British markets, were it ever contemplated, might have the same result.

If state law was absent, law in a different form was an unspoken presence in the London and Liverpool markets. It entered in relation to the way that the markets were constituted and governed; the controls over those using them; the system of rules for transactions on them and how these were cleared and settled; the standard form contracts used for dealings and the standard units of delivery and grades; and the arbitration procedures for dispute settlement. It was not state law; instead, it was the private law-making of the markets themselves. Traders, brokers and merchants devised rules, contracts and institutions for commodity transactions within the capacious framework the law offered. This was done without much contact with the law's practitioners or institutions. Commercial practices evolved along certain lines and became norms in rules and standard form contracts. Clever traders like Caesar Czarnikow anticipated future risks and so additional provisions addressed them.[347] If developments such as futures contracts or a clearing house were thought desirable, these were formulated in rules and contracts, with borrowings from elsewhere.[348]

Until the twentieth century, lawyers were not regularly engaged in the work of formulating the rules and contracts of the London and Liverpool commodity markets or in advising on how disputes were to be settled or arbitrated. For much of our period lawyers' involvement was more with drafting the requisite documents to carry on business (articles of partnership, business leases, company formation) than with how business itself was

---

[345] J. Smith, Organised Produce Markets, *op cit*, 4–5. See also C. Kulp, 'Possibilities of Organized Markets in Various Commodities' (May 1931) 155 *Annals Amer Acad Pol & Soc Sci*, 176–178 on the need for markets to be also free from domination by interests.

[346] See M. Blair, G. Walker & S. Willey (eds.), *Financial Markets and Exchanges Law*, 2nd ed., Oxford, Oxford University Press, 2012.

[347] 103 above.   [348] As with the German influence in clearing and settlement: 90 above.

carried on.[349] When asked for advice, as with Gore-Browne's opinion over the establishment of a LCTA clearing house, lawyers might not prove especially helpful in facilitating what was thought to be a commercially desirable development.[350] With more complex matters, as with the operation of novation in a clearing house, lawyers would be called upon, as they were when litigation raised its head. Generally speaking, however, lawyers were incidental rather than central to the private law of the markets.

When the private law of the markets rubbed up against formal law in the occasional dispute which made its way to court,[351] the commodity markets generally found a sympathetic audience, on the whole ready to give a judicial stamp of approval to commercial practice. That was either through the recognition of the trade usage on a market or through the working out of the well-accepted philosophy (evidenced in the extract from a judgment of Lord Wilberforce at the beginning of this conclusion) that the courts should not allow the ordinary law to stand in the way of freely contracted bargains on these markets. Equally the courts adopted a hands-off approach to matters such as the internal affairs of market organisations and the decisions of the arbitrators appointed to settle disputes between their members. In some cases, such as futures transactions, the courts appeared on the scene so late in the day that their influence was bound to be marginal. When statutory law stood in the way of the operation of market practices, the courts were accommodating, as with the passage they steered for futures dealings, or the course market contracts had charted around the rocks of the Gaming Act 1845.[352]

The view from the ground was that conflicts of interest in the commodity markets were rife.[353] There were high-level fiduciary duties for brokers when acting as agents, but that seemed to have little purchase in practice. Market abuse could lead to losses, indeed the bankruptcy of those dealing there, as with the practice of cornering. Nonetheless, the common law did not emulate popular morality and remained aloof.[354] The courts drew the clear distinction between law and morality.[355] Lord Bramwell's view had much support, even if only at the unconscious level: market speculation may be thought distasteful, but it was through this 'that we now have so many railways and other useful undertakings'.[356] If steps were to be taken against practices like cornering, that was mainly through self-regulation by the markets and the trade associations themselves. Only the most egregious frauds attracted the attention of the criminal law. Then, as with the great pepper corner of the 1930s, since there

---

[349] see 90 above. [350] 92 above.

[351] On the whole English courts were insulated from the waves of litigation washing into United States courts. So the chances of untoward decisions were fewer. Partly that is because of the healthy systems of arbitration, partly by the limited category of speculators on the London and Liverpool commodity markets who were potential litigants if deals went wrong for them.

[352] 86, 118, 120–123 above.

[353] T. Croker, *Advice to Merchants*, London, the author, 1863, 25. The author claimed to be a clerk in a colonial broker's office in Mincing Lane.

[354] 114 above. [355] 114 above. [356] *Thacker v. Hardy* (1878) 4 QBD 685, 692–693.

was no specific law against market abuse, resort had to be made to other offences, the law of theft or the prospectus offences under the Companies Acts.

Perhaps most importantly, when doctrinal stumbling blocks proved insuperable, drafting around the problem in the standard form contracts and rules of a market to perpetuate a market practice was almost always possible. The response to *Cooke & Sons* v. *Eshelby*[357] is an example of how obstacles could be surmounted in this way. *Robinson* v. *Mollett*[358] provides another. All this – the freedom to engage in private law-making, the imprimatur which the courts generally gave to market practice, the ability to surmount legislative and doctrinal obstacles – enabled the markets to mould contracts and rules to their liking, making commercial law with little hindrance in areas such as futures trading and financial architecture, clearing and settlement systems being a good example. As a result, the law facilitated commercial dealing and profit-making on the London and Liverpool commodity markets in the ways commercial parties desired.

[357] (1887) 12 App Cas 271; 75–76 above. [358] (1875) LR 7, HL 802; 78–79 above.

3
Agents, 'Agents' and Agency

3.1 Introduction

> He was met at the station by Kopeikin, the company's representative in Turkey. Kopeikin had arrived in Istanbul with sixty-five thousand other Russian refugees in 1924, and had been, by turn, card sharper, part owner of a brothel, and army clothing contractor before he had secured – the managing director alone knew how – the lucrative agency he now held. (Eric Ambler, *Journey into Fear*, 1940)

Agents play a variety of roles in the early twentieth-century thriller. In Eric Ambler's *Journey into Fear*,[1] most of the action takes place around the Italian steamship *Sestri Levante* on its journey to Genoa after the naïve engineer Graham leaves Turkey and Kopeikin, his company's agent there. Kopeikin seems more knowing than might be expected, and that sets the scene as German secret agents attempt to thwart the Turkish–British alliance in which Graham's company is playing a part. Then, in Graham Greene's *Our Man in Havana*,[2] James Wormold is an agent in two senses, not only a secret agent but also the agent in Cuba selling his firm's Atomic Pile vacuum cleaners. A further example is Dorothy L. Sayers' novel *Murder Must Advertise*,[3] where Lord Peter Wimsey goes undercover in the advertising agency Pym's Publicity Ltd to investigate the murder of one of its copywriters. He discovers that the weekly advertisements Pym's publishes for a client are used to signal to the 'agents' (Sayers' term) of a drugs gang how to collect the next delivery.

As in literature, so in commercial life, agents had a chameleon character. In 1829 the *Law Magazine* noted that it was desirable, if not indispensable, to have agents resident abroad to receive consignments of goods exported and to purchase and ship foreign commodities as may be wanted in return.[4] As we saw in Chapter 1, the practice of international trade changed as the century progressed, and by the middle of the nineteenth century sending goods to merchants abroad for sale on consignment was no longer common. With the improvements from mid-century in transport (railways and steam ships) and

---

[1] London, Stodder & Stoughton, 1940.   [2] London, Heinemann, 1958.
[3] London, Victor Gollancz, 1933.
[4] 'Mercantile Law' (1829) 1 *Law Magazine*, at 261–262. See 12 above.

communications (the telegraph), the number of independent agents along commodity supply chains diminished. Importers could more easily deal with the producers or the agents acting for them.

Despite this, agents at home and abroad remained essential to trade, but with enhanced roles, with additional functions and in new guise. Brokers, as we have seen, were central to the increasingly sophisticated commodity markets in London and Liverpool. Trading companies abroad performed agency services for shipping, insurance and banking interests, as well as dealing in goods. Agents also came into their own in various parts of the world as so-called managing agents of plantations, mines and factories, and in the result became the fulcrum of powerful business groups.[5]

In its pure form agency involves a person, the principal, authorising another, the agent, to bind her in dealings with third parties. The agent 'drops out' of the picture once the principal and the third party are brought together in contract. But part 3.2 of the chapter shows that it was sometimes difficult in practice to identify the true agent and that to meet commercial need agency law in its pure form required adaptation. There were also the so-called agents who distributed the motor-vehicles and similar products of the modern age. For marketing reasons these were described as the agents of manufacturers and producers, but they were not true agents in law. The story of these agents is resumed in Chapter 4 in considering the distribution of manufactured goods.[6] Part 3.2 of this chapter also touches on fraudulent agents and what in the book are called local agents.

Parts 3.3 and 3.4 take the narrative further to examine how through doctrines such as undisclosed principal and reasonable compliance with a principal's instructions, and through devices such as commission, del credere and confirming agents, the law went further in meeting commercial need. English law recognised that an agent should not always 'drop out' of the picture. Rather, the agent was to bear some responsibility for the underlying principal–third party contract and could be legally liable for its performance. In these cases the agent remained an agent vis-à-vis the principal but might be treated as a principal vis-à-vis the third party. The commercial benefit was that both the principal and the third party had someone against whom to claim, that someone usually within the jurisdiction, if a transaction went wrong.

The chapter changes tack in part 3.5 to consider how three businesses, described in various ways as agents – Czarnikow & Company, Lewis & Peat and Jardine Matheson – performed a variety of functions as agents but also acted on their own behalf. The niceties of agency law, and the neat categories of the legal treatises, were not for them as they went about the business of serving clients and pursuing profit through their own dealings. Managing agents are the subject of part 3.6. There agency and company law overlapped. The managing agents were true agents in law, providing services to plantation,

---

[5] G. Jones, *Merchants to Multinationals*, Oxford, Oxford University Press, 2002.   [6] 266 below.

mining and processing companies, many of which they had incorporated or promoted. In some of the companies being managed there were minority shareholders, independent of the managing group, who on occasion agitated because of the way the company was being run or its profits distributed. Resort was sometimes had to legal weaponry.

Touched on in this chapter, and elsewhere in the book, is another dimension to agency: principals needed agents to contract with third parties when they were unable to give personal attention to a matter or to act themselves. An important province for this was the company, a form of business enterprise which began to proliferate from the second half of the nineteenth century.[7] Companies could only contract with third parties through the actions of natural persons. Their directors and employees acted as agents. The corporate context threw up a range of new issues for agency law, although these are not for this book, which is centred on transactions rather than institutions.

Nor are the doctrinal dimensions of agency law for extended treatment here. One general point about the English law on the subject should, however, be made at this point. From what has been said so far, it is obvious that agency law performed its role in many different contexts. It did this largely by enunciating broad principles, to be applied in specific contexts, not by developing separate strands of agency law for different types of agents.[8] In commercial circles, however, talk was of specific agents, the shipping agent, insurance agent, stock and station agent, motor manufacturer's agent and so on.

If this chapter is not an extended doctrinal history of agency law, it draws on the not inconsiderable body of case law to help explain how different types of agents operated. The story from the case law is part of a piece with what emerges from business archives. As might be expected, there was little case law in England dealing with the relationship between the commission agent abroad and the overseas buyer. Litigation in Britain tended to involve parties within the jurisdictions. That between overseas agents and buyers occurred in the courts of the jurisdiction where they were based. (There are examples of the reverse situation featuring a British party and a foreign commission merchant based in Britain.[9]) To present a more complete picture, there is resort to a little of the case law of some other common-law courts, notably India. Wherever it originated, however, the case law can only take the story so far. The daily practices of agents demand a wider compass.

---

[7] 423 below.
[8] Good accounts of doctrinal history include S. Stoljar, *The Law of Agency: Its History and Present Principles*, London, Sweet and Maxwell, 1961; R. Munday, 'A Legal History of the Factor' (1977) 6 *Anglo-Amer LR* 221; F. Reynolds & B. Davenport (eds.), *Bowsted on Agency*, 13th ed., London, Sweet & Maxwell, 1968 (this edition contains more historical material than later editions).
[9] e.g., *Cassaboglou v. Gibb* (1883) 11 QBD 797; 155 below. See D. Hill, 'The Commission Merchant at Common Law' (1968) 31 *MLR* 623, 631.

3.2 Agents and Agency Law

Let us take, for example, a bale of cotton produced in North America. The bale passes from the hands of the planter into those of the agent on some station or other on the Mississippi and travels down the river to New Orleans. Here it is sold – for a second time, for the agent has already bought it from the planter – sold, it might well be, to the speculator, who sells it once again, to the exporter. The bale now travels to Liverpool where, once again, a greedy speculator stretches out his hands towards it and grabs it. This man then trades it to a commission agent who, let us assume, is a buyer for a German house. So the bale travels to Rotterdam, up the Rhine, through another dozen hands of forwarding agents, being unloaded and loaded a dozen times, and only then does it arrive in the hands, not of the consumer, but of the manufacturer. (Frederick Engels, 1845)[10]

The complexity during our period of transferring commodities from producer to customer, with or without processing or manufacture, demanded the services of intermediaries.[11] With the passage of time the chains of intermediaries in trade were shortened and the agent was more likely than previously to be the broker in the commodities markets, or the representative of a large trading or manufacturing organisation. Whatever their character, middlemen in trade were not always popular figures, as illustrated by Engels' description of the movement of cotton from the American south to a German manufacturer. It was in the context of the many different types of intermediaries during our period – to take Engels' mid-century example, Southern selling agents, Liverpool brokers, shipping and forwarding agents on both sides of the Atlantic – that the general principles of agency law took shape.

The power-conferring aspect of agency law, where all these different agents were vested with the authority to alter their principal's liabilities, and the consequences of this for third parties, became a key factor from the nineteenth century as business organisations dealt with others over longer distances, grew in size or took corporate form.[12] It is a major concern of this chapter. The discussion is largely of agency law in the context of the trade in goods, but agency law applied to services as well. Shipping and insurance agents are two important figures, mentioned in the chapter, but not addressed at length. Agency in the context of banking services will be encountered in Chapter 6.

The first systematic treatment of agency law was in 1812 by William Paley in his *A Treatise on the Law of Principal and Agent: Chiefly with Reference to Mercantile Transactions*.[13] More influential than Paley, and the later English textbooks published in the nineteenth century, was *Commentaries on the Law of Agency* by Joseph Story, professor of law at Harvard Law School and

---

[10] Speech, Elberfeld, 8 February 1845, *Karl Marx & Frederick Engels Collected Works*, vol. IV, 243.
[11] A. Shaw, 'Some Problems in Market Distribution' (1912) 26 *Q J Econ* 703.
[12] F. Dowrick, 'The Relationship of Principal and Agent' (1954) 17 *MLR* 24, 36–38; E. Orts, *Business Persons. A Legal Theory of the Firm*, Oxford, Oxford University Press, 2013, 59–62.
[13] London, J. Butterworth and J. Cooke, 1812.

associate justice of the US Supreme Court.[14] Story's more adventurous exposition, attempting to fill gaps and to enunciate principle, meant that he was cited throughout the nineteenth century in important agency cases as the English judges sought answers to new problems or a justification for the conclusions they drew.[15]

In nineteenth-century accounts agency law took some time to work free of the law of master and servant.[16] It was also bedevilled for a while with definitional issues, the distinction between 'factors' and 'brokers' being one. In the early part of the nineteenth century, in litigation involving parties whose names lived on well into the twentieth century, *Baring* v. *Corrie*,[17] Abbott CJ said that a factor was a person to whom goods were consigned for sale from abroad (or from a distance), usually in his own name, without disclosing his principal, whereas a broker was not entrusted with the possession of the goods and ought not to sell in own name.[18] Over time, the rigidity of these definitions was doubted, no doubt in part because of commercial practice.[19] Thus, on the commodities markets, as we saw in Chapter 2, brokers often dealt as principals and not simply as agents.[20] In 1883 Cotton LJ considered the position of an agent entrusted with the possession of goods for the purpose of sale, and acting under special instructions from his principal to sell at a particular price and in the principal's name. He held that the agent in those circumstances did not lose his character as a factor, and to the consequent right of lien (security) over the goods.[21]

While the focus in the present discussion is on agents contracting with third parties – the external aspects of agency – its internal aspects deserve mention. One internal aspect concerned the rights of agents vis-à-vis their principals, crucially their right to commission.[22] More important for our purposes was the agent overreaching himself or worse, acting contrary to instructions, and the principal's

---

[14] Boston, Charles C Little & James Brown, 1839. The book went through various editions.
[15] e.g., *Salomons* v. *Pender* (1865) 3 Hurl & C 639, 643–644, 159 ER 682, 684, per Martin B (agent's commission); *Ireland* v. *Livingston*, (1872) LR 5 HL 395, 410–411, per Blackburn J (agent's authority); 'the considered opinion of a most distinguished lawyer'; *Lloyd* v. *Grace, Smith & Co* [1912] AC 716, 736, per Lord Macnaghten (at 737, citing Blackburn J's endorsement of Story in *McGowan & Co* v. *Dyer* (1873) LR 8 Q B 141, at 145)(fraud of agent); *Thomas Gabriel & Sons* v. *Churchill & Sim* [1914] 3 KB 1272, 1278, per Buckley J (del credere agency).
[16] As late as 1891, Holmes J was insisting it was an application of master–servant principles: 'Agency' (1891) 4 *Harv LR* 345, 346.
[17] (1818) 2 B & Ald 137, 143, 106 ER 317, 319. On Baring Brothers & Co, see 24–25, 29 above. Corrie MacColl & Son was a firm of commodity traders, particularly in copra, rubber and vegetable oils.
[18] at 143, 319 respectively (50 hogsheads of Surinam sugar per *Active*). See also '*The Matchless*' (1822) 1 Hagg 97, 166 ER 35. See W. Evan, *The Law of Principal and Agent*, London, William Maxwell & Son, 1878, 3.
[19] e. g., J. Russell, *A Treatise on the Laws relating to Factors and Brokers*, London, S. Sweet, 1844.
[20] 74–76 above.
[21] *Stevens* v. *Biller* (1883) 25 Ch D 31, 37. Lindley LJ agreed. See J. Cotton (revised M. Curthoys), 'Cotton, Sir Henry (1821–1892)', *Oxford Dictionary of National Biography*.
[22] W. Evans, *The Law Relating to the Remuneration of Commission Agents*, 2nd ed. by W. Herbert, London, Horace Cox, 1900, esp chs 1 & 2; H. Giveen, *Law Relating to Commission Agents*, London, Clement Wilson, 1898, Ch 2.

position in these circumstances. Those giving evidence to a Parliamentary Select Committee in 1856 gave examples. T.M. Weguelin, of the merchants Thomson, Bonnar & Co, which had a large trade with Russia, referred to brokers assuming an authority they did not really possess in concluding contracts.[23] He added that many such cases were resolved without litigation. Germain Lavie, of the solicitors Oliverson, Lavie and Peachey,[24] gave evidence of brokers drawing contracts which conferred unauthorised powers. 'In one case the man actually went to law; but he gave it up .... My clients in each case ... proved that they never gave the broker any such authority as he assumed.'[25]

Over time the courts enunciated principles to protect against agent abuse. The dishonest agent was straightforward; he had to account for illicit profits if still around.[26] The agent's fiduciary duties needed time in the making. In the commercial sphere, cases such as *Aberdeen Railway Co* v. *Blaikie*[27] took a strong line. There the House of Lords held that a contract for the purchase of iron railway chairs by a railway company was unenforceable because of the conflict of interest of one of its directors, who was also a member of the iron-founders contracted to manufacture them. 'So strict was the principle', said Lord Cranworth, 'that no investigation could be allowed as to the fairness or unfairness of the contract'.[28] To avoid this consequence, the agent was bound in a conflict of interest situation to disengage or to make full disclosure of the interest and obtain the informed consent of the principal to the situation.[29]

1 Agent or Principal?

Dear Sir, – In answer to your of the 6th inst., I beg to inform you that in consequence of an arrangement with the Swedish firms, by which barrel-staves will be trimmed and finished to three standard lengths before shipment, we are entitled to offer an additional discount of five per cent for the coming season on orders of five thousand staves and upwards. (Q [Arthur Thomas Quiller-Couch], *Shinning Ferry*, 1905)[30]

---

[23] House of Lords, *Report from the Select Committee of the House of Lords on the Mercantile Law Amendment Bill [HL]* (on re-commitment), Session 1856, No 294, 18 June 1856, 21.

[24] At the time, solicitors to prominent clients such as the Chartered Bank of India, Australia and China.

[25] House of Lords, Report from the Select Committee of the House of Lords on the Mercantile Law Amendment Bill [HL], *op cit*, 30.

[26] e.g., *Nitedals Taendstikfabrik* v. *Bruster* [1906] 2 Ch 671 (British agent of Norwegian match company substituting own invoices, with higher price, with the shipping documents).

[27] (1854) 17 D (HL) 20. See D. Kershaw, *The Foundations of Anglo-American Corporate Fiduciary Law*, Cambridge, Cambridge University Press, 2018, 313–315.

[28] at 21.

[29] On the development of fiduciary law: P. Finn, *Fiduciary Obligations 40th Anniversary Republication with Additional Essays*, Sydney, Federation Press, 2016; D. Kershaw, op cit, 28–33. See also 76 above.

[30] London, T. Nelson & Sons, 1905. See A. L. Rowse, *Quiller Couch A Portrait of 'Q'*, London, Methuen, 1988, 92–93. Barrel staves were the subject matter of a leading case in sales, *Arcos* v. *Ronaasen* [1933] AC 470; 208–209 below.

One of Quiller-Couch's Cornish novels opens with John Rosewarne dictating this letter to his clerk to send to a Plymouth correspondent. In the novel, Rosewarne's ancestors had built up a successful business as shipowners, traders, bankers and agents. Despite the ambiguity in the letter, his Plymouth correspondent would probably have appreciated through the course of dealing in which capacity Rosewarne was acting, principal or agent. That was not always the case. A broker or trader might be acting as principal one moment, agent the next. The capacity in which he acted would be of little, if any, concern in most cases. Transactions would be entered, bargains fulfilled. The parties would move to the next deal. It was only when something went wrong, or one of the parties sought to renege on a deal, that the distinction between those acting as agent and those buying or selling on their own account loomed large.

Illustrative are a number of cases in the Indian courts in the first part of the twentieth century where agents there received indents (orders) from Indian customers to purchase goods in Britain and elsewhere.[31] In *Holmes Wilson and Co. Ltd v. Bata Kristo*[32] the standard form indent of the agents, Holmes Wilson & Co, was typical of those used by buying agents in Calcutta (Kolkata). They were completed by the buyer and were to purchase 'on my (our) account and risk the whole or any part of the undermentioned goods on the terms and conditions stated'.[33] The goods were steel plates, and Holmes Wilson & Co ordered them from the United States Steel Products Co. The buyer refused to take delivery and pay since the exchange rate had moved against him. When Holmes Wilson & Co sued, he contended that the sale was between United States Steel and himself, and that Holmes Wilson & Co as agent could not sue. In the Calcutta High Court Page J found for Holmes Wilson & Co. As a matter of fact, he held, the buyer had approved Holmes Wilson & Co following the well-established practice in the indent trade in Calcutta with 'CIF/commission nil' orders, whereby an agent made its profit by buying from the supplier at one price and selling to the buyer at the indent price.[34] No doubt Page J regarded the defendant's behaviour as unmeritorious. Merits were also near the surface in at least one of a number of Bombay (Mumbai) cases where an Indian buyer reneged on its indent.[35]

---

[31] cf. the charterparty cases in the Indian courts in the late nineteenth century as to whether those acting as shipping agents were liable as principals: *Soopromonian Setty v. Heilgers*, 1879 ILR 5 Calc 71 (held, P W Heilgers and Co were agents); *Mackinnon Mackenzie & Co v. Lang Moir & Co*, 1881 ILR 5 Bom 584 (held, Mackinnon not principals); *Hasonbhoy Visram v. Clapham*, 1882 ILR 7 Bom 51 (held, Finlay, Muir & Co not principals – had signed charterparty as agents, but were liable under Art 237 of Indian Contract Act for their representation). cf. *Schiller v. Finlay*, 8 Bom LR 544 (held, Finlay Muir & Co were principals – had signed 'acting for ...' without mentioning expressly that they were agents. Case decided before Indian Contract Act).

[32] AIR 1927 Cal 668.

[33] Orders to a buying agent might specify the name of the manufacturer from whom goods were to be obtained, might be open orders for goods to be purchased in the best market and in any event might specify a maximum price and the timing for the order to be fulfilled.

[34] Rather naively, Page J lamented the casual attitude of merchants to legal principles.

[35] *Mahomdally Ebrahim Pirkhan v. Schiller, Dosogne and Co* ILR (1889) Bom 470. See also *N. Roy & Co v. Surana, Dalai and Co* (1919) 23 Bom LR 1119; *Gordhandas Nathalal v. Gorio Limited*

The issue of whether an agent was acting as principal arose in a different context when a decision in the Madras High Court reached the Privy Council in 1925.[36] There a Madras (Chennai) firm exported groundnuts, castor seeds and other commodities. It did this through London merchants. When a cargo of groundnuts never arrived, the merchants paid compensation for non-delivery on an onward sale of the groundnuts to a Marseilles buyer. The issue was whether the merchants had acted as principals in the French sale so they could then recover from the Madras firm. In the Privy Council, Lord Phillimore said that it was possible that the London merchants were agents 'according to the modern business extension of the phrase'. In other words, they were really buyers from the Madras firm selling as principals at the best price they could get.[37] On examining the correspondence between the Madras firm and the London merchants from 1913, he concluded that with the mention of commission and a blank against 'buyer' in the standard contract form, the London merchants were, in the strict sense, agents, so that their claim against the Madras firm was unsuccessful.[38]

2 Agent or 'Agent'?

> There is great force in the observations . . . upon the extension which modern business has given to the terms 'agent' and 'agency'. In many trades – particularly, for instance, in the motor-car trade – the so-called agent is merely a favoured and favouring buyer. (Lord Phillimore, 1925)[39]

Writing in 1933, the author of what was said to be a practical guide to the subject of sales management warned manufacturers that, because of the legal consequences, sales through agents was a step to be taken warily.[40] One such consequence, he explained, was that a manufacturer could be directly liable to the ultimate purchaser under the Sale of Goods Act 1893 for faults in the goods. Notwithstanding this danger agency, while not dominant, was used throughout our period in the commercial sale of manufactured goods.[41] With mass-produced consumer goods, however, the retailer was rarely the agent of

---

(1934) 36 Bom LR 834. cf. *Paul Beier* v. *Chhotalal Javerdas*, ILR (1904) Bom 1, 6 Bom LR 948 (usage in the Bombay market).

[36] *Hope Prudhomme & Co* v. *Hamel & Horley Ltd* [1925] UKPC 23, (1925) 49 ILR Mad 1, AIR 1925 PC 161, (1925) 6 LR PC 129.

[37] [1925] UKPC 23, 4.

[38] Ibid., 8–9. The Privy Council also rejected the High Court's decision that the Madras firm had ratified the London merchants acting as principals in the particular contract: at 9–12.

[39] *Hope Prudhomme & Co* v. *Hamel & Horley Ltd* [1925] UKPC 23, 4. Bigham J made the same point about the sole agent for Talbot cars in Yorkshire (*Pye* v. *British Automobile Commercial Syndicate Ltd* [1906] 1 KB 425, 427), as did Atkin J regarding distribution of the Model T Ford (*Ford Motor Company (England) Ltd* v. *Armstrong* (1914) 30 TLR 400, 400; on appeal (1915) 31 TLR 267).

[40] C. Bolling, *Sales Management*, 2nd ed., London, Pitman, 1933, 111.

[41] e.g., *L Schuler AG* v. *Wickman Machine Tool Sales Ltd* [1974] AC 235 (German manufacturer of panel presses; British agent appointed in 1963 for their sale to UK vehicle manufacturers).

the manufacturer. Inquiries of a hardware merchant in the Midlands in the early 1960s revealed that, within the memory of its directors, on only one occasion, with a very special lawn-mower, had the firm marketed a product on other than its own account.[42] Yet it was sometimes commercially advantageous to describe the retailer as the manufacturer's 'agent', as with Lord Phillimore's motor-car and lorry dealers, even if as a matter of law the dealer was not a 'Ford agent', an 'Austin agent' or a 'Morris agent'.

In some cases it was the economic realities which led to a transformation in the legal character of the retailer from a true agent to an 'agent'. Petrol is an example. In the early years of the twentieth century it was sold in Britain in sealed tin cans by cycle repairers, kerosene suppliers and so on. The General Petroleum Co Ltd of London distributed Shell petrol to customers.[43] General Petroleum's standard agreement and the associated signage made clear that local retailers sold the company's petroleum as agents of, and in the name of, the company.[44] Property in the petroleum spirit remained in the company 'until actually delivered' to customers. The same applied to the tin containers. Agency in this context could not survive. The increased demand for petrol and the introduction of the mechanical petrol pump meant that it was no longer appropriate. The retailer became a seller, albeit that its garage might be plastered with the name of the relevant oil company.[45]

In 1931 Scrutton LJ referred to the 'many difficulties' which this practice of calling retailers 'agents' had caused.[46] Evidence of that is hard to come by. In practice it was only when things went wrong that the issue became relevant. The English courts approached the matter pragmatically, recognising that use of the term 'agent' in commercial practice did not necessarily mean an agency in law.[47] That did not mean that legal characterisation was always easy, especially if there was no written contract. In that situation the courts had to impose a legal character on the relationship by reasoning from the circumstances, such as the course of dealing between the parties, as well as from the

---

[42] C. Parker, 'Book Review' (1962) 25 *MLR* 608, 611. See also S. Stoljar, The Law of Agency, *op cit*, 123.

[43] S. Howarth, *A Century in Oil: The 'Shell' Transport and Trading Company*, London, Weidenfeld, 1997, 69.

[44] WMRC, MSS 198/M/9/1, Thomas Moscrop and Company Ltd, 'Agency agreement with General Petroleum Company Limited 17 April 1905'. This was General Petroleum's standard form, with gaps for matters such as the agent's name, the area of its agency and its commission. Previous arrangements between the parties seem to have been set out in letters: ibid. For a lengthy US agreement, dated 31 May 1905, under which Californian Petroleum Refineries appointed Jardine Matheson as sole agents on commission for China, Japan, etc.: CUL, Jardine Matheson Archive, Agreements and Contracts, JM/F1/106.

[45] see 277–279 below.

[46] W. T. Lamb and Sons v. Goring Brick Company Ltd [1932] 1 K.B. 710, 717. See also N. Isaacs, 'On Agents and "Agencies"' (1925) 3 *Harv Bus R* 265.

[47] *International Harvester Co of Australia Pty Ltd v. Carrigan's Hazeldene Pastoral Co* (1958) 100 CLR 644, canvassed the authorities: 652–653. See also *Wilson v. Darling Island Stevedoring & Lighterage Co Ltd* (1956) 95 CLR 43, 70.

implications of their choice.[48] A written contract might state the nature of the 'agent', but in a vacuum that could mislead without an appreciation of the commercial context.

The House of Lords was almost led into error in a case involving the tyre trade, *Michelin Tyre Co Ltd v. Macfarlane (Glasgow) Ltd (in liquidation)*.[49] It arose when Michelin claimed against the liquidator of one of its dealers, now insolvent, for the unpaid price of tyres. Michelin contended that the dealer was an agent so that it had to account to Michelin for what customers had paid for the tyres. In the agreements of 1913 and 1915 there was a retention of title clause (the tyres were to remain the property of Michelin until sold), and the dealer was subject to the typical restrictions in distribution arrangements as to whom and at what price it sold.[50] It described the dealer as 'stockists' and 'consignees', but the word 'agent' was used when referring to Michelin's obligation to place the dealer's name in a prominent position in its famous 'Guide to the British Isles'.[51] The Sheriff Court in Glasgow, and on appeal the First Division of the Court of Session, held that the tyre dealer was not Michelin's agent and that the relationship between the two was one of buyer and seller.[52] The Lord President described the language of the agreements as 'uncouth', but nonetheless clear. He referred to the course of dealing between the parties in which the dealer did not furnish Michelin with a list of its customers, rendered invoices and accounts in its own name, and used moneys received from customers for the general purposes of its business.[53] In the era of high formalism the House of Lords made no reference to these factors.[54] Fortunately, the practical implications of Michelin's argument were not lost on Lord Finlay LC – if Michelin was correct, as a matter of law it would be a party to every retail sale of its tyres in the country – and the appeal was, by majority, dismissed.[55]

3 Fraud

[T]he practice of merchants ... is not based on the supposition of possible frauds. The object of mercantile usages is to prevent the risk of insolvency, not

---

[48] An early case was *John Towle & Co v. White* (1873) 29 LT 78 (HL) (London 'cotton agent' not true agent of Derbyshire textile manufacturer; see esp Lord Selborne LC's reasoning: 80). See *London Gazette*, 7 August 1868, 4422 on the firm. See also *Wheeler and Wilson Manufacturing Co v. Shakespear* (1869) 39 LJ Ch 36 (US sewing machine manufacturer; generally understood in trade that its 'agents' purchased and then on-sold and not true agents: at 39); *Dramburg v. Pollitzer* (1873) 28 LT 470 (distributor of gelatine paper 'Sole agent for Kneppers & Co of Vienna'; jury entitled to find distributor selling in own right).
[49] 1917 2 SLT 205.   [50] 275–276 below.
[51] See H. Lottman, *The Michelin Men: Driving an Empire*, London, I.B. Tauris, 2003, 95–96; S. Harp, *Marketing Michelin*, Baltimore, Johns Hopkins University Press, 2001, 21.
[52] 1916 2 SLT 221.   [53] 1916 2 SLT 221, 227. Other members of the Court of Session agreed.
[54] On high formalism: P. Atiyah, *The Rise and Fall of Freedom of Contract*, Oxford, Oxford University Press, 1979, 661.
[55] 1917 2 SLT 205, 209. Lords Haldane and Parmoor dissented.

of fraud; and any one who attempts to follow and understand the law merchant will soon find himself lost if he begins by assuming that merchants conduct their business on the basis of attempting to insure themselves against fraudulent dealing. The contrary is the case. (Bowen LJ, 1883)[56]

Fraud committed by agents was a concern, although the focus was not so much on independent agents but on the directors, managers and other employees of a company who, in law, were its agents.[57] Action against the fraudulent agent was theoretically possible, but in practice he would have disappeared or depleted his ill-gotten gains and was not worth suing. The issue then became which of the two innocent parties, the principal or the third party, should bear the loss. The courts struggled to enunciate a principle for these situations. The issue was approached on a case-by-case basis. It was not until 1912 that it was authoritatively established that the principal was liable for an agent's fraud acting within the scope of his authority, even when the agent acted for its own benefit.[58] That was an advance, but only part of the picture. Doctrine, a sense of which party was most responsible for the agent's fraud and a concern with trying to reach a commerce-friendly result all entered the mix as courts addressed the circumstances and consequences of agent fraud in specific circumstances.[59]

A good illustration of how judges could disagree as to who should bear the loss caused by a fraudster is provided by a case involving the Liverpool cotton exchange, *Hollins* v. *Fowler*.[60] There in a typical transaction early in December 1869 Fowler & Co, the plaintiffs, instructed their brokers, Rew & Freeman, to sell American cotton 'ex *Minnesota*'. About a fortnight later another cotton broker, HK Bayley & Co, offered to buy thirteen bales of the *Minnesota*'s cotton, falsely stating it was on behalf of Thomas Seddon of Bolton.[61] Seddon knew nothing about the transaction. Bayley took possession of the cotton and fraudulently sold it to another cotton broker, the defendants, Francis Hollins & Co. Hollins obtained a delivery order from Bayley, collected the cotton and had it dispatched by rail to its own customer, a mill in Stockport. Hollins paid Bayley in cash. Fowler had not been paid, and on 10 January 1870 his lawyers

---

[56] *Sanders Brothers* v. *Maclean & Co* (1883) 11 QBD 327, 343.
[57] e.g., 'Fraudulent Agents' (1874) JP 419; 'Agent's or Servant's Frauds' (1888) 52 JP 193; 'Fraud by an Agent' (1932) 173 Law Times 3.
[58] *Lloyd (Pauper)* v. *Grace, Smith & Co* [1912] AC 716.
[59] e.g., *Jacobs* v. *Morris* [1902] 1 Ch 816 (London agent of Melbourne tobacco merchant with no power to borrow; cigar merchant who lent him money liable since 'more to blame': at 834); *Swire* v. *Francis* (1877) 3 App Cas 106 (PC; Britain's Supreme Court at Shanghai) (Butterfield & Swire's local agent in Kiukiang (Jiujiang) to bear loss; it had chosen the sub-agent who defrauded payments to Chinese merchants). Note that Butterfield & Swire was in turn acting as general agents at Shanghai of the China Navigation Company. On its trading activities: G. Jones, Merchants to Multinationals, *op cit*, 36–37, 129–131, 164–165, 242).
[60] (1875) LR 7 HL 757.
[61] Fowler made inquiries as to Seddon and agreed to sell on discovering there was a firm of that name. Seddon seems to have had two cotton mills: *Grace's Guide to British Industrial History*, online edition, searched 14 February 2018.

(stating Bayley's fraud) demanded that Hollins return the cotton. Hollins replied that it had long since been made into yarn. At the Liverpool Assizes in Spring 1870, the jury gave affirmative answers to the two questions Willes J posed – whether the thirteen bales were bought by Hollins in the course of their business as brokers, and whether they dealt with the cotton only as agents to their principals – and found for Hollins. When the judges of Queen's Bench (Mellor, Lush and Hannen JJ) considered the matter in November 1871, they entered judgment for Fowler. On appeal to the Exchequer Chamber, in June 1872 the six judges were equally divided, although the reasoning within each group varied.[62]

Over five years after the fraud had been committed the case reached the House of Lords. It summoned the judges for their advice. The opposing views were represented by Blackburn J and Brett J. Blackburn J opined that Fowler should succeed however hard it was on Hollins. Albeit that Hollins was innocent of Bayley's fraud, he had converted Fowler's cotton. Established principles of law could not be departed from to meet the hardship of the case, and if there was inconvenience to business, Parliament should alter the law.[63] Brett J took the contrary view: Hollins according to the jury's findings had acted as an agent and as such could not be liable for conversion. The question, he said, was 'a most important one for Liverpool', since it would mean additional precautions in the despatch of cotton to the mill towns.[64] Ultimately the House of Lords found for Fowler. All of the law lords were impressed by the fact that when Hollins purchased the cotton he had no principal, albeit that Bayley knew that he was acting as a broker. As such Hollins acted as principal and was caught by the rule that a person was guilty of conversion if, however innocently, he obtained possession and disposed of goods of a person who has been fraudulently deprived of them.[65] Doctrine trumped what Brett J regarded as the most commercially sensible result.

Agent fraud could cause untold damage. In the early 1900s fraud by an agent (in law) of Dodwell & Co, a large trading house in Asia, was thought to threaten its future; ironically, the law of agency then played a role in recovering its losses. The firm was prominent in the tea trade with China and Japan, with branches engaged in trading, shipping and processing in Asia and the Pacific.[66] The branch in Colombo, Ceylon (Sri Lanka), was established in 1897 for the tea trade, but later acquired tea and coconut plantations. During 1905–1906, and then 1909–1910, the price of rubber rose sharply. Booms attract speculators, and one of these was the manager of Dodwell's Colombo branch, R. H. Williams, in law one of the firm's agents. He speculated on his own account

---

[62] (1872) LR 7 QB 616. See 'The Doctrine of Conversion' (1873) 54 *Law Times* 359.
[63] at 765.   [64] at 780.
[65] See 'The Law of Conversion as applied to Sales by Purchasers without Notice of the Fraud' (1875) 59 *Law Times* 366.
[66] G. Jones, Merchants to Multinationals, *op cit*, 54–55, 58, 104, 138, 149; F. King, 'Dodwell, George Benjamin (1851–1925)', *Oxford Dictionary of National Biography*.

during these booms, but in the second boom also used the company's bank account with the connivance of the branch's bookkeeper. When the second boom inevitably burst, the losses to the firm were considerable, some £90,000. At one point it was feared that the firm's future as a whole was threatened, although concerns were allayed when its bankers, the Hong Kong and Shanghai Bank (HSBC), advised that there were sufficient reserves.[67]

After the fraud was discovered in October 1911, Williams was convicted in criminal proceedings. Dodwell & Co. obtained judgment against Williams in his bankruptcy, but the dividend of 2 ¼ percent was little consolation. In early 1913 the firm commenced legal proceedings against the rubber brokers, E. John & Co, who had acted for Williams.[68] Dodwell's claim was in relation to four cheques Williams drew on its account with HSBC in favour of the brokers, two in 1909 and two in 1910, signed 'Dodwell & Co Ltd, R H Williams, Manager'. The District Judge in Colombo held that the brokers knew that Williams was dealing on his own account, not always as the firm's agent, but had taken the four cheques honestly. He found in Dodwell's favour in relation to part of the fourth cheque.[69]

On appeal to the Supreme Court in Colombo, Pereira and Shaw JJ found in Dodwell's favour on the basis that Williams had no authority as agent to draw the cheques, and had the brokers looked at them they would have seen that Williams was writing them to pay for his own speculations.[70] The brokers appealed to the Privy Council, and the opinion of the board was given by Viscount Haldane.[71] He reasoned that Williams had paid over Dodwell's property in breach of his fiduciary duty as an agent of the firm, and that the brokers had notice of this. The brokers were, in turn, under a fiduciary duty to account to their principal, Dodwell, for what in effect was trust money.[72] However, Dodwell's claim in relation to the 1909 cheques was time barred. In that respect the brokers were partly successful. In fact the money the firm lost was almost completely recovered since other brokers had meanwhile paid Dodwell because of potential litigation against them.[73]

4 Local Agents

Superior classes, as traders, compradors, better shopkeepers etc. wear decent, grave long robes of blue or black, stockings & shoes of white or blue, like canoes . . .. Visit to Ap-pong, one of the wealthiest Chinese here. House very

---

[67] S. Jones, *Two Centuries of Overseas Trading*, Basingstoke, Macmillan, 1986, 182.
[68] See LMA, CLC/B/123/MS27520, Dodwell & Company Ltd, 'News cuttings relating to a court case concerning embezzlement of company funds in Colombo, Ceylon'.
[69] His reasoning is at *John v. Dodwell & So Ltd* [1918] AC 563, 564–565.
[70] *Dodwell & Co Ltd v. John et al* (1915) 18 NLR 133. Ennis J dissented because he held that Dodwell's claim was time barred.
[71] *John v. Dodwell & Co Ltd* [1918] AC 563. [72] at 569–70.
[73] E. Warde, *The House of Dodwell A Century of Achievement, 1858–1958*, Exeter, Dodwell & Co Ltd, 1958, 89.

large, with sev[eral] foreign pictures & engravings... Visit to house of Wo Lung, another leading merchant. His is a new house & very beautifully furnished, with European pictures, & a piano. (Richard Henry Dana Jr, Journal, China, 1860)[74]

When the Massachusetts lawyer and legislator Richard Henry Dana Jr visited China in 1860, he met and observed through foreign eyes some of the Chinese agents which the overseas trading firms needed to buy and sell for them in local markets. They distributed the imports like opium (from India), textiles and metal products, and obtained the silk and tea from inland China for the trading houses to export. China proved remarkably resistant to penetration by Westerners, and without the Chinese agents the trading companies would have achieved little.[75] A key figure for the foreign trading houses and the banks in China was the comprador, a Chinese in their employ entering transactions as agent on their behalf.[76] Compradors could be powerful figures, employing staff, controlling funds, investing on their own behalf in trading firms and also conducting their own commercial operations, possibly from premises away from the European trading house.

In India, Indian merchants were also indispensable for British trading firms, initially in the port cities but later outside.[77] For financing and managing a crop like cotton, a series of Indian agents were essential so that it reached the Calcutta (Kolkata) agency houses for export to Europe.[78] Unlike China, the extension of British rule and the railway network built in the second half of the nineteenth century altered the organisation and finance of trade as leading foreign firms like the Ralli Brothers and Volkart Brothers established buying organisations in the interior.[79] Agency chains were truncated, but despite this remained vital to the import–export business. As in China and India, the local agent was vital in other places like the Straits Settlements (Singapore), where

---

[74] R. Lucid (ed.), *The Journal of Richard Henry Dana, Jr*, Cambridge, MA, Harvard University Press, 1968, vol. III.

[75] J. Osterhammel, 'British Business in China 1860s-1950s', in R. Davenport-Hines & G. Jones (eds.), *British Business in Asia since 1860*, Cambridge, Cambridge University Press, 1988, 192; W. Cheong, *Mandarins and Merchants: Jardine Matheson & Co, a China Agency of the Early Nineteenth Century*, London, Curzon Press, 1979; T. Rawski, 'Chinese Dominance of Treaty Port Commerce and Its Implications, 1860-1875' (1970) *Explorations in Economic History* 451. cf. G. Allen & A. Donnithorne, *Western Enterprise in Far Eastern Economic Development: China and Japan*, 2nd ed., London, Allen & Unwin, 1962, 45-46.

[76] K. Abe, 'Intermediary Elites in the Treaty Port World: Tong Mow-chee and his Collaborators in Shanghai, 1873-1897' (2015) 25 *Journal of the Royal Asiatic Society* 461; Yen-Ping Hao, *The Comprador in Nineteenth Century China Bridge between East and West*, Harvard, Harvard University Press, 1970.

[77] C. Bayly, 'Inland Port Cities in North India: Calcutta and the Gangetic Plains 1780-1900', in D. Basu (ed.), *The Rise and Growth of the Colonial Port Cities in Asia*, Lanham, University Press of America, 1985, 13-17.

[78] C. Bayly, *Rulers, Townsmen and Bazaars: North Indian Society in the Age of British Expansion 1770-1870*, Cambridge, Cambridge University, 1983, 277-278, 283-284, 299, 301-302.

[79] R. Ray, 'Asian Capital in the Age of European Domination: The Rise of the Bazaar, 1800-1914' (1995) 29 *Modern Asian Stud* 449, 493.

the large agency house Guthrie & Co. bought and sold everything through local Chinese agents.[80]

By the twentieth century, if not earlier, the agency relationship between the larger foreign trading organisations and banks on the one hand and their local agents on the other might be formalised in Western-style agreements. Thus, clause 6 of the 1920 agreement between HSBC and its comprador at the head office in Hong Kong (which seems to have reflected the agreements the bank had with its compradors elsewhere) provided that he guaranteed all the transactions entered into by the bank with Chinese parties and was answerable for their solvency and reliability.[81] That meant that his obligations to the bank as his principal were more onerous than would otherwise be the case with an agent. Other obligations in the agreement were perhaps more straightforward, for example that he act in accordance with the custom and usage regarding compradors and keep the bank's secrets.[82]

As ever there was the issue in which capacity an agent was acting. The issue reached the Privy Council in 1885 in *David Sassoon Sons & Co v. Wang Gan-Ying*.[83] The evidence of David Sassoon & Sons' comprador at Tientsin, Hoo Mei Pin, was that he repeatedly informed the third party, Wang Gan-Ying, that he was acting independently in the relevant transaction. The case was an appeal from a decision of the Chief Justice of Britain's Supreme Court for China and Japan.[84] In the Privy Council Lord Monkswell was distinctly unimpressed with both the judgment of the Chief Justice and that of the consular judge who had heard the matter at first instance.[85] Where were their reasons for asserting that it was improbable that Hoo Mei Pin would have been trusted if acting independently and not as an agent? To the contrary, Lord Monkswell said, the evidence was that Hoo Mei Pin had an extensive business, conducted from establishments in a great number of places, facts

---

[80] S. Cunyngham-Brown, *The Traders*, London, Newman Neame, 1971, 94.

[81] C. Smith, 'Compradors of the Hong Kong Bank', in F. King (ed.), *Eastern Banking: Essays in the History of the Hong Kong and Shanghai Banking Corporation*, London, Athlone, 1983, 94.

[82] For judicial characterisation of a bank's comprador, see *Russo Chinese Bank v. Li Yau Sam* [1910] AC 174, 175 (PC, Britain's Supreme Court at Hong Kong). See also the role of the comprador in *Hip Foong Hong v. H. Neotia & Co* [1918] AC 888, a case involving the opium trade, on appeal from Britain's Supreme Court at Shanghai.

[83] [1885] UKPC 42. As well as China, David Sassoon & Sons had extensive interests in India, along with the rival (though family related) firm, E. D. Sassoon & Co: see S. Jackson, *The Sassoons*, London, Heinemann, 1968, 39–44, 60–64, 98–107; C. Roth, *The Sassoon Dynasty*, New York, Arno Press, 1977, 95–107.

[84] Like other imperial powers, Britain established this court (and the consular courts below it) to exercise jurisdiction over Westerners. See *Imperial Japanese Government v. Peninsular and Oriental Steam Navigation Co* J [1895] A.C. 644. See J. Norton-Kyshe, *The History of the Laws and Courts of Hong Kong from the earliest period to 1898*, London, T. Fisher Unwin, 1898; C. Tarring, *British Consular Jurisdiction in the East*, London, Stevens & Haynes, 1887; R. Chang, *The Justice of the Western Consular Courts in Nineteenth-Century Japan*, Westport, Greenwood Press, 1984; P. Cassel, *Grounds of Judgment: Extraterritoriality and Imperial Power in Nineteenth-Century China and Japan*, New York, Oxford, 2012.

[85] On Monkswell and his commercial experience: D. Pugsley, 'Collier, Robert Porrett, first Baron Monkswell (1817–1886)', *Oxford Dictionary of National Biography*.

which were well known to the Chinese traders at Tientsin (Tianjin), including Wang Gan-Ying. That gave rise to an inference of trust. In favour of his finding that Hoo Mei Pin was acting as an agent, not independently, the Chief Justice had also relied on the fact that he had given receipts which bore the chop (sign) of David Sassoon & Sons. However, said Lord Monkswell, the consular judge's assessors (who had dissented) had stated that compradors commonly did that in their own transactions, as well as those of their firms. The upshot was that the Privy Council advised that a finding be entered that Hoo Mei Pin had acted on this own account, not as agent, in the relevant transaction.[86]

As in this case, the courts applied the ordinary rules of agency law to local agents. However, in the case of India, the courts identified special categories of local agent, who were held as a result of trade usage to carry heavier responsibilities than agents usually would at common law. One category comprised agents acting for up-country Indian constituents on what were known as *cutcha adatia* terms, who dealt as principal in relation to both their constituents and the trading houses.[87] More important was the trading house's banyan. By law he carried double liability. First, and importantly for the trading houses, he was presumed to be a del credere agent to them. That meant that if a trading house had a banyan sell goods in the market, he guaranteed the price. The justification was market usage.[88] Second, the banyan was treated as a principal as regards third parties. Consequently, in a case in 1859 a banyan employed by W.R. Paterson & Co negotiated the purchase of 243 bags of saltpetre. The firm credited him with the amount, but he absconded. In the Calcutta High Court Peacock CJ held that, in the absence of specific contractual terms, local custom meant that the banyan, not Patersons, was personally liable to the sellers for the price so that Patersons did not need to pay twice.[89]

3.3 Law Facilitating Agency

> The law of principal and agent is one of the greatest importance in a mercantile country. (*The Law Times*, 30 May 1874)

English law facilitated in various ways the role of agents in the numerous commercial environments in which they operated. In doing so it needed to

---

[86] See also *Grant Smith & Co v. Juggobundhoo Shaw* (1865) Bourke's Rep (VII) 17; 2 Hyde 129, where the Calcutta High Court rejected the evidence of the firm's principal, taken on commission in Scotland, about the capacity in which Ramcomul Mitter acted in the Calcutta (Kolkata) market in purchasing jute for the firm and arranging for its packing, pressing and shipment. Norman CJ held that ordinary rules of English law applied: 27.

[87] *Sobhagmal Gianmal v. Mukundchand Balia* [1926] UKPC 79, 1–2; (1926) 28 Bom LR 1376.

[88] See T. Pearson, *The Law of Agency in British India*, Calcutta, WH Allen & Co, 1890, 9–10. On the village bania in the network linking producers to trading houses: D. Cheesman, 'The Omnipresent Bania': Rural Moneylenders in Nineteenth-Century Sind' (1982) 16 *Modern Asian Stud*, 445, 450.

[89] *Pallyram v. W.R. Paterson & Co* (1859) 2 Boulnois 203. See also *Faizulla v. Ramkamal Mitter* (1868) 2 Bom LR(OC) 7.

address a range of problems. The 1874 *Law Times* article from which the quotation at the outset of this part is taken concerned the need for the courts to secure principals against the unauthorised acts of their agents, and also to secure the public against the acts of agents ostensibly authorised, but bound in reality by secret instructions.[90] As early as 1825, Best CJ recognised that the third party should be protected in the case of the fraudulent agent, at the expense of the principal, where the agent had been held out by the principal as having authority in previous, similar transactions.[91] 'Holding out' did not mean that the third party was to be protected as a matter of course. As we will see, legislative intervention in the form of the Factors Acts was necessary to confer greater protection on third parties in certain transactions, although there is a good argument that English law was commercially deficient in failing to protect them to the extent offered by the civil law.[92]

English law consciously attempted to fashion a commercially sensible approach to many of the problems presented. One was through the doctrine of undisclosed principal. Under the doctrine a principal could conceal his existence from the third party at the time of a bargain yet later sue to enforce it. Although criticised as doctrinally incoherent, which no doubt it was, the courts justified the doctrine of the undisclosed principal as commercially convenient. As we saw in Chapter 2 this was not the view of the commodity markets, where the rules excluded its operation. Another area where the courts sought to be helpful to trade was that they recognised that in the absence of instantaneous communications, it was reasonable in some circumstance for agents to set their own course, without checking with their principal.[93] As we see that principle outlived its usefulness.

1 The Agent's Authority

Most straightforward when an agent's authority was questioned was that the matter was spelt out clearly in a written contract. Written contracts appointing agents became increasingly common. They were a notable feature for selling agents appointed by manufacturers of machinery and equipment, and those selling chemicals and bulk minerals.[94] Typical was the ten-year agreement

---

[90] 'The Authority of Masters of Ships' (30 May 1874) 57 *The Law Times* 76.
[91] *Gillman* v. *Robinson* (1825) 1 C & P 642, 171 ER 1350.
[92] I. Brown, 'The Significance of General and Special Authority in the Development of the Agent's External Authority in English Law' (2004) *JBL* 391, 395.
[93] Similarly, the Privy Council on appeal from the Lahore High Court upheld a commission agent's reasonable efforts to collect his principal's debts from third parties for purchases of sugar: *Gokal Chand-Jagan Nath (Firm)* v. *Nand Ram das-Atma Ram (Firm)* [1939] AC 106.
[94] e. g., GRO, D4791/43/9, Gloucester Railway Carriage and Wagon Co, 'Agreement for Messrs. Perrins Ltd. of London to act as sole agents for the Republic of China and Manchuria', 12 December 1931; LMA, CLC/B/123/MS27728, Gray Mackenzie and Company Ltd, 'Agency agreement concluded with Imperial Chemical Industries Ltd relating to the sale of "heavy" chemicals in the Persian Gulf, 1950'.

Jardine Matheson & Co entered in 1886 with M. Decauville, a French engineer: Jardine Matheson were appointed as exclusive agents in China, Hong Kong and Korea to find markets for his railway rolling stock and bridges; they undertook to use their best endeavours to obtain contracts and 'to push their sale'; they were forbidden from introducing or constructing any similar equipment during the course of the agreement; commission was 15 per cent on the value of sales and 10 per cent if purchasers in those areas bought business direct; and the agreement could be terminated by twelve months' notice on either side.[95]

From the first part of the twentieth century, standard agreements were published for British manufacturers appointing selling agents abroad.[96] In broad terms these reflected the type of clauses in the Jardine Matheson agreement: appointment as agent covering a specific geographic area, their obligations in prompting sales, commission and termination. If there was a written agreement, the focus was to interpret its terms to decide issues such as whether the agent had actual authority to enter the transaction at issue,[97] or whether his authority could be or had been properly revoked.[98]

If the agent's acts did not fall within the scope of his actual authority, the courts developed notions of usual and apparent authority which could protect third parties by imposing liability on the principal for the agent's actions. Usual authority was enunciated in an 1865 decision by Cockburn CJ concerning the appointment of a London agent by a straw-hat manufacturer in Luton. He referred to 'the well-established principle, that if a person employs another as an agent in a character which involves a particular authority, he cannot by a secret reservation divest him of that authority'.[99] That principle was invoked in *Watteau v. Fenwick*[100] where the court (Lord Coleridge CJ and Wills J) referred to the principal's liability for all the acts of the agent 'which are within the authority usually confided to an agent of that character, notwithstanding limitations, as between the principal and the agent put upon that authority'.[101] In a number of cases apparent authority was held to derive from the position an agent occupied.[102]

---

[95] CUL, MS JM/F1/93, Jardine Matheson Archive, 'Agreement ... dated Petit-Bourg, 13 November 1886'.

[96] *Encyclopædia of the Laws of England with Forms and Precedents*, London, 1st ed., London, Sweet & Maxwell, 1902, vol. I, 322; *An Export Handbook*, London, Institute of Export, 1939, 18–27.

[97] e.g., *Jacobs v. Morris* [1902] 1 Ch 816 (London agent of Melbourne tobacco merchant); *International Paper Co v. Spicer* (1906) 4 CLR 739 (US paper manufacturers appointed an Australian agent to sell).

[98] e.g., NBAC, Australian Agricultural Company (London Office), 160/74/65, 'Legal opinions, powers of attorney, calls on proprietors and dividends declared', vol. I, 1834–1924, 'Agreement with Agent for Sale of Coal [in Scotland]', Advice from Mr Freshfield on termination, 25 October 1880.

[99] *Edmunds v. Bushell* (1865) LR 1 QB 97.   [100] [1893] 1 QB 346.   [101] at 348–349.

[102] e.g., *Smethurst v. Taylor* (1844) 12 M & W 545, 152 ER 1314 (commission agent purchasing shirtings through agent of Manchester manufacturer for Liverpool merchants engaged in consignment trade with India and China); *Smith v. M'Guire* (1858) 157 ER 589, (1858) 3 Hurl & N 554 (person purchasing oats and chartering ship per procuration).

It is fair to say that neither *Watteau v. Fenwick* nor the concept of usual authority stood the test of time.

Apparent (or ostensible) authority came to the fore. It was often said to turn on estoppel, although that rationale was subsequently rejected.[103] Whatever the doctrinal basis, it applied where the principal by words or deeds held out the agent as having a particular type of authority, and as a result the third party was induced to enter a transaction. The principal was not permitted to point to any limitations on the actual authority of the agent but was bound by what the agent had done. Since apparent authority depended on how the principal had allowed the agent to act in certain ways, or had represented his authority, the agent's authority had to be traceable to the principal.[104] After our period this led to English law at its worse, decisions which were conceptually arid and commercially surprising, where third parties, acting in a commercially reasonable manner, lost out, although the agent they had dealt with had, to all appearances, the principal's authority despite that not being the case.[105]

In the context of trade, apparent authority could arise where a person was in possession of goods, or a document of title to goods, and purported to deal with them as owner, even fraudulently. Apparent authority might follow from a course of dealing with a third party being protected despite an unauthorised agent. There were many cases.[106] For apparent authority to work, however, there had to be a holding out to the third party. In *Farquharson Brothers & Co v. C. King & Co*[107] timber merchants, who warehoused imported timber at Surrey Commercial Docks on the Thames, instructed the dock company to accept transfer and delivery orders signed by its clerk. The clerk had their authority to make limited sales to known customers but fraudulently gave orders for the transfer of timber to a business he had established. From that address and under that name he sold the timber to packing-case manufacturers. Reversing the Court of Appeal, the House of Lords held that the manufacturers never knew of the merchants, so there had been no holding out by the timber merchants to them. The merchants could recover the price of their property stolen from them, and the third-party manufacturers had to bear the loss of the fraud. Lord Macnaghten observed that simple inquiries by the manufacturers as to the bona fides of the clerk's business would have unmasked the fraud.[108]

---

[103] W. Evans, *A Treatise upon the Law of Principal and Agent*, London, William Maxwell & Son, 1878, 136–137.
[104] *Freeman & Lockyer v. Buckhurst Park Properties (Mangal) Ltd* [1964] 2 QB 480.
[105] e.g., *Armagas Ltd v. Mundogas SA ('The Ocean Frost')* [1986] AC 717; *British Bank of the Middle East v. Sun Life Assurance Co of Canada (UK)* [1983] 2 Lloyd's Rep 9.
[106] e.g., *Pickering v. Busk* (1812) 15 East 38, 104 ER 758 (seller who transferred hemp in warehouse into broker's name had to bear loss when broker wrongly sold to third party; broker had apparent authority); *Manchester Trust v. Furness* [1895] 2 QB 539 (owners' representation through their agent, the master of a vessel, to the bank holding bills of lading as to ownership of cargo). See G. Spencer Bower, *The Law relating to Estoppel by Representation*, London, Butterworth, 1923, 1st ed., 197–208; F. Reynolds & B. Davenport (eds.), Bowsted on Agency, 13th ed., *op cit*, 261–266.
[107] [1902] AC 325.   [108] at 335.

2 Doctrine of Undisclosed Principal

Under the doctrine of undisclosed principal, developed in the eighteenth century, an agent with actual authority, and intending to do so, could bring his principal into contractual relations with a third party, even though the fact of the agency was kept secret. Third parties, although they thought they were dealing with a principal, might find an undisclosed principal coming forward to sue on the contract.[109] Often this had no practical effect if the principal chose not to act. The agent might sue and be sued on the contract, although any recovery by the agent would be held for the principal. Later the doctrine was held to work the other way, so that the third party could sue the undisclosed principal.[110] There were situations where the undisclosed principal could not intervene, as where it was inconsistent with a written contract. That might be the case with a contract which contained an express term that the agent and third party were the only parties to the agreement.[111]

The doctrine of undisclosed principal was unsuited to the commodity markets where brokers often acted without identifying any principal or that they were dealing on their own account.[112] The concern of their counterparties was with those named in the transaction, not with who might be behind them. The approach of the House of Lords in *Isaac Cooke & Sons* v. *Eshelby*[113] was that it was common knowledge that brokers dealing on the Liverpool Cotton Exchange might be trading on their own account as well as for others. If a third party desired to deal with a broker as principal (thus having the right of set off), they should inquire whether that person was acting for an undisclosed principal.[114] That was commercially impractical when brokers desired to close their deals without fuss. Following the case the rules of the Liverpool Cotton Exchange were amended to limit the scope for undisclosed principals. Other markets followed suit.[115]

Judges gave commercial convenience as the rationale of the undisclosed principal doctrine.[116] It could favour both principal and agent.[117] In certain circumstances, if the principal's existence was to be disclosed at the time of a transaction, his interests might be adversely affected. For example, if it were

---

[109] e.g., *Fred Drughorn Ltd* v. *Rederiaktiebolaget Transatlantic* [1919] AC 203.
[110] e.g., *Teheran-Europe Co Ltd* v. *S T Belton (Tractors) Ltd* [1968] 2 QB 545 (Iranian importers able to sue British supplier for defective air compressors, although its English agent did not reveal the supplier's identity at time of contract).
[111] The rule in *Humble* v. *Hunter* (1848) 12 QB 310, 116 ER 885.
[112] See S. Stoljar, op. cit., 209, who cites two cases involving coffee brokers: *Waring* v. *Favenck* (1807) 1 Camp 85, 170 ER 886; *Kymer* v. *Suwercropp* (1837) 1 Camp 109, 170 ER 894.
[113] (1887) 12 App Cas 271. See 75 above.   [114] at 277.   [115] 76 above.
[116] e.g., *Keighley Maxsted & Co* v. *Durant* (t/a *Bryan Durant & Co*) [1901] AC 240, 261–262, per Lord Lindley. Lindley had a Chancery, not a commercial practice, but would have picked up much in Common Pleas and the Court of Appeal. See G. Jones & V. Jones, 'Lindley, Nathaniel, Baron Lindley (1828–1921)', *Oxford Dictionary of National Biography*. The case was part of a long running dispute: *In Re An Arbitration between Keighley, Maxsted & Co and Bryan Durant & Co* [1893] 1 QB 405.
[117] Tan Cheng-Han, 'Undisclosed Principals and Contract' (2004) 120 *LQR* 480, 482–485.

known that he was behind a commodity purchase, the price might escalate, or competitors might be able to gain an advantage. In practice the agent's name might carry more weight than that of the principal when goods were being bought or sold in foreign markets. Likewise, agents might prefer their principal not to know the third parties they were dealing with for fear of being bypassed. If also dealing for themselves, they might wish to switch between roles without third parties knowing what role they were playing in a transaction.

Armstrong v. *Stokes*[118] was illustrative of how the doctrine might apply. J. & O. Ryder & Co was a commission merchant in Manchester. It sometimes acted for itself as well as filling orders for others. Armstrong was another merchant in Manchester who had had previous dealings with the firm. In mid-June Ryder & Co placed an order for 200 pieces of grey, unbleached shirtings. A month later Armstrong sent the cloth but before it was paid Ryder & Co failed. When its books were examined, Armstrong learnt that the firm had ordered the cloth as a commission agent for Stokes & Co. Since Ryder & Co were not manufacturers, it was obvious that they bought in the shirtings from elsewhere, but Stokes & Co had never had contact with the suppliers or bleachers.[119] Armstrong's case was that, in the circumstances, it was entitled to demand payment from Stokes & Co as the undisclosed principal of Ryder & Co in the transaction. In giving the court's judgment, Blackburn J acknowledged the controversial nature of doctrine but said that any doubts about it came too late. If a vendor discovered that there was an undisclosed principal on the failure of the person with whom it believed itself to be contracting, it could take advantage of this 'unexpected godsend' and recover the price direct from the principal. However, in this case an exception applied: Stokes & Co had paid Ryder & Co at a time when Armstrong knew of no one else as principal.

In *Armstrong* v. *Stokes* Blackburn J's view was that in some cases there was an 'intolerable hardship' of double payment if a principal had already paid his agent, who had not in turn paid the third party but was now bankrupt or had disappeared.[120] To avoid this Blackburn had introduced the gloss that the doctrine did not apply if it caused such injustice. That was resisted, perhaps because of its uncertainty. A few years later, in *Irvine & Co.* v. *Watson & Sons*,[121] at the time of sale the sellers of palm oil knew the broker was buying not on his own account but for a principal, albeit unknown. Ignorant that the sellers had not been paid – the terms were cash on or before delivery – the buyers paid the broker. The Court of Appeal held that this did not preclude the sellers from suing them for the price when the broker became insolvent. The one qualification to this result was if the sellers had by their conduct

---

[118] (1872) LR 7 QB 598.
[119] The evidence was that Stokes & Co gave orders to Ryder & Co for white and grey shirtings. When as in this case white shirtings were ordered, Ryder & Co bought grey shirtings and had them bleached, charging the price it had bought from Armstrong, the cost of bleaching, one per cent on top, along with handling charges.
[120] at 610. [121] (1880) 5 QBD 414 (sale on terms of Liverpool General Brokers Association).

induced the buyers to believe that the broker had already paid them for the goods.[122] *Mitchell's Maritime Register* noted unsympathetically that the buyers in *Irvine & Co. v. Watson & Sons* 'are in the position of men – unfortunately a very common one – who have placed themselves in a false position from not understanding an elementary principle of commercial law. Payment to one man for account of another is no payment as regards the latter, unless payment is made with knowledge and consent.'[123]

To legal purists the doctrine of undisclosed principal was anomalous and unsound, although in commercial contracts there was nothing novel about the idea of a third party coming in to enforce a contract.[124] Commenting on *Cooke v. Eshelby*[125] in 1887, Sir Frederick Pollock launched a strong attack in an editorial note in the *Law Quarterly Review*, including the coup de grâce that law on undisclosed principal 'is inconsistent with the elementary doctrines of the law of contract'.[126] Despite a wealth of criticism, attempts to curb its reach proved abortive. The irony was that its critics often offered alternative theories to explain and save it.[127] That did not mean, as we have seen, that the doctrine was always consistent in its application or necessarily acceptable in the outcomes it produced.[128] But as a shortcut to liability in situations where it was merited, the English courts might use it to achieve a pragmatic result over that dictated by theory. This was not the only example of this approach.[129]

3 Reasonable Compliance with Principal's Instructions

One aspect of the duties of an agent was to obey the lawful instructions of their principal. But too rigid an application of this principle was commercially impractical when the state of communications across continents meant that agents might not be able to obtain a variation in their instructions when circumstances demanded a change. The courts helpfully held that reasonable behaviour on the part of an agent in this situation was all that was necessary.

---

[122] Bramwell and Brett LJJ distinguished *Armstrong* v. *Stokes* as turning upon the peculiar character of Ryder and Manchester commission merchants: 417, 420.
[123] 'Agents and Principals', *Mitchell's Maritime Register*, 25 June 1880, 813.
[124] *Pyrene Co. LD.* v. *Scindia Navigation Co Ltd* [1954] 2 QB 402, 422, per Devlin J, a leading commercial practitioner and judge: Tony Honoré, 'Devlin, Patrick Arthur, Baron Devlin (1905–1992)', *Oxford Dictionary of National Biography*. See P. Devlin, *Taken at the Flood*, East Harling, Taverner Publications, 1996, 156–160 on the beginning of his commercial practice.
[125] (1887) 12 App. Cas 271.
[126] (1887) 3 *LQR* 358, 359. See further (1896) 12 *LQR* 204; (1898) 14 *LQR* 2.
[127] S. Stoljar, The Law of Agency, *op cit*, 228. See J. Ames, 'Undisclosed Principal-His Rights and Liabilities' (1909) 18 *Yale LJ* 443; W. Lewis, 'The Liability of the Undisclosed Principal in Contract' (1909) 9 *Col LR* 116; F. Mechem, 'The Liability of an Undisclosed Principal' (1910) 23 *Harv LR* 513; W. Seavey, 'The Rationale of Agency' (1920) 29 *Yale LJ* 859; A. Goodhart & C. Hamson, 'Undisclosed Principals in Contract' (1932) 4 *CLJ* 320; W. Müller-Freienfels, 'The Undisclosed Principal' (1953) 16 *MLR* 308.
[128] F. Reynolds, 'Practical Problems of the Undisclosed Principal Doctrine' (1983) 36 *CLP* 119.
[129] e.g., 389–398 below.

Depending on the circumstances, substantial compliance with a principal's order was sufficient.

Ireland v. *Livingston*[130] was the leading case. A Liverpool principal wrote to Mauritius commission agents that they may ship 500 tons of sugar at 26s 9d to cover freight and insurance, adding that 50 tons more or less was of no moment if it enabled engagement of a suitable vessel. The instructions also included the principal's preference for sending the vessel to London, Liverpool or the Clyde. Five hundred tons of sugar could not be purchased in one lot in Mauritius, and it was the customary course of business there to purchase an amount of this size in smaller quantities from different suppliers. The agent was able to procure some 400 tons at the price, from different sources, and shipped the cargo in one vessel to Liverpool. The principal sought to avoid the transaction because prices had fallen. The Queen's Bench judgment held that it could not,[131] but was reversed in June 1870 by a divided Court of Exchequer Chamber.[132] The Exchequer Chamber was in turn reversed by the House of Lords in April 1872. It held that the Liverpool principal was bound to accept the cargo. In advising the House of Lords, Blackburn J referred with approval to Story's analysis, followed in *Johnston* v. *Kershaw*.[133] The judgment of Lord Chelmsford LC was short and to the point. The instruction to the Mauritian agent was patently ambiguous as demonstrated by the differences about what it meant among the judges hearing the case. In cases of ambiguous or uncertain instructions, if the agent acted reasonably and in good faith he was within his authority, even if what was done was not the course the principal intended.[134]

The rule enshrined in *Ireland* v. *Livingston* was commercially convenient at the time: an agent was not in breach of his principal's instructions in reasonably interpreting them in one of two plausible ways. As Lord Salmon explained much later, 'in 1872 there were no means by which an agent, at the other end of the world, receiving ambiguous instructions, could communicate with his principal in London to clear up any doubt about their meaning before carrying out his duty to act upon them promptly'.[135] The rule was applied in other

---

[130] (1872) LR 5 HL 395.
[131] (1866) LR 2 QB 99. It reasoned that the order was not a limitation of the quantity to be purchased but designed not to fetter the agent's discretion: per Cockburn CJ & Mellor and Shee JJ.
[132] (1870) LR 5 QB 516. It held that the order letter was unambiguously for a single cargo of 500 tons in a single ship.
[133] at 410–411. Blackburn's advice won high praise: K Llewellyn, 'The First Struggle to Unhorse Sales' (1939) 52 *HLR* 873, 904. In *Johnston* v. *Kershaw* (1867) LR 2 Ex 82 agents in Pernambuco, Brazil, bought and shipped 94 bales of Paraiba first cotton when their Liverpool principals had ordered 100 bales. There was a heavy fall in the price of cotton in Liverpool, and the Liverpool principal sought to avoid the deal. The court accepted the argument of Quain QC and Judah Benjamin, based on a passage in Story, that an agent could still be said to act within his authority when it was impossible to buy the exact amount the principal had ordered at the specified price.
[134] Lord Chelmsford LC was unimpressed with the merits of the principal's position: 416. Lords Westbury and Colonsay agreed: 417–418.
[135] *Woodhouse AC Israel Cocoa Ltd SA* v. *Nigerian Produce Marketing Co Ltd* [1972] AC 741, 772.

contexts as well, for example, when an ambiguous telegram was sent to the captain of a chartered ship.[136] Within a few decades of the decision in *Ireland* v. *Livingston*, all the continents were linked by overseas cable. Admittedly, this did not enable instantaneous communication, which might be necessary if instructions were to be clarified so action could be taken on a rapidly changing market.[137] With the advent of the telephone and telex, however, it became more feasible for an agent to seek clarification of ambiguous instructions before acting. Nonetheless, the principle in *Ireland* v. *Livingston* still held sway until after our period ended.[138]

4 The Factors Acts

Although generally adopting a pragmatic approach, in some cases the English courts were willing to go only so far. When it came to disputes between the rights of an owner of goods and the third parties to whom a factor (an agent with possession of goods) had wrongly sold or pledged them, preference tended to be given to the owner. That was expressed in the well-established *nemo dat* principle – that no third party could obtain a better title to goods than the person from whom they were obtained. Yet it was often impractical for merchants to satisfy themselves as to the ownership of goods before dealing with a factor, especially if the factor was sometimes dealing as agent, sometimes on his own account. At common law an agent could not readily pledge the goods of his principal for his own debts.[139] Yet that was a restraint on the expansion of credit, since banks and others making advances wanted protection when mistakenly taking as collateral a pledge of documents of title to goods (e.g., bills of lading, dock warrants) which the pledgor held as agent, not as owner.[140]

The matter came to a head in the early part of the nineteenth century. In 1817, in *Graham* v. *Dyster*,[141] the plaintiffs, merchants in Liverpool, had hides consigned to them from Brazil. They transmitted the bill of lading to their London brokers, Battye and Pilgrim, instructing them to sell the hides. As on previous occasions, they drew a bill of exchange on Battye and Pilgrim, who accepted it – and were therefore liable on it – in anticipation of being able to

---

[136] *Miles* v. *Haslehurst* (1906) 23 TLR 142. See also *Weigall & Co* v. *Runciman & Co* (1916) 85 LJ KB 1187. There was earlier authority to the same effect: *Boden* v. *French* (1851) 10 CB 886, 138 E.R. 351 (instruction for sale of coal at Neale's Wharf, Blackfriars, ambiguous as to whether it could be sold on customary two months' credit).

[137] 5, 11–12, 72, 127–128 above.

[138] *Midland Bank Ltd* v. *Seymour* [1955] 2 Lloyd's Rep 147. Limited to letters of credit by Lord Diplock in *Commercial Banking Co of Sydney Ltd* v. *Jalsard Pty Ltd* [1973] AC 279, 286 (PC, on appeal from New South Wales). The doctrine was finally challenged in *European Asian Bank AG* v. *Punjab & Sind Bank (No.2)* [1983] 1 WLR 642, 656, per Robert Goff LJ.

[139] 'The Factors Acts. The Existing Rules of Common Law' (1877) 63 *LT* 303. A leading case was *Paterson* v. *Tash* (1742) 2 Str 1178, 93 ER 1110.

[140] 405–409, 428, 461 below.   [141] (1817) 6 M & S 1, 105 ER 1143.

pay it on sale of the hides.[142] The brokers placed the hides in the hands of the defendant to sell and handed over the bill of lading, without informing him that the hides belonged to others. The defendant paid before the brokers paid on the bill of exchange. The brokers became insolvent. The court held that plaintiffs were entitled to recover the proceeds of sale from the defendant. The brokers had no authority to pledge the hides. Abbott J opined that the principle that a factor could not pledge goods was sacrosanct: it 'be much for the benefit of commerce to hold this principle sacred'.[143]

To the contrary the court's conclusion was out of touch with commercial opinion and contrary to commercial need. Parliament intervened. A committee of the House of Commons identified two issues: first, that a merchant making advances in the regular course of commerce to agents or factors, upon the security of merchandise, could lose out when ignorant that the agent or factor was not the owner; and, second, that a purchaser of merchandise from an agent or factor was liable to pay a second time, when ignorant that the agent or factor had no power in the particular circumstances to sell.[144] The committee found that the mercantile community was in favour of law reform to offer protection in both cases, as were almost all those representing traders abroad. To facilitate credit and foreign trade, the majority of the committee recommended legislation.[145] There was opposition from some legal members, especially Sir James Scarlett MP (later Lord Abinger, chief baron of the Exchequer).[146] Notwithstanding the opposition, in 1823 Parliament enacted the first of the Factors Acts, its preamble stating that mercantile men considered that the state of the law was conducive to fraud, produced frequent litigation and proved in its effects highly injurious to the interests of commerce. In broad terms the legislation protected those taking goods shipped in a factor's name as ostensible owner, where it was not obvious that he did not own them.[147] The 1823 Act was followed by further legislation in 1825 and 1842. The 1842 Act protected those like a bank advancing money to agents who pledged a document of title to goods in the ordinary course of business, which had been 'entrusted' to them, and which they seemed to have the authority to pledge.[148]

In 1923 Scrutton LJ described the history of the Factors Acts in the nineteenth century as being the 'restriction of their language by the Courts in favour of the true owner, followed by reversal of the Courts' decisions by the Legislature'.[149] An example of this restrictive interpretation concerned the

---

[142] On bills of exchange: 386 passim below.   [143] at 6, 1145 respectively.
[144] *Report from the Select Committee on the Law relating to Merchants, Agents or Factors etc,* House of Commons Papers, no 452, 13 June 1823. The committee received a memorandum on the law, including foreign law, from the solicitor, Mr James Freshfield: at 25–32.
[145] at 6.
[146] S. Thomas, 'The Origins of the Factors Acts 1823 and 1825' (2011) 32 *J Leg Hist* 151, 177–185.
[147] 4 Geo IV, c.83, s.1; H. Boyd & A. Pearson, *The Factors' Acts (1823 to 1877)*, London, Stevens & Sons, 1884, 27–29.
[148] 6 Geo IV, c 94, s.2; 5 & 6 Vict, c 39, s. 1. See S. Stoljar, The Law of Agency, *op cit*, 117–118.
[149] *Folkes v. King* [1923] 1 KB 282, 306.

concept in the legislation of an agent being 'entrusted' with goods or the documents of title to goods. The courts held that an agent obtaining a dock warrant on the back of having the bill of lading was not entrusted with the dock warrant.[150] The 1842 Act sought to remedy that. Similarly, the 1877 Act sought to remedy decisions at odds with commercial practice where the courts on an interpretation of 'entrustment' had held that the statutory protection did not extend to (i) a third party who did not know that the selling agent's authority had been revoked when the latter pledged dock warrants for Montilla wine; (ii) a bank, where a purchaser of tobacco in bond in the warehouses of the St. Katharine Dock Company left the dock warrants with the seller, who pledged them for an advance; and (iii) another bank, to which a Liverpool wool broker and warehouse keeper had pledged wool received by him from abroad for the plaintiffs in London, the plaintiffs as usual forwarding him the bills of lading so he could receive and store the wool until they gave him instructions to sell.[151]

Therefore legislation resulted from the unsatisfactory manner in which the courts interpreted the legislation. The culmination was the Factors Act 1889, a consolidating and amending measure. Its provisions were reflected in sections of the Sale of Goods Act 1893. The concept of a mercantile agent was substituted for that of the agent 'entrusted' with goods or documents of title to goods. In broad terms protection was given to a bona fide third party where, with the consent of the owner, a mercantile agent was in possession of goods or the documents of title to them, and sold, pledged or otherwise disposed of them. The mercantile agent had to act in the ordinary course of business as a mercantile agent, and the third party could not have notice of the agent's lack of authority at the time of the disposition.[152] The protection of the Factors Acts extended only when goods were in England and Wales. Similar legislation was enacted in other common-law jurisdictions.[153] The effect of the Factors Acts and its counterparts was to afford a wide protection to a third party like a bank dealing with a mercantile agent and making an advance to him on a pledge of a document of title.[154] We see the importance of this for commercial credit in Chapter 6.[155] By contrast with the nineteenth-century experience, courts in the twentieth century worked more

---

[150] *Phillips v. Huth* (1840) 6 M. & W 572, 151 ER 540; *Hatfield v. Phillips Court* (1845) 14 M & W 665, 153 ER 642.

[151] *Fuentes v. Montis* (1868) LR 3 CP 268; (1868) LR 4 CP 93; *Johnson v. Credit Lyonnais Company* (1877) 2 CPD 32; (1877) 3 CPD 32; *Cole v. North Western Bank* (1875) LR 10 CP 354; 40 & 41 Vic c 39. See A. Pearson-Gee, *The New Factors Act*, London, Wildy & Sons, 1890, 13–18; P. Blackwell, *Law relating to Factors*, London, Effingham Wilson, 1897, 92–103; W. Evans, 'Agency – Unauthorised Sales, Pledges, and Exchanges – The Factors Acts' (1877) 63 *LT* 390; N. Miller, 'Bills of Lading and Factors in Nineteenth Century English Overseas Trade' (1957) 24 *U Chi LR* 256, 283–289; *Oxford History of the Laws of England, vol.12, 1820-1914, Private Law*, Oxford, Oxford University Press, 2010, 1123, 1124 (M. Lobban).

[152] ss. 2(1), 25.

[153] e.g., D. Allen & J. Johnston, 'Mercantile Agents. A Comparison of English and New Zealand Statutes' (1937) 13*NZLJ* 20.

[154] 400 passim below.   [155] 388–390, 394 below.

readily with the grain of the legislation to protect third parties over owners when engaged in common commercial dealings.[156]

3.4 Agents as Principals

The Noble House [Struan & Co] and Brock & Sons had always bought teas and silks and spices on their own account. But being canny, the Struans and Brocks also carried cargo for others and acted not only as shippers but as brokers and bankers and commission agents, both inbound to England and outbound. Outbound they would carry cargo for others – cotton goods, cotton yarn and spirits. (James Clavell, *Tai-Pan A Novel of Hong Kong*, 1966)[157]

Where agents acted in a variety of capacities, as with Struan & Co and Brock & Sons in James Clavell's popular novel, we have seen that the courts might hold that in the circumstances of a specific case they were acting not as an agent in their dealings with a third party but on their own account as a principal. In this part of the chapter, we are concerned with how, in certain situations, English law forged rules so that an agent had liabilities in matters relating to the payment, quality and delivery of goods. That contrasted with how agents normally dropped out of the reckoning once a transaction had been negotiated. A consequent advantage to the principal or the third party if a case fell into one of these categories was that, if a transaction turned sour, the dispute could be localised in the jurisdiction convenient to the complainant. Although that did not solve completely which system of law was to be applied to a dispute,[158] it did mean that the problems associated with suing a party in courts elsewhere in the world were mitigated.[159] None of this affected the relationship and the liabilities as between principal and agent: the agent continued to owe duties of loyalty to the principal, and the principal had to perform its obligations to the agent, especially to pay commission.

As a matter of law the agent's liability in such cases had various justifications.[160] Trade usage (custom) was one. In Chapters 1 and 2 we saw that on various

---

[156] Much of the case law the Acts generated in the twentieth century concerned individuals dealing wrongfully with motor vehicles: *Folkes v. King* [1923] 1 KB 282; *Heap v. Motorists' Advisory Agency Ltd* [1923] I KB 577; *Staffs Motor Guarantee Ltd v. British Wagon Company* [1934] 2 K.B. 305; *Pearson v. Rose & Young Ltd* [1951] 1 KB 275.

[157] London, Hodder & Stoughton, 1966.

[158] Spanish law was considered but not applied where the plaintiffs, merchants in Cuba, shipped a cargo of tobacco to the defendants, undisclosed London merchants, through shipping agents in Havana, later insolvent: *Mildred, Goyeneche & Co v. Maspons Y Hermano* (1883) 8 App Cas 874; (1882) 9 QBD 530.

[159] In *FW Green & Co Ltd v. Brown & Gracie Ltd* [1960] 1 Lloyd's Rep 289 (HL), Australian 'mercantile agents' in Melbourne (respondents) purchased food in Australia for Scottish importers (appellants) and were paid commission. '[T]hough in a sense the respondents were intermediaries, they were, in law, principals as between themselves and the appellants', at 292, per Viscount Simonds.

[160] See F. Reynolds & B. Davenport (eds.), *Bowsted on Agency*, 13th ed., op cit, 248–253; C. Schmitthoff, *Agency in International Trade: A Study in Comparative Law*, Leiden, Sijthoff, 1970, 151–153.

markets brokers were personally liable to those with whom they dealt, whether acting for themselves or others, initially as the custom and later as a result of specific rules of a market.[161] Contract was another basis for the agent's liability, in the case of the confirming agent considered shortly, a collateral contract.[162] Exceptionally, the agent's liability might be based in statute, as with the broker's responsibility to the insurer for premiums payable under a policy of marine insurance.[163] In none of the three categories of case examined here – the commission agent, the del credere agent and the confirming agent – was the position completely clear, either as a matter of law or practice.

1 Commission Agents and Foreign Principals

(i) The Commission Agent

A common practice in the nineteenth century was for a British-based business to export-import through commission agents resident in a foreign jurisdiction or for trading houses abroad to employ an agent in Britain to buy and sell.[164] The commission agent or trading house might have a partner or representative in Britain. The courts recognised that the commission agent may be acting as a principal. For example, in obtaining manufactured goods from a British exporter for an Indian principal, it would stand as principal vis-à-vis the exporter, and there would be no privity of contract between its principal and the exporter.[165] Vis-à-vis its principal, however, the commission agent remained an agent and was required to act with due care, diligence and loyalty in fulfilling the tasks entrusted to it. One rationale of an agent–third party contract, instead of a principal–third party contract, was given by Blackburn J in *Armstrong* v. *Stokes*,[166] the obvious inconvenience of privity of contract, he said, 'between a Liverpool merchant and the grower of every bale of cotton which is forwarded to him in consequence of his order given to a commission merchant at New Orleans'.[167] The court was justified in treating it as a matter of law, he added, that in the absence of evidence of express authority to that effect, the commission agent could not pledge his foreign principal's credit.

Blackburn J applied this approach the following year, when giving the judgment of the Queen's Bench Division in *Hutton* v. *Bulloch*.[168] There, in a typical arrangement, Halliday Fox & Co, merchants in London, had a partner (by then deceased), Halliday, carrying on business in Rangoon (Yangon) in the firm Halliday Bulloch & Co. The firms were distinct and Bulloch in Rangoon, the defendant, was not a partner in the London firm. Four parcels of goods

---

[161] 73–74 above.
[162] e.g., *Sobell Industries Ltd* v. *Cory Bros & Co Ltd* [1955] 2 Lloyd's Rep 82. See also *Perishables Transport Co* v. *Spyropoulos (N) (London) Ltd* [1964] 2 Lloyd's Rep 379 (air freight).
[163] Marine Insurance Act 1906, s. 54(1).
[164] R. Munday, 'A Legal History of the Factor' *op cit*, 233.
[165] *Ireland* v. *Livingston* (1872) LR 5 HL 395, 408, per Blackburn J.   [166] (1872) LR 7 QB 598.
[167] at 605.   [168] (1873) LR 8 QB 331.

(manufactured by yet someone else) were supplied by the plaintiffs, and by arrangement between the plaintiffs and Halliday Fox & Co sent on joint account to Rangoon. The plaintiffs had no knowledge of Bulloch or that the Rangoon firm was in any way interested in the transaction until after the goods were supplied and Halliday Fox & Co failed. The court held that the plaintiffs could not sue Bulloch for the price. The Rangoon firm had not given authority to the London firm to establish privity of contract and pledge its credit with the English suppliers of the goods, the plaintiffs. The Exchequer Chamber upheld Blackburn J's analysis.[169] Then in *Robinson v. Mollett*,[170] an important case about organised markets, Blackburn J reiterated these points, justifying them as a matter of principle. The analysis, he added, in no way interfered with the existence of a fiduciary relation, or the consequent obligation of the agent not to put his own interest in conflict with that of his principal.[171]

A body of law grew up around the nineteenth-century commission agent. It was not straightforward. A considerable effort was spent in distinguishing commission agents from factors.[172] There was also a difficulty since Blackburn J in *Armstrong v. Stokes*[173] had labelled the commission agent's position as a 'matter of law'. It was later regarded as a matter of custom and not applicable if, under the contract, the foreign principal was directly liable to the third party with whom the agent dealt.[174] Additional remarks by Blackburn J in *Ireland v. Livingston* – suggesting the effect of the transaction between a commission merchant and its principal was of a contract of sale passing property in the goods from the one to the other, so that the commission merchant had the right of stoppage in transit[175] – also gave rise to temporary difficulty until *Cassaboglou v. Gibb*[176] quashed the notion of a vendor–purchaser relationship.

(ii) Doctrine of Foreign Principal

Closely associated with these rules about commission agents was the doctrine of foreign principal. This was the presumption that where a foreign principal employed an agent, the agent assumed personal responsibility and could not create privity of contract between the principal and any third party (or, as it

---

[169] (1874) LR 9 QB 572. [170] (1875) LR 7 HL 802. see 78–79 above. [171] at 810.
[172] R. Munday, 'A Legal History of the Factor', *op cit*, 233–234. [173] (1872) LR 7 QB 598.
[174] *Miller Gibb & Co v. Smith & Tyrer Ltd* [1917] 2 KB 141. [175] (1872) LR 5 HL 395, 409.
[176] (1883) LR 11 QBD 797. The case involved Gibb, Livingston & Co, a commission agent in Hong Kong, obtaining opium for English buyers. On the firm and T. A. Gibb & Co in London: S. Jones, Two Centuries of Overseas Trading, *op cit*, 17–18, 184–187; C. Crisswell, *The Taipans: Hong Kong's Merchant Princes*, Oxford, Oxford University Press, 1981, 103, 191. The firm was involved in the China trade (e.g., importing textiles, opium for a time; exporting tea); was agent for many businesses – shipping, insurance (e.g., Lloyd's agent in Shanghai); for a while had its own tea clippers and steamships; and in the early twentieth century branched into engineering and manufacturing. It incorporated in 1920. As well as in opium dens, opium was widely used in nineteenth-century medicines such as laudanum, a popular painkiller before aspirin: see V. Berridge, 'Victorian Opium Eating: Responses to Opiate Use in Nineteenth-Century England' (1978) 21 *Victorian Stud* 438. Berridge also explains its importation and sale through brokers.

was sometimes expressed, to pledge the principal's credit). The doctrine was established before our period.[177] It was applied in a number of nineteenth-century cases. Thus, in 1873 it was the basis for holding that the 'sole agent' in London of an Austrian manufacturer was liable to the buyer for non-delivery.[178] To Bramwell B in 1874 the rationale of the foreign principal doctrine was largely that given in *Armstrong* v. *Stokes*: given the distance, it was 'eminently improbable' that the Rangoon merchant in the case before him should have authorised the London merchant to pledge his credit so as to make him a party to contracts with the British supplier.[179] A year earlier Blackburn J had been blunter: the British manufacturer 'does not trust the foreigner, and so does not make the foreigner responsible to him, and does not make himself responsible to the foreigner'.[180] That was a case where the court held that the German buyer could not sue the British manufacturer for late delivery of some of the sets of railway wheels and axles ordered, since its contract was with its London agent who arranged the deal. However, it was false logic to assume that under the foreign principal doctrine the overseas buyer should be deprived of its ordinary rights to sue the manufacturer just because the manufacturer could hold the agent liable in the other direction.

(iii) Doctrine Faces Commercial Reality

Commercial realities were reducing the risks for the British importer, manufacturer and supplier. By the turn of the twentieth century there were further improvements in communications and transport. As well there were organisational changes – import merchants buying on their own account; manufacturers' export agents providing facilities in a foreign country for one or more manufacturer; overseas 'agents', usually acting as principals and often holding stock; the establishment of import and export departments in British enterprises which bought and sold direct; and the growth of confirming agents, confirmed credits and government-backed export guarantees.[181]

Judges began to reflect the new realities. Although the learning surrounding commission agents and foreign principals remained, in practice they found that on the facts it did not apply. That was justified on the basis that the words of the contract or the dealings between the parties indicated that the agent was an ordinary agent and had the authority to establish privity of contract

---

[177] S. Stoljar, The Law of Agency, *op cit*, 238; R. Munday, 'A Legal History of the Factor', *op cit*, 237–238.
[178] *Dramburg* v. *Pollitzer* (1873) LT 470 ('a well established rule', at 471, per Bovill CJ).
[179] *Hutton* v. *Bulloch* (1874) LR 9 QB 572, 573 (thus the British supplier could not sue the Rangoon merchant when the London merchant failed).
[180] *Die Elbinger Actien-Gesellschaft* v. *Claye* (1873) LR 8 QB 313, 317.
[181] S. Chapman, *Merchant Enterprise in Britain*, Cambridge, Cambridge University Press 1992, 195, 198, 201–202, 229, 232; P. Payne, *British Commercial Institutions*, 4th ed., London, Harrap 1964, 78–85. See also R. Steffen & F. Danziger, 'The Rebirth of the Commercial Factor' (1936) 36 *Colum LR* 745, 745–746; W. Hillyer, 'Four Centuries of Factoring' (1939) 53 *Q J Econ* 305, 310.

between, say, the principal and the English supplier.[182] Similarly, the Indian judges found the presumption of foreign principal in section 230(1) of the Indian Contract Act to be rebutted if the contract was made in the name of the foreign principal, not that of the agent.[183] By July 1917 Scrutton LJ was expressing the view that one could not attach the same importance as forty or fifty years previously to the fact that the principal was a foreigner.[184]

A few months earlier Bray J had observed that trade had changed greatly since Blackburn J had stated the liability of commission agents: British firms made contracts with foreign firms directly and British agents were loath to make themselves personally responsible for their foreign principals.[185] In New Zealand, one of the great Commonwealth judges, Salmond J, held that an agent would only be liable to an English manufacturer if it bought goods and onsold them to the New Zealand importer, or if the agent's engagement provided that he was to contract with, and assume liability to, the English manufacturer.[186] In the books, however, the doctrine of foreign principal limped on, despite judicial disapproval,[187] until finally killed off in England in 1968.[188] It was a different era, the judges said, and overseas business was not conducted as it was a century previously. Foreign buyers might open a banker's commercial credit so that goods were paid for as they were shipped, and exporters could gain cover through an export guarantee.[189]

2 Del Credere Agents

A seller's agent might undertake to guarantee their principal that the buyers with whom it dealt on behalf of the principal would pay for the goods. The agent was known as a del credere agent, a term derived from the Italian. As

---

[182] e.g., Glover v. Langford (1892) 8 TLR 628. See W. Evan, *The Law of Principal and Agent*, London, William Maxwell & Son, 1878, 446–448; H. Fegan, 'Foreign Principals' (1932) 80 *U Penn LR* 858, 867; C. Picciotto, 'Rights of Agents Acting for Foreign Principals' (1920) 4 *Minn LR* 244, 245.
[183] *Tutika Basavaraju, v. Parry & Co* (1903) 27 M 315; *Arunachalam Chettiar vs Kasi Nevenda Pillai* (1914) 24 Ind Cas 1007. And see post-Independence: *V.R. Mohanakrishnan v. Chimanlal Desai & Co*, AIR 1960 Mad 452.
[184] *HO Brandt & Co v. HN Morris & Co* [1917] 2 KB 784, 797.
[185] *Miller Gibb & Co v. Smith & Tyrer Ltd* [1917] 2 KB 141, 162.
[186] *Bolus & Co Ltd v. Inglis* [1924] NZLR 164, 174–175 per Salmond J. (Salmond J was New Zealand's outstanding jurist: A. Frame, 'Salmond, John William', *Dictionary of New Zealand Biography*, 1996.) See also *Downie Bros v. Henry Oakley L Sons* [1923] NZLR 743.
[187] *Holt & Moseley (London) v. Sir Charles Cunningham and Partners (1949)* (1949) 83 Ll L Rep 141 (no presumption that home agents contracted personally when acting for foreign principal); *Anglo African Shipping Co of New York Inc v. J Mortner Ltd* [1962] 1 Lloyd's Rep 610, 621, per Diplock LJ (on Diplock: R. Stevens, *Law and Politics: The House of Lords as a Judicial Body 1800–1976*, London, Weidenfeld & Nicolson, 1979, 562–567.) cf. *Maritime Stores v. HP Marshall & Co* [1963] 1 Lloyd's Rep 602 (not too much weight to be attached to fact of foreign principal). See also A. Hudson, 'Agency-Foreign Principal' (1957) 35 *Can Bar R* 336; A. Hudson, 'Agent for Foreign Principals' (1966) 29 *MLR* 353.
[188] *Teheran-Europe Co Ltd v. ST Belton (Tractors) Ltd (No1)* [1968] 2 QB 545.
[189] at 553, 559 and 563.

Mellish LJ put it in 1871, a del credere agent 'guarantees that those persons to whom he sells shall perform the contracts which he makes with them'.[190] One reason that an agent might take on this additional liability was if it knew more about third-party buyers than its principal, and was thus in a position to undertake responsibility for their contractual performance. The del credere agent usually charged an additional commission, the so-called commission del credere, to cover its potential liability.[191] As with other agents, there was no reason for the del credere agent to reveal the identity of its principal to a buyer.

Del credere commissions operated in the London corn (and linen) market from at least the late eighteenth century.[192] In 1796 the House of Lords held that a London corn trader, instructed to sell wheat on del credere terms, was liable to his unpaid principal.[193] There were then some doctrinal wobbles.[194] By the beginning of our period, however, the law on the subject was broadly clear: agents taking a del credere commission were guarantors, and they could only be sued by their principals when the buyers failed (through insolvency) to pay.[195] As agents of the seller, the implication for del credere agents was that they could not be sued by a buyer for their principal's failures and that they did not deal with their principal, the seller, as principals themselves – although as we shall see both these points were subject to challenge. As regards the guarantee point, the del credere agent was different from the confirming agent, whose undertaking (the confirmation) to the seller gave rise to a primary liability.[196]

Del credere terms featured in *Couturier v. Hastie*,[197] the leading case in nineteenth-century sales law on goods which had perished at the time of sale.[198] There merchants at Smyrna (İzmir) shipped a cargo of Indian corn from Salonica (Thessaloniki), arranging for the defendant merchant to sell it on the London market, which he did. Meanwhile the ship had been caught in a storm, and the cargo had become heated and fermented. The ship put into Tunis Bay and the master disposed of the cargo. The buyer refused to accept the shipping documents or to pay. He later became bankrupt. The Smyrna

---

[190] *Ex parte White. In re Nevill* (1871) LR 6 Ch App 397, 403.
[191] e.g., S. Chapman, Merchant Enterprise in Britain, op cit, 65.
[192] Matthew Bacon, *A New Abridgement of the Law*, 5th ed (by Henry Gwillim), London, A Strahan, 1789, vol. IV, 602.
[193] *Mackenzie and Lindsay v. Scott* (1796) VI Brown 280, 2 ER 1081.
[194] See R. T. S. Chorley, 'Del Credere' (1929) 45LQR 221, 223–224.
[195] W. Paley, *A Treatise on the Law of Principal and Agent*, 3rd ed. by J. Lloyd, London, Saunders & Benning, 1833, 111–114; J. Chitty, *A Practical Treatise on the Law of Contracts*, 2nd ed., London, S. Sweet, 1834, 171; J. Chitty, *The Practice of the Law in all its Principal Departments*, 3rd ed., London, S. Sweet, 1837, vol. I, 83; J. Storey, op cit, para. 33. cf. Chitty's earlier view: *A Treatise on the Laws of Commerce and Manufactures and the Contracts relating thereto*, London, H. Butterworth, 1824, vol. III, 83, 194, 202–203, 211.
[196] The case was the basis of Sale of Goods Act 1893, section 6: i.e., a contract for the sale of specific goods is void where without the knowledge of the seller they have perished at the time when the contract is made.
[197] (1856) 5 HL Cas 673, 10 ER 1065; (1853) 9 Ex Rep 102, 156 ER 43.
[198] HH Judge Chalmers, *The Sale of Goods Act 1893*, 2nd ed. revised, London, William Clowes & Sons, 1894, 17.

sellers sued the defendant merchant on his del credere commission.[199] In construing the contract, the Exchequer Chamber and the House of Lords held that the buyer was not liable to pay because, at the time of sale, there was nothing to be sold. Since a precondition to the defendant's liability on his del credere commission was the buyer's liability, the sellers' action failed.

It appears that del credere commissions continued to be used in the London grain and cattle feed markets well into the nineteenth century.[200] However, a spectacular failure of a buyer, and subsequently its agent, in the cattle-food market led to the abandonment of the practice in both this and the grain trade market.[201] Del credere commissions existed in trades other than grain. They were an established feature in importing timber, where London merchants sold on del credere terms for Scandinavian and Russian dealers.[202] There is an 1853 case where a Halifax manufacturer arranged for a Liverpool merchant to sell its products on del credere terms through the merchant's foreign houses at Lima and Valparaiso,[203] and an 1870 decision where a London tobacco broker sold on del credere terms for a large importer of cigars.[204] It does Antony Gibbs & Sons no credit that mid-century it was charging the Peruvian government del credere commission on the sales of guano (seabird excrement) that it arranged. It was long after the commission was merited, since the demand for the fertiliser was so high that buyers paid cash for purchases.[205]

By the end of the nineteenth century, it seems that del credere commission had had its day in the sun. Prepared on the eve of the First World War, but published in 1916, *The Exporter's Handbook and Glossary*[206] noted that the del credere system was for markets where British manufacturers had to entrust sales to merchants who were not financially strong enough to purchase outright themselves, but who nevertheless had the requisite knowledge of export markets and sufficient capital to assume the responsibility of guaranteeing payment by buyers. The handbook asserted that the system was necessary only in markets where credit conditions were doubtful, and orders could not be

---

[199] Evidence at trial was of a 3½ percent commission: *Couturier v. Hastie* (1852) 9 Ex Rep 40, 155 ER 1250, at 45, 1253. The Exchequer Court held that the del credere undertaking was not to pay the debt of another within section 4 of the Statute of Frauds, so did not require writing.

[200] A. Pulling, *A Practical Treatise on the Laws, Customs, Usages and Regulations of the City and Port of London*, London, Stevens & Norton, 1842, 470–471; *Tamvaco v. Lucas* (1861) 1 B & S 185, 121 ER 683, aff'd (1862) 3 B & S 89, 122 ER 34 (wheat shipped from Taganrog, Russia, sold in London). cf. *New Zealand and Australian Land Company v. Watson* (1881) 7 QBD 374 (New Zealand wheat sold by London brokers not on del credere terms).

[201] D. Hill, 'The Impact of Trade Usage on Commercial Agency at Common Law', in *New Directions in International Trade Law*, Dobbs Ferry, New York, Oceana, 1977, vol. II, 533. Details are sketchy. Professor Hill did much work on the commodity markets just before their demise.

[202] See *Hoare v. Dresser* (1859) 7 HL Cas 290; 11 E.R. 116.

[203] *Graham v. Ackroyd* (1853) 10 Hare 192, 68 ER 894.

[204] *Bramwell v. Spiller* (1870) 21 LT 672.

[205] W. Mathew, 'Antony Gibbs & Sons, the Guano Trade and the Peruvian Government, 1842–1861', in D Platt (ed.), *Business Imperialism 1840–1930*, Oxford, Clarendon, 1977, 369.

[206] F. Dudeney, *The Exporter's Handbook and Glossary*, London, Pitman, 64–65.

confirmed by a reputable finance house. Drawing on his experience at the bar and as a judge in the Commercial Court, Bray J observed in 1917 that the conditions of trade had changed, so that British firms and companies were more ready to make contracts directly with those abroad. Further, he said, British agents were loath to make themselves personally responsible to their foreign principals so that anything in the shape of a del credere commission was rare.[207] By the late 1920s, Professor Chorley opined that apart from the timber trade, del credere commissions no longer appeared to be in very general use, replaced for British exporters by the confirmation system.[208]

The exceptional case of the del credere agent in the timber trade survived well into the twentieth century. It gave rise to two leading cases.[209] Both involved Churchill & Sim, established in 1813 and specialising in timber imports from its early days. Until the Second World War, Churchill & Sim sold imported timber through auctions. (In the mid-nineteenth century these were conducted on conditions that the commission was a shilling a lot and that the timber was sold 'without any allowance for Faults or Defects'.[210]) The first of these cases, *T. Thomas Gabriel & Sons v. Churchill & Sim*,[211] was decided on the very eve of the First World War. Churchill & Sim had sold for the plaintiff timber merchants about 380 loads of blackbutt scantlings to Millar's Karri and Jarrah Company Ltd, CIF London, but the loads were late. The Court of Appeal held that Churchill & Sim was not liable to the plaintiff on its del credere commission, since that did not cover the buyer's refusal to pay for non-performance, only its failure to pay through insolvency or similar reason. Then in 1937, in the second leading case on del credere agency involving Churchill & Sim, the Court of Appeal confirmed in *obiter* remarks that the liability of del credere agents should not be extended to contractual performance.[212]

If it did not cover non-performance, how far did the liability of the del credere agent extend? It was a matter which concerned Wallace Brothers – the London arm of a trading firm with wide interests in India and elsewhere[213] – because of its business in exporting teak from Burma (Myanmar). Wallace Brothers paid close attention to del credere agency

---

[207] *Miller, Gibb & Co. v. Smith & Tyrer Ltd* [1917] 2 KB 141, 162.
[208] 'Del Credere', *op cit*, 223. Chorley subsequently opined, on the basis of an unreported case decided in Manchester in 1923, *Dukinfield Mill Co Ltd v. Shorrock*, that they still appeared usual in the Lancashire yarn trade: (1930) 46 *LQR* 11.
[209] *Thomas Gabriel & Sons v. Churchill & Sim* [1914] 3 KB 1272; *Churchill & Sim v. Goddard* [1937] 1 KB 92.
[210] A. Muir, *Churchill and Sim, 1813–1963: A Short History*, London, N. Neame, nd but c.1963, 39, 63, 77. See also D. Platt with R. Michie & A. Latham, *Decline and Recovery in Britain's Overseas Trade 1873–1914*, London, Macmillan, 1993, 39.
[211] [1914] 1 KB 449.
[212] *Churchill & Sim v. Goddard* [1937] 1 KB 92. There buyers had rejected Finnish timber, rightly as it turned out in an arbitration: see *Goddard v. Raahe O/Y Osakeyhtio* (1935) 53 Ll L Rep 208.
[213] 182–183 below.

law from the 1920s.[214] In 1934 it sought advice from Johnson Jeeks & Colclough, City of London solicitors, when Italian buyers of their teak had difficulty obtaining sterling to pay them. The brokers Foy Morgan & Co had charged Wallace Bros a del credere commission on the sale, but claimed to be under no liability for the resulting inconvenience.[215] The solicitors replied by return that the brokers were liable to pay, once payment was due, even if the difficulty was attributable to foreign government exchange control, but that no interest was due for late payment without the court ordering it.[216] Wallace Bros decided on the generous course. It informed Foy Morgan & Co that although they could sue, they would not pursue the matter for the time being, only to be met by the brokers' assertion that the custom in the timber trade was that del credere commission did not cover this problem.[217]

In the immediate post–Second World War years, del credere agency was still acknowledged as a possibility where an exporter was not sufficiently in touch with an overseas market to judge the financial soundness of a buyer.[218] Del credere commissions continued in the timber trade. The justification was that when timber was sold in Britain, the sellers and buyers were separated by thousands of miles, and most sellers needed the assistance of an agent in Britain to import and market it, coupled with an assurance of payment.[219] In other areas confirmations and guarantees took over. There was also a wider utilisation of credit insurance through the Exports Credits Guarantee Department of the Board of Trade[220] and of confirmed letters of credit. Under these a bank on the instructions of a buyer undertook to pay the seller on its presentation of the appropriate shipping documents.[221] These techniques provided alternative avenues to ensuring that sellers were paid. By the 1970s del credere commissions did not rate a mention in a standard work for bankers on trade financing,[222] although they seemed to survive to an extent with imported timber.[223]

---

[214] LMA, CLC/B/207/MS40132, Wallace Brothers, Correspondence relating to brokers' liability, particularly with regard to 'del credere' terms under which a broker guarantees the solvency of a buyer of goods, 'Del credere agency'. In October 1919 the solicitors Coward & Hawksley, Sons & Chance asked the firm to give expert evidence before the registrar in Admiralty about del credere commission. As late as 1954 there is an internal note about what the firm understood del credere commission to mean (dated 14 October 1954).

[215] LMA, CLC/B/207/MS40132, Wallace Brothers, ibid., letter 9 November 1934.

[216] Ibid., letter 9 November 1934.   [217] Ibid., letters 12 November 1934, 13 November 1934.

[218] C. Schmitthoff, *The Export Trade A Manual of Law and Practice*, London, Stevens, 1948, 90.

[219] J. Leigh, *The Timber Trade*, 2nd ed., Oxford, Pergamon, 1980, 14–15.

[220] e.g., Overseas Trade (Credits and Insurance) Act, 1920; Trade Facilities Act, 1921; Export Guarantees Act 1937; Export Guarantees Act 1939; Overseas Trade Guarantees Act 1939; Export Guarantees Act 1945. see D. Aldcroft, 'The Early History and Development of Export Credit Insurance in Great Britain, 1919–1939' (1962) 30 *The Manchester School* 69.

[221] 391 passim below.

[222] A. Watson, *Finance of International Trade*, London, Institute of Bankers, 1976.

[223] *Bank Negara Indonesia 1946 v. Taylor* [1995] CLC 255.

3 Confirming Agents/Confirming Houses

By the eve of the First World War British firms, variously described as confirming agents, confirming houses or import-export agents, furnished services to a foreign buyer. (The term 'confirming agent' will be used here.) As its agent, confirming agents guaranteed ('confirmed') that a British exporter would be paid, usually on presentation of its invoice and the shipping documents. Bankers' letters of credits did that, but the confirming agent also guaranteed the exporter more widely, for example against the buyer's non-acceptance of the goods. In performing services for the foreign buyer, the confirming agent remained its agent.[224] Although it was slow coming, legal analysis, such as it was, saw the confirming agent's liability to the exporter as based on a separate contract between the two.

The system of confirming overseas orders was recognised in *The Exporter's Handbook and Glossary*, prepared in 1914.[225] It seems that around this time the practice was used with the sale abroad of British motor cars and motor cycles, and with the export of piece goods (fabrics in standard widths and lengths) to India and elsewhere in the British Empire.[226] The practice continued in the interwar years. Those studying the syllabus of the Institute of Export, established in 1935, were informed of keen competition between 'export commission houses' in guaranteeing overseas sales. The overseas buyer, the student was told, paid for the service by a commission, a percentage value of the merchandise shipped. Confirming agents also performed multifarious duties for a manufacturer in the execution of its overseas principal's orders – shipping, insurance, the preparation of invoices, banking 'and, by no means of least importance, the acceptance of credit risks'.[227]

In the post–Second World War period, the London confirming agent continued, often as part of a larger organisation.[228] Some confirming agents employed agents abroad to solicit prospective buyers, whose orders they would then confirm.[229] In *James Shaffer v. Findlay Durham & Brodie*[230] the confirming agent undertook to obtain orders in continental Europe for the plaintiff manufacturer's products (e.g., taps, bibcocks). As well as confirming purchases from British manufacturers, London confirming agents might confirm purchases by

---

[224] *Scott v. Geoghegan & Sons Pty Ltd* (1969) 43 ALJR 243, 245 (a customs prosecution in the High Court of Australia).

[225] op cit.

[226] R. Church, 'Markets and Marketing in the British Motor Industry Before 1914' (1982) 3 *J Trans Hist* 1, 9; Chorley, 'Del Credere', *op cit.*, 223.

[227] G. T. MacEwan, *Overseas Trade and Export Practice*, London, Macdonald and Evans, 1938, 152. The book was written to cover the syllabus of the Institute by its vice-chairman.

[228] e.g., B. Rosenbloom & T. Andras, 'Wholesalers as Global Marketers' (2008)15 *J Marketing Channels* 235, 240; N. Alexander, 'British Overseas Retailing, 1900–60: International Firm Characteristics, Market Selections and Entry Modes' (2011) 53 *Business History* 530, 543.

[229] In *J. M. Wotherspoon & Co Ltd v. Henry Agency House* (1962) 28 MLJ 86, J. M. Wotherspoon had engaged the defendant to do this, the latter's commission apparently being paid by the suppliers.

[230] [1953] 1 WLR 106. The issue was whether they had done sufficient to fulfil their contractual obligation to obtain orders: see 281 below.

Commonwealth buyers of goods sourced from manufacturers elsewhere in Europe.[231] The confirming agent had a foothold in New York.[232] London confirming agents might also give confirmations to a foreign supplier of those importing into Britain, as well as providing finance to the importers' customers.[233] In the early 1960s, a textbook endorsed by the editor-in-chief of *Financial News* stated that a significant part of the British export trade passed through the hands of confirming agents, particularly from medium-sized manufacturers.[234] Confirming agents might self-insure (perhaps easier if part of a larger organisation), but in some cases they protected themselves through the government's export credit guarantee arrangements.[235]

Even in the late 1960s and early 1970s it was unclear from the written standard form contracts whether commission agents were accepting a wider liability than that the beneficiary of the confirmation (the British exporter) would be paid. In practice, whatever interpretation could be placed on the contracts, commission agents undertook liability when, without justification, their foreign principals cancelled an order.[236] In the absence of a special contractual provision, however, they did not undertake liability for the quality of the goods supplied. Their responsibility in that regard was limited to the exercise of reasonable care in sourcing the goods. In some cases, buyers might have a buying agent, additional to the confirming agent, with responsibilities for doing that.[237]

It was not until the mid-1950s that there was any legal analysis of what confirming agents were doing. One suggestion was that they were like a bank confirming a letter of credit and thereby guaranteeing payment to the seller if the proper documents were tendered.[238] As a matter of legal theory, the commission agent's undertaking to the exporter could have had legal force in two ways. First, the confirming agent could itself be the buyer of the goods, selling them on to the overseas buyer; second, it could make itself independently responsible to the exporter for payment, while remaining an agent vis-à-vis the overseas buyer, its principal. The first was

---

[231] e.g., *Stunzi Sons Ltd* v. *House of Youth Pty Ltd* [1960] SR (NSW) 220 (Hawkes & Co of London confirming order by Australian purchaser of women's dresses from a Swiss manufacturer); the *Wotherspoon case* (1962) 28 *MLJ* 86 (plaintiff confirming agent in London confirming sale of Dutch confectionary to buyer in Kuala Lumpur).

[232] *Anglo African Shipping Co of New York Inc* v. *J. Mortner Ltd* [1962] 1 Lloyd's Rep 610 (NY confirming agent confirming purchase of vinyl sheeting from US manufacturer).

[233] e.g., *Tellrite Ltd* v. *London Confirmers Ltd* [1962] 1 Lloyd's Rep 236.

[234] P. Payne, *British Commercial Institutions*, 4th ed., London, Harrap 1964, 80, 194.

[235] Ibid., 334–335.

[236] D. Hill, 'Confirming Agent Transactions in Commonwealth Countries' (1972) 3 *J Maritime L & Commerce* 307, 330.

[237] e.g., *J. S. Robertson (Aust.) Pty. Ltd.* v. *Martin* (1956) 94 CLR 30 (Australian importer had subsidiary in London to buy, the London confirming agent being limited to providing financial confirmation of purchase orders and arranging shipping etc.).

[238] C. Schmitthoff, 'Conflict Avoidance in Practice and Theory' (1956) 21 *Law and Contemporary Problems* 429, 448–449; C. Schmitthoff, 'Confirmation in Export Transactions' [1957] *JBL* 17.

straightforward, since, as a buyer, the confirming agent would assume primarily liability to the exporter. In the early 1960s it was said that commission agents bought from exporters, shipping the goods under their own invoice.[239] But this may have involved a misunderstanding by a non-lawyer of the legal character of the relationship. The function of a confirming agent was not to buy and sell goods, unless there was a specific reason for doing so. One such reason was where exchange control regulations in the foreign buyer's country prevented it from paying commission to the confirming agent, so that the latter's remuneration for providing financial confirmation derived from reselling goods to the buyer at a higher price than what it paid the exporter.

The second legal basis of the confirming agent's liability was that, while it remained an agent vis-à-vis of the overseas buyer, its undertaking to the British manufacturer was under an independent contract. That analysis required some legal creativity. The first part of the relationship was straightforward: the confirming agent as part of its obligations to its principal, the buyer, would undertake that the exporter was paid. But what was the legal character of the confirming agent's unilateral undertaking vis-à-vis the manufacturer? In the 1950s the judges simply assumed that the confirming agent was liable on its promise. In *Rusholme & Bolton & Roberts Hadfield Ltd v. S. G. Read & Co. (London) Ltd.*[240] Pearce J asserted that Manchester manufactures of shirting material could claim damages against the London confirming agent when Australian buyers cancelled their order prior to delivery, owing to import restrictions and a trade recession in Australia. In *Sobell Industries Ltd v. Cory Bros & Co*[241] *Ltd* McNair J held that the confirming agent was liable on the basis that it had guaranteed payment by the Turkish importer, who had withdrawn its order for radio sets. He did not address the point about how the unilateral undertaking was binding under the doctrines of English law.

Later there was academic criticism of the courts' legal analysis of the functions confirming agents performed, the confusion in terminology, and even of the judges' understanding of the commercial operations entailed.[242] Whatever the deficiencies, the court's recognition of the binding nature of a confirming agent's undertaking accorded with commercial need. The legal basis of the undertaking was never properly tested before commercial practice moved on and the system was overtaken by other forms of export finance such as bankers' confirmed credits and export guarantees.[243] This is yet one more example of commercial practice ploughing ahead irrespective of supporting legal analysis. While the system was in vogue, confirming agents regarded their undertakings to pay in accordance with a confirmation as binding, they paid without demur and that was enough.

---

[239] P. Payne, *op cit.*   [240] [1955] 1 WLR 146.   [241] [1955] 2 Lloyd's Rep 82.
[242] e.g., D. Hill, 'The Impact of Trade Usage on Commercial Agency at Common Law', in *New Directions in International Trade Law*, Dobbs Ferry, N.Y., Oceana, 1977, vol. II, 534–539.
[243] 161 above.

3.5 Varieties of Agent

The journey took the best part of a month, since the ship stopped at a number of islands in the Malay Archipelago ... sometimes for an hour of two, sometimes for a day, to take on or discharge cargo. It was a charming, monotonous and diverting trip. When we dropped anchor, the agent come out in his launch. (W. Somerset Maugham, *The Four Dutchman*, 1928).[244]

The nineteenth-century law books on agency generally presented their analysis along abstract legal lines. Perhaps it is not surprising that the best discussion of the different categories of agent appeared in a text published in India: the agent in the sub-continent had an obvious institutional presence in the form of the trading (agency) houses, and agency law there had to grapple with a range of practical issues including those associated with the activities of local agents such as the banyan.[245] Generally speaking, the particular features of agency law relating to specialist agents like Somerset Maugham's shipping agent were found in the treatises on the relevant subject areas such as shipping and insurance, or specialist texts on institutions such as the stock market or banking.[246]

As we have seen, the one business organisation might perform multiple functions including acting as agents. The stock and station agents in Australia such as Dalgety & Co, Elder Smith & Co and Goldsbrough Mort & Co performed a range of services for farmers. They were their agents in consigning wool for sale, but with time diversified their services to offer finance, marketing (such as acting as auctioneers), information (e.g., on market prices) and advice. For the farmer, acting through the single intermediary of a stock and station agent not only reduced transaction costs but also increased the likelihood of receiving 'free' services such as technical and business advice.[247] In the discussion of Jardine Matheson in this part, and in part 3.6 of the chapter, we consider further the multi-functional trading firms of India and Hong Kong: as well as acting on their own account, they might be shipping, insurance and banking agents, as well as managing agents for plantations, mines and factories.[248]

---

[244] W. Somerset Maugham, 'The Four Dutchmen', in *More Far Eastern Tales*, London, Vintage, 2000 (1928).

[245] e.g., T. Pearson, *The Law of Agency in British India*, Calcutta, W H Allen & Co, 1890, 8–17.

[246] E. Macgillivray, *Insurance Law relating to All Risks other than Marine*, London, Sweet & Maxwell, 1912, 343–344, 355–358, 349–350; T. Carver, *The Law relating to Carriage by Sea*, London, Stevens & Sons, 1885, 51–52, 132–137.

[247] S. Ville, *The Rural Entrepreneurs A History of The Stock and Station Agent Industry in Australia and New Zealand*, Cambridge, Cambridge University Press, 2000, 20, 73; R. Hartwell, *The Dalgety and New Zealand Loan Company*, unpublished manuscript, Ch. 9. See *Goldsbrough Mort & Co Ltd v. Maurice* [1937] HCA 71; (1937) 58 CLR 773 (report contains terms of contract for its wool-broking services); *Gray v. Dalgety & Co Ltd* [1916] HCA 35; (1916) 21 CLR 509 (financial services).

[248] e. g., the many agencies of Gillanders, Arbuthnot & Co in Rangoon (Yangon): *Venice Steam Navigation Co Ltd v. Ispahani* (1930) 36 Ll. L. Rep. 135, 137 (PC, on appeal from the High Court at Fort William (Kolkata)).

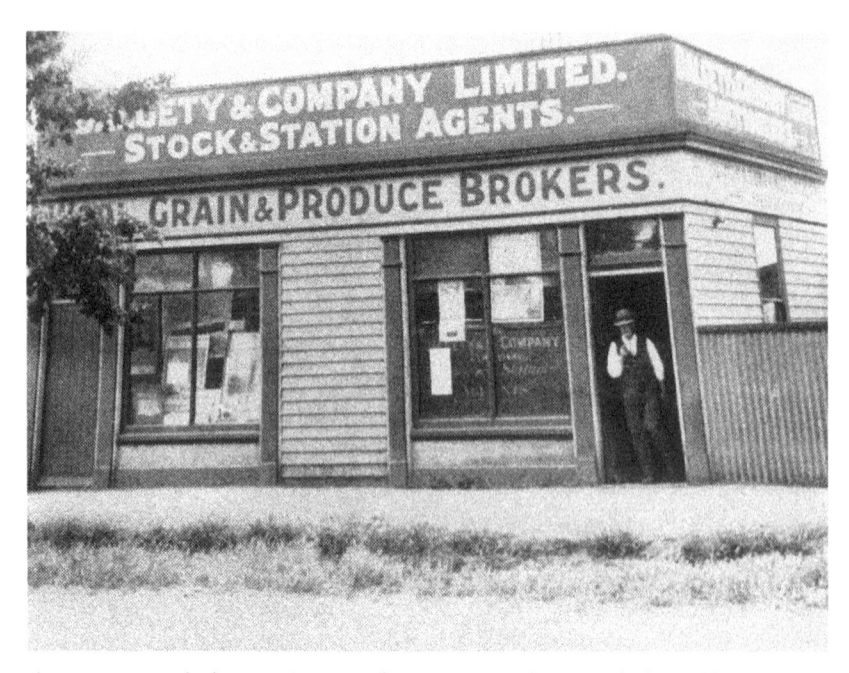

Figure 3.1 Agents, brokers, auctioneers: Dalgety & Co., Australia, c.1930 (Dalgety plc)

Commercial accounts of agency often featured buying and selling agents and how they went about their business. Buying and selling agents might be appointed for their expertise in a line of business. Henry R Merton & Co Ltd was one. It was a leading metal trader in London; a major supplier to British industry; involved in forming the London Metal Exchange; and, together with its associate company Metallgesellschaft AG, in control of the American Metal Company in the United States.[249] Who better for Great Cobar Ltd to list as its selling agent, and to impress the market, when in 1906 the company was being promoted to exploit mines working copper, silver and gold in Cobar, western New South Wales?[250] Under its contract with Great Cobar, Henry R Merton & Co was to act for fifteen years as its sole selling agent, for the whole world, undertaking that at all times it would use its best endeavours to promote the sale of its minerals, on the best terms obtainable, at prices not less than those for the time being which Great Cobar fixed.[251]

---

[249] S. Becker, 'The German Metal Traders before 1914', in G. Jones (ed.), *The Multinational Traders*, London, Routledge, 1998, 70–72; M. Wilkins, *The History of Foreign investment in the United States, 1914–1945*, Cambridge, MA, Harvard University Press, 2004, 18; R. Gibson-Jarvie, *The London Metal Exchange*, Cambridge, Woodhead-Faulkner, 1976, 76.

[250] G. Blainey, *The Rush That Never Ended: A History of Australian Mining*, 3rd ed., Carlton, Melbourne University Press, 1978, 134–135, 271, 284–285.

[251] *In Re Great Cobar Ltd* [1915] 1 Ch 682. The company being in receivership the court ordered that the receiver and manager might disregard the agreement.

What follows are some examples of the range of agents encountered in our period and of the law's bearing on their activities.

1 Brokers and their Services: Czarnikow and CSR

The broker featured in the last chapter, which focused on his role on organised markets.[252] The general brokers in commodities of the eighteenth century became the specialised brokers of the nineteenth.[253] The essential feature was that rather than trading as principals and profiting from the difference, if any, between a buying and selling price, the broker traded on behalf of buyers and sellers, taking no financial risk, but earning a commission on the transaction. Presumptive legal rules grew up around the broker's activities: the broker could not sell in his own name; payment to him was not good discharge; he avowedly acted for a principal, even if unnamed; and so on.[254] In fact, little if anything of this held for brokers dealing on organised markets, since their usages, practices or rules could and often did provide the opposite.[255] Brokers dealt in their own names, often for themselves; clients continued to deal with their brokers (and paid them) and not with the other side; and brokers made themselves liable in addition to, if not lieu of, their principals. All this was, of course, according to contract.[256]

When *Hollins v. Fowler* was in the Exchequer Chamber,[257] as prominent a commercial lawyer as Brett J (later Lord Esher MR) could opine that the 'mercantile characteristics' and legal duties of a broker was that he was an agent who was, properly speaking, 'a mere negotiator between the other parties'.[258] Whether Brett J's limited view represented the law, it certainly did not reflect the 'mercantile characteristics' of brokers. First, brokers ignored the legal niceties and not infrequently labelled themselves as both brokers and

---

[252] 71 passim above.
[253] G. Rees, R. Craig & D. Jones, Britain's Commodity Markets, London, *op cit*, 46–49.
[254] e. g., *Baring* v. *Corrie* (1818) 2 B & Ald 137; 106 ER 317; *Linck Moeller & Co* v. *Jameson & Co* (1885) 2 TLR 206; *Armstrong* v. *Stokes* (1872) LR 7 QB 598, 610, per Blackburn J.
[255] On usages and practices: e.g., *Cropper* v. *Cook* (1868) LR 3 CP 194 (sale of 1200 bags of Donskoi (Russian) wool, to arrive *per Stamboul*; usage in Liverpool wool trade for broker to make himself personally responsible for price); *Hollins* v. *Fowler* (1875) LR 7 HL 757 (sale of 13 bales of American cotton per *Minnesota*; practice of broker making himself liable; to be treated as principal); *Fleet* v. *Murton* (1871) L.R. 7 QB 126 (sale by fruit brokers of raisins to arrive from Trieste; custom in fruit and colonial market that brokers personally liable); *Irvine & Co* v. *Watson & Sons* (1880) 5 QBD 414 (payment to broker for oil might, by custom and usage, be good discharge). cf. *Southwell* v. *Bowditch* (1876) 1 CRD 374 (sale note for 5 tons of anthracene was clear; thus no custom or usage effective to make broker personally liable); *Flatau Dick & Co* v. *Keeping* (1931) 39 Ll L Rep 42 (in the circumstances buyer not responsible in Baltic hardwood trade to broker for price). On market rules: 76 above.
[256] e.g., *Gadd* v. *Houghton* (1876) 1 Ex D 357 (fruit brokers in Liverpool; sold note showed intention that foreign principals, not brokers, were to be liable).
[257] (1872) LR 7 QB 616.
[258] at 623. The 'negotiator' language was picked up by legal commentators: e.g., W. Evans, 'Agency-Some Preliminary Questions' (1878) 64 *LT* 186.

agents, a fact recorded in a number of cases in the law reports.[259] As such they were indicating that they were prepared to go beyond the function of mere negotiator and the limited duties Brett J identified. Second, as we have seen, brokers might deal on their own behalf – nowadays known as proprietary trading – for purposes of both trade and speculation. We have seen that proprietary trading could cause difficulty when it was unclear in which capacity brokers were acting. Further, in engaging in 'mere negotiation', brokers might bring buyers and sellers together in a variety of different ways. There was no law that transactions had to be channelled through brokers and no one else, although in the interwar period attempts were made to enforce this as the practice for the grain trade on the Baltic Exchange. That was to thwart the large millers and food manufacturers, who were increasingly buying directly.[260]

Third, brokers might provide services to their clients such as extending credit to them on transactions. In other words, the approach of brokers to valued principals was not simply to act as the 'mere negotiator' in a series of isolated transactions. Clients were to be cultivated. As well as financial accommodation, brokers offered information about the state of world markets as regards the commodities in which a principal instructed them to deal. Bulletins were produced from the end of the eighteenth century and evolved in the nineteenth century with increasingly detailed and specialised information such as the state of supply and demand at London auctions.[261] The client newsletter was born.

An illustration of the extended services brokers could provide to clients was the relationship between the London sugar broker Czarnikow & Co and the Colonial Sugar Refinery Ltd in Australia. Czarnikow, describing itself as 'colonial brokers', was by the end of the nineteenth century London's leading sugar broker, with offices in Liverpool, Glasgow and New York. Until his death in 1909, the firm's founder, Caesar Czarnikow, was the dominant force in the firm. On the eve of the First World War the firm's capital exceeded that of most of the merchant banks.[262] In the 1930s Czarnikow & Co was probably the

---

[259] e.g., *Brookman v. Rothschild* (1829) 3 Sim 153, 195, 57 ER 957, 973 ('brokers and agents' in foreign securities); *Gregson v. Ruck* (1843) 4 QB 737, 736, 114 ER 1075, 1076 (colonial merchants selling East India rums through 'agents and brokers'); *Laming v. Cooke* 175 ER 602, (1858) 1 F & F 9 (sale of St Petersburg tallow through 'brokers and agents'); *Mitsui v. Mumford* [1915] 2 KB 27 (Japanese company in London carrying on timber business at Antwerp through 'brokers and agents' there); *Mehmet Dogan Bey v. G. G. Abdeni & Co Ld* [1951] 2 KB 405 (freight under charterparty to be paid to owner's 'brokers and agents' in London).

[260] LMA, CLC/B/103/MS23, 172/9, LCTA, Minutes of executive committee, 15 December 1936, 312. see H. Barty-King, *The Baltic Exchange*, London, Hutchinson Benham, 1977, 330–333; G. Rees, R. Craig & D. Jones, *Britain's Commodity Markets*, op cit, 155.

[261] M. Aldous, 'Rehabilitating the Intermediary: Brokers and Auctioneers in the Nineteenth-century Anglo-Indian trade' (2017) 59 *Business History* 525, 536, 539–540.

[262] H. Janes & H. Sayers *The Story of Czarnikow*, London, Harley Publishing, 1963, 80, 107; S. Chapman, Merchant Enterprise in Britain, *op cit*, 78, 210; P. Chalmin, *The Making of a Sugar Giant : Tate and Lyle, 1859–1989*, London, Harwood Academic, 1990, 19, 110; J. Orbell, '(Julius) Caesar Czarnikow (1838–1909)', *Oxford Dictionary of National Biography*. Czarnikow was instrumental in the formation of the London Produce Clearing House.

world's largest sugar broker.[263] As for the Colonial Sugar Refinery Company (CSR), it was formed on 1 January 1855 and expanded rapidly in the later part of the nineteenth and early twentieth centuries. It had sugar mills in Australia and Fiji, and interests in sugar refineries in Australia and New Zealand.[264] As a company it loomed large in the South Pacific. In some circles its dominance was a cause of political resentment. It supplied the Australian domestic market, but it also imported and exported raw sugar. In dealings with buyers in Britain, Canada, Indian, Ceylon, South Africa and elsewhere, CSR mainly used Czarnikow as its broker.[265] As would be expected, Czarnikow charged CSR commission on the transactions it arranged.[266]

The relationship between the two parties appears relatively uneventful. Legal disputes between the two did not even appear on the horizon. Czarnikow would negotiate on price and to which port sugar was to be shipped. It would introduce CSR to new buyers and sellers.[267] It would attempt to reach an accommodation when parties dealing with CSR wanted to change the contractual terms relating to matters such as shipping and insurance.[268] On occasion it advised CSR to adopt an unpalatable course, for example to agree to the repurchase of sugars ('your interests are best served by this').[269] CSR would not necessarily agree with the price Czarnikow suggested for a transaction and might cable its refusal.[270] In 1912 Czarnikow chose to remind CSR that if CSR bid less than the price it had accepted, Czarnikow could not guarantee that it would obtain the sugar, and 'you would, I presume, not hold me responsible'.[271] Sometimes Czarnikow felt the need to apologise that the price negotiated was not what CSR wanted.[272] On the whole it seems that CSR was content to leave the price of its deals to Czarnikow.[273]

That did not mean that from time to time there were no upsets. For example, in 1905 CSR visited buyers of its refined sugar in Ceylon (Sri Lanka) and a few months later dealt with another firm, Blyth Greene Jourdain & Co Ltd, over

---

[263] P. Chalmin, *Traders and Merchants: Panorama of International Commodity Trading*, 2nd ed., New York, Harwood Academic Publishers, 1987, 23.

[264] Initially an unlimited partnership, it incorporated in New South Wales in 1887: see C. Turnbull, 'Widening the Field', in A. Lowndes, *South Pacific Enterprise*, Sydney, Angus & Robertson, 1956; B. Richardson, *Sugar: Refined Power in a Global Regime*, Basingstoke, Hampshire, Palgrave Macmillan, 2009, 59.

[265] J. Dixon, 'Sugar Marketing Operations', in A. Lowndes (ed.), ibid., 153. CSR had other agents in London, notably Parbury Henty & Co.

[266] There are examples in NBAC, CSR Ltd, HO and Dep Correspondence, 142/2299, Czarnikow to CSR, September 1909-June 1911.

[267] e.g., ibid., 142/2230, letter Czarnikow to CSR, 8 March 1912.

[268] e.g., ibid., 142/2299, letter Czarnikow to CSR, 31 December 1909.

[269] Ibid., 142/2299, letter Czarnikow to CSR, 17 March 1911.

[270] Ibid., 442/2579, pp. 37, 42, 60, cables CSR to Czarnikow, 18 & 21 May 1912, 6 June 2012.

[271] Ibid., 142/2300, letter Czarnikow to CSR, 26 January 1912.

[272] Ibid., 142/2301, letter Czarnikow to CSR, 24 December 1914. It explained that it had consulted Parbury Henty & Co.

[273] Ibid., 142/2578, p. 429, letter CSR to Czarnikow, 6 March 1912.

Mauritian sugar.[274] Caesar Czarnikow took umbrage and insisted that business should be through him: '[I]t is impossible for your representative [visiting Ceylon] to know what passes between buyers and myself, or between them and their London house here. Confusion may arise when business matters are discussed.' CSR stood its ground and continued to deal with Blyth Greene Jourdain & Co Ltd as regards Mauritius.[275] In July 2012 Czarnikow made clear that it accepted no responsibility for any loss of quality of sugar during the voyage: that was a matter for the buyer and seller.[276] One aspect of quality is the polarisation value of raw sugar, its sucrose content. It seems that as a matter of course CSR paid buyers' agents for excess polarisation of the sugar it had shipped.[277]

In June 1904 Czarnikow sent CSR pro forma contracts for futures dealings. There was some variation in detail between the contracts: thus the contracts for raw sugar provided for a quality floor (expressed in terms of polarisation for a minimum amount of the cargo on arrival, in some cases the matter to be determined by an authorised chemist). Disputes were to be settled by arbitration in London.[278] Over time, these pro forma contracts had to be modified, for example to take into account the law in particular jurisdictions and market developments.[279] A war clause had been inserted in contracts some time before the outbreak of the First World War, defining liability in event of war.[280] A hallmark of the contracts was simplicity. As an example, contract number 1468 of 1905 stated that it was a sale for CSR's account to Ralli Bros of 50 tons 1A Australian granulated, at 16/3 per hundredweight, C & F Calcutta, for shipment within a fortnight, to be packed in double bags containing 70 pounds net, with payment in 3 months by confirmed credit,[281] marine insurance from shore to shore to be effected by the buyers, and brokerage to be ½ per cent. Disputes arising out of the contract were 'to be settled by Arbitration of London brokers in the usual manner, and this submission may be made a rule of the High Court'.[282]

For CSR, Czarnikow was more than a broker buying and selling on its behalf. It was a crucial source of information and advice. Czarnikow was renowned for collecting and distributing information about world sugar markets. CSR received its printed reports, *Weekly Price Current*, later known as the

---

[274] Ibid., 142/2296, letters Czarnikow to CSR, 4 July 1905; 20 October 1905.
[275] Ibid., 142/2579, p. 260, letter CSR to Czarnikow, 22 October 1912 (see also p. 251).
[276] Ibid., 142/2300, letter Czarnikow to CSR, 5 July 1912.
[277] e.g., ibid., 442/2579, p. 74, cable CSR to Erdman & Sielcken, 19 June 1912.
[278] Ibid., 142/2296, the pro forma contracts dated 10 June 1904.
[279] e.g., ibid., 142/2300, 142/2305, 142/2305, letters Czarnikow to CSR, 12 March 1915, 9 April 1919, 27 September 1920 respectively.
[280] Ibid., 142/2300, letter Czarnikow to CSR, 7 August 1914; 103 above.
[281] In a letter of 20 April 1905 Czarnikow explained Ralli Bros' standing, if CSR were not aware of it, and that Ralli never gave bank credits: ibid., 142/2296. On Ralli Bros: *History and Activities of the Ralli Trading Group Commodity Merchants for 160 years*, London, Bowater, 1979.
[282] Ibid., 142/2296, dated 20 April, 1905.

Czarnikow Sugar Review. But there was more to it than that. CSR received regular letters from Czarnikow, commenting on the demand and price for sugars around the world, containing information on specific events and markets.[283] Czarnikow offered advice and commentary, for example, on the samples of sugars CSR had sent it, concerning the negotiability of draft bills of exchange drawn on particular London banks, and regarding customs regulations in destination countries. Information on time-sensitive matters was sent by cable, in code, so that it remained confidential. Czarnikow sent CSR samples of sugars produced elsewhere in the world for the purpose of comparison. Although CSR reciprocated by providing information to Czarnikow on the situation in Australia and the Pacific region, it was evident that CSR regarded the much greater flow of information in its direction as invaluable, 'as it is only on rare occasions that the cables from our London agents contain information of this nature'.[284] However powerful CSR might have been in the South Pacific region, it was no wonder that it did not want to imperil its relationship with Czarnikow, let alone have any upset or quibble degenerate into a legal dispute.

2 Chameleon Brokers and Agents: Lewis & Peat

In the real world the successful agent did not fit the neat categories of the legal treatise; it followed new lines of business and took on new forms as profit dictated. A case in point is Lewis & Peat, a firm based in the City of London and Singapore. The firm traced itself back to 1775, when Robert Lewis began trading spices in the City. When he entered into partnership with William Peat in 1846, the firm was established as brokers in Mincing Lane, arranging the auctioning of a wide variety of commodities from the Far East. By the 1880s it was engaged in the forward trading of commodities. Before the First World War rubber had become the largest and most profitable part of its business, but it still dealt in other commodities such as spices.[285] It was said, at its demise in 2000, to be the largest rubber trading house in the world.

In its earliest appearance in the law reports, the firm was described as 'brokers', as indeed it was.[286] The case dates from the 1880s.[287] Kaltenbach and Fisher & Co, a firm in Singapore, consigned produce for sale in London to Charles Meyer, a merchant and commission agent. Meyer engaged Lewis & Peat as brokers not only to sell the consignments but also for speculative transactions on his own account. In relation to a consignment of pepper, which formed the agency aspect of the case, Meyer had pledged the shipping

---

[283] e.g., 'It may seem strange to you, but ... the British Workman does not eat the cheapest [sugar] ...': ibid., 142/2299, letter Czarnikow to CSR, 23 December 1909.
[284] Ibid., 142/2578, p. 225, letter CSR to Czarnikow, 29 August 1911.
[285] A. Mason, *Two Centuries of Lewis & Peat*, London, Lewis & Peat, 1975, 8, 16, 21–23, 29.
[286] R. Michie, 'The City of London and International Trade 1850–1914', in D. Platt (ed.), *Decline and Recovery in Britain's Overseas Trade 1873–1914*, London, Macmillan, 1993, 39.
[287] *Kaltenbach Fischer & Co v. Lewis & Peat* (1883) 24 Ch D 54; (1885) 10 App Cas 617.

documents to Lewis & Peat, which then made an advance to him in anticipation of the expected sale. Lewis & Peat sold the pepper on six months' credit. Before the buyers had taken delivery or paid, Meyer died insolvent, heavily indebted to both Kaltenbach and Lewis & Peat. At that point, Lewis & Peat learnt of Kaltenbach's interest. Reversing the Court of Appeal on this aspect of the claim, the House of Lords upheld Kaltenbach's claim to the surplus proceeds on the sale of the pepper, after deducting Lewis & Peat's advance to Meyer. Lewis & Peat, it said, did not have a lien or set off for the whole of Meyer's indebtedness to it. The result was justified on the basis first that Kaltenbach and Lewis & Peat had been brought into privity of contract by Meyer's agency, so Kaltenbach was the seller and Lewis & Peat their agent; second, Kaltenbach still had property in the pepper and its proceeds; and, third, as a result of section 7 of the Factors Act 1842, Kaltenbach as the true owner of goods could recover from Lewis & Peat as pledgee the balance of the proceeds of sale after satisfying any lien.[288]

By 1909 Lewis & Peat's turnover was some £6 million, mainly in rubber.[289] In the 1920s it was the largest produce broker in the City of London.[290] In that capacity it appeared in several cases, arising from arbitrations, as seller of pepper in one case[291] and copra cake in another.[292] It had established a branch in Singapore in 1918. That became the most profitable part of the business.[293] It became selling agents there for rubber estates and had other rubber consigned to it for sale. In that role it arranged for the collection, storage and shipment of the rubber. In the 1920s and 1930s it entered agreements with the Borneo Company Ltd to perform these tasks on behalf of that company.[294] (It seems it may have done this by informal arrangement prior to the written terms.) The agreements provided for the payment by Lewis & Peat of godown (warehouse) charges, for the Borneo Company to insure against fire, for shipping arrangements (if the Borneo Company should undertake this) and for the selection and sampling of the rubber should this be required. Under the agreements, the Borneo Company undertook to make advances of up to $50,000 to the estates which supplied the rubber. Lewis & Peat agreed to indemnity the company for any losses incurred in this financing. As regards

---

[288] See A. Goodhart & C. Hamson, 'Undisclosed Principals in Contract' (1932) 4 *CLJ* 320, 333–334.
[289] R. Michie, 'The City of London and International Trade 1850–1914', *op cit*.
[290] P. Chalmin, Traders and Merchants: Panorama of International Commodity Trading, op cit, 23.
[291] *In re Arbitration between Lewis & Peat Ltd and Catz Amercian Co (Inc) (Nos 1 & 2)* (1926) 26 Ll L Rep. 263; (1927) 28 Ll L Rep. 51.
[292] *Pinnock Brothers v. Lewis and Peat Ltd* [1923] 1 KB 690. In *WE Marshall & Co v. Lewis & Peat (Rubber)* [1963] 1 Lloyd's Rep 562 it was selling rubber through brokers.
[293] A. Mason, Two Centuries of Lewis & Peat, *op cit*, 38.
[294] LMA, CLC/B/123/MS 27232A/16, Borneo Company Ltd, Agreements 24 March 1921; 10 September 1924; 10 April 1931.

the Borneo Company's own rubber, Lewis & Peat guaranteed the solvency of any buyer to whom it was sold.

The 1931 agreement was more detailed than previous agreements, covering more eventualities. It is likely that the previous agreements were drafted by the parties themselves, but the 1931 agreement was drafted by the Singapore law firm Drew & Napier, which no doubt explains its enhanced form.[295] One thing it did was to formalise the payment mechanism: the Borneo Company had to invoice and collect payment for the rubber in accordance with the rules of the Singapore Chamber of Commerce Rubber Association, although it remained responsible for payment unless it took steps to notify Lewis & Peat if a buyer did not pay promptly. The 1931 agreement was also the first to provide a governing law clause, the law of the Straights Settlements (Singapore). In 1931 it was also agreed that the Borneo Company should auction rubber on behalf of Lewis & Peat, the auctions being conducted under the auspices of the Singapore Chamber of Commerce.[296] In July 1939, Lewis & Peat wrote to the Borneo Company reminding it that it was essential when doing this that the Lewis & Peat name should appear on sale statements and auction samples since, with its larger clients, it was assuming the risk.[297] That must have been under special arrangements with them. After the independence of Malaysia and Singapore in the 1960s, Lewis & Peat continued as leading commodity brokers until its demise some two decades later.[298]

3 Multifunctional Agents: Jardine Matheson

Jardine Matheson & Co was formed in 1832 in Canton (Guangzhou), became a large Hong Kong trading house and remains an important conglomerate based in Hong Kong. It is said to be the model for Struan & Co, the trading house at the centre of James Clavell's novel *Tai-Pan*, quoted at the outset of part 3.4 of this chapter. Initially involved in the import/export trade with China, including until the late 1860s/early 1870s the importation of opium from India, it expanded its activities before the First World War to encompass shipping, manufacturing (e.g., cotton mills) and construction (e.g., Chinese railways). Its activities spread geographically to Japan and elsewhere in Asia.[299] Its affairs in

---

[295] There is a brief history of the firm, *The History of Drew & Napier 1889–1989*, Singapore, Drew & Napier Ltd, 1989.
[296] LMA, CLC/B/123/MS 27232A/21, Borneo Company Ltd, Agreement 10 April 1931.
[297] Ibid., letter July 1939.
[298] N. White, *British Business and Post-Colonial Malaysia 1957–70: Neo-Colonialism or Disengagement?* New York, Routledge Curzon, 2004, 141.
[299] see e.g., R. Grace, *Opium and Empire: The Lives and Careers of William Jardine and James Matheson*, Montreal, McGill-Queen's University Press, 2014; M. Keswick, *The Thistle and the Jade: A Celebration of 175 years of Jardine Matheson*, London, Octopus, 1982; R. Blake, *Jardine Matheson: Traders of the Far East*, London, Weidenfeld & Nicolson, 1999; W. Cheong, *Mandarins and Merchants: Jardine Matheson & Co, A China Agency of the Early Nineteenth Century*, London, Curzon Press, 1979; E. Le Fevour, *Western Enterprise in Late Ch'ing China;*

Britain were in the hands of the Scottish house Matheson & Co, which had extensive investments in Asia.[300] Jardine Skinner & Co conducted business from Calcutta (Kolkata). Jardine Matheson & Co and Jardine Skinner & Co acquired Matheson & Co just before the First World War.

In the course of its trading, service and other activities, Jardine Matheson & Co acted as agent in various ways, notably as selling agents, manufacturers' agents, and shipping and insurance agents. As selling agents, the trend over time was away from commission sales. Jardine Matheson became the distributor in the region, on an exclusive basis, of a range of mass-produced goods. By the 1930s, its selling agencies included Seagram's rye whisky, White Horse whisky, Fry's chocolate, Sharps toffee, Pears soap, Remington typewriters and Nobel's explosives.[301]

Typical legal questions arose in the conduct of Jardine Matheson's agencies. Advice was sought from a variety of legal sources. Thus in the early days, the Advocate General of Bengal advised[302] that, with qualifications, Jardine Matheson could set off claims on the bankruptcy of a London firm: Jardine Matheson had not only purchased and shipped silk to it from China but also sold goods in China which the London firm had consigned to it.[303] In 1851, a barrister in Bombay (Mumbai), John Howard, was asked to advise after 1,100 chests of opium en route from Calcutta to China on the P&O steamer *Erin* were damaged in a collision at sea and sold in Singapore. The underwriters disputed liability, asserting that whoever had authorised their sale in Singapore – the master or P&O's Singapore agent – had no authority to do so. Ignoring any liability of P&O's agent, Mr Howard opined that the master had been wrong to authorise the sale.[304] In 1879 Jardine Matheson sought an opinion as to whether the lien (security) over coal being delivered to a buyer in Nagasaki would be lost if the coal was transhipped to shore by an agent in its principal's vessels, at the principal's expense. No, was the opinion of Montague Smith, a lawyer in Hong Kong, so long as the agreement made clear that the coal was being handed over for that limited purpose. However, he advised, there was a risk that the lien could be lost as against third-party purchasers for value, since the coal would be in the apparent control of the principal.[305]

Questions of agency law also arose when Jardine Matheson dealt with third parties where there were doubts as to their authority to act. Thus, in 1884 it

---

A Selective Survey of Jardine, Matheson and Company's Operations, 1842–1895, Cambridge, MA, East Asian Research Center, Harvard University, 1968.

[300] S. Chapman, Merchant Enterprise in Britain, *op cit*, 237–239
[301] G. Jones, Merchants to Multinationals, *op cit.*, 246.
[302] Until well into the twentieth century law officers could, in addition to their official duties, take private clients: see J. Edwards, *The Law Officers of the Crown*, London, Sweet & Maxwell, 1964, 71–79.
[303] CUL, Jardine Matheson Archive, Legal Opinions, JM/F15/3, 1 December 1834 (a slight twist was because at some point the London firm had established a 50/50 business in Guangzhou).
[304] Ibid., JM/ F15/8, 30 September 1851. He cited *Freeman v. The East India Company* (1822) 5 B & Ald 617, 106 ER 1316.
[305] Ibid., JM/F15/1, Opinion, 20 June 1879 (the opinion seems wrongly catalogued as 1829).

sought advice as to whether Wong Yat Sun could convey legal title to a ship. He was on the register as its owner, but his title derived from a bill of sale given by a Chinese company, and there was a risk, albeit small, that the company' partners might attempt to upset the deal.[306] The most extraordinary case of this nature occurred in 1900 when, after their comprador introduced a Hong Kong broker, Jardine Matheson signed a document under which the revolutionary government of the Philippines was to give them the monopoly to purchase all the unsold hemp produced in that country that season. The request for counsel's opinion, prepared by the solicitors Deacon & Hastings, set out the story of how the plenipotentiary of the revolutionary government was supposed to sign the final agreement, but then authorised one Vincente Ilustre as sub-agent to do so.[307] Things became even fishier after the signing ceremony, attended by a delegation said to include the plenipotentiary and Illustre, when documents which they had produced were examined. One was purportedly signed by the Prime Minister, Lord Salisbury. Suspicions were heightened when Jardine Matheson was asked for a substantial advance by way of promissory notes.

In annotations to Deacon & Hastings' brief, the response of counsel (Mr Francis QC and Mr Pollock) was far from complimentary about Jardine Matheson's failure to request documents earlier, both as to the bona fides of those purporting to act as the agents of the revolutionary government, and as to the approval of both the United States and British governments to the deal. In response to Jardine Matheson's fear of legal action, at least by the broker whose claim was to 50 percent of the net profits, counsel advised that Jardine Matheson should abandon the agreement, even though on its face it was perfectly valid. They opined that Vincente Ilustre would never dare claim, but since the broker might, they should settle with him. Counsel gave short shrift to Deacon & Hastings' suggestion that the agreement might be illegal through immorality.[308] That was based on the argument that enforcing the monopoly against reluctant growers might lead to a loss of life if there was civil strife. The hard-edged character of English contract law came through in counsel's response: 'If on high moral grounds one of the parties repudiates [the contract] he must pay for it ... Dealing in opium is immoral but nevertheless contracts for the sale and purchase of it are valid and binding. There is no illegality on the face of the contract. None necessarily involved in carrying it out.'

Often the legal advice given to Jardine Matheson as regards agency issues was as much practical as it was legal. An example in 1859 concerned Jardine Matheson's agency for Alliance Insurance. Dunstan & Co requested insurance of its property, and a cover note was issued without the usual practice of

---

[306] Ibid., JM/F15/30, 18 January 1884, Advice of Hon E. L. O'Malley. Chinese companies were partnerships.
[307] Ibid., JM/F15/31, Messrs Jardine Matheson & Co and Mr V. Ilustre & Others, Case for Counsel's Opinion.
[308] See J. Chitty, *The Law of Contracts*, London, Sweet & Maxwell, 1896, 563–565.

inspection. Under its agreement with Alliance, Jardine Matheson was prohibited from insuring ship chandler stores at ordinary rates. That was Dunstan's line of business. Dunstan insisted that Jardine Matheson should insure at the lower rate in accordance with the note. Insuring with Alliance was 'out of the question', advised Mr W. S. Bridges, counsel whom Jardine Matheson had instructed to advise. In his opinion two courses were open to Jardine Matheson. First, it could pay the higher rate itself. Second, it could take the risk that there would be no fire in the twelve months until the policy ended, although if there was a fire during that period Jardine Matheson would be liable. It was not for him to tell his client what to do, but if he were in the same shoes, 'I would sacrifice the difference of rates of premium to avoid the possibility of a law suit even though I considered as I certainly do my case at least as good as that of the other side.'[309]

In its role as shipping, insurance and general agents, Jardine Matheson was involved in various disputes leading to arbitration. Sometimes its involvement was to protect the interests of its principals,[310] but sometimes the claims involved it directly. One example occurred in 1874 when the consignees in Hong Kong of a cargo of saltpetre from Calcutta (Kolkata) found that it had been damaged by sea water. Jardine Matheson as their agents had taken delivery from the godowns of the ship's agents. Before the arbitrator it was accepted that the immediate cause of the damage was the poor state of the vessel Jardine Matheson had hired for the task. So obviously it was liable to its principals, the consignees. The arbitration arose when Jardine Matheson claimed that the loss was covered by insurance. The Union Insurance Society denied liability. In his award the arbitrator found in the insurance company's favour. It was an implied term of the insurance contract, he held, that a suitable vessel would be employed. Despite Jardine Matheson's arguments that the vessel it hired was properly licensed and regularly employed in this type of work, the plain fact was (he decided) that the vessel was unsuitable.[311] A second example occurred in 1878 when Jardine Matheson agreed to the arbitration of a dispute (including over their fees), when it acted as agents for the sale of property in Yokohama belonging to an insolvent firm.[312] A final example involved claims by Jardine Matheson that French merchants in Lyon, to whom it had consigned silk for sale, had not followed its instructions, with the result that there were heavy losses.[313]

---

[309] Another example of practical advice concerned the steps Jardine Matheson should take when a ship was consigned to it for sale in Hong Kong by its Melbourne owners: ibid., JM/F15/13, 9 February 1863.
[310] e.g., CUL, Jardine Matheson Archive, Arbitration Papers, JM/F24/1, 16 January 1833 (insurance); JM/F24/6, 21 April 1863, (Shanghai, dispute over freight/demurrage); JM/F24/9, 4 September 1868 (Hong Kong shipping).
[311] Ibid., JM/F24/10, 11 June 1874.
[312] Ibid., JM/F24/11, 4 December 1878. The Attorney-General of Hong Kong, George Phillipps, acted as arbitrator.
[313] Ibid., JM/F24/12; F24/13.

Despite its multifarious activities, Jardine Matheson seemed not to have been engaged in litigation in a significant way.[314] That was partly because some of the disputes it was involved in went to arbitration. No doubt in some cases it also received advice that the law was unfavourable, so that it was better not to pursue a claim.[315] In other cases it may have been that the threat of legal proceedings by its lawyers produced a favourable result and there was no need to take matters further. For example, in 1859 Mr Bridges of counsel advised Jardine Matheson, acting as a ship's agent, that the purchaser of a cargo of coal – in fact the naval store-keeper – should take full delivery, and that if he did not do so the remainder should be sold on his account and legal proceedings commenced.[316] There is no record of any proceedings being taken, and it is reasonable to assume a positive outcome. Finally, the firm had some unhappy experiences with litigation, which may have had a dissuasive effect. Thus, on one occasion the firm ended up in the Privy Council when it petitioned for the bankruptcy of another Hong Kong firm.[317] On another occasion it initiated criminal proceedings in the Mixed Court against three Chinese over money allegedly owed. The proceedings fizzled, and the firm's subsequently stated intention of proceeding against one of them in the civil courts seems to have come to nothing.[318]

However, the firm took proceedings in 1867 against the master of a British ship in Britain's Supreme Court for China and Japan, Summary Division.[319] The explanation appears to lie in Jardine Matheson's own claim that it was a test case. The facts in outline were that the master had engaged Jardine Matheson when the ship arrived in Shanghai as its agent. In addition to other tasks such as discharging the cargo, Jardine Matheson found him a possible further charter, which he rejected. Later, however, when the agency was still in existence, he chartered his vessel directly to the same shipper for a voyage to Amoy (Xiamen) on more favourable terms. The firm asserted that, with further negotiations, it could have obtained those better terms. The court held that the firm was entitled to its commission, since the charterparty entered was the direct result of its effort. To hold otherwise would encourage trickery and collusion between a vessel and a shipper.[320] In supporting the result, the

---

[314] In 1868 it was taken to Britain's Supreme Court of China and Japan when tea it shipped from Shanghai arrived damaged at its destination: *Ivanoff Oberin & Co v. Jardine Matheson*: F23/44, 31 January 1868. On the court: 141 above.
[315] e.g., CUL, Jardine Matheson Archive, Legal Opinions, JM//F15/25, 12 November 1870, advice of Julian Paunceforte, the Attorney-General of Hong Kong: see *Law List*, London, Stevens and Sons, 1879, 910.
[316] Ibid., JM/F15/12, 17 December 1859.
[317] *Lyall v. Jardine, Matheson, & Co* (1870) LR 3 PC 318.
[318] *Jardine Matheson & Co v. Kin Cheu Quai, Kah Yan Koau, Wei Tsung Yuan*, Supreme Court & Consular Gazette, v1, 4 May 1867, 218; 29 June 1867, 321.
[319] *Jardine Matheson & Co v. Burke*, Supreme Court & Consular Gazette, vol. II, 14 December 1867, 240–241. See also *Jardine Matheson & Co v. Jones* [1876] ColConC 20 (Consular Court, Yokohama: claim by firm for commission when acting as ship brokers).
[320] *Burnett v. Bouch* (1840) 9 Car & P 620, 173 ER 982 was cited as analogous.

Supreme Court & Consular Gazette[321] editorialised that the rule should extend further, to situations where the charter was one which, in the ordinary circumstances, an agency house might be expected to procure.

The firm's apparent reticence in taking legal proceedings did not preclude actions taken against it. Thus in 1889 the firm was sued in Britain's Supreme Court for China and Japan when a cask of claret it carried on one of its steamers from Shanghai to Tientsin (Tianjin) arrived empty.[322] There was a lucky escape from litigation in Britain in *White* v. *Munro*,[323] when Jardine Matheson, acting through Matheson & Co in London, purchased a steamer, *Europe*, for the China Merchants Steam Navigation Company. The ship broker employed for the task sued for brokerage in the Sheriff Court at Glasgow. But he sued the sellers, not his principals, with the argument that, according to custom in the ship-broking trade, they were liable. On appeal the majority of the Court of Session thought that the custom was unclear. In any event it held that the sale which ultimately took place was not in consequence of anything done by the broker, so that he was not entitled to brokerage.

3.6 Managing Agents

30 August: Sir N. N. Sircar, Law Member: The European group would probably oppose him ... He had, however, reason to believe that some who were very bitter against managing agents during the passage of the Companies Bill had now developed tenderness for Managing Agents ...

20 September: Dr. Ziauddin Ahmed's amendment evoked a lively, sometimes heated, debate which had not concluded when the House rose. The amendment was to the effect that no insurance companies started after the Act shall have managing agents ...

Mr Satyamurthi elaborated the point and defined the Congress attitude ...

Mr. Jinnah expressed strong opposition to managing agents for any kind of insurance business. They were, he said, parasites. (India, Legislative Assembly, Debate on the Insurance Bill, 30 August, 20 September, 1937)[324]

Managing agents were an important feature of British overseas business activity during our period. However, as we see from these few extracts in the Indian Legislative Assembly in 1937, their role became bitterly contested by the independence movements. Managing agents were a novel form of business enterprise combining the commercial expertise of the trading firms with the

---

[321] Vol. II, 14 December 1867, 235.   [322] *Ritter* v. *Jardine Matheson & Co* [1887] ColConC 19.
[323] (1876) 3 R 1011. The China Merchants Steam Navigation Company was a Chinese company: see Chi-Kong Lai, 'China's First Modern Corporation and the State: Officials, Merchants, and Resource Allocation in the China Merchants' Steam Navigation Company, 1872–1902' (1994) 54 *J Econ History* 432.
[324] The Indian Annual Register, July–December 1937, vol. II, 87, 103.

finance available through the joint stock company.[325] Trading firms became investors (along with others) in companies running plantations, mines and manufacturing operations, as well as their managers.[326] The larger managing agents became investment groups, enabling trading firms to build up a diversified portfolio of corporate interests. Among the larger managing agents which appear in the following account, focused on India, Singapore and Hong Kong, are Jardine Matheson & Co, Jardine Skinner & Co, James Finlay & Co, Binny's, the Borneo Company, Mackinnon Mackenzie, Shaw Wallace & Co, Andrew Yule & Co, Parry & Co and Thomas Duff & Co.[327]

Typically, managing agents started life as trading firms, acting as commission agents importing manufactured products and exporting raw or partly processed goods. The improvements in communications with the telegraph and steamship in the second half of the nineteenth century meant the need for a chain of middleman decreased. That fall in business was offset by the firms expanding their activities to manage companies producing primary products like tea, jute and rubber, and manufacturing a range of products.[328] In many cases the import–export side became secondary, the 'pots and pans' part of the business as Sir John Hay of the large Singapore agency house Guthrie & Co. disparagingly described it.[329] Managing agents might perform only limited functions for a company, such as shipping its output and purchasing its machinery and supplies, but typically they performed all aspects of a company's business.

Managing agents commonly managed companies which they themselves had promoted. They provided both management and technical expertise, as well as investment funds. The key was control. In floating the companies, they earned underwriting and other fees at the outset, followed by dividends, commissions and other charges which the managed companies paid for their services once they were up and running. Managed companies might be incorporated in Britain, drawing on the capital available there, with the

---

[325] C. Jones, *International Business in the Nineteenth Century*, Brighton, Wheatsheaf, 1987, 136.
[326] M. Aldous, 'Avoiding "Negligence and Profusion": The Ownership and Organization of Anglo–Indian Trading Firms, 1813–1870' (2016) 17 *Enterprise & Society* 752.
[327] For India: T. Roy & A. Swamy, *Law and the Economy in Colonial India*, Chicago, University of Chicago Press, 2016, 152–156; M Manton, *The Rise of The British Managing Agencies in North Eastern India 1836–1918*, SOAS, University of London, MPhil thesis, 2008; D. Tripathi, *The Oxford History of Indian Business*, New Delhi, Oxford University Press, 2004, 331; S. Jones, *Merchants of the Raj: British Managing Agency Houses in Calcutta Yesterday and Today*, Basingstoke, Macmillan 1992; B. Tomlinson, 'British Business in India 1860–1970', in R. Davenport-Hines & G. Jones (eds.), *British Business in Asia since 1860*, Cambridge, Cambridge University Press, 1988, 96–100; P. Agarwala, *The History of Indian Business*, New Delhi, Vikas, 1985, 289–293.
[328] Jardine Matheson's ice-making factory had a cameo role in *Hong Kong Milling Co Ltd v. Arnold Karberg & Co* (1910) 5 HKLR 45, 48.
[329] S. Cunyngham-Brown, *The Traders*, London, Newman Neame, 1971, 250. See also C. Marshall, *A History of Modern Singapore 1819–2005*, Singapore, National University of Singapore Press, 2009, 105. On Hay, J. Orbell 'Hay, Sir John George (1883–1964)', *Oxford Dictionary of National Biography*.

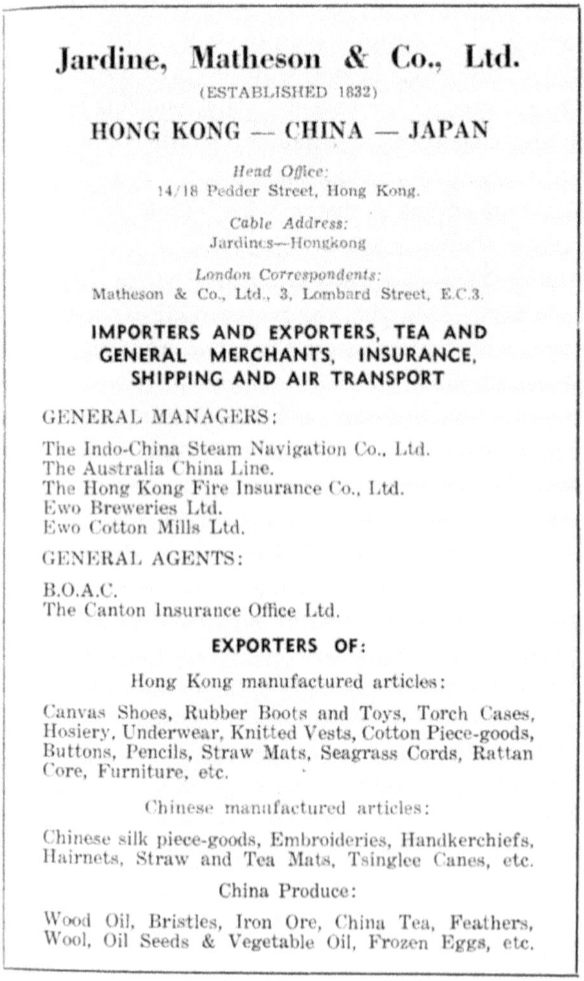

> **Jardine, Matheson & Co., Ltd.**
> (ESTABLISHED 1832)
>
> **HONG KONG — CHINA — JAPAN**
>
> *Head Office:*
> 14/18 Pedder Street, Hong Kong.
>
> *Cable Address:*
> Jardines—Hongkong
>
> *London Correspondents:*
> Matheson & Co., Ltd., 3, Lombard Street, E.C.3.
>
> **IMPORTERS AND EXPORTERS, TEA AND GENERAL MERCHANTS, INSURANCE, SHIPPING AND AIR TRANSPORT**
>
> GENERAL MANAGERS:
>
> The Indo-China Steam Navigation Co., Ltd.
> The Australia China Line.
> The Hong Kong Fire Insurance Co., Ltd.
> Ewo Breweries Ltd.
> Ewo Cotton Mills Ltd.
>
> GENERAL AGENTS:
>
> B.O.A.C.
> The Canton Insurance Office Ltd.
>
> **EXPORTERS OF:**
>
> Hong Kong manufactured articles:
>
> Canvas Shoes, Rubber Boots and Toys, Torch Cases, Hosiery, Underwear, Knitted Vests, Cotton Piece-goods, Buttons, Pencils, Straw Mats, Seagrass Cords, Rattan Core, Furniture, etc.
>
> Chinese manufactured articles:
>
> Chinese silk piece-goods, Embroideries, Handkerchiefs, Hairnets, Straw and Tea Mats, Tsinglee Canes, etc.
>
> China Produce:
>
> Wood Oil, Bristles, Iron Ore, China Tea, Feathers, Wool, Oil Seeds & Vegetable Oil, Frozen Eggs, etc.

Figure 3.2 Managing and general agents: Jardine Matheson & Co. Ltd, Hong Kong, 1953 (Hugh Farmer and the Industrial History of Hong Kong Group)

offices of the managing agent in, say, London and Glasgow providing minimal secretarial and treasury services to their boards.[330] Companies might also be floated locally, for example in Calcutta (Kolkata) or Hong Kong, with expatriate but also local investors.[331] The form of managed company

---

[330] S. Chapman, Merchant Enterprise in Britain, *op cit*, 123–125; J. Drabble, *Rubber in Malaya 1876–1922*, Kuala Lumpur, Oxford University Press, 1973, 78–85. We can note in passing that the firms' reputations generally meant the absence of hopeless or fraudulent company flotations, a feature of company promotions at the time: J. Drabble, Rubber in Malaya 1876–1922, op cit, 83. cf. *Wills v. Jimah Rubber Estates Ltd* (1911) 7 Straits Settlements LR 112 (malpractice in allotment of shares).

[331] W. Malenbaum, *Prospects for Indian Development*, London, Allen & Unwin, 1962, 161.

sometimes changed with time. In the period 1914–19 sterling companies involved with jute were refloated as rupee companies, in order to reduce their tax liabilities and to take advantage of the boom in jute share listings in Calcutta.[332] Local entrepreneurs, such as the Tatas in India, also entered the managing agent business and either formed or acquired interests in managed companies.[333]

Managing agents sometimes managed no more than one company.[334] An example is the appointment in 1913 in a two-page document of L. G. Attenborough as managing agent of Ipoh Tin Dredging Ltd, a company incorporated in London under the Companies Acts to carry out operations in the Federated Malay States.[335] The larger managing agents managed a range of companies, engaged in different activities and economic sectors. For example, by 1902 Andrew Yule & Co managed four jute mills, an inland navigation company, a cotton mill, fifteen tea estates, four coal companies, two flour mills, an oil well, a small railway, a jute press house and a zamindary company. There later followed managing agencies for more jute mills, a power company, a paper mill, a sugar refinery, chemical factories and a brickworks.[336] While the businesses they managed were companies, many managing agents remained as unincorporated firms themselves until well into the twentieth century.[337] In India after the Second World War managing agents became public companies with an increasing fraction of the shareholding owned by Indian shareholders. From the mid-1950s the large financial reserves held by the successful managing agents in India made them a target for takeovers.[338]

1 Legal Structure

There was nothing new for English law to the concept of an agent being appointed to manage a principal's business.[339] However, the term 'managing

---

[332] A. Wearmouth, *Thomas Duff & Co and the Jute Industry in Calcutta, 1870–1921; Managing Agents and Firm Strategy,* University of Dundee, PhD thesis, 2015, 94.

[333] see *Tata Hydro-Electric Agencies Ltd Bombay v. Commissioner of Income Tax* [1937] UKPC 36; [1937] A.C. 685 (PC) (Tata as managing agent of various Indian hydro-electric companies). See also e.g., *Shanti Prasad Jain v. Director of Enforcement,* 1962 AIR 1764, 1963 SCR (2) 297; G. Jones, Merchants to Multinationals, *op cit,* 137, 315; B. Tomlinson, *The Economy of Modern India,* Cambridge, Cambridge University Press, 2013, 120, 123–124; T. Roy, *The Economic History of India,* 3rd ed., New Dehli, Oxford University Press, 2011, 202.

[334] A. Brimmer, 'The Setting of Entrepreneurship in India' (1955) 69 *Quarterly J Econ* 553, 566 (over three quarters in sample managed only one company); R. Nigam, *Managing Agencies in India, First Round: Basic Facts,* India, Department of Company Law Administration, 1957.

[335] LMA, CLC/B/123/MS27232A/13, Borneo Company Ltd, Deed of appointment.

[336] *Andrew Yule & Co Ltd 1863–1963,* Edinburgh, privately published, 1963, 9–12, 18. See also the lists in H. Townend, *The History of Shaw Wallace & Co,* Calcutta, Shaw Wallace, 1965, 142, 201–203.

[337] G. Jones, Merchants to Multinationals, *op cit,* 125.

[338] G. Tyson, *Managing Agency,* Calcutta, Hooghly Printing Co, 1961, 20–23.

[339] e.g., *Trueman v. Loder* (1840) 11 Ad & El 589, 113 ER 539.

agent' began to be used abroad for those who managed a principal's business in a particular area of business or region. The 1936 amendment to the Indian Companies Act 1913 defined a managing agent as a person, firm or company entitled 'to the management of the whole affairs of that company by virtue of an agreement with the company and under the control and direction of the directors except to the extent, if any, otherwise provided for in the agreement'.[340] That definition did not accord with what had become the reality. Although the legislation suggested that a managing agent might act under the control of the company's directors, in truth it was the other way around: managing agents had the whip hand over the company and its directors were placemen. Instead of the principal directing the agent, as with ordinary agency, the position was reversed. Not only might the managing agent have promoted the company, it might have a substantial investment in it. If not held by the managing agent's principals, shares in a managed company were often owned by their relatives or those closely allied by business or personal relationships. Thus, the managing agent would be able to appoint its own people to the board of a managed company, or those willing to do its bidding, and thus be in a position to control it.[341] If they existed, minority shareholders were at an obvious disadvantage, an issue which boiled over on several occasions. Even if a managing agent and its associates did not hold the majority of shares in a company being managed, they might still be able to control it through the managing agent contract.[342]

Central to the operation of the managing agent system was the legal control the managing agent had over the company being managed. That might be contained in the constitution of the managed company.[343] This was clearly an atypical notion of agency. It meant that a managing agent could continue indefinitely and might also have entitlements in a winding up in priority to other shareholders. An example is provided by the managing agent relationship in India between Wallace & Co and the Bombay Burmah Trading Company Ltd (Bombay Burmah). Wallace & Co, East India merchants, was formed as a partnership between Lewis and George Wallace in London in 1862.[344] Earlier in Bombay (Mumbai) Lewis Wallace, and an elder brother William, had been shipping agents and traders in commodities, notably cotton

---

[340] Act No XXII of 1936, s.2(1).
[341] C. Nomura, 'The Origin of the Controlling Power of Managing Agents over Modern Business Enterprises In Colonial India'; (2014) 51 *Indian Econ & Soc Hist R* 95.
[342] R. Goel, 'Managing Agents: Their Powers and Function: A Historical Review' (1961) *J Indian Law Institute* 389, 400.
[343] S. Basu, *The Managing Agency System*, Calcutta, World Press, 1958, 7, 76, 91, 97–98.
[344] A. Pointon, *Wallace Brothers*, Oxford, Oxford University Press, 1974, 9, 22, 98; G. Jones, Merchants to Multinationals, op cit, 40. Incorporated in 1911, the company later developed merchant banking, commodity broking and other interests. Its merchant banking arm was eventually acquired by Standard Chartered Bank. J. A. Bryce, brother of the Regius Professor of Civil Law at Oxford (later Viscount Bryce), was a partner 1881–1906: I. Russell, 'Bryce, (John) Annan (1843–1923)', *Oxford Dictionary of National Biography*.

and cotton goods, and that became the Indian arm of the enterprise. Over time Wallace & Co acquired wide interests in Asia. Bombay Burmah was one of the many companies floated during the speculative boom Bombay experienced during the American Civil War, when India became an important source of cotton in lieu of the US southern states. It was incorporated in 1863 to acquire Wallace & Co's business in Burma of forests, teak concessions, sawmills, godowns and elephants. Payment for the business was cash and the allotment of one hundred preferential shares.[345]

When initially incorporated under the Indian Companies Act XIX of 1857, and later when registered under sections 224–225 of the Indian Companies Act 1882, the memorandum and articles of Bombay Burmah provided that, at its option, Wallace & Co should be the perpetual secretary, treasurer and manager of the company in return for a share of the net profits of the business.[346] The position of Wallace & Co as managing agent was underpinned in other articles. Its powers as secretary, treasurer and manager of the company were, under the general control of the directors, and subject to any board resolutions, to 'manage all the business of the company, and do all things which they should think fit for carrying out its objects'.[347] The articles also provided that the chairman of the company should be the senior or only resident partner or representative in India for the time being of Wallace & Co, who 'shall, at his option, be and continue the chairman of the Company of the board of directors, notwithstanding any clause or regulation of the Company or in these presents to the contrary'.[348] Control was almost complete since the articles of the company relating to the disqualification, rotation and dismissal of directors by special resolution in a general meeting 'shall not apply to the chairman of the board of directors being at the time the senior or resident partner or representative of Messrs Wallace & Co, at Bombay'.[349]

If enshrined in the managed company's constitution as with Bombay Burmah, the position of the managing agent was well entrenched. Attempts to oust it without changing the memorandum and articles would be ultra vires and void.[350] Otherwise, control relied on the contract between it and the company setting out the arrangements between the two. That made it more vulnerable, if the company was taken over, although the view of a solicitor in what was then the leading Indian firm, Orr Dignam & Co, was that the contracts 'were still excessively in favour of the managing-agency houses

---

[345] R. Macaulay, *History of the Bombay-Burmah Trading Corporation Ltd*, London, Spottiswoode Ballantyne & Co, 1934; A. Pointon, *The Bombay Burnah Trading Corporation Limited 1863–1963*, Southampton, Millbrook, 1964; G. Barton & B. Bennett, 'Forestry as Foreign Policy: Anglo-Siamese Relations and the Origins of Britain's Informal Empire in the Teak Forests of Northern Siam 1883–1925' (2010) 34 *Itinerario* 65.

[346] Articles LXXV, LXXVII. The memorandum and articles are in *Bombay Burmah Trading Corporation Ltd v. Dorabji Cursetji Shroff* [1904] UKPC 79.

[347] Article LXXIV.   [348] Article LXXI.   [349] Article XC.

[350] *Nusserwanji Merwanji Panday v. Gordon* (1881) 6 Bom 266 (but Sargent J recognised that ultimately the majority shareholders could remove the managing agent).

themselves, and the companies had little comeback'.[351] These contracts between the managing agent and the company varied, depending in part on the history of the relationship. Where the company was the creature of the managing agent, the contract could be succinct.

A representative case is provided by the 1912 managing agent agreement under which the British India Steam Navigation Company Ltd (the BIN) appointed the firm Mackinnon Mackenzie & Co to be its managing agent for the company's shipping business.[352] The BIN had its origins in a small, limited liability company established in 1856, which Mackinnon interests came to dominate by the end of the decade, enabling William Mackinnon to restructure and rename it as the BIN in 1861.[353] Clause 2 of the 1912 agreement provided that the firm should act as managing agents, 'and as such shall conduct their entire agency business' at the different places where the company's steamers traded. The remainder of the agreement was given over to financial matters. The company was obliged to pay, and the firm was entitled to retain out of the moneys it received on the company's account, the expenses of acting as such – wages and salaries, the repair of vessels and machinery, the loading and unloading of vessels, coal purchases, shed rents, port charges, gratuities, advertising, pilotage, rebates on freight or primage to shippers or shippers' agents, but not brokerage, except where, according to the custom of the port, it formed a charge against the ship or freight (clause 3). Remuneration for the firm acting as managing agent was calculated as a percentage of gross earnings of the company (clause 5). Special payments were to cover matters such as dry dock and workshop operations in Calcutta and Bombay (clauses 6–7, 9). Sub-agents were to be appointed by, and were under the control of the firm, but were subject to the company's veto (clause 8).

By contrast, the agreement under which the firm Jardine Matheson & Co became 'general managers' of the Indo-China Steam Navigation Company Ltd reflected its less than total control of the company and consequently its greater accountability to shareholders. The firm had promoted the company in London in 1881, but of its paid-up capital the two largest shareholders were the principals of Scottish firms (one, the founder of the Glen line). Of shares held by the investing public,[354] some £150,000 was raised in China and Hong

---

[351] H. C. Waters, quoted in S. Jones, Merchants of the Raj, *op cit*, 67. cf. C. Nomura, 'The Origin of the Controlling Power of Managing Agents over Modern Business Enterprises in Colonial India', *op cit*, 112–113.

[352] LMA, CLC/B/123/MS27818, Mackinnon, Mackenzie & Co. It followed earlier agreements dating back to 1861. It in turn was replaced by agreements of 1918 and 1924 on essentially the same lines as the 1912 agreement.

[353] J. Munro, *Maritime Enterprise and Empire*, Woodbridge, Suffolk, 20003, 37–42. Mackinnon Mackenzie & Co had engaged in import–export business in Calcutta since 1847, with William Mackinnon & Co its Glasgow counterpart and Gray Dawes & Co its London arm. Through the driving force of (Sir) William Mackinnon, and after his death in 1893 James Mackay (Lord Inchcape), Mackinnon firms were spawned in India, the Gulf, East Africa and Australia. In 1914 BIN merged with P & O to become the largest shipping group in the world.

[354] See *In re Indo-China Steam Navigation Company* [1917] 2 Ch 100.

Kong.[355] Under the agreement, dated 20 April 1882,[356] the firm was to manage the business of the company 'with fidelity and reasonable skill and diligence', and subject to the instructions and control of the company's directors (clause 2). The firm was to keep the books and accounts as directed by the company and was to permit their inspection by the company at all reasonable times (clause 3). The firm could employ sub-agents where it had no operations itself, but was to be responsible for their acts and defaults as if these were its own and was responsible for their remuneration (clauses 5, 7). At least twice a year the firm was to render an account of all receipts and expenditure connected with its management of the company's business (clause 6). The firm was entitled to commission at 5 percent on the gross receipts of the company (with, until 1896, an additional 3 percent on the gross amount of freight and passage money received through sub-agents) and to office expenses and advertising costs (clauses 7–8). Disputes were to be referred to arbitration (clause 11).

These managing agent agreements concerned shipping services. Examples from other areas of business activity are provided by those entered by the Borneo Company Ltd. Incorporated under the Limited Liability Act of 1855, and reregistered under the Joint Stock Companies Act 1856, the company finally sought a stock exchange listing in 1922.[357] In the mid-nineteenth century it acquired the trading activities of a firm, MacEwen & Co, in Singapore, Batavia, Jakarta and Manila, which it extended to Calcutta, Hong Kong and Siam.[358] But from early on, the company also engaged in production – mines in Borneo, brickworks in Singapore, jute and sugar mills in India, teak forests in Siam and, in the 1920s, a rubber plantation in Sumatra.[359] For this purpose it entered managing agent agreements with the operating companies.

---

[355] M. Keswick, *The Thistle and the Jade. A Celebration of 150 Years of Jardine Matheson & Co*, London, Octopus Books, 1982, 114, 142; Kwang-ching Liu, 'Steamship Enterprise in Nineteenth-Century China'; (1959) 13 *Journal of Asian Studies* 435, 439; G. McMillan 'Trading on Chinese Shores: The Indo-China Steam Navigation Company and Change in the China Coastal Shipping Market, 1880–1900' (2016) *Int'l J Maritime Hist* 291, 295. The new company acquired the ships of Jardine's China Coast Steam Navigation Company and the Yangtze Steamer Company (which had been established largely with local capital). Until its demise in the 1970s, the fleet served China (in particular the Yangtze), Japan, India (see *Indo-China Steam Navigation Co v. Jasjit Singh*, 1964 AIR 1140, 1964 SCR (6) 594), the Philippines and Australia.

[356] CUL, Jardine Matheson Archive, Agreements and Contracts, F1/81.

[357] In 1925 the company incorporated a subsidiary, Borneo Motors Ltd, in Singapore, to further the distribution of motor vehicles, the activity with which its name became widely associated in the region. cf. Chapter 4.5, 4(i).

[358] P. Griffiths, *A History of the Inchcape Group*, London, Inchcape, 1977, 129–31. In 1862 the company's Singapore manager introduced Anna Leonowens as governess to the Thai royal family, giving to rise various books and the 1951 musical *The King and I* by Richard Rogers and Oscar Hammerstein: E. Baigent & L. Yorke, 'Leonowens [née Edwards], Anna Harriette" (1831–1915)' *Oxford Dictionary of National Biography*.

[359] P. Griffiths, ibid., 132–137; S. Jones, *Two Centuries of Overseas Trading*, Basingstoke, Macmillan, 1986, 19–20, 199, 203–205, 2110; H. Cox & S. Metcalfe, 'The Role of Networks in the Early Development of Borneo Company Ltd' (1998) 4 *Asian Pacific Bus Rev* 53; S. Metcalfe, 'The Structure and Evolution of an Operational Network: The Borneo Company Ltd 1850–

The agreements of the Borneo Company with the Bruseh Tin and Rubber Estates Ltd in 1911 and 1946,[360] and the Alexandra Brickworks Ltd from 1900 to 1946,[361] are illustrative. Under them the Borneo Company was appointed as the agent and secretary to each company and was obliged to provide their boardroom and secretarial services. It was charged with using its best endeavours to dispose of the produce of the enterprise or to cause it to be disposed of to the best advantage and at the best prices which could be obtained.[362] Pending sale, the Borneo Company was obliged to store and insure the product. As a gesture to the legalities, and perhaps with the change in the political climate, by 1946 the agreements contained an additional provision, that the Borneo Company should act under the general control of the company being managed and should comply with the directions of its board. Moreover, there was a clause that the Borneo Company had to deal with money received on account of the company as directed, and had to pay what was owed on its dealings on the company's behalf.

These were agreements with companies which the Borneo Company had itself promoted and continued to dominate. But it also entered into managing agent agreements with companies quite independent of itself, for example, to run the Swedish Match Company's factory in Bangkok.[363] Of interest are the arrangements with the Pahang Consolidated Co Ltd, which matured over time. Early agreements, from 1906, were for the Borneo Company to 'undertake the management and supervision of the company's mines and property'.[364] With the growth of Pahang Consolidated to be one of the largest tin lode mines in the world,[365] the relationship with the Borneo Company changed. It became the company's agent in Singapore, to arrange the shipment of the tin and to purchase and deliver the plant and machinery needed for the mines. Under the agreements Borneo Company was entitled to commission and remuneration in the ordinary way, although it was obliged to keep accounts, to use its best endeavours to promote the company's business and to maintain confidentiality about its affairs.[366]

1919' (2000) 7 *Asia Pacific Bus Rev* 17, 30; H. Longhurst, *The Borneo Story*, London, Newman Meame, 1956, 34–35, 45, 61, 65, 89–90.

[360] LMA, CLC/B/123/MS27232/6, CLC/B/123/MS27232A/27A; CLC/B/123/MS27233, Memorandum Book, 35–38, 45–54, 76–77. On Bruseh, see J-F. Hennart, 'Transaction Cost Theory and the Free Standing Firm', in M Wilkins & H Schroeter (eds.), *The Free Standing Company in the World Economy 1830–1996*, Oxford, Oxford University Press, 1998, 76–77. On the role of the agency houses in Malayan tin: Yip Yat Hoong, *The Development of the Tin Mining Industry in Malaya*, Singapore, University of Malaya Press, 1969, 372–373.

[361] LMA, CLC/B/123/MS27232/1. The brickworks were in Singapore.

[362] For some reason this provision was not in the 1946 Bruseh Agreement.

[363] LMA, CLC/B/123/MS 27232A/6A, dated 26 November 1931.

[364] LMA, CLC/B/123/MS 27232/22.

[365] Wong Lin Ken, *The Malayan Tin Industry to 1914*, Tucson, Arizona, 1965, 169.

[366] LMA, CLC/B/123/MS/27232/22. See agreements 22 September 1936, 18 April 1946, 16 April 1953, 6 August 1958. See also *A History of the Pahang Consolidated Company Limited 1906–1966*, London, Pahang Consolidated Co Ltd,1966, 23, 48–49; Pahang Consolidated Company

2 Managing Agents as Agents

In law managing agents were agents. When issues arose, the same type of legal arguments could be deployed as in ordinary agency cases. Authority was one such issue: how far could the managing agent go in binding the company, whose business it was managing, to transactions with third parties? Early on the courts applied the rule that the authority of a managing agent was to do what was usual in the ordinary conduct of that type of business. If the managing agent acted within that remit, the principal was bound even if the particular transaction with the third party was not specifically authorised. The managing agent itself was not liable on the transaction.[367]

In line with agency law, the authority of a managing agent did not extend to entering transactions which had nothing to do with the managed company's business. That was underlined in *Oriental Bank Corporation v. Baree Tea Company, Limited*,[368] where the principal of the managing agent, Mr. Nicholls, falsely told his bank manager that he wanted an advance to carry on the tea estate which his firm managed. The moneys were not spent on the tea estate, Nicholls & Co failed, and the bank sued the tea company. The Calcutta High Court held that the bank failed in its claim because Nicholls & Co had no authority to enter this type of transaction for purposes other than the tea estate.[369]

The presumption of foreign principal in section 230 (1) of the Indian Contract Act 1872 created a potential problem for managing agents, even if they had acted within their authority. Contrary to the ordinary rule, it meant that an agent was liable (and could also sue) whenever it entered a sale or purchase contract for a merchant resident abroad.[370] That could mean the inconvenience, or worse, of a managing agent being personally liable on contracts made to sell the products of the company it managed. Although its business would be in, say, India, as a matter of law the company managed was resident in Britain, often the case when it had been incorporated there, and its affairs (albeit minimal) were conducted from there.[371] That problem was solved by the Madras High Court in 1903, where Benson and Bhashyam Ayyangar JJ found that the presumption in section 230(1) was readily rebutted.[372]

Limited v. *State of Pahang* (1931–1932) FMS LR 131; on appeal [1932] UKPC 86; [1933] 2 MLJ 247 (PC) (unsuccessful litigation by company over its concession).

[367] see 144–145 above.

[368] (1883) ILR 9 Cal 880. See also *In re Cunningham & Co Ltd* (1887) LR 14 Ch D 317 (Buenos Aires managing agent of company exporting canned meat had no authority to give promissory note).

[369] at 886. *Jumma Dass* v. *Eckford* (1883) ILR 9 Cal 1 was another claim arising from the insolvency of Nicholls & Co.

[370] The section codified the foreign principal rule: see 155–157 above.

[371] See *Calcutta Jute Mills Co Ltd* v. *Nicholson* (1876) Ex D 428, a tax case – the company had jute mills in Bengal.

[372] *Tutika Basavaraju* v. *Parry & Co* (1903) ILR 27 Mad 315. See H. Brown, *Parry's of Madras*, Madras, Parry, 1954, 142, 144, 164, 168–170.

Agency law was a weak reed in curbing the conflicts of interest rampant in the operation of the managing agent system. As we have seen a managing agent earned a commission on sales, as well as the remuneration set out in the agreement for management and secretarial services. In addition, a managing agent could earn additional income from the multiple services provided to a managed company. For example, the large managing agents were often shipping and insurance agents as well and earned commission on the freight and insurance cover they arranged on a managed company's behalf. Managing agents might also lend money to a company or guarantee a bank advance. The potential conflicts of interest in these arrangements were patent.[373] The commissions charged by managing agents could be higher than market rates. The fees for management services might be fixed irrespective of the level of sales, although in practice during a slump the managing agent might reduce or waive its fees. In addition shipping, insurance and banking could be placed with those with whom the managing agent had established relationships when more advantageous rates were available elsewhere. In some cases, conflicts of interest took the form of insider trading in a managed company's shares. Since managing agents typically managed a number of companies the resultant cross-directorships were another potential source of conflict as one managed company was advantaged over another. Ultimately, such conflicts played out to the disadvantage of a managed company's shareholders and employees.

Yet legal disputes were relatively few, notwithstanding how widespread the system of managing agents was and the multiple conflicts of interest entailed. One factor was that managing agents aimed to avoid trouble. They needed to maintain a reputation for honesty and good management both to retain existing contracts with companies which they did not dominate and to attract new business. As a result they might tread more warily than they otherwise would have with the fees and commissions charged. Another possibility is that conflicts were quickly settled so as to avoid attracting other disgruntled parties to the fray.[374] Whatever the reason, even where a managing agent did dominate a managed company it might avoid blatantly disadvantaging the minority shareholders and attempt to damp down disputes behind the scenes. Indeed, managing agents sometimes expressed a moral or legal responsibility to the shareholders of the companies they managed, a mixture of paternalism and self-interest.[375] Good dividends might be important to the wider family of shareholders associated with the principals of a managing agent, indeed even to the principals themselves when they retired. Occasional disputes erupted, however, with discontented shareholders; we return to the topic in the next section.

---

[373] G. Jones, Merchants to Multinationals, *op cit*, 182–183, 88–89.
[374] J. Drabble & P. Drake, 'British Agency Houses in Malaysia', *op cit*, 310 (Kajang Rubber Estates Ltd accused Guthries of making an unjustified profit on goods supplied to the estate).
[375] G, Jones, Merchants to Multinationals, *op cit*, 186.

A managing agent might terminate an unprofitable agency. '[T]he duties of an agent are in the nature of personal service, and as such incapable of being enforced in equity.'[376] That was said in a case where the court refused the directors of a company an order preventing its managing agent from resigning, even though his agency was a condition in the company's prospectus and expressly provided for by its articles of association. Conversely, a company might terminate a managing agent's services. If that was not opposed it was relatively straightforward, albeit damages might be payable for breach of contract.

Illustrative from the early history of BP is the 10-year managing agency agreement entered in May 1914 between Anglo-Persian Oil Company Ltd and Strick Scott & Co Ltd (previously called Lloyd Scott & Co Ltd).[377] Under it the latter was appointed as managing agents of the company's business, in particular 'to effect and carry out the sale of petroleum and other products of the Company and generally to act as their agents in Persia and the East'.[378] By the early 1920s it had become evident, both economically and politically, that the oil company itself should assume control over all aspects of production and marketing. In particular, the commission payable to Strick, Scott & Co had become well in excess of the amount ever anticipated. In October 1922 the oil company cancelled the managing agent's agreement in return for a payment of £300,000 in compensation. In a separate agreement its assets were transferred to the oil company for £1 million.[379]

3 Shareholders of Managed Company v Managing Agent

The architecture of the managing agent system contained an inherent tension between the interests of the shareholders of the managed company on the one hand and those of the managing agent on the other. A typical source of conflict arose over commission and other payments to the managing agent. These provided a source of growth through retained earnings, but the other side of that coin was a reduction in the dividends payable to shareholders. Conflicts of interest also arose through a managing agent managing a diversity of companies, or having other potentially conflicting interests such as insurance or shipping agencies. There was the potential to favour one managed company

---

[376] *Mair v. Himalaya Tea Company* (1865) L R 1 Eq 411.
[377] The latter's original directors were drawn from Shaw Wallace & Co and the Finlay Fleming group: See R. Ferrier, *The History of the British Petroleum Company. The Developing Years 1901–1932*, Cambridge, Cambridge University Press, 1982, 129.
[378] The agreement is set out in *Anglo-Persian Oil Company* Ltd v. *Dale (Inspector of Taxes)* [1932] 1 KB 124, 126.
[379] [1934] 1 KB 124, 128–129; R. Ferrier, ibid., 307–309, 318. cf. the post-Independence termination of the managing agent agreement for Austin cars in India, considered in *Commissioner of Income-tax* v. *Ashok Leyland Ltd*, 39 Comp Cas 180 (192) (Mad), which seemed to turn on payment alone: discussed in V. Rao, *Law of Agency*, 2nd ed., Allahabad, Law Book, 1986, 734–735.

over another, or to allocate business inside the group when it might be better placed elsewhere. As a result, shareholders of the managed company could lose out.[380] On various occasions disgruntled shareholders objected to what the managing agents of their companies were doing, although many disputes were settled or fizzled out.[381]

Occasionally the tensions erupted into full-blown legal disputes. One involved James Finlay & Co as managing agent of the Champdany Jute Company.[382] Established in Glasgow in the mid-eighteenth century as a textile manufacturer, James Finlay & Co gradually built up trading activities in England, the continent and abroad. The firm had connections with India, leading to the establishment of Finlay Clerk & Co in Bombay (Mumbai) in 1862 and Finlay Muir & Co in Calcutta (Kolkata) in 1870. Later there were branches in Karachi, Chittagong (Chattogram), Colombo, Rangoon (Yangon) and Java.[383] In India the firm diversified into jute mills and tea estates by promoting and managing companies in which it held the majority of shares, but attracting additional capital from outside investors because of the firm's high reputation. A dominant figure in Finlay from the 1860s was John (later Sir John) Muir, who considered shareholders as a necessary evil. To ensure control he stuffed his boards with compliant relatives.[384]

The Champdany Jute Company Ltd was incorporated by Finlay in Scotland in 1873 to manufacture jute in Calcutta. At the time outside investors in jute companies saw them as a source of quick returns and high profits.[385] By contrast a managing agent like Finlay was more concerned with the long term through the income from commission and the other returns as agent. In 1882 the tension between Muir and the non-Finlay directors and shareholders erupted over plans for the investment of Champdany funds in building a further jute mill. The outside investors saw this as subtracting from the profits available for dividends, but associated with this were their concerns over depreciation provisions, the treatment of capital expenditure and how

---

[380] G. Jones & J. Wale, 'Merchants as Business Groups: British Trading Companies in Asia before 1945' (1998) 72 *Bus His R* 367, 396–399; G. Jones, Merchants to Multinationals, *op cit*, 184–185.

[381] e.g., T. Corley, *A History of the Burmah Oil Company 1886–1924*, London, Heinemann, 1983, 112–114 (the company's shareholders objecting to Finlay Fleming & Co as managing agent).

[382] R. Stewart, *Scottish Company Accounting 1870 to 1920. Selected Case Studies of Accounting in its Historical Context*, University of Glasgow, PhD thesis, 1986, 327–325, which draws on the James Finlay & Co Ltd archives at the University of Glasgow. Unfortunately Stewart makes no reference to the reported case law, considered below. See *Champdany Jute Co Ltd, Petitioners* 1924 SC 209 on the Champdany company.

[383] *James Finlay & Company Ltd: Manufacturers and East India Merchants, 1750–1950*, Glasgow, James Finlay & Co, 1951; J. Scott & M. Hughes, *Anatomy of Scottish Capital*, London, Croom Helm, 1980, 34–35.

[384] M. Clough, 'Muir, Sir John, first baronet (1828–1903)', *Oxford Dictionary of National Biography*.

[385] T Sethia 'The Rise of the Jute Manufacturing Industry in Colonial India: A Global Perspective' (1996) 7 *J World History* 71, 90.

rupee accounts were converted into sterling.[386] Muir reacted badly to the opposition. The company's law agent, Professor Robertson, advised that Muir's suggestion to reduce the directors' decision that year, recommending a 10 per cent dividend, might be unlawful.

In the following years Muir was determined to avoid a repetition and ensured that outside directors were replaced by persons sympathetic to the Finlay interest. By the early 1890s there was only one non-Finlay director remaining.[387] Thus the only avenue for dissident shareholders about management decisions was the court. Led by Maxwell Hannay, a Glasgow merchant, they challenged the level of Finlay commission in high-profile litigation in 1895. No dividend had been paid since 1893, yet the firm had earned very considerable amounts in commissions on sales, banking services, salaries, directors' fees and other sources of profit.[388] In their petition the dissident shareholders claimed for repayment to Champdany of three separate sums: £16,250, said to be fraudulently charged as excess commission; £8,160, said to be improperly charged as commission on advances obtained for Champdany, when this was already covered by the contractual commission payable; and £8,000, said to be interest which the firm should have paid on as moneys of the company but which the firm used for its own purpose.[389] The summons further claimed against Sir John Muir and the other directors for repayment of £9,850, said to have been distributed out of capital to the shareholders as dividend in 1893, when no dividend was earned. It was alleged that the accounts of the company had been falsified and manipulated to conceal the fraudulent payments, and that the Glasgow auditors had never had access to the books of Champdany in India.

In a hearing before Lord Low in the Outer House of the Court of Session, the defenders invoked conventional company law doctrine, notably the rule in *Foss* v. *Harbottle*,[390] that since the complaint was against the conduct of those managing the affairs of the company it could only be advanced by the company itself. In his judgment in early March 1896, Lord Low held that the claims for the three sums fell within one of the exceptions to the rule in *Foss* v. *Harbottle*, that if a company is defrauded by a person with a majority of votes who stifles inquiry, the shareholders can sue. However, the Court held that the fourth claim should be dismissed: it did not appear that dividends were not paid out of profits previously accrued. At the hearing, to meet the shareholders' allegation that they were unable to make their claims more specific, the firm agreed to allow their books to be examined by a jointly nominated accountant. As a result the shareholders attempted to amend the

---

[386] R. Stewart, *op cit*, 297, 302–303, 309–312. Champdany had poorer dividend performance compared with others in the Calcutta jute industry: A. Wearmouth, Thomas Duff & Co and the Jute Industry in Calcutta, 1870–1921; Managing Agents and Firm Strategy, *op cit*, 125–126. At this point only 40 percent of the shares were owned by Finlay interests.
[387] Ibid., 310, 313.   [388] Ibid., 259.   [389] *Hannay* v. *Muir* (1896) 3 SLT 295.
[390] 2 Hare 461; 67 ER 189.

record by restricting the first claim to a sum of £1,306, the second to £5,300 and the third to £3,544.

Finlay raised several objections to this when the case went on appeal to the Inner House. Judgment was given in mid-December 1898 by Lord Low, by then Lord President. He identified 'the true question between the parties [as] whether the agents have taken too much and given the company too little'.[391] The court limited the pursuers' claims but allowed some to go to trial. The trial was due to take place in October the following year. However, the pursuers withdrew the action. It appears that they realised the difficult task of proving their allegations. By this time a capital reorganisation of Champdany had come into effect. As a result ordinary shareholders could convert to holding preference shares at a price double the market value for ordinary shares, provided they gave no support to the ongoing legal action. That led to a reduction in the non-Finlay interest in Champdany. Moreover, to avoid future criticism, the Finlay directors began to abstain from voting at the board on matters concerned with the commission payable to James Finlay in Britain, and Finlay Muir in Calcutta, and the services provided for the company.[392]

A few years later another dispute was litigated between the shareholders of a company and its managing agent, leading to an appeal from the High Court of Bombay to the Privy Council.[393] The case arose out of Wallace & Co acting as managing agent of the Bombay Burmah Trading Company Ltd.[394] The litigation was triggered when in 1895 Wallace & Co proposed a change in the memorandum and articles of Bombay Burmah. (Wallace & Co took the amendments in draft to C. B. Lynch and F. A. Owen, partners in the solicitors Craigie Lynch, for them to revise and settle.[395]) Later R. H. Macaulay, the Wallace partner at the centre of the litigation, portrayed the amendments as a sensible tidying-up exercise to make clear that the existing company's activities were intra vires. In his view this commendable effort by the managing agent was met by wholly unreasonable opposition, led by Dorabji Cursetji Shroff, 'a sort of professional agitator, always looking out for opportunities of giving trouble to the directors of any company of which he was a shareholder'.[396] So much for shareholder rights, especially if they were Indian shareholders. Shroff was far from being the professional agitator. Although not opposed to some expansion in the company's powers, he viewed the proposed amendments to

---

[391] *Hannay v. Muir* (1898) 1 F 306, 313.
[392] R. Stewart, *op cit*, 306; G. Jones & J. Wale, 'Merchants as Business Groups: British Trading Companies in Asia before 1945', *op cit*, 398–399.
[393] *Bombay Burmah Trading Corporation Ltd v. Dorabji Cursetji Shroff* [1904] UKPC 79; [1905] AC 213 (PC); *Re Bombay Burmah Trading Corporation*, ILR 1904 27 Bom 73.
[394] 182–183 above.
[395] LI, *Privy Council, Printed Cases, Judgments and Appeal Documents*, 'Bombay Burmah Trading Corporation Ltd v. Dorabji Cursetji', vol. 499, 61–62. Advice was also sought from Owen on the advertising and timing of the amendments and the petition itself was settled by counsel.
[396] R. Macaulay, *History of the Bombay-Burmah Trading Corporation Ltd*, London, Spottiswoode Ballantyne, 1934, 35.

the company's powers as too wide and too risky. Until then, Shroff noted, there had been no complaint that the company had not been able to expand its business beyond timber but, he added, the kernel of his complaint was that the departures from this business 'had most of them been a source of loss to the shareholders'.[397]

Legal advice to the company had been that its powers were wide enough to cover its proposed activities. In 1892 the company had obtained the advice of John (later Lord Justice) Rigby QC, who in August that year confirmed in writing the advice he had given earlier in the year. That was that if the company acquired a timber concession in Sumatra, and supplied the timber for sleepers on the Indian railways, it would be within its powers.[398] A year after the earlier consultation, in May 1893, Rigby was consulted again: he recorded a short opinion that it would not be ultra vires for Bombay Burmah to acquire a concession of oil wells in Sumatra and to work it and deal in oil.[399] Until 1912 Shroff had the support of a sufficient number of Bombay Burmah shareholders to thwart the special resolution which was needed to make the necessary amendments to the memorandum and articles. But at meetings of the company in May and June 1902, the special resolutions were passed. If the proxies Macaulay held had not been counted, however, the resolutions would have been lost.

At the hearing Shroff contended that some of the proxies which Macaulay as chairman of the company had used to pass the special resolution were invalid. In October 1902 the High Court (Jenkins CJ and Batty J) held that, indeed, Macaulay had not been properly appointed as a proxy in compliance with the company's articles. The company sought permission to appeal to the Privy Council, which the High Court granted given, it said, the importance of the issue for the financial and commercial position of the company and for Indian companies generally.[400] Before the Privy Council the company was successfully represented by Richard Haldane KC, later Lord Haldane LC, at the time an acknowledged leader of the bar.[401] Wallace & Co's position as managing agent was central to Lord Lindley's rejection of the High Court's reasoning; Macaulay had been properly appointed as a proxy.[402]

4 Regulation and Demise

A justification of the managing agent system was that it maximised the impact of limited managerial and financial resources. Overhead costs were

---

[397] *Times of India*, 30 March 1896, extracted ibid., 133–134.
[398] *Record of proceedings, op cit*, 78–79.   [399] Ibid., 79.
[400] *Record of Proceedings*, ibid., 227.
[401] see R. Heuston, *Lives of the Lord Chancellors 1885–1940*, Oxford, Clarendon, 1964; H. Matthew, 'Haldane, Richard Burdon, Viscount Haldane (1856–1928)', *Oxford Dictionary of National Biography*.
[402] at 218–219.

economised and technical and specialist services were provided of a standard which the average-sized business might have had difficulty in securing for itself. Since countries like India did not have mature capital markets until well into the twentieth century, the large and successful managing agents were able to finance the development of mills, mines, plantations and transport systems from their own resources, or they facilitated access to the London capital market for this purpose.[403] On the other hand, the managing agent system extracted excessive profit from businesses in various ways, through fees, commissions and dividends. The returns of some managing agents became a scandal. Development was not its goal, since it oriented enterprises to export markets. There was a network of interlocking directorships of the companies being managed. The system led to a concentration of economic power in a relatively few, mainly foreign, hands. It was not surprising that Indian nationalists regarded the managing agent system as an instrument of British imperialism and that its regulation became a plank of the independence movement.[404]

India led the way in the regulation of managing agents. The 1936 amendments to the Indian Companies Act VII of 1913 attempted to boost the rights of shareholders in managed companies. The initial appointment, reappointment, or variation of appointment of any managing agent had to be approved by a resolution of the managed company passed at a general meeting.[405] Managing agents could only be appointed for a period of 20 years, although they could be reappointed.[406] They were limited to appointing one-third of the directors of a board of a managed company.[407] The amendments also sought to curb excessive returns to managing agents. Section 87C limited the remuneration of managing agents, with provision for a minimum payment where profits were inadequate or non-existent. Additional remuneration was possible if the company passed a special resolution.[408] Generally speaking the funds of a managed company could not be used for loans to its managing agent or to assist other companies being managed by the same managing agent. There were similar restrictions on the granting of guarantees by a managed company.[409] Managing agents could not exercise a power to issue debentures in a managed company or to invest its funds without specific authority.[410] Managing agents were forbidden completely in the case of banks,[411] a restriction soon extended to insurance companies.[412]

---

[403] G. Tyson, *Managing Agency*, Calcutta, Houghty Printing, 1956, 3–4. As late as the mid-1950s, of a total paid up capital of Rs 970.8 crores in joint stock companies operating in India, Rs 464.4 crores represented the paid up capital of companies managed by managing agents: R. Nigam, *Managing Agencies in India: First Round, Basic Facts*, New Delhi, Department of Company Law Administration, 1957; P. Lokanathan, *Industrial Organization in India*, London, Allen & Unwin, 1935.

[404] T. Roy, 'Trading Firms in Colonial India' (2014) 88 *Bus Hist R* 9, 13.   [405] s. 87B(f).
[406] s. 87A (i).   [407] s. 87I.   [408] s. 87C(ii).   [409] s. 87D-87E.   [410] S. 87G.   [411] s. 277H.
[412] Insurance Act 1938, s.32.

After Indian independence the pressure for further restrictions on managing agents grew. In any event their future was far from bright with partition dividing businesses and markets, and government policy favouring tariffs, exchange control and high taxes.[413] The process of control went through many twists and turns. A government memorandum on amending the Indian companies legislation in 1949 proposed that no company should be allowed to act as a managing agent; no private company should be managed by a managing agent; managing agents should draw no commission on sales, turnover or purchases and should be paid no office allowance; and the managing agent system should be banned in specified industries or companies designated by the government. The government rejected these radical recommendations.[414]

A Companies Bill was introduced to Parliament in September 1955. That was amended significantly during the course of the parliamentary process so that the Companies Act of 1956 contained more detailed regulation of managing agents than initially proposed. Nonetheless, the Act was a damp squib.[415] Section 324 conferred on the central government a power to make a notification declaring that no company engaged in a specified industry or business should have a managing agent. Where managing agents were permitted, the Act provided that government approval would not be accorded unless it was satisfied that it was not against the public interest for a managing agent to be appointed, that the managing agent was fit and proper and that the conditions of the agreement were fair and reasonable.[416] Under section 348, the ceiling set for remuneration of a managing agent was ordinarily ten percent of the net profits. Shortly after its enactment the Bombay High Court commented that it was 'unfortunate that a law which is intended to help in the development of companies in our country and also to put down abuses ... should not have been couched in clear and more precise language'.[417]

Managing agents such as Wallace & Co, and the companies it managed like Bombay Burmah, considered the steps to be taken to ensure compliance. Partly the advice derived from the Bombay Chamber of Commerce and the Mill Owners' Association, but Mr Aitken of the Bombay (Mumbai) law firm Crawford & Bayley was also consulted.[418] The concern was not only with the changes to the managing agent system but also with the requirement that the

---

[413] T. Roy, 'Trading Firms in Colonial India'; (2014) 88 *Bus Hist Rev* 9, 41–42.
[414] National Council of Applied Economic Research New Delhi, *The Managing Agency System*, London, Asia Publishing House,1959, 21–23; U. Varottil, 'The Evolution of Corporate Law in Post-Colonial India: From Transplant to Autochthony' (2016) 31 *Amer U Int'l LR* 253, 277.
[415] D. Tripathi, The Oxford History of Indian Business, *op cit*, 285.   [416] s. 326.
[417] *Thanawala v. Jyoti Ltd*, AIR 1958 Bomb 214, [1].
[418] LMA, CLC/B/207/MS40076, Wallace & Bros, Correspondence (Bombay Burmah to London, 20 February 1956; 14, 15, 17, 28 March 1956. The file also contains correspondence regarding what became the Companies (Amendment) Act 1960: the Bill was not anticipated to affect Wallace greatly, although it was thought that it could affect the Tatas. See also A. Pointon, *Wallace Brothers*, Oxford, 1974, 86, 112.

appointment of sole selling agents be approved by a company's general meeting.[419] Resolutions drafted by Mr Aitken to accord with these requirements were placed before the board and shareholders of the Bombay Burmah Co, relating to its appointment of Wallace & Co as managing agent.

There had been a growth of Indian managing agencies such as the Tatas, Birlas, Dalmias, Singhanias, Thapars and Goenkas.[420] Throughout the 1950s there were a series of hostile takeovers of European managing agents, which consequently led to a transfer of control of the companies being managed. Often this was driven by speculation, and the firms taken over ended in insolvency or left their core business.[421] Ultimately India abolished the managing agent system with the insertion in 1969 of section 324A into the Companies Act 1956. Elsewhere governments were slower to act. In the Gulf, Gray Mackenzie & Co was affected by the policy introduced by Kuwait in 1965, under which 51 percent of the shares had to be owned locally.[422] There was a commission of inquiry in Sri Lanka, which questioned the future of the managing agent system.[423] In Singapore and Malaysia the system continued into the 1970s. Localisation occurred as agency houses domiciled abroad were registered in these two jurisdictions, and shares were issued on the Singaporean and Kuala Lumpur stock exchanges and taken up in the domestic market.[424]

3.7 Conclusion

> No word is more commonly and constantly abused than the word 'agent'. A person may be spoken of as an 'agent', and no doubt in the popular sense of the word may properly be said to be an 'agent', although when it is attempted to suggest that he is an 'agent' under such circumstances as create the legal obligations attaching to agency that use of the word is only misleading. (*Kennedy v. De Trafford*, 1897, per Lord Herschell)[425]

Truly, during our period, as one writer has expressed it, agency was everywhere, and its legal web enmeshed all.[426] The courts had developed the general principles of agency law by the end of the eighteenth century. In the nineteenth century many of these were refined and given new application in the context of

---

[419] s. 294, amended by the Companies (Amendment) Act 1960, s. 101. See *Shalagram Jhajharia v. National Co Ltd* 1965 35 Comp Cas 706 (Calcutta).
[420] P. Agarwala, *The History of Indian Business*, New Delhi, Vikas Publishing House, 1985, 274.
[421] T. Roy & V. Swamy, *Law and the Economy in Colonial India*, op cit, 155.
[422] LMA, CLC/B/207/MS27734A, Gray Mackenzie & Co, 'History of the Company ...'.
[423] *Report of the Commission of Inquiry on Agency Houses and Brokering Firms*, Sessional Paper No XII, 1974.
[424] J. Drabble & P. Drake, 'British Agency Houses in Malaysia' (1981) 12 *J Southeast Asian Stud* 297, 299, 322.
[425] [1897] AC 180, 188. See to similar effect other judicial remarks at 134 above.
[426] S. Issacharoff & D. Ortiz, 'Governing Through Intermediaries' (1999) 85 *Virginia LR* 1627, 1635.

the rapidly changing patterns of trade and commerce. This context also led to the elucidation of new principles. With the changing commercial context during our period, some businesses turned their back on agents as the appropriate technique for their activities and used agency principles in different ways. The law's approach was in the main pragmatic, trying to match principle with commercial convenience, albeit that on occasion the pull of doctrine, precedent and property rights proved too strong.[427] Some of the problems faced were familiar, for example, which of two innocent parties (in the typical case, the principal or third party) should bear the loss in the case of fraud (the agent in our example). At the other end of the spectrum were the new, and special, problems thrown up by the dependence in foreign lands on local agents, such as the comprador in China or the banyan in India, to collect, distribute and finance products.

Agency in practice did not always fit the neat categories of existing legal principle, nor (as illustrated in the extract from Lord Herschell's judgment) did the term in ordinary usage always match legal precision. The 'agent' was not always an agent as the law defined it. Terminological inexactitude, however, was good marketing: car dealers, as an example, could portray themselves as carrying the authority of the manufacturer. In practice agency relationships were fluid and not according to the legal model. As ever commercial parties pursued profit in whatever way was convenient. There might be a hierarchy of agents transmitting commodities and products across oceans.[428] Even the true agent in law could perform many commercial functions. Brokers bought for themselves as well as others. Those acting as agents might provide finance to their principals in the way of credit or quicker payment. Agents acted as a source of market information and advice. And an agent might hold multiple agencies; as we have seen, trading houses overseas might buy and sell abroad as agent or for themselves, might act as well as a shipping, insurance and forwarding agent, and might manage as agents the business of plantations, mines and factories.

Commercial convenience was at the fore in the notion of apparent (ostensible) authority, allowing the third party to rely on appearances despite the agent lacking actual authority, although there is much in the view that the law should have gone further to protect third parties. Despite the strictures of doctrinal purists like Sir Frederick Pollock, the editor of the *Law Quarterly Review*, the notion of undisclosed principal was developed because it was conceived by the courts (however doubtfully) as commercially convenient. And commercial convenience (and commercial morality) underlay the courts' recognition that, in the absence of instantaneous communications, agents could not be expected to comply strictly with their principal's orders when it

---

[427] As the story of the Factors Acts demonstrates: see 153 above. See also 138 (doctrine of conversion trumping Liverpool practices for distributing cotton to textile mills).

[428] e.g., *New Zealand and Australian Land Company* v. *Watson* (1881) 7 QBD 374 (import of wheat through agent and sub-agent).

was reasonable to secure something other than what the principal had ordered. However, there was a long struggle around the Factors Acts and the problem of the agent wrongfully disposing of a principal's goods or obtaining an advance from a bank by wrongfully pledging a document of title to goods. The courts were protective, in the main, of the principal's property rights, whereas Parliament was more inclined to defend innocent third parties and banks carrying out beneficial commercial and financial functions.

In a variety of ways, the English judges laid the classic concept of agency law to one side – that agents brought their principal and a third party together into a contractual relationship but then 'dropped out' of the picture. Depending on the type of arrangement and its context, they recognised that agents could be liable as principals when the one side had failed to perform. It was a recognition of commercial need – to have someone in the jurisdiction responsible if a foreign deal turned sour – albeit that the common law did not (unlike the civil law) enunciate general principals of commercial agency to accommodate the problems associated with international sales and transportation.[429] The quest proceeded pragmatically and flexibly. Del credere agents, who guaranteed their seller-principal that the buyer would pay, were well known at the beginning of our period and limped on into the twentieth century. The confirming agent guaranteed third-party exporters that its buyer-principal would pay. When the confirming agent finally reached the courts doctrinal difficulties were brushed under the carpet and commercial needs met.

In the first part of the nineteenth century trading at a distance demanded that importers and exporters of goods appoint agents abroad in the true legal sense, someone who could forge legal relationships on their behalf with third parties. With time some of these agents transformed themselves into trading houses, buying and selling on their own account. Through the managing agent system some took a further step, embarking on fixed capital investments in mills, plantations and industry. With that they transformed into investment groups, managing the companies which they, in many cases, had floated, either in London or locally. A criticism is that the law was deficient in allowing the directors and shareholders of managed companies to lose control to the managing agent.[430] Another is that 'the legal fiction of agency' meant that 'the agency houses were not agents at all but private partnerships that contrived to control public companies by the device of using the prestige of their name and the British legal system to have permanent control written into the articles of association of various companies'.[431] From a legal perspective these criticisms are not entirely accurate. The managing agent system may have disadvantaged minority shareholders in the managed companies; it may have

---

[429] D. Hill, 'The Commission Merchant at Common Law', *op cit*, 624–625. Quaere whether as suggested the civil-law approach was more commercially conducive.
[430] T. Roy & V. Swamy, Law and the Economy in Colonial India, *op cit*, 142, 152–155.
[431] S. Chapman, Merchant Enterprise in Britain, *op cit*, 271.

led to economic inefficiencies because of the absence of shareholder control over management; and, most importantly, it may have perpetuated foreign domination of an economy. Whatever fictions were involved in this, it was exactly what those in control of the managing agents wanted: it was not the law which was deficient, but the context of Empire which it executed.

4

Sale, Hire and the Distribution of Manufactured Goods

4.1 Introduction

The commonest form of contract is the contract of sale. (*The Law Times*, 1895)[1]

English sales law was at the centre of commercial law during our period. It had evolved in the Middle Ages. By the end of the fourteenth century, as a practical response to commercial needs, its perspective had moved firmly out of the focal plane of property into that of contract.[2] In subsequent centuries the common law of sale developed in a context of rules of pleading and precedent, and mainly of domestic transactions, 'the facts of horses and a majestic ignorance of commerce', as Karl Llewellyn characterised it.[3] In the nineteenth century modern sales law emerged, addressing problems arising from the export of products of the industrial age and the import of commodities for food and manufacture. But that law was not always, or even mainly, the law of the courts. Through the vagaries of litigation the judges often saw sales through the lens of the relatively small-scale or abnormal transaction.[4] In practice, the law of sales was in important respects made by commercial parties and contained in the contracts they drew up for the sale of particular manufactured products or in the standard form contracts drafted by trade associations for selling commodities and raw materials across continents.

This chapter and the next explore how sales law was moulded to the demands of the industrial age. In the main the subject-matter of the present chapter is manufactured goods; that of Chapter 5, commodities, specifically 'soft' commodities like cotton, wheat, wool and tea. As with other parts of the book, these chapters are not concerned with detailed doctrinal history. Cases

---

[1] E. Jelf, 'Where to Find Your Law' (1895) 98 *LT* 372, 373.
[2] D. Ibbetson, 'From Property to Contract: The Transformation of Sale in the Middle Ages' (1992) 13 *J Legal Hist* 1, 13.
[3] K. Llewellyn, 'Across Sales on Horseback' (1939) 52 *Harv LR* 725, 738. Llewellyn was a prime mover in the US Uniform Commercial Code: e.g., W. Twining, *Karl Llewellyn and the Realist Movement*, London, Weidenfeld and Nicolson, 1973; Z. Wiseman, 'The Limits of Vision: Karl Llewellyn and the Merchant Rules' (1987) 100 *Harv LR* 465. See also L. Friedman, *Contract law in America: A Social and Economic Case Study*, Madison, University of Wisconsin Press, 1965, 52–60 As we will see Llewellyn's analysis was somewhat exaggerated.
[4] M. Bridge, 'The Evolution of Modern Sales Law' [1991] *LMCLQ* 52, 53.

are examined, but in large part to understand the factual background to the trading in goods and how it was conducted. The focus is on commercial, not consumer, transactions. To put it another way, the chapters are concerned with deals between commercial parties, not between shopkeepers and consumers, the supply of plant, engines and grain, not that of pots, pans or biscuits. From the late nineteenth century retail transactions in these latter items were transformed by the advent of the department stores and multiple shops, and by the new techniques of advertising and branding. It is a separate story.[5]

A recurrent theme of the discussion is that the common-law rules of sale, later codified in the Sale of Goods Act 1893, were altered, ignored or replaced if they failed to accord with commercial need. Parties could and did write their own contracts, with their own rules regarding matters such as where liability fell if things went wrong, what remedies would obtain, and how disputes were to be settled. As Karl Llewellyn recognised many years ago, sales law would lie 'in the hands of the draftsman, of the negotiator, and of the arbitrator'.[6] Some appreciation of the default rules of sales law is necessary, however, for an understanding of how things were done differently in commercial practice.

Part 4.2 of the present chapter therefore offers a partial overview of the development of sales law from the early nineteenth century through the lens of quality, how the law defined it, what it applied to and the remedies available if goods were not up to scratch. The case law mentioned centres around the subject matter of this and the following chapter, manufactured goods and commodities.

Part 4.3 of the chapter considers how these rules applied with heavy manufactured goods such as plant and machinery, chemicals and locomotives. Here we see that in some cases the default rules of sales law could have purchase, such as the obligation on the seller to provide goods fit for purpose. At the end of the day, however, the terms of any written contract between the parties tended to be determinative, although its ramifications in practice had to be seen in the context of the relationship between the manufacturer and purchaser whether, for instance, it was long term and trust remained or had evaporated.

These written contracts were vital if the contract contained detailed specifications as to how an item was to be made. What would happen should it not match them in terms of remedy and aftersales service might be more informal, without resort to lawyers or law. In this part of the chapter we encounter iconic

---

[5] Partly covered in R. Cranston, *Consumers and the Law*, 1st ed., London, Weidenfeld &Nicolson, 1978. See also W. Fletcher, *Powers of Persuasion The Inside Story of British Advertising 1951–2000*, Oxford, Oxford University Press, 2008; R. Church, 'Advertising Consumer Goods in Nineteenth-Century Britain: Reinterpretations' (2000) 53 *Econ Hist Rev* 621; T. Corley, 'Consumer Marketing in Britain 1914-60' (1987) 29 *Bus Hist* 65; T. Nevett, *Advertising in Britain*, London, Heinemann, 1982; W. Fraser, *The Coming of the Mass Market 1850–1914*, London, Macmillan, 1981; A. Adburgham, *Shops and Shopping 1800–1914*, London, Allen & Unwin, 1964.
[6] 'On Warranty of Quality and Society' (1936) 36 *Col LR* 699, 706–707.

British manufacturers (or their predecessors) during our period, for example Robert Stephenson and Hawthorns, Unilever, Imperial Chemical Industries (ICI), Cammell Laird and Ferranti.

There is a contemporary concern with the 'death' of sales law and its adequacy for the twenty-first century.[7] There is no need to enter that debate here. The reality, as explored in Part 4.4 of the chapter, is that from the mid-nineteenth century manufactured goods were being supplied to the market not only through sales contracts but also through hire and deferred (hire) purchase. On the one side, customers obtained manufactured goods on credit; on the other, suppliers had some protection through a form of quasi-security if customers defaulted in their payments, or the goods were wrongly disposed of.

In the second half of the nineteenth century hire and hire purchase were especially important in supplying railway wagons to collieries and manufacturers to enable them to distribute their products through the rail network. (Coal of course had become the key source of power and was to become the main source of light through electricity generation.) In the twentieth century the techniques of hire and hire purchase took a hold in the distribution of retail and commercial products. Hire and hire purchase were a significant factor in the rise of the motor car, bus and lorry for the transport of people and goods. Asset finance, a modern form of these techniques, is now widely employed to supply aircraft, plant, motor vehicles, photocopiers and computers.

In Part 4.5 of the chapter we turn to the distribution through commercial channels of manufactured and processed goods, motor vehicles, tyres and petrol. An essential point here is that if these goods were being distributed for onward sale to further customers, distributors were bound by contract to market them in specific ways. For example, they might be obliged to confine their efforts to specified geographic areas and to 'push' the product or to use their 'best endeavours' in marketing it.

Distribution contracts might go further and oblige distributors to supply the goods to customers at prices set by the manufacturer (retail price maintenance) and to market them in particular ways. In Britain the common law was a weak reed in controlling restrictive trade practices and legal regulation was slow in coming. When it did arrive, towards the end of our period, it lacked bite. In this part of the chapter, names well known at the time make an appearance – Austin Motor Company, Standard Motor Company (later Standard-Triumph International) and Dunlop Rubber – as well as some which survive (Selfridges and Esso Petroleum).

---

[7] e.g., L. Gullifer, 'The Vanishing Scope of the Sale of Goods Act 1979 in the Twenty-first Century', in C. Mitchell & S. Watterson (eds.), *The World of Maritime and Commercial Law*, Oxford, Hart, 2020; L. Gullifer, '"Sales" on Retention of Title Terms: Is the English Law Analysis Broken?' (2017) 133 *LQR* 244. Llewellyn had raised the issue in 1936: ibid., at 706.

4.2 Sales Law in Outline: Quality

> You are doubtless aware that the whole of English mercantile law is ultimately founded on commercial usage ... Mercantile usage is the raw material; the decided cases are the manufactured article ... In mercantile matters I imagine that the certainty and definiteness of a rule are of more importance than a very nice and exact adjustment of conflicting interests in each particular case. (Mackenzie Chalmers, 1880, 1881)[8]

This part of the chapter outlines some limited aspects of sales law as it developed in the nineteenth century. In important respects these were incorporated in Chalmers' Sale of Goods Act 1893. The codified rules were then applied by the courts through the lens of the 1893 Act. The discussion is not a comprehensive account of the law. The focus is on representations in sale contracts about price and quality and the implied terms relevant to quality. Important issues in practice such as a seller's failure to deliver goods (including short and late delivery), the self-help remedy sellers had when their buyer failed (stoppage in *transitu*) and what could be done in the case of a buyer's non-acceptance of goods are referred to only in passing.[9]

Since this book is not a doctrinal history the discussion does not track nuances in the law's development, although key decisions are encountered. As in other parts of the book, the cases are used to illustrate the evolution of rules relevant to the marketing of manufactured goods, the subject matter of this chapter, and the trade in commodities, the topic of Chapter 5. Throughout the discussion we see that while there was a corpus of sales law, codified in the 1893 Act, there were other legal rules relevant for sales and related transactions.

The story of Mackenzie Chalmers' drafting of what became the Sale of Goods Act 1893, after earlier success with the Bills of Exchange Act 1882, and subsequent work on the Marine Insurance Act 1906, is well known.[10] At the forefront of his codifications of English commercial law was a philosophy of facilitating commerce. That is evident in the quotation at the head of this part of the chapter, coming at the outset of his codification efforts. It was

---

[8] M. Chalmers, 'On Some Points of Difference Between the English and Foreign Systems of Law Regarding Bills of Exchange, and their Relative Merits', (February 1880) 1 *J of Institute of Bankers* 239, 241; M. Chalmers, 'On the Codification of Mercantile Law with Especial Reference to the Law of Negotiable Instruments', ibid., vol. 2, March 1881, 113, 121–123.

[9] e.g., S. Thomas, 'The Development of the Implied Terms on Quantity in the Law of Sale of Goods' (2014) 35 *J Leg Hist* 281 (history of law re short delivery); M. Bridge, 'Markets and Damages in Sale of Goods Cases' (2016) 132 *LQR* 405 (references nineteenth-century law on non-performance).

[10] There was mixed enthusiasm in England for comprehensive codification, as advocated by Bentham and introduced in India: A. (Lord) Rodger, 'Codification of Commercial Law in Victorian Britain', (1993) 80 *Proceedings of the British Academy* 149; M. Lobban, *The Common Law and English Jurisprudence 1760–1850*, Oxford, Clarendon, 1991, 185ff; G. Bower, 'Codification of English Law: Retrospect' (1884) 121 *Westminster Review* 450; G. Bower, 'Codification of English Law: A Prospect' (1884) 122 *Westminster Review* 1.

a theme which Chalmers reiterated on various occasions. In an address to the American Bar Association in August 1902 he asserted that business required certainty in the rules and wanted to avoid expensive litigation.[11] He added that it was difficult for lawyers to grasp the point, but commerce 'would rather have a somewhat inconvenient rule clearly stated than a more convenient rule worked out by a series of protracted and expensive litigations'.[12] Chalmers' sentiments do not convey the full picture: nineteenth-century codification was driven as well by a legal ideology of progress through rationalisation.[13] Nor do they tell whether in practice commercial interests were furthered by his codifications.[14]

Chalmers drafted the Sale of Goods Bill in 1888 and it was introduced into Parliament the following year. Subsequently, he made much of the influence of Pothier's *Traité du contrat de vente* of 1772, but in his approach to codifying he was guided by how it had been done in India.[15] He published his digest of existing sales law in 1890. That was the basis of his 1894 textbook, which ran to many editions.[16] In the introduction to the first edition, Chalmers stated that his former pupil master Lord Herschell had advised him to reproduce as exactly as possible the existing law.[17] Reintroduced after consideration by a Select Committee and groups outside Parliament,[18] the Bill finally became law after amendments to it in both the House of Commons and the House of Lords.[19]

The early years of the 1893 Act were uncontroversial.[20] Later criticisms were that Chalmers misunderstood the case law, failed to incorporate important aspects of the common law and introduced rigidities (the strict division between conditions and warranties being one).[21] Whatever the truth of these criticisms they seem to miss at least two points, first, Chalmers' intention that the 1893 Act should contain default rules, for use only where the parties

---

[11] M. Chalmers, 'Codification of Commercial Law' (1903) 19 *LQR* 10, 14   [12] Ibid., 15.
[13] While there was commercial support in England, it was stronger in Scotland: A. Rodger, *op cit*, 151, 160–161, 163–167.
[14] R. Ferguson, 'Legal Ideology and Commercial Interests: The Social Origins of the Commercial Law Codes' (1977) 4 *Brit J L&S* 18.
[15] See G. Pearson, 'Relevance of Mackenzie Chalmers to Australian Law' (2011) 65 *ALJ* 97, 104.
[16] *The Sale of Goods 1893*, London, William Clowers & Sons, 1894. The last was by Michael Mark and Lord Mance (ed.), *Chalmers' Sale of Goods*, 18th ed., London, Butterworths, 1981.
[17] He accepted that Scots law was amended more. On Herschell's influence: S. Hedley, 'Chalmers, Sir Mackenzie Dalzell (1847–1927), judge and civil servant'; P. Polden, 'Herschell, Farrer, first Baron Herschell (1837–1899)', *Oxford Dictionary of National Biography*.
[18] e.g., Report of a Special Committee of the Council of the Incorporated Law Society, *Sale of Good Bill 1891*, Committee Reports, vol. 8, 1891 (Law Society library).
[19] e.g., Report from the Select Committee on Sale of Goods Bill [HL], HC 374, 15 August 1893. See P. Mitchell, 'The Development of Quality Obligations in Sale of Goods' (2001) 117 *LQR* 645, 656–661.
[20] J. Christie, 'The Sale of Goods Act 1893 and Recent Cases' (1897) 9 *Judicial Review* 275, 276.
[21] e.g., Lord Diplock, 'The Law of Contract in the Eighties' (1981) 15 *U Brit Col LR* 371, 375; S. Stoljar, 'Conditions, Warranties and Description of Quality in Sale of Goods – II' (1953) 16 *MLR* 174, 177.

themselves did not make provision in their contract, and secondly, that commercial practice regularly modified the Act's terms.

1 Express Warranties, Misrepresentation and Fraud

While there were twists and turns in the doctrinal history, by the beginning of our period express representations in a contract for the sale of goods about matters such as their price and quality were actionable if untrue.[22] Thus a buyer selling to third parties on the basis of an express warranty given to it by its seller might successfully claim what it had fairly and reasonably paid out to the third parties when the product did not come up to the mark.[23] Not every statement on the occasion of a sale constituted a warranty, however, because, as the *Law Times* explained in 1856, 'it is usual for [a seller] to speak well of the goods he has to sell ... and, therefore, a mere representation of their value, or assertions generally in praise of their goodness, do not amount to a warranty ... [T]he rule of *caveat emptor* applies.'[24]

Express warranties might require the court to construe the contract to determine if the seller was, in fact, warranting the goods, and in relation to which aspect. In *Hopkins* v. *Hitchcock*[25] sixty-seven tons of iron were sold by a Middlesbrough manufacturer, through its London commission agent, for export to Bremen. The contract was for 'S & H' (crown) common bars. That was because the manufacturer had been Snowden & Hopkins, and its iron marked 'S & H' with a crown was highly valued. Snowden had retired, and the business continued under the name Hopkins & Co., the mark of the new firm being 'H & Co' with a crown. The Court of Common Pleas held that the buyer had wrongly rejected the iron because the mark 'S & H' in context was for iron not of a particular brand but of a known quality, which this was.[26] Willes J accepted that in other situations a particular brand might be of value, especially in a foreign market, 'as a guarantee for its excellence', and it would be a breach not to provide it.[27]

There was much case law about whether statements about quality not spelt out in the contract itself could be incorporated into the contract.[28] These might

---

[22] *Mondel* v. *Steel* (1841) 8 M & W 858, 151 ER 1288 (ship not built to specification; became evident on London–New South Wales voyage). On the doctrinal history, D. Greig, 'Misrepresentation and Sale of Goods' (1971) 87 *LQR* 179, 179–190.
[23] *Dingle* v. *Hare* (1859) 7 CB (NS) 145, 141 ER 770 (sale of 20 tons of superphosphates; did not contain 30 per cent phosphate of lime as warranted).
[24] 'The Law of Warranty on the Sale of Personal Chattels' (1856) 27 *LT* 158. See also 'The Mercantile Law Amendment Act, Warranty' (1857) 29 *LT* 277, 301, 313.
[25] (1863) 14 CB (NS) 65, 143 ER 369. cf. *Dickson* v. *Zizinia* (1851) 10 CB 602, 138 ER 238 (grain shipped fob at Orfana (Greece) to be of good and merchantable condition; it did not make sense that this was a warranty that it be in that condition on arrival).
[26] Erle CJ, Willes, Byles, Keating JJ. [27] at 71, 371, respectively.
[28] e.g., *Stucley* v. *Baily* (1862) 1 Hurl & C 405, 158 ER 943 (sale of vessel). As ever with nineteenth-century sales law horses (the equivalent of course of the modern motor vehicle) frequently featured: e.g., *Wood* v. *Smith* (1829) Mood & M 539, 173 ER 1250; *Street* v. *Blay* (1831) 2 B & Ad

be oral representations at the time of sale or advertisements.[29] In the early twentieth century the House of Lords set a high threshold. The implication of *Heilbut, Symons & Co. v. Buckleton*[30] – a case involving the sale of shares, not goods – was that a statement about the quality of goods had to be made with contractual intent if it was to be an express warranty.[31] In that case Lord Moulton had referred to the possibility that a representation, if not part of the contract, might constitute a collateral contract.[32] There was a scarcity of reported cases about them.[33]

Although a case involving shares, the headnote to *Seddon v. North Eastern Salt Company Ltd*[34] boldly stated that the court would not grant rescission of an executed contract for the sale of a chattel or a chose in action on the ground of an innocent misrepresentation. Doubts persisted as to the availability of rescission in these circumstances.[35] At the end of our period the Law Reform Committee recommended abolition of the rule in *Seddon's case* for sales of goods and that damages be available for innocent misrepresentations, along with rescission.[36] Those changes were finally adopted in the Misrepresentation Act 1967.[37]

Absent fraud, a buyer could not sue on a representation not part of a contract.[38] Yet fraud in sales transactions was difficult to prove. *Horsfall v. Thomas*[39] was the high-water mark. In that case the Mersey Steel and Iron Company made the defendant a cannon so he could conduct tests for future business with the War Office. Although he had the opportunity, he did not inspect the cannon beforehand. It worked well at first but then burst. He refused to meet the bill of exchange he had accepted for payment.[40] The company sued. The defendant's case was that the bill was obtained by the company's fraud in telling him that the gun had no weak points they were aware of, when they knew that a metal plug had been inserted at one point of the barrel. In the Court of Exchequer Bramwell B – an arch-exponent of the free market – held that there was no fraud when a manufacturer did not tell

---

456, 109 ER 1212; *Hopkins v. Tanqueray* (1854) 15 CB 130, 139 ER 369; *Foster v. Smith* (1856) 18 CB 156, 139 ER 1326.

[29] As in *Freeman v. Baker* (1833) 5 B & Ad 797, 110 ER 985; *Taylor v. Bullen* (1850) 5 Ex. 779, 155 ER 341 (sales of ships).

[30] [1913] AC 30.

[31] For the history: M. Bridge, *The Sale of Goods*, 4th ed., Oxford, Oxford University Press, 2019, 472–474,

[32] at 47.

[33] K. Wedderburn, 'Collateral Contracts' [1959] *CLJ* 58; 'Warranty Collateral to a Written Contract' (1913) 77 *JP* 171. See 267 below.

[34] [1905] 1 Ch 326.   [35] *Leaf v. International Galleries (A Firm)* [1950] 2 KB 86.

[36] *Tenth Report of the Lord Chancellor's Law Reform Committee*, Cmnd 1782, 1962.

[37] P. Atiyah & G. Treitel, 'Misrepresentation Act 1967' (1967) 30 *MLR* 369.

[38] *Kain v. Old* (1824) 2 B & C 627, 107 ER 517 (sale of ship),

[39] (1862) 1 Hurl & C 90; 158 ER 813.

[40] On payment by bills of exchange: 383 below.

the buyer about a known, patent defect, but merely said that he should judge for himself.[41]

2 Nature and Quality of Goods: The Implied Terms

With no express representation in a contract, or fraud, buyers needed to take protective measures to ensure the quality of the goods they purchased. But the principle of *caveat emptor* was never as foundational as sometimes supposed.[42] Early on the courts implied terms about the nature and quality of the goods sold. These implied terms were codified in the Sale of Goods Act 1893.[43] Described as conditions, the Act stated that a buyer could reject goods in the event of non-compliance with these implied terms in sections 13–15. In practice, however, other provisions in the Act meant that buyers were in many instances limited to a claim in damages. The ambit of the implied terms changed over time: for example, the courts narrowed the implied term that goods should comply with their description.[44]

(i) Compliance with Description

Compliance of goods with their contractual description was a precondition to the buyer's obligation to take delivery and pay for them, said Pollock CB in *Nichol v. Godts*.[45] There the broker's sold note recorded a sale of 33 tons of foreign refined rape oil, warranted equal to sample at £35 per ton. Although the oil matched the sample, it was not foreign refined rape oil as described but a mixture of hemp and rape oil. Consequently, the buyer was not bound to accept it. In another commodity sale, merchants at Calcutta (Kolkata) and London sold through brokers a quantity of 'Calcutta linseed, tale quale', per the vessels *Gloriosa*, *Albatross* and *Highlander*. The Court of Common Pleas held that the contract was not satisfied by the delivery of linseed, though coming from Calcutta, which contained so large an amount of other inferior seeds as to prevent its passing in the market by the commercial name, Calcutta linseed.[46]

---

[41] at 101, 818, respectively. The ruling was controversial: see *Oxford History of the Laws of England*, Oxford, Oxford University Press, 2010, vol. XII, 411 (M. Lobban).

[42] P. Atiyah, *The Rise and Fall of Freedom of Contract*, Oxford, Oxford University Press, 1979, 471–475. cf. W. Hamilton, 'The Ancient Maxim Caveat Emptor' (1931) 40 *Yale LJ* 1133.

[43] In an earlier draft there had been an additional implied term, that in a sale by a manufacturer the goods were of the seller's own manufacture: G. Wilton, 'Commercial Morality' (1909) 21 *Jud Rev* 237, 242.

[44] see M. Bridge, 'Description and the Sale of Goods: the *Diana Prosperity*', in C. Mitchell & P. Mitchell (eds.) *Landmark Cases in the Law of Contract*, Oxford, Hart Publishing, 2008.

[45] (1854) 10 Ex 191, 156 ER 410 (Platt, Martin and Parke BB agreed). The doctrinal ins and outs of nineteenth-century sale by description law are discussed in S. Stoljar, 'Conditions, Warranties and Description of Quality in Sale of Goods – I' (1952) 15 *MLR* 425, 438–445; 'Conditions, Warranties and Description of Quality in Sale of Goods – II' (1953) 16 *MLR* 174, 174–183.

[46] *Wieler v. Schilizzi* (1856) 17 CB 619, 139 ER 1219 (Jervis CJ and Cresswell, Crowder and Willes JJ).

Nichol v. Godts was applied in a case of a sale of oxalic acid.[47] After the contract had been in existence for some time the acid was analysed and found to contain sulphate of magnesia. This seriously impeded the conversion process for which it was needed, as well as diminishing the quantity produced. The jury was instructed that the seller could only perform his part of the contract by delivering that which in commercial language might properly be described as oxalic acid. The jury awarded the buyer damages; the Court of Common Pleas refused to interfere. The decision was a clear advance: there was no warranty that it was oxalic acid, and the purchaser had inspected it beforehand (albeit that inspection would not have detected the defect). In effect, the seller was being made liable for a latent defect.

Chalmers codification of the implied term that goods must correspond with their description was in section 13 of the 1893 Act. It protected commercial purchasers of manufactured products and those dealing on the commodity markets.[48] It sometimes enabled buyers to avoid the operation of exemption clauses in standard written contracts. In 1923 Roche J held that an exemption clause for 'defects' contained in a contract for the sale of imported East African copra cake[49] did not apply. The copra cake was not 'defective' but so mixed with castor beans that it could not properly be described as copra cake.[50]

Correspondence with description as regards measurement or weight was strictly applied.[51] If the parties wanted a margin, they needed to incorporate it into the contract; otherwise the court would apply a bright-line rule. In *Arcos v. Ronaasen*[52] Wright J at first instance had held on a special case stated from an arbitration that the buyer was entitled to reject a cargo of staves from Archangel (Arkhangelsk), Russia.[53] They had been shipped on the White Sea 1928 CIF form and purchased to manufacture cement barrels.[54] Ostensibly

---

[47] *Josling v. Kingsford* (1863) 13 CB (NS) 447, 143 ER 177.

[48] For manufactured goods: e.g., *Bostock & Co Ltd v. Nicholson & Sons Ltd* [1904] 1 KB 725 (sulphuric acid, sold as commercially free from arsenic to sugar manufacturers, but containing arsenic).

[49] On a London Cattle Food Trade Association standard form – 100 bags of East African copra cake at £7 per ton CIF, fair average quality, sound delivered, net cash in London against shipping documents on arrival of steamer. See 295 above.

[50] *Pinnock Brothers v. Lewis and Peat* [1923] 1 KB 690. See also *Wallis v. Pratt* [1911] AC 394; 218 below.

[51] The same applied to time of performance: e.g., *Bowes v. Shand* (1877) 2 App Cas 455 (Madras rice to be shipped March/April; held, non-compliance, since most bags on board in February).

[52] [1933] AC 470. On Arcos Ltd: C. Andrew, *The Defence of the Realm: The Authorized History of MI5*, London, Allen Lane, 2009, 153–155. It organised USSR trade to Britain.

[53] (1932) 42 Ll L Rep 163. The buyer was taking every point to avoid the contract: it had been unsuccessful in an earlier arbitration that the shipment was not, in accordance with its terms, a summer shipment: at 167. Wright was a leading commercial judge of the first part of the twentieth century: see N. Duxbury, 'Lord Wright and Innovative Traditionalism' (2009) 59 *U Toronto L J* 265.

[54] Under a CIF (cost, insurance and freight) contract, the price includes the cost of the goods, as well as their insurance and transport to destination. Once shipped, and having provided the shipping documents to the buyer, the seller's duties are fulfilled: *Tregelles v. Sewell* (1862) 7 H & N 575, 158 ER 600 (300 tons of iron rails shipped by iron merchants in London CIF to

they had been rejected because the staves did not conform to the contractual measurement of half an inch thickness, but there are hints in the judgment that the buyer was seeking to buy cheaper elsewhere. Both the Court of Appeal and the House of Lords dismissed appeals: even if the staves were fit for the purpose of barrel-making and merchantable, they did not match the contractual description.[55]

(ii) Fitness for Purpose

Fitness for purpose was the term the courts implied when goods were sold for a particular purpose, as long as that purpose had been made known to the seller.[56] In the leading case of *Jones v. Bright* Best CJ said that the principle 'will teach manufacturers that they must not aim at underselling each other by producing goods of inferior quality', and that the law would protect purchasers 'who are necessarily ignorant of the commodity sold'.[57] This was a 'sweeping doctrine', a commentator in the Law Magazine wrote, 'more suitable, it is said, to modern times'.[58] The rule was enunciated against a background of industrial products being transported beyond where they were made and being sold to strangers.[59] An advocate of *caveat emptor*, Lord Abinger CB (sitting in the Exchequer Chamber) attempted to distinguish the rule out of its separate existence in *Chanter v. Hopkins*.[60] There the buyer ordered one of the seller's patented 'Chanter's smoke-consuming furnaces'. He received cold comfort when it was found not to be of any use in his brewery. Without referring to *Jones v. Bright* by name, Lord Abinger said it was a case where there was a failure of the seller to comply with his contractual obligation, not properly a warranty case. He concluded that the buyer had the misfortune to order an item, on the supposition that it would answer a particular purpose but found that it did not. Parke B put it slightly differently: the seller performed his part of the contract by sending a well-known machine, and it was the defendant's responsibility whether it answered his desired purpose.[61]

The Court of Common Pleas was having none of this and continued to apply the separate rule, that goods had to be fit for purpose.[62] In *Brown v. Edgington*

Harburg); *Ireland v. Livingston* (1872) LR 5 HL 395, 406–407, per Blackburn J. See H. Goitein, *The Law as to C.I.F. Contracts*, London, E. Wilson, 1924.

[55] (1932) 43 Ll L Rep 1 (Scrutton, Greer, Slesser LJJ); [1933] AC 470.
[56] For the earlier cases M. Bridge, *The Sale of Goods*, Oxford, Oxford University Press, 1997, 318–319; *Oxford History of the Laws of England*, Oxford, Oxford University Press, 2010, vol. XII, 481 (M. Lobban).
[57] (1829) 5 Bing 533, 130 ER 1167, at 546, 1173.
[58] 'Mercantile Law Contract of Sale' 6 *Law Magazine* 114, 123.
[59] See G. Pearson, 'Reading Suitability against Fitness for Purpose – The Evolution of a Rule' (2010) 32 *Sydney LR* 273, 275–276.
[60] (1838) 4 M & W 399, 150 ER 1484, esp at 405, 1487, where Abinger refers to the facts of the case.
[61] at 406, 1487. On Abinger and Parke and the different approach in the two courts, see P. Atiyah, *The Rise and Fall of Freedom of Contract*, *op cit*, 368.
[62] (1841) 2 Man & G 279, 133 ER 751 (dealer in rope visited warehouse and took measurements; to be used for a crane; manufacture subcontracted; dealer liable when it broke).

Tindal CJ had drawn a distinction between a sale where a party relied not on his own judgment but that of the seller, having informed him of the use to which the article was to be put.[63] He applied the distinction when ordering a new trial in *Shepherd* v. *Pybus*.[64] There the plaintiff, a manufacturer of cement at Faversham in Kent, bought a new barge from the defendant bargebuilder to carry cement up the Thames to his wharf in London. The barge leaked and cargoes of cement damaged. The jury found for the cement manufacturer, but the court was not satisfied without evidence that the bargebuilder had notice of the precise service for which the barge was purchased.[65]

Two decades on from Lord Abinger and Parke B, the Exchequer Chamber in *Bigge* v. *Parkinson*[66] endorsed the statement in *Chitty on Contracts*, that '[w]here a buyer buys a specific article, the maxim *"caveat emptor"* applies; but where the buyer orders goods to be supplied, and trusts to the judgment of the seller to select goods which shall be applicable to the purpose for which they are ordered, there is an implied warranty that they shall be reasonably fit for that purpose'.[67] In the first edition of his treatise on *Sale of Personal Property* in 1868, Benjamin stated the fitness for purpose rule boldly – consistently with the book being not simply a compendium of case law but an attempt to elucidate principle[68] – that if a person bought an article for a particular purpose made known to the seller at the time of the contract, and relied on the seller's skill and judgment to supply what was wanted, there was an implied warranty that the thing was fit for that purpose.[69] In 1877 the Court of Appeal held that fitness for purpose operated even in the case of latent, undiscoverable defects.[70]

The implied term of fitness for purpose was codified in section 14(1) of the Sale of Goods Act 1893. It was given a wider application than the implied term regarding merchantability in section 14(2) since it was not confined, as was merchantability, to sales by description and (in effect) to goods which could not be examined. The courts gave it a wide application. Much later it was said that this was to compensate for the narrow ambit of section 14(2).[71] It also extended to the containers in which a product was sold.[72] The proviso in

---

[63] at 290, 756.   [64] (1842) 3 Man & G 868, 133 ER 1390.
[65] at 881–882, 1395. cf. at 871, 1391, the reporter's statement that the seller knew the purpose.
[66] (1862) 7 Hurl & N 955, 158 ER 758, 961, 760 (contract to supply provisions for London to Bombay (Mumbai) voyage of *Queen Victoria*).
[67] 6th ed., 399, as stated by Cockburn CJ.
[68] C. MacMillan, 'Judah Benjamin: Marginalized Outsider or Admitted Insider?' (2015) 42 *J L & Soc* 150, 168.
[69] J. Benjamin, *Sale of Personal Property*, London, Henry Sweet, 1868, 488. Mellor J stated the rule in less clear terms in *Jones* v. *Just* (1868) LR 3 QB 197, 203. cf. Lord Blackburn, *The Contract of Sale*, 2nd ed. by J. Graham, London, Stevens & Sons, 1885, 205ff, which concentrated on merchantability, even though at the time less important. Unsurprisingly, Blackburn's book died; Benjamin's thrived and lives on, albeit in much altered form, to the present day.
[70] *Randall* v. *Newson* (1877) 2 QBD 102 (pole for carriage purchased from carriage builder).
[71] *Henry Kendall & Sons (A Firm)* v. *William Lillico & Sons Ltd* [1969] 2 AC 31, 79, per Lord Reid.
[72] *Geddling* v. *Marsh* [1920] 1 KB 668.

section 14(1) – that there was no implied condition in the sale of a specified article under its patent or other trade name – was read down to cases where the buyer bought on the basis of the trade name alone, clearly indicating (in the court's view) the absence of any reliance on the seller's skill and judgment.[73] The subsection required that the goods be of a description which it was in the course of the seller's business to supply. In *Spencer Trading Co Ltd v. Devon*[74] the court held that goods should be fit for the purpose even though something new for the manufacturer.[75]

The courts also adopted a generous approach to the requirement in section 14(1) that the buyer make known to the seller the particular purpose for which the goods were required. Where goods by their nature had an obvious purpose, they held that a buyer did not need to communicate expressly why they were being bought. This was more likely with mass-produced consumer goods, as in the leading case of *Priest v. Last*,[76] where the court held that the purpose of the US-made water bottle which had burst and scalded the buyer's wife was obvious. The Privy Council took the same approach when it reversed the High Court of Australia in *Grant v. Australian Knitting Mills Ltd*.[77] The purpose of wearing woollen underpants was obvious – to wear next to the skin – so the retailer was liable when the customer contracted dermatitis because of excess sulphites negligently left in them in the process of manufacture.[78] By contrast with goods for the retail market, those sold commercially might serve a variety of purposes. There the buyer generally needed to make express which of these fitted the bill. Whether that had been done depended on the evidence. In *Bristol Tramways etc Carriage Company Ltd v. Fiat Motors*[79] there were orders sent to Fiat Motors for 'the 24/40 hp Fiat omnibus ... which we inspected' and 'six 24/40 hp Fiat omnibus chassis without tyres'. The evidence was that Fiat had been informed that the vehicles were for heavy passenger traffic in hilly Bristol. The Court of Appeal had no difficulty in holding that the implied condition in section 14(1) applied and that the buses should have been reasonably fit for that type of transport.

(iii) Merchantability

Merchantability, the second implied condition in section 14 of the 1893 Act, did not amount to much by comparison with fitness for purpose. It, too, was conjured by nineteenth-century courts for the needs of the new age. In *Gardiner v. Gray*[80] the buyer had purchased in London twelve bags of 'waste

---

[73] *Bristol Tramways etc Carriage Company Ltd v. Fiat Motors* [1910] 2 KB 831; *Baldry v. Marshall* [1925] 1 KB 260, 266–267, per Bankes LJ; *Wilson v. Rickett Cockerell & Co* [1954] 1 QB 598.
[74] [1947] 1 All ER 284 (adhesive substance supplied to fly paper manufacturer). [75] at 286.
[76] [1903] 2 KB 148.   [77] [1936] AC 85; (1933) 50 CLR 387.
[78] cf. the idiosyncratic buyer with abnormally sensitive skin: *Griffiths v. Peter Conway Ltd* [1939] 1 All ER 685 (CA).
[79] [1910] 2 KB 831. cf. *Jones v. Padgett* (1890) 24 QBD 650 (cloth wanted for special purpose of making uniforms).
[80] (1815) 4 Camp 144, 171 ER 46. See also *Laing v. Fidgeon* (1815) 6 Taunt 108, 128 ER 974.

silk'. When it was sent on to Manchester it proved to be of such poor quality that it could not be sold under that description. Lord Ellenborough held that where there was no opportunity to inspect, the maxim *caveat emptor* did not apply. Goods had to be saleable in the market under the contractual description, although a buyer without an express warranty could not insist that they be of any specific quality or fitness. He put the rationale for the implied warranty pithily: 'The purchaser cannot be supposed to buy goods to lay them on a dunghill.'[81]

When in 1868 in *Jones* v. *Just*[82] Mellor J summed up the law as to the implied terms in sales contracts, he expressed the merchantability requirement as meaning that goods sold under a specific description had to be saleable under that description, but only if the buyer had no opportunity to inspect them beforehand.[83] That was essentially how Blackburn J had directed the jury in the case, which had awarded damages to the plaintiffs. There had been a CIF sale to the plaintiffs, through their Liverpool broker, of bales of Manilla hemp, expected to arrive on four named ships from Singapore. On arrival 200 of the bales had been damaged. It seemed that the hemp had become wet during the voyage from Manilla to Singapore, where it had been dried and repacked. It could not be sold as Manilla hemp, but had been successfully auctioned as 'Manilla hemp with all faults' for about 75 per cent of the price it would otherwise have fetched. The Court of Common Pleas refused to interfere with the jury's award.

The implied term of merchantability was codified in section 14(2) of the 1893 Act. It applied where goods were bought by description from a seller who dealt in goods of that description. The proviso was that if the buyer had examined the goods there was no implied condition as regards defects which such examination ought to have revealed.[84] Goods would not be merchantable if they were of no use for the one purpose for which goods complying with the contractual description would normally be used. That was the conclusion as regards the first two propellers made for the *Athelfoam* in the *Cammell Laird* case, discussed below; they were made specifically for that vessel, but since they did not work properly and were only fit for scrap they could not be merchantable.[85]

The difficulty was if goods under the contractual description were reasonably capable of ordinary use for several purposes. If that was the position the law regarded them as being of merchantable quality 'if they are reasonably

---

[81] at 144, 47. The implied term did not extend to containers in which goods were marketed: *Gowerr* v. *Von Dedalzen* (1837) 3 Bing NC 717, 132 ER 587 (CIF sale of good, merchantable Gallipoli oil, cargo of *Fortuna* to arrive, its containers said to be below standard).
[82] (1868) LR 3 QB 197.
[83] at 202–203. Mellor J was giving the judgment of Cockburn CJ, Blackburn J and himself.
[84] e.g., *Thornett & Fehr* v. *Beers & Son* [1919] 1 KB 486 (unmerchantable glue; buyer in rush; examination would have revealed that it was defective).
[85] [1934] AC 402, 430, per Lord Wright. See also *Grant* v. *Australian Knitting Mills Ltd* [1936] AC 85, 99–100.

capable of being used for any one or more of such purposes, even if unfit for use for that one of those purposes which the particular buyer intended'. That was said by Lord Wright in *Canada Atlantic Grain Export Company Inc v. Eilers*,[86] a case of a CIF sale of barley under the London Corn Trade Association (LCTA) Contract No. 30. That standard form contract provided that an official certificate of inspection was to be final as to quality, the grain 'not [being] warranted free from defect, rendering the same unmerchantable, which would not be apparent on reasonable examination ... '. Although certified by US government inspectors, the barley was affected by *fusarium roseum*, which the sellers did not know about and which was only discoverable on bacteriological examination. Wright J held that there was no basis for upsetting the arbitrators' award that the barley was merchantable, since it was still saleable under its description. Further, he held, the clause in the LCTA contract was effective in limiting the extent of the sellers' liability for quality.[87]

In the years immediately after passage of the Act, the metes and bounds of merchantability seemed to be not as unclear as was later thought. Acceptability to reasonable buyers, acting reasonably, after a full examination of the goods, was the rather sensible template Farwell LJ invoked in *Jackson v. Rotax Motor and Cycle Company*.[88] There a dealer had ordered some 600 motor horns of slightly varying descriptions and prices from a French manufacturer. When they arrived, many were dented or badly finished through defective packing and bad workmanship. Damaged in this way the horns were not acceptable, and thus the Court of Appeal held that they were not of merchantable quality. That was so, even though they could easily have been improved at trifling cost.[89] Usability was another approach, which Lord Wright applied in the *Canada Atlantic Grain Export Company case*.[90]

(iv) Sale by Sample

Sale by sample, and the implied warranty that the quality of the bulk should match it, was the first of the implied warranties Benjamin addressed in his treatise *Sale of Personal Property*.[91] That was no doubt because of its importance in the commodity sales of the first part of the nineteenth century. For example, Liverpool cotton brokers took to buying by sample instead of inspecting the bales. More careful packing, and the increased volume of trade, facilitated this development. Brokers interested in buying specific cotton

---

[86] (1929) 35 Ll L Rep 206, 213. German importers were suing the American exporters. See earlier *Jones v. Padgett* (1890) 24 QBD 650: cloth merchantable, since no evidence that unfit for other ordinary purposes.
[87] 'The grain is to be free ... from defects rendering it unmerchantable if discoverable by reasonable examination', at 211. See 346–347 below.
[88] [1910] 2 KB 937.   [89] See esp Kennedy LJ at 950.
[90] (1929) 35 Ll L Rep 206. See also *Cammell Laird & Co Ltd v. Manganese Bronze & Brass Co Ltd* [1934] AC 402, 430–431.
[91] *op cit*, 482.

were able to inspect the samples at the offices of selling brokers.[92] The common law of sale by sample was codified in section 15 of the Sale of Goods Act 1893. There was a rich case law behind it. Conditions of sale 'per sample', said Abbott CJ in 1821, 'have the same effect as if the seller had, in express terms, warranted that the goods sold should answer the description of a small parcel exhibited at the time of the sale'.[93] The following year he held that the buyer of a parcel of wheat, by sample, had a right to inspect the bulk at a convenient time, so that if the seller refused the contract might be rescinded.[94] His reasoning, to discourage the sale of a commodity not yet acquired, did not survive in the new age of sales to arrive.[95]

Compliance of the sample with the bulk did not preclude the implication of a further term such as merchantability, as in *James Drummond & Sons v. E H Van Ingen & Co*, where both the samples and the bulk contained the same latent defect which was not discoverable by customary and diligent inspection.[96] To the suggestion that the buyer should have subjected the sample to detailed examination, Lord Macnaghten observed that that was not the way in which business was done: a sample could not 'be treated as saying more than such a sample would tell a merchant of the class to which the buyer belongs'.[97] Conversely, use of a sample in the course of a sale did not necessarily mean that there was a sale by sample; the contract and circumstances had to demonstrate this.[98] *Russell* v. *Nicolopulo*[99] was a case where they did. A cargo of Russian wheat from the Black Sea, afloat on the vessel *Barticola*, was sold by brokers in the London market to Irish buyers. In accordance with contemporary practice, given the length of the voyage the sellers, Nicolopulo & Co., had an agent, Scott & Co., examine samples of the grain. The bought note stated that the wheat was 'accepted on the report and samples of Messrs. Scott & Co.' The Court of Common Pleas rejected the argument that all that this amounted to was that the samples were in truth drawn by the agents.

Sale by sample fell by the wayside with commodities once they were sold according to the standards set by the trade associations. With LCTA, samples were taken to constitute the standards applicable for different grains.[100] This was no longer sale by sample as contained in the 1893 Act. An observer of sales of foreign grain at the London Corn Exchange in the 1920s noted how the character of the exchange had changed: 'At one time the floor of the market was knee-deep in corn, for a buyer when he handled a sample was not allowed

---

[92] S. Chapman, *Merchant Enterprise in Britain*, Cambridge, Cambridge University Press, 1992, 76; N. Buck, *The Development of the Organisation of Anglo-American Trade 1800–1850*, New Haven, Yale University Press, 1925, 60.

[93] *Parker* v. *Palmer* (1821) 4 B & Ald 387, 106 ER 978, at 391, 980 (rice). See earlier *Parkinson* v. *Lee* (1802) 2 East 314, 102 ER 389 (hops).

[94] *Lorymer* v. *Smith* (1822) 1 B & C 1,107 ER 1 (wheat). [95] 306, 318 passim below.

[96] (1887) 12 App Cas 284. [97] at 297.

[98] *Gardiner* v. *Gray* (1815) 4 Camp 144, 171 ER 46. See also *Dawson* v. *Collis* (1851) 10 CB 523, 138 ER 208.

[99] (1860) 8 CB NS 362, 141 ER 1206. [100] 306–307 below.

to return it to the bag ... Now, however, most of the corn is sold on standard type sample, and therefore there are scarcely any sweepings.'[101]

3 Remedies for Breach of the Quality Standards

When the implied terms about description, fitness for purpose, merchantability and compliance with sample were incorporated in sections 13–15 of the Sale of Goods Act 1893, they were stated to be conditions. In nineteenth-century contract law a term labelled as a condition entitled a party to terminate the contract, however trivial the breach. If not a condition, a term was regarded as a warranty and the buyer could only obtain damages for breach. The law took the view that the motive of the buyer in terminating the contract and rejecting goods was irrelevant, captured in Lord Atkin's judgment in *Arcos v. Ronaasen*.[102] There are other cases in the books where buyers rejected goods on technicalities because of a falling market and the possibility of purchasing elsewhere more cheaply.

Absent an express term, the matter of rejection for breach of one of the implied conditions was complicated by the concept of 'acceptance' in the 1893 Act. In brief outline, section 11(1)(c) of the Act meant that buyers could lose the right to reject, and were limited to a claim for damages, once they 'accepted' the goods under contracts which were not severable. Albeit that buyers who had not previously examined goods prior to delivery were by section 34(1) not deemed to have accepted them until they had had a reasonable opportunity of doing so, section 35 provided that they were deemed to have accepted goods first, if they intimated acceptance, secondly, did an act inconsistent with the seller's ownership, or thirdly, said nothing to the seller about rejection after retaining the goods for a reasonable period. The rules about acceptance were unnecessarily rigid. In some cases the courts mitigated the strictness of the rules, for example finding a contract was severable. In *Jackson v. Rotax Motor and Cycle Company*[103] the buyer, after accepting the first instalment of motor horns, rejected later instalments. Upon its construction of the contract, the court held that acceptance of the first instalment did not preclude rejection of later, defective instalments.

Rejection as a remedy was a recurrent theme of sales talk. Scrutton LJ canvassed the matter on several occasions, pointing out the practical, as well as the legal implications. One aspect, he said, was that foreign buyers could reject goods for trivial breaches and use that and the fact that the goods were a long way off to extort from sellers a reduction in price.[104] There were also

---

[101] *The City of London*, London, Times Publishing, 1927, 187. On the market in grain in London see: 6–7, 9, 61–62 above.
[102] [1933] AC 480. See 42 above.   [103] [1910] 2 KB 937.
[104] *Szymanowski & Co v. Beck & Co* [1923] 1 KB 457, 467–468 (a case turning on the contract, not the 1893 Act). See also his comments in *Montague L Meyer Ltd v. Kivisto* (1929) 35 Ll L Rep 265, 266 (sale of Finnish timber).

cases where goods arrived from abroad and importers began distributing them to sub-buyers before defects were discovered. Because the buyers were treated as having accepted the goods by acting inconsistently with the seller's ownership, they were confined to a claim in damages.[105] In Chapter 5 we see that the commodity trade associations opted out of the 1893 Act's rules about rejection in their standard form contracts.[106] After our period both the courts and Parliament modified the law of rejection for defective goods.

4 The Reach of Sales Law: 'Sale' or 'Work and Materials'?

In 1934 Lord Wright said in *Cammell Laird and Co Ltd* v. *Manganese Bronze and Brass Co Ltd* that there was no general rule that the implied term as to fitness for purpose was excluded where a manufacturer agreed to make a machine to the design of the buyer.[107] In other words, although there may have been a great deal of work involved in its making, the contract could still be one of sale as opposed to one for work and materials. In a case in 1926, involving a contract where Blyth Shipbuilding and Dry Docks Co. (in Northumberland) agreed to build a steel motor vessel according to the specifications of the Italian shipping line (the Cosulich Line, based in Trieste) ordering it, Romer J concluded that this was 'unquestionably a contract for the sale of future goods within the meaning of the Sale of Goods Act, 1893, this expression being defined by s. 62 (1) of the Act as meaning goods to be manufactured or acquired by the seller after the making of the contract of sale'.[108]

English law had reached this point of sales law having an imperial reach in a typically English way, testing various approaches as litigants presented specific facts and arguments. The issue of where sale ended had first arisen with section 17 of the Statute of Frauds 1677.[109] That provided that a contract for the sale of goods for £10 or more was only good if the buyer accepted and received part of the goods; made part payment or gave something to bind the bargain; or there was a signed note or memorandum.[110] In that context Blackburn J – unsurprisingly perhaps as the author of a treatise on sale – took an expansive view of the subject matter.[111] The test, he held, was whether the contract was to result in a sale of goods; if so, it was a sale, not a contract for

---

[105] *Hardy & Co* v. *Hillerns & Fowler* [1923] 2 KB 490 (not Rosario and/or Santa Fé wheat as per contract but Entre Rios variety); *E. & S. Ruben Ltd* v. *Faire Brothers & Company Ltd* [1949] 1 KB 254 (crinkly rubber, unsuitable for use in sub-buyer's footwear machinery, and not up to sample). The nineteenth-century case law is examined in S. Stoljar, 'The Doctrine of Acceptance' (1958) 1 *Melb ULR* 483. See also J. Honnold, 'Buyer's Right of Acceptance' (1949) 97 *U Penn LR* 457.

[106] 347–348 below.   [107] [1934] AC 402, 426.

[108] *Re Blyth Shipbuilding and Dry Docks Company Ltd* [1926] Ch 494, 499. Romer J's conclusion was undisturbed on appeal and approved in the *Cammell Laird case* [1934] AC 402, 420–421.

[109] 29 Car 2 c.3.   [110] Section 17 was later enacted as section 4(1) of Sale of Goods Act 1893.

[111] *Lee* v. *Griffin* (1861) 1 B & S 272, 121 ER 716.

work and materials, despite the skill and the substance of the work entailed in their manufacture.[112]

In reaching this result the court had distinguished *Clay* v. *Yates*,[113] where Pollock CB had said that the issue was what was the essence of the contract, and that was to be determined by considering the relative importance of, on the one hand, the work and, on the other, the materials. In 1935 the Court of Appeal seemed to revive the *Clay* v. *Yates* test, looking at the substance of the contract to determine how much skill and labour went into the production process.[114] However, the facts were such – a contract for the painting of a portrait – that the Blackburn J line of authority remained unscathed as regards goods manufactured to specifications. It was the approach of Romer J in *Blyth Shipbuilding and Dry Docks case* and, to return to where we began, it was also the situation in *Cammell Laird & Co Ltd* v. *Manganese Bronze & Brass Co Ltd*, where the House of Lords held that the contract to manufacture propellers for a particular ship, according to specifications provided by the ship-owner, was to be analysed according to sales law.[115]

5 Excluding the Implied Conditions as to Quality

Perhaps the most important aspect of sales law was that the parties could exclude the common law, and later the implied rules as codified in the Sale of Goods Act 1893. Section 55 of that 1893 Act was clear about that. The courts imposed some limits on the extent to which parties could contract out. First, those wanting to take advantage of an exclusion clause had to make sure that it was brought home to the other side, in other words, was part of the contract. That rule was most clearly developed not with sales but in the context of the liability of carriers such as the railways, and their attempt to limit their liability to customers for loss and damage.[116] Secondly, the courts interpreted exclusion clauses narrowly against those inserting them in a contract, the so-called *contra proferentem* rule. That had an obvious application to sellers inserting exclusion clauses in their standard form contracts.[117]

---

[112] at 277–276, 718, respectively. Crompton and Hill JJ were to similar effect.
[113] (1856) 1 Hurl & N 73, 156 ER 1123.   [114] *Robinson* v. *Graves* [1935] 1 KB 579.
[115] [1934] AC 402; 223 below. Earlier cases like *Mondel* v. *Steel* (1841) 8 M & W 858, 151 ER 1288 involved ships not being built to specification, but whether this was a sale contract did not arise.
[116] e.g., *Clark* v. *Gray* (1802) 4 Esp 177; 170 ER 682; *Peek* v. *Directors, etc. of the North Staffordshire Railway Company* (1863) 10 HL Cas 473; 11 ER 1109; *Parker* v. *South Eastern Railway Company* (1877) 2 CPD 416. See B. Coote, *Exception Clauses*, London, Sweet & Maxwell, 1964, 21–33; J. Adams, 'The Standardization of Commercial Contracts or the Contractualization of Standard Forms' (1978) 7 Anglo-Amer L Rev 136; *Oxford History of the Laws of England*, vol.12, 1820–1914, Private Law, Oxford, Oxford University Press, 2010, 473–475, 912–915, 967–968 (M. Lobban), who discusses both the case law and the special statutory regimes.
[117] An early case: *Shepherd* v. *Kain* (1821) 5 B & Ald 240; 106 ER 1180 (sale of a ship, described as 'copper-fastened vessel', 'to be taken with all faults', but only partially copper-fastened so words did not protect seller for breach of warranty).

Beck & Co v. Szymanowski & Co[118] is an example. Manchester textile manufacturers sold 2,000 gross of '200 yard reels of sewing cotton fob English Port' to the plaintiffs, merchants carrying on business at Petrograd (St Petersburg) and also at Manchester.[119] The contract contained an exemption clause, clause 5, providing the 'goods delivered' were 'deemed to be in all respects in accordance with the contract, and the buyers shall be bound to accept and pay for the same' unless they gave notice of defects within fourteen days after the reels arrival. The buyers received complaints from their Russian customers that the reels delivered to them were not of the contract length, but notice was not given within the fourteen days. Clause 5 meant that the buyers could not reject the goods, but was it wide enough to exclude a claim for damages? The House of Lords held not: the language had to be clear and it did not cover short delivery; it applied to 'goods delivered' – in effect their quality – not to those not delivered.

A leading case on the *contra proferentem* rule under the 1893 Act was *Wallis* v. *Pratt*.[120] It was a case of a sold note given at the London Corn Exchange, Mark Lane,[121] for what was said to be common English sainfoin seed. The note stated on the reverse side that sellers gave 'no warranty express or implied as to growth, description, or any other matters'. Although the seed was equal to a sample the buyer had inspected, when planted it proved to be inferior giant sainfoin. It was common ground that there had been a breach of the implied condition in section 13. The majority of the Court of Appeal held that since the buyer had accepted the seed by reselling it, under section 11(1)(c) the breach was to be treated as a breach of warranty, to which the exemption clause applied.[122] The House of Lords allowed the appeal: the obligation to supply English sainfoin seed remained a condition, whatever the remedial consequences of subsection 11(1)(c), and the words of the exemption clause did not cover a breach of a condition, only of a warranty.[123] What followed the decision was a mass checking, and if needs be redrafting, of contracts to ensure that liability for a breach of a 'condition' was excluded, as well as of a 'warranty'.[124]

---

[118] [1924] AC 43.
[119] Free on board (FOB) English port meant that the risk passed to the buyer on shipment at an English port. See *Wackerbarth* v. *Masson* (1812) 3 Camp 268, 170 ER 1378 (sugar sold 'free on board a foreign ship'; seller only bound to put on board ship, which it was the duty of the buyer to name).
[120] [1911] AC 394.
[121] The market for seed was conducted separately from that for grain in the Corn Exchange building: F. Dolman, 'Where Merchants most do Congregate. The Corn Exchange' (1895) 8 *The Ludgate Illustrated Magazine* 406, 412.
[122] [1910] 2 K B 1018 (Vaughan Williams and Farwell LJJ, Fletcher Moulton LJ dissenting).
[123] In his reasoning Lord Shaw placed heavy emphasis 'in a commercial contract of construing the meaning of two businessmen' at the time the bargain was made: at 400–401.
[124] 'Sale by Description' (1947) 204 *LT* 130, 131.

4.3 Heavy Manufactured Goods: Plant and Machinery, Chemicals, Locomotives

> Passepartout had woken up and watched, unable to believe that he was crossing India on the Great Peninsular Railway. It all seemed made-up to him. And yet noting could be more genuine! The locomotive, with a British engine-driver and burning British coal, threw its smoke out over the plantations of red pepper, cotton, coffee, nutmeg, and cloves. (Jules Verne, *Around the World in Eighty Days*, 1873)[125]

During most of our period British-made heavy manufactured goods – plant and machinery, chemicals and locomotives – were marketed in considerable volume, both at home and abroad. When disputes arose over their quality, contract law, rather than the specific rules of sales law, often had the whip hand, especially if they had been manufactured to the detailed specifications in a contract. Given their expense and complexity, the express terms of the contract might indicate what the buyer anticipated, how an item was to be tested, as well as the consequences if expectations fell short. An example is furnished by a contract in the 1870s governing the sale of Dick & Stevenson's steam digger for railway construction.

In some cases, the default rules of the common law of sale, later incorporated in the Sale of Goods Act 1893, came into their own. That was because the parties had not agreed relevant terms or anticipated in their express terms the turn of events they now faced. Even in cases where relevant terms had been agreed, sales law might have a heavy bearing on the courts' analysis of the contract when disputes arose. The House of Lords decisions in the *Cammell Laird* and *Silica Gel* cases are illustrative.

When heavy plant and machinery was supplied over a period, the parties to the contract (or contracts) would typically address quality defects by negotiation, price adjustments or after-sales service to put things right.[126] Lawyers might be in the background advising, but the courts were generally only troubled as a last resort. How the Central Electricity Board dealt with Ferranti's short-circuiting transformers in the 1930s shows how, in a long-term relationship, commercial parties might resolve issues amicably. Inspection, monitoring and on-site assessment by a buyer during the construction phase of heavy manufactured goods – all worked to nip quality issues in the bud, especially when coupled with a good relationship between the buyer and seller and after-sales service to put any problem right. We see this on the occasion of British-made steam locomotives being sold abroad in the late 1940s.

---

[125] Jules Verne, *Around the World in Eighty Days*, transl. William Butcher, Oxford, Oxford University Press, 1995.

[126] S. Macaulay 'Non-Contractual Relations in Business: A Preliminary Study' (1963) 28 *Amer Soc Rev* 55 is the seminal study. See further at 290n below.

However, an accommodating attitude might not last forever in a long-term buyer–seller relationship. For various reasons a breaking point might be reached, and legal proceedings initiated. The behaviour of one of the parties might be so bad that it could no longer be excused. That is what occurred in 1924–1925 with the sale of chemicals by Brunner Mond to Lever Bros, companies already powerful, but destined shortly after to become two of the largest British companies in the twentieth century: in 1926 Bruner Mond, along with the United Alkali Company, the British Dyestuffs Corporation and Nobel Explosives, was transformed into Imperial Chemical Industries (ICI), in its time British's largest manufacturer; in 1929 Lever Brothers became the multinational Unilever on its merger with Margarine Unie of the Netherlands.[127]

1 Heavy Machinery: Express Terms about Performance

Sales law had a background role in Britain's industrial revolution. By 1800 there were some 1,200–1,330 steam engines in operation in Britain, including 500 of James Watt's make.[128] In the eighteenth century steam engines had been used for pumping in mines and canals, but more was to come as they spread to powering cotton mills and were harnessed for ships and railways.[129] Law facilitated the sale of Watt's revolutionary design, in part through the patent protection it afforded from competition.[130] Partly it also enabled Watt and his partner, Matthew Boulton, to mould the terms on which the engines were marketed to customers. In lengthy contracts, with long recitals and a mode of expression drawn from real property transactions, Watt and Boulton offered the engines on instalment terms over several years, with a substantial down-payment. They also undertook to assist erect the engine. The contract represented that the engines 'when completed and finished and in good and proper order shall be able to work the said machinery' with a specified horsepower. Reflecting the terms of a real

---

[127] G. Jones, *Renewing Unilever*, Oxford, Oxford University Press, 2005, 7–9; W. Reader, *Fifty Years of Unilever 1930–1980*, London, Heinemann, 1980, 1–10.

[128] P. Mathias, *The First Industrial Nation*, 2nd ed., London, Methuen, 1983, 122–123; P. Hudson, *The Genesis of Industrial Capital A Study of The West Riding Wool Textile Industry c1750-1850*, Cambridge, Cambridge University Press, 1986, 139–140.

[129] There is no need to enter the debate among historians about the impact of steam power: e.g., K. Bruland & K. Smith, 'Assessing the Role of Steam Power in the First Industrial Revolution: The Early Work of Nick von Tunzelmann' (2013) 42 *Research Policy* 1716; G. von Tunzelmann, *Steam Power and British Industrialization to 1860*, Oxford, Clarendon, 1978. See also R. Hills, *Power in the Industrial Revolution*, Manchester, Manchester University Press, 1970.

[130] *Hornblower & Maberly v. Boulton & Watt* (1799) 8 Term Rep 95, 101 ER 1285; *Boulton and Watt v. Bull* (1795) 2 H Bl 463, 126 ER 651. See E. Robinson, 'James Watt and the Law of Patents' (1972) 13 *Technology and Culture* 115. See also C. Beauchamp, *Invented by Law: Alexander Graham Bell and the Patent That Changed America*, Cambridge, Mass, Harvard University Press, 2014, 10.

property lease, the contracts conferred on Watt and Boulton a power of inspection when payments were outstanding.[131] But if the law was predominantly enabling, it might occasionally constrain. Early in the sale of their steam engines abroad Watt and Boulton were advised that it would be rash to rely on any foreign guarantee of payment because of enforcement problems in non-English courts abroad.[132]

With time the plant and machinery of the industrial era became more sophisticated, often made to specifications agreed with or advanced by the buyer. The issue of quality control became more acute once products were supplied in this way.[133] In keeping with the briskness and efficiency of the industrial age, the contracts drawn to govern the sale of plant and equipment, and products such as chemicals, moved away from the excessive verbiage of the Watt-Boulton model drawn from property law. Sometimes commercial practice was to set the terms out in an exchange of letters.[134] Even written contracts could be relatively short, although with the specifications appended the resultant documentation might be lengthy.[135]

Whether there was a breach of a contract might first require an interpretation of its express terms. One such case was *Mackay v. Dick*.[136] There a railway contractor, Mackay, had undertaken to construct a branch line for the Caledonian Railway Company. In the main the railways of nineteenth-century Britain were constructed by the railway navvies, undertaking back-breaking work with pick and shovel.[137] To assist with the excavation of an extensive cutting, the Wishaw Cutting, with the Carfin Cutting at one end, the Garriongill Cutting at the other, Mackay decided to buy a steam excavator,

---

[131] BA & C, LS/15/91, Boxes, 28/8 and 31/46, Boulton and Watt, Indenture dated 1 March 1786 between Watt & Boulton and Liptrap & Ors, Whitechapel, London; Indenture dated 1 March 1796 between Watt & Boulton and Nevins & Gatliff, clothiers of York. See H. Dickinson & R. Jenkins, *James Watt and the Steam Engine*, 2nd ed., Ashbourne, Moorland, 1981, 139. On the baleful influence of land law on sales transactions: K. Llewellyn, 'The First Struggle to Unhorse Sales' (1939) 52 *Harv L Rev* 873, 873–874.

[132] S. Chapman, *Merchant Enterprise in Britain: From the Industrial Revolution to World War I*, Cambridge, Cambridge University Press, 1992, 135.

[133] M. Casson, 'Contractual Arrangements for Technology Transfer: New Evidence from Business History' (1986) 28 *Bus Hist* 5, 17.

[134] e.g., GRO, GWWC, D4791/27/1, contract for sale of some 300 wagons and carriages by Gloucester Wagon Co. Ltd for Santa Fe & Reconquista Railway, Argentina, February 1887 (the letters referred to specifications). See also 'A Contract in Letters' (1890) 54 *JP* 675.

[135] e.g., GRO, GWWC, D4791/27/10, D4791/27/18, contracts for sale by Gloucester Wagon Co. Ltd to (i) Indian Midland Railway Co. Ltd, metalwork for 135 covered wagons, 28 June 1900; (ii) Canton Kowloon Railway, 4 passenger car underframes and bogies, 9 January 1933 (both with specifications attached). See also the precedents in *Encyclopaedia of the Laws of England with Forms and Precedents*, 1st ed., London, Butterworths, 1906, vol. XI, 583 ('Agreement between Wholesale Manufacture and Retailer for Sale'), 591 ('Agreement for the Manufacture and Supply of Frames for Chairs').

[136] (1881) 6 App Cas. 251. See also *Millar's Machinery Co Ltd v. David Way & Son* (1935) 40 Comm Cas 204 (gravel cleaning machine).

[137] T. Coleman, *The Railway Navvies: A History of the Men Who Made the Railways*, London, Hutchinson, 1965; D. Brooke, *The Railway Navvy*, London, David & Charles, 1983.

invented by Dick & Stevenson. In September 1876 Mackay and Dick & Stevenson entered negotiations and reached an agreement set out in an exchange of letters. Under the contract (as the House of Lords interpreted it) Dick & Stevenson were to bring one of their steam excavators to the Carfin Cutting and try it out on a properly 'opened-up face' before February 1877. Both sides agreed that if the machine answered the test, Mackay was to keep it and pay the agreed price.

The railway company changed its plans, so that when the excavator arrived it was taken to the Garriongill cutting where it broke down. After repair, it was sent to the Carfin Cutting. There it was tried, and broke down again, but not while working a properly 'opened-up face'. Upholding the First Division of the Court of Session, the House of Lords held that Dick & Stevenson was entitled to be paid for the price of the excavator. Mackay had never enabled the machine to be properly tested in line with the contract on a properly 'opened-up face' at Carfin Cutting. In general, Lord Blackburn said, where in a written contract both parties agreed that something should be done which could not effectually be done unless both concurred, each impliedly agreed to do all that was necessary for it to occur. That had not happened.[138]

Mackay v. Dick was not the only dispute reaching the courts where the outcome turned on the express terms of the contract rather than the default rules in the common law, later the Sale of Goods Act 1893. In a leading case on damages, *Victoria Laundry (Windsor) v. Newman Industries*,[139] the court awarded the buyers (launderers and dyers) lost profits when the second-hand 'vertical Cochran boiler of 8,000 lb per hour capacity heavy steaming' arrived late, the buyers having stated in a letter its intention to put the boiler promptly to use 'at the very moment when a concluded contract emerged'.[140] In *Saint Line Limited v. Richardsons, Westgarth & Co Ltd*[141] the marine engineers, who sold a set of unsatisfactory engines to the plaintiff shipping line for one of its vessels, the *Saint Germain*, had to compensate it for direct and immediate losses when the relevant clause in the sale contract only protected it against claims for indirect and consequential damages. There are other examples, touched on below.

2 Goods Manufactured to Specification

During our period, as we have seen, English law adopted an imperial view of sale. Sales law encompassed a wide range of contracts, including those involving work and materials to manufacture what the buyer wanted.[142] Therefore when goods were manufactured to specifications provided by the buyer, the contract generally fell under sales law. That had important ramifications. If this type of contract had been regarded as a contract for work and materials, the

---

[138] (1881) 6 App Cas 251, 263. Lord Selborne LC and Lord Watson agreed.
[139] [1949] 2 KB 528.   [140] at 533–534, per Asquith LJ.   [141] [1940] 2 KB 99.
[142] 216–217 above.

manufacturer would only have been required to exercise reasonable care and skill in making the goods.[143] Sales law set a higher bar: what the manufacturer made had to be fit for the purpose which the buyer required. It did not matter that the manufacturer had exercised reasonable care and skill in making goods if they did not meet this standard.

Cammell Laird and Company Ltd v. *Manganese Bronze and Brass Company*[144] was a strong case in extending yet further the reach of sales law and the implied condition of fitness for purpose in section 14(1) of the 1893 Act. The plaintiff, Cammell Laird, based on the River Mersey in Birkenhead, was one of Britain's leading shipbuilders.[145] The defendants, Manganese Bronze, made ships' propellers.[146] The dispute arose over a contract for Manganese Bronze to manufacture two propellers for the *Athelfoam* and her sister ship, the *Athelbeach*, which Cammell Laird was building for the owner, the United Molasses Company Ltd. The ships had been ordered by the company to carry either petroleum or molasses. Cammell Laird provided detailed specifications and working drawings for the propellers, which included the dimensions, the pitch ratio, the total developed area and the maximum horsepower. Other aspects were left to Manganese Bronze, which was not provided with details of the ships' diesel engines, including their differing critical periods. The contract for the propellers stated that they were to be to the 'entire satisfaction' of Cammell Laird and the ships' owners.

When fitted, the propeller of the *Athelfoam* caused excessive vibration and noise at the critical period of the vessel's engines. Two replacement propellers and long and expensive trials were necessary to get things right. Cammell Laird claimed for the cost of the delay and of the trials. Its claim was based on express warranty, as well as sections 14(1) and (2) of the 1893 Act. Manganese Bronze counterclaimed for the cost of the replacement propellers. In the Commercial Court, Roche J held that there had been a breach by Manganese Bronze of the implied condition of fitness for purpose under section 14(1).[147] Reversing Roche J, the majority in the Court of Appeal (Scrutton and Lawrence JJ) held that Cammell Laird had no case under

---

[143] The general principle was stated by Willes J in *Russian Steam-Navigation Trading Company* v. *Silva* (1863) 13 CBNS 610, 617,143 ER 242, 245. The materials, however, had to comply with Sale of Goods standards and their common law predecessors: *G. H. Myers & Co* v. *Brent Cross Service Co* [1934] 1 KB 46.

[144] [1934] AC 402. The only reference in the minute book of the Cammell Laird directors 1932–1934 (Wirral Archives, ZCL 5/45) is 10 April 1934: 'It was resolved that the thanks of the Board be conveyed to the Management, Staff and Legal Advisers on the result of the action against the Manganese Bronze & Brass Co. Ltd.' I am grateful to William Meredith of the Wirral Archives Service for this information. The litigation was closely followed in the *Birkenhead News*: 9, 16, 30 July 1932; 18 & 21 January 1933; 7, 10, 14 & 17 February 1934.

[145] K. Warren, *Steel, Ships and Men: Cammell Laird, 1824–1993*, Liverpool, Liverpool University Press, 1998.

[146] It also made motorcycles and the iconic London black taxi.

[147] (1932) 43 Ll L Rep 466. He rejected separate claims that the propeller was made of defective material and that its blades were negligently shaped.

section 14(1).[148] Both judges invoked a passage in *Benjamin on Sale*[149] to support their conclusion that Manganese Bronze's only liability was to make the propellers according to the plans supplied and in a workmanlike manner.[150]

The House of Lords allowed Cammell Laird's appeal.[151] First, it held, there was a breach of the express warranty. Albeit made in accordance with the plans and made with good workmanship and materials, the two propellers initially provided for the *Athelfoam* were unsatisfactory. Therefore Manganese Bronze had failed to comply with the contractual term that it would supply a propeller to the entire satisfaction of the owner's representatives. Secondly, the court recalled, the first requirement of section 14(1), making known the particular purpose, had been given a liberal interpretation.[152] Here Cammell Laird had satisfied this precondition, in that the propellers had been ordered for use on specific vessels, the *Athelfoam* and its sister ship.[153] Actual reliance on the seller's skill and judgment, a further requirement of section 14(1), meant bringing home to the mind of Manganese Bronze that is was being relied on in such a way that it could be taken to have contracted on that footing. Reliance under the section 14(1) could be partial.[154] In this case, even though Cammell Laird provided the specifications, it still relied on Manganese Bronze manufacturing something that would function as a propeller.

3 The Silica Gel Case: Plant for an Oil Refinery

Cited in the *Cammell Laird case* was the largely unreported House of Lords decision *Medway Oiland Storage Co v. Silica Gel Corporation*.[155] Although it involved a contract to provide a key part of the plant for an oil refinery, it was treated as a contract for the sale of goods to which section 14 (1) applied. Unlike the conclusion in the *Cammell Laird case*, the House of Lords held that there was no reliance and that that was confirmed by the express terms of the contract. The background was the post–First World War period when petroleum was in increasing demand, especially with the number of commercial and

---

[148] [1933] 2 KB 141. They rejected express warranty since the problem was not the propeller but its use with the ship's engine.
[149] 7th ed., 662–663.
[150] [1933] 2 KB 141, 165, 183. As to section 14(2) both held that the propeller was merchantable as a propeller.
[151] [1934] AC 402.
[152] Citing *Manchester Liners Ltd. v. Rea Ltd* [1922] 2 AC 74 (shipowners ordering coal to bunker their steamship, the *Manchester Importer*, which proved unsuitable for the vessel).
[153] per Lord Wright at 422. Lords Tomlin, Warrington and Russell agreed.
[154] at 425, 427. See Lord Macmillan at 419 (despite specifications there was still margin for Manganese Bronze's skill and judgment as shown by the three different propellers made for the *Athelfoam*). cf. *Teheran-Europe Co. Ltd. v. S. T. Belton (Tractors) Ltd* [1968] 2 QB 545. (Iranian importers of air compressors relied upon own skill and judgment that suitable for resale in Persia as new and unused.)
[155] Part of the judgment is at (1928) 33 Comm Cas 195.

private motor vehicles growing. Headed by an American, Charles de Ganahl, the Medway Oil and Storage Company bought land on the Isle of Grain in the Thames estuary in Kent in 1923 to build a facility for the storage, refining and marketing of oil.[156] In January 1924 Medway Oil entered a contract with the Silica Gel Corporation of Maryland for a silica gel refining unit and the supply of silica gel to service it.[157]

Medway Oil had decided to acquire a licence for the Cross patent cracking process to refine the Russian oil in its new plant. When investigating the process in the United States, Medway Oil had learnt of the potential use of silica gel. Through Silica Gel's London agent, it obtained samples and information. On two occasions de Ganahl's son, who had just completed a chemical engineering degree in Massachusetts, visited Silica Gel in Maryland with other Medway officials to inspect the process. Young de Ganahl suggested the introduction into the process of bubble towers between the Cross cracking and silica gel processes, then a novel method in refining petroleum. Silica Gel's representative did not disagree. The contract between the parties was relatively short, covering just five clauses. Clause 2 provided, in part: 'Should the plant fail to fulfil the conditions of work [Silica Gel] shall proceed to put same in order but should the plant then totally fail [it] shall take back the plant and refund ... the price thereof and [it] shall not be under any further or other liability.'[158]

The refinery began using the process in July 1924, but it was abandoned as a failure the following month when the petrol it produced clogged the engines of vehicles using it. Medway Oil claimed for breach of section 14(1) of the Sale of Goods Act 1893 on the grounds that the silica gel refining unit was not fit for the purpose for which it was acquired. After a thirteen-day trial, Rowlatt J held that Medway Oil was entitled to damages, but that it could not reject the plant. Silica Gel, he reasoned, was the expert and the proponent of the product. Medway Oil had communicated the purpose of the plant to it, showing that it relied on Silica Gel's skill and judgment.[159] The silica gel plant was not reasonably fit for that purpose. The Court of Appeal (Lord Hanworth MR, Scrutton and Sargant LJJ) allowed Silica Gel's appeal. As Scrutton LJ put it in relation to section 14(1), 'in an experimental plant after making all the enquiries they thought necessary, [Medway Oil] relied on their own judgment'.[160] Further, the court held that clause 2 of the contract excluded any implied term in Medway Oil's favour such as that in section 14(1) of the 1893 Act.

---

[156] J. Smith, *Isle of Grain, Hoo Peninsula, Kent*, Swindon, English Heritage, Research Report Series no. 1-2014, 13. The oil refinery closed within the decade (HC, *Hansard*, v. 272, 29 November 1932, cc.624–625). Later BP had a refinery there: J. Bamberg, *The History of the British Petroleum Company*, Cambridge, Cambridge University Press, 1984, vol. 2, 290.

[157] Silica Gel Corporation eventually became part of W. R. Grace & Co: T. Votteler, *International Directory of Company Histories*, London, St James, 1988, vol. 50, 522.

[158] The contract is in LI, Printed Cases, Judgments and appeal documents, House of Lords, *Medway Oil & Storage Company Ltd v. The Silica Gel Corporation*, vol. 740, 1928, 703–705.

[159] Ibid., 617–618. [160] Ibid., 675.

The House of Lords dismissed Medway Oil's appeal. Lord Sumner, with whom the others agreed, said that there had to be evidence showing that reliance on the seller's skill and judgment had been brought home to the seller, albeit that substantial (not total) reliance would be sufficient. Here this was the first large-scale operation undertaken with silica gel in refining petrol. Medway Oil had taken its own precautions. In the circumstance no seller would understand that a buyer was relying on its skill and judgment. In effect reducing the scope for reliance claims, Lord Sumner said that reliance on another was not a course which was always either obvious or probable, 'it may be so far from what prudence would dictate as to be neither'. Further, Lord Sumner held, clause 2 did not suggest reliance, especially when compared with earlier drafts of the clause where Medway Oil had put forward wording dealing expressly with warranties and damages in a form more favourable to itself than Silica Gel.[161]

4 Ferranti and the Central Electricity Board: Short-Circuiting Transformers

Ferranti International plc was in the post–Second World War period one of Britain's most successful companies in electrical engineering and defence electronics – developing airborne navigation systems, computers and microelectronic chips – before its demise in the early 1990s. The company had begun in the late nineteenth century under the inspired leadership of Sebastian de Ferranti, born in Liverpool of an Italian father.[162] Ferranti's early success was in manufacturing meters and transformers for electricity supply, but before the First World War he was also manufacturing generators, steam valves, high-voltage cables and switchgear.[163]

In the 1920s the government's decision to create a national electricity grid provided an important opportunity for Ferranti's transformer department, managed by Ferranti's son, Vincent. The Electricity (Supply) Act 1926 had created the Central Electricity Board, the CEB, to orchestrate the national grid out of a patchwork of independent and municipal suppliers.[164] Ferranti was one of the few firms capable of manufacturing large, three-phase transformers, which it had persuaded the CEB to use in place of the planned single-phase equipment. By the end of 1930 the Board had awarded Ferranti 32 per cent of the contracts for supplying 66Kv and 132Kv transformers.[165] The contracts for

---

[161] The full judgment is in ibid.
[162] J. Wilson, 'Ferranti, Sebastian Ziani de (1864–1930), electrical engineer and inventor', *Oxford Dictionary of National Biography*. Vincent Ferranti succeeded his father, who died suddenly in 1930, in running the business.
[163] J. Wilson, *Ferranti A History, Building a Family Business 1882–1975*, Lancaster, Carnegie Publishing, 2000, 1.
[164] s. 1. See L. Hannah, *Electricity before Nationalisation*, London, Macmillan, 1979, 105–155.
[165] J. Wilson, *Ferranti and the British Electrical Industry 1864–1930*, Manchester, Manchester University Press, 1988, 132–134. Unfortunately, Wilson does not refer to the dispute outlined here, except to say that Ferranti's contracts with the Board were completed in 1932: 134.

the supply of the transformers contained many pages of specifications and incorporated by reference the 1926 edition of the Model Form of General Conditions of the Institution of Electrical Engineers for the United Kingdom.

Important in Ferranti's role in supplying transformers to the CEB was the relationship between Vincent and Johnstone Wright, deputy chief engineer and, after 1933, chief manager of the CEB. Difficulties between the two were settled by negotiation and compromise. In 1931 there had been a difference over the price for lagging the transformers at the Southwark transforming station, Vincent explaining to Wright that the higher price than anticipated was because of the experimental work that had had to be performed. A compromise was reached: the CEB would have one lagged transformer to begin.[166] Then in 1932, to the irritation of the CEB, there were delays in delivering the transformers for the north-west and south-west regions. Wright urged speed, adding that as 'an inducement to yet further improvements of the delivery dates' given for the two stations, he 'might be prepared to dangle a further 30,000Kv transformer before your eyes'.[167] A few months later Wright made a personal plea to Vincent ('the fountain head', he flattered) for early delivery for the Barton station, which supplied Warrington, a major industrial centre. Vincent obliged.[168]

This background of accommodation and compromise was important when, in late 1933, a design fault was discovered in the 132Kv transformers – they short-circuited when subject to surges. That was in breach of the contract specifications, which required the transformers to meet certain levels of pressure. There were meetings between Vincent and Wright and their respective teams.[169] Investigations were undertaken. Ferranti asked the CEB for information about the phases on which flash-overs occurred, although the CEB replied that it was difficult to answer the question.[170] Given what appeared to be a clear breach of contract, Ferranti obtained legal advice on the question whether its liability was limited by the terms of the contract. It sought advice from its solicitors, Skelton & Co. of Manchester, who engaged William Gorman QC (later a High Court judge).

In an opinion dated 8 May 1934 Gorman considered relevant clauses of the contract.[171] First, the contract provided that the CEB would conduct tests contained in its Schedule F, including a short-circuit test. Whether those tests were conducted was irrelevant, said Gorman, since clause 13(3) of the contract

---

[166] MSI, YA1996.10/1/7/427, Ferranti, Correspondence, General, C4, letters between Wright and Vincent, 9, 15. 16, 21, 28 April 1931.
[167] Ibid., letter Wright to Vincent, 26 April 1932. Vincent replied on 2 May 1932 that if the dangling took effect he might manage another conjuring trick.
[168] Ibid., letters, 20, 30 June, 2 July 1932.   [169] Ibid., letter, Vincent to Wright, 29 January 1934.
[170] Ibid., letter, Ferranti to Vincent, 28 February 1934.
[171] MSI, YA1996.10/2/3/361, Ferranti, 'Ferranti Ltd and Central Electricity Board, Opinion, 8 May 1934.' There had been an opinion the previous year by J. E. (later Lord Justice) Singleton about Ferranti's liability in the event of lightning strikes: MSI, YA1996.10/2/3/360, Opinion, 16 December 1933.

provided that no approval by the engineer of work, plant or materials should relieve Ferranti from liability to complete the contract in accordance with its terms. The tests, as he put it, were an additional safeguard but did not affect Ferranti's liability. Secondly, Gorman explained, the various clauses provided for the engineer appointed under the contract to issue certificates. There was a distinction, he said, between the type of certificate under clause 25 of the Model Form, a precondition to payment, and the certificate referred to in clause 34, issued when the transformers were 'taken-over' by the Board. Once there was a 'taken-over' certificate the CEB lost its right of rejection. However, Gorman added, clause 36 of the Model Form made Ferranti responsible in the twelve months following the plant being taken over for materials, design or workmanship below the standard in the specification. Under the clause, Gorman concluded, Ferranti had to remedy such defects once the engineer had required it to do so and had specified in writing the nature of the fault.

The CEB did not attempt to reject the transformers, even if it could have done so. Whatever the legal position that was no doubt a practical decision, based in part on the availability of substitutes and the track record of Vincent and the Ferranti team addressing problems. At some point, in accordance with the contract, the engineers required Ferranti to make repairs and modifications at four transformer stations, 'under your contract' (in other words, clause 36), 'so that re-erection and putting into service of the transformers shall be carried out without any avoidable delay'.[172] Ferranti undertook the necessary remedial work. There had been a hitch, but one which was satisfactorily resolved. As the CEB put it in its annual report for 1934, 'minor troubles inevitably [are] associated with the initiation of a system of the magnitude of the national grid'.[173] The relationship between Ferranti and the CEB continued in the following decade, with Ferranti providing the Board further services and advice, and the good relationship between Wright and Vincent being maintained.

5 Ensuring Quality by Specification, Inspection and Monitoring: Steam Locomotives

The British steam locomotives of the nineteenth and first part of the twentieth centuries were in the main hand-built, precision made, and of a high standard of engineering, but characterised by a lack of standardisation in their design and manufacture.[174] Stiff competition between the railways companies for

---

[172] MSI, Ferranti, Correspondence, General, YA1996.10/1/7/427, C4, 1931–1948, Draft instruction; letter Vincent to Wright, 9 June 1934. There is no final instruction in the file. Nor does there seem to be anything in the CEB files: MSI, Electricity Council Archive, YA1989.338. I am grateful to Emma Burgham, archivist at the Science and Industry Museum, for checking this.
[173] Central Electricity Board, *Seventh Annual Report*, 1st January to 31st December 1934, 7.
[174] M. Kirby, 'Product Proliferation in the British Locomotive Building Industry, 1850–1914: An Engineer's Paradise?' (1988) 30 *Business History* 287; D. Drummond, 'Building a Locomotive: Skill and the Work Force in Crewe Locomotive Works 1843–1914' (1987) 8 *J Transport Hist* 1,

business, coupled with technical innovations such as iron (rather than steel) rails, continuous braking and block signalling, meant locomotives could become faster and more powerful. There were regular improvements in their design and construction, introduced in new models and when locomotives were rebuilt after being in service.[175] Systematic on-road testing to foster better service came later.[176]

(i) The Engine Manufacturers

The locomotives used by British railway companies were mainly built in-house, partly through a desire for speedy delivery, and partly to ensure quality. What became the large railway company workshops in Swindon, Crewe, Derby and Doncaster developed a momentum of their own in the manufacture of locomotives. Standardisation was facilitated.[177] After nationalisation of the railways in 1948 and the creation of what became known as British Rail, the policy of in-house manufacture became entrenched.

Independent of the railway companies were many railway locomotive and carriage manufacturers. In 1875 the locomotive manufacturers formed themselves into the Locomotive Manufacturers' Association (the LMA) to protect their interests.[178] Around this time Beyer, Peacock & Co., Robert Stephenson & Co., and R. & W. Hawthorn & Co. were, together with the Baldwin Locomotive Works in Philadelphia and Borsig in Berlin, the five largest locomotive manufacturers in the world.[179] At the end of the Second World War the leading locomotive firms in Britain were, first, the North British Locomotive Co. Ltd, the largest and based in Glasgow.[180] It sold some 12,000 locomotives during its existence – 28,000 if production of the earlier firms was considered – mainly abroad.[181] Secondly, there was Beyer Peacock & Co. Ltd, which began in the

---

21; R. Samuel, 'Workshop of the World: Steam Power and Hand Technology in Mid-Victorian Britain', *History Workshop*, No 3, Spring, 1977, 41–42; P. Bagwell, *The Railway Clearing House in the British Economy 1842-1922*, London, Allen & Unwin, 1968, 212–215.

[175] M. Kirby, 'Technological Innovation and Structural Division in the UK Locomotive Building Industry 1850-1914' in C. Holmes & A. Booth (eds.), *Economy and Society European Industrialisation and its Social Consequences*, Leicester, Leicester University Press, 1991.

[176] e.g., W. Goss, *Locomotive Performance*, New York, John Wiley, 1909; W. Dalby, *Steam Power*, London, Longmans, Green & Co, 1915; J. Warren, 'Early Railway History and the Evolution of the Locomotive', Great Western Railway (Bristol) Lecture and Debating Society, Session 1928-1929, No 94; 'Locomotive Testing' in J. Simmons & G. Biddle, *Oxford Companion to British Railway History from 1603 to the 1990s*, Oxford, Oxford University Press, 1997.

[177] J. Simmons, *The Railway in England and Wales 1830-1914*, Leicester, Leicester University Press, 1978, 182–183.

[178] On the LMA: J. Simmons & G. Biddle (eds.), *op cit*, 414.

[179] L. Hannah, 'Corporations in the US and Europe 1790-1860' (2014) 56 *Business History* 865, 870.

[180] *Locomotives*, PEP Engineering Reports III, London, Political & Economic Planning, 1951, 18–19; R. Campbell, 'The North British Locomotive Company Between the Wars' (1978) 20 *Business History* 201.

[181] A. Fleming, S. McKinstry & K. Wallace, 'The Decline and Fall of the North British Locomotive Company, 1940–62: Technological and Financial Mismanagement or Institutional Failure?' (2000) 42 *Business History* 67, 68.

1850s and was based in Gorton, Manchester. From the outset it exported most of its locomotives.[182] Next was Vulcan Foundry Ltd, which began with steam locomotives in 1833 and during its life time manufactured over 6,000, about half for India and Ceylon.[183] Fourth there was what in 1937 became Robert Stephenson and Hawthorns Ltd, which had been the first steam locomotive works in the world in 1823.[184] Historically there had always been a close association between Vulcan Foundry Ltd and Robert Stephenson and Hawthorns Ltd and in 1944 they amalgamated, and a joint managing director appointed.[185]

Locomotive manufacturers such as these were largely excluded from the domestic market since the railway companies attempted to meet their needs in-house. In the late nineteenth century the locomotive manufacturers resorted to legal action in an attempt to prevent the railway companies from limiting further the home market they dominated.[186] It was a victory of sorts since the decision was interpreted as limiting the railway companies, under their constitutive statutes, to manufacturing for their own needs and selling only surplus engines and rolling stock.[187] It was in places such as India,

Figure 4.1 Locomotives for export: Robert Stephenson & Hawthorns Ltd engines bound for India (National Railway Museum and Alstom)

---

[182] R. Hills & D. Patrick, *Beyer Peacock: Locomotive Builders to the World*, Glossop, Transport Publishing, 1982. Its most successful locomotive, the Beyer Garrett, was articulated, with the boiler frame and cab between two steam engines on separate frames: R. Grantham, 'Spanning the World', *Professional Engineering*, May 2013, 26.
[183] J. Lowe, *British Steam Locomotive Builders*, Barnsley, Pen & Sword Books, 2014, 629–634.
[184] Ibid., 609–616.   [185] At the time, Mr G. Collingwood: see 236–237 below.
[186] *Attorney General* v. *Great Eastern Railway Co* (1880) 5 App Cas 473.
[187] J. Browne & H. Theobald, *The Law of Railway Companies*, 4th ed., London, Stevens & Sons, 1911, 94.

Australasia and South Africa that the locomotive manufacturers found a large market, although they also sold in China, East and West Africa and South America. The manufacturers built a wide range of locomotives to cope with the diversity in local track gauges, gradients and the availability of fuel and water. The lack of standardisation was later to place them at a disadvantage with foreign manufactures such as Baldwin. It was said that British locomotives were too perfect technically, were subjected to unnecessarily strict testing procedures and were made yet more expensive because of limited standardisation.[188] With time the British manufacturers tried to steer buyers in the direction of existing designs.[189] Catalogues of locomotives already made were of some assistance in encouraging this. The demise of the companies came with the 1960s with technological change (electrification and diesel engines) and wider political and economic changes (newly independent countries like India determined to build their own).

(ii) Ensuring Quality: Specifications, Inspection, Monitoring and After-sales Service

To ensure the quality of the railway locomotives, sales contracts entered by British manufacturers adopted a four-pronged approach. First, the specifications to which the locomotives were to be built were detailed, especially when coupled with the drawings incorporated by reference. For example, in December 1929 the Bengal Nagpur Railway ordered sixteen N class Beyer Garratt engines. At one time privately owned, the railway had the heaviest traffic in coal and ores to be found in India.[190] The specifications for Order 1152 was for ten engines and covered requirements for their arrangement; the type, standard and source of the various parts; the marking of parts; the name and number plates; boiler pressure and how it was to be tested; the livery and how it was to be executed; and the methods of testing and weighing.[191] The specifications under Orders 1153 and 1154 of the same date for six more N class Beyer Garratt engines were shorter, as variations on Order 1152.[192] There were drawings for the orders, which stated that the dimensions given in them should not be exceeded.

Secondly, as well as internal controls the work was subject to inspection by buyers. Inspection had come early. In 1856 R. & W. Hawthorn entered an agreement with the Stockton and Darlington Railway Company – the world's

---

[188] S. Saul, 'The American Impact on British Industry 1895–1914' (1960) 2 *Bus Hist* 19, 20–21.

[189] C. Heap, 'Nineteenth Century Production and Pricing at Beyer, Peacock & Company, Locomotive Manufacturers, Manchester', in N. Cossons, *Perspectives in Railway History and Interpretation*, York, National Railway Museum, 1992, 32.

[190] O. Nock, *The British Steam Railway Locomotive 1925–1965*, London, Ian Allan, 1966, 87. See also D. Boughey, 'British Overseas Railways as Free-Standing Companies 1900–1915' (2009) *Business History* 484, 491.

[191] MSI, YA1966.24/3/4/5/4, Beyer, Peacock & Co. Ltd, Garratt Locomotive Order Book Nos 1146–1161, p. 80.

[192] Ibid., pp. 98, 103.

first railway to use steam[193] – to supply six mineral locomotives and tenders, the first by May, the remainder at two a month after that, with an option for ordering two or four more engines on the same terms by 1 February 1857.[194] The terms were short but draconian. First, the locomotives were to be in accordance with the pattern of one of the railway company's existing engines and the instructions given by one of its representatives. Second, the price for each engine was only payable when it had run 1,000 miles and the workmanship and materials had been inspected and certified as satisfactory by the railway company's engineers.[195] With time the task of inspection for those ordering locomotives from abroad was undertaken on their behalf by independent consultant engineers in Britain.

Third, buyers could also monitor the progress of the work. Initially, progress reports might be required on the stages of construction, and engineers might visit the manufacturer's factory. This ad hoc monitoring evolved into a more formal system where contracts included clauses allowing the railway companies ordering the engines to inspect all the work and materials whenever they liked, as well as having the power to reject any which they regarded as inferior or imperfect. It was also practice to specify that unless specifically approved sub-contracting was forbidden, and that there would be a financial penalty for late delivery. These attempts at monitoring contracts 'evolved during the century as the locomotive itself became more complex, as design could be more closely specified, and as railway companies became more knowledgeable of the engineering involved and of the [manufacturers]'.[196]

Finally, on the manufacturers' side they would conduct on-site visits once the locomotives had arrived at their destinations to obtain first-hand information about their running. No doubt these visits were also aimed at building good relations for the future. Even if this form of after-sales service was not incorporated into the contract, it seems to have been a customary understanding with some locomotive manufactures that they would sort out problems which arose.[197] Thus in 1946 Beyer, Peacock & Co. had their consultant engineers in South Africa travel the country to report back details to Britain on the workings of the first twenty GEA class Beyer Garratt engines in service there. Various problems were identified, some of which could be

---

[193] M. Kirby, *The Origins of Railway Enterprise: The Stockton and Darlington Railway, 1821–1863*, Cambridge, Cambridge University Press, 1993.
[194] NA, Rail 667/331, Agreement for 6 loco engines, R & W Hawthorne and Stockton and Darlington Railway Company, 4 January 1856. cf. NA, Rail 667/336, Agreements with Stephen Carlton for building of railway carriages, 7 January 1852, 14 August 1853, where the railway company's representatives could enter Carlton's works to inspect progress.
[195] NA, Rail 667/331, ibid.
[196] D. Boughey, 'The Internalisation of Locomotive Building by Britain's Railway Companies during the Nineteenth Century' (1999) 28 *Business and Economic History* 57, 62.
[197] cf. J. Wightman, 'Beyond Custom: Contract, Contexts, and the Recognition of Implicit Understandings', in D. Campbell, H. Collins & J. Wightman (eds.), *Implicit Dimensions of Contract*, Oxford, Hart Publishing, 2003, 164.

rectified by better handling of the engines, but the engineers reported in congratulatory mode that 'the engine itself is practically perfect in every respect', and there 'has not been a single complaint regarding the workmanship or material'.[198]

(iii) The Post-Second World War Tasmanian Tender for Locomotives

This four-pronged contractual approach to ensure quality – specifications, inspection, monitoring and on-site assessment – can be illustrated with the Tasmanian Government's purchase of eighteen steam locomotives in the immediate post–Second World War period. Although coming on-line, diesel engines were considered but ruled out by the government because of the difficulties of obtaining the fuel from abroad. The tender for the engines was announced on 23 December 1948 – ten light 4-6-2 type locomotives of 20,000lb tractive effort, and eight heavy 4-8-2 type locomotives of 28,000lb tractive effort – for service on the 3'6"-gauge Tasmanian railways, in conformity 'with the specifications attached'. The notice also stated: 'The lowest or any tender [will] not necessarily be accepted.'[199]

No tenders were received from Australian manufacturers. However, there was interest in Britain. The chief mechanical engineer for Tasmanian Railways travelled there to negotiate with those who had tendered. North British Locomotive Co. Ltd. and Beyer, Peacock & Co. Ltd. submitted offers, but he recommended ruling them out on the grounds of expense and the time it would take to fulfil the orders. The tenders of Vulcan Foundry Ltd. for the heavy-duty locomotives and of Robert Stephenson & Hawthorns Ltd. for the light-duty locomotives were chosen.[200] As we have seen, the companies were related, and the proposed standardisation of many of the parts between the two types of locomotive was an attraction.[201] The Vulcan Foundry locomotives were to be of a type listed in their catalogue for mixed traffic, and the Robert Stephenson and Hawthorns engines were to be similar to what had been supplied to Nigerian Railways.

Negotiations began over the contracts. Sometimes these were conducted directly, sometimes via the Tasmanian Agent-General in London. (Very occasionally the companies' Australian agent, the Steel Company of Australia, was involved.) In response to the tender Robert Stephenson and Hawthorns offered the locomotives dismantled or fully made. Ultimately, the government chose the latter. Delivery was to commence in October 1950, to be completed in December 1950. A fixed price of £19,750 was quoted, payment to be in

---

[198] MSI, YA1966.24/5/2, Beyer, Peacock & Co. Ltd, File of letters and reports relating to South African Railways, Letter Fraser & Chalmers (SA) Ltd to Beyer, Peacock & Co. Ltd, 11 June 1946. (See also ibid., Letters 13 June 1946, 15 June 1946 and 2 September 1946.)
[199] TA, 48/2051, Supply of heavy, light and goods-type locomotive engines with double bogie tenders from England – specifications, contracts and enquiries.
[200] *Examiner Newspaper* (Launceston), 24 February 1949.
[201] TA, 48/2051, *op cit*, Memorandum, Chief Mechanical Engineer to General Manager and others, 7 February 1949.

pounds sterling in London. Payment terms were proposed as 50 per cent of the price on steaming of each boiler, 40 per cent on certification by an inspector of the steaming of each locomotive at the company's works and the remaining 10 per cent on delivery of each locomotive FOB at a British port (but payment to take place in any event after a specified period if there were shipping delays).[202]

Both companies insisted on inserting in the contract the so-called safeguarding clause, which had been adopted by the Locomotive Manufacturers' Association in 1948 against the background of post-war economic and political uncertainty. The clause conferred a right to adjust the price at the time of delivery in the event of changes in (i) the costs of materials before sub-contracts were executed; (ii) rates of wages and laws on working conditions; and (iii) 'any other costs direct or indirect whether resulting from Government Legislation and the conditions arising therefrom or otherwise'. The clause provided that claims for additional costs were to be substantiated 'where necessary' by the manufacturer's auditors. The safeguarding clause also contained protection in the event of delays and cancellation. Sub-clause (4) stated that delivery periods were given in good faith, but no guarantee could be given or liability accepted for any penalty, whether as liquidated charges or otherwise. As to cancellations, this had to be with the manufacturer's consent, and then only on terms which would indemnify it 'in respect of the cost of all drawings, tooling, material, labour and other costs and charges attributable to the order'.[203]

The Tasmanian government's specifications were relatively short. For the 4–8–2 type goods locomotives, the nature of the service specified was 'the manufacture, erection and testing at the maker's works, packing for shipment and delivery fob at an English port of the eight 4–8–2 type goods locomotives ... in strict accordance with this specification, the conditions of contract and to the entire satisfaction of the chief mechanical engineer ... and his inspecting engineer'.[204] The locomotives were described as generally in accordance with the Vulcan Foundry specification dated 14 March 1949 for mixed traffic locomotives. Clauses in the specification then required that the different parts had to comply with the Tasmanian rolling stock gauge ('shown on drawing No F-9P-4'); be of a certain measurement (e.g., distance between wheels to be 3'3" in all cases except for flangeless tyres which were to be 3'2 1/2" apart); be fitted in a certain manner (e.g., standard buffers and drawgear to be as shown on drawings Nos 100 and 101 and fitted in positions shown in drawing No E-25 L-3); be of a certain type (e.g., Hasler speed indicator and recorder) and colour; and be marked and numbered in a particular way (e.g.,

---

[202] Ibid., letter Robert Stephenson and Hawthorns Ltd to Agent General for Tasmania, 31 January 1949.
[203] The clause is set out in ibid., letter, Agent General for Tasmania to General Manager, Railway Department, Transport Commission, 7 February 1949.
[204] Ibid., Transport Department – Tasmania, Railway Branch, 'Specification No 94', 5 May 1949.

axles to be branded with maker's names and date of manufacture). The specifications also contained a general clause that although details might not be mentioned the locomotive was to be complete in every way, and no advantage was to be taken of any error or omission in them.

The general conditions of the contract accompanying the specifications for the locomotives were more detailed.[205] A preliminary clause provided that the conditions were to be inspected to give the widest effect to their intention 'as if forming headings of or instructions for a contract for works to be carried out to the satisfaction of the [chief mechanical] engineer'. None of the conditions were to be varied, waived, discharged or released, either at law or equity, except by express consent in writing given by the Tasmanian Transport Commission. Among the clauses was a deposit clause, under which a manufacturer had to lodge with the Transport Commission a security deposit on signing the contract. That would be forfeited in the event of a failure to fulfil the terms and conditions. Security money, the clause stated, 'shall be considered to be compensation for damages sustained due to breach of contracts'. There was a penalty clause for payment of a specified amount ('by way of liquidated damages') in case of delay or late delivery.

The expected quality standard of the locomotives was addressed in the general conditions in various ways. Under clause 5(5), headed 'Contract and mode of carrying out same', the Transport Commission and the chief mechanical engineer were to be able to inspect the factory, machinery, materials and work in progress at all times. Clause 6, entitled 'Quality and Workmanship', required that the work should generally be 'of the best material and finished in the highest class of its respective kind', and 'in every respect to the entire satisfaction of the engineer'. It conferred on the chief mechanical engineer the power to inspect work and materials; to test materials and workmanship in any way considered necessary; and to reject any work or material which in his opinion was not up to the standard of the specifications. In that event the manufacturer should, within twenty-four hours, 'at his own expense, commence to remove or amend the same with work or materials to the satisfaction of the engineer'.

Central to the general conditions was a system of inspectors' certificates. The staged payments set out in the payment clause could only be made after the inspector had certified that each boiler had passed the steaming test (for the first payment of 50 per cent of the price) and each locomotive had passed the steaming test for the second payment (40 per cent of the price).[206] Even if a certificate had been given, payment was to be withheld under clause 8 on the occurrence of default, defined as a refusal, failure or delay to carry out the conditions in any material particular, of which the engineer was to be the sole

---

[205] Ibid., Transport Department of Tasmania, Railway Branch, 'General Conditions of Contract Accompanying Specifications number 94 and 96', undated.

[206] The issue of an inspector's certificate transferred property in the materials and work to the Transport Commission.

judge. Further, clause 10 provided that the grant of a certificate or the acceptance of any works or their use did not preclude the engineer from rejecting any unsound materials, improper workmanship or defective works. The clause continued that the Transport Commission and the chief mechanical engineer could require the manufacturer 'to take back, replace or resend any work not performed in accordance with the contract'. The responsibility of the manufacturer for defective work and materials was to continue for twelve months from the date of delivery.

(iv) Completing the Contract, Manufacturing, Inspections and After-Sales Service

In June 1949 the government hit a legal snag. It seemed that until then no lawyer had been involved. Now that the contracts were to be drawn up, a government lawyer was asked to advise. The lawyer pointed out that since the acceptance of the tender had not been made subject to the general conditions, the usual provisions contained in Transport Department contracts could not be included in the contracts unless the manufacturers agreed. That included the clause requiring the lodging of a security deposit and the penalty clause for late delivery.[207] It appears that the Tasmanian authorities let the matter go and the manufacturers were not approached. The usual conditions were not incorporated into the contracts.

Draft contracts were sent to the manufacturers on 22 July 1949. On the whole the manufacturers agreed to the Tasmanian drafts.[208] Among the amendments they suggested were words to make clear that the 1948 safeguarding clause had effect. Tasmania as the governing law was rejected. In accordance with 'international usage', was the rather far-fetched reply, contracts such as these should be subject to English law. '[We] are executing orders for all parts of the world and in every single case, the contracts are under English law.' As to the position of the chief mechanical engineer, the reply said, his powers should be more limited than proposed. Finally, the companies said, they would prefer wording as regards defective material and workmanship which 'had generally been accepted between us and other customers'. This established free-of-charge replacement of defective material and workmanship for twelve months after delivery. The draft clause the companies proffered ruled out liability for other expenditure incurred and for consequential damages.

The Tasmanian Government agreed to the manufacturers' suggestions, although there were further tweaks to the drafts over matters such as a change in the type of lighting.[209] The contracts were eventually signed in the first part of 1950. The government appointed London consultant engineers Preece Cardew & Rider to conduct the inspections provided for in the contract.

---

[207] Ibid., Legal Officer, Department of Transport to General Manager, 15 June 1949.
[208] Ibid., G. Collingwood, Vulcan Foundry Ltd to General Manager [Tasmania], Transport Department, 1 September 1949.
[209] Ibid., letter, Manager of Railways to G. Collingwood, 27 October 1949; letter, Robert Stephenson and Hawthorns to Transport Department, 21 December 1949.

The firm pressure-tested the boilers; as we have seen successful testing was required for interim payment.[210] On completion of each locomotive Preece Cardew & Rider then tested the boilers, cylinders and tender, examined alignments (e.g., of the engine frames) and tested the pressing, assembly and machining of the wheels and axles.[211] In mid-1952, they reported that there had been issues with the sanding gear and clearances on the bearings of the 4–8–2 type engines, but that these had been resolved.[212] On the whole inspection occurred without incident as work on the locomotives proceeded.

Meanwhile, in February 1951 arrangements had been made for Mr Collingwood, the joint managing director of the manufacturers, to visit Tasmania. The Transport Department requested several modifications during the production process (for example, extra clearance with the axle box on the driving wheels; fitting plates on the side rods). The parties reached a compromise and split the cost.[213] On several occasions, the manufacturers' accountants, Deloitte, Plender, Griffiths and Co., certified increases in cost under the safeguarding clause. The Tasmanian Government paid without quibble.[214]

The engines arrived in Tasmania. The locomotives from the Vulcan Foundary works went into service from November 1951. When the Robert Stephenson & Hawthorns engines arrived, corrosion was identified in the roller bearings of the engines. Apparently, this occurred during the sea voyage to Australia because steel and brass particles had been left in the bearings during the initial assembly in the factory. The bearings were replaced under the contract. The two classes of engines provided a decade or so of satisfactory service before being replaced on Tasmanian railways by diesel engines.

6 Brunner Mond's Sale of Alkali to Lever Bros: Fraudulent Representation

With commercial sales, misrepresentation claims did not feature regularly in the case law; when they did, they tended to involve commodities dealings.[215] It was highly unusual with heavy manufactured goods for large commercial parties to be associated with a claim of misrepresentation. Even rarer did a commercial purchaser of such goods make allegations of fraud. All this

---

[210] Ibid., Letter, Preece Cardew & Rider to Agent General Tasmania, 6 June 1951, for third and fourth locomotives ('found satisfactory').
[211] Ibid., e.g., Letter from Preece Cardew & Rider, 27 September 1951 that Nos 8 & 9 of 4-6-2 type were satisfactory and accepted for shipment, enclosing 'Report on Inspection of Plant and Materials', 6 September 1951 and 'Final Inspection and Test', 26 September 1951.
[212] Ibid., Letters, Preece Cardew & Rider to Agent General Tasmania, 13 June 1951, 26 July 1951.
[213] Ibid., Memorandum, Chief Mechanical Engineer, 'Re Modifications "M" and "H" Class Locomotives', 11 June 1954.
[214] e.g., ibid., Memorandum, Chief Mechanical Engineer, 'Contract for 4-6-2 Locomotives and Spares', 23 April 1952.
[215] e.g., *Brown Jenkinson & Co Ltd* v. *Percy Dalton (London) Ltd* [1957] 2 QB 621 (bill of lading fraudulently stating orange juice shipped in good order and condition); *Wells (Merstham) Ltd* v. *Buckland Sand and Silica Ltd* [1965] 2 QB 170 (sand noncompliant with warranted analysis).

underlines how extraordinary was the successful claim in fraud brought in 1924 by one of the country's leading manufacturers against another.

The claim arose out of a contract of October 1919 governing the sale by Brunner Mond and Company Ltd to Lever Brothers Ltd of alkali for use in the manufacture of soap. By the time of the dispute Lever Brothers had a reputation in Britain and abroad for its 'Sunlight' soap, which was the market leader and made largely from vegetable oils. Its other leading products were 'Lux' soap powder and 'Vim' household cleaner.[216] The business was run in effect by William Lever, a dynamic but somewhat mercurial entrepreneur who in 1917 became Lord Leverhulme. As for Brunner Mond, it had begun as manufacturers in 1873 and through drive and innovation hit the British chemical industry hard with its efficient production of soda ash, alkalis and ammonia.[217] Among its acquisitions was Joseph Crosfield & Sons, which made soap and alkali. Brunner Mond was allied with Solvay & Cie, a Belgium company with chemical factories across Europe.

The relationship between Lever Brothers and Brunner Mond predated the contract at issue in the 1924 fraud claim. It had not been altogether smooth. First, when in 1909 the 1904 contract for the sale of alkali had to be renegotiated, Lever had been in a position of weakness. Newspapers controlled by Lord Northcliffe had carried out a campaign defaming Lever Brothers with accusations about the standard of its product, business and employment practices. Northcliffe feared losing advertising revenue as a result of Leverhulme's attempt to rationalise the soap trade. Lever Brothers' products and profits suffered significantly.[218] Brunner Mond took advantage of Leverhulme's weakness. Under the 1907 contract Lever Brothers agreed to buy all their alkali needs from Brunner Mond and to keep out of alkali manufacturing until the contract came to an end in 1916. There was counterpart undertaking by Brunner Mond not to enter soap manufacturing. The one benefit for Lever Brothers in the new contract was that Brunner Mond was not to supply any other soap-maker with alkali at a lower price. There was one exception: under an existing agreement Crosfield paid half a crown a ton less for their alkali than Lever Brothers.[219]

---

[216] B. Lewis, *'So Clean' Lord Leverhulme, Soap and Civilization*, Manchester, Manchester University Press, 2008.

[217] W. Reader, *Imperial Chemical Industries A History*, London, Oxford University Press, 1970, vol. I, 94–95.

[218] Lever sued and there was a very substantial settlement in his favour: see C. Wilson, *The History of Unilever*, London, Cassel & Co., 1954, vol. I, 84–88; *Lever Bros* v. *Associated Newspapers* [1907] 2 K.B. 626 and *Lever Brothers Ltd* v. *The 'Daily Record' Glasgow Ltd*, 1909 SC 1004. After negative advice from one KC, Lever took the advice of F. E. Smith, later Lord Birkenhead, who (the story goes) worked through the night and advised succinctly the following morning: 'There is no answer to this action for libel, and the damages must be enormous'. See J. Campbell, *F. E. Smith First Earl of Birkenhead*, London, Jonathan Cape, 1983, 174.

[219] W. Reader, Imperial Chemical Industries A History, *op cit*, 236–237.

A second and more recent cause of ill-will concerned Crosfield and Gossages & Company. As soap-makers both were rivals to Lever Brothers. As part of that rivalry, Lever Brothers had successfully objected before the registrar, Swinfen Eady J, and the Court of Appeal to Crosfield's attempt to register the word 'perfection' as a trademark for its soap.[220] In 1911 Leverhulme acquired the Lymm estate in Cheshire and its salt deposits. That placed him in a position to manufacture his own alkali. In retaliation Brunner Mond acquired Crosfield and Gossages through generous offers for their shares.[221] Leverhulme's solicitors advanced the legally dubious argument that those acquisitions were in breach of an implied term in the 1907 sale contract by which Brunner Mond would not enter the soap trade or become competitors in it of Lever Brothers.[222] The matter seemed to rest there. Then in 1913 Crosfield lost an important patent case concerning its hydrogenation process of converting unsaturated fatty acids. Lever Brothers was on the other side.[223] Negotiations between Lever Brothers and Brunner Mond followed which led to heads of agreement dated 5 June 1913. Under these Brunner Mond agreed not to engage otherwise in soap manufacture, and that the business of Crosfield and Gossages would be carried out for the mutual benefit of both parties.

Next, there was business in China. In 1916 one of the Lever Brothers companies, Associated Enterprises Ltd, obtained an interim injunction to restrain Brunner Mond from taking steps said to be in breach of the 1913 agreement relating to the formation of a company for selling soap in China, to which the China business of Crosfield, Gossages and Price's Patent Candle Company Ltd would be transferred.[224] In early 1917 Associated Enterprises sought a writ of sequestration against Brunner Mond for allegedly breaching that injunction. Rowlatt J refused the application and on appeal the Court of Appeal made no order.[225] On 20 June 1917 Associated Enterprises returned to court with an application for a declaration and an injunction with respect to Brunner Mond's promoting a Chinese soap business. With two other KCs and a leading junior in support, Sir John Simon KC opened the case before Atkin J in the Commercial list.[226] Unbeknown to counsel, the parties met and a settlement was announced after 10 days of the trial. Under the settlement Lever Brothers could nominate two directors to the Crosfield and Gossage

---

[220] *In Re Joseph Crosfield & Sons Ltd* [1910] 1 Ch 118, [1910] 1 Ch 130.
[221] A. Musson, *Enterprise in Soap and Chemicals: Joseph Crosfield & Sons Limited 1815–1965*, Manchester, Manchester University Press, 1965, 240–244.
[222] Unilever Archives, File 632, Brunner Mond & Co., letter Simpson North & Co. [solicitors, Liverpool] to Brunner Mond, 26 June 1912, 2–3.
[223] *Joseph Crosfield & Sons Ltd* v. *Techno-Chemical Laboratories Ltd* (1913) 30 RPC 297 ('The Plaintiffs are substantially Brunner Mond & Co. and the real Defendants are Lever Bros Ltd', at 302, per Sir S. Cripps KC for the plaintiffs). See A. Musson, Enterprise in Soap and Chemicals: Joseph Crosfield & Sons Limited 1815–1965, *op cit*, 250–252.
[224] *Associated Enterprises Ltd* v. *Brunner Mond & Co Ltd, The Times*, 6 February 1917.
[225] Ibid.   [226] *Associated Enterprises Ltd* v. *Brunner Mond & Co Ltd, The Times*, 21 June 1917.

boards.[227] Lever Brothers prepared a draft agreement to give effect to the settlement. Brunner Mond rejected it, one reason being that Lever-appointed directors would have access to commercially sensitive information from what were effectively its competitors.

Then in 1919 Lever Brothers returned to the fray, this time in its own name and not that of Associated Enterprises. Its main action involved an application for a declaration that the directors it nominated to Crosfield and Gossages should be full directors and not denied access to information. As a side wind it also sought an injunction preventing Crosfield from increasing its capital on the basis that this might thwart the main action. The Court of Appeal refused the injunction: increasing Crossfield's capital was a bona fide scheme in the interests of that company, in any event not to be challenged by a party (Lever Brothers) not even a shareholder. As to the main action, Lever Brothers' counsel, Sir John Simon KC, submitted that under the 1917 agreement its nominated directors could not be 'mere dummies'.[228] Lord Leverhulme gave evidence the morning of the second day of the trial. Apparently he was an unimpressive witness, for after the luncheon adjournment it was announced that, following discussions with his counsel, the application would be withdrawn.[229] There were further negotiations between the parties. Earlier Leverhulme had suggested that Brunner Mond should sell its interest in Crosfield and Gossages to him. After much internal debate in Brunner Mond, the transfer was agreed. Leverhulme remained bitter about the price of £4 million he had to pay, £1 million more than he thought the companies were worth.[230]

With this background of hostility between Brunner Mond and Lever Brothers, things did not augur well for the 1919 alkali contract, albeit that it was dated the same day, 8 October, as the contract for the transfer of Crosfield and Gossages to Lever Bros.[231] Under clause 2 of the alkali contract Brunner Mond was to sell all the alkali Lever Brothers required from time to time for its business. It was to be in the form of soda ash guaranteed 58 per cent. Under clause 3 Lever Brothers was not to purchase alkali in any form from anyone other than Brunner Mond unless, for the reasons specified in clause 12 of the contract (fire, accidents, war, strike, lockouts, etc.), Brunner Mond could not meet its requirements. Nor was Lever Brothers or its associated companies to sell alkali to anyone: clause 5. The prices payable for light- and heavy-quality alkali were spelt out in clauses 6 and 7. After 31 December 1920 they were to be mutually agreed, but failing agreement were to be in accordance with the method of calculation set out in the contract. Clause 7 contained the important

---

[227] *Associated Enterprises Ltd v. Brunner Mond & Co Ltd*, The Times, 13 July 1917.
[228] *Lever Bros Ltd v. Brunner Mond & Co Ltd*, The Times, 25 February 1919.
[229] *Lever Bros Ltd v. Brunner Mond & Co Ltd*, The Times, 26 February 1919.   [230] Ibid., 298.
[231] Key clauses of the contract are in *Lever Bros Ltd v. Brunner Mond & Co Ltd*, Amended Statement of Claim, High Court of Justice, King's Bench Division, 1924, L No 1337 ('Levers' 1924 Amended Statement of Claim').

proviso that after 31 December 1920 'the basis prices for alkali delivered for consumption in any country shall never be higher than the basis prices for the time being charged by [Brunner Mond] to any soapmaker in such country'. For these purposes, clause 8 provided that the certificate of Brunner Mond's auditors was to be taken as conclusive evidence of the prices charged.

Unknown to Lever Brothers, and in breach of the 1919 alkali contract, Brunner Mond had continued to supply the Cooperative Wholesale Society (CWS), Lever Brothers' main retail competitor, with alkali at less than the prices set out in its contract. At the time the contract was entered Lever Brothers had asked for and believed it had received assurances on a number of occasions, identified in Levers' 1924 Amended Statement of Claim, that the CWS would pay the increase Lever Brothers had to pay and would not get its alkali any cheaper.[232] Brunner Mond's auditors were kept in the dark as was most of the Brunner Mond board. The situation began to unravel when, in early 1923, a Lever Brothers associate company in Australia bought a small soap company there, Lewis & Whitty, and found that under a 1920 contract it was paying Brunner Mond for its alkali less than that set by the 1919 Lever Brothers–Brunner Mond contract. Lever Brothers accepted compensation for the overcharges incurred during the currency of the Lewis & Whitty contract. As one of Lever Brothers' solicitors advised in February 1924, the settlement meant that it had waived any breach of the 1919 contract. But that was not an end of the matter, he added, since in November 1923 Lord Leverhulme had written to Brunner Mond that he wanted an assurance that there were no other contracts in breach of the 1919 contract, and in the meanwhile that he reserved all Lever Brothers' rights. '[T]his is now the point upon which we must pin them down.'[233]

Pinning Brunner Mond down Leverhulme certainly did. After express denials that there were other contracts where it was supplying alkali at lower rates, Brunner Mond's chairman, Roscoe Brunner, finally confessed: although the CWS invoices for alkali showed one thing (hence deceiving Brunner Mond's own auditors), the company was giving the CWS rebates on silicate of soda to bring down the price of alkali. Lever Brothers' writ was issued on the 4 June 1924. Its Amended Statement of Claim sought a declaration that Lever Brothers was induced to enter the 1919 sales contract by fraudulent representations and was not binding, as well as damages. The trial was listed for November 1925. Brunner Mond's lawyers advised that there was virtually no defence and a trial would cause reputational loss. Eventually the case was settled with the payment of £1 million and a new sale contract. Roscoe Brunner resigned the chairmanship and later shot his wife and himself.[234] It

---

[232] W. Reader, Imperial Chemical Industries A History, *op cit*, 298.
[233] Unilever Archives, GB1752/LBC/147, Brunner Mond & Company Ltd, Alkali Contract, Letter 'Brunner Mond & Company Ltd Re Lewis & Whitty's Contract', 19 February 1924.
[234] W. Reader, Imperial Chemical Industries A History, *op cit*, 374–375. Reader notes that the Brunner Mond files were purged, probably in the late 1930s, of documents about the long dispute (p. 237).

was said that Leverhulme regarded the £1 million as a quid pro quo for what he thought was the excessive price he had paid for the purchase of Crosfield and Gossages a few years earlier.

4.4 Hire, Hire Purchase and Asset Finance

> Compared with his financial prospects, his emotional future was barren and bleak. Even his financial future was mortgaged. With the help of the HP he would pay that mortgage off. But there was no way of buying happiness on the HP – monthly instalments of unhappiness would not win happiness in the end. (L. P. Hartley, *The Hireling*, 1957)[235]

Selling on credit was as old as sale itself. From the late eighteenth century steam engines were supplied on terms allowing several years' payment, in yearly or six-monthly instalments.[236] Competition between Boulton & Watt and other steam engine manufacturers dictated credit terms to promote sales.[237] In the cotton industry machine manufacturers in the very late eighteenth and early nineteenth centuries sold on up to six months' credit, with a 5 per cent discount for payment with bills of exchange at three months.[238] As we will see, credit was central to international commodity sales through the use of trade-related bills of exchange.[239] Credit had been available to the wealthy but became a more general feature of retailing in the department stores, furniture stores and other retail outlets of the twentieth century.[240]

From the mid-nineteenth century hire and hire purchase became important credit techniques with commercial and consumer goods. Later it was called asset finance, since finance was been provided to fund the acquisition of an asset. It grew out of credit sales and was available to the less wealthy, albeit not the poor.[241] Hire and hire purchase were also used to extend credit in commercial sales for some of the manufactured products of the industrial age. In Hartley's novel *The Hireling*, hire purchase was the means by which the First World War veteran Leadbitter obtained an expensive vehicle for his chauffeuring business. Lorries were supplied on hire purchase to businesses transporting goods.

English law did not permit a seller to recover goods once they were in the buyer's possession, even if provided on credit. In this regard English law

---

[235] L. P. Hartley, *The Hireling*, London, Hamish Hamilton, 1957.
[236] D. Jenkins, *The West Riding Wool Textile Industry 1770–1835*, Edington, Pasold Research Fund, 1975, 191–192.
[237] See 220–221 above.
[238] M. Edwards, *The Growth of the British Cotton Trade 1780–1815*, Manchester, Manchester University Press, 1967, 202–203.
[239] 242 below.
[240] e.g., H. Barty-King, *The Worst Poverty A History of Debt and Debtors*, Stroud, Alan Sutton, 1991, 164–165.
[241] R-M. Gelpi & F. Julien-Labruyere, *The History of Consumer Credit: Doctrines And Practices*, Basingstoke, Macmillan, 2000, 129–131.

differed from that of other European countries, which permitted a seller to recover goods supplied to an insolvent buyer but not paid for.[242] During our period English law took the view that a seller providing goods on credit was in the same position as any other creditor, having to prove in the insolvency. The transformation came after our period in the mid-1970s with the recognition of the continental retention of title clause.[243] The problem of the insolvent buyer was one incentive for sellers to adopt a variant to sale on credit. The first step was when manufacturers began to supply plant and machinery on hire. The hirer needed to maintain the rental payments if plant and machinery was not to be reclaimed by the owner, who might be the supplier or the financier. The technique took hold with railway wagons.[244] In such cases the hirer never obtained property in the goods and had to return them at the end of the hire period.

What was initially deferred purchase, later hire purchase, took matters further. The plant, machinery or equipment was hired but at the end of period the customer purchased it. The reality was that it was being sold on credit terms even though, as a matter of law, hire purchase was not a credit sale. The supplier or the financier remained the owner during the hire period and so, as with hire, obtained protection in the event of the hirer's bankruptcy, or if the hirer wrongfully disposed of the goods, provided they could be found. Thus a second reality was, as was said in relation to the supply of printing machinery in the 1890s, that the hire purchase system 'is a means of giving credit with a certain amount of security; in other words a capitalist manufacturer finances a printing concern with the least liability to himself'.[245]

With commercial goods hire purchase was most developed with the railway wagon. As well, it was used to supply gas engines,[246] printing presses,[247] steam engines and other industrial machinery like cranes.[248] The first edition of the *Encyclopaedia of Forms and Precedents*, published before the First World War, contained hire purchase precedents for industrial goods.[249] Shop fittings in the

---

[242] *Oxford History of the Laws of England, 1820–1914*, Oxford, Oxford University Press, 2010, vol. XII, 790 (M. Lobban).

[243] J. Davey & C. Kelly, 'Romalpa and Contractual Innovation' (2015) 42 *JL&S* 358; S. Wheeler, *Reservation of Title Clauses: Impact and Implications*, Oxford, Oxford University Press, 1991.

[244] *Railway Times*, 12 July 1856, 817 (wagons offered by 'The Railway Carriage Company, Oldbury, near Birmingham'). Hotel furniture was also hired: *In re Parker* (1885) 14 QBD 636.

[245] 'A Printer on the Hire System', *Hire Traders' Guide and Record*, 1 September, 1894, 82 (reprinting a letter in the *Printers' Register*).

[246] *McEntire v. Crossley Brothers Ltd* [1895] AC 457. On the Otto gas engine – an internal combustion engine – and the role of Crossley Brothers in improving and distributing it: J. Ortiz-Villajos, 'Patents, What For? The Case of Crossley Brothers and the Introduction of the Gas Engine into Spain c. 1870–1914' (2014) 56 *Bus Hist* 650, 651.

[247] *Ex p Hughes and Kimber Ltd, Re Thackrah, The Times*, 4 July 1888.

[248] *In Re Barnett* (1885) 15 QBD 169, 170; *Allchin, Linnell & Co Ltd* (public inquiry ordered by Kekewich J), *The Times*, 26 Nov 1891, 3; *Anchor Line (Henderson Bros) Ltd (No1)* [1937] Ch. 1.

[249] *Encyclopaedia of the Laws of England with Forms and Precedents*, 1st ed., London, Butterworths, 1908, vol. VI, 455, 459, 462.

jewellery trade were also supplied this way.[250] At the turn of the century motor vans were being marketed on hire purchase.[251] In the 1920s and 1930s a prominent finance house, United Dominions Trust (UDT), provided hire purchase facilities to small businesses for vehicles (trucks and vans) and machinery (laundry, textile and baking equipment). Plans backed by the Bank of England for UDT to use hire purchase to extend the electricity system and to fund the canning industry had limited success.[252] After the Second World War hire purchase was used to supply businesses with equipment like automatic machines.[253]

For tax and other reasons, the finance lease became popular in the United States after the Second World War to provide commercial credit to businesses needing capital equipment.[254] The technique spread elsewhere, including Britain, encouraged from the 1960s by the tax advantages. There was also aggressive marketing by the leasing companies, which were prepared to tailor the pattern of rental payments to customer needs.[255] As a matter of law it was hire. A range of equipment was supplied under finance leases – fork-lift trucks, manufacturing plant, motor vehicles, aircraft, and later photocopiers and computers. Whereas operating leases were for a relatively short period, the finance lease might be for a period covering most, if not all, of the equipment's useful life. The lessee paid the full value of the equipment, plus interest, and had the obligation to maintain, repair and insure it. Sale and leaseback – a variation on hire and hire purchase – was another form of asset finance. A business wanting working capital or to refinance its existing debt sold its assets to a finance house or bank, and then leased them back under a hire or hire purchase agreement.

1 Hire and Deferred Purchase: Railway Wagons

> ... when the engine brought its load of waggons to a standstill, and a smart, metallic bump, bump, bump ran *diminuendo* from waggon to waggon, one might have fancied that some leviathan game was being played. (Arnold Bennett, *A Man from the North*, 1898)[256]

---

[250] A. Edwards, *Approbation, Sale or Return, and Hire Purchase*, London, Unwin, 1905, 18 (reprinted from *Jeweller and Metalworker*, 15 September, 1905).
[251] *Times*, 17 February 1897, 6B
[252] S. Bowden & M. Collins, 'The Bank of England, Industrial Regeneration, and Hire Purchase between the Wars' (1992) 45 *Econ Hist R* 120, 131.
[253] *Independent Automatic Sales Ltd* v. *Knowles & Foster* [1962] 1 WLR 974.
[254] Comment, 'Acquisition of Industrial and Commercial Equipment through Leasing Arrangements' (1957), 66 *Yale LJ* 751, 751–752; H. Cleveland & T. Huertas, *Citibank 1812–1970*, Cambridge, MA, Harvard University Press, 1985, 270.
[255] J. Clark, 'Equipment Leasing – Some Tax Thoughts' [1977] *BTR* 282; I. Davies, 'Equipment Leasing: a Decade of Growth' [1983] *LMCLQ* 631; T. Clark, 'The World of Leasing', in T. Clark (ed.), *Leasing Finance*, London, Euromoney, 1985, 1.
[256] London, John Lane & Bodley Head, 1898.

From hire and hire purchase for furniture in the early nineteenth century, through railway wagons mid-century, pianos and sewing machines in the latter part of the century, and motor vehicles and other consumer durables in the twentieth century, to modern asset finance – perhaps *crescendo*, rather than Arnold Bennett's *diminuendo*. Railway wagons were crucial to the story. This section examines how modern-day asset finance emerged from the need to finance the simple railway goods wagon on the rapidly expanding railways of the nineteenth century.

(i) Railways, Railway Wagons and the Wagon Companies

Unlike other countries, the railways in Britain were private affairs. Until grouped in 1923 into four main companies, there were over a hundred railway companies, many struggling financially.[257] When it came to operate the railways, the companies allowed those wanting to transport goods to furnish their own wagons. Apart from the capital required to fund the wagons, the railway companies faced fluctuating demand and the opportunity cost if wagons lay idle in railway sidings. Legislation exempted them from the obligation they would have had as common carriers to provide wagons for materials such as coal, coke, gravel, slag, sand, stone, lime, silt in bulk, ammoniac liquor, coal tar and gas water if their carriage would damage the wagons, as it generally would.[258] Many private Railway Acts establishing the railway companies, and then section 92 of the Railway Clauses Consolidation Act 1845 recognised the right of persons and other railways to run wagons and carriages over a railway company's lines.[259] When this occurred the Railway Clearing House collated information and apportioned the receipts between the different railway companies.[260] Private wagons had to be registered. In the period 1888–1917 over half a million newly built private wagons were registered, about 45 per cent of total wagon production.[261] Wagons for carrying coal were an important component.

Compared with the modern railway wagon of steel construction, with suspension and continuous braking, the goods wagon which the British railway companies operated was typically small, four-wheeled, and mainly of wooden construction. The use of timber meant wagons were relatively inexpensive and could be readily repaired and modified. Wagons were often open,

---

[257] Railways Act 1921.
[258] Railway Rates and Changes Order Confirmation Acts 1891 and 1892. See E. Williams, *An Epitome of Railway Law*, London, Stevens & Haynes, 1912, 86–87; R. Essery, D. Rowland & W. Steel, *British Goods Wagons from 1887 to the Present Day*, Newton Abbot, David & Charles, 1970, 22.
[259] See *Powell Duffryn Steam Coal Co v. Taff Vale Railway Co* (1874) LR 9 Ch App 331.
[260] P. Bagwell, *The Railway Clearing House in the British Economy 1842–1922*, London, George Allen & Unwin, 1968. See also R. Edwards, '"Keeping unbroken ways": The Role of the Railway Clearing House Secretariat in British Freight Transportation, c.1923–c.1947' (2013) 55 *Bus Hist* 479, 482–483.
[261] R. Davenport-Hines, *Dudley Docker*, Cambridge, Cambridge University Press, 1984, 32.

possibly with a tarpaulin cover. There were also vans, cattle wagons, hoppers and guard's vans. The most important commodity carried during this period was coal, the major source of energy for Britain well into the twentieth century. The issue of the private ownership of railway wagons became charged with arguments that it was an obstacle to the most efficient use of railway rolling stock.[262] Those arguments over the use of private wagons continue to the present day.[263] Collieries had large numbers of private wagons, but many other companies also had their own wagons for transporting goods. Some of the private wagons would be in a business's own livery, an early form of display advertising.

Railway wagons were manufactured by specialist wagon companies. The wagon companies were sometimes also involved in manufacturing other rolling stock, railway engines and railway signalling.[264] By the 1880s there were over 200 wagon companies.[265] In 1886 the Wagon Owners' Association was formed primarily, it would seem, to bind members to charge minimum rates for wagons they leased on hire or hire purchase terms.[266] Five wagon companies feature in the following account. First, the Birmingham Wagon Company, based in Smethwick in the West Midlands. Founded in 1856 as a deed of settlement company,[267] it became a limited company under the Limited Liability Act 1855. With counsel's advice W. H. Reece, a Birmingham solicitor, arranged the incorporation, as well as an early agreement with Marshall, a wagon builder.[268] In 1878 the company changed its name to the Birmingham Railway Carriage and Wagon Company and continued in business until the 1960s.[269] Second, the Gloucester Wagon Company was incorporated in 1860 by Gloucester merchants with a capital of £100,000, which was oversubscribed. Its market was initially the collieries and mines in South Wales and the Black Country. By 1865 the company had

---

[262] see H. Ross, *British Railways*, London, Edward Arnold, 1904, 158–160; L. Kenworthy, *Private Wagon Ownership*, London, Harper, 1930, 1–21.

[263] V. Van Vleck, 'Delivering Coal by Road and Rail in Britain: The Efficiency of the "Silly Little Bobtailed" Coal Wagons' (1997) 57 *J Econ Hist* 139; P. Scott, 'The Efficiency of Britain's "Silly Little Bobtailed" Coal Wagons: A Comment on Van Vleck' (1999) 59 *J Econ Hist* 1072; V. Van Vleck, 'In Defense (Again) of "Silly Little Bobtailed" Coal Wagons: Reply to Peter Scott' (1999) 59 *J Econ Hist* 1081.

[264] See *Saxby v. Gloucester Waggon Co* (1881) 7 QBD 305 (interlocking railway points and signals).

[265] GRO, GWWC, D4791/10/1, 'The Gloucester Wagon Company', from the *Gloucester Journal*, 13 December 1884.

[266] GRO, GWWC, D4791/59/1, 'Agreement for the Formation of "The Wagon Owners' Association"', 1 February 1886.

[267] On deed of settlement companies: L. C. B. Gower, 'The English Private Company' (1953) 18 *L & Contemp Prob* 535.

[268] SRO, BRCWC, D831/1/2/2, D831/1/2/2, Draft directors' meetings minutes, 8 November 1855. Reece continued to be retained in the following years, mainly for debt collection.

[269] J. Hypher, C. Wheeler & S. Wheeler, *Birmingham Railway Carriage & Wagon Company*, Cheltenham, Runpast Publishing, 1995, 5–8. It later extended beyond wagons to railway coaches, then buses, diesel railcars and diesel electric locomotives, supplying such items in Britain and abroad.

an order for 560 sets of wagon iron-work for the Great Indian Peninsula Railway Company, on which Phileas Fogg and his valet, Passepartout, travelled in Jules Verne's *Around the World in Eighty Days*.[270] Within twenty years it had workshops in Riga and St Petersburg.[271] Third, the North Central Wagon Company was established in Rotherham in 1861; it became a joint stock company in 1894. Also in Rotherham was, fourth, the British Wagon Company, established in 1869. Fifth, there was the largest of the wagon manufacturing companies, and the second largest employer in the West Midlands that, in 1912, was named the Metropolitan, Carriage, Wagon and Finance Company, forged in 1902 by Dudley Docker – a powerful entrepreneur in early twentieth-century Britain – by the merger of five large rolling-stock companies, a merger emblematic of the move to industrial concentration.

The wagon companies could simply have sold the wagons they manufactured, and sometimes did. But providing credit to those needing wagons was a source of profit and met commercial need. In 1919 Docker told his shareholders that 'we have found as much money can be made of finance as by manufacture'.[272] Winning a reputation for its credit facilities, and providing wagons on advantageous deferred purchase terms, were important elements in Docker's success. Indeed, some of the wagon companies were financiers from the outset rather than wagon makers.[273] The wagon companies were able to use their deferred purchase agreements as security to borrow themselves.[274] The other side of the coin was that from the point of view of businesses needing wagons and locomotives, the obvious advantage of hire and deferred (hire) purchase was that capital did not have to be laid out immediately for they obtained their wagons on credit. As we have seen, businesses could also use the wagons and locomotives they owned to refinance themselves by selling them to the wagon companies, then leasing them back on hire or deferred purchase terms for continued use (sale and leaseback).

(ii) Hire, Conditional Sale and Hire Purchase

The Birmingham Wagon Company has been credited with being the first finance leasing company in the world.[275] The earliest mention of deferred

---

[270] When tendering in 1867–1868 for rolling stock for the Orel-Vitebsk Railway (Russia), concerns over its agent's authority led it to engage a London solicitor: GRO, GWWC, D4791/6/2, Directors' Minute Books, 294–295, 309, 311, 317, 339.

[271] Anon, *The History of the Gloucester Railway Carriage Wagon* Company, London, Weidenfeld & Nicolson, 1960. Like the Birmingham Company it continued making railway rolling stock until the 1960s.

[272] R. Davenport-Hines, *Dudley Docker, op cit*, 32.

[273] R. Harris, *Hire Purchase in a Free Society*, 3rd ed., London, Hutchinson, 1961, 22–23. See *Lincoln Waggon and Engine Company* v. *Mumford* (1880) 41 LT (ns) 655, 655.

[274] e.g., GRO, GWWC, D4791/45/7, 'Equitable Mortgage for 780 wagons', November 1915. See 262n below.

[275] T. Clark, *Leasing*, London, McGraw-Hill, 1978, 6; H. Rosen, 'The Luxembourg Rail Protocol: A Major Advance for the Railway Industry' (2007) 12 *Uniform LR (ns)* 427, 427.

payment arrangements seems to be in its records for 30 September 1858, when an offer of four wagons was made to Mr Lyalton 'on terms of ultimate purchase'.[276] In the directors' records in the following years there are regular references to the 'DP principle', the deferred purchase principle – two agreements submitted in August 1859 for affixing the company's seal and two other agreements considered; an agreement before the 29 November 1860 meeting for six wagons on deferred payment over five years, yielding a return of 12 ½ per cent interest; and consideration on 3 November 1863 of the lowest price at which wagons could be furnished on deferred purchase to Mr Isaac Marshall.[277]

Wagon companies might simply hire wagons, rather than disposing of them under deferred purchase arrangements. In the mid-1860s the general manager of the Gloucester Company, Isaac Slater, reported to the directors that hire yielded a higher return than deferred purchase (sometimes called a 'purchase lease' or 'hire and purchase' in the records), an average return of 10 per cent compared with 7½ per cent for deferred purchase. Deferred purchase also required that a wagon company have a larger amount of capital, and Slater noted that in its first five years the company had increased its capital on three occasions.[278] However, deferred purchase was the favoured method of supplying wagons for the Gloucester company because of the lower risks associated with it. That was because a prospective purchaser under hire purchase took greater care of the wagons and kept up payments until finally purchasing them.

The directors made explicit their preference for deferred purchase over hire in their report to shareholders for the year ending 31 December 1862, after some shareholders had challenged the policy.[279] At an ordinary meeting in early 1864 the board spelt out the position: with deferred purchase the purchaser tended to do the repairs, and since the wagon company's name plate was clearly on the wagons the only risk was insolvency and the consequent loss of the expected return.[280] When a shareholder again raised the issue at another ordinary meeting later that year, the chairman replied robustly, to general acclamation, that there 'was no doubt that wagons let on hire paid a larger rate of interest, but the plan was less safe than the deferred payment principle'.[281]

In practice the wagon companies used both simple hire and deferred purchase, the split no doubt reflecting what customers could be persuaded to

---

[276] SRO, BRCWC, D831/1/2/2, Draft Directors' Meetings Minutes, 30 September 1858.
[277] SRO, BRCWC, D831/1/2/3, Agenda Book for Directors' Meetings, 25 August 1859, 29 November 1860; D831/1/2/2, Draft Directors' Meetings Minutes, 11 August 1863, 5 November 1863. See also D831/3/1/1, Finance Journal, 379ff (September 1860-); 493ff (September 1861-).
[278] GRO, GWWC, D 4791/6/2, 'Financial Report by Mr Slater', 9 May 1865, 38–39, 41.
[279] GRO, GWWC, D 4791/2/3, Directors' Reported Accounts, 31 December 1862.
[280] GRO, GWWC, D 4791/3/3, Report of Proceedings of the Fourth Ordinary Meeting held on 16 February 1864.
[281] GRO, GWWC, D 4791/3/4, Report of the Proceedings of Fifth Ordinary Meeting, held on 23 August 1864.

accept and what they would agree. In its early years the number of deferred purchase agreements for the Gloucester company seems always to have exceeded the number of simple leases: in 1866–1867, 6,633 and 1,888, respectively; and in 1868–1869, 7,403 and 2,766, respectively.[282] By the 1870s the picture had changed and leases became more important: in 1875–1876, 4,185 wagons were on deferred purchase, with 6,722 being hired. The figures for 1883–1884 were 3,566 and 5,765; for 1888–1889, 3,148 and 5,458, respectively.[283] For the Birmingham company in 1909, there were some 1,400 wagons leased (albeit 1,000 of them to one customer) as against 312 on deferred purchase. The representative figures for 1913 were 275 leased, 123 on deferred purchases and for 1921, 147 leased, 22 on deferred purchases.[284] The relatively small numbers were because, as we have seen, the Birmingham company exported a great deal of its output, which tended to be sold outright. After the First World War the Gloucester company sold all its simple hire wagons, together with the benefit of the associated tenancy agreements, and discontinued its business of providing wagons on hire.[285] It seems that there was a shortage of wagons because of the war and they could be sold at a good price. Simple hiring was later resumed.[286]

On the demand side, deferred purchase seems to have been especially attractive to less-well-capitalised companies such as collieries and mining operations. The Birmingham company published its initial prospectus in the *Mining Journal*, no doubt with an eye on advertising for business as well as to attract investors. However, deferred purchase was not confined to smaller customers.[287] The Gloucester company supplied the Great Western Railway (GWR) with wagons on deferred purchase terms in March 1865, and later that year the GWR's great rival, the Midland Railway Company, paid cash for 1,000 wagons against monthly deliveries.[288] The GWR contract gave rise to considerable legal activity the following year when the company refinanced the deal by assigning the contract to Warner, Burnett and Dowling of London. The Gloucester company received £40,900 for the £49,050 of instalments outstanding, although it had to pay broker's commission. Warner, Burnett and Dowling insisted that GWR should be a party to the deed of assignment, but the Gloucester company was against it. It called in a solicitor, Mr Simpson of Messrs Helps & Sons, to advise. Eventually GWR entered a separate deed of covenant for due performance vis-à-vis Warner, Burnett and Dowling of all the covenants it had given under its agreement with the Gloucester company.[289]

---

[282] Directors' Reports and Accounts, 1860–1960, D 4791/2/4; D 4791/2/6; D 4791/2/13.
[283] GRO, GWWC, D 4791/2/13; D 4791/2/21, D 4791/2/26.
[284] SRO, D 831/1/5/6, Registration of Agreements 1904–1949.
[285] *Gloucester Railway Carriage and Wagon Company Ltd* v. *Commissioners of Inland Revenue* [1925] AC 469, 471.
[286] GRO, GWWC, D 4791/2/53, 31 May 1935.
[287] e.g., SRO, D 831/1/5/9, Lapsed Deferred Purchase Agreements, 1915–1934.
[288] GRO, GWWC, D 4791/6/2, Directors' Minute Books, 14 March 1865, 9 May 1865.
[289] GRO, GWWC, D 4791/6/2, Directors' Minute Books, 1860–1962, 92, 109, 137.

The idea of deferred purchase for railway wagons was borrowed, it was said at the time, from the operation of building and land societies.[290] Each member of these contributed by subscription; each, in due course, acquired a home. Originally they were terminating societies: they would be wound up upon all the homes being built and legal title to the land would be conveyed to the member-tenants.[291] There were other examples of contracts for a lease, coupled with a right to purchase the freehold at the end of the rental period.[292] What is certain is that the language and substance of deferred purchase agreements for wagons were resonant of a lease of land – 'rent', 'tenants', the obligation to repair (fair wear and tear excepted) and so on.

To give just one example, under an agreement dated 9 January 1877 the Gloucester Company agreed to 'let and ultimately ... to sell' to Powell Duffryn Steam Coal Co. Ltd ('the Tenants') – and the tenants 'agree to hire and ultimately to purchase' 744 ten-ton wagons over a ten-year period, at a yearly rental of £9.50 per wagon, payable quarterly (clauses 1–2).[293] There was no provision for the tenants to terminate the agreement, a later feature of hire purchase agreements. Typical of deferred purchase agreements, the bulk of it was concerned with the care, repair and (excessive) loading of the wagons by the tenants.[294] As to the financial aspects, clause 3 provided for an interest charge of 8 per cent per annum in the event of late payment (clause 3). Failure to pay meant the wagon company could seize the wagons, 'seize and distrain' and 'sell and dispose' the goods in them, and terminate the agreement, all without prejudice to taking legal action (clause 12). This remedy for a tenant's default also applied if they assigned, sub-let or otherwise parted with possession of the wagons without the Gloucester company's consent, or allowed its name plate to be removed or defaced. Most importantly, clause 13 provided that once the tenants had paid the rent over the ten-year period, and any outstanding interest or other charges, they could remove the Gloucester company's name plates 'and all rights, title and interest of the Wagon Company to and in the said wagons shall cease and determine and the same shall be vested in the Tenants' (clause 13). Disputes were to be referred to arbitration (clause 14).

By the late 1880s some of the wagon companies had adopted what was later to become characteristic of hire purchase agreements, the option to purchase. Instead of an agreement to hire and obligations ultimately to sell and purchase

---

[290] GRO, GWWC, D4791/10/1, 'The Gloucester Wagon Company', from the *Gloucester Journal*, 13 December 1884.
[291] E. Cleary, *The Building Society Movement*, London, Elek Books, 1965, 21–22.
[292] e. g., *Green v. Low* (1856) 22 Beav 625, 52 ER 1249.
[293] GRO, GWWC, D4791/45/1, Wagon Leases and Sales 1877–1960. The agreement is in manuscript. It was cancelled on full payment in October 1886. Powell Duffryn Steam Coal Co. Ltd. grew to become the largest coal producer in South Wales.
[294] Reflecting landlord–tenant-law, the Gloucester company was responsible for 'fair wear and tear'; other repairs were for the tenant: cl 4–5. Clause 10 addressed reputed ownership: wagons had to display the Gloucester Company's name and number plate 'as owners'.

as with the 1877 Gloucester–Powell Duffryn agreement, the British Wagon Company's standard printed form provided that wagons were let for a number of years, and at the end of the period the 'tenants' had to deliver up the wagons in a good state of repair and working order: clause 13.[295] However, clause 15 provided that if the tenants had paid all they owed, and the additional sum of one shilling for each wagon within 14 days of the end of the hiring period, the wagons would become 'the absolute property of the said Tenants'. This was hire purchase, hiring with a right, but not an obligation to purchase.

By the first part of the twentieth century the Birmingham Wagon company had two standard deferred purchase forms, one for domestic, the other for foreign transactions.[296] It is difficult to know how much it used deferred purchase in foreign sales. With its large export business, it sold its rolling stock outright in India, China, Japan, the Federated Malay states, Turkey, Egypt, Africa and South America.[297] However, it used deferred purchase terms in 1931 for three postal vans for the Argentine North Eastern Railway Co. Ltd, along with an arbitration clause.[298] It might agree to variations for important customers.[299] The standard form for domestic hire purchase was of some thirteen clauses.[300] Details could be written in, for example the date of the agreement, the name of the 'tenants' (still called that), the number of wagons and their identifying features and the terms for rental. Under the default clause, clause 12, the wagon company could terminate the agreement and seize the wagons if the tenants were in arrears with payments; committed an act indicating insolvency; without the wagon company's consent permitted the wagons to leave their possession; or allowed the wagon company's name plate to be removed or defaced. Clause 13 provided that the agreement should not be construed as a purchase, but on payment of all the rent there was a right to purchase. There was no arbitration clause.

(iii) The Law's Role: Default, Disposal, Sale and Leaseback

Early on the law mitigated some of the risks facing the wagon industry. With some two hundred wagon companies by the 1880s, and many

---

[295] GRO, GWWC, D4791/45/5, Memorandum of Agreement British Wagon Company Ltd and Will Edgar, William Prestage & Edward Smith t/a William Smith & Co., dated 24 January 1888. The British Wagon agreement is in the Gloucester company's archives with a note that the latter completed the purchase. It seems it had bought this and other agreements when British Wagon wanted to raise money.

[296] SRO, BRCWC, D831/1/5/9, Lapsed Deferred Purchase Agreements, 1915–1934.

[297] SRO, BRCWC, D831/1/5/3–5, Contract Books 1926-.

[298] SRO, BRCWC, D831/1/5/7, Wagon Hire Agreements 1924–1932. The Gloucester company used deferred purchase for rolling stock built at its Riga and St Petersburg factories: GRO, GWWC, D4791/2/8, Directors' Reports and Accounts, 1860–1960.

[299] SRO, D 831/1/5/9, Lapsed deferred purchase agreements, 16 January 1934, amendment giving San Paulo (Brazilian) Railway the right to repay at any time.

[300] See also standard printed form of North Central in LI, Printed Cases, judgments and appeal documents, House of Lords, 'Manchester Sheffield and Lincolnshire Railway Co v. North Central Wagon', 1888, vol. 398, 737–739.

undercapitalised, one dimension was the collapse of a wagon company. Under English law contract rights were assignable in equity and, after passage of the Judicature Acts, in law as well.[301] Assignment enabled solvent wagon companies to take over the agreements of less stable businesses without disruption to hirers. The courts were quick to quash attempts by hirers in this situation to avoid payment by arguing that hire agreements could not be assigned because they required personal performance by the original wagon company of contractual obligations such as repair. Repair of wagons by the assignee company, it was held, was sufficient performance.[302]

Financial difficulties and the hirer's inability to pay rent, and ultimately its insolvency, were also obvious risks. There are instances where in such circumstances the lease was assigned to a replacement tenant, who would pay according to the original terms. For a time doubts were cast over this technique for the Gloucester Company. One of its tenants purported to assign its wagons to the GWR and the company resolved to accept the GWR as its new tenant and to discontinue proceedings to recover the rent from the original tenant. However, GWR failed to pay as well. The view of the Gloucester company's solicitor, and of Mr G. M. Dowdeswell QC who was called on to advise, was that GWR had not become the tenants of the wagons. Further, Mr Dowdeswell unhelpfully continued, it would be necessary for the company to repossess the wagons from GWR and to sue it for damages for their unlawful detention. Eventually GWR paid, and it never came to that.[303]

Apart from non-payment of rent on the wagons, a hirer's other creditors, or its landlord, might attempt to seize the wagons because it had not paid them. In these circumstances the wagons on hire or deferred purchase remained the wagon company's property and could be reclaimed if seized.[304] Protection for wagon companies extended to the hirer's insolvency. If under the agreement property in the wagons remained in the wagon company until payment of the final instalment, the wagon company was entitled to an order of the Bankruptcy Court that the wagons be delivered to it.[305] The doctrine of reputed ownership was no threat, despite railway wagons carrying the livery of the hirer, because 'it is so notorious that the true ownership ... is indicated by the metal owner-plates affixed [which]

---

[301] Judicature Act 1873, s. 25 (6).
[302] *British Waggon Company and the Parkgate Waggon Company v. Lea & Co* (1880) 5 QBD 149, 154.
[303] GRO, GWWC, D4791/6/2, Directors' Reports and Accounts, 1860–1960, 14 May 1867, 9 July 1867, 8 October 1867.
[304] e.g., *Lancashire Waggon Company (Limited) v. Fitzhugh* (1861) 6 Hurl & N 502, 158 ER 206; 'Railway Insolvency', *The Times*, 29 December 1866, 4 (extract from *Solicitors' Journal*). Parliament also offered protection against other creditors: Railway Companies Act 1867, s. 4; Railway Rolling Stock Protection Act 1872, s.3.
[305] *McEntire v. Crossley Brothers Ltd* [1895] AC 457.

prevents the circumstances of [a hirer's] possession being such as to make him the reputed owner of them'.[306]

An area of potential risk for the wagon companies was the hirer wrongfully disposing of the wagons to a third party. This type of risk was a major issue when hire purchase became a prominent feature in the marketing of furniture, consumer durables and motor vehicles. In practice it was not a major risk for the wagon companies. When in the early 1880s one of the hirers from the Gloucester Wagon Company disposed of some wagons, the company was able to reach an agreement that the third party still owed the rent.[307] One reason that the wrongful disposal of wagons was not a common problem was that they would have the name plates of the wagon company attached, albeit that these could always be removed by the fraudulent. Moreover, it was notorious that wagons were often on hire or deferred purchase terms so that third parties would be wary about purchasing them without being given assurances about their true ownership.

A further area of risk loomed larger for the wagon companies. That concerned sale and leaseback, where a company in financial straits would raise capital by selling its wagons and other rolling stock to a wagon company and then leasing them back for continued use. There are various examples of what appear to be cash-strapped collieries and other businesses doing this. One dimension was the power of a company to enter a sale and leaseback. In *Yorkshire Railway Wagon Co v. Maclure*[308] when first proposed the transaction was presented as a loan on security, but after doubts were raised the Cornwall Minerals Railway Company took the advice of counsel.[309] As a result the proposal was altered to one in which the Cornwall company sold the rolling stock and hired it back from the wagon company over a period of five years, when it would have the option to purchase the rolling stock. The wagon company sued for non-payment of hire but was met with the argument that the transaction was ultra vires as exceeding the railway's borrowing power.[310] At first instance Kay J held that 'common sense' dictated the transaction to be a borrowing on security, that the repurchase was a 'fiction' and that to find otherwise would allow the railway company to exceed the limits on its powers Parliament had imposed.[311] The Court of Appeal had a different view of common sense and strongly disagreed with Kay J's analysis. All three judges regarded the transaction not as a borrowing, but as a 'real' transaction involving the sale and hiring of the rolling-stock.[312] It was therefore valid against

---

[306] H. Taynton, *An Outline of the Law Relating to the Private Ownership of Railway Rolling Stock*, Lincoln, Horace Cox, 1893, 60. Property of a bankrupt divisible amongst its creditors included goods in its possession with permission of the true owner, where it was the reputed owner: Bankruptcy Act 1883, s. 44(2)(iii).
[307] GRO, GWWC, D4791/45/2, Memorandum of Agreement between the Gloucester Wagon Company and Andrews & Baby, 17 November 1882.
[308] (1882) 21 Ch D 309.   [309] at 312, per Jessel MR.
[310] Railway Regulation Act 1844, 7 & 8 Vict, c.85, s.19.
[311] (1881) 19 Ch D 478. He held nonetheless that the directors' guarantees were valid.
[312] (1882) 21 Ch.D 309.

Figure 4.2 Asset finance: the beginnings with North Central Wagon Co. (Grace's Guide to British Industrial History)

both the railway company and the guarantors. No doubt the court was unimpressed that the railway company was now arguing that the form of the transaction which its lawyers had proposed was void.

Another dimension to sale and leaseback was the legal risk that it might be registerable under the Bills of Sale Acts as a chattel mortgage. The complexities of Bills of Sale law, and the practical difficulties of registration, meant that commercial parties generally tried to avoid its clutches.[313] The issue arose in *Manchester, Sheffield, and Lincolnshire Railway v. North Central Wagon Company*[314] in what the court recognised as a test case.[315] A colliery in financial straits, the Blacker Main Coal Company, had raised finance in 1884 by selling for £1,000 to North Central Wagon Company one hundred of the railway wagons it used to deliver coal to its customers.[316] The wagon company then leased the wagons back to the Blacker company for three years, the rent (payable quarterly) pitched at a level to repay the £1,000 with interest at 7 per cent, Blacker then having the option of purchasing them for a nominal sum. In accordance with practice North Central had its name plates fixed to the wagons along with that of the colliery.

---

[313] 255, 259 below. [314] (1888) 13 App Cas 554. [315] (1886) 32 Ch D 477, 493.
[316] The wagons actually belonged to another wagon company, the Sheffield Waggon Company, which was paid directly the £257 still owing under the hire purchase agreement between it and the Blacker company so the North Central deal could proceed.

The case emerged, as do so many commercial cases, on insolvency, in this instance of the Blacker company. North Central claimed that it owned the wagons and repossessed those it could. The defendant railway company, which had not been paid the tolls Blacker owed it for running the wagons on its lines, claimed that it had a statutory right under section 97 of the Railways Clauses Consolidation Act 1845 to sell the nine wagons it had laid its hands on. North Central had the advice of Phipson Beale of Lincoln's Inn that the railway company could not do this and sued it for the return of the wagons. The judge at first instance was Sir James Bacon V-C, a judge who 'showed some of the foibles of an old practitioner confronted with a new order'.[317] He held, first, that the invoice and receipt between North Central and the colliery constituted a bill of sale, creating in substance a loan advanced on the security of the wagons, which was void as unregistered under section 9 of the Bills of Sale Act 1882;[318] and second, that in any event the railway company had a statutory right to detain and sell the wagons for the unpaid tolls. As a result of the judgment Mr Beale advised that in future sale and leaseback transactions the wagon company would need to take actual delivery of the property before leasing it out again.[319]

What of an appeal? North Central called a meeting of the Wagon Owners' Association. The Association briefed counsel, Edward Macnaghten QC (soon to be appointed directly as a law lord) and Reginald Bray. In a relatively long opinion, distributed to association members, they were doubtful about the chances on appeal.[320] In response North Central explained that its case had been put 'indifferently' to them, which explained their pessimistic opinion.[321] It obtained a more positive opinion from its counsel before Bacon VC, John Rigby QC and Phipson Beale, which was also distributed to association members.[322] Still the association's solicitor opined that an appeal was ill-advised and likely to do more harm than good 'by minimising the already strong judgments favourable to the association'.[323] The association's members supported their solicitor and were against the appeal. The writing was on the wall for North Central's request that the Association support the legal costs of an appeal.

North Central's board was having none of this negativity from the trade. It resolved to appeal without delay; it would bear the cost itself. In February 1887 its steadfastness was vindicated when the Court of Appeal allowed its appeal.[324] It was now the railway company's turn to appeal. Argument in the House of Lords was heard in April 1888. In July that year, it dismissed the

---

[317] J. Rigg & H. Mooney, 'Bacon, Sir James (1798–1895)' *Oxford Dictionary of National Biography*.
[318] See 259 below. At 495 Bacon VC distinguished the hire purchase of furniture.
[319] RBS, NCF/1/9, Directors' Meeting Minute Book, 17 March 1886.
[320] RBS, NCF/16, Record of Special Trials, 'Opinion', 30 March 1886.
[321] RBS, NCF/1/9, Directors' Meeting Minute Book, 1 April 1886.
[322] RBS, NCF/1/9, Directors' Meeting Minute Book, 12 May 1886.
[323] RBS, NCF/1/9, Directors' Meeting Minute Book, 7 June 1886.
[324] (1887) 35 Ch D 191 (Cotton, Lindley, and Lopes LJJ).

appeal.[325] The law lords reasoned that the transaction was not a mortgage or a loan on the security of the wagons and the documents did not have to be registered under the Bills of Sale Acts. As to any right of the railway company to detain the wagons for unpaid tolls, that could only apply in respect of the coals being carried in the wagons, not to the wagons themselves which the Blacker company did not own. The overturning of Bacon V-C's decision was acclaimed as 'in the interests of trade'.[326]

2 The Hire Purchase Boom

> After my work in the City, I like to be at home ... Carrie and I can manage to pass our evenings together without friends ... Carrie is not above ... practising the 'Sylvia Gavotte' on our new cottage piano (on the three years' system), manufactured by W. Bilkson (in small letters) and from Collard and Collard (in very large letters). (George Grossmith & Weedon Grossmith, *The Diary of a Nobody*, 1892)[327]

From the late nineteenth century hire purchase came into its own for the purchase of the consumer durables of the new age like sewing machines and pianos, and then in the twentieth century, motor cars and lorries. In the main the boom in hire purchase was for non-commercial use, as with Mr and Mrs Pooter's piano bought on the three-year system. However, we have seen it was used commercially, and especially so with vans and lorries. In the late 1950s about one-sixth in amount of hire purchase funds was for commercial items, in the main commercial vehicles and industrial and farming equipment.[328] One disincentive to financing plant and machinery through hire purchase was the rule of property law that when attached to land, say in a factory, items could become part of the land as so-called fixtures and thus subject to any mortgage held, for example, by the owner's bank.[329]

(i) The Rise and Rise of Hire Purchase

On the eve of the Second World War, Simonds J (later Lord Chancellor) expressed a widely shared ambivalence, that while hire purchase played a very large part in commercial and social life, and 'is an enormous business in the City of London and elsewhere', that was '[f]or good or for evil'.[330] This

---

[325] (1888) 13 App Cas 554.
[326] H. Taynton, An Outline of the Law Relating to the Private Ownership of Railway Rolling Stock, *op cit*, 57.
[327] George Grossmith & Weedon Grossmith, *The Diary of a Nobody*, Bristol, J. W. Arrowsmith, 1892.
[328] F. Oliver, *The Control of Hire-Purchase*, London, George Allen & Unwin, 1961, 21. See also C. Bolling, *Hire-Purchase Trading*, London, Pitman, 1928, 41.
[329] *Hobson v. Gorringe* [1897] 1 Ch 182 (11 hp Stockport gas engine on hire purchase affixed by bolts and screws to prevent rocking; held to be a fixture). In the trade press the decision received mixed appraisal: 'The Gas Engine Case', *Hire Traders' Record*, 1 June, 1897, 52.
[330] *Transport and General Credit Corporation Ltd v. Morgan* [1939] Ch 531, 551.

was said in a case where the court rejected a defence that a finance house involved in hire purchase was carrying on an unlicensed business of moneylending which would have meant that the transaction was invalid under the Moneylenders Acts 1900 to 1927. With a touch of hyperbole Lord Chorley commented at the time that if the argument had succeeded, it would have knocked away the foundation 'upon which the whole superstructure of modern hire-purchase selling has been erected'.[331]

In the first part of the nineteenth century hire purchase had been used to a limited extent for furniture.[332] From the 1860s it enabled the expanding middle and skilled working classes access to items like sewing machines. By 1913, Singer's sales of sewing machines were over two and a half million per annum, some 90 per cent of the market, the first mass-produced, mass-marketed consumer durable, with the world's first global brand.[333] Crucially for our story was that the machines were hired under the Singer instalment scheme, the generous terms being the hallmark of Singer marketing.[334] Early on the courts recognised that the Singer Company's property interest generally trumped that of other creditors when it repossessed them from defaulting customers.[335] Hire purchase was also the means many families used to obtain a piano, as a badge of respectability as well as for use.[336] It was a piano which featured in the leading case on hire purchase, *Helby v. Matthews*,[337] to which we return. In the 1860s, the 'three-year system' had developed, which Mr & Mrs Pooter used to obtain their Bilkson cottage piano. Under it customers could obtain an instrument by hiring it over a three year period and purchasing it at the end.[338] But there were drawbacks; in 1868 the *Musical Standard*

---

[331] R. Chorley, 'The Future of Hire-Purchase Agreements' (1940) 3 *MLR* 239. 240.

[332] See *Consumer Credit Report of the Committee ('Crowther Report')*, Cmnd 4596, London, HMSO, 1971, 42.

[333] e.g., A. Godley, 'American Multinationals in British Retailing 1850–1962', in H. Bonin & F. de Goey (eds.), *American Firms in Europe 1880–1980*, Geneva, Droz, 2009, 315–316; M. Casson & A. Godley, 'Revisiting the Emergence of the Modern Business Enterprise: Entrepreneurship and the Singer Global Distribution System' (2007) 44 *J Management Stud* 1064, 1071–1072; A. Godley, 'Selling the Sewing Machine Around the World: Singer's International Marketing Strategies 1850–1920' (2006) 7 *Enterprise & Society* 266; R. Davies, *Peacefully Working to Conquer the World: Singer Sewing Machines in Foreign Markets 1854–1920*, New York, Arno Press, 1976, 76–77, 96–97, 104–104: M. Wilkins, *The Emergence of Multinational Enterprise American Business Abroad from the Colonial Era to 1914*, Cambridge, Mass, Harvard University Press, 1970, 41–45.

[334] e.g., 'Handling the Asset in Large Cities', *Red S [Singer] Review*, vol. 1, n.1, September 1919, 18; vol. 1, n.2, October 1919, 20. Singer's terms are outlined in *Singer Manufacturing Co v. The London and South Western Railway Co* [1894] 1 QB 833.

[335] *Singer Manufacturing Company v. Clark* (1879) 5 Ex D 37; *Singer Sewing Machine Co v. J. Wright (Irvine's Trustee)* (1896) 4 SLT 16. See also *Singer Sewing Machine Company Ltd v. Galloway and Beasley*, 1909 1 SLT 525.

[336] F. Carnevali & L. Newton, 'Pianos for the People: From Producer to Consumer in Britain, 1851–1914' (2013) 14 *Enterprise & Society* 37, 59–60, 62–63.

[337] [1895] AC 471.

[338] *In re Blanshard ex parte Hattersley* (1878) 8 Ch D 601 (evidence that three-year system widespread).

lamented that hire purchase meant that an incalculable number of inferior instruments were being marketed.[339]

As well as sewing machines and pianos, by 1891 the official organ of the Hire Traders' Protection Association listed as suitable for 'the hire trade' bedsteads, bicycles, knitting machines, furniture, musical instruments, mangles and wringers and perambulators.[340] In the twentieth century the financing of motor vehicles came to dominate, although the technique was also used for supplying items such as radio sets, gramophones, vacuum cleaners and washing machines. Hire purchase was a major factor in the rapid growth in the interwar period of the multiple shops in the furniture trade.[341] Hire purchase was making the products of the modern age affordable. In 1938 it accounted for three-quarters of the sales of vacuum cleaners.[342] By 1961 the Hire Purchase Trade Association's register of those with items on hire purchase contained more than a million names.[343] Despite the wide penetration of hire purchase in society, there was a stigma associated with its use – a form of class snobbery – which survived the Second World War.[344] The boom in hire purchase meant that controls on its use (e.g., requiring minimum deposits) became an effective tool of macro-economic policy,[345] albeit that controls had serious ramifications for industry. The popularity of hire purchase as a legal form of instalment credit spread to places like Australasia.[346]

---

[339] C. Ehrlich, *The Piano A History*, 2nd ed., Oxford, Clarendon, 1990, 99–100.
[340] *Hire Traders' Guide and Record*, 2 March 1891, 1–2.
[341] J. Jefferys, *Retail Trading in Britain 1850–1950*, Cambridge, Cambridge University Press, 1954, 426–427.
[342] P. Scott, 'Managing Door-to-Door Sales of Vacuum Cleaners in Interwar Britain' (2008) 82 *Business History Review* 761, 771.
[343] M. Share, 'Some Problems of Finance Companies' (1962) 112 *LJ* 759, 761.
[344] 'The Hire Purchase System', *Red S [Singer] Review*, vol. 1, n.10, June 1920, 17; 'The Hire Purchase System', *Red S [Singer] Review*, vol. 18, n.5, January 1937, 19; 'Hire Purchase v. Cash', *Red S [Singer] Review*, vol. 18, n.8, April 1937, 15; 'Hire Purchase' (1955) 119 JP 158 ('still deeply distrusted by ... ordinary prudent type'). See P. Scott, 'The Twilight World of Interwar British Hire Purchase' (2002) 177 *Past & Present* 195; S. O'Connell, *The Car and British Society. Class, Gender and Motoring 1896–1939*, Manchester, Manchester University Press, 1998, 31.
[345] e.g., Hire-Purchase and Credit Sale Agreements (Maximum Prices and Charges) Order 1950. See M. Artis, 'Monetary Policy and Financial Intermediaries: The Hire Purchase Finance Houses' (1963) 25 *Oxford Bull Econ & Statistics* 27–29; 'Evasion of the Hire-purchase and Credit-sale Control' (1960) 110 *LJ* 505.
[346] R. Goode & J. Ziegel, *Hire Purchase and Conditional Sale A Comparative Survey of Commonwealth and American law*, London, British Institute of International and Comparative Law, 1965, 19–25 (but note the New Zealand variation); P. van der Eng, 'Consumer Credit in Australia during the Twentieth Century' (2008) 18 *Accounting, Business and Financial History* 243. In North America conditional sale and chattel mortgages were used: see J. Logemann, 'Different Paths to Mass Consumption: Consumer Credit in the United States and West Germany during the 1950s and '60s' (2008) 41 *J Soc Hist* 525.

(ii) The House of Lords' Imprimatur in Helby v Matthews

In the late 1870s and 1880s there was criticism of what was described on one occasion in the musical trade press as the tangled state of hire purchase law. The position on the hirer's bankruptcy and the extent to which the landlord had a right to seize the goods for unpaid rent were causes for concern.[347] There seemed to be uncertainty as well as to whether the implied obligations of sellers for the quality of goods applied to hire and hire purchase.[348] Another issue was whether hirers might be able to confer good title on a third party to whom they purported to sell or pledge the goods (notwithstanding a prohibition in the hire purchase agreement against doing this). There was the further question whether hire purchase was caught by the Bills of Sale Acts.[349]

The legal status of hire purchase came before the courts in *Lee* v. *Butler*.[350] There the hirer of furniture from the plaintiff under a 'hire and purchase' agreement sold it to the defendant before the last payment (called 'rent') was made. The defendant received the furniture in good faith and without notice that it was under a hire purchase agreement. The agreement provided that when all the rental payments had been made, 'thenceforth [it should] be and become the sole and absolute property of the said hirer'. Section 9 of the Factors Act 1889 (equivalent to section 25(2) of the Sale of Goods Act 1893) provided that a buyer in possession of goods on credit could pass good title to a bona fide purchaser. The Court of Appeal held that the section applied: the hirer was a person who had agreed to buy furniture and had possession of it with the consent of the plaintiff, so that (as here) its disposition was effective when made to a third party acting in good faith. In other words, the plaintiff's title was trumped by that of the innocent third-party purchaser. Lord Esher MR said that it was a very plain case.[351]

Lee v. *Butler* placed the future of hire purchase in jeopardy. The Hire Traders' Protection Association, which had been formed in 1891, took up the issue. Its object was protecting the interests of the hire trade.[352] H. E. Tudor was its solicitor and the *Hire Traders' Record* became its official journal.[353] At a meeting of its general committee on 15 August 1893 the Association considered whether to support an appeal in *Lee* v. *Butler* and allocated £20 for the purpose of publicising the issue and taking the matter forward.[354] On receiving

---

[347] C. Ehrlich, The Piano A History, *op cit*, 100–101. Conflicting decisions are noted in 'The Legal Aspect of the Hire System of Purchase' (1878) 65 *LT* 429.

[348] 'Implied Warranty on Sale or Hire of Chattels' (1881) 26 *Sol J* 136.

[349] *McEntire* v. *Crossley Brothers Ltd* [1895] AC 457 decided it was not. There was an unsuccessful campaign in the 1880s–1890s by larger businesses and some banks that by legislation it should be: R. Bennett, *Local Business Voice: The History of Chambers of Commerce in Britain, Ireland, and Revolutionary America, 1760-2011*, Oxford, Oxford University Press, 2011, 28–32, 556–558.

[350] [1893] 2 QB 318. [351] at 321. [352] *Hire Traders' Guide and Record*, 1 June 1892, 5.

[353] In later years Tudor appeared in many courts on behalf of many hire traders.

[354] The following is based on an unpublished summary of the minute books of the Association's executive committee, kindly provided to me in 2009 by Chris Oakes, then chief executive of the

counsel's advice at its September 1893 meeting, however, the Association decided that it was useless to pursue that course. Instead, it resolved to support Charles Helby, a manufacturer and retailer of pianos in London, in a case he had litigated in the County Court. The Association's support was to pay for counsel for the hearing. The following month, on Helby's request, the Association gave him an indemnity for his legal costs to the extent of £50, but subject to that sum being increased.

In the hire purchase agreement at issue in Helby's case, dated 23 December 1892, he as 'owner' had agreed to let a piano on hire to Charles Brewster, the 'hirer', who agreed to pay the 'owner' a monthly 'rent or hire instalment' of ten shillings and sixpence, on the terms that, if the hirer punctually paid all the monthly instalments, the piano should become his property. Until the full amount was paid, the agreement provided that the piano should remain the property of the owner. There was a further clause that if the hirer did not perform his obligations, the owner might repossess the piano by entering Brewster's home. Moreover, the hirer might terminate the hiring by returning the piano, in which case the hirer remained liable for the arrears of hire up to the date of return and was not entitled to any allowance for what had already been paid. Helby was suing because Brewster, after paying some of the instalments, had pledged the piano with the defendant pawnbrokers to secure a loan. When Helby discovered this he sued the pawnbrokers, but they refused to return the piano. Their defence was that they had received the piano in good faith and without notice of Helby's claim and that Brewster, having 'bought or agreed to buy' it, they were protected by section 9 of the Factors Act 1889.

Both the County Court and the Divisional Court rejected the defence, but the Court of Appeal applied *Lee* v. *Butler*[355] and found in favour of the pawnbrokers.[356] The general committee of the Hire Traders' Protection Association resolved at meetings in May 1894 to fund an appeal to the House of Lords and to raise £4,000 for that purpose. The appeal was heard in late April 1895 and judgment in favour of Helby given a month later.[357] For Lord Herschell the contract was 'in reality' one for hire, not sale, even if it was likely both parties contemplated that it would end in a purchase. *Lee* v. *Butler* was distinguishable because there the customer had no right to return the goods and the transaction would necessarily result in a sale.[358] Whilst in popular language Helby's obligation might be described as an agreement to sell, said Lord Watson, it was in law nothing more than a binding offer to sell which could be accepted when all instalments were paid.[359] Lord Macnaghten added to this formalism the policy of freedom of contract.[360]

Association's successor body, the Consumer Credit Trade Association. It seems that the minute books have since been 'lost'.
[355] [1893] 2 QB 318.   [356] [1894] 2 QB 262.   [357] [1895] AC 471.   [358] at 475, 477–478.
[359] at 480. See also Lord Shand at 483–484.   [360] at 482.

Helby v. *Matthews* gave the green light to hire purchase transactions.[361] Cases in the pipeline were decided in accordance with the ruling.[362] The first of a number of books on hire purchase law was published.[363] To reinforce the point that hirers had no obligation to purchase, standard form agreements following the case provided explicitly that hirers had to exercise an option to do so, typically on a nominal payment. In addition, hire purchase agreements introduced a minimum payment clause, providing that if the hirer returned the goods or the agreement was terminated by the owner on the hirer's breach before a specified portion of the hire-purchase price had been paid, the hirer was liable for the difference between that amount and the payments already made.[364] That clause was open to abuse, with hirers in financial difficulties having to pay a substantial 'minimum' sum, even though the goods were in their possession for only a short time before being returned to the owner. For many years the courts refused to assist hirers. At the end of our period, in the 1960s, the courts began to take a less benign approach and struck down such clauses under the rule against penalties.[365]

(iii) Hire Purchase Techniques and Regulation

Once hire purchase evolved in the twentieth century, there would be three parties involved in a transaction, the customer, the retailer and the finance house (either an independent entity or an associated company of the retailer). In a lecture on hire purchase in 1938 the barrister Hugh Boileau set out two methods for tripartite hire purchase.[366] In the first the customer would choose the item from the retailer and would sign a form addressed to the finance house. If the customer's credit was sound, the finance house would purchase the goods from the retailer to become their owner. It would then hire them to the customer under a hire purchase arrangement. The customer would need to pay a deposit, but that was a bookkeeping transaction since the amount would be deducted

---

[361] There were some minor hiccups with reputed ownership under the Law of Distress Amendment Act 1908 and Bankruptcy Act 1914.
[362] *Payne* v. *Wilson* [1895] 2 QB 537.
[363] W. Russell, *A Practical Manual of Hire-Trade Law for Lawyers and Hire-Traders*, London, Stevens & Sons, 1895. See also R. Dunstan, *The Law Relating to the Hire-purchase System*, London, Sweet & Maxwell, 1910; W. Earengey, *The Law of Hire Purchase*, London, Stevens, 1930.
[364] The clause made its first appearance in the courts in *Elsey & Co. Ltd* v. *Hyde*, unreported, 1926: see J. Ziegel, 'Retail Instalment Sales Legislation: A Historical and Comparative Survey' (1962) *U Tor LJ* 143, 163.
[365] e. g., *Associated Distributors, Limited* v. *Hall* [1938] 2 KB 83 (hirer returned tandem bicycle after one payment; CA held clause not a penalty). cf. *Bridge* v. *Campbell Discount Co Ltd* [1962] AC 600 (hirer returned car after one payment; clause operated as a penalty); *Anglo Auto Finance Co Ltd* v. *James* [1963] 1 WLR 1042 (clause a penalty because whatever time during the hiring the hirer defaulted in payment, the finance company to recover 100 per cent of hire-purchase price). See E. Campbell-Salmon, 'Hire-Purchase: Damages or Penalty' (1963) 234 *LJ* 629.
[366] 'Hire-Purchase' (1938) 85 *Law Journal* 248.

from the price the finance house paid the retailer. From the legal point of view, Boileau argued, this was the best kind of hire purchase transaction.

The second of Boileau's method was for the hirer to enter the hire purchase agreement with the retailer, and for the hirer to give it promissory notes for each instalment. The retailer would then discount the notes with the finance house, although it would continue to collect payments from the hirer as the finance house's agent.[367] Boileau said that this second system had the 'high approval of Roche J', by then a law lord. There were variations on these techniques. With the first method, the finance house might have a right of recourse (or partial recourse) against the retailer should the hirer default. The retailer might also have a repurchase obligation if goods were repossessed on the hirer's default. As an encouragement to retailers, finance houses might pay them a commission calculated as a percentage of the hire purchase charge.[368] Retailers might serve as agents of the finance house to collect instalments.

Block discounting was another approach, where a retailer 'sold' (assigned) hire purchase agreements to a finance house.[369] It was thought appropriate with a large ('block') of small agreements.[370] The technique was examined in the Court of Appeal when George Inglefield Ltd went into voluntary liquation with the Great Depression.[371] Its business consisted largely in letting out furniture on what Lord Hanworth MR described as the *Helby v. Matthews* form.[372] Under a master agreement with a finance house, the Industrial Discount Company, it sold the property in hired goods to the finance house and assigned it the benefit of all rights and remedies under the hire purchase agreements. Until default no notice was given to a hirer of any assignment. The liquidator contended that the assignments were by way of charge and therefore void for non-registration under the Companies legislation.[373] The Court of Appeal held that they were genuine and not designed to evade the registration provisions. Lord Hanworth MR said that the court ought not to approach the agreements with a sinister view but on the basis that parties had freedom to enter the contracts they pleased.[374]

---

[367] cf. H. Tudor, 'Credit System as applied to Cycles', *Hire Traders' Guide and Record*, 1 December 1891.
[368] M. Share, 'Some Problems of Finance Companies' (1962) 112 *LJ* 759, 760.
[369] Money might be advanced on the deposit of blocks of hire purchase agreements, without assignment: C. Gordon Jones & R. Proudfoot, *Notes on Hire Purchase Law*, 2nd ed., London, Butterworth, 1937, 65ff.
[370] 'Problems of Hire-Purchase Finance' (1940) 89 *LJ* 206, 206. See R. Harris, Hire Purchase in a Free Society, op cit, 64: R. Goode, Hire-Purchase Law and Practice, *op cit*, 657–670, 1209–1214.
[371] *In Re George Inglefield Ltd* [1933] Ch 1. See *Olds Discount Co v. John Playfair Ltd* [1938] 3 All ER 275 (application of money-lending legislation).
[372] at 18. See W. Earengey, *The Law of Hire Purchase*, London, Stevens & Sons, 1930, 3. On *Helby v. Matthews* [1895] A C 471, see 260 above.
[373] Companies Act 1929, s. 79; Companies (Consolidation) Act 1908, s. 93.
[374] at 22. Romer LJ thought the legislation should be amended to require registration: 27.

Despite the widespread use of hire purchase, there was intense criticism of the practices of some hire purchase traders and finance companies. One dimension to the criticism was typified by the remarks of William Booth, founder of the Salvation Army, who in the early twentieth century wrote of the high effective rates of interest being charged to customers.[375] Apart from high interest rates there was also the scandal of the so-called snatch back, where some firms would repossess the goods after the bulk of the instalments had been paid when one was not met on time.[376] In these circumstances the hirer would get no credit for what had already been paid. The higher courts were not always sympathetic.[377] There was outright abuse by some in the trade.[378] Recognising that such abuses might jeopardise the future of the trade, the Hire Trader's Protection Society condemned oppressive agreements and practices.[379] As early as the 1890s it attacked snatch back, 'the name "legal" strikes us as very absurd'.[380] The official line was that there was a stark division between the respectable trade and the unscrupulous.[381] In fact abuse was not always confined to marginal traders.[382] County court judges became prominent critics. In the 1930s some even suggested that hire purchase should be illegal.[383] Hire traders knew that they should avoid bringing their cases before certain county courts because of the hostility they might face.[384]

The campaign to regulate hire purchase eventually bore fruit with the Hire Purchase Act 1938, a private members' bill which confined the remedies exercisable against defaulting hirers.[385] To address snatch back, hirers on paying a third of the total price were protected against repossession without an order from the County Court.[386] Hirers were given the right to terminate on payment of one-half of the hire purchase price without further payment.[387] The court was empowered to make a postponement order under which the hirer could remain in possession of the goods on paying smaller instalments.[388] An intending hirer had to be given certain information, and

---

[375] W. Booth, *In Darkest England and the Way Out*, London, International Headquarters of the Salvation Army, 1890, 184.
[376] 'The Hire Purchase Act 1938' (1939) 187 *LT* 116, 117.
[377] *Cramer v. Giles* (1883) Cab & El 151.
[378] R. Harris, Hire Purchase in a Free Society, *op cit*, 26.
[379] E.g., 'A Form of "Legal" Hire Agreement', *Hire Traders' Record*, 1 June 1896, 55.
[380] *Hire Traders' Record*, 1 June 1896, 56.
[381] H. Labouchere MP, 'The Rights and Wrongs of Hire Purchase', *Hire Traders' Guide and Record*, 1 September 1894, 81, 81–82.
[382] e.g., *Hynds v. Singer Sewing Machine Company Ltd*, 1909 1 SLT 512.
[383] P. Polden, *A History of the County Court 1846–1971*, Cambridge, Cambridge University Press, 1999, 130.
[384] E.g., 'Tales of the Courts', *Red S [Singer] Review*, vol. 2, no. 3, November 1920, 10; 'Legal Reminiscences', ibid., vol. 2, no 10, June 1921, 9.
[385] On background and for the bill in committee see A. Vallance, *Hire-Purchase*, London, Thomas Nelson & Sons, 1939, 91ff.
[386] s. 11.   [387] s. 4(1).   [388] s. 13.

there were also conditions of quality implied in a hirer's favour along the lines of those in the Sale of Goods Act 1893.[389]

County court judges implemented the 1938 Act's protections with vigour. In some cases a finance house thought to be acting unreasonably would have its monthly repayments set at a very low amount, effectively denying it repayment.[390] Criticism by County Court judges survived the Second World War. To those aligned with the trade, the judges took too favourable a view when customers offered excuses for non-payment and gave customers the benefit of the doubt far too readily. By the 1960s the higher courts were also taking an unfavourable view of the practices of finance houses,[391] and of the wide exemption clauses they used in their standard form agreements to limit their liability.[392] Finance houses in Britain began extending personal loans to consumers beyond the reach of the Hire Purchase Acts.[393] Following the report of the Crowther Committee in 1971, the Consumer Credit Act 1974 introduced a more comprehensive approach to regulating the different forms of consumer credit. That is another story.

4.5 Distribution: Controlling the Market

The products of the industrial age were generally distributed through intermediaries (at the time, the term middlemen was popular).[394] In the interwar period the overall trend was a reduction in their number in the distribution chain. The multiple shops, department stores and motor-vehicle dealerships were the most visible sign of how this was occurring.[395] At common law and as codified in the Sale of Goods Act 1893, there was no distinction between sales to an intermediary like a wholesaler or retailer on the one hand, and those to an ultimate purchaser like a consumer on the other. (Legislation after our period like the Consumer Credit Act 1974 and the Unfair Contract Terms Act 1977

---

[389] ss. 2, 8. See *Lowe v. Lombank Ltd* [1960] 1 WLR 196. cf. *Drury v. Victor Buckland Ltd* [1941] 1 All ER 269.
[390] A. Vallance, Hire-Purchase, *op cit*, 181.
[391] e.g., *Wickham Holdings Ltd v. Brooke House Motors Ltd* [1967] 1 WLR 295, [1967] 1 All ER 117.
[392] e.g., *Charterhouse Credit Co v. Tolly* [1963] 2 QB 683 (overruled in *Photo Production Ltd v. Securicor Transport Ltd* [1980] AC 827); *Lowe v. Lombank Ltd* [1960] 1 WLR 196; *Yeoman Credit Ltd v. Odgers* [1962] 1 WLR 215.
[393] M. Share, 'Credit-Sale Agreements and the Hire-Purchase Acts' (1958) 102 *Sol J* 497; *Crowther Report*, 64, 69.
[394] C. Chisholm, *Marketing and Merchandising*, London, Modern Business Institute, 1924, 15. See *W. T. Lamb and Sons v. Goring Brick Company Ltd* [1932] 1 KB 710, 712, per Wright J.
[395] P. Scott & J. Walker, 'Barriers to "Industrialisation" for Interwar British Retailing? The Case of Marks & Spencer Ltd' (2017) 59 *Bus Hist* 179; A. Godley, 'Foreign Multinationals and Innovation in British Retailing 1850–1962', R. Church & A. Godley (eds.), *The Emergence Of Modern Marketing*, London, Cass, 2003; A. Briggs, *Marks &Spencer 1884–1984*, London, Octopus, 1984; W. Fraser, *The Coming of the Mass Market 1850–1914*, London, Macmillan, 1981, 111–121, 128–133; D. Alexander, *Retailing in England during the Industrial Revolution*, London, Athlone Press, 1970, 112–117, 131; A. Briggs, *Friends of the People; The Centenary History Of Lewis's*, London, B. T. Batsford, 1956; J. Jefferys, *Retail Trading in Britain 1850–1950*, Cambridge, Cambridge University Press, 1954.

began to take seriously the imbalance in bargaining strength in business-to-consumer sales and to fashion different standards.)

Manufacturers, producers and wholesalers often sought to control those down the distribution chain as to how their goods were to be marketed. In some cases they could do this through the financial power they exercised in providing credit to a distributor or in financing its stock in trade.[396] As a matter of law, the sales contract might oblige the distributor to market the goods at a particular price (resale price maintenance), to display or advertise them in particular ways, to confine their efforts within territorial limits, and to offer associated services to a prescribed standard. In return the distributor might be entitled to describe itself as an 'agent' or 'authorised dealer' of the manufacturer or producer. The distributor consequently benefitted from the goodwill generated by the latter's advertising and sales promotion and might become the preferred source in an area of a sought-after product.

After an outline of the different types of intermediary, this part of the chapter focuses on the nature and content of these distribution arrangements. As we see, first, they might be quite informal, not even contractual, but with the aim of having distributors in different geographical areas take a product and sell it at approved prices. Typically, however, the arrangements were contractual. Distributors might be given the exclusive right to market in a geographic area and be bound, in return, not to market competing products there. Illustrative are the contracts Ferranti used for marketing its electrical equipment abroad in the 1920s.

The bargaining power of manufacturers and producers led to tighter controls in the distribution of the mass-market goods of the late nineteenth and twentieth centuries, bicycles, motor bikes and motor vehicles. Resale price maintenance became an essential component of the distribution contract: the dealer should only use the manufacturer's list prices or face penalties or blacklisting. The same attempt to control marketing occurred with vehicle accessories like tyres and petrol. Distribution contracts might impose on a wholesaler or retailer an obligation to 'push' or use its 'best endeavours' to obtain orders for a product. The meaning of th terms for distributors is examined through the story of hard-fought litigation about what it meant for the sale of Watson's whisky in New South Wales in the interwar period. Finally, there is a brief discussion of how a manufacturer or producer, unhappy with a distributor's performance, could terminate the contract. As we see through the distribution of a British sports car in New York just after the Second World War, because of the legal and practical difficulties this was not always an easy option and that it might be better for the manufacturer to wait for the contractual arrangement with the distributor to lapse through the effluxion of time.

---

[396] R. Goode, *Fundamental Concepts of Commercial Law*, Oxford, Oxford University Press, 2018, 3–4; N. Isaacs, 'The Dealer-Purchaser' (1927) 1 *U Cincinnati LR* 373, 375–376.

1 Distributors in Many Forms

As we saw in Chapter 3, distributors might be described as agents and be paid a commission on sales.[397] This did not necessarily mean that they were agents in the legal sense.[398] The sales contract with a buyer was with them, not with the manufacturer or producer. To take just one example: the Oldham-based manufacturer Platt Bros & Co. Ltd supplied textile machinery to the world, installing it and training the workforce if needed. To do so it used 'agents'.[399] Under a contract dated 13 July 1895, it appointed Jardine Matheson & Co. as its sole agent in China and Hong Kong for the sale of spinning machinery. Jardine Matheson & Co. was confined to sourcing such machinery from the company and obliged to use best endeavours to obtain orders. Commission was payable on orders, less if they came to Platts directly. But clause 5 of the contract recognised that since payment had to be made in cash on shipment, Jardine Matheson & Co. was 'practically in the position of principals for orders sent though them'. Jardine Matheson & Co. was at liberty to make such financial arrangements with its customers as it deemed prudent, although it undertook to work generally to Pratt's prices.[400] In other words, Jardine Matheson & Co. was not a true agent in law.

With products like textiles, wholesalers remained a major channel of distribution to retailers. They bought from manufacturers (sometimes a number) to sell on to retailers.[401] For many years wholesalers were also vital in the export of textiles and their distribution in overseas markets.[402] Even within Britain wholesalers could be the distributor of choice for manufacturers.[403] For example, Nettlefold & Chamberlain built up a near monopoly in woodscrews in Britain and as well a large export business. From the early days it eschewed selling directly to shops and from acquiring ironmongery outlets itself. Instead, it chose to distribute its products through major wholesalers and used a system of varying discounts to retain their loyalty.[404]

---

[397] see C. Bolling, *Sales Management*, London, Pitman & Sons, 1933, 110. [398] 134–136 above.
[399] D. Farnie, 'The Marketing Strategies of Platt Bros & Co. Ltd of Oldham, 1906–1940' (1993) 24 *Textile Hist* 147, 159.
[400] CUL, Jardine Matheson Archive, Agreements and Contracts, F1/102.
[401] C. Chisholm *Marketing and Merchandising*, London, Modern Business Institute, 1924, 89ff; E. Levinson, 'Wholesale Marketing', in R. Lemmon et al, *Some Problems of Marketing*, Melbourne, Melbourne University Press, 1928, 39. See also G. Porter & H. Livesay, *Merchants and Manufacturers*, Baltimore, Johns Hopkins University Press, 1971, 3–5, 10.
[402] M. Prat, 'Between the Firm and the Market: An International Comparison of the Commercial Structures of the Cotton Industry (1820–1939)' (2009) 51 *Business History*, 181, 183–184; G. MacEwan, *Overseas Trade and Export Practice*, London, MacDonald & Evans, 1938, 169.
[403] S. Chapman, *Hosiery and Knitwear Four Centuries of Small-scale Industry in Britain*, Oxford, Oxford University Press, 2002, 158–165; S. Chapman, 'The Decline and Rise of Textile Merchanting 1880–1990' (1990) 32 *Bus Hist* 171.
[404] E. Jones, 'Marketing the Nettlefold Woodscrew by GKN 1850–1939', in R. Davenport-Hines (ed.), *Markets and Bagmen*, Aldershot, Gower, 1986, 132–135. The 'Chamberlain' in the firm name was that of the eminent Midlands political family.

Wholesalers were in the decline from the interwar years. Advocates for the greater integration in Britain of the marketing and distribution process contended that retailers could perform their own wholesaling, especially the multiples and department stores. Manufacturers, it was also said, should sell directly to retailers and customers.[405] With consumer goods the integration of mass production and mass distribution under the same roof was unusual. As we have seen, a notable exception was the Singer Sewing Machines Co. With entrepreneurial flair it began using its own retail outlets in the last quarter of the nineteenth century and engaged in direct marketing to customers through instalment agreements under its canvasser–collector system.[406]

The relationships in a distribution chain tended in practice to be linear, from the manufacturer or producer through intermediaries to the ultimate customer. In that context it is perhaps not surprising that English law was slow in finding that the ultimate customer could attribute liability for defective products to their manufacturer. The law, in a sense, reflected the commercial reality. There was a breakthrough in legal doctrine with what the *Law Times* described as the 'revolutionary' case of *Donoghue* v. *Stevenson*.[407] With reference to Cardozo J's decision in the New York Court of Appeals in *MacPherson* v. *Buick Motor Co*,[408] the House of Lords held that even where a manufacturer sold goods through distributors, it might be under a duty to the ultimate customer to take reasonable care that they were free of defects. In the following years the principle was applied in different contexts.[409] Once manufacturers began using brand advertising extensively, and other marketing tools such as manufacturers' guarantees, there was a closer relationship with the ultimate customer.[410] Potentially that could have acquired a legal character, enabling ultimate customers to sue manufacturers on a collateral contract.[411] That potential was never properly exploited, either by lawyers or

---

[405] E. Elbourne, *The Marketing Problem*, London, Longmans Green, 1926, 175.
[406] 257 above.
[407] [1932] AC 562. See 'Manufacturer and Consumer' (1932) 173 *LT* 411, 412. See also 'Consumer's Action against Retailer and Manufacturer' (1935) *Sol J* 952; M. Chapman, *The Snail and the Ginger Beer: The Singular Case of Donoghue v Stevenson*, London, Wildy Simmonds & Hill, 2010; J. Kleefeld, 'The Donoghue Diaries: Lord Atkin's Research Notes in Donoghue v Stevenson' [2013] *Jur Rev* 375; A. Rodger, 'Lord Macmillan's Speech in Donoghue v Stevenson' (1992) 108 *LQR* 236. See also D. Ibbetson, 'George v Skivington (1869)' in C. Mitchell & P. Mitchell (eds.), *Landmark Cases in the Law of Tort*, Oxford, Hart Publishing, 2010.
[408] 217 NY 382 (1916).
[409] 'Reasonable Care as between Manufacturer and Consumer' (1938) 185 *LT* 123 reviewed a number.
[410] G. Borrie & A. Diamond, *The Consumer, Society and the Law*, London, Penguin, 1964, chapter 4; H. Sales, 'Standard Form Contracts' (1953) 16 *MLR* 318, 333.
[411] As in the famous *Carlill* v. *Carbolic Smoke Ball Co* [1893] 1 QB 256. see A. Simpson, *Leading Cases in the Common Law*, Oxford, Oxford University Press, 1996. See also *Wood* v. *Lectrik Ltd*, *The Times*, 13 January 1932, 4; *Shanklin Pier Ltd* v. *Detel Products Ltd* [1951] 2 KB 854; *Wells (Merstham)* v. *Buckland Sand and Silica Co* [1965] 2 Q.B. 170. cf. *Lambert* v. *Lewis* [1982] AC 225.

the courts, and the prime remedy for the ultimate customer remained against her immediate supplier under sales or hire purchase law.[412]

2 Informality in Distribution Arrangements

Although by the turn of the twentieth century written distribution agreements were becoming more common, they could still be remarkably informal. One example were the arrangements in *Rose and Frank Co v. J. R. Crompton and Brothers Ltd*,[413] a well-known case in English contract law concerning the intention to create legal relations. Rose & Frank was a New York firm which imported from Crompton carbon tissue paper manufactured in Britain.[414] The first arrangement between the parties was contained in a letter of 1905 to Rose & Frank, which confirmed the arrangement to 'confine the sale of it to you for the United States and Canada for the 12 months ending March 31, 1906'.[415] In a further letter in 1908 Crompton continued the arrangements. Rose & Frank pressed for a formal agreement to which the British manufacturer of much of the paper Crompton exported to them, Brittains Ltd, would also be a party. An agreement to this effect was drafted but never executed.[416]

Instead there was a document signed by the three parties in 1913 in which the British companies expressed their willingness that the present arrangements with Rose & Frank should continue on the same lines, initially for three years, determinable on six months' notice. It set out the agreement of the British companies to confine the sale of carbon paper in the case of the United States exclusively to Rose & Frank (with one specified exception). The document contained what was termed an 'honourable pledge' clause, whereby the 'arrangement' was not entered as a legal agreement, and was not subject to the jurisdiction of courts in either the United States or England, but was only an expression of the three parties 'to which they each honourably pledge themselves', to be carried out 'with mutual loyalty and friendly co-operation'.

In May 1919, Rose & Frank sued the British companies. The background was that the British companies had become discontented with the way in which Rose & Frank was setting prices for its customers which, in their view, were so high as to encourage competition. They telegrammed, inviting a representative of Rose & Frank to visit England to discuss matters. The invitation was rejected. The British companies then terminated the arrangement without notice and began supplying other firms in North America, at lower prices. Rose & Frank sued for both breach of contract and for non-delivery under several orders which had been accepted. In the Commercial

---

[412] J. Stannard, 'The Road to Shanklin Pier, or the Leading Case That Never Was' (2006) 57 *N Ireland LQ* 375.
[413] [1925] AC 445. See D. Allen, 'The Gentleman's Agreement in Legal Theory and in Modern Practice' (2000) 29 *Anglo-American LR* 204, 205.
[414] Carbon paper was used to make copies as documents were typed or written.
[415] See [1923] 2 KB 261, 263.   [416] It is set out at [1923] 2 KB 261, at 299–301.

Court Bailhache J gave judgment for Rose & Frank. Because of the honourable pledge clause the Court of Appeal disagreed, and by majority (Bankes and Scrutton LJJ; Atkin LJ dissenting) also reversed the judge on the enforceability of the orders which had been accepted.[417] The House of Lords agreed that because of the honourable pledge clause the 1913 arrangement was not a legally binding contract, but accepted the conclusion of Bailhache J and Atkin LJ that the accepted orders constituted enforceable contracts of sale.[418]

Informality in Crompton's case was its desire for flexibility as regards US distribution. By contrast Rose & Frank wanted the greater commitment which a formal agreement offered. Formal agreements had also come to characterise contract documentation in American legal and commercial practice. At the time the balance of power was in Crompton's favour so it could impose informality.[419] Informality in distribution arrangements seems also characteristic of smaller-sized British manufacturers. For example, Gannow Engineering Co. Ltd of Manchester took only a few sentences to confer 'sole selling-rights' to its pulverising granulator machines on a New Zealand distributor, setting out commission of 10 per cent by way of deduction from the invoice value, less freight, with payment to be made against shipping documents from the distributor's English agent (i.e., a bank or export house).[420] Informality was less evident with the more expensive mass-produced goods. An agreement for the New Zealand distribution of UK-made ABC motorbikes – negotiated for the New Zealand distributor by a London agent – ran to over a dozen clauses: the New Zealand distributor had exclusive rights to sell on the North Island and would take 150 motorbikes over a six-month period; it had to maintain a specified stock of spare parts and to pay in London; and it took responsibility for the motorbikes as soon as they left the manufacturer's works.[421] Trade associations such as the British Cycle and Motorcycle Manufacturers and Traders Union Ltd may have had a hand in this greater formality.[422] Certainly once the Institute of Export was established, it encouraged British exporters to incorporate appropriate protective provisions in their distribution agreements.[423]

---

[417] [1923] 2 KB 261.   [418] [1925] AC 445.
[419] Some law lords speculated that the honourable pledge clause was Crompton's desire to avoid United States anti-trust law see [1925] AC 445, 451.
[420] *Gannow Engineering Co Ltd* v. *Richardson* [1930] NZLR 361, 368.
[421] *Bolus & Co Ltd* v. *Inglis Bros Ltd* [1924] NZLR 164, 170–171.
[422] S. Koerner, 'The British Motor-Cycle Industry during the 1930s' (1995) 16 *J Transport Hist* 55. 59–60.
[423] G. MacEwan, Overseas Trade and Export Practice, *op cit*, 161. (MacEwan was vice-president of the Institute.) See also C. Schmitthoff, *Agency Agreements in Export Trade*, London, Institute of Export, 1980.

3 Selling Electrical Equipment Abroad in the 1920s/1930s: Ferranti

Ferranti provides an example of how larger British manufacturers designed their distribution arrangements to sell their products abroad. In the main it did so through distributors appointed in different parts of the world, although exceptionally in Canada it had its own subsidiary. In the 1920s for India and China it used Callenders Cable & Construction Co. Ltd, a British manufacturer of insulated cable with offices in Bombay and Shanghai.[424] In eastern Australia it appointed an established importer of electrical equipment, Noyes Brothers. For Russia, Poland, the Baltic and northern Manchuria it chose Becos Traders Ltd, an industrial and financial grouping concerned with trade with the Soviet regime.[425] Elsewhere agent houses were used such as Tozer Kemsley & Milbourne in Japan and Korea; Lewis Lazarus & Sons in the Straits Settlements (Singapore), the Federated Malay States and southern Siam (Thailand); and Cox & King (Agents) Ltd for Egyptian government tenders. In European countries local firms were generally appointed; they were to cover the colonies of each European country as well. In the interwar period most of Ferranti's exports went to countries in the British Empire.[426]

The arrangements Ferranti had with these distributors were on what it described as a 'merchant agent' basis. This had nothing to do with agency in the legal sense: the agent bought on its own account and then sold the product in its geographic market.[427] Exceptionally in France, Belgium and Spain commission agents were appointed, although even there a number of specified items were supplied on a merchant agent basis. This seemed to be for smaller items, perhaps where the commission payable was not high enough to cover the expense of the orders.

Pricing loomed large in the arrangements which Ferranti had with its distributors. The prices at which it sold on a merchant agent basis were generally at a discount to those set out in its current catalogues and schedules (the discount varying between agents), often with a further reduction if payment was made against shipping documents in London. In a clause entitled 'agent's selling prices' in the 1926 agreement for electrical protective gear entered with the Skoda Works in Pilsen (Plzeň), Czechoslovakia (the Czech Republic), Ferranti reserved the right if the Skoda Works on-sold to charge not less than its standard export prices. It further reserved the right to control maximum selling prices when items were sold in such a way that its prices were

---

[424] MSI, YA1996.10/2/3/7, Ferranti, Finance & Control, 'Summaries of Agents Agreements 1921–1935'. See R. Morgan, *Callender's, 1882–1945*, Prescott, BICC, 1982.

[425] A. Williams, *Trading with the Bolsheviks: the Politics of East-West Trade*, Manchester, Manchester University Press, 1992, 75.

[426] J Wilson, *Ferranti and the British Electrical Industry 1864–1930*, Manchester, Manchester University Press, 1988, 104, 135

[427] MSI, Ferranti, Finance & Control, YA1996.10/2/3/7, 'Summaries of Agents Agreements 1921–1935'. The only full agreement in the file seems to be that in 1926 with the Skoda Works. I have assumed, as seems likely, that the agreements summarized here, if indeed reduced to writing, were no more detailed.

disclosed to the customer.[428] Delivery under the arrangements Ferranti had with distributors was almost always FOB at a British port.

As for other terms in the arrangements, Ferranti's distributors were generally appointed for a fixed term, then continued from year to year, terminable on one, three, or six months' notice. In the 1926 agreement with the Skoda Works, Skoda agreed not to offer to sell any goods of another make competing with Ferranti's, except where that was specified by the customer. Under the arrangements with its distributors, Ferranti reserved the right to deal with any orders coming directly to itself from the territory covered by the agency. In that case the distributor was entitled to a commission on the price charged to the buyer. The commission varied in amount and might also be amended by mutual agreement 'to prevent loss of business'. To protect a distributor in the case of direct orders from its territory, Ferranti agreed that it would quote prices in such cases which included the commission payable to the agent.

4 Controlling Distributors: Motor Vehicles, Tyres and Petrol

The marketing of mass-produced motor vehicles (initially, Ford's Model T) and accessories such as tyres, and the concomitant need to supply petrol throughout the country were associated with formal, detailed and standardised distribution agreements. Manufacturers sought to control how their product was marketed by those down the chain of distribution, especially the retailers who were supplying it to the public. Distribution agreements also sought to limit the liabilities of manufacturers and producers should there be defects in their products. Exemption and limitation clauses might confine the remedy of rejection which the Sale of Goods Act 1893 provided to buyers of goods which were not reasonably fit for purpose. For example, the 'Main Dealers' Agreement' from 1931 for one Coventry-based motor car manufacturer provided that 'all conditions, warranties and liabilities implied by statute, common law or otherwise are excluded'. The so-called warranty in the agreement provided that if a defect was disclosed in any part of a new vehicle within twelve months of the date of delivery, that part would be repaired or replaced free of charge.[429]

(i) Motor Vehicles

The Motor Trade Association was formed in 1910, as a branch of the Society of Motor Manufacturers and Traders, to curb dealers from price cutting in their distribution of motor vehicles.[430] From 1911 it enforced manufacturers' prices

---

[428] MSI, YA1996.10/2/3/8, Ferranti, 'Finance & Control'. On the Skoda Works, A. Skřivan 'Arms Production in Interwar Czechoslovakia'; (2010) 23 J *Slavic Military Stud* 630–631, 632.
[429] *Andrews Brothers (Bournemouth) Ltd v. Singer & Co Ltd* [1933] 1 KB 17, 18. See D. Thoms & T. Donnelly, *The Motor Car Industry in Coventry since the 1890s*, Beckenham, Croom Helm, 1985, 90–94.
[430] R. Church, 'Markets and Marketing in the British Motor Industry before 1914' (1982) 3 *J Transport Hist* 1, 11.

initially by denying supplies to dealers who were undercutting through the operation of a 'stop list', and later by imposing a 'fine' for less serious offending. The courts upheld the practice in several challenges by dealers.[431] Their assumption was that the association was promoting the legitimate interests of the trade. Retail price maintenance was therefore one aspect of the manufacturer-dealer relationship.

Even before the First World War Ford dealers in Britain had to agree relatively comprehensive standard terms with Ford. Fixed prices were especially important to Ford's marketing.[432] In 1919 Ford also prohibited dealers from stocking other firms' cars, leading to the departure of a number of its dealers.[433] The retail price maintenance in Ford's 1913 dealer agreements received a public airing in an unsuccessful claim in the High Court against a dealer who had undercut the retail price Ford set. Under the agreement, the distributor was to pay £250 as agreed damages for every breach of its undertakings. In the High Court Atkin J applied the Court of Appeal decision in *Dunlop Pneumatic Tyre Company, Limited* v. *New Garage and Motor Company Ltd*[434] and held that the £250 Ford claimed on each of the dealer's sales was a penalty and could not be enforced.[435] Different breaches of the list prices might have the most varying effects, he reasoned, and the sale of one small spare part might have no effect on the company at all. Following the reversal of the *Dunlop Pneumatic Tyre Company* case in the House of Lords,[436] it was argued that Atkin J's decision was wrong. By majority the Court of Appeal upheld his decision: breach of different obligations in the agreement were all visited by payment of the same fixed sum, £250. It was an arbitrary amount, fixed *in terrorem* and payable for varying breaches differing in kind, not a genuine pre-estimate of loss.[437]

Ford's direct control over its dealers was matched by that exercised by other United States motor vehicles manufactures and, after the Second World War, by Volkswagen and the Japanese manufacturers. It contrasted with the more attenuated model adopted by British manufacturers.[438] To

---

[431] *Ware and de Freville Ltd* v. *Motor Trade Association* [1921] 3 KB 40; *Thorne* v. *Motor Trade Association* [1937] AC 797. See also *Sorrell* v. *Smith* [1925] AC 700; K. Johnson-Davies, *Control in Retail Industry with Particular Reference to the British Motor Industry*, London, Trader Publishing, 1945.

[432] A. Nevins, *Ford. The Times, the Man and the Company*, New York, Charles Scribner's & Sons, 1954, 493, 509–510; H. Bonin, Y. Lung & S. Tolliday, *Ford 1903-2003 The European History*, Paris, PLAGE, 2003, 11.

[433] M. Wilkins & F. Hill, *American Business Abroad Ford on Six Continents*, Detroit, Wayne State University Press, 1964, 100–101; R. Church, 'The Marketing of Automobiles in Britain and the United States before 1939', in A. Okochi & K. Shimokawa (eds.), *Development of Mass Marketing The Automobile and Retailing Industries*, Tokyo, University of Tokyo Press, 1981, 71; P. Scott, *The Market Makers Creating Mass Markets for Consumer Durables in Inter-war Britain*, Oxford, Oxford University Press, 2017, 274.

[434] [1913] 2 KB 207.

[435] *Ford Motor Company (England) Ltd* v. *Armstrong* (1914) 30 TLR 400.   [436] [1915] AC 79.

[437] (1915) 31 TLR 267, 267–268.

[438] T. Whisler, *The British Motor Industry 1945-1994*, New York, Oxford University Press, 1999, 245–246, 248–249, 254–259. See also K. Richardson, *The British Motor Industry 1896-1939*,

reduce costs they used many dealers, operating at different levels, who could stock other makes of motor vehicles as well. The disadvantages of these arrangements were increased transaction costs, less market feedback, and dealers able to pursue their own, not the manufacturer's interests. In 1928 a report of the US Bureau of Foreign & Domestic Commerce noted that dealer contractual arrangements in Britain were respected more in the breach than in the observance, that some of the English manufacturers furnished dealers on a consignment basis, and that if the contract could not be lived up to because of economic conditions it was rare that the manufacturer took measures against the dealer.[439] Attempts by British car manufacturers to end the historic fragmentation in vehicle distribution in the 1960s and 1970s largely failed.[440]

Any impetus to change which competition law might have brought to vehicle distribution agreements in Britain was stifled by the feeble nature of the legislation and its interpretation by the courts.[441] Under the Monopolies and Restrictive Practices (Inquiry and Control) Act 1948 the Monopolies Commission could inquire whether anti-competitive practices were against the public interest, but only when matters were referred to it by the Board of Trade. The Board then had discretion whether to take action. From 1948 to 1956 there were relatively few referrals, and those that were lasted on average over two years to complete. Motor vehicles were not included.[442] Then the Restrictive Practices Act 1956 provided, in broad terms, that restrictive trade practices were presumed contrary to the public interest.[443] Agreements restricting competition had to be registered, and the Registrar of Restrictive Trading Agreements could make references to the Restrictive Practices Court (a division of the High Court).[444] If the court found a restriction to be against the public interest, it was void.[445] However, resale price maintenance at the individual level was

---

London, Macmillan, 1977, 220–222. cf. the earlier control of Morris: M. Adeney, *Nuffield*, London, Robert Hale, 1993, 68–69. In the United States, state legislatures introduced regulation of car dealerships to overcome the inequality of bargaining power in the manufacturers' favour: R Smith, 'Franchise Regulation: An Economic Analysis of State Restrictions on Automobile Distribution' (1982) 25 *J L & Econ* 125, 130–133.

[439] quoted in P. Scott, *The Market Makers: Creating Mass Markets for Consumer Durables in Interwar Britain*, Oxford, Oxford University Press, 2017, 275.

[440] e.g., T. Donnelly, J. Begley & C. Collis, 'The West Midlands Automotive Industry: The Road Downhill' (2017) 59 *Business History* 56; R. Church, *The Rise and Decline of the British Motor Industry*, Basingstoke, Macmillan, 1994; P. Dunnett, *The Decline of the British Motor Industry*, London, Croom Helm, 1980.

[441] A. Scott, 'The Evolution of Competition Law and Policy in the United Kingdom', in P. Mehta (ed.), *The Evolution of Competition Laws and their Enforcement*, New York, Routledge, 2012; T. Sharpe, 'British Competition Policy in Perspective' (1986) 1 *Ox Rev Econ Policy* 80.

[442] H. Mercer, *Constructing a Competitive Order*, Cambridge, Cambridge University Press, 1995, 105.

[443] s. 21. See R. Wilberforce, A. Campbell, N. Elles & R. Gresham-Cooke, *The Law of Restrictive Trade Practices and Monopolies*, London, Sweet & Maxwell, 1957.

[444] s. 20(2)(a).   [445] s. 20(3).

enforceable.[446] The upshot was that while it disappeared in some areas, it actually extended into new fields such as hardware, footwear, branded textiles and electrical appliances.[447] It was only with further legislation such as the Resale Prices Act 1964 – which rendered individual retail price maintenance arrangements unlawful – that the practice of manufacturers fixing retail prices gradually disappeared.[448]

An illustration of the contractual networks consequent on the British approach to motor vehicle distribution, and of the impact of the law, was provided when the Austin Motor Company[449] was referred to the Restrictive Practices Court in the mid-1950s. Until 1956, Austin had entered annual agreements with its so-called 'distributors', which were bound to purchase a specified number of Austin cars at the retail price, less a discount of 17½ per cent, and to use their best endeavours to market them and generally to promote the sale of the company's vehicles.[450] Most of these cars were for resale in the trade. Below the 'distributors' were 'dealers', who were also bound to obtain a specified number of cars each year, with a proportion to be available to the trade. Dealers were invoiced at the full retail price, less a discount of 17½ per cent. (Austin paid the distributor an additional discount of 4 per cent on such sales.) Next in the hierarchy came the 'retail dealers', who also had annual written agreements, to which their distributor and dealer were generally also parties. Retail dealers were not appointed in respect of any area but took a specified number of Austin motor cars every year for retail purposes, which they obtained at a discount of 17½ per cent off the list price.[451]

So the distribution chain comprised a complex and inefficient set of contractual arrangements, albeit designed to control those in the chain. Austin sought to avoid registration under the 1956 Act by taking advantage of an exemption for bilateral contracts.[452] It transformed the existing multipartite agreements into bilateral agreements between itself and each distributor and dealer. There was no legal nexus between the distributors and the dealers, although the terms of the new agreements remained largely the same. One difference was that in the new agreements dealers were appointed as agents of Austin. In the pre-Act agreements the dealer was to appoint retail dealers in its territory either in accordance with Austin's nomination or in accordance with

---

[446] s. 25.
[447] H. Mercer, 'Retailer–Supplier Relationships Before and After the Resale Prices Act, 1964: A Turning Point in British Economic History' (2014) 15 *Enterprise and Society* 133, 135.
[448] H. Mercer, 'The Making of the Modern Retail Market: Economic Theory, Business Interests and Economic Policy in the Passage of the 1964 Resale Prices Act' (2017) 59 *Business Hist* 778, 779.
[449] See R. Church, *Herbert Austin The British Motor Car Industry to 1941*, London, Europa, 1979.
[450] *Re the Austin Motor Co Ltd's Agreements* [1958] Ch. 61.
[451] There was at least one other category, 'registered dealers', typically distributors of other makes of car as well, who received a discount of 10 per cent on the list price.
[452] s. 8(3).

its own choice, although Austin had a veto. In the new agreements a dealer had the power to appoint retail dealers 'as agent and on behalf of the company'.

The referral of the new agreements to the Restrictive Practices Court was a test case.[453] The Registrar of Restrictive Trading Agreements submitted that Austin might be regarded as an agent of the distributors and dealers to ensure that, through this network of bipartite agreements, the mutual interdependence of the agreements was maintained. Upjohn J rejected this: 'Austin was not in any sense acting as agents for its own dealers. Austin called the tune.'[454] Reference to the earlier history was irrelevant, Upjohn J held, when the terms of the new agreements were clear: now there were no mutual arrangements between distributors and dealers, and each of the new agreements fell within the statutory exemption. As a contemporary observer noted, the decision drove a coach and horses through the Act's registration requirements.[455]

(ii) Tyres

An issue which arose with distribution agreements was whether manufacturers could bind those further down the chain when there were a series of bilateral contracts and those in the chain were not in a direct contractual relation with the manufacturer. (Before 1956 Austin achieved this by requiring that all in the distribution chain sign the contract.) One technique was to require each party in the chain to have the party immediately below bind itself by contract to enforce the manufacturer's terms as with pricing. Then the issue arose: how could a manufacturer enforce the obligation in the contract to which it was not a party given the English doctrine of privity of contract? Agency law was invoked, with the argument that those down the chain were acting as agents for the manufacturer in having their buyers sign up to the pricing policy. With respect to this attempt at control tyre manufactures were in the lead.

Before the First World War the rubber tyre manufacturer Dunlop Pneumatic Tyre Co. Ltd required a distributor buying tyres from it, 'as agents for' Dunlop, to obtain from those buying from it, in turn, a written undertaking that they also would observe Dunlop's list prices, and that they would not allow trade discounts without previously obtaining a written agreement to that effect.[456] Selfridges, a large department store in Oxford Street in London, sold motor tyres, covers and tubes made by various manufacturers, including

---

[453] *Re the Austin Motor Co Ltd's Agreements* [1958] Ch. 61.   [454] [1958] Ch 61, 74.
[455] R. Stevens, 'The Duke, the Intentional Arousing of Expectations in Others, and the Registrar of Restrictive Trading Agreements' (1963) 26 *MLR* 547, 549–551. See also K. Wedderburn, 'Restrictive Trade Practices—Resale Price Maintenance—Registration of Agreements' (1957) 15 *CLJ* 121. Upjohn J was the orthodox Chancery judge: see H. Magnus, revised S. Cretney, 'Upjohn, Gerald Ritchie, Baron Upjohn (1903–1971)', *Oxford Dictionary of National Biography*.
[456] *Dunlop Pneumatic Tyre Co Ltd* v. *Selfridge & Co Ltd* [1915] AC 847, 849. See generally J. McMillan, *The Dunlop Story: The Life, Death and Re-Birth of a Multi-National*, London, Weidenfeld & Nicolson, 1989; L. Woodhead, *Shopping, Seduction and Mr Selfridge*, London, Profile, 2012.

Dunlop. Over the Christmas–New Year period 1911–1912, they advertised Dunlop tyre covers to customers at less than the Dunlop list price. To fill the orders they bought the tyre covers from A J Dew & Co, a dealer in motor tyres and motor accessories in London. Consistently with their agreement with Dunlop, Dews sent a 'price maintenance agreement' with the order, dated 2 January 1912, which they requested Selfridges to sign. About a week later Selfridge's manager signed and returned the agreement.

Early the following month, February 1912, Dunlop commenced an action against Selfridges for an injunction and damages for breach of the 2 January agreement. Dunlop claimed that it was an agreement which it had with Selfridges through Dews as agent. In their re-amended defence Selfridges alleged that the agreement was with Dews, not Dunlop. In February 1913 Phillimore J found in favour of Dunlop, awarded it damages and granted an injunction, but in January 1914 that decision was reversed by the Court of Appeal, which accepted Selfridge's argument that their contract was with Dews, not Dunlop.[457] The House of Lords heard the case in March 1915. The following month it dismissed the appeal, with different reasoning from the Court of Appeal: even if Dunlop was an undisclosed principal, and Dews was acting as its agent, Selfridges were not bound since Dunlop's contract lacked the English law requirement of consideration and was thus unenforceable.[458]

That defeat did not lead Dunlop to abandon its attempts to control price cutting with its tyres. The contractual undertakings it imposed on distributors like Dews were clearly enforceable. Indeed, the year before the *Selfridges case*, the House of Lords had held that Dunlop could impose under its contract with distributors a fixed payment for every tyre sold in breach of its current price list. That, the House of Lords held, was by way of liquidated damages and did not constitute a penalty.[459] In the interwar years Dunlop went further and took the lead to establish the Tyre Manufacturers' Conference, which enforced price maintenance among tyre distributors through fines and stop lists administered by the Motor Trade Association. By 1939 common price lists were used by most tyre manufacturers; these were Dunlop's lists.[460] Then in 1955 the Monopolies Commission found that resale price maintenance in the tyre trade was against the public interest.[461] Coupled with the implications of the Restrictive Trade Practices Act 1956 for collective restraints, and the arrival of other brands of tyres, Dunlop's strategy broke down. Within the decade it was facing a highly competitive market for tyres, and its market position had declined.

---

[457] [1913] WN 46; [1914] WN 59.
[458] Dunlop Pneumatic Tyre Company Ltd v. Selfridge & Co Ltd [1915] AC 847.
[459] Dunlop Pneumatic Tyre Company Ltd v. New Garage and Motor Company Ltd [1915] AC 79.
[460] T. McGovern, 'Why Do Successful Companies Fail? A Case Study of the Decline of Dunlop' (2007) 49 *Bus Hist* 886, 889.
[461] Monopolies Commission, *Supply and Export of Pneumatic Tyres*, London, HMSO, 1955.

(iii) Petrol

Distribution arrangements for the sale of petrol, compared with those for motor vehicles and accessories like tyres, took longer to mature. In part that reflected the bargaining strength of the distributors, which at the outset was the reverse of where it ended up. That was because petrol was initially distributed in two-gallon cans by cycle shops and ironmongers.[462] In 1920 Anglo-American Oil Co. Ltd, the British distributing subsidiary of the Standard Oil Company of America (later Esso), introduced the first hand-operated petrol pumps with underground storage tanks. Other petrol companies followed. Any site which had previously sold petrol in cans was regarded as a potential distributor. Little initial capital was required. The dispensing equipment was obtainable from the oil companies on payment of a small deposit, with very generous repayment periods. The oil companies competed to sign up distributors. Generally, the oil companies placed no limit on the number of retailers they would supply in any area. Prices were fixed by agreements between the oil companies, and they and the Motor Trade Association combined to prevent price cutting through use of the stop list system.[463] In Britain, unlike the United States, these anti-competitive arrangements were lawful.[464] For their part the oil companies agreed to stop discrimination against retailers who sold independent brands. Until the Second World War most British petrol retailers were independents and sold more than one brand of petrol.[465]

Early in 1950 import quotas on petrol ceased and the rationing of consumption, in force from the start of the Second World War, was removed. Esso had experimented with company-owned petrol stations in the 1930s and initiated the move to solus arrangements, whereby distributors sold its brand exclusively.[466] Over the summer of 1950 there was intense competition between Esso and the main oil companies in Britain – Shell (the Shell-Mex-British Petroleum group), and Regent (Texaco/Caltex) – to obtain solus contracts with retailers. By April 1951 the so-called exclusivity war meant that over a half of petrol retailers had signed such agreements.[467] One inducement for

---

[462] See the advertisement at J. Jonker, J. van Zanden, S. Howarth & K, Sluyterman, *A History of Royal Dutch Shell*, Oxford, Oxford University Press, 2007, 8.

[463] D. Dixon, 'Petrol Distribution in the United Kingdom 1900–1950' (1963) 6 *Bus Hist* 1, 6, 13: D. Dixon, 'Inter-War Changes in Gasoline Distribution: A US- UK Comparison' (1997) 26 *Bus & Econ Hist* 632, 633.

[464] 272 above. See H. Heathcote-Williams, E. Roberts & R. Bernstein, *The Law of Restrictive Trade Practices and Monopolies*, London, Eyre & Spottiswoode, 1956.

[465] Monopolies Commission, *Petrol. A Report on the Supply of Petrol to Retailers in the United Kingdom*, HC 264, 1965 ('MC Petrol 1965'), paras. 41, 44, 48.

[466] The story was in evidence in *Bolam v. Regent Oil Co Ltd* (1956) 37 TC 56, 58-59. See also *MC Petrol 1965*, paras. 87-88; A. Godley, 'Foreign Multinationals and Innovation in British Retailing, 1850-1962' (2003) 45 *Bus Hist* 80, 87.

[467] That figure was 80 per cent by 1953, 95 per cent by the 1960s: *MC Petrol 1965*, paras. 59, 397. see also D. Dixon, 'The Development of the Solus System of Petrol Distribution in the United Kingdom, 1950-1960' (1962) 29 *Economica* 40; J. Bamberg, The History of the British Petroleum Company, *op cit*, vol. 3, 229–232.

them was an 'exclusivity payment', calculated by reference to the estimated volume of petrol to be supplied over the following years. Because of competition, solus contracts soon extended up to five or six years and provided for lump-sum payments in advance.[468]

Another inducement to exclusivity was for a retailer to lease a site to an oil company for a term of years at a nominal rent, in return for a premium, with the oil company granting a sublease back to the retailer at a nominal rent for the same term of years (less a few days). In addition to the covenants for payment of rent and repair usual in a lease, the sublease would contain covenants tying the retailer so that it took all its supplies from the oil company. It would also undertake to carry on business at the petrol station.[469] A clause for re-entry in the case of any breach of covenant had the advantage in preserving the petrol station for the oil company in the event of the retailer getting into financial difficulty or wishing to sell the business. There was some uncertainty about the validity of that clause as against a receiver or liquidator.[470]

From 1953 the bargaining strength of petrol retailers diminished. The financial resources of the oil companies enabled them to purchase stations outright and to let them to retailers of their choice, on the basis of exclusive supply. This method of acquiring a tie was the most preferred, but because of planning restrictions good sites were difficult to acquire outright.[471] There were also a small number of solus arrangements between petrol companies and large multiple retailers, some involving loans to the retailer to establish a petrol business. In at least one case the oil company took shares in a company controlling a chain of petrol stations. Some multiple retailers spread their business between two or three suppliers, making solus arrangements with each of them for different stations.[472]

Under the typical solus agreement, in consideration of the oil company supplying its current products to the petrol retailer, the latter undertook to buy all its petrol from the company, to sell that at retail prices fixed by the company, to market no other petrol, to use only the company's lubricants in the lubricating bay, to exhibit only the company's advertising, and to carry on the petrol business while the agreement remained in force. The retailer was required to place orders for the largest possible loads, or for a stated minimum quantity, and usually also had to give reasonable notice of its requirements. Purchases were at the bulk wholesale prices ruling when it was delivered, less

---

[468] Ibid., 60–61.
[469] *Cleveland Petroleum Co Ltd* v. *Dartstone Ltd* (No 1) [1969] 1 WLR 116; *Alec Lobb (Garages) Ltd* v. *Total Oil (Great Britain) Ltd* [1985] 1 WLR 173 (1969 agreement).
[470] see *Regent Oil Co Ltd* v. *Strick (Inspector of Taxes)* [1966] AC 295, 297-299, a case about the tax implications of the payment. In fact Regent used this technique very little: see at 300.
[471] see Monopolies and Mergers Commission, *Petrol. A Report on the Supply of Petrol in the United Kingdom by Wholesale*, Cmnd 7433, 1979, para. 30.
[472] MC Petrol 1965, para.104.

appropriate discounts and rebates, and were to be in cash on delivery unless other terms were agreed. Rebate was paid in arrear, usually quarterly.

The retailer also agreed to keep the petrol station open during reasonable hours and to provide an efficient service. There might also be restrictions on the retailer's trade in lubricants, tyres, batteries and accessories. Under other clauses the retailer might also agree not to dispose of the premises without first offering them to the oil company, and not to transfer them to a third party without first having the third party agree to observe the solus obligations. If the oil company had lent money to the petrol retailer, its position was strengthened.[473] There was growing criticism, advanced in part by the Motor Agents Association representing the petrol stations, that the oil companies were engaged in anti-competitive practices: they refused to supply petrol stations which did not sign a solus agreement, and to those selling petrol from less than a stated number of pumps, those in areas where in the company's view their brand was already adequately represented, and those in breach of their solus tie.[474]

The courts were hesitant in assisting distributors. In early 1962 a petrol retailer sought a declaration in the High Court that he was entitled to repay a 1956 loan, which he had borrowed from an oil company to purchase the premises. Under the terms of the mortgage it was repayable by instalments over twenty years, but not earlier, and during that period he was bound to buy the company's petrol. Russell J held that the twenty-year tie was not oppressive and that it was not unconscionable to enforce it. Ignoring the patent inequality of bargaining power involved in the relationship, he said that there was no basis for interfering with a bargain freely arrived at by the parties.[475] Another petrol retailer was more successful, however, when he invoked the common-law doctrine of restraint of trade. In 1963, Petrofina had applied for an injunction against a petrol retailer who, to stay afloat financially, had breached his solus agreement and began selling the Esso brand as well. Buckley J heard the case in February 1965, and in March gave judgment that the petrol retailer was not in breach of the agreement. With a twelve-year tie, he held, the contract was unenforceable as a common-law restraint of trade.[476] But in June that year Mocatta J distinguished *Petrofina* in a case where Esso sought injunctions against a defendant who was selling petrol other than the Esso brand in circumstances where the oil company had a mortgage over the retailer's land for the twenty-one- year period of the tie.[477]

---

[473] see *Petrofina (GT. Britain) Ltd* v. *Martin* [1966] Ch 146, 150-152; MC Petrol 1965, paras. 80-84, 93, 143-144.
[474] MC Petrol 1965, paras. 252-257.
[475] *Hill* v. *Regent Oil Co* (1962) 106 SJ 220. See also *Regent Oil Co Ltd* v. *Aldon Motors Ltd* [1965] 1 WLR 956.
[476] *Petrofina (Gt Britain) Ltd* v. *Martin* [1965] Ch 1073.
[477] *Esso Petroleum Co Ltd* v. *Harper's Garage (Stourport) Ltd* [1965] 3 WLR 469; [1965] 2 All ER 933.

Then on 23 July 1965 the Monopolies Commission reported that the solus agreements between the oil companies and the petrol distributors were against the public interest if the periods were too long or too wide, for example, covering lubricating oil and accessories such as tyres as well as the petrol. The Commission recommended that the period of any solus agreement for petrol should generally not exceed five years, although it might be continued on an annual basis if neither party wished to terminate it. When an oil company made a loan to a retailer for a period exceeding five years, however, the Commission accepted that a solus tie might extend to the latest date for repayment. The tie should be for a definite period and not contingent on the purchase of a specified volume of petrol, with the retailer having the option to repay the loan at any time after five years.[478] In light of the Commission's recommendations, the oil companies entered non-legal undertakings to observe them, which later had added force as a result of European Community law.[479]

In the wake of the Monopolies Commission's report the courts followed suit: solus agreements for too long a period could be a common-law restraint of trade and unenforceable, even when coupled with a mortgage. Not only that, the courts also adopted the benchmark of a five-year period suggested by the Monopolies Commission. In December 1965 the Court of Appeal upheld the Petrofina decision: restraints had to be reasonable as between the parties and not injurious to the public interest.[480] Early the following year, in February 1966, it allowed an appeal in the *Esso case* and held that the doctrine of restraint of trade applied to mortgages.[481] The *Esso case* reached the House of Lords in December that year and judgment was given in February 1967. While it did not wholly endorse the Court of Appeal's judgments in the *Petrofina* and *Esso* cases, it held that the doctrine of restraint of trade applied since the distributor in the case had given up its previous right to sell other petrol. The House of Lords also held that the doctrine applied notwithstanding the existence of a mortgage, and that the tie of twenty-one years was void. A five-year period for a solus agreement was not in the circumstances longer than necessary to afford adequate protection to Esso's legitimate interests in maintaining a stable system of distribution.[482] There was reference in argument and in the speeches of Lords Reid, Hodson and Pearce to the report of the Monopolies Commission and to the five-year period recommended there.[483]

---

[478] MC Petrol 1965, paras. 383, 388, 390, 415. The report noted that by the end of 1963 resale price maintenance for petrol had virtually ceased, replaced by recommended retail prices: para. 25.

[479] T. Daintith, 'Vital Fluids: Beer and Petrol Distribution in English Law', in C. Joerges (ed.), *Franchising and the Law*, Baden-Baden, Nomos, 1991, 148.

[480] *Petrofina (Great Britain) Ltd v. Martin* [1966] Ch 146.

[481] *Esso Petroleum Company Ltd v. Harper's Garage (Stourport) Ltd* [1966] 2 QB 514. Applied in *Regent Oil Co Ltd v. J T Leavesley (Lichfield) Ltd* [1966] 1 WLR 1210.

[482] [1968] AC 269. See D. Heydon, *The Restraint of Trade Doctrine*, London, Butterworths, 1971, 219.

[483] at 281, 282, 301, 320–321, 322.

The combined effect of the Monopolies Commission report and these decisions was that the large oil companies generally restricted the length of solus arrangements to five years.[484] Even during a five-year period the courts began to look more sceptically at solus arrangements. Thus in 1976 the Court of Appeal prevented Shell from taking advantage of its solus contract with a small garage when it had refused to give the retailer the benefit of the price support scheme it had introduced to assist other Shell garages in the area during a price-cutting war.[485] The reduction in solus periods led the oil companies to seek ownership of sites whenever possible, managed by short-term licensees. It also meant a fall in the market share of the large oil companies, as other suppliers arrived on the scene. By the early 1980s almost a quarter of petrol stations in Britain were distributing independent British brands.[486] The law ran in parallel with market forces to produce these changes in distributing petrol.

5 Contractual Performance of Distributors: A Case of Whisky

British producers could impose on their distributors an obligation to push a product or to use best endeavours to market it. These obligations were uncertain in scope. In the case of a London-based agent appointed for Britain, India and the colonies to use best endeavours to obtain orders for a company's cotton goods, the court held (rather vaguely) that it was an undertaking to get all the orders it could.[487] What these obligations to use best endeavours or to push a product meant in any particular case seemed a matter of impression.

That was evident in a protracted and an over-lawyered case in the 1930s, which ended in the Privy Council, on appeal from the Supreme Court of New South Wales.[488] The case concerned a 1929 agreement involving on the one hand the plaintiff company, B. Davis Ltd, which on incorporation had taken over the business of Herbert ('Boydie') Davis.[489] Distillers Ltd held 29,000 shares in the company, Davis 19,000, with the remaining 12,000 being held by three others. Distillers Ltd listed the company as a subsidiary. Davis was the managing director. He was

---

[484] cf. *Alec Lobb Garages Ltd* v. *Total Oil Great Britain Ltd* [1985] 1 WLR 173 (the lengthy period there was exceptional: the oil company entered a sale and leaseback which had enabled the petrol station to continue in business).

[485] *Shell UK Ltd* v. *Lostock Garage Ltd* [1976] 1 WLR 1187. And see other cases: e.g., *Esso Petroleum Co Ltd* v. *Mardon* [1976] QB 801 (Esso liable on representation as to prospective throughput of petrol station).

[486] N. Ritson, I. Byrne & D. Cohen, 'A Dixonian Analysis of Petrol Retailing in the UK 1880-2000' (2017) 27 *Int'l Rev Retail, Distribution and Consumer Research* 390, 395.

[487] *Reigate* v. *Union Manufacturing Company (Ramsbottom) Ltd* [1918] 1 KB 592, 600, per Pickford LJ (later Lord Sterndale MR).

[488] *B. Davis Ltd* v. *Tooth & Co Ltd* [1937] UKPC 87, [1937] 4 All ER 118.

[489] He was also known as 'Whistler' Davis, since it was said that he would whistle encouragement to his race horses, even at Ascot.

a flamboyant UK-based wine and spirit merchant who ran a Rolls-Royce, had many servants and gambled.[490] Boydie Davis' personality is an important explanation for the failure to settle the dispute. His company had been appointed as the sole selling agent for the export of Watson's whiskies to various parts of the world, including New South Wales. Watson's whisky was blended in Dundee. Watson's No 10 was a brand name used for the export market before the sale of the product at home.[491] Watson's whiskies had not been marketed in New South Wales for some time.

The other party to the 1929 agreement, the defendant, Tooth & Co. Ltd, was a brewer and merchant of liquors in New South Wales. It owned or controlled some 1,200 hotels (public houses) in the state. During the first part of the twentieth century Tooth operated the largest brewery in New South Wales, the landmark Kent brewery on Parramatta Road, Sydney. It had some 80 per cent of the market and ranked as one of Australia's largest companies.[492] In 1929 it acquired Resch's Ltd, another brewer.

There had been previous agreements between the Davis company and Tooth in 1924 and 1926 for the distribution of other whiskies. The 1929 agreement was drawn up without the involvement of lawyers. Davis had travelled from England to Sydney, and in January 1929 negotiated with Mr Cleary, Tooth's general manager. Under the agreement Tooth assumed for the period of 10 years 'the sole agency' in New South Wales for the sale of Watson's whiskies, with the option of a further five years. Tooth also agreed that it would not assume the agency for any other Scotch whisky, but it could sell proprietary brands of other whiskies in response to specific orders and dispose of existing stocks.[493] The agreement also dealt with the supply and bottling by Tooth of bulk whisky supplied under the agreement.[494] Under clause 4(c) of the agreement Tooth undertook to 'devote the principal part of their energies so far as Scotch whisky is concerned by means of themselves, their travellers and others pushing the sale of Watson's No 10 in bottle and Watson's Special Scotch

---

[490] NBAC, Tooth & Co, Z136, Box 33, Re B. Davis and DCL [Distillers Co. Ltd], Notes on B. Davis Ltd etc.; Memo R. C. Middleton [deputy manager] to Tom Watson [manager], 26 September 1934.

[491] R. Wilson, *Scotch The Formative Years*, London, Constable, 1970, 412–413, 425, 430; R. Weir, *The Distilling Industry of Scotland in the Nineteenth and early Twentieth Centuries*, University of Edinburgh, PhD thesis, 1974, 539; M. Moss & J. Hume, *The Making of Scotch Whisky*, Edinburgh, James & James, 1981, 118, 150.

[492] M. Westcott, 'Markets and Managerial Discretion: Tooth & Co & Co., 1970–1981' (2008) 50 *Business Hist* 602, 607; B. Stubbs, 'Tied Houses, Taxes, and Technology: Concentration in the Brewing Industry of New South Wales, 1882 to 1932' (1999) 39 *Aust'l Econ Hist R* 87, 89, 91.

[493] Popular proprietary brands of whisky in New South Wales at the time were Dewar's and White Horse, but another newcomer to the market, McCallum's Perfection, also sold well. Dalgety & Co. were agents for White Horse and Goldsbrough Mort for McCallum's: [1937] 4 All ER 118, 122. See 165 above. On marketing of Scotch whisky abroad through agents: N. Morgan & M. Moss, 'The Marketing of Scotch Whisky: An Historical Perspective', in R. Tedlow & G. Jones (ed.), *The Rise and Fall of Mass Marketing*, London, Routledge, 1993.

[494] Key parts of the agreement are at [1937] 4 All ER 118, 119-120.

whisky in bulk throughout New South Wales'. There was also provision for the company to provide £2,000 for advertising. Newspaper advertising had ceased in July 1930. Further, the special traveller Tooth employed to promote Watson's whiskies had finished his employment in March 1930. However, other methods of advertising, by window displays and on mirrors and other articles bearing Watson's name, were employed throughout the whole period of the agreement.

Davis was dissatisfied with the volume of orders received for Watson's whisky – notwithstanding the economic depression – and with Tooth's promotion of the product.[495] There was also a separate issue about the way Tooth had bottled and stoppered the bulk whisky. Of a new design, the stoppers it used proved defective. Instead of a tin lining, the stoppers from Tooth's suppliers were made of lead. When the bottles were laid flat the stoppers disintegrated, causing discoloration of the whisky and the deposit of sediment in the bottles. The whisky had to be unbottled, filtered and re-bottled with proper stoppers. The evidence was that this had a detrimental effect on sales, although there was disagreement as to the precise degree.

Davis travelled to Sydney in August 1932. There were discussions over 4–5 weeks, which on his evidence at the later trial were sometimes heated. Davis had access to his lawyers during the negotiations, including counsel.[496] Among the proposals and counterproposals was that Tooth should take specific orders of whisky. Davis said that the current management of Tooth did not understand the contract, since they had not made it; Tooth responded that it was simply a matter of reading it.[497] In late September settlement terms seemed to have been agreed.[498] However, in November 1932 Davis informed Tooth that these had not been accepted by his board in London. Tooth suspected that it was Davis rather than Distillers who was making the running. Further efforts at settlement that month came to nothing.[499]

In February 1933 the Davis company issued a writ in England. The issue of the English writ seemed to stimulate expenditure by Tooth on a renewal of newspaper advertising. In May 1933 Davis returned to Australia. He now wanted Tooth to buy out his 29,000 shares in the Davis company at £2 a share.[500] He informed Tooth's general manager, Thomas Watson, that his English counsel, Sir Leslie Scott KC (later Scott LJ), had advised that his company's position was unassailable

---

[495] NBAC, Tooth & Co, Z136, Box 43, Davis 1932.
[496] NBAC, Tooth & Co., Privy Council, Judicial Committee, Printed Cases of Appellants and Respondents, No 31 of 1936, B. Davis Limited v. Tooth & Company Limited, Record of Proceedings, vol. 1, 23ff (evidence of Davis); 501ff (evidence of Watson).
[497] NBAC, Tooth & Co, Z136, Box 43, 'Brief outline of Mr Davis' conversations with me [Watson] in 1932', 2.
[498] NBAC, Tooth & Co., Privy Council, Judicial Committee, Printed Cases of Appellants and Respondents, No 31 of 1936, B. Davis Limited v. Tooth & Company Limited, Exhibits, vol. I, 159–160; vol. III, 424–425, 430–431.
[499] NBAC, Tooth & Co, Z136, Box 43, cable, 11 November 1932.
[500] NBAC, Tooth & Co, Z136, Box 43, 15 May 1933.

since Tooth's fiduciary duty was to do everything Davis would do if he were in New South Wales selling the whisky.[501] Later that month the Tooth board rejected further terms. Davis told them that legal action would continue, would cost them £30,000 and would 'smash' them. As long as Tooth put their hand in their pocket, he added, he would be satisfied.[502] In the High Court in London Talbot J ordered that the English writ be served. There were further negotiations. In early June 1933 Tooth proffered a draft agreement in return for the writ being discontinued.[503] That did not happen. Tooth applied to the English High Court through the London agents of its Sydney solicitors for the writ to be set aside. Sir Leslie Scott KC appeared for Davis. Roche J held that London was not the appropriate forum for any trial, a decision upheld by the Court of Appeal in early November 1933.

The Davis company then issued a writ for breach of contract in the New South Wales Supreme Court. In the New South Wales litigation both sides were represented by a bevy of legal talent. The Davis side retained Windeyer KC, Abrahams KC and Mr Henery; Tooth retained Monahan KC, Weston KC and Mr Alroy Cohen. In the New South Wales Supreme Court in July 1934, Halse Rogers J gave judgment on preliminary matters.[504] Tooth had contended that its obligation to push Watson's whisky under clause 4(c) was satisfied so long as it did more for it than it did for all other brands combined. It argued that a term might properly be implied that it would carry on its business in Scotch whisky as before, with such modifications as might be reasonable in the circumstances. The judge rejected these submissions: clause 4(c) was not ambiguous and meant that Tooth was actively to market Watson's whiskies. The phrase 'nor take any interest in any other brand or brands' was intended to cover activity which might tend to prevent Tooth from devoting the principal part of its energies to pushing Watson's whisky.[505]

Following the ruling on preliminary matters, Halse Rogers J tried the claim as a commercial cause over fourty-five days. He heard evidence on a wide range of matters such as sales methods, advertising, the use of travellers, tied houses and managed houses. In his substantive judgment handed down on 7 March 1935, the judge held that in relation to clause 4(c) there had been a breach. On the stopper issue for the bulk whisky, he held that Tooth had been negligent in not conducting any test of the stoppers it had bought in, and in failing to have the damaged whisky analysed.[506] At a later hearing, damages were set at £A9,305, the judge adopting figures taken by the parties in their abortive settlement negotiations.[507]

---

[501] NBAC, Tooth & Co., Z136, Box 43 'Brief outline of Mr Davis' conversations with me [Watson] in 1932', 4.
[502] Ibid., Box 43, 17 May 1933, 2 [Davis 1933].
[503] Ibid., Box 43, letter 6 June 1933 and draft agreement.
[504] NBAC, Tooth & Co., Privy Council, Judicial Committee, Printed Cases of Appellants and Respondents, No 31 of 1936, B. Davis Limited v. Tooth & Company Limited, Record of Proceedings, vol. 1, 142. On Monahan QC: *Sydney Morning Herald*, 26 July 1944.
[505] Ibid., 144.   [506] Ibid., vol. 2, 914.   [507] Ibid., vol. 2, 987.

Adopting an expression used by counsel for the plaintiff company on the clause 4(c) issue, the judge held that on the evidence Tooth had not 'featured' Watson's No 10 or the Watson's Special, that is to say, had not made it prominent in its whisky business and put it to the forefront. Instead of pushing Watson's, it had adopted a policy of laissez-faire. The evidence of some of Tooth's licensees was that they had never heard of Watson's whiskies, and that some of Tooth's travellers never mentioned it. Particularly telling for the judge was the arrogance exhibited in the evidence of Watson, Tooth's general manager, that the whisky business was only an infinitesimal part of his company's business, and that Tooth was not going to 'cloud a good beer trade for the sake of a few gallons of whisky'.[508]

Both parties appealed, Davis as to the level of damages, Tooth as to the adverse findings. Just before the appeal was heard it appeared that Davis might settle.[509] That was not to be and the Full Court heard the appeal over a period of several weeks. Further documents were adduced. Judgment was given on 17 September 1935, and there was a further hearing that month on costs. Davidson J (with whom Maxwell J agreed) allowed the appeal on the clause 4 (c) issue; there was no breach of contract if Tooth conducted its business as it had done before the agreement, or conducted it in the manner it thought best in the bona fide exercise of its discretion, giving to Watson's whiskies more of its energies than it gave to others. Stephen J dissented. All agreed that there was no negligence on the stopper issue.[510]

There had been some discussion on the Tooth side whether an appeal should be taken to the High Court of Australia,[511] but Davis sought permission to appeal to the Privy Council. Final leave to appeal was granted in January 1936. At this point the parties had spent £50,000 in litigation.[512] But money was not to be spared, and leaders of the English bar were briefed for the appeal. However, judicial appointments intervened. Davis had briefed William Greene KC after Sir Leslie Scott KC went to the bench in 1935 but shortly after Greene, too, was appointed to the Court of Appeal, becoming Master of the Rolls two years later. Tooth's case was to be advanced by Gavin Simonds KC, but he was appointed to the Chancery Division of the High Court (eventually becoming Lord Chancellor in 1951).[513] Ultimately the Davis side was represented by Sir Stafford Cripps KC and two juniors; on the Tooth side there was Sir William Jowitt KC, WW Monahan KC, Mr (later Sir) Valentine Holmes

---

[508] Ibid., vol. 2, 930–931.   [509] NBAC, Tooth & Co., Z136, Box 33, Watson's No 10.
[510] NBAC, Tooth & Co., Privy Council, Judicial Committee, Printed Cases of Appellants and Respondents, No 31 of 1936, B. Davis Limited v. Tooth & Company Limited, Record of Proceedings, vol. 2, 1000.
[511] NBAC, Tooth & Co, N/20, 2676A Memos, 4 June 1935.
[512] *Sydney Morning Herald*, 10 March 1937.
[513] Simonds gave advice in conference: NBAC, Tooth & Co., N/20, 2676, letters, Middleton to Watson, 19 June 1936. Middleton was Tooth's deputy manager, who spent over twenty months abroad for the case, interspersed with visits to breweries etc. around the UK, Europe and the US.

and another junior.[514] In Sydney the Tooth board was astounded at Jowitt's fees but decided it was too late to change its leader.[515]

Comprising Lords Russell and Roche, and the Chief Justice of Canada, Sir Lyman Duff, the Privy Council heard argument on seventeen days over a four-week period in June and July 1937. Judgment was given in late October. The Board was persuaded to restore the trial judge's finding: Tooth had broken their contract to 'push' Watson whiskies. They had not made sufficient efforts to sell it, nor had they done their best to promote its sales in their tied and managed houses.[516] There was activity, but also comparative passivity, as it suited Tooth for its own business purposes. Efforts to sell Watson's whisky were partial and spasmodic. As the Privy Council put it: 'That was mainly due to the absence of effort to sell. The higher management of the defendant company failed ... to appreciate that they were bound, under the contract, to see that all travellers and all licensees were active in the matter.' As well, the Privy Council disagreed with the Full Court majority about the stoppers, being especially unimpressed with the use of lead. Tooth were held to be in breach of its duty of care in failing to exercise common prudence in testing what was a new stoppering device.[517] The damages Halse Rogers J had awarded were restored.

Unsurprisingly, Tooth was unhappy at the outcome. Could not more have been made of the depressed economy in New South Wales, was one issue it raised with its lawyers. Its London solicitors attempted to assuage the hurt: Davis's expenses would be in excess of the amount of the damages he was awarded.[518] In early 1938 Tooth paid its solicitors £13,000 sterling to cover damages, costs and interest.[519] Davis had threatened further litigation, and English counsel gave further advice.[520] Nothing came of Davis's threat. Court approval of the costs of the case continued into the 1940s, after Davis had died. The case is a salutary example of how expensive and lengthy commercial litigation is sometimes driven in a wholly uncommercial manner by the arrogance and pig-headedness of the parties' principals.

---

[514] Tooth accepted the advice of the leading Sydney solicitor, (Sir) Norman Cowper, that it was an elementary precaution to send Australian counsel: see NBAC, Tooth & Co, N/20, 2676A, letters, Middleton to Watson, 16 January 1936.
[515] NBAC, Tooth & Co., Z136, Box 33, Middleton, Watson to Middleton, 1 June 1937. Jowitt's brief fee was 2,500 guineas, with refreshers of 200 guineas a day; the combined fees for junior counsel were slightly higher: NBAC, Tooth & Co., Z136, Box 25, File 6, Bell Brodrick & Gray [BBG] to Stephen Jacques & Stephens [SJS, Tooth's Sydney solicitors], 11 May 1937. Both Cripps and Jowitt had been law officers in Labour governments (Cripps, Solicitor-General, Jowitt, Attorney-General); and both were to be members of the post-war Attlee government, the first as Chancellor of the Exchequer, the second as Lord Chancellor.
[516] [1937] 4 All ER 118, at 128G-130G.
[517] at 131A-G. By the 1930s the dangers of lead poisoning were better known.
[518] NBAC, Tooth & Co., Z136, Box 25, File 6, BBG to SJS, 22 October 1937.
[519] Ibid., Tooth & Co. to SJS 7 January 1939.
[520] Ibid., SJS to BBG, 30 March 1939; BBG to SJS, 4 May 1939.

6 Termination of a Distributor's Contract: The Triumph TR2 Sports Car in New York

It was unusual for disputes about the performance of a distributor to end up in litigation. Termination of the contract was usually the most effective course. Under English law parties to a contract could take a wide, discretionary power to terminate, with few limits on how their discretion was to be exercised.[521] Thus a termination clause in a distribution contract could contain a relatively short notice period and no need to show cause for ending it. The threat of termination could provide a powerful incentive for good performance, obviating the need to take action. There might also be good economic reasons for termination being the last resort: with a car dealership there was likely to be a disincentive on the part of both the manufacturer and the dealer to terminate since there could be considerable sunk costs which both would lose if the contract was brought to an end.[522] Although legally straightforward, ending a distributor contract pursuant a termination clause might not be so easy in practice. The practical difficulties came to the fore in a dispute in the 1950s between Standard-Triumph of Coventry and one of its US distributors, the New York-based Fergus Motors Inc.

Standard-Triumph was part of the Standard Motor Company Ltd, which in the early 1950s began producing its TR series of sports cars for export, mainly to the US market.[523] Fergus Motors Inc. was a New York-based importer of foreign sports cars.[524]

Under a 1953 distribution agreement between the two, Fergus had to use best endeavours to enhance in every way possible the goodwill of Standard-Triumph and the reputation of its sports cars.[525] The agreement was to continue from year to year but was terminable by Standard-Triumph on three months' notice. The agreement was governed by New York law. It conferred on Fergus a non-exclusive right to sell vehicles and accessories in 'metropolitan New York' (defined to include the counties of New York, New Jersey and Connecticut).[526] Under it, Standard-Triumph had considerable

---

[521] H. Collins, 'Discretionary Powers in Contract', in D. Campbell, H. Collins, & J. Wightman, *Implicit Dimensions of Contract: Discrete, Relational, and Network* Contracts, Oxford, Hart Publishing, 2003, 248–249.

[522] H. Beale, D. Harris & T. Sharpe, 'The Distribution of Cars: A Complex Contractual Technique', in D. Harris & D. Tallon, *Contract Law Today : Anglo-French Comparisons*, Oxford, Clarendon Press, 1989, 330–334.

[523] T. Whisler, 'Niche Products in the British Motor Industry: A History of MG and Triumph Sports Cars, 1945-81' (1993) 22 *Bus & Econ Hist* 19, 20.

[524] The cars were shipped to Standard-Triumph, a wholly owned Delaware subsidiary: *Fergus Motors Inc. v. Standard-Triumph Motor Company Inc*, 130 F Supp 780, 781 (SDNY 1955).

[525] WMRC, Standard Motor Company, MSS.226 ST/3/0/US/3/1/5.

[526] Ibid. A 1939 agreement between the Standard and Fergus, to be construed in accordance with English law, made Fergus the distributor of Standard's products for the whole of the United States, Fergus appointing sub-dealers to assist in the task: WMRC, Standard Motor Company, MSS.226 ST/3/0/US/3/1/4.

discretion in filling orders from Fergus – it 'may reject any order such or accept a part only thereof'.[527]

Unhappy with Fergus' performance, Standard-Triumph ceased supplying it in 1954 and began using other American dealers in New York to distribute its vehicles, especially the Triumph sports car, the TR-2. Fergus sued in the New York state courts for some $1 million in damages for lost profits, expenses of advertising and the cost of other investments it had incurred in undertaking the dealership.[528] Standard's New York lawyer, John F. Sonnett of the Wall Street firm Cahill, Gordon, Reindel and Ohl, also a director of Standard-Triumph, advised against undue optimism regarding the action. He cautioned that, whatever the legal merits of Fergus' claim, litigation by a former dealer was always dangerous in the United States, particularly in jury cases where dealers would be favoured.[529] Sonnett also warned that Fergus had experience in this type of litigation, having once sued Ford. The case might be settled if Standard were prepared to offer Fergus a franchise for Manhattan. The British company was keen to see the back of Fergus and would not contemplate a settlement where Fergus would continue as a distributor.

Sonnett's strategy turned to setting aside the service of process on the UK company on the basis that the Delaware subsidiary, not it, conducted Standard's business in New York.[530] When one of Standard's directors visited New York in March 1955, the prospects for the litigation seemed better. His report noted that, under English law, the agreement would be a complete answer to the claim, but because of United States litigation methods it would have small effect.[531] Cases of dealers suing manufacturers after termination of their agreement almost invariably went in favour of the dealer, he explained, mainly because of sympathy for the dealer, considered to be in an unequal bargaining position. The report added that the New York state courts had the disadvantage from Standard's point of view of more extensive discovery and leaving less time for settlement negotiations.

Standard's application to transfer the matter to the Federal Court was successful. Standard then applied for the British company, Standard, to be removed from the litigation, since it was the subsidiary, Standard-Triumph, which was conducting business in the United States. In May 1955, that motion

---

[527] The 1939 agreement was said to be in substitution for previous 'agency or similar' agreements: WMRC, Standard Motor Company, MSS.226 ST/3/0/US/3/1/4.

[528] WMRC, Standard Motor Company, MSS.226 ST/3/0/US/3/1/6, Complaint, undated, Supreme Court, State of New York.

[529] see S. Macaulay, *Law and the Balance of Power. The Automobile Manufacturers and their Dealers*, New York, Russell Sage Foundation, 1966, 25, 67. See also S. Macaulay, 'Long-Term Continuing Relations: The American Experience Regulating Dealership Franchises' in C. Joerges, *Franchising and the Law*, Baden-Baden, Nomos, 1991; F Kessler, 'Automobile Dealer Franchises: Vertical Integration by Contract' (1957) 66 *Yale LJ* 1135.

[530] WMRC, Standard Motor Company, MSS.226 ST/3/0/US/2, letter, 30 September 1954.

[531] WMRC, Standard Motor Company, MSS.226 ST/3/0/US/2, Report on Visit to the United States of America Re Fergus Motors Inc, 14 March 1955.

came before Judge Murphy in the United States District Court for the Southern District of New York.[532] Fergus' defence was that the British company was doing business in New York for the purposes of jurisdiction and venue through the agency of its subsidiary, Standard-Triumph, and on its own behalf. Applying a 1925 United States Supreme Court precedent, involving a domestic transaction between two American corporations,[533] the judge held that the Fergus defence should be dismissed. Standard-Triumph had a real existence in the jurisdiction, whereas the British parent was not doing business there: it had no directors or officers in residence, held no books, records, property or bank accounts, and undertook no advertising.[534] An appeal to the Second Circuit Court of Appeals was dismissed in August. As Standard's New York lawyers had forecast, Fergus' defeat at this interlocutory stage induced it to settle, for the princely sum of $12,000.

4.6 Conclusion

Sales occurred within the framework of the law. The courts fashioned nineteenth-century sales law in the course of deciding the cases which parties litigated. That meant that while the sale of heavy machinery and of cargoes of commodities from abroad featured, relatively small-scale commercial transactions were a regular feature. The courts' task was a pragmatic one. In spelling out the rules of trade the judges drew on the answers to questions they had posed to juries, the parties' arguments, practical reasoning, their own experience and the philosophies of the age. Judges like Blackburn, Bramwell, Sumner, Scrutton, Atkin and Wright had experience of commercial cases at the bar, in the case of some of them commercial experience themselves or perhaps family connections to business. They brought that knowledge and sentiment to bear.

With the implied terms in sales contracts regarding correspondence with description (as well as the requirement that the bulk should correspond with the sample), contract loomed large: parties should supply what they said they would.[535] The same applied, in extended form, with fitness for purpose, although in that regard there were added twists such as whether the buyer had made known the purpose and had relied on the seller's skill and judgment. When a buyer had not examined the goods, as with plant and machinery to be manufactured or with imported commodities, from early in the nineteenth century there was also the implied term of merchantability. As a requirement of saleability, it did not have the same purchase in commercial sales as the implied term of fitness for purpose but came into its own with mass-produced consumer durables.

---

[532] *Fergus Motors Inc* v. *Standard-Triumph Motor Company Inc,* 130 F Supp 780 (SDNY 1955).
[533] *Cannon Manufacturing Co* v. *Cudahy Packing Co,* 267 US 333 (1925).   [534] at 782.
[535] Professor Carey, 'A Course of Lectures on the Law of Contracts' (1846) 7 *LT* 127, 127. See also Oxford History of the Laws of England, *op cit,* vol. 12, 477 (M. Lobban).

By the end of the nineteenth century, when Chalmers came to codify sales law, there was a corpus of rules governing the implied terms relevant to quality – compliance with description, fitness for purpose, merchantability and conformity of the bulk with any sample. In codifying these and the other rules in what became the Sale of Goods Act 1893, Chalmers' stated aim was to further 'certainty and definitiveness' and to facilitate commerce. As he put it, the law was not for lawyers but for businesspeople, who would rather an inconvenient but certain rule than one conducive to protracted and expensive disputes. Importantly, Chalmers saw his codification as containing default rules, which only applied when the parties had not formed an intention or failed to express it. Following the common law, section 55 of the 1893 Act allowed parties to opt freely out of the implied terms about quality contained in the Act.

In practice, that is precisely what the parties to the sale of heavy industrial goods like plant and machinery did: they did not leave quality issues to the open-textured standards of the common law or the 1893 Act. At the least, the parties' contract required as a precondition that plant and machinery be given the opportunity to show its mettle or to perform to the satisfaction of the buyer (Dick & Stevenson's excavator; the Silica Gel plant). Typically, a sales contract went further with specifications of what was to be manufactured and how – often detailed, and possibly coupled with drawings of its design. The buyer might provide the specifications, they might be implied if ordering from the seller's catalogue or they might be mutually agreed (the propellers for the *Athelfoam*; the 1948 Tasmanian contract for steam locomotives). In some cases, there was an added assurance of quality with the powers the contract conferred on purchasers to scrutinise the manufacturing process, and to monitor and test what was being made during the production process and following delivery.

That did not mean that disputes did not arise. With commercial parties these were typically resolved by negotiation.[536] That might occur in the context of a long-term relationship. This was the story in the interwar period of Ferranti's contract to supply transformers to the Central Electricity Board. When a problem emerged with short-circuiting, Ferranti asked its lawyers about its legal responsibility, but its aim was to find a solution and to maintain its reputation and standing with the Board.[537] What is striking are those

---

[536] The seminal study is S. Macaulay, 'Non-Contractual Relations in Business: A Preliminary Study' (1963) 28 *Amer Sociological Rev* 55. Later empirical research includes H. Beale & T. Dugdale, 'Contracts between Businessmen: Planning and the Use of Contractual Remedies' (1975) 2 *Brit LJ&S* 45, 51, 53, 55–57; L. Bernstein, 'Private Commercial Law in the Cotton Industry: Creating Cooperation through Rules, Norms, and Institutions' (2001) 99 *Michigan LR* 1724, 1744, 1748; W. Konradi, 'The Role of Lex Mercatoria in Supporting Globalised Transactions: An Empirical Insight into the Governance Structure of the Timber Industry', in V. Gessner (ed.), *Contractual Certainty in International Trade*, Oxford, Hart, 2008, 56–57.

[537] On relational contracts see e.g., H. Collins, *Regulating Contracts*, Oxford, Oxford University Press, 2002, 141–142, 327–328; D. Campbell, 'Good Faith and the Ubiquity of the "Relational" Contract' (2014) 77 *MLR* 475; H. Collins, 'Is a Relational Contract a Legal Concept?', in

exceptional cases where in a long-term relationship one of two equally matched parties resorted to legal weaponry and a dispute ended in court. Explaining these cases is not always easy. In the absence of records, Cammell Laird's litigation with Manganese Bronze is difficult to fathom. By contrast, the reason for Lever Brothers' writ against Brunner Mond in June 1924 is fairly obvious – a long and discordant relationship, finally fractured with the discovery of Brunner Mond's deceit. In other cases, we can safely speculate. If Selfridges got away with breaching Dunlop Rubber's resale price maintenance, other retailers would follow and the system would collapse. The whisky case in the Privy Council in 1937 is a salutary example of how expensive and lengthy commercial litigation could be driven in a wholly uncommercial manner by the emotions, arrogance and pig-headedness of the parties' principals.

As well as dispute resolution, lawyers and courts were engaged to test the boundaries of commercial contracting when new techniques of marketing arrived on the scene. Skirmishes with hire purchase culminated in the case of *Helby* v. *Matthews*,[538] which the Hire Traders' Protection Association funded in the House of Lords to establish (in broad terms) that hire purchase was different from sale. Its success set hire purchase on its expansive path as an alternative avenue to sale in the distribution of manufactured goods. On the back of the instalment credit system it approved, the motor car became as transformative in the twentieth century as the railways had been in the nineteenth.

Just as important as *Helby* v. *Matthews* were the cases establishing that hire purchase was not a chattel mortgage, and thus not registerable as a bill of sale. That point had already been made in the Court of Appeal,[539] but was confirmed by the House of Lords in *McEntire* v. *Crossley Brothers Ltd*, decided just a fortnight earlier than the judgment in *Helby* v. *Matthews*.[540] The two decisions were part of a piece; the highest court gave its judicial imprimatur to hire purchase as a mode of distributing the manufactured products of the new age, the domestic piano in one case, the internal combustion engine in the other.

Another decision, litigated as a test case, was *North Central*.[541] Sale and leaseback, it held, was not a loan on the security of what was sold and, like hire purchase, did not need registering as a bill of sale. Legally speaking, businesses could raise finance on their existing assets relatively smoothly as an addition to other forms of funding such as the bank advance.

Helby v. *Matthews* and the *North Central* case reflected a regular feature in the history of English commercial law: innovative techniques were developed

S. Degeling, J. Edelman & J. Goudkamp (eds.), *Contract in Commercial Law*, Sydney, Thomson Reuters, 2016.
[538] [1895] AC 471; 259–261 above.   [539] *In re Robertson* (1878) 9 Ch D 419.
[540] *McEntire* v. *Crossley Brothers Ltd* [1895] AC 457; 243 above.
[541] *Manchester Sheffield and Lincolnshire Railway Co* v. *North Central Wagon Co* (1888) 13 App Cas 554; 254–255 above.

(sometimes with the assistance of lawyers); these were reduced to contractual form and widely adopted in commercial practice; the technique was eventually litigated in court, often following an insolvency or fraud, but sometimes collaterally or in a test case; and the technique then received the judicial stamp of approval. In other words, the courts were not in the vanguard. Because of the nature of litigation, their intervention came after a commercial practice was underway, sometimes after it was well entrenched. That created at the very least a psychological barrier to the courts upsetting the apple cart.

That was evident when in 1939 Lord Simonds recognised what had become the two sides of the hire purchase coin – 'for good or for evil, a necessary part of our social life ... now a recognized mercantile service' – when quashing the suggestion that it constituted unregistered moneylending, an obstacle to its unbridled commercial success.[542] In *Helby* v. *Matthews* Lord Macnaghten, as we saw, justified the result as a consequence of the freedom of parties to make the arrangements they wanted.[543] As Lord Simonds acknowledged, however, freedom of contract was Janus-faced. It enabled many to benefit from the products of the industrial age, radio sets, vacuum cleaners, motor vehicles and so on. When full-blown, however, the freedom it conferred on the hire purchase trade led to many abuses in consumer transactions, Lord Simonds' evil. The abuses led, eventually, to the Hire Purchase Act 1938, a private members' bill, which sought to curb some of the worst excesses. Until then hire purchase had been a regulation-free zone, as was sale, legislation like the Merchandise Marks Acts having a limited purchase.[544]

Another dimension to party autonomy in contracting was that it enabled manufacturers and producers to control those in the distribution chain as to how products were to be marketed. Retail price maintenance was one example. The rule against penalties and the restraint of trade doctrine were very much outer boundaries in English law to free contracting. They were invoked with limited success against some of the more egregious practices the oil companies employed to bind the distributors of their petrol. Manufacturers and producers acted in concert through trade associations like the Motor Trade Association to enforce restraints on distributors. The courts saw nothing wrong in this.[545] When challenged, they upheld the systems of fines and stop lists as legitimate business practices. It was not until the competition legislation of the post–Second World War period that such behaviour vis-à-vis distributors came under a cloud.

Overall, legal regulation of marketing techniques had little relevance during our period. The exception was hire purchase, but regulation was in the main for consumer sales.[546] The impact of the consumer movement in other areas

---

[542] *Transport and General Credit Corporation Ltd* v. *Morgan* [1939] Ch 531, 551; see 256 above.
[543] at 482.   [544] 36 above.   [545] 272 above.
[546] The Hire Purchase Act 1954 raised the price for agreements covered to £300: s. 1(1)(b).

was felt after our period. As regards the regulation of distribution practices, the contrast with the United States was stark. There to protect distributors was a staggering amount of legislation at the state level, prompted by political pressure from those like car dealers to curb manufacturers' and producers' contract-making.[547] Procedural differences also entered. As the Standard Motor Company learnt in the early 1950s, when it wished to rid itself of the New York distributor of its Triumph TR2 sports car, it would face a civil jury if it litigated in the state Supreme Court, which would be sympathetic to the dealer.[548] By this time in Britain the civil jury in commercial cases was a thing of the past. It was only near the end of our period that competition law in Britain started to have some impact. The *Esso Petroleum case* in 1967[549] was a watershed, when the courts fell into line with the approach of the regulator, the Monopolies Commission, in the ties that the oil companies could legitimately impose on their petroleum distributors.

---

[547] T. Daintith, 'Vital Fluids: Beer and Petrol Distribution in English Law', *op cit*, 144; 273n above.
[548] 288 above.   [549] [1968] AC 269. See 280 above.

5

International Commodity Sales

5.1 Introduction

> I heard the waggons, loaded high-up with coffee-sacks, twelve to a ton, with sixteen oxen to each waggon, starting on their way to Nairobi railway station ... Now we had done what we could do. The coffee would be on the sea in a day or two, and we could only hope for good luck at the big auction-sales in London. (Karen Blixen, *Out of Africa*, 1937)[1]

Sale, as that term is generally understood, has always been thought to be the basic relationship in commercial dealings, although we discovered in Chapter 4 how it had to concede ground to new techniques of supplying goods, hire and hire purchase. During our period agents facilitated sale, as we learnt in Chapter 3, and distributors, as we have just seen, marketed the products of manufactures and importers (Chapter 4, part 4.5). The London and Liverpool commodity markets had sale at their base, although the relationship of sale with physical commodities became increasingly tenuous as they evolved as futures markets (Chapter 2, part 2.4). When we turn to bank finance in the following chapter, part 6.2 will explore how the international sale of commodities was funded.

The focus of this chapter is the sale of goods from the primary sector, rather than of manufactured goods, the subject-matter of the previous chapter. Moreover, the focus is on what the market describes as 'soft' commodities, those grown such as grain, cotton, coffee, cocoa, sugar and palm oil, rather than 'hard' commodities such as minerals and oil. Karen Blixen's coffee is just one example of primary products being grown, harvested and then transported for sale on the commodity markets of London. Earlier we saw that from the nineteenth century trade across oceans and continents expanded beyond luxury goods to bulk commodities from primary producing areas in North America, the steppes of Russia, Asia and the southern hemisphere to satisfy an industrialising and industrialised Britain, and later other parts of Europe. Markets in goods became globalised. It is this aspect of sale – the international sale of commodities, to feed the industrial workers and the new middle classes

---

[1] Karen Blixen (Isak Dinesen), *Out of Africa, 1937*, New York, Random House, 1937.

of industrialisation, and to provide raw materials for industry – which is our current concern.

Sales of commodities in the nineteenth century were by dealings on physical markets and by auction; they were relatively straightforward (parts 5.2 and 5.4 of this chapter). Auctions lived on into the twentieth century for the disposal of commodities such as tea and wool. What becomes quickly evident in the story, outlined in part 5.3 of the chapter, is how the trade associations like the London Corn Trade Association (LCTA)[2] formed from the mid-nineteenth century had as a major aim the formulation of standard form contracts to govern the international sale of the commodities in which their members had an interest. Sale in this way was not on physical markets or by auction, it was over a distance and formalised in documents, the standard form contracts for international sales. These sales contracts are the precursors of contracts used world-wide today for trading not undertaken on a private or in-house basis. With international dealings in grain and animal feed the preferred basis is the contracts of the London-based Grain and Feed Trade Association (Gafta), formed from LCTA in 1971.[3] Much of the world's cotton is traded internationally under the rules and by-laws of the International Cotton Association, previously the Liverpool Cotton Association.[4]

The discussion in parts 5.5 and 5.6 of the chapter trace the evolution from the nineteenth century of these standard form contracts issued by bodies like the LCTA. It explores how the various trade associations went about the work of private law-making through standard form contracts within the framework of the law. For historical reasons, taken up in Chapter 1 of the book, this was the law of England, although because the contracts were adopted internationally the forces behind their formulation came from other countries as well. Particular attention is given to the process of how these standard form contracts were drawn up, and the way they were moulded by and accommodated to the law. Few disputes about commodities ever reached court, and then as issues on arbitration awards. Part 5.7 deals with the way most commodity disputes, if they got that far, were settled by arbitration.[5]

---

[2] 'Corn' in English parlance included all grains except rice. See also *Scott v. Bourdillion* (1806) 2 Bos & P NR 213, 127 ER 606 (rice not 'corn' within the meaning of insurance policy).
[3] M. Atkin, *The International Grain Trade*, Cambridge, Woodhead, 1992, 107; M. McGarry & A. Schmitz, *The World Grain Trade*, Boulder, CO, Westview Press, 1991, 475; *Bunge SA v. Nidera BV* [2015] UKSC 43, [2015] Bus LR 987; [2015] 2 Lloyd's Rep 469, [1]. Gafta was formed in 1971 as an amalgamation of LCTA and the London Cattle Food Trade Association (LCFTA).
[4] See its website: www.ica-ltd.org. see also L. Bernstein, 'Private Commercial Law in the Cotton Industry: Creating Cooperation through Rules, Norms, and Institutions' (2001) 99 *Mich LR* 1724, 1725.
[5] Earlier versions of parts 5.2, 5.3, 5.5, and 5.6 appeared in R. Cranston, J. Ramberg & J. Ziegel (eds.), *Jan Hellner in memoriam Commercial Law Challenges in the 21st Century*, Stockholm, Stockholm Centre for Commercial Law, 2007.

5.2 Origins: Bought and Sold Notes

> [A] ticket passes from the factor to the purchaser, stating the quantity sold him; as well as an order of delivery to the captain or the warehouse-keeper, to deliver such a quantity of grain ... but there is no contract signed on the part of the purchaser.[6]

This was the evidence given to a House of Commons Select Committee in 1834 at the beginning of our period. 'Sold notes', but not formal contracts, were mandatory in the spot market for grain in London. The notes were in a simple, standard form setting out the date, parties, quantity and price for the grain:

> Corn Exchange, 1834
> Sold Messrs. C. & D.
> About 1,000 Qrs. Of Wheat, at 50s per Qr
> For W.G.
> No refusal will be accepted unless sufficient reason be given at my Stand before Ten o'Clock, next Market Day.[7]

There was one additional term to what was essential, a right to reject. So parties would need to inspect the grain, to decide if it was of the quality they wanted. The term was subject to opportunistic behaviour, for buyers could renege on a bargain if in the meanwhile they could obtain the grain elsewhere at a better price. At the base of the form was a delivery order, also identifying where the grain was lying.

> 'Corn Exchange, 1834
> The Ship *Gray*   }
>   Lying at Brewer's Quay
> Captain A.B.   }
> Deliver the Bearer for Messrs. C. & D.
> 1,000 Qrs. Of Wheat.[8]

All this related to spot sales. But the merchant giving this evidence, someone involved in the foreign grain trade, added briefly that 'a contract often passes when purchases are effected of grain at a distance'. The terms of that type of contract, he said, were:[9]

---

[6] House of Commons, *Select Committee on Sale of Corn*, HC No 517, 1834, 79.
[7] Ibid., 81. See also A. Pulling, *A Practical Treatise on Laws ... of the City and Port of London*, 2nd ed. London, V & R Stevens, 1844, 471. The Corn Exchange was in Mark Lane in the City of London: see 62 above. In the Imperial system of measurement, a quarter (qr) is a quarter of a hundredweight i.e. 28 lbs. or two stone (nearly 13 kilograms). Twenty hundredweight are a ton. There were 20 shillings (s) in a £.
[8] On delivery orders: 351 below. Brewer's Quay was near the Tower of London and destroyed during the Second World War: see *London Riverscape*, London, London's Found Riverscape Partnership, 2000, 7.
[9] Ibid., 80.

London, 183[]
Sold to (or Bought of) Mr [] through Mr. [] of this city,
Shipment to be effected to [] with all possible dispatch.
Freight [] per Q., with [] per cent primage.
Payment by []
    Witness [] [] Signed.

Here we see the bare bones of the later standard form contracts for international commodity sales – the parties are stated and the note contains the destination, the shipment period and freight and payment details.[10] Agency is also evident with the transaction occurring through a broker.

On the surface little seemed to have changed twenty years later. Evidence to the Mercantile Law Commission in 1854 was that in important commercial centres like Manchester written contracts for sale were the exception rather than the rule.[11] A similar picture was painted two years later to a Parliamentary committee by a young John Hollams, a commercial solicitor in the City of London, and a driving force behind the law firm now known as Clifford Chance.[12] Hollams' evidence was that written contracts were unusual in mercantile transactions in London. While they might be used in the sale of land, there would be at most a bought and sold note with dealings in commodities through brokers, at auctions, and even for sales of entire floating cargoes.[13] It might be prudent to have written contracts, said Hollams, but in his view merchants conducted their business in a careless manner and did not have time to sit down carefully and express accurately the terms of their dealings in writing.[14]

A more senior solicitor, J. W. Freshfield, whose firm still bears the name, also gave evidence. Freshfield's firm were solicitors to the Bank of England and to mercantile houses in the City.[15] In apparent contradiction to Hollams' evidence he began by telling the committee that contracts used in the City of London were in writing and that, indeed, it would be very unsafe, especially given that business was transacted through brokers, not to have written contracts.[16] But it is clear that the writing he was referring to was contained in standard form bought and sold notes, at least for sales of floating cargoes, which 'state all the terms of the contract just as they are stated in the broker's

---

[10] An example of a FOB contract, for sale of sugar, is in *Wackerbarth v. Masson* (1812) 3 Camp 270, 170 ER 1378.

[11] *Royal Commission on Assimilation of Mercantile Laws in the United Kingdom ... Second Report*, C1977, 1854–1855, 6.

[12] Hollams (later Sir John) was with the firm now known as Clifford Chance. He was later president of the Law Society: J. Slinn, *Clifford Chance*, Cambridge, Granta Editions, 1993, 19, 23. Hollams' memoirs were *Jottings of an Old Solicitor*, London, John Murray, 1906.

[13] *Select Committee of House of Lords on the Mercantile Law Amendment Bill*, HL No 294, 1856, 41, 43, 45.

[14] Ibid., 52

[15] J. Slinn, *A History of Freshfields*, London, Freshfields, 1984, 91–93, 128, 130; J. Slinn, 'Freshfield, Charles Kaye (1808–1891)', *Oxford Dictionary of National Biography*.

[16] *op cit*, 4–5.

book'.[17] Together the two notes were adequate, in Freshfield's view, as the note or memorandum in writing of the contract as demanded by the Statute of Frauds.[18]

Hollams' view, that merchants tended not to reduce the terms of their dealings to writing, echoed the conventional wisdom of the judges. In *Humfrey v. Dale*[19] Lord Campbell CJ contrasted what he said were the different attitudes of lawyers and merchants to written contracts: the former desired certainty, and would have a written contract express all its terms, but merchants and traders, with a multiplicity of transactions pressing upon them, and moving in a narrow circle and meeting each other daily, would leave unwritten what they took for granted. In a vast majority of cases, of which courts of law heard nothing, he added, their mode of dealing was advantageous, even at the risk of occasional litigation.[20] That case concerned a sale between brokers on the Baltic Exchange of linseed oil.[21] The sold note, sent by the selling broker to its principal, and the bought note, sent by the buying broker to the selling broker, mirrored each other. Their brevity is striking and there are few differences from the 1834 notes quoted earlier.

Humfrey v. Dale was a contract on the Baltic Exchange between brokers, albeit with respect to a commodity to be sourced abroad six months hence. With transactions for importing specific commodities there was a need for more detail. Before the House of Lords Select Committee in 1857, evidence was given by T. M. Weguelin, the senior partner of a firm, Thomson, Bonnar and Company, and a governor of the Bank of England.[22] Weguelin's evidence was that his firm did a considerable trade, one part of which was importing Russian produce such as tallow and hides. Sales of these commodities were effected through brokers and Weguelin quoted what he described as one of the simplest broker's notes for the sale of tallow by a St Petersburg merchant. Among the terms were the price and quality of the tallow; the time of its shipment (FOB at Cronstadt – St Petersburg's port – on or before the 31st of July next); and the method of payment (against presentation of the bill of lading, by draft of the seller on the buyer payable at three months from that date).[23]

That there was greater detail in brought and sold notes for imports was evident in one of the great nineteenth-century cases on sales law, *Jones v. Just*.[24]

[17] Ibid., 15. The practice of brokers entering contracts in their books continued at the end of the century: H. D. Bateson, 'Forms of Mercantile Contracts' (1895) 11 *LQR*, 266, 270.
[18] Ibid., 16.   [19] (1857) 7 El & Bl 266; 119 ER 1246.   [20] at 278; 1250, respectively.
[21] Linseed was used in paint and linoleum: see J. & C. Bibby, *A Miller's Tale A History of J. Bibby & Sons Ltd Liverpool*, Liverpool, J. Bibby & Sons Ltd, 1978, 18.
[22] On the firm's Russian trade forty years earlier: D. Fisher, 'Poulett Thomson', D. Fisher (ed.), *The House of Commons 1820-1832*, Cambridge, Cambridge University Press, 2009, 856, 857.
[23] *op cit*, 20. For similar contracts for Burmese rice: *Simond v. Braddon* (1857) 2 CB (NS) 324, 140 ER 441 and *Vernede v. Weber* (1856) 1 H&N 311, 156 ER 1222. Traders had standard form contracts for Russia grain: S. Fairlie, *The Anglo Russian Grain Trade 1825-1861*, PhD thesis, University of London, 1959, 229.
[24] (1868) LR 3 QB 197. See K. Llewellyn, 'On Warranty of Quality, and Society' (1936) 36 *Columbia LR* 699, 719-720, 725-726. See 212 above.

The case confirmed that when the buyer had no opportunity of inspecting the goods, they had not only to answer the contract description but also to be saleable (or merchantable) under it.[25] From the point of view of the present discussion the interest of the case is that the contract the plaintiffs entered in 1865, through brokers, to purchase Manilla hemp from the Far East, was evidenced by a sold note with what were becoming familiar terms – the quantity; that it was Manilla hemp; the names of the ships, their intended destination and when they were expected to arrive; the price; that the sale was on CIF terms; how the weight was to be determined ('shipping weights'); and payment terms ('cash against shipping documents on 21st October 1865, less 2½ % discount').

5.3 Trade Associations and Standard Form Contracts

I think it may be fairly claimed for our contracts that they have become a means of standardising terms and conditions, in connection with articles which formerly were more or less subject to various ideas put forward either by buyer or seller, and this must necessarily have an influence for good and for the convenience in the conduct of transactions which are so largely made in these days, through the medium of telephone and telegraphic. (President, London Oil and Tallow Trades Association, 1913)[26]

Standard form charterparties and bills of lading were in existence at the beginning of the nineteenth century.[27] Standardisation of the contracts for the international sale of commodities came later. Trade associations were formed in London and Liverpool in the last part of the nineteenth and early twentieth centuries, specifically to promote standard contract terms. These associations managed to impose a uniformity beyond the standardisation which traders could impose through use of their own standard contract terms to cover the bulk of transactions in particular commodities. That did not mean that variety in contract terms for commodities was eliminated since the conditions under which each was produced, shipped and discharged turned on a multiplicity of factors. Almost from the outset, the standardised contract terms of some of these associations were adopted internationally, whatever was the origin or destination of the commodity. Their international reach is attributable to the leading role of the City of London during this period in finance, insurance and shipping, and the outward-looking nature of those engaged in these activities.

---

[25] See *Gardiner* v. *Gray* (1815) 4 Camp 145, 171 ER 46; *Tye* v. *Fynmore* (1813) 3 Camp 462, 170 ER 1446.

[26] LMA, CLC/B/103-04/MS23234, London Oil and Tallow Trades Association, Annual General Meeting, 28 January 1913.

[27] An example of the former from 1813 is reproduced: H. Barty-King, *The Baltic Story Baltic Coffee House to Baltic Exchange*, London, Quiller Press, 1994, 5. See O. Prausnitz, *Standardization of Commercial Contracts in English and Continental Law*, London, Sweet & Maxwell, 1937, 13–18.

1 Liverpool Cotton and Grain

[The association] arose out of the need which was felt by brokers for definite information respecting the position of the market ... The growth of the business – speculation some people will call it – in 'futures' has greatly enlarged the functions of the association, rendering necessary the formation of a code of laws and usages by which all its members in their dealings with each other agreed to be bound. (*The Ludgate Illustrated Magazine*, The Liverpool Exchange, 1895)[28]

The breakthrough in the history of standard form contracts occurred with the cotton trade in Liverpool. In the 1840s sales among cotton brokers in Liverpool were conducted on the basis of sample and without written contract, the invoice referring simply to amount and price.[29] The speculation in cotton accompanying the American Civil War in the early 1860s shook cotton traders out of their complacency. The Cotton Brokers' Association drew up a set of rules for the conduct of forward transactions drawing largely on the existing practices of the trade.[30] These rules could be incorporated into particular transactions by reference but were soon, if not from the very outset with some traders, printed on the contract.[31]

By 1869 the association had drawn up two sets of rules, Rules Relating to Cotton Sold to Arrive and Rules Relating to Cotton Sold for Delivery. Neither set of rules was designed for spot transactions, although that could not prevent spot sales being expressed subject to the rules and regulations of the association.[32] The first set of rules was of a familiar kind in overseas commodity sales, for cotton to arrive in Liverpool, to be shipped during the period set out in the contract from a named port or ports abroad.[33] The second set of rules, for cotton sold for delivery, became the basis of futures trading.[34] Instead of a specific shipment these rules governed the sale of cotton of a particular type to be delivered in Liverpool during a particular period, which in practice was one of two named months. It may have been technological innovation, the ability to telegraph accurate estimates of when cotton would be delivered in Liverpool, that was the origin of the delivery contract.

---

[28] F. Dolman, 'Where Merchants most do Congregate. The Liverpool Exchange' (1895) 9 *The Ludgate Illustrated Magazine* 599, 603–604.

[29] N. Buck, *The Development of the Organisation of Anglo-American Trade 1800–1850*, New Haven, Yale University Press, 1925, 620.

[30] T. Ellison, *The Cotton Trade of Great Britain*, London, E. Wilson, 1886, 274; N. Hall, 'The Governance of the Liverpool Raw Cotton Market, c 1840–1914' (2016) 53 *Northern History* 98, 100–101.

[31] e.g., *Thorburn v. Barnes* (1867) LR 2 CP 384. See also *Fairlie v. Fenton* (1870) LR 5 Ex 169. cf. *Neill v. Whitworth* (1866) LR 1 CP 684.

[32] Judicature Commission, Third Report of the Commissioners, C 957, 1874, Appendix, Evidence of the Liverpool Cotton Brokers' Association, 2. See *Hollins v. Fowler* (1875) LR 7 HL 757, 758.

[33] A.W.B. Simpson, 'The Origins of Futures Trading', in P. Cane & J. Stapleton (eds.), *Essays for Patrick Atiyah*, Oxford, Oxford University Press, 1991, 185n.

[34] Ibid., 198–200. See 86 above.

Within a decade the Liverpool Cotton Brokers' Association had printed contracts, with the rules on the back, dated October 1878 for an American Cotton, Arrival Contract and American Cotton, Delivery Contract.[35] As well as being on the terms of the rules on the back, the contracts were also expressed as subject to the clearing house regulations. For obvious practical reasons these were not set out on the printed forms but contained in the association's handbook.[36] When the forms were revised yet again in November 1879, brokers were recommended to exchange existing contract forms at once for the new forms 'where practicable', and as far as possible to make all contracts from that date on the new form. To carry this into effect invitations were sent out for a special meeting of the association.[37] As well as the contracts for American cotton to be shipped to Liverpool, the association had a general form for sale of cotton CIF, to be shipped by identified ships from named ports to any destination (not necessarily Liverpool) during a specified shipment period.[38]

No doubt inspired by the example of the cotton traders in the town, the Liverpool Corn Association drew up a standard form contract for spot rules in grain. In evidence to the Royal Commission examining court reform in March 1873, the association claimed that its form of contract was 'invariably' used in the trade there.[39] The form of contract was rudimentary, obliging one of the parties to set out whether it had bought or sold ('Agreeably with the Printed Rules of the Association'), the nature of the grain, and the terms of payment ('allowing interest equal to three months from – '). The only express terms on the face of the contract were a default clause (either party could repurchase or resell within the next two market days, the defaulter having to make good any loss) and an arbitration clause.

Incorporated by reference, the rules of the contract were more comprehensive.[40] They addressed sales of specific grain, flour and feed, such as ex ship, and obliged sellers to approve the bulk as early as possible after the purchase, so that should no written notice be sent to the seller by six o'clock of the day of sale, or stating the causes why it could not be examined within that time, the purchase was to be binding. Under the rules the seller's responsibility ceased on delivery and there were a number of provisions about the buyer's obligation in taking delivery and as to matters such as risk if it had not done so. The arbitration rule was relatively elaborate. Many of these terms and rules for

---

[35] LRO, Liverpool Cotton Brokers' Association Ltd, 380 COT 4/42–43.
[36] e.g., *Constitution, Laws and Usages of the Liverpool Cotton Brokers Association 1881*, Liverpool, 1881, 40–45. See N. Hall, 'The Governance of the Liverpool Raw Cotton Market c. 1840–1914', *op cit*, 102.
[37] LRO, 380 COT 4/50, Liverpool Cotton Brokers' Association Ltd.
[38] Constitution, Laws and Usages . . ., *op cit*, 38–39.
[39] *Judicature Commission, Third Report of the Commissioners*, C 957, 1874, Appendix, Evidence of the Liverpool Corn Trade Association, 3.
[40] Ibid.

Liverpool grain contracts drawn up by the association reflected the practice in international trade.

2 The Role of the London Trade Associations

> The shipping business of the Exchange would be extremely limited in its scope were it not for the presence of the merchants and brokers in grain ... These form the most important element of 'The Baltic' ... [It]is the place where cargoes, as well as parcels of foreign grain, either on passage or for future shipment, are bought and sold ... Generally the guarantee of quality is 'fair average' of the month's shipments, and samples are kept at the offices of the London Corn Trade Association. (*The Windsor Magazine*, 1900)[41]

The formation of the London Corn Trade Association (LCTA) in 1878, with the express object of initiating new standard form contracts for dealings in grain, was a breakthrough. Standard form contracts, issued by individual firms, were increasingly difficult to handle given the multiplicity of transactions in the grain markets in London. Deals could be done orally on the Baltic Exchange, but on the terms of the standard form contracts issued by the association. That reduced transaction costs by an agreed nomenclature and set of conditions, greater uniformity in the practices for shipment and payment, and an industry-wide procedure for dispute resolution.[42] In reporting on the inaugural meeting of the association, and its object of initiating new forms of contract to protect the interests of the trade, *The Times* also noted the 'crowded attendance', the support of 'the most eminent firms in London', and the statement by its proponents that the association was in the national interest, not only of the grain trade, but also of shipowners, insurance companies and Lloyd's.[43] Being drawn from all sections of the grain trade was one ingredient in LCTA's future success.

Until then, despite the progress in standardising contracts in Liverpool, the pace in London had been slower. A notable development had been with linseed, a relatively small, albeit important, commodity in international trade.[44] The background was that the linseed imported from the Black Sea and Calcutta (Kolkata) was mixed with rape and other seeds. In 1848, then in 1857, linseed importers had tried to adopt a united front to curb adulteration, but disputes were still being arbitrated on a regular basis.[45] In 1862 three leading members of the trade convened a meeting of importers, crushers, exporters and brokers. Initially efforts were focused on a system of analysis to detect adulteration, along

---

[41] W. Mackenzie, '"The Baltic": Its History and Work' (1900) 12 *The Windsor Magazine*, 559, 563.
[42] H. Barty-King, *Food for Man and Beast*, London, Ebury Press, 1978, 18–19. Barty-King suggests that the banks might have a had role pressing for standard contracts (ibid., 17).
[43] *The Times*, May 16, 1878, 6. The National Federation of Corn Trade Associations was formed in 1918 to carry out the representation function to government, leaving LCTA to concentrate on the contracts.
[44] 6, 66, 68 above.   [45] see *Wallis v. Hirsch* (1856) 1 CB (NS) 316, 140 ER 131; 298 above.

the lines of that used in Marseilles. When the 'Committee of the Linseed Association' met in 1862 – it became the Incorporated Oil Seed Association in 1881 – it established a sub-committe to draw up proposed rules, by-laws and standard contracts. There resulted contracts for Black Sea, Azov and Danube linseed, East Indian linseed, and linseed from St Petersburg and Archangel.[46] By the 1930s the association had some fifty standard form contracts.[47]

Other trades began to organise to reduce risks with international transactions and to handle disputes when they arose. The litigation in *Bowes* v. *Shand*,[48] containing important dicta of Lord Blackburn on sale by description,[49] was generated by a dispute over two contracts of sale each of 300 tons of Madras rice, 600 tons in total, to be shipped at Madras (Chennai) or coast to London during March and/or April 1874, per *Rajah of Cochin*. The contracts were in standard and fairly detailed form, and it seems fairly clear (albeit not stated) that they were a product of the London Rice Brokers' Association; the association was mentioned in the contract as the appellate body if either party was dissatisfied with the arbitrator's award.[50]

Following the formation of LCTA, there was a profusion of trade associations on similar lines.[51] Their mandate – and this was the attraction to potential members – was to draw up standard form contracts to facilitate transactions and deal with disputes. At a meeting of the London Oil and Tallow Trades Association in July 1910, in a pitch to persuade all the relevant firms to join, the first president spoke of how the standardised contracts in the trade increased confidence. '[H]ouses [i.e. traders] abroad anxious to do business in London will feel more secure in their dealings if they know they are dealing in contracts which are common to the trade.'[52] At the third annual general meeting he linked the need for standardisation with the advent of modern ways of conducting trade through telephone and telegram in the passage quoted at the beginning of this part of the chapter.

By 1912, two years after it was formed, the London Oil and Tallow Trades Association had thirty-two standard contracts, and by 1913, thirty-seven

---

[46] H. Barty-King, *The Baltic Exchange*, London, Hutchinson Benham, 1977, 144–146; G. Rees, *Britain's Commodity Markets*, London, Paul Elek, 1972, 311.

[47] J. Bahl, *Oilseed Trade of India*, Bombay, New Book Co,1938, 145.

[48] (1877) 2 App Cas 455. It was one of Judah Benjamin's many successes: see C. MacMillan, 'Judah Benjamin: Marginalized Outsider or Admitted Insider?' (2015) 42 *JL&S* 150, 169–170. *Benjamin's Sale of Goods* survives to this day: M. Bridge (ed.), London, 11th ed., Sweet & Maxwell, 2021.

[49] at 480.

[50] The contracts are set out in LI, *House of Lords Printed Cases, judgments and appeal documents*, 'Bowes v Shand', vol. 312, 1877, 805–810 (33–38). Archives of the London Rice Brokers' Association do not seem to have survived.

[51] 9–10 above.

[52] LMA, CLC/B/103–04/MS23234, London Oil and Tallow Trades Association, Minutes, 21 July 1910.

standard contracts.[53] Associations to promote standard form contracts were still being formed in the 1920s. The Cocoa Trade Association began in 1928 because of the felt need for a contract specifically for sales of cocoa – the basis of chocolate making – in place of the Liverpool General Produce Association Contract, on which until then nearly all cocoa had been traded. An important factor was that under the latter arbitration was in Liverpool, but this was increasingly inconvenient with the growing importance of London as the cocoa market for Europe. The Gold Coast FOB Contract A.1 was launched in 1929, the West Africa CIF Contract A2 in 1930. In the 1930s Contract No. A8 was designed for futures dealings.[54]

3 Standardising Contract Terms

From the outset the standard form contracts of the commodity trade associations contained a number of basic terms. In brief, there was the date and place where the contract was made, with the names of the parties – the one typically at the head of the contract ('Sold to' or 'Bought of'), the other at the foot. If the transaction was effected by a broker the signature would be its signature, not the principal's. The sale might be expressed to be according to the printed rules on the contract, and this division between terms, usually on the front, and rules, usually on the back, was widely adopted. It probably derived from the need that in market transactions brokers bought and sold notes had to be brief and therefore incorporate the more detailed rules by reference. There was no difference in legal effect between the terms and the rules.

After this there followed the type of commodity and its quantity. The commodity would usually be said to be shipped in good condition, the ship being identified either specifically or as falling within a defined class of vessel. The port or ports from which the commodity was to be despatched might be identified. With quantity the form might allow the seller to ship a standard variation (e.g., two per cent more or less). The date of the bills of lading, or the period during which they might be dated, would be set out. There would be space for the price in terms of a unit of quantity printed on the form. If a CIF contract its nature might be indicated specifically as part of the destination clause – 'shipped, including freight and insurance, to'. Provision might be made for payment for any deficiency, although the printed clause might exclude from scope any deficiency through sea accident (covered by the insurance). From the time of the first standard contracts a payment clause

---

[53] FOSFA International – the Federation of Oils, Seeds and Fats Associations – was formed in 1971 as a result of the amalgamation of four predecessor associations – the Incorporated Oil Seed Association, the London Oil and Tallow Trades Association, the London Copra Association and the Seed Oil, Cake and General Produce Association (founded 1935). See J. Mark & R. Strange, *The Food Industries*, London, Chapman & Hall, 1993, 236.

[54] Cocoa Association of London and London Cocoa Terminal Market Association, *'Their Nibs' First 50 Years of CAL and LCTMA*, London, 1979, 1–3.

was invariably present. Brokerage, the rate and by whom payable, might be stated to be due, even if the contract was cancelled. There was invariably an arbitration clause, often developed at much greater length than other terms or rules.

In addition to these basic terms were other clauses such as the appropriation (or declaration), *pro rata* and default clauses. These are discussed further below.[55] What is striking is the huge variety in standard contract forms. Forms were not only for different commodities but also for the same commodity in different contexts. As early as 1888 LCTA had thirty contracts covering grain from India (2), Australia (2), California (3), elsewhere in north America (2), Chile (1), La Plata, Argentina (4), Egypt (1), the Black Sea and Danube (13), and St Petersburg and the Baltic (2). Only two of these specifically mentioned London as the port of destination, indicating that even at this stage the contracts had an international character.[56] The contracts were designed either for whole cargoes or large quantities in the holds on a ship (called 'parcels'). Contracts were also divided as regards the condition of the grain on arrival. A contract labelled 'tale quale' (as found) meant that, provided the grain was shipped in good condition, the buyer had to accept its condition on arrival. By contrast, under 'rye terms' the seller was responsible for damage occurring during the voyage and effectively gave an assurance that the grain was sound on arrival. In both cases the grain had to be shipped in good condition.[57]

Eight years later the number of contracts was up to forty-eight, with new contracts specifically for Oregon and Washington sales, and additional contracts for each of the other places already mentioned in exporting grain.[58] By 1929 there were seventy-five different contracts. No other association could match this range of standard form contracts. The number of contracts, even for the same type of grain, demonstrated that while bringing about a uniformity in the contractual terms between different traders it was necessary to acknowledge the different conditions under which grain was exported in various parts of the world. Take a basic term like 'shipped in good condition'. Given the difficulties in the early years with ensuring the quality of Californian wheat, the early LCTA Californian contract forms omitted the term, although it was a feature in later years in all contracts. The difference was justified by the circumstances and accepted by a Sub-committee appointed by the LCTA Executive Committee in June 1885, even though the committee's terms of reference were to revise the white wheat contracts and to bring them into unison with the rules and regulations of other contracts.[59] A decade later,

---

[55] 345, 309–310, 349–350 respectively.
[56] London Corn Trade Association, *Forms of Contracts in Force*, London, LCTA, 1888. I have only been able to find the contents page.
[57] A. Hooker, *The International Grain Trade*, 2nd ed., London, Pitman, 1939, 29. See also O. Klenav, 'Argentine Grain Trade', *Corn Trade News*, vol. 92, 27 December 1924, 2.
[58] London Corn Trade Association, *Forms of Contracts in Force*, London, LCTA, 1896.
[59] LMA, CLC/B/103/MS23175, LCTA, Sub-committee to revise white wheat and other contracts, 13 November 1885.

LCTA accepted that 'shipped in good condition' could not be inserted as a term in all its 'rye terms' forms used for maize, once its Black Sea Grain Committee pointed out the problems this would involve with Russian grain.[60]

Similarly, there were problems in unifying the classification term for vessels, designed to give an assurance to the buyer of the soundness of the ship bringing the grain to its destination. As mentioned, the classification clause in the contracts provided that shipment was to occur in a vessel which the standard wording asserted would not fall below a certain class (e.g., 'classed not lower than 90 A1, or British Corporation BS, or equal classification in American, French, Italian, Norwegian or other equal Register'). Again local conditions might demand a variation: thus the classification clause in the LCTA Chinese No. 4 contract was varied in 1929 to cover shipments from ports up the River Yangtsze, by lighters being towed by a river tug or steamer.[61]

4 The Central Issue of Quality

The quality of grain varied and LCTA became what has been termed a quality assurance centre with its contracts and its system of arbitration.[62] While North American and Australian wheat was clean and of good quality, with a limited number of grades, Russian and Indian wheat typically had a high mix of impurities.[63] In the nineteenth century a not inconsiderable proportion of grain was sold by sample, without any description as to quality.[64] In the contract the sample would be identified as marked in a particular way and in the possession of a named person. Sale by sample was facilitated as the postal system and quicker transport meant the samples could be sent for examination more efficiently. Later, commodities like grain were described in terms of fair average quality. Whether grain was of fair average quality (faq) could be determined by sampling the bulk. In the contract the term might empower arbitrators to decide faq in their discretion in the event of a dispute. Otherwise the clause might define fair average quality by comparison with an official faq standard, for example for the month's grain when the bill of lading was dated.

The LCTA had rules for how faq samples were to be made up.[65] Essentially, samples were taken from arriving cargoes and the faq sample drawn proportionately from all those samples. As the American and Australian Grain Committee of the LCTA explained in 1894, 'we get all the samples we can,

[60] LMA, CLC/B/103/MS23175, LCTA, Black Sea Grain Committee, Minutes, 19 June, 11 December 1896.
[61] LMA, CLC/B/103/MS23185/002, LCTA, China and Manchurian Feeding Stuffs Committee, Minutes, 3 March, 18 April 1929.
[62] A. Velkar, *Markets and Measurements in Nineteenth Century Britain*, Cambridge, Cambridge University Press, 2012, 191.
[63] e.g., P. Herlihy, *Odessa: A History, 1794–1914*, Cambridge, Mass, Harvard University Press, 1986, 207–208.
[64] 213–215 above.
[65] e.g., London Corn Trade Association, *Contracts in Force*, London, LCTA, 1896.

and the Committee mix them together, after rejecting those which are palpably too good or palpably too inferior'.[66] In the case of Californian wheat, the LCTA relied on the samples forwarded by the San Francisco Produce Exchange to set standards. In 1883 the committee decided by majority to set standards for wheat from New York, even though the New York Produce Exchange had not set standards itself.[67] In 1912 the LCTA Sub Committee re Sampling Rules warned that despite the rules it was still up to sellers and buyers to protect their interests and to prevent tampering with samples.[68]

From the mid-nineteenth century grading was developed in the United States to ensure quality. That was because grain arrived from large numbers of small producers and was mixed together in warehouses and grain elevators. As wheat was presented for storage it was inspected and classified according to established grades. To protect the reputation of the trade the produce exchanges in various centres undertook the grading. Later important wheat markets like Chicago, Minneapolis, St Louis and Duluth were subject to state regulation to prevent abuses.[69] *Munn v. Illinois*[70] was the great case when the US Supreme Court held that states could regulate grain elevators and warehouses, and other similar facilities clothed with the public interest.

In its early days US inspection was not always reliable. In 1906 there was a conference between European buyers and delegates from the United States on what was said to be the lax and unsatisfactory certification of grain from some US ports.[71] Earlier that year there had been a decision by LCTA to exclude from new contract forms the Virginian ports of Newport News and Norfolk, since there was no produce exchange or public authority there responsible for inspection.[72] The so-called embargo on certificates issued in these ports was removed in mid-September 1908.[73] President Roosevelt's proposal to Congress to put certification on a federal basis was followed with interest in London. Finally, in 1916 the Grain Standards Act enabled the US Department of Agriculture to establish grades and inspection for cereals transported in interstate or foreign commerce.[74] Increasingly, therefore, LCTA's role was to indorse the standards of others.

[66] LMA, CLC/B/103/MS23177/001, LCTA, American Grain Committee, Minutes, 31 July 1894. On the uniform quality of Australian wheat: H. Darling, 'The Marketing of Wheat', in R. Lemmon et al, *Some Problems of Marketing*, Melbourne, Melbourne University Press, 1928.
[67] LMA, CLC/B/103/MS23177/001, LCTA, American Grain Committee, Minutes, 13 March 1883.
[68] LMA, CLC/B/103/MS23174/003, LCTA, 19 September 1912.
[69] W. Cronin, *Nature's Metropolis. Chicago and the Great West*, New York, Norton, 1991, 141–142. See also W. Brown, *American Colossus: The Grain Elevator, 1843 to 1943*, Brooklyn, New York, Colossal Books, 2009; G. Lee, 'The Historical Significance of the Chicago Grain Elevator System' (1937) 11 *Agricultural History* 16.
[70] 94 US 113 (1876).   [71] *Corn Trade News*, 10 November 1906, 1323.
[72] LMA, CLC/B/103/MS23172/002, LCTA, American Grain Committee, *Annual Report 1905-6*.
[73] LMA, CLC/B/103/MS23172/004, LCTA, American Grain Committee, Minutes, September 1908.
[74] 'The Federal Grain Standards Act' (1917) 17 *Col LR* 177; J. Smith, *Organised Produce Markets*, London, Longmans, Green & Co., 1922, 12–13; L. Hill, 'Effects of Regulation on Efficiency of Grain Markets' (1985) 17 *Case W Res J. Int'l L* 389, 406–409.

In Canada federal government inspection and grading of grain began in the 1880s. Wider jurisdiction was taken over storage facilities under the Manitoba Grain Act 1900. Legislative control was consolidated in the Canada Grain Act 1912, to be administered by the Board of Grain Commissioners (later the Canadian Grain Commission).[75] In both the United States and Canada grain inspectors would certify that a particular quantity of grain, of a specified quality, had been loaded into a named ship (or one of its holds if it did not constitute the whole cargo). Under the contracts the certificate was determinative of the quality issue. With a formal mechanism for determining and certifying standards, the control of grain quality could be administered more easily.[76]

Variations in quality could be even greater with commodities other than wheat. In May 1910, the number of Chinese exporters wrote to the LCTA China and Manchurian Feeding Stuffs Committee including Craig & Co. Ltd of Shanghai, the agency of the East-Asiatic Co. Ltd, Schwarz Gaumer & Co., Fuhrmeister & Co., David Sassoon & Co. Ltd and Samuel McGregor & Co. Ltd. The committee explained that it was impossible to ship exactly to sample, because of variations in crop and climatic conditions. To overcome the 'endless claims and arbitrations' they proposed that the quality clause of the Chinese Horse Beans Parcel Contract No. 26 should read 'of fair average quality at time and place of shipment *about* as per standards deposited by Chinese shippers' with the LCTA. After consultation with importers and others, the LCTA agreed to the variation, although not to an additional sentence to the clause which would have rendered any claim for variation in size or colour 'inadmissible'.[77] As we see later the association saw itself as balancing the interests of buyers and sellers in the type of standard terms adopted.

5 Contractual Networks: The Pro Rata Clause and the Bill of Lading

A standard form contract for commodity sales did not stand alone but as part of a contractual network.[78] Most obviously the one cargo of a commodity

---

[75] J. Blanchard, *A History of the Canadian Grain Commission, 1912–1987*, Winnipeg, Canadian Grain Commission, 1987.
[76] A. Velkar, Markets and Measurements in Nineteenth Century Britain, op cit, 210–212; R. Risk, 'The Golden Age: The Law about the Market in Nineteenth-Century Ontario' (1976) 26 *U. Toronto LJ* 307, 314.
[77] LMA, CLC/B/103/MS23185/001, LCTA, China and Manchurian Feeding Stuffs Committee, Minutes, 2 July 1910.
[78] On contractual networks: G. Teubner, 'Piercing the Contractual Veil? The Social Responsibility of Contractual Networks', in T. Wilhelmsson (ed.), *Perspectives of Critical Contract Law*, Aldershot, Dartmouth, 1993; H. Collins, *The Law of Contract*, 4th edn., Cambridge, Cambridge University Press, 2008, 170; M. Amstutz & G. Teubner (eds.), *Networks. Legal Issues of Multilateral Cooperation*, Oxford, Hart, 2009; R Brownsword, 'Contracts with Network Effects: Is the Time Now Right?', in S. Grundmann, F. Cafaggi & G. Vettori (eds.), *The Organizational Contract*, Farnham, Surrey, Ashgate, 2013.

could be subject to a string of transactions as it was sold on in the market. How a string was formed through the mechanism of a notice of appropriation (or declaration) set out in the standard form contracts is examined later.[79] Another way that contracts were networked to each other was through the *pro rata* clause of the standard forms. This clause dealt with a classic problem in the sale of goods. Say a ship loaded wheat of the same type and quality in the one hold, one part consisting of a sale from A to B and the remainder a sale from C to D. Say there was an excess or deficiency in the quantity or the wheat was damaged during the voyage. How was any excess to be paid for or loss to be shared when it was impossible to say whose wheat was involved? The answer was by means of a *pro rata* clause. It provided that the difference in quantity or damage was to be shared among the various buyers, in our example B and D, in the proportions of wheat they had in the hold. If B or D received more or less than its *pro rata* share – which could easily happen if the excess or deficiency in quantity or damage was not discovered until B had unloaded and taken its part of the wheat – the clause provided the receivers must settle with each other in cash at the market price on the day of the vessel's arrival.

The *pro rata* clause took its modern form in LCTA contracts in 1908, during a major exercise of revising existing contracts. The committee entrusted with the task asked their solicitor, Mr Tilleard, about the *pro rata* clause. He replied that there would be no difficulty in drafting a short clause to bind all interested parties.[80] We return to how this was done in a moment. His draft was met with various objections from members but eventually an amended version was agreed on and inserted.[81] When the North American Contracts Committee discussed Contract No. 19 in 1921, its *pro rata* clause was said to conform to the custom of the trade.[82] But this could not be the case, except in the sense of the North American trade. In early 1930 the Contracts Committee found it impossible to incorporate a uniform *pro rata* clause in all UK contracts.[83] Moreover, as late as the 1930s there was no *pro rata* clause in the standard forms issued by another grain association, the Liverpool Corn Trade Association. The LCTA Standing Contracts Committee recorded that in one case a ship with Manitoba wheat was first discharged in Liverpool and then in Glasgow, when damage was found. The buyers there refused to share the loss on the basis they had bought the wheat under the standard form of the Liverpool association, which did not cover this eventuality.[84]

---

[79] 343–345 below.
[80] Tilleard was from the firm J. & A. A. Tilleard, 10 Gracechurch Street in the City of London: *The Law List 1908*, London, Stevens & Sons, 1908, 605.
[81] LMA, CLC/B/103/MS23174/002, LCTA, Sub-committee re Revision of Contract Forms, Minutes, 18 March, 23 March, 7, 14 April, 10 December 1908.
[82] LMA, CLC/B/103/MS23174/006, LCTA, North American Contracts Committee, Minutes, 29 September 1921.
[83] LMA, CLC/B/103/MS23174/008, LCTA, Contract Committee, Minutes, 1930.
[84] LMA, CLC/B/103/MS23 174/009, LCTA, Standing Contracts Committee, Minutes, 19 January 1933.

The *pro rata* clause exhibited the flexibility of English contract law and the inventiveness of lawyers. As a matter of technique, it achieved the sharing of the damage, or of the excess or deficiency in quantity, by deeming that the parties to the contracts containing the *pro rata* clause had entered into mutual agreements with each other to that effect. Consequently, in *Berry, Barclay & Co. v. Louis Dreyfus & Co*,[85] Wright J, a leading commercial judge and later a law lord, described the *pro rata* clause as providing for a 'super-added contract' between the various sellers and buyers which they were deemed to have entered into by the fact that each entered their own particular contract with knowledge that there might be others entering into other contracts in identical terms.[86]

The case involved the shipment of two parcels of wheat from Australia, both under the LCTA Contract No. 14, one between Berry, Barclay & Co. and W. H. Pim, Junr & Co., the other between Louis Dreyfus & Co. and Spillers Ltd. The quantities under the two contracts were 1,000 tons and 1,500 tons. The wheat was in bags and in a number of holds of the ship. The ship discharged the wheat in Antwerp and Liverpool, and it was discovered that some had come loose from the bags in No 4 hold. The argument was whether, as found by the arbitrators, apportionment for *pro rata* purposes should be in the ratio 1,000/1,500. After expressing his reluctance to do so, Wright J disagreed with the arbitrators and held that apportionment was to be in relation to the different quantities of the respective parties in No 4 hold alone, where the loss had occurred.

As well as being linked to each other standard form contracts were networked to other contracts, notably the 'shipping documents'. The shipping documents would include a bill of lading (the receipt of the goods on board, the document of title to them, and evidencing the contract of carriage), a policy of marine insurance and an invoice for the goods. The payment clause would make presentation of these shipping documents a prerequisite to payment. As to the bill of lading, the typical shipment clause in an LCTA contract would provide that the goods had been shipped 'as per bill or bills of lading dated or to be dated ... The bill of lading to be dated when the goods are actually on board.' It was usual to give as the date two months such as July/August, which meant all bills of lading had to be dated within that period.

The conditions and rules of the standard contract provided that the bill of lading date was generally to be considered proof of the date of shipment. A simple illustration arose with a sale of China white peas, 1919 crop, on a LCTA contract.[87] The contract had the word 'accordingly' inserted in the blank 'shipment to be made per river and/or ocean-going vessel or vessels, and Bills of Lading or Bills of Landing to be dated [accordingly]'. The sellers tendered two bills of lading by the *Polyphemus*, Shanghai to Rotterdam, dated

---

[85] (1929) 35 Ll L Rep 173.   [86] at 180.
[87] *Weis & Co. Ltd. v. Produce Brokers' Company* (1921) 6 Ll L Rep 164.

29 January, although the ship did not in fact arrive at Shanghai until 30 January, and loading did not begin until February 2 (although the peas were delivered for shipment on January 29). Sankey J held that the sellers had not complied with the sale contract. The clause meant that the bills of lading had to be dated according to the date of shipment, not when the goods were ready for shipment. In his reasoning Sankey J said that this was not a mere technical objection: bills of lading passing as documents of title from hand to hand and buyers had no wish to take documents which on resale on the same form of contract 'might be thrown back on their hands'.[88]

Freedom of contract in standard form terms was confined by this networking to bills of lading. In 1921 the LCTA North American Contracts Committee tried to have the destination clause in grain contracts amended.[89] This provided for shipment to the place identified in the contract but allowing deviation ('direct or indirect'). The committee wanted to limit the liberty of ships from North American ports to call at intermediate ports en route, unless this was in geographical order. The situation, where vessels from North America were known to have proceeded to Hamburg and Scandinavian ports, before arriving in the United Kingdom, was regarded as unacceptable. The committee acknowledged that the trade might accept bills of lading which gave the ship owners more flexibility but argued that this was a survival of war conditions.

Change, however, did not occur. The First World War had transformed the balance of power between the United States and Europe. The LCTA had to accept for North American contracts the position proposed by the North American Export Grain Association.[90] Under this, LCTA North American contracts allowed ships to proceed indirectly, 'as per customary bill of lading'. The committee's proposal that deviation be explicitly limited to geographical order was trumped. In 1924 the International Convention for the Unification of Certain Rules of Law Relating to Bills of Lading (the Hague Rules) permitted reasonable deviation, offering some limitation on the ability of ship owners to proceed at their convenience to discharge cargoes.[91]

---

[88] at 166. Sankey was a fine judge and Lord Chancellor but not naturally a commercial lawyer: see R. Heuston, *Lives of the Lord Chancellors, 1885-1940*, Oxford, Clarendon, 1964; R. Stevens, *Law and Politics: the House of Lords as a Judicial Body 1800-1976*, London, Weidenfeld & Nicolson, 1979, 226–228.

[89] LMA, CLC/B/103/MS23174/006, North American Contracts Committee, minutes, 8 September 1921.

[90] LMA, CLC/B/103/MS23174/007, North American Contracts Committee, minutes, 22 November 1922, 16 January, 3 May, 24 July 1923.

[91] Article IV, r.4. See R. Temperley & F. Vaughan, *Carriage of Goods By Sea Act 1924 including the Rules Relating to Bills of Lading (the Hague rules)*, 4th ed., London, Stevens and Sons, 1932, 71–78.

6 Adoption of Standard Form Contracts

Standard contract terms having been drawn up the issue was would they be widely adopted. The answer was resoundingly positive. Early figures are not available, but those from later periods demonstrate that large numbers of contract forms were sold.[92] The annual reports of the LCTA from 1925–1926 to 1928–1929 record that sales of contract forms were over a quarter of a million annually, ranging from 261,000 in 1925–1926 to a high point of 291,000 in 1927–1928. Fluctuations in sales from year to year might have reflected the disruptions in trade during the 1920s as a result of fairly violent currency fluctuations; otherwise it might simply have been because forms were revised or new forms introduced in particular years.

The depression in international trade in the 1930s was reflected in a fall in the number of standard form contracts sold, with a steady decline from 189,000 in 1932–1933 to 110,000 in 1938–1939 (there was a slight bounce to 155,000 in 1936–1937). In the 1950s and early 1960s sales of the forms hovered around the 100,000 mark (although 1954–1955 was a good year, with 135,000 being sold). As would be expected, with a less widely traded commodity like copra, sales of standard form contracts were fewer. Nonetheless, the figures which the London Copra Association reported to its annual general meetings in the 1920s are impressive; 14,962 in 1921–1922; 24,168 in 1922–1923; 23,360 in 1923–1924; 21,979 in 1924–1925; 14,892 in 1925–1926; 20,842 in 1926–1927; and 11,790 in 1927–1928.[93]

While encouraging the use of their standard contract forms – sales of the forms were an important source of income – the trade associations needed to protect the forms' integrity. When in late 1889 it was learnt that J. Henry Schröder & Co. had added additional clauses to the LCTA forms they had purchased, the association insisted these be in different print type to make obvious that they were not original.[94] There was no obligation on members, or anyone else, to use an association's forms. But when a South African trader in Durban started to use modified LCTA terms, which it headed 'London Corn Trade Association, Limited', as in the printed forms, the LCTA solicitor advised that this could be an infringement of copyright through the implied representation that it was an association form.[95] Similarly in 1914 the president of the London Oil and Tallow Trades Association warned members about using their own forms but bringing them within the rules of association by impressing a rubber stamp on the contract to that effect.[96]

---

[92] That contract forms were sold was recognised in *Aune v. Cauwenberghe & Fils* (1938) 60 Ll L Rep 389, 392.
[93] LMA, CLC/B/103/MS 23224/003 – MS 23224/005, London Copra Association, Minutes of general meetings.
[94] LMA, CLC/B/103/MS 23172/001, LCTA, Executive committee minutes, 14 & 21 November 1891.
[95] LMA, CLC/B/103/MS23174/004, letter Tilleards, Solicitors, to LCTA, 27 June 1910.
[96] LMA, CLC/B/103/MS23234, London Oil and Tallow Trades Association, 'Scrapbook', 27 June 1914.

After the First World War the trade associations tried to address the issue more systematically. The London Copra Association resolved to sell contracts only to members and instructed their printer not to sell them without the name of a member printed on them.[97] LCTA went further. A special sub-committee agreed on a three-point directive to be circulated to members. First, members' standard forms could be used by members for contracting whether as principals, brokers or agents with other members or non-members; secondly, members might supply forms to their accredited non-member agents for use solely in connection with the member's business; and thirdly, an application to purchase forms carried with it an implied undertaking that the forms were required for sole use of the member and would not be supplied for a non-member except as provided for under the first and second points.[98] The development of copying and other electronic processes in the second half of the twentieth century meant that hard-copy contract forms were no longer called for, although the associations' contractual terms were still used.

7 Global Reach of London/Liverpool Standard Contract Terms

In a paper read to the International Law Association in The Hague in 1921, Dr H. Craandyk, a Dutch lawyer, referred to the powerful role of trade associations, and to how (he claimed) international trade was not possible, or at least not as efficient, without them. In his paper it was the standard form contracts of British-based trade associations which Dr Craandyk identified as crucial: the LCTA contracts for grain (he mentioned that a German–Dutch contract for grain sales from the Baltic and Russia had existed before 1914 but was apparently no longer used); the contracts of the Cotton Brokers' Association of Liverpool; and those of the London Rubber Trade Association, the Copra Trade Association, the Oil Seed Association and the Produce Broker's Association. Dr Craandyk commented that if two persons agreed to a sale of one or all these commodities, the only thing left for them to do was to make a choice of the contract, type of commodity and price. Or, if that was too much trouble, he added that they could simply send a contract note, also issued by one of the associations, containing the clause: 'All the terms, conditions, and rules contained in contract form No. – shall be deemed to be incorporated in and to form part of this contract note.'[99]

Indications of the international use of the standard form contracts issued by the London trade associations are apparent in the figures on their sales.[100] The

---

[97] LMA, CLC/B/103/MS23224/004, London Copra Association, 85, 99 (February 1925).
[98] LMA, CLC/B/103/MS23174/007, LCTA, Sub-committee re members and on-members contract forms, 7 December 1927.
[99] H. Craandyk, 'International Rules Relating to the Sale of Goods', in International Law Association, *Report of the Thirtieth Conference*, London, ILA, 1922, vol. 1, 447.
[100] There are also cases indicating international use e.g., *Thalmann Frères & Co v. Texas Star Flour Mills* (1900) 5 Com Cas 321, 82 LT 833 (sale by Galveston dealers to Paris corn merchants on LCTA form; Court of Appeal interpreting US statute to decide case); *Karberg and Co v. Blythe,*

president of the LCTA told the annual general meeting in 1928–1929 that sixty per cent of its contract forms were sold in continental Europe, 'which shows that our friends on the other side of the Channel look upon the London Corn Trade Association as the ruling authority in the grain trade of Europe, and perhaps I might say of the world'.[101] Complacency was not the order of the day. At a conference called by the Baltic Exchange in March 1927 a future president of the LCTA had warned that there were now rival contracts issued in Hamburg, Antwerp and Rotterdam, and the LCTA forms could no longer be said to be paramount.[102]

LCTA had introduced a short form of contract for continental importers, followed in the late 1920s by a short confirmation as an alternative, which simply incorporated the relevant continental contractual terms by reference.[103] In the 1930s sales of this short form to continental Europe ranged per annum from 24,000 (1935–1936) to 56,000 (1930–1931). The figure of 40,000 in 1934–1935 was a sign, said that year's LCTA annual report, that its forms still continued to serve as a basis for international grain trading.[104]

How was it that the standard form contracts of some of the London and Liverpool associations which Dr Craandyk mentioned in his 1921 paper became so dominant in world trade? Partly it was a result of Britain's economic position in the nineteenth century as a major importer and a centre, in the City of London, for banking, shipping and insurance.[105] But that was only a start. There were other factors in the paramountcy of these standard form contracts throughout the twentieth century. War was one. Dr Craandyk described the demise of the German–Dutch form with the advent of war in 1914. In the interwar years other contracts for commodities with a continental European destination were available. By the mid to late 1930s, buyers in a politically resurgent Germany were using standard form contracts for grain providing for arbitration and analysis in Hamburg. The German contracts were C&F rather than CIF because the German government had control over the country's trade and was writing its own insurance.[106] Efforts by LCTA to persuade the grain associations in exporting countries to continue to use only its standard form contracts failed for continental European destinations.[107] Again war, and the defeat of Germany in 1945, put an end to this challenge to the LCTA standard

> Green, Jourdain and Co Ltd [1916] 1 KB 495 (sales of Chinese horse beans on LCTA form to continental buyers; but both sales made on London market).

[101] LMA, CLC/B/103/MS23172/008, Annual general meeting, 1928–1929, 322.
[102] H. Barty-King, *Food for Man and Beast*, London, Ebury Press,1978, 54; J. Sgard, 'A Tale of Three Cities: The Construction of International Commercial Arbitration', in G. Mallard &. J. Sgard (eds.), *Contractual Knowledge*, Cambridge, Cambridge University, 2016, 160.
[103] LMA, CLC/B/103/MS23172/008, LCTA, Minutes of executive committee and of annual general meetings, 258.
[104] LMA, CLC/B/103/MS23172/009, LCTA, Minutes of executive committee and of annual general meetings, 246.
[105] 4, 29 above.
[106] LMA, CLC/B/103/MS23172/010, Executive committee minutes, 367, 369, 376.
[107] Ibid., 9.

form contracts. Once again they ruled the roost, at least between independent buyers and sellers.

Empire was another factor. It should not be a shock that when Canada and Australia became substantial grain exporters at the end of the nineteenth century their traders should be content to use LCTA standard forms. There was an element of cultural cringe in the report of an Australian Royal Commission in the 1930s that sales of wheat overseas were concluded under the form of contract 'specially provided for the Australian trade by the London Corn Trade Association'.[108] The politics of standard form contract use was underlined by the qualification which the Royal Commission added: sales to Japan, by then an expanding and powerful imperial power, did not use LCTA contracts: they were made through Japanese branch offices in Australia, the commodities were carried in Japanese ships and the transactions were on a FOB basis.[109]

Rubber provides another example. By the 1920s ninety per cent of the world's total rubber production was from plantations – the balance from the wild – with approximately two-thirds of that coming from the British Empire, notably Malaya (Malaysia) and Ceylon (Sri Lanka), the remainder from the Dutch East Indies (Indonesia). So again, contracts drawn up by a London-based trade association, in that case the Rubber Trade Association, had an edge.[110] But here the competitive pressures were greater and that association missed a trick. The huge demand for rubber from the US automobile industry undermined the grip of the London rubber market. Moreover, the standard form contract of the association did not cover the increasing amounts of rubber auctioned in Colombo and Singapore.[111] The association's forms lost out.

Crucial, perhaps, was that to varying degrees trade associations such as the LCTA began to see themselves as international in character. This reflected the self-image of the City of London and, for a period but to a lesser extent, Liverpool. Association members traded in commodities on the international markets of London (commodities generally) and Liverpool (cotton and wheat). Especially in London they were in contact with bankers, insurers and others who were also dealing internationally. The Baltic Exchange was during the nineteenth and well into the twentieth century a commodities market

---

[108] *Royal Commission on the Wheat, Flour and Bread Industries, 2nd Report*, Australian Parliamentary Papers, Session 1934–1935, No.83, vol. IV, 161. See also H. Darling, 'The Marketing of Wheat', in R. Lemmon et al, *Some Problems of Marketing*, Melbourne, Melbourne University Press, 1928, 28.

[109] Ibid., 162, 168.

[110] S. Dowling, *The Exchanges of London*, London, Butterworth & Co, 1929, 119. The contract is reprinted ibid., 114–116.

[111] A. Coates, *Commerce in Rubber*, Singapore, Oxford University Press, 1987, 148–149, 174, 180–181; C. Barlow, *The Natural Rubber Industry*, Kuala Lumpur, Oxford University Press, 1978, 343.

(notably grain, flour, oilseeds and tallow) as well as an international market for chartering and selling ships.[112]

Continental associations did not seem to have had the same international outlook or ambition. As for the North American Export Grain Association, established in 1912, it had the aim of promoting the commercial export of grain and oilseeds from the United States. Its membership eventually encompassed nearly all those private, publicly owned and cooperative bodies in the United States engaged in this activity. But given its aim it is not surprising that, when it first drew standard contract forms, these were limited to FOB transactions at US ports.

The composition of the membership of the London and Liverpool associations, most notably in the case LCTA, was another component in their international character.[113] Although the majority of LCTA members were domiciled in the United Kingdom, there was always a substantial foreign membership, hovering at just less than a third. Moreover, member firms domiciled in the United Kingdom included those which were, or had been, of foreign origin, reflecting the international character of the City of London and, to a degree, Liverpool. Figures given in the LCTA annual reports show that in the early 1930s, 338 members were domiciled in Britain, 156 abroad; in 1954 the figures were 287 and 127; and in 1963, 222 and 129. (Overall membership declined over time, reflecting especially after the Second World War the demise of the smaller trader and the amalgamation of firms.)

Continental membership was interrupted, of course, during the world wars. In the hysteria which followed the outbreak of the First World War in 1914, the LCTA executive decided that those of German or Austrian nationality should be requested not to enter the premises of the association, although on legal advice, so that arbitrations would not be upset, that was later amended so as not to extend to those 'of enemy nationality' attending arbitrations.[114] On the whole, however, from an early period foreign membership was encouraged. That was the case, too, with the other associations. For example, the London Copra Association amended its articles before the First World War to admit foreign traders to full membership and, by 1926, of its 175 members 44 were foreign.[115]

In the 1930s there was pressure on the LCTA to admit members of recognised foreign associations. That pressure was partly because of competition from a German–Dutch contract, with Rotterdam as the venue for arbitration. In response to the threat, LCTA expressed the hope that 'having regard to its past services to the Trade, [it] confidently relies upon the continuation of the unswerving support of shippers [sellers] and their Associations'.[116] While conceding the pressure to be more universal in membership, LCTA asserted that it 'has always been the only

---

[112] 61, 77–78, 82 above.
[113] M. Rothstein, 'Multinationals in the Grain Trade 1850–1914' (1983) 12 *Bus & Econ Hist* 85, 88.
[114] LMA, CLC/B/103/MS23172/006, LCTA, Executive committee minutes, 1914–1915.
[115] LMA, CLC/B/103/MS23224/001, 71, 74; CLC/B/103/MS23224/004, 29 January 1926, 195.
[116] LMA, CLC/B/103/MS23172/009, Annual report, 1931–1932, 89.

great International Corn Trade Association. Its contracts, standards and arbitration are in almost world-wide use'.[117] Nevertheless in 1934 representatives of continental grain trade associations were invited to become full members of the Standing Contracts Committee, which was responsible by then for overall supervision of the association's contracts. The invitations were accepted.[118] The response to the foreign threat was to head it off by co-option. After the Second World War that policy continued, and is reflected in the international character of Gafta today.[119]

5.4 Commodity Auctions

> From thence Mr. Creed and I to Wilkinson's, and dined together, and in great haste thence to our office, where we met all, for the sale of two ships by an inch of candle (the first time that ever I saw any of this kind), where I observed how they do invite one another, and at last how they all do cry, and we have much to do to tell who did cry last. (Pepys diary, 1660)[120]

Auctions had long been used in Britain for the sale of land and later art.[121] Pepys had observed the frenzied bidding ('crying') for two ships in the middle years of the seventeenth century. Sale by candle, as he described it, was so called because a candle with pins stuck evenly down the side was lit and the last bid before each pin dropped out was successful. The description 'sale by candle' continued to be used into the nineteenth century, well after candles were no longer employed.[122]

During the nineteenth century, and into the twentieth, auctions (sometimes termed 'public sales') played a significant role in the story of the sale of imported commodities to Britain. These would be auctioned in London, often setting world prices. After a description of the London commodity auctions, this part of the chapter sketches the relevant law, its limited reach and how through auction conditions the commercial community itself determined how things would work. First, there is an account of how the common law of sales was much modified by the conditions drawn up for conducting these auctions (part 5.4, 2). The final section addresses how the law gave considerable latitude to

---

[117] LMA, CLC/B/103/MS23172/009, Annual general meeting, 30 May 1933.
[118] LMA, CLC/B/103/MS23172/009, Executive committee, minutes, 10 July 1934. In the post–Second World War era the executive of the LCTA included representatives of foreign grain interests.
[119] In 2020 Gafta had over 1,900 members in 98 countries: see www.gafta.com. FOSFA (the Federation of Oils, Seeds and Fats Associations) had 1,169 members in 88 countries: see www.fosfa.org.
[120] *The Diary of Samuel Pepys*, 6 November 1660. Although there was some debate, the better view was that ships were goods: Behnke v. Bede Shipping Company Ltd [1927] 1 KB 649, per Wright J.
[121] D. Fitz-Gibbon, 'The London Auction Mart and the Marketability of Real Estate in England, 1808–1864' (2016) 55 *J British Stud* 295; F. Etro & E. Stepanova, 'Art Auctions and Art Investment in the Golden Age of British Painting' (2017) 64 *Scottish J Pol Econ* 191.
[122] J. Findlay, *The Baltic Exchange*, London, Witherley & Co, 1927, 32; B. Cowan, *The Social Life of Coffee: The Emergence of the British Coffeehouse*, New Haven, Yale University Press, 2005, 134.

manipulation, which in the absence of state law those associated with the London commodity auctions contained through their own practices (part 5.4, 3).

1 The Rise and Fall of London Commodity Auctions

> Grannie greeted him cordially as 'Harold, my boy' – he was a great favourite with her. She and uncle Julius monopolized him for the evening. There was great talk of trucking sheep, the bad outlook as regarded the season, the state of the grass in the triangle, the Leigh Spring, the Bimbalong, and several other paddocks, and of the condition of the London wool market. (Miles Franklin, *My Brilliant Career*, 1901)[123]

Miles Franklin's family followed the condition of the London wool auctions since they indicated world prices. On arrival in London, wool from Australia would be warehoused, including at the London Docks' wool floor and nearby warehouses.[124] Samples would be available to the selling brokers for their

Figure 5.1 Auctioning colonial wool, Wool Exchange, London, 1889 (Alamy Ltd)

---

[123] Edinburgh, William Blackwood & Sons, 1901. Written at the age of 16, Miles [Stella] Franklin's autobiographical novel tells of her growing up on a sheep station in rural New South Wales. See J. Roe, 'Franklin, Stella Maria Sarah Miles (1879–1954)', *Australian Dictionary of Biography*, Melbourne, Melbourne University Press, 1981, vol. VIII.

[124] Greater London Industrial Archaeology Society, 'New Street Wool Warehouse, London EC2', *Notes and News*, April 1984; Anon, 'Where Merchants most do Congregate. The Wool Exchange' (1895) 9 *The Ludgate Illustrated Magazine* 501, 502.

assessment of the quality and value. The selling brokers were acting for the importers, often a bank which had provided advances on consignments of the wool. Catalogues would be prepared, sometimes containing a hundred pages of particulars – where the wool was stored, its quality, the number of bales and the mark and name of the ship. The bales would be arranged for inspection by potential buyers during a morning. The auction would then take place in the afternoon at the Wool Exchange in Coleman Street.[125]

Sugar and spices were early products sold by auction.[126] Tallow (for candles) and indigo (for dying) were also sold in this way in the first part of the nineteenth century. The advent of gas lighting and chemical dyes respectively reduced the demand for these commodities.[127] Tea was freely auctioned in Mincing Lane from 1834, initially from China after the East India Company's monopoly was removed, later from India, Ceylon (Sri Lanka), Java (Indonesia) and East Africa, when tea was grown for export in those parts of European empires.[128] Mincing Lane became the physical and financial centre for the world trade in tea.[129] By the late nineteenth century tea had become an immensely important import to Britain, replacing beer as the main beverage, partly as a result of campaigning by the Temperance movement. By 1910 Britain had forty per cent of the world consumption and it also acted as an entrepôt for other national consumers.[130]

Rubber was initially sold in London in 1876 on the strength of samples over brokers' counters or else by auction. The market grew with the advent of rubber tyres for bicycles and motor vehicles and other uses. Auctions were conducted at the Rubber Exchange in Mincing Lane. They were sometimes marred by lots being suddenly withdrawn in anticipation of a rise in prices.[131] The boom in rubber shares in the early twentieth century derived from the high world price for the product.[132] Rubber shares were traded in Mincing Lane as well as on the

---

[125] see 8 above; 320–322 below.

[126] J. Stobart, *Sugar and Spice Grocers and Groceries in Provincial England, 1650-1830*, Oxford, Oxford University Press, 2013, 66. See also *Hinde v. Whitehouse* (1806) 7 East 558, 103 ER 216 (sugar auctioned). Sugar was still auctioned in the early twentieth century: A. Jenkins, *The House of Man*, London, E. D. & F. Man Ltd, 1985, 97, 108.

[127] *The City or the Physiology of London Business*, London, Groombridge & Sons, 1852, 140, 157; House of Lords, *Select Committee on the London Docks, St Katharine Docks, and Victoria (London) Dock Amalgamation Bill*, Minutes of Evidence, 19 April, 1864, 8; M. Aldous, 'Rehabilitating the Intermediary: Brokers and Auctioneers in the Nineteenth-Century Anglo-Indian Trade' (2017) 59 *Business History* 525, 534–535.

[128] A. Webster, 'The Strategies and Limits of Gentlemanly Capitalism: The London East India Agency Houses, Provincial Commercial Interests, and the Evolution of British Economic Policy in South and South East Asia 1800–50' (2006) 59 *Econ Hist Rev* 743, 744.

[129] E. Rappaport, *A Thirst for Empire How Tea Shaped the Modern World*, Princeton, Princeton University Press, 2017, 149; D. Courtney, *From Forum to Futures*, London, Hindsight Books, 2004, 73–78.

[130] D. Forrest, *Tea for the British: The Social and Economic History of a Famous Trade*, London, Chatto & Windus, 1973.

[131] A. Coates, *The Commerce in Rubber*, Singapore, Oxford University Press, 1987, 52–53.

[132] W. Huff, 'Boom-or-Bust Commodities and Industrialization in Pre-World War II Malaya' (2002) 62 *J Econ Hist* 1074, 1078(table 2): D. Kynaston, *The City of London The Golden Years*, London, Pimlico, 1995, 518–523.

Stock Exchange. The rapid promotion of rubber companies was inevitably accompanied by scandal.[133] In the years running up to the First World War almost all rubber imported to Britain was sold at fortnightly auctions. By that time, however, it was becoming accepted that it was unnecessary to catalogue and auction standard grades of plantation rubber which were recognized by name as regular in quality. After the war rubber auctions were abandoned and it was sold by description after inspection of samples at brokers' salesrooms.[134]

After the First World War the London commodity auctions were not as extensive as previously.[135] First there was the growth of auctions abroad. From 1890 an important point of sale for the foremost producer of apparel wool, Australia, had become the auctions held there, principally in Brisbane, Sydney and Melbourne.[136] Tea had begun to be auctioned in Calcutta (Kolkata) in 1861 and Colombo (1883), a sign of things to come.[137] Next, commodities were no longer being routed through Britain to the same extent as previously. Exporters dealt directly with those in a commodity's ultimate destination rather than through the London markets. Thus Singapore, where rubber was the mainstay of the economy, began marketing that commodity straight to the American west coast rather than through London brokers.[138] Further, of those commodities which were still shipped to London, some were disposed of in other ways. To continue with the rubber example, the adoption of standard grades led to the replacement of auctions with sales through brokers, on the conditions in the standard form contracts of the Rubber Trade Association for spot and CIF transactions.[139]

The same decline in London auctions as with wool and rubber was experienced by other commodities. Spices had always been sold at auction, but that became less frequent due to a significant increase in business done on a CIF basis.[140] Brazilian coffee was handled on CIF contracts or contracts registered with the London Produce Clearing House, albeit other varieties of coffee continued to be sold at auction. (The coffee which was sold at auction was displayed shortly before the auction in small trays in brokers' sale rooms, specimens being available to the

---

[133] see e.g., *Heilbut, Symons & Co v. Buckleton* [1913] AC 30.
[134] H. Hotchkiss, 'The Evolution of the World Rubber Situation' (1924) 2 *Harv Bus Rev* 129, 133–134.
[135] *The City of London*, London, The Times, 1927, 187.
[136] D. Merrett & S. Ville, 'Institution Building and Variation in the Formation of the Australian Wool Market' (2013) 53 *Aust Econ Hist R* 146, 147; S. Ville, 'The Relocation of the International Market for Australian Wool' (2005) 45 *Aust Econ Hist R* 73; S. Ville, *The Rural Entrepreneurs*, Cambridge, Cambridge University Press, 2000, 134.
[137] *Centennial Year of the Colombo Tea Auction 1883-1983*, Colombo, Ceylon Chamber of Commerce, 1983.
[138] *Allen & Gledhill Centenary*, Singapore, Allen & Gledhill, 2002, 18–19; R. Maclean, *A Pattern of Change The Singapore International Chamber of Commerce*, Singapore, SICC, 2000, 161.
[139] G. Rees, Britain's Commodity Markets, London, *op cit*, 270.
[140] Department of Commerce, Bureau of Foreign and Domestic Commerce, *Market Methods and Trade Usages in London*, Washington, Government Printing Office, 1923, 66.

wholesale dealers for roasting and tasting.[141]) Imported timber was still sold at auction with the use, as in other trades, of catalogues. Inspection of lots beforehand occurred mainly at the Surrey Commercial Docks on the Thames, where the timber was often kept in ponds to limit drying out.[142]

Although diminished, in the 1920s and 1930s tea and imported wool continued to be sold at auction. The preconditions still obtained: there was a range of types and varieties of tea and wool; there was still an abundant supply into London; this was channelled through a limited number of importers; and there was a significant number of competing buyers prepared to purchase in this way.[143] But the future was clear. While wool was still being auctioned at the Coleman Street wool exchange, in the interwar period some 80 per cent of the Australian and New Zealand wool clip was being auctioned in the Antipodes.[144] By the 1930s tea from China was sold privately by brokers and not generally auctioned.[145] The tea auctions at Calcutta and Colombo were turning over about a quarter as much as the auctions of London and were growing fast.[146] Given the large domestic demand in Britain, however, teas were still auctioned in London in considerable quantities. In the 1930s there were auctions in Mincing Lane on Monday and Wednesday for Indian teas, on Tuesday, Ceylonese, and on Thursday, Javanese, Sumatran and others. Selling brokers sent their inspectors to the warehouse where the tea was being stored after discharge from the ship to check that each consignment was of uniform quality and to value it. A selling broker would thus know the approximate price it should attract when auctioned. When prospective buyers received the auction catalogue, they would have teas tasted themselves and give orders to the brokers acting for them as to the prices to bid.[147] Overproduction and the world depression in the 1930s hit tea prices, and international efforts by producers to improve them were only moderately successful.[148]

After the Second World War the pace of decline in the London commodity auctions quickened. London was no longer a major entrepôt. With tea, newly independent countries promoted their own centres for its packaging,

---

[141] J. Smith, *Organised Produce Markets*, London, Longmans, Green & Co, 1922, 179; J. Smith, *Produce Exchanges*, London, Modern Business Institute Ltd, 1924, 482–492. See also C. Duncan, *Marketing: Its Problems and Methods*, New York, D. Appleton & Co,1920, 152–155.

[142] T. Stobart, *The Timber Trade of the United Kingdom*, London, Crosby Lockwood & Son, 1927, vol. I, 59, 67–72.

[143] Ibid., 167–168.

[144] O. Hobson, *How the City Works*, London, News Chronicle Publications, 1938, 133–136; A.G. Linney, 'What London Stores for the World – I Wool', *PLA Monthly*, November 1925, No 1, 13.

[145] O. Hobson, ibid., 128.

[146] G. Rees, 'The London Commodity Markets and Commonwealth Trade' (1981) 129 *Royal Soc of Arts J* 88, 94.

[147] C. Maughan, *Markets of London*, London, Pitman, 1931, 97–102; F. Staveacre, *Tea and Tea Dealing*, London, Pitman, 1929, 52–58; A.G. Linney, 'What London Stores for the World – II Tea', *PLA Monthly*, January 1926, No 3.

[148] B. Gupta, 'The International Tea Cartel during the Great Depression 1929-1933' (2001) 61 *J Econ Hist* 144.

warehousing and auctioning. Governments introduced controls over the total quantity of tea that could be exported annually and, in the case of India and Ceylon, also over the amount that could be sent to London for initial sale. In 1938, 62 per cent of all Ceylon and Indian tea sold by auction was sold at the London auctions; in 1954 the proportion was 33 per cent.[149] Much 'common tea' was disposed of by private sale, and the auctions conducted in places like Calcutta, Colombo and Mombasa meant that by the 1960s London tea auctions were in terminal decline.[150] Direct sales of tea were also facilitated by new methods of communication.[151] It was the same story with wool. By 1959 only about a tenth of the world's wool was sold in London. Not long after, perhaps symbolically, the Wool Exchange in Coleman Street, the centre for wool auctions, was demolished.[152] With commodities generally, standardisation and the development of reliable lot samples meant that it was no longer necessary to inspect them to gauge the quality. Coupled with quicker transport and communications these developments undermined the raison d'être of auctions and warehouses as links in the distribution chain. Their replacement was trade conducted mainly on a CIF basis.[153]

2 Sales Law and Auction Conditions

There is no more curious sight in the City than one of the wool auctions which are now being held every afternoon in the Wool Exchange, Coleman Street... Five minutes before four nearly every seat is occupied... [The auctioneer] has to sell a hundred thousand pounds' worth of wool before six o'clock, 'Lot 213, ten bales', he says. Simple words, but the signal for a very tempest of excitement... It is a bear-garden, a Babel, a scene of indescribable confusion... But the auctioneer speaks one word, and the storm is stilled ... That word is 'Tomkins'. The lot has been knocked down to Tomkins. Without drawing breath, the selling broker goes on to the next lot. Spectator, 'London Wool Auctions'. (*The West Australian* (newspaper), 1 November 1884)

The underlying legal principle of commodity auctions was freedom of contract. Sellers and auctioneers could by contract exclude themselves from liability for the conduct of the auction and the quality of the goods sold. Consequently, buyers concerned about the quality of what they were bidding

---

[149] The Monopolies and Restrictive Practices Commission, *Report on the Supply of Tea*, HC 15, 1956, 12. See *Health & Tea. A Convention to Mark 125 Years of Ceylon Tea*, Colombo, 1992, 19.
[150] E. Rappaport, A Thirst for Empire How Tea Shaped the Modern World, *op cit*, 347–348; G. Rees, The History of the London Commodity Market, *op cit*, 61. Tea auctions moved to Plantation House in 1938, later to Upper Thames Street.
[151] D. Forrest, *The World Tea Trade*, Cambridge, Woodhead-Faulkner, 1985, 199. The last London tea auction was in 1998: 'Curtain Falls on Final London Tea Auction', *Financial Times*, 30 June 1998. See also G. Corea, *Taming Commodity Markets*, Manchester, Manchester University Press, 1992, 196.
[152] D. Kynaston, *The City of London A Club No More 1945–2000*, London, Pimlico, 2001, 124.
[153] G. Rees, Britain's Commodity Markets, *op cit*, 171, 413–415.

for needed to inspect the goods, or a sample of them, beforehand. Sellers wanting protection on price could set a reserve price.

The courts gave the conduct of auctions a wide berth when the occasional dispute arose; it was the free market at work. Parliament rarely interfered. Under the Auctioneers Act 1845, brokers had to obtain an annual licence for £10 from the Commissioners of Customs and Excise to conduct an auction. The Act also required that brokers should display their name and address at the auction.[154] But that was all. The legislation was essentially a revenue-raising device, not an attempt to regulate trade.[155]

In practice, the London commodity auctions were invariably conducted on a set of conditions governing their sales. With some modification, the conditions in the first part of the nineteenth century were based on those used by the East India Company in its auctions.[156] Initially these conditions were displayed at the auction premises, but later they were spelt out in the catalogues of the lots to be sold. The courts had no difficulty in holding that the conditions were to be treated as incorporated in any contract of sale, even though they were not otherwise communicated to a bidder.[157] For a while, however, there was uncertainty about a ruling of the King's Bench that the requirement of writing contained in the Statute of Frauds 1677 applied to auctions.[158] A simple solution was approved in *Bird* v. *Boulter*: the record by the auctioneer's clerk in the sale book as each lot was knocked down was sufficient, since he had implied authority at that point from all attending to make the entry.[159]

The practice in the London commodity markets was that the goods went to the highest bidder. In 1856 a City of London solicitor, John Hollams, was asked by a Select Committee of the House of Lord about when there was uncertainty as to who in fact had made the highest bid.[160] At least to the outside observer of the hectic and unfathomable atmosphere of the London wool auction quoted at the outset of this section, it might sometimes have been difficult to identify the person, although in that case the auctioneer seemed to have no problem in marking the lot down to 'Tomkins'.[161] Hollams' answer was that usually, 'to avoid litigation', one of the conditions for auctions was that the biddings were to be recommenced in the event of a

---

[154] s. 7. [155] Repealed Finance Act 1949, Sch 11 Pt I.
[156] A. Pulling, *A Practical Treatise on Laws . . . of the City and Port of London*, 2nd ed., London, V & R Stevens, 1844, 464. See O. Prakash, *European Commercial Enterprise in Pre-Colonial India*, Cambridge, Cambridge University Press, 1998, 78.
[157] *Mesnard* v. *Aldridge* (1801) 3 Esp 271, 170 ER 612 (auctioneer pasting conditions on his box and declaring them as usual was sufficient notice). See J. Bateman, *A Practical Treatise on the Law of Auctions*, 3rd ed., London, A. Maxwell & Son, 1846, 59.
[158] *Kenworthy* v. *Schofield* (1824) 2 B & C 945, 107 ER 633.
[159] (1833) 4 B & Ad 443, 110 ER 522. See *Halsbury's Laws of England*, 2nd ed., London, Butterworth, 1931, vol. I, 700.
[160] On Hollams, 97 above.
[161] e.g., '[T]he difficulty is to 'spot' the highest bidder': Spectator, 'London Wool Auctions', *op cit.*

dispute (although he acknowledged that buyers may not have read the condition to this effect).[162]

Later some commentators cast doubt on how as a matter of contract law a condition like this could be binding on those bidding at an auction.[163] This seemed to be because of the English law doctrine that a contract derives from an offer and acceptance. Whether at an auction the offer was made by the seller, and accepted by the highest bidder, or made by the buyer, and accepted by the seller,[164] that did not result in a contract to which others attending the auction became a party. A century on from Hollams' evidence there was still a dearth of legal authority about how at a commodity auction disputes about the highest bidder were to be resolved.

The explanation was that the practice of commodity auctions nipped disputes in the bud. One aspect was the condition for the immediate re-auctioning of goods if there was a dispute about the highest bidder. That as a condition for the auctioning of goods was recommended in the first edition of the *Encyclopaedia of Forms and Precedents* published in the early 1900s.[165] It was the practice in the London wool market; the lot was auctioned again whenever there was any dispute, although the relevant condition providing for this at the Coleman Street auctions was somewhat more complicated than that recommended in the *Encyclopaedia*.[166] There were variations on this theme, one being a show of hands or the decision of the auctioneer to be final. A condition to this effect persisted in some auction sales in the City of London throughout the nineteenth century and was carried over to the twentieth.[167] Another approach was a condition that the decision of the selling broker was final, coupled with an option on his part to put the lot up again.[168]

As with any contract for a sale of goods, the law implied terms in auction sales as to description and quality. These were codified in the Sale of Goods Act 1893, with its implied terms of correspondence with description and sample, fitness for purpose and merchantability.[169] With auction sales the implied term regarding description would be particularly important. However, as in other areas of commercial dealing the implied terms were excluded or modified by the conditions governing auctions. Caveat emptor was the default rule: buyers

---

[162] *Select Committee of House of Lords on the Mercantile Law Amendment Bill*, Parl. Papers, XIV.1 (294), 1856, 43–44.
[163] see E. George, 'Auctioneer's Refusal to Accept Highest Bid' (1949) 65 *LQR* 310, 312.
[164] see Blackburn J in *Harris v. Nickerson* (1873) LR 8 QB 286, 288.
[165] *Encyclopaedia of Forms and Precedents*, London, Butterworth, 1908, vol. XI, 575.
[166] S. Dowling, *The Exchanges of London*, London, Butterworth & Co, 1929, 196–201 (a dispute 'shall be decided by the brokers, unless one of the claimants will advance, in that case the lot shall be put up again').
[167] e. g., Department of Commerce, Bureau of Foreign and Domestic Commerce, Market Methods and Trade Usages in London, *op cit*, 10 (rules of the Coffee Trade Association).
[168] *Royal Commission . . . into Operation and Constitution of . . . Courts in England and . . . Present Separation and Division of Jurisdictions between Courts*, Third Report, Parliamentary Papers, XXIX.I, 13, C957, 1874, Appendix, 3 (conditions of Liverpool General Brokers).
[169] ss. 13, 14, 15. See 207–215 above.

took the goods as they were and it was up to them to protect themselves by inspection and testing prior to the auction.[170] Conditions in the catalogue for the sale of tea in the Commercial Sale Rooms at Mincing Lane on 2 April 1838 included the provisions that no allowance would be made on account of 'any damage, rubbish, false package, or unequal goodness, found or alleged to be found after the Goods have been taken from the Warehouse', and that teas were to be 'at the risk of the Sellers till the Prompt Day, unless paid for previously' when they would be at the buyer's risk.[171]

Similarly, some sixty years later in the early 1900s Eastwood & Holt, prominent brokers at Mincing Lane, highlighted the following condition in their auction catalogues: goods were to be taken 'with all faults and errors of description whatever as they now lie in the warehouses mentioned in the Catalogue'.[172] In the 1920s a typical condition for wool auctions in London was that the wool was to be 'taken away by the buyers at their own expense within fourteen days, with all faults and defects of whatever kind (including defect or error of description)'.[173] For some commodities, however, there was a gloss on this approach. Leading coffee brokers Carey & Browne stated in their conditions around the same time that successful bidders were to take a lot at its landing weights (with customary allowances) as it lay in the warehouse, a damaged portion with all faults. Any objection as to quality or description was not to be entertained unless made within ten days of sale.[174]

What if the catalogue was unclear and a bidder made a mistake as to what he was buying? *Scriven Brothers & Co* v. *Hindley & Co*[175] arose from a typical auction of commodities at the Commercial Sale Rooms in Mincing Lane just prior to the First World War. The plaintiffs were employed to sell a large quantity of Russian hemp and tow for the bank, which had made advances on it. They employed one Northcott, an auctioneer and broker. The goods were still at the docks, but as usual sample bales were on view at the Cutler Street showrooms of the Port of London Authority. On the floor in front of the bales was written in chalk 'SL 63 to 67' for the hemp, 'SL 68 to 79' for the tow.

---

[170] In Singapore in 1893 a judge held that one of Drew & Napier's clients, Tan Chong, had no case despite the coffee he bought at auction being contaminated by arsenic: *The History of Drew & Napier 1889–1989*, Singapore, Drew & Napier, no date but 1989, 57.

[171] H.A. Antrobus, *A History of the Assam Company 1839–1953*, Edinburgh, Constable, 1957, illustration facing p. 264. The prompt day was when final payment had to be made.

[172] MLD, PRA, Eastwood & Holt Catalogues, 1902, 'Public Sale at the London Commercial Sale Rooms Mincing Lane on Monday, July 14th, 1902'.

[173] The full conditions are in Ministry of Agriculture and Fisheries, *Report of Wool Marketing in England and Wales*, London, HMSO, 1926. The condition had been there from the outset of London wool auctions: NBAC, AA Co, Despatches, 1/18, 'For Sale by Auction by J. T. Simes & Co at Garraway's Coffee-House', Change-Alley, Cornhill, Thursday, 23rd August, 1838, Conditions of Sale, cl. 2.

[174] C. Woodhouse, *The Woodhouses, Drakes and Careys of Mincing Lane*, London, self published, 1977, 29 (June 1899 conditions). See also Department of Commerce, Bureau of Foreign and Domestic Commerce, Market Methods and Trade Usages in London, *op cit*, 9 (conditions of Coffee Trade Association).

[175] [1913] 3 KB 564.

Northcott's catalogue contained the shipping mark 'SL', and the numbers of the bales in two lots, 63 to 67, 47 bales, and 68 to 79, 176 bales, but did not distinguish between the hemp and the tow. When the manager of the defendant broker inspected the samples of 'SL' hemp, his attention was not called to the fact that the tow was also marked 'SL'. The defendants successfully bid for the 47 bales at just over £24 per ton, and then for the 176 bales at £17 per ton. The tow was in fact very inferior, 'mere rubbish' as several witnesses put it at trial. When they discovered this the defendants refused to pay.

The plaintiffs sued, the defendants claiming that the tow had been knocked down to them under a mistake of fact. The plaintiffs contended that the mistake was only a mistake as to value. Witnesses on both sides said that Russian hemp and Russian tow were never landed from the same ship under the same shipping marks. The case went before a judge and civil jury.[176] The jury answered questions put to them. A. T. Lawrence J found for the defendants.[177] The parties were never *ad idem* as to the subject-matter of the proposed sale, and therefore there was no contract of sale. Since Russian hemp was never known to be consigned or sold with the same shipping marks as Russian tow from the same cargo, it was natural for the person inspecting the 'SL' goods and being shown hemp to suppose that the 'SL' bales represented that commodity. The judge added that the auctioneer was under a duty to make clear to the bidder either upon the face of the catalogue or in some other way which lots were hemp, which tow. To rely upon a buyer discovering chalk marks upon the floor at the show room 'seems to me unreasonable as demanding an amount of care upon the part of the buyer which the vendor had no right to exact'.[178]

3 Manipulation, 'Puffers' and Rings: The Law's Lop-sided Approach

Asked whether there were abuses in the auctions conducted in Mincing Lane, he said that he did think there were, 'because a new broker without goodwill, that is to say, not being of a respectable nature, would get no business by selling in auction or in any other way'. As to whether there were any rules or regulations needed, he answered: 'I do not really think there are. They are perfectly straightforward rules and regulations which are printed on the front of every catalogue'. (Evidence, President, London

---

[176] Juries had been used from the nineteenth century to resolve cases of mistake: C. MacMillan, *Mistakes in Contract Law*, Oxford, Hart, 2010, 92–93. Civil juries were abandoned shortly after the First World War: *Gregory* v. *Commissioner of Police of the Metropolis* [2014] EWHC 3922 (QB), [2015] 1 WLR 4253, [14]; 55n above.

[177] For a short time Lord Chief Justice: see R. Stevens, *The Independence of the Judiciary*, Oxford, Oxford University Press, 1993, 30. '[A]n adequate rather than distinguished judge', appointed for his political connections: N. Davidson, revised R. Stevens, 'Lawrence, Alfred Tristram, first Baron Trevethin (1843–1936)', *Oxford Dictionary of National Biography*.

[178] at 569.

General Produce Brokers' Association, House of Lords Select Committee, 1935)[179]

Foreign producers sometimes thought that the London auction sales were manipulated to their detriment.[180] Manipulation of a sorts occurred with Australian wool, in London and at home. In the nineteenth century it would be held back from the London auctions to influence price, and in some cases importers withdrew their clients' wool from the auctions if it appeared that there would be a glut on the market. In the 1920s Australia growers and brokers attempted to influence price by regulating the supply of wool going to auction.[181] On the buyers' side there were rings, particularly by smaller buyers to secure lots too large for individual use, although the practice probably had little effect on price.[182]

With tea, the Food Council reported in the 1920s that speculative operations occurred at the London auctions but that overall this did not affect price.[183] In 1956 the Monopolies and Restrictive Practices Commission found that from time to time selling and buying brokers in combination regulated the amount of tea being auctioned, which had the effect of restricting competition in its availability in Britain. The Commission concluded that this was not against the public interest because of its advantage to even out sales over the year without, it seemed, an overall impact on price.[184]

One exception to the general hands-off approach of the common law to auctions was because Lord Mansfield had held – after discussions, he said, with non-lawyers about the 'morality and rectitude' of the practice – that sellers bidding in an auction for their own goods, either themselves or through agents, was a fraud upon the public. It was against good faith, he said, and would lead good men in the way of the dishonest. No one would bid in auctions if the price could be artificially inflated in that way. However, it was legitimate for sellers to impose a reserve price or to insert a condition allowing themselves the liberty to bid.[185] Morality and good faith were not the soundest basis for a rule in the era of freedom of contract, but Mansfield's ruling remained firm. Serjeant Wilde unsuccessfully challenged it before Best CJ and the Court of Common

---

[179] *Report by the Select Committee of the House of Lords upon Auctioneers', House Agents' and Valuers' Licences*, vol. 98, 18 July 1935. The Association was based in Mincing Lane but did not represent all brokers selling there.

[180] Song Ong Siang, K. Tan, G. Uma Devi & Kua Bak Lim, *One Hundred Years of the Chinese in Singapore*, annotated ed., Singapore, National Library Board, 2016, 613.

[181] M. Keneley, 'Woolgrowers, Brokers and the Debate over the Sale of the Australian Wool Clip 1920–1925' (2001) 41 *Aust Econ Hist Rev* 35, 47.

[182] A. Barnard, *The Australian Wool Market 1840–1900*, Melbourne, Melbourne University Press, 1958, 125–127; A. Barnard, 'A Century and a Half of Wool Marketing', in A. Barnard (ed.), *The Simple Fleece*, Melbourne, Melbourne University Press, 1962, 481.

[183] Food Council, *Report . . . to the President of the Board of Trade on Wholesale Tea Prices*, London, HMSO, 1926, 14–16.

[184] Monopolies and Restrictive Practices Commission, Report on the Supply of Tea, op cit, 39, 40–41.

[185] *Bexwell* v. *Christie* (1776) 1 Cowp 395, 98 ER 1150, at 397, 1151 respectively. Aston, Willes and Ashhurst JJ agreed.

Pleas in early 1826 with the argument that such 'puffery' was commonplace and purchasers were not deceived.[186] Best CJ was an old-fashioned judge with an eighteenth-century sense of morality, and given that the rule was Mansfield's was able to carry the court against a change.[187]

But doubts continued to be expressed about Mansfield's rule against a seller's employment of 'puffers' at auctions.[188] Before the Court of Appeal in Chancery in 1865, counsel contended that the common-law cases supporting the rule were mainly out of date. However, the attack on Mansfield's rule was unsuccessful and it remained the law.[189] It could be justified doctrinally in that a seller employing a puffer to bid would be in breach of his representation that the highest bidder would have the goods knocked down to him. The rule's soundness was put beyond doubt when Chalmers incorporated it in what became section 58 of the Sale of Goods Act 1893: a buyer could treat a sale at auction as fraudulent if the seller bid himself, or his agent bid, or if the auctioneer knowingly took a bid from the seller or any such person.[190] However, the statute went on to provide that a seller could expressly reserve to himself the right to bid.[191]

The other side of the coin to puffing was the practice of buyers forming a ring to bid. It might have been expected that given the rule disfavouring puffing, the law would require that at auctions there would be open competition by bidders. Indeed in 1833 Gurney B had directed a jury that a so called 'knock-out' agreement would be an indictable conspiracy, that is, where a group (or 'ring') agreed among themselves that only one would bid at an auction, and they would afterwards divide the spoils resulting from the lower price obtained.[192] In an era of freedom of contract, however, Gurney B's direction was soon ignored. The rule became that there was nothing illegal for potential bidders at an auction to form a ring to agree that only one of them should bid for a lot, with the intention of obtaining a lower price.[193] Purchases could be subsequently shared among those in the ring by dividing them in a prearranged manner, each member paying the appropriate part of the purchase price. With non-fungible goods, a more complicated share-out might be necessary. A further, informal auction was a common solution so that the spoils could be divided.

There is some evidence of price-depressing agreements among buyers in the commodities auctions. Collusive arrangements among buyers were particularly complex in Australian wool auctions.[194] They took a mutated form in a case

---

[186] *Crowder* v. *Austin* (1826) 3 Bing 368, 130 ER 555.
[187] P. Atiyah, *The Rise and Fall of Freedom of Contract*, Oxford, Oxford University Press, 1979, 169.
[188] J. Bateman, A Practical Treatise on the Law of Auctions, *op cit*, 145–153.
[189] *Mortimer* v. *Bell* (1865) LR 1 Ch App 10. If a rule existed in equity that the vendor of land might employ a single 'puffer', it was abolished by the Sale of Land by Auction Act 1867 (sometimes called the Puffer's Act). See also *Gilliat* v. *Gilliat* (1869) LR 9 Eq 60.
[190] s. 58(3).   [191] s. 58(4).   [192] *Levi* v. *Levi* (1833) 6 Car & P 239, 172 ER 1224.
[193] *Galton* v. *Emuss* (1844) 1 Coll 243, 63 ER 402.
[194] R. Cassidy, *Auctions and Auctioneering*, Berkeley, University of California Press, 1967, 187–189.

where local merchants in Bombay entered wagering contracts as to the price that Patna opium would fetch at auction. The Privy Council held on appeal that there was nothing to prevent those merchants from bidding at the auction themselves, or employing others to bid, so as to bring about the price by which a wager was to be won.[195] Parke B said that however much the judges might disapprove of such wagering transactions (which the Indian legislature had since declared void), and however disreputable these wagers might be, 'still we cannot pronounce them to be fraudulent in contemplation of law, which only seeks to lay down broad rules for the government of human conduct applicable to all classes of persons, and does not exonerate parties from their contracts (which it is its primary duty to enforce) on the ground of fraud, except where they are distinctly shown to be in violation of the ordinary rules of morality'.[196]

The law permitting rings was revisited after the First World War in a case involving army surplus, *Rawlings* v. *General Trading Co.*[197] At first instance Shearman J ventured that a ring agreement was contrary to public policy and unenforceable. The majority in the Court of Appeal would have none of it: the agreement was not illegal. Bankes LJ applied the precedents.[198] Atkin LJ said that the seller could have obtained a higher price by inserting a reserve price in the conditions of sale. There is no evidence, he added in freedom of contract mode, that the price was not satisfactory to the seller or to the auctioneer.[199] Scrutton LJ dissented: though reasonable as between the parties, the agreement was contrary to public policy as a restraint of trade and thus unenforceable.[200] It was only with the passage of the Auctions (Bidding Agreements) Act 1927 that rings and knockouts were made unlawful. The Act was a private members' Bill introduced by Lord Darling, who had sat as a judge with Scrutton LJ, and aimed explicitly at reversing *Rawlings* v. *General Trading Co.*[201] In practice the Act was a damp squib.[202] If a copy of a bidding agreement was deposited with the auctioneer beforehand, no breach occurred.[203] A major prosecution failed for non-compliance with the requirements in the Act.[204]

Meanwhile, the London commodities markets had begun to address the possibility of rigged bidding. Clauses in the conditions for some commodity auctions allowed brokers to refuse to recognise any bid, without giving reasons.[205] That enabled them to take preventive action if they suspected rigging. It is difficult to know at this distance the extent to which the London

---

[195] *Doolubdass Pettamberdass* v. *Ramloll Thackoorseydass* (1850) 5 Moo Ind App 109, 18 ER 836.
[196] at 135, 846, respectively.
[197] [1920] 3 KB 30. Shearman J was prepared to limit the rule to where the goods were public property.
[198] [1921] 1 KB 635, at 640–641.   [199] at 646–647.   [200] at 648.
[201] *Hansard*, HL Deb, 20 July 1926, vol. 65, cc86–88.
[202] B. Yamey, 'Bidding Agreements at Auctions' (1955) *Butterworths S African L Rev* 73, 77.
[203] s. 1(1).   [204] *R* v. *Barnett* [1951] 2 KB 425.
[205] e.g., coffee, furs: Department of Commerce, Bureau of Foreign and Domestic Commerce, *Market Methods and Trade Usages in London*, Washington, Government Printing Office, 1923, 9, 23.

commodity auctions were manipulated and if so whether this produced the desired outcomes. The 1927 Act, one Labour MP asserted, was aimed at small dealers, but the 'great brokers in Mincing Lane dealing in thousands of tons of tea, the rubber brokers and the other dealers in raw commodities ... are apparently ignored, yet they have rings'.[206] The evidence of the president of the General Produce Brokers' Association in 1935 (quoted at the beginning of this section) about the absence of abuses in the Mincing Lase commodity auctions seems unduly complacent. What can be said with greater certainty is that the well-established practices operating in the London commodity auctions made the 1927 Act an irrelevance one way or the other.

5.5 Private Law-Making: The Processes of the Trade Associations

'Shall I tell you what I've noticed: People are quite on the wrong tack in offering less than they can afford to give; they ought to offer more and work backward.' Soames raised his eyebrows ... 'Try buying pictures on that system', said Soames; 'an offer accepted is a contract—haven't you learned that?' Young Mont turned his head to where Fleur was standing in the window. 'No', he said, 'I wish I had. Then there's another thing. Always let a man off a bargain if he wants to be let off.' 'As advertisement?' said Soames dryly. 'Of course it is; but I meant on principle.' 'Does your firm work on those lines?' 'Not yet', said Mont, 'but it'll come.' 'And they will go.' (John Galsworthy, *To Let*, London, William Heinemann, 1921)

The central figure in Galsworthy's *Forsyte Saga*, Soames Forsyte, asserts at various points in the novels an intense belief in contract, property and vested rights, including over people. In this passage, Michael Mont, whom Soames' only child, Fleur, will marry, takes the contrary view about the sanctity of contract: parties when entering a contract should not aim to maximise their advantage at the expense of others, and once entered contractual terms should be applied flexibly and if needs be the other side excused from contractual performance. That was certainly not the approach of English law once contracts were entered. However, Mont's more flexible approach applied at the private law-making stage in the different commodity trade associations, where commercial realities and the balance of the different interests had to be accommodated.

At one level drafting standard contract terms was an intensely practical exercise. Although no records survive it seems highly likely that the first standard form contracts of the leading trade associations were plagiarised from the existing contracts of member firms. The records of the London Copra Association offer an analogy. When its general committee decided in 1916 that a simple spot contract was needed, it took the spot contract of a member firm, Corrie, MacColl & Co., changed the title and a few key words,

[206] *Hansard*, HC Deb, 25 February 1927, v 202, c2094.

but did little else.[207] The one obvious addition in the new association contract was the clause that disputes were to be settled by arbitration in accordance with the rules of the London Copra Association.[208]

Similarly, once a trade association had a number of standard form contracts, it was easy enough to lift clauses from one for use in another, and even to incorporate whole chunks to create additional contracts covering matters such as different means of shipment, new sources of an existing commodity or different commodities altogether. Thus in 1909 a LCTA sub-committee quickly approved a form which Australian exporters had drawn up on the basis of the existing LCTA cargoes form.[209] Similarly, in 1920 the Chinese and Manchurian Cereals Contract was transformed, with some minor amendments, into a Japanese Cereals Contract, the Chinese and Manchurian contract being simultaneously amended so the payment clause was common to both.[210]

At another level the process of contract formulation was more complex. In a sense the trade associations needed to react to events. These might be immediate and pedestrian, as with a query raised by a member, or as the result of an arbitration award or court judgment which threw new light on the meaning of a contract term or identifying a problem never anticipated. At the other end of the spectrum the events might be long term, as with changing economic conditions, with no immediate implications for contract terms, but with an impact on the players in the market and their relative bargaining power. Ultimately changed bargaining power as between importers and exporters and between nations could influence contractual terms because, as with democratic law-making generally, the decision was, to varying degrees, a product of conflicting interests. Along the spectrum were events such as war and the impact of new technologies.

Just how the different interests manifested their influence, and to what effect, are by no means completely clear at this distance in time. The occasions when the records are explicit about it are few and far between. One such example was a meeting of interests involved in the Persian Gulf grain trade in early 1950, which was told that vendors were now strong enough to insist on the use of a new LCTA contract in preference to the existing Dutch contract.[211] However, there are glimpses of how competing importer interests, conflicting interests in importing and exporting countries, and the contrast between commodity and ship-owner interests rubbed up against each other in the adoption of some standard contracts and their terms. From this one inference

---

[207] Corrie, MacColl & Son began as importers and brokers in commodities in the late eighteenth century and in the early twentieth century were in importing copra for the manufacture of soaps and margarine. The firm still operates in commodities like rubber.
[208] LMA, CLC/B/103/MS23224/002, London Copra Association, Minutes, 24 October 1916, 44–45.
[209] LMA, CLC/B/103/MS23174/002, LCTA, Sub-committee re Australian Steamer Contract Form, 14 December 1909; 6 January 1910.
[210] LMA, CLC/B/103/MS23185/001, LCTA, China and Manchurian Feeding Stuffs Committee, minutes, 19, 24 August 1920.
[211] LMA, CLC/B/103/MS23174/011, LCTA, Minutes of sub-committees, 9 February 1950.

is certain: the formulation of standard form contracts was not some neutral exercise, where Soames' contractual principles were sacrosanct, and the enterprise of contract formulation devoid of values and the clash of interests.

1 Events and Changed Circumstances

[There is] the necessity to bring up to date the repeatedly occurring needs for adjustments of contract conditions, which the ever-restless evolution of trade presents from time to time. (President of LCTA, Annual General Meeting, 27 May 1926)[212]

Generally speaking the trade associations kept separate the tasks of contract formulation in the light of changed conditions, and the need to respond to the impact of immediate events. If questions were raised about the meaning of a contract term because of an event, for example a dispute about a contract's ramifications for a particular cargo, that was regarded as a matter for future clarification, or for the parties to resolve between themselves or by arbitration. It was not for the trade association, or its relevant committees, to issue an authoritative interpretation. Occasionally the trade associations might proffer a view about what a term meant, or at least what market sentiment took it to mean.[213] Against adopting that as a general practice, however, were the pressures of time and institutional specialisation. As the Standing Contracts Committee of the LCTA put it in 1931, it was for arbitrators to rule about the meaning of contractual terms. If parties were unhappy about an interpretation, they could always appeal.[214] Occasionally an association might vary a contract to achieve what it regarded had always been intended. The LCTA decided to add 'including [Great] lake ports' to the North American contracts when Louis Dreyfus & Co. Ltd – later one of the so-called 'merchants of grain' – raised doubts as to whether shipments from these ports were covered.

Neither did the associations have any inclination, let alone the legal power, to modify contracts retrospectively, or to control contractual performance in the light of specific events. Thus in 1932 typhoons in Japan, and consequent flooding, meant a disruption to exports. The Japan Cereals Export Association and the Japanese Embassy in London requested the LCTA to arrange for an extension of the period of shipment. However, LCTA replied, this was a matter of contract between sellers and buyers, although it did offer to arrange a meeting of interested parties to attempt to arrive at an equitable solution in the light of

---

[212] LMA, CLC/B/103/MS23172/008, Minutes of executive committee and of annual general meetings, 206.

[213] e.g., LMA, CLC/B/103/MS23177/001, LCTA, American and Australian Grain Committee, minutes, 26 November 1896; MS23174/008, Standing Contracts Committee, minutes, 5 June 1930.

[214] LMA, CLC/B/103/MS23174/008, LCTA, 1 October 1931, LMA, CLC/B/103/MS23174/009, LCTA, Standing Contracts Committee, 22 October 1931.

what had occurred.[215] Similarly, in the late 1950s associations of grain importers in continental Europe complained that some sellers were abusing the 'extension of shipment clause', which enabled them to claim an additional period to fulfil a contract following a strike or similar event. Again LCTA responded that it could not intervene in particular cases of the abuse of contractual rights. However, it sent a letter to grain exporting associations in various parts of the world. Four months after the matter was first raised the Standing Contracts Committee was told that no further complaints of abuse had been received.[216]

Changed circumstances in the longer term were a different matter. The events demanding adjustments in contract terms were enormously varied. Some were on their face relatively simple, the emergence of new nations or products, and the opening up of new sources or destinations for a commodity. Thus the creation of the Irish state required contracts to be amended in relation to their domiciliary and arbitration clauses.[217] At the request of the North American Export Grain Association, LCTA agreed in 1933 to amend contracts No. 28 and 29 to include shipments from Albany, New York.[218] The growing power of the labour movement – 'the spread of socialistic tendencies of the labouring classes', as it was put at the annual general meeting of the London Oil and Tallow Trades Association in 1912[219] – led to the insertion of strike clauses in commodities contracts, giving exporters the benefit on an extended time for shipment should there be labour disruption.

Another driver of adjustments was engineering and technological innovation, especially in shipping and communications. The tendency to ship commodities in bulk rather than bags was reflected in basic clauses such as those concerned with quality and price. For some commodities containerisation towards the end of our period meant new contracts.[220] As regards notices, the nineteenth-century commodity contracts recognised that these could be given by cable or telegram (e.g., claims for an additional period to ship under a strike clause, or to re-sell or re-purchase under a default clause). In the mid-twentieth century contracts were amended with the advent of telex – 'or other similar method of rapid written communication' as LCTA contracts put it – as an additional means of giving or passing on the notices referred to in them.[221]

Yet technological change did not always produce contractual alterations in the face of strong interests favouring the status quo. The advent of air mail meant that the shipping documents for a cargo could arrive well in

---

[215] LMA, CLC/B/103/MS23185/002, LCTA, China and Manchurian Feeding Stuffs Committee, Minutes, 29 September 1932.
[216] LMA, CLC/B/103/MS23174/012, LCTA, Contracts Committee, 25 November 1959; 23 March 1960.
[217] LMA, CLC/B/103/MS23174/007, Contracts Committee, Minutes, 3 November 1927.
[218] LMA, CLC/B/103/MS23174/009, 18 May 1933. See also LMA, CLC/B/103/MS23174/003, London Committee, Minutes, 16 May 1912 (opening of new London docks).
[219] LMA, CLC/B/103/MS23234, 'Scrapbook', 23 January 1912.
[220] LMA, CLC/B/103/MS23172/013, LCTA, Executive Committee, Minutes, 378.
[221] LMA, CLC/B/103/MS23172/012, LCTA, Executive Committee, Minutes, 58.

advance of the goods. If an importer took up the documents as soon as they arrived and paid cash, it meant that it could be laying out money well in advance of receiving the goods. The maturity dates of bills of exchange used for payment – and hence the credit extended – had an impact on the returns for exporters. In 1930 the LCTA Contracts Committee recommended amendments to the payment clauses in contracts. For example, it proposed for the Californian and Oregon and Washington contracts that payment be by sixty-day drafts, rather than the existing thirty-day period at which point importers had to make payment. A meeting in London of those involved in the Californian, Oregon and Washington business decided that the case for change had not been made out.[222] No doubt the idea of changing payment terms was unpalatable to many on the exporting side, since they would be taking larger discounts when selling the bills of exchange drawn to pay for the wheat.[223]

Wars, or at least the threat of conflict, also shaped some of the clauses in standard form contracts. War clauses, agreed with the North American Export Grain Association, were printed in red on the back of the United States and Canadian contracts from January 1916.[224] But in the run up to the First World War LCTA had resisted pressure from the North American Association that under its contracts buyers should be compelled to cover war risk: sellers, said the LCTA, should continue to insure for their own account.[225] After the outbreak of war in August 1914 that line could no longer be maintained and a special committee of the LCTA, together with the Institute of London Underwriters, devised a compromise. Under its proposed war risk clause, for insertion in all contracts, the seller was obliged to have insurance not only on Lloyd's conditions but also in accordance with LCTA's war risk and strike risk clauses. Any expense of the insurance covering war and strike risk exceeding one-half of one per cent of the invoice amount was to be paid by the buyer.[226]

Then there were the changes in market operations such as the development of futures trading examined in Chapter 2 (part 2.4). Existing contracts were unsuitable for this. In the early 1900s, there were a number of changes in the contracts for wheat in the Liverpool market to enable dealings in futures.[227] In London a standard clause in LCTA contracts provided that should their fulfilment be rendered impossible by a government prohibition on export, or a blockage or hostilities, it should be cancelled. In futures contracts, however,

---

[222] LMA, CLC/B/103/MS23174/008, LCTA, Contracts Committee, Minutes, 6 November, 16 December 1930; 19 February, 30 April 1931.
[223] 383 below.   [224] See LMA, CLC/B/103/MS23172/007, LCTA.
[225] LMA, CLC/B/103/MS23172/006, Minutes of Executive Committee. See also *The Times*, 2 February 1912, 18. cf. *C Groom Ltd v. Barber* [1915] 1 KB 316 (contract of UK Jute Goods Association – 'war risk for buyer's account').
[226] LMA, CLC/B/103/MS23174/007, LCTA, War Risk Insurance Committee, Minutes, 7 March, 28 March 1922.
[227] The story is told in G. Rees, *Britain's Commodity Markets, op cit*, 142.

cancellation was not appropriate; what happened instead was that contracts were closed out and differences paid according to the settlement price. Consequently, when LCTA's executive committee decided to modify existing contracts for use in futures trading in 1936, the prohibition of export clause was dropped.[228] Once clauses like this were stripped out of the existing contracts, their standardised versions for futures trading in a particular grain were identified by an 'A' after the number. For daily futures trading there was a short form, incorporating by reference both the clauses of the longer version, and LCTA's by-laws. It was printed in two parts, one for the seller, and one for the buyer, perforated in the middle.

Despite the modifications, futures trading could still raise issues for standard form contracts. For example, as a result of a claim for cancellation of a contract by reason of frustration of a venture involving Iraqi barley per *Kohistan* in 1957, the futures executive redrafted the default clause so that it and its closing-out provisions applied to a failure to fulfil its terms by either party, whether by reason of the impossibility of performance or otherwise.[229] LCTA called in legal assistance to advise on the shape of the relevant clause. Calling in the lawyers was to become more common in the post–Second World War era.

2 Principles Underlining Trade Association Law-making

As a framework for reacting to new circumstances, and for periodically reviewing their standard form contracts, the trade associations worked to a number of principles. First, was the principle of certainty. This bright-line approach was consistent with the principles of English commercial law.[230] It seemed also to be a principle valued by trade interests abroad. When it was proposed in 1958 to introduce the word 'about' into the LCTA contract for shipments from Iraq, the Danish association of grain importers protested: shipments were faq (fair average quality) or they were not, and any margin introduced in that contract would spread to others, impairing confidence in London contracts.[231] Achieving certainty was implicit in all LCTA's work both in the original drafting of terms and in redrafting them when problems were exposed by experience, an arbitration award or the occasional court judgment. An open-textured clause was to be avoided in the interests of certainty. When the Exporters Association of Shanghai suggested in 1932 that a general *force majeure* clause should be inserted in Form No 4, the Standing Contracts Committee of LCTA pointed out the danger of uncertainty should such a clause be inserted in any grain contract. Ultimately strike and prohibition clauses were adopted along the lines

---

[228] LMA, CLC/B/103/MS23172/009, LCTA, Executive Committee, Minutes, 279.
[229] LMA, CLC/B/103/MS23205/002, London Grain Futures Association, Minute Book No 2, 110–111.
[230] 41–43 above.
[231] LMA, CLC/B/103/MS23174/012, Contracts Committee, Minutes, 2, 18 December 1958.

of comparable clauses in other LCTA contracts, which specified the circumstances giving rise to permissible interruptions in performance.[232]

Another example in relation to *force majeure* comes from the 1950s and LCTA's Australian contracts.[233] The Australian exporters wanted the strike clause to be extended to cover not only instances of named vessels being withdrawn by ship owners but also providing for extension and cancellation in cases of forward shipments. A sub-committee found that the shippers' proposals went too far for buyers. However, it agreed to a clause allowing the unshipped portion of a consignment to be cancelled where the loading of a named vessel was prevented by strikes and other causes such as plant failure. The continental associations of importers in Germany, Holland, Belgium and Denmark then raised objections to the language proposed – interruption caused by 'combination of workmen' was too vague. The matter dragged on and eventually a compromise was reached.

A second principle in the drafting and redrafting of standard form contracts was that the associations should represent the trade as a whole. In promulgating contractual terms, the stated objective was to strike a balance between the interests of buyers and sellers, importers and exporters.[234] At a minimum, that meant feeding in the views of the different interests into the process. Illustrative is that in the early years LCTA contracts were revised regularly. Suggestions for alternatives came from a range of organisations across the spectrum – exporters (e.g., Adelaide Chamber of Commerce), shipping interests (e.g., the UK Chamber of Shipping), associations of importers (e.g., the Berlin Produce Exchange; the Chamber of Commerce, Berlin) and customer groups (the National Association of British and Irish Millers). Views also came from a range of individual exporters (e.g., S. Wolberg, Odessa), importers elsewhere (e.g., H. Neumann, Antwerp), importers in Britain, including local and foreign houses (L. Dreyfus & Co., J. H. Friedland, Payne & Routh, Praschauer & Co.), and individual customers (Spillers & Bakers Ltd.).[235]

With time both exporting and importing interests were consulted more systematically as contracts were drawn and redrawn. But that did not mean that contract formulation was a level playing field. Individual exporters might have agents or branches in London, but their collective interests were

---

[232] LMA, CLC/B/103/MS23174/009, Contracts Committee, Minutes,16 August 1932, 30 March, 17 October 1933.

[233] LMA, CLC/B/103/MS23174/012, LCTA, Sub-committee re frustration and prevention of shipment.

[234] LMA, CLC/B/103/MS23224/001, London Copra Association, 24 March 1914, 49; LMA, CLC/B/103/MS 23234, London Oil and Tallow Trades Association, 'Scrapbook', 31 January 1911.

[235] e.g., Suggested Alterations of Contract Forms, 1895 revision; and revisions for years 1896 to 1909. LMA, CLC/B/103/MS23175. Other examples include the London Cattle Food Trade Association seeking agreement of American exporters (LMA, CLC/B/103/MS23220, LCFTA, 12 September 1912, 12–13; 17 April 1913, 25; 15 January 1914, 36), and the London Copra Association being pressed by French importers (Union des Fabricants d' Huile de France) and Dutch East Indies exporters (LMA, CLC/B/103/MS23224/004, 207; CLC/B/103/MS23224/005, 36, 88, 298).

expressed through their trade associations, located at least an ocean away and in some cases on the other side of the world. *A priori* their sway would be more tenuous than that of importer interests. Moreover, amongst importers there was a gradation of influence: without compensating mechanisms, those with a presence in London would have a greater chance of their voice being heard than those in continental Europe, simply because social and other mixing in London would reinforce influence. We return to this issue later.

Uniformity as far as possible between standard form contracts was a third principle underlying the associations' work in drafting and redrafting contractual terms. In 1908 the periodic review of LCTA contracts were said to be 'to simplify, by reducing the number of, and bringing about greater uniformity among the various Forms'.[236] The period following the First World War was an occasion for a revision of all LCTA contracts, with the aim 'to get all our clauses standardized as much as possible'.[237] These general expressions of concern with uniformity took concrete form. Among the many examples is that by the early 1920s LCTA contracts for all countries except the United States included a war risk insurance clause. That was a good reason to LCTA to bring United States contracts into line.[238]

3 Interests and the Changing Balance

These were the principles in the drafting of standard form contracts by associations – certainty, balancing interests and as much uniformity as possible – but drafting was never an exercise devoid of commercial realities. From the outset there were conflicting interests, most notably between importers and exporters. Exporters would want early payment; importers would like to defer payment as long as possible. Exporters wanted the option of walking away from a contract if their country imposed an export ban; importers would want compensation if this occurred. Exporters would want the possibility of more time to fulfil a contract in the event of a labour strike; importers would often just want the commodity or to walk away. And both sides would want to take advantage of rising or falling markets.

The associations had to take a line on such issues in clauses relating to payment, labour strikes and so on. Importers and exporters were not, however, an undifferentiated lump. While the concerns, say, of importers throughout Europe were similar on an issue like commodity quality, there were other issues over which trade associations in places like London, Hamburg and Rotterdam could differ. Moreover, there were outside interests to which both importers and exporters were subject. At LCTA's annual general meeting in

---

[236] LMA, CLC/B/103/MS23172/004, LCTA, Annual Report 1907–1908.
[237] LMA, CLC/B/103/MS23172/007, Annual General Meeting, 20 May 1920. See also Annual Report 1931–1932: CLC/B/103/MS23172/009, 89.
[238] LMA, CLC/B/103/MS23174/006, North American Contracts Committee, Minutes, 29 September 1921.

1901 the president noted the 'monster combinations of American railroads with Atlantic steamship lines' which, he opined, must affect trade.[239] The need to negotiate solutions with ship owners, insurance markets and other third parties is a regular occurrence in the association's records.

The trade associations mediated these various interests. While taking them into account, the stronger associations like LCTA could generally impose the solution they thought best, although at times they had to bend in the wind. Other associations were not in a strong position and were bounced along by forces. In the early 1920s the exporters of branded tallow, predominantly Australian, insisted on selling on terms which included a strike clause. Importers objected. Attempts by the London Oil and Tallow Trades Association to reach a compromise having failed, all it could do was to inform importers of the new position.[240] Sometimes the compromise reached between the different interests was the product of horse-trading. From late 1912 through 1913, the LCTA Australian contracts were revised by a specially appointed sub-committee with both seller and buyer representation. At one meeting in January 1913 the sellers' representatives agreed that if the then rule on standard Contract No. 7 should be retained, they for their part would undertake that rule 1 in standard Contract No. 8 would be carried out in practice by sellers.[241]

The perception held in exporting countries of some of the trade associations was that they had been captured by the importing interest. This was the case with LCTA, at least in the eyes of American exporters. In 1881, as the first of the North American standard form contracts was being drawn up, a large meeting of grain exporters held in New York denounced it as one-sided, onerous and favouring importers. Over the following months LCTA made amendments to the draft. Still exporters in New York, Philadelphia and Baltimore rejected it and framed a contract of their own.[242] The LCTA contracts won the day but resentment still continued.

Sometimes irritation was more because of the way the contracts were used. For example, LCTA's North American contracts required insurance on Lloyd's conditions with approved British or United States underwriters or companies, but if insurance was written in America, losses were to be payable in England. That importers in England would not purchase cargoes unless insured with Lloyd's was a particularly sore point on the west coast of the United States. The fact was that before the First World War American grain exporters were not in

---

[239] LMA, CLC/B/103/MS23172/002, LCTA, 30 May 1901. See also LMA, CLC/B/103/MS23174/006, LCTA, North American Contracts Committee, 22 September 1921.

[240] LMA, CLC/B/103/MS23233, Minutes of Contracts Committee, 26 April, 5, 12 May, 29 September 1921, 40, 46.

[241] LMA, CLC/B/103/MS/23174/003.

[242] *The Times*, November 28, 1881, 5; 1 May 1882, 5; 13 May 1882, 7; 29 May 1882, 6.

a strong enough position to carry the day on such matters.[243] After the First World War the balance changed.

How different interests played out over time is illustrated by the story of the payment clause in North American contracts in the early twentieth century. Under the existing clause payment was by means of cash in London (through a bank) in exchange for the shipping documents.[244] Once the importer had the shipping documents it could control the consignment, since one of the documents was the bill of lading, recognised by the common law as a document of title. Alternatively, payment was by way of acceptance by the importer of the exporter's bill of exchange, with the shipping documents attached, the bill maturing sixty days after 'sight' (i.e., the point of acceptance of the bill, making the importer liable on the instrument as well as under the contract of sale). The second option had the disadvantage to exporters that not only might they be giving considerable credit to importers – the sixty days to maturity of the bill – but they were also bearing the risk if the importer became insolvent before paying under it.[245] Although in theory under the contracts North American exporters could exclude the second method of payment, in practice it seems that their bargaining power did not enable them to do this. Much better, from their point of view, if this possibility were to be excluded from the contract altogether so that importers always had to pay cash against documents.

In early 1908 the chairman of the Baltimore Chamber of Commerce wrote to LCTA of a meeting of grain interests there where numerous complaints were raised that importers 'frequently failed to live up to the spirit of the London grain contract by deferring the payment of bills until after the arrival of the vessel and even after the discharge of the grain'. With high interest rates, many of the best American banks were refusing to handle the usual sixty-day sight documentary bills drawn on buyers in the United Kingdom. There had been a recent case, the president continued, where an importer had failed before paying on the bill, showing clearly 'that present conditions of the London Contract are inadequate and unjust to the Shipper [exporter]'. Sixty-day sight bills dated from a time when the voyages were much longer than they now were with steam ships. Quite apart from the fact that all continental sales were net cash terms only, the letter continued, American exporters had to pay their suppliers in the United States either on delivery or long before delivery.[246]

The balance of bargaining power at the time favouring buyers, LCTA was able to give the complaint short shrift: it replied that the contract was drawn

---

[243] W. Bates, *American Marine. The Shipping Questions in History and Politics*, Boston, Houghton Mifflin, 1892, 162, quoting a letter from the Californian Institute of Bankers to the *Bankers Magazine*. London, 12 March 1891.

[244] 386 below.

[245] Exporters wanting early payment could 'sell' the bill of exchange but at a discount because the buyer would only be paid on maturity of the bill and was assuming the risk of non-payment. See 388–390 below.

[246] LMA, CLC/B/103/MS23172/004, Letter, 20 February 1908.

providing a double option to sellers, for payment either by cash less discount on or before arrival of the ship, or by a buyer's acceptance of a seller's draft at 60 days.[247] The powerful New York Produce Exchange returned to the issue in more emphatic terms some four and a half years later with a 'unanimous opinion' of grain exporter members that LCTA American contracts must be amended to read 'payment by cash in exchange for shipping documents'. LCTA batted this away with a polite reply that, having carefully considered the matter, they could not see their way to make the alteration.[248]

In early 1913 there was intensified pressure from the newly formed North American Grain Export Association. Cables were exchanged across the Atlantic and a special conference was held in April with other grain associations in Britain. In May 1913 LCTA attempted to persuade British firms not to buy American grain except on the compromise terms which by this time it was offering the North American Grain Export Association.[249] The matter became serious enough that there was a visit by an American delegation. In the result LCTA amended its North American contracts to reduce the sixty-day period for payment on any bill of exchange to seven days for shipments from north-eastern and comparable ports, and a longer period for other American ports.[250]

Half a century later American grain exporters had the upper hand. The realignment of power was evident in a dispute about the extension of shipment clause in North American LCTA contracts in the early 1950s. That clause enabled sellers to claim up to an additional eight days within which bills of lading needed to be dated, in other words, another eight days to ship a consignment, provided they gave the requisite notice to the buyer. Under the clause sellers had to make an allowance to the buyer, to be deducted from the contract price, and based on the number of additional days. It was the amount of the allowance which gave rise to the disagreement. In 1950 American exporters represented by the North American Export Grain Association called for a reduction in the allowances payable. They justified this in terms of the high price and narrow margins then payable on grain.[251] They were able to invoke the support of the Hamburg grain traders' association for a reduction.[252]

Initially LCTA refused to budge, so the American association advised its exporters to insert a new extension of shipment clause in all offers of CIF and C&F grain.[253] If the Europeans wanted American grain, they would have to accept this new clause in the standard contract. In response LCTA decided to omit any form of extension of shipment clause from its contracts. But LCTA

---

[247] LMA, CLC/B/103/MS23172/004, Executive Committee, Minutes, 17 March 1908.
[248] LMA, CLC/B/103/MS23172/005, Executive Committee, Minutes, 26 November 1912.
[249] LMA, CLC/B/103/MS23174/004, Minutes of sub-committees, 21 April, 22 April, 2 May 1913.
[250] LMA, CLC/B/103/MS23172/005, Annual Report 1913–1914.
[251] LMA, CLC/B/103/MS23174/011, Standing Contracts Committee, Minutes, 20 July 1950; CLC/B/103/MS23172/011, Executive Committee, Minutes, 137, 11 July 1951.
[252] LMA, CLC/B/103/MS23172/011, 101–102.   [253] Ibid., 142. 152.

could not maintain this line. In an era of post-war reconstruction Europe needed American grain, and continental importers were soon accepting the American clause.[254] LCTA's position was further undermined as the war-time and post-war controls on private grain trading were removed.[255] Over two years after the dispute began, a compromise was reached: the LCTA extension of shipment clause would be amended to reduce the allowances for buyers when grain was shipped late, but not as low as the American association originally proposed.[256]

As well as simple economic strength – the American example – interests could threaten to take their business elsewhere, in other words, could threaten to contract on other standard forms. This occurred before the First World War as Russian exporters sought to use the rival German contract for Russian and Danube grain sales as a bargaining chip with LCTA. At the first formal conference in London between Russian and British grain interests in 1910, the Russians pointed out that they had been meeting with German grain importers over the previous six years. They then identified the advantages for them of the German contract over the LCTA equivalent. For example, the strike clause in the German contract gave sellers up to 21 additional days after the termination of the strike, lock-out or riot to effect shipment when the disruption occurred at the end of the contract period.[257] LCTA refused to bring their contract into line. The argument about maintaining uniformity between the Russian and other LCTA contracts – the Plate (Argentinean) contracts were cited – was unlikely to carry much weight with the Russians: after all, there were always some differences between contracts covering shipments from different jurisdictions. Perhaps more persuasive was the advantage of the LCTA strike clause in relation to coverage, for it included not only the prevention of shipment through strikes at the port, but elsewhere, such as on the railway to the port. 'You must take the good with the bad', the Russian delegates were told.[258] In the event, the matter was unresolved before the First World War, and the war and its aftermath adversely affected both Russian grain exports and the German contract.

4 The Role of Lawyers: On Tap, Not on Top

Where were the lawyers as the trade associations reacted to the events and pressures affecting their standard contract provisions? Drafting the associations' contracts was a practical exercise, undertaken in the main by association members themselves. They knew the trade, the purpose behind a clause and the result they wanted to achieve. Lawyers were involved, but generally reserved for tricky issues and those with an obvious legal connotation such as

---

[254] Ibid., 165.   [255] Ibid., 198(2).   [256] Ibid., 202.
[257] LMA, CLC/B/103/MS23172/004, LCTA, 'Conference between Russian Delegates and British Delegates. Held at the Offices of the London Corn Trade Association, 15–17 February 1910'.
[258] Ibid., 10.

the arbitration clauses in the contracts. Each association appointed solicitors, an outside law firm. Occasionally counsel would be briefed to give advice on particularly difficult matters. For example, E. W. Roskill QC, a leading commercial lawyer and later a law lord, redrafted LCTA's appropriation clause in the 1950s.[259]

When lawyers were called upon, this was mainly to assist with the interpretation and drafting of specific contractual terms. If questions were posed these were sometimes basic. In 1908, LCTA's solicitor was asked by the sub-committee charged with revising all contract forms whether there was an advantage for parties to sign on the back instead of, as customary, on the front. It will be recalled that the format of the contracts was that terms were set out on the face but further terms, described as conditions and rules, were on the back. The face of the LCTA contracts began 'bought of/sold to' – enabling the parties to insert the names, 'on the printed conditions and rules endorsed on this contract'. So it is not surprising that when the question of signing on the back was raised, given this explicit cross-reference, the association's solicitor gave the monosyllabic response, 'No'.[260]

Legal opinion was sometimes a surprise to trade association members. The advice to LCTA in April 1912 of Leslie Scott KC (later Solicitor-General and judge of the Court of Appeal), that 'strikes, riots and civil commotions' were not covered by the ordinary Lloyd's insurance policy called for by its contracts, was quite unexpected.[261] For the time being LCTA decided that if buyers wanted insurance to cover these risks, they should pay an additional premium. Ultimately the contracts were amended to oblige sellers to supply insurance policies which included LCTA's strike risk clauses.

The contractual provisions relating to strikes and similar disruptions also illustrate another point about legal advice: the trade associations might not accept it. Under the typical strike clause, as we have seen, sellers had a right to claim an extension of time for shipment. To claim that right, they had to give notice to the buyers. Against legal advice, LCTA's executive committee accepted that such notice could be given up to two days after the last guaranteed time of shipment in relation to Plate (Argentinean) contracts – a period which subsequently became standard in strike clauses in other LCTA contracts.[262] Another example was that in 1921 LCTA's North American Contracts Committee endorsed a new payment clause, drawn up by one of its members in conjunction with the association's solicitor, to cover the eventuality of the vessel arriving before the shipping documents. However,

---

[259] e.g., LMA, CLC/B/103/MS23174/011, LCTA, 20 July 1955. On Roskill's background in commercial law, Lord Templeman, 'Roskill, Eustace Wentworth, Baron Roskill (1911–1996)', *Oxford Dictionary of National Biography*.

[260] LMA, CLC/B/103/MS23174/002, 23 March 1908.

[261] LMA, CLC/B/103/MS23172/005, LCTA, 23 April 1912 (Executive Committee); 21 May 1912 (Annual Report).

[262] See the contracts in A. Hooker, *The International Grain Trade*, 2nd ed., London, Pitman, 1939.

the proposal was rejected by LCTA's executive committee in favour of its own draft for the clause.[263] Sometimes the problem was that the lawyers did not understand the practical implications of a contract term. For example, in 1956 LCTA's solicitor had to redraft an amendment to the default clause when it was pointed out that it was likely to lead to disputes in the event of there being no market in the grain covered by the contract.[264]

Although the drafts proffered by LCTA's solicitors for contractual terms might be rejected, at least initially, on the whole the two sides engaged in a constructive dialogue. It was a world of practical men, knowing what they wanted in their standard form contracts, and generally confident they were able to express this, but increasingly aware, as clauses became more complicated and the case-law built up, that legal advice needed to be taken to get things right. In the early years of LCTA legal advice seems to have been sought mainly about the arbitration clause. By 1908, however, when the LCTA Sub-Committee Re Revision of Contracts engaged in a major exercise of updating all standard form contracts, the association's lawyer helped with the drafting of the *pro rata* and appropriation clauses as well.[265] Four years later, as we have seen, lawyers were being consulted about the implications of a war risks clause. The range of advice increased in the interwar years, to include strike clauses, circle clauses and bill of lading issues.[266] Matters were no longer confined to England, if they ever had been. There are records in the 1920s of the solicitor to the London Copra Association preparing an affidavit on the meaning of the word 'afloat' in its contracts for a firm in Marseilles, and of obtaining advice from a Rotterdam firm on a point of Dutch law.[267]

An example of how lawyers could prove their worth arose in 1929, when LCTA's Contracts Committee was considering redrafting its tender of policies clause for CIF contracts. Despite earlier thoughts, it decided that nothing needed to be done with the clause after the association's solicitor drew its attention to a recent court decision which confirmed that the existing provisions were sound.[268] Similarly, in 1922 an issue arose with the circle clause of the London Copra Association. Circle clauses addressed the situation where because cargoes might be traded several times before arrival at their destination, a string of sales could end up with a seller later appearing as the buyer of the same goods. Once the contracts in a string were tied together by notices of appropriation, the same party appeared more than once. Circle clauses

---

[263] LMA, CLC/B/103/MS 23174/006, 3, 15, 23 February 1921.
[264] LMA, CLC/B/103/MS 23172/0011, 394(2), CLC/B/103/MS23172/012, 5.
[265] LMA, CLC/B/103/MS 23174/002, 28 February, 18, 23 March, 7, 14 April, 25 November, 10, 15, 31 December 1908.
[266] e.g., LMA, CLC/B/103/MS23174/006, 29 September, 11 October 1921; CLC/B/103/MS23174/008, 6 December 1929, 26 February 1931.
[267] LMA, CLC/B/103/MS23224/003, 4, 18 January 1922, 39, 49, 53; CLC/B/103/MS23224/005, 5 October 1931.
[268] LMA, CLC/B/103/MS23174/007, 14 March 1929. The case was *Loders & Nucoline Ltd* v. *Bank of New Zealand* (1929) 33 Ll L Rep 70.

provided for the payment of financial differences between buyers and sellers in the circle formed by the string of contracts returning to the party who appeared twice. Goods, or documents representing the goods, did not need to pass between those in the circle.[269] For many years discussions in LCTA about having a circle clause in their contracts got nowhere.[270]

The London Copra Association had adopted a circle clause relatively early in its history.[271] When the copra contracts were being revised in the early 1920s, the general committee suggested a revised version of the circle clause as follows: 'If the goods are not declared the accounts shall be settled between each buyer and each seller in a Circle by a payment ... by the buyer to his seller of the excess of the Seller's invoice amount over the lowest invoice amount in the circle and no buyer should be entitled to call for documents.' The association's solicitors were consulted, just as they had been on the original drafting. They gave the sensible advice that the opening part of the clause should be amended to read 'If the goods are not declared, *or having been declared are not delivered*'.[272]

5.6 The Legal Framework: Contract-Making and the Courts

> From this organisation into trade associations resulted (a) Standard contracts (b) Conditions (c) Arbitration, each of which has had a very strong effect on the law of contract as well as on the judicature ... Of the freedom of contract parties make a continuous and ample use ... [T]he institution of arbitration has not only succeeded in gaining a place by the side of the official judicature, it even has repelled it from the field of commercial case. (Dr H. Craandyk, International Law Association, *Annual Meeting*, The Hague, 1921)[273]

The legal framework for the London and Liverpool trade associations in drawing their standard form contracts was English law. In the nineteenth century it was simply assumed that it applied and there was no close analysis of the issue. Later, the contracts provided that arbitration would be in London. By the beginning of the twentieth century the LCTA contracts stated that they were deemed to be made in England and performed there; the courts of England or arbitrators appointed in England had exclusive jurisdiction over all disputes which might arise under the contract (except for enforcement); and such disputes were to be settled according to English law. Drafting the contracts was a practical exercise and law was not in the forefront.

---

[269] For a modern discussion: M. Bridge, *International Sale of Goods*, 4th ed., Oxford, Oxford University Press, 2017, 541–542.
[270] e.g., LMA, CLC/B/103/MS23174/008, 26 February 1931.
[271] See discussion of draft rule 17: LMA, CLC/B/103/MS23224/001, 17 March, 31 March 1914, 47, 51, 106–109.
[272] LMA, CLC/B/103/MS23224/002, 27 July 1922, 123. See also 132–137.
[273] H. Craandyk, 'International Rules Relating to the Sale of Goods', *op cit*, 447–448, 451.

1 Fitting Standard Contracts with the Law

In his 1921 paper Dr Craandyk, the Dutch lawyer, pointed out that the upshot of the detailed contractual provisions and the arbitration of disputes under them resulted in 'a very strong effect on the law of contract as on the judicature'.[274] As to the standard form contracts used in the commodity markets, these were drawn against a backdrop of English common and statutory law. The law did not impose much in the way of obstacles for trade associations as they undertook the task. English common law was generally facilitative of commercial transactions and the courts were reluctant to upset what was decided for a market by the association of merchants dealing there. Freedom of contract meant that in drawing up their standard form contracts the trade associations had a largely unencumbered hand. They could create their own system of rights and liabilities to accommodate the way transactions were to be effected.

Take an example. Early on, CIF sales of commodities could take place in general terms and down a chain of buyers and sellers as parties hedged and speculated. Standard form contracts adapted to these arrangements (and variations of them) by introducing the notion of 'appropriation' (or 'declaration').[275] At some point the seller would be obliged to earmark the goods to fulfil its obligations under a particular contract. This would be done by serving a notice on the buyer naming the ship, the date of the relevant bill of lading and the quantity of the commodity shipped. Failure to do so would constitute default on the part of the seller and sellers down the line.[276] Contracts were connected together in a string as notices were given for the different buy and sell transactions along its length, which until then the only thing they had in common was that they were for the same type of commodity to be shipped from the same port or range of ports in the same shipment period. Provided the notice concerned goods which conformed to the contract, it was understood that it could not then be withdrawn. The seller was bound to deliver those goods (or the related shipping documents) and not sell to anyone else. In 1873, the Liverpool Cotton Brokers' Association sought the opinion of Judah Benjamin QC as to whether a seller could make an in-time second declaration when the buyer had objected to the first because (as the seller accepted in that case) it was not compliant with the contract.

---

[274] Ibid., 447.
[275] Distinct from appropriation in sales law, where by an act of unconditional appropriation 'property' (and thus risk) passed in unascertained goods (e.g., commodities in bulk) or future goods (a commodity not yet acquired): *T.D. Bailey, Son & Co* v. *Ross T Smyth & Co Ltd* [1940] 3 All ER 60, 65–66; (1940) 67 Ll L Rep 147, 154–156. For a modern treatment: M. Bridge, *Sale of Goods*, 4th ed., Oxford, Oxford University Press, 2019, 133–135.
[276] LCTA American Grain Contract, Cargoes, No.12, 1896 in *Forms of Contract in Force*, London, LCTA, 1896. In 1896 appropriation clauses were not yet introduced into most LCTA standard forms.

Benjamin's short opinion in the affirmative was printed and made available to the association's members.[277]

Not only could those drafting an association's standard form contracts establish procedures not recognised in the common law of sale. They also had great leeway in modifying the common law rules if these did not fit the desired way of doing things. The same applied with statute, since in the commercial context Parliament rarely imposed mandatory rules which could not be avoided. As we have seen in Chapter 4 (part 4.2), when the common law of sale was codified in the Sale of Goods Act 1893 freedom of contract was explicitly recognised in section 55. That enabled any right, duty or liability which would arise under a contract of sale by implication of law to be negatived or varied by express agreement. As for foreign legislation, because the trade associations' contracts provided for London (or Liverpool) arbitration and English law as the proper law and England as the place of performance, this could generally be ignored or dealt with by way of a contractual term. Thus in LCTA's contracts the United States Harter Act and the carriage of goods by sea legislation of other jurisdictions were accommodated by specific clauses.

2 Moulding the Law to Commercial Need: Quality, Rejection and Default

There were several areas where trade associations in the commodity markets took advantage of this freedom to modify or reject the common law and statutory rules in drawing up their standard form contracts. Three areas bear closer examination: first, the terms the law implied in sales contracts regarding the quality of goods; secondly, the right of buyers to reject goods which did not match their description, or were not merchantable or fit for the purpose; and thirdly, the remedies the law made available to buyers on default by a seller in fulfilling its contractual obligations.

From early in the nineteenth century the English courts implied a term of merchantability in sales contracts when there was no opportunity to inspect a commodity beforehand.[278] From the outset, however, the standard form contracts of the trade associations in the commodity markets rendered much of this law irrelevant by defining the quality standard (e.g., fair average quality of the season's shipment at the time and place of shipment)[279] and setting out a mechanism for evaluating whether it had been met (e.g., comparison with samples kept by the relevant trade association; an official certificate of inspection as to quality was final as regards North American grain).

Moreover, the standard form contracts might exclude merchantability expressly. After the enactment of the Sale of Goods Act 1893 this was a standard practice in LCTA contracts, which took advantage of the power

---

[277] LRO, Liverpool Cotton Brokers' Association Ltd, 380 COT /1/5/1, 5 April 1873. The opinion was sought after *Tetley* v. *Shand* (1873) 10 WR 206, 207.
[278] *Gardiner* v. *Gray* (1815) 4 Camp 144, 171 ER 46. See 212–213 above.
[279] LCTA, *American Grain Contract No.1*, 1879.

conferred in section 55 of the Act to do this. To quote a heavily used standard term of the time: 'The grain is not warranted free from defect, rendering the same unmerchantable, which would not be apparent on reasonable examination, any statute or rule of law to the contrary notwithstanding.'[280] The rationale of this type of clause was recognised by Sellers J in a case concerned with the sale of rubber: sellers should be liable only for defects which could be detected by visual inspection, the normal practice for examining goods for quality in the commodities markets.[281] The application of this type of provision arose in a dispute between American sellers and German buyers over a consignment of barley sold CIF Bremen, on Contract No. 30 of the LCTA, when it was discovered that the barley was affected by a fungus. The buyers refused to accept delivery. Dutch buyers, who then bought the barley under the same description at the ruling market price, raised no objection. Wright J upheld the finding of the arbitrators that the barley was merchantable and added, against the background of the standard term quoted: 'In any case, their finding that the defects were not discoverable on reasonable examination is enough to support their award.'[282]

The implied terms as to quality in the Sale of Goods Act 1893 could be excluded by contract, so long as the intention to do that was clear.[283] In line with the notion of freedom of contract, there were no compulsory implied terms in ordinary sales. However, section 2(2) of the Fertilisers and Feeding Stuffs Act 1926 took a different tack. It required that when certain specified commodities were sold for use as food for cattle or poultry, there was an implied warranty, notwithstanding any contract or notice to the contrary, that they were suitable to be used as such, and did not contain specified ingredients. Inconsistently with this, standard form No 6 of the London Cattle Food Trade Association (LCFTA) stated that the products were not warranted free from latent defect, but were warranted to be free from castor seed and husk. In *C. E. B. Draper & Son Ltd v. Edward Turner & Son Ltd*[284] the Court of Appeal held that section 2(2) did not apply: the sale had taken place abroad, since the seller had transferred the bills of lading to the buyer with the intention of passing the property in the goods before the ship reached Britain.[285]

Another area where the common law was modified by standard form contracts in the commodities markets concerned the remedy of rejection. At common law, codified in the Sale of Goods Act 1893, falling short in relation to

---

[280] e.g., LCTA, *American Grain Contract, Cargoes, No.12*, 1896.
[281] *Steels & Busks Ltd v. Bleeker Bik & Co Ltd* [1956] 1 Lloyd's Rep 228, applying *F E Hookway & Co Ltd v. Alfred Isaacs & Sons* [1954] 1 Lloyd's Rep 491, a sale of shellac. Sometimes this was known as 'look-sniff' inspection.
[282] *Canada Atlantic Grain Export Company (Inc) v. Eilers* (1929) 35 Ll L Rep 206.
[283] 217–218 above.   [284] [1965] 1 QB 424 (Lord Denning MR, Danckwerts and Diplock LJJ).
[285] The court relied on (1) the common-law presumption that legislation does not apply outside the UK; (2) s. 2(2) applied to sales, not contracts for sale. Finding (2) was overruled in *Henry Kendall & Sons v. William Lillico & Sons Ltd* [1969] 2 AC 31 (s. 2(2) applied since CIF shipping documents transferred in UK i.e., UK place of sale where title transferred).

quality standards could mean that sellers faced having the contract terminated and their goods rejected.[286] With international sales this could lead to difficulties. Foreign sellers would have to dispose of rejected goods in a distant market. Unless they had a branch or trusted agent at the port of destination, they might not obtain the market price to cover their losses. Moreover, as Scrutton LJ recognised, they might also be vulnerable to an unscrupulous buyer who rejected goods unreasonably to extort a reduction in price.[287] Consequently, standard form contracts for commodities typically ruled out rejection and obliged buyers to pay against documents, confining their remedy to financial compensation such as an allowance on price for shortcomings in quality.

However, the courts could read non-rejection clauses to keep them in bounds. The non-rejection clause in *J Aron & Co v. Comptoir Wegimont Societe Anonyme*[288] was wide, 'whatever the difference of the shipment may be in value from the grade, type or description'. The case involved a sale in London of cocoa powder CIF Antwerp from United States ports during October. McCardie J held that the buyers were entitled to reject the documents because, although the goods were at the docks in New York on 8 October, they were not shipped during October because of a strike. Reading the clause *contra proferentum* and invoking a US Supreme Court judgment,[289] McCardie J reasoned that the non-rejection clause did not apply because it did not extend to shipment at a particular time, which was more a condition precedent to liability than a description.

By 1896 all forty-eight LCTA standard form contracts provided, with slight variations in wording: 'Difference in quality should not entitle the Buyer to reject, except under the award of arbitrators or the Committee of Appeal, as the case may be.'[290] That modest phraseology, not extending to the failure of the goods to match their description, was maintained well into the twentieth century, although with some embellishment. For example under the 1938 Contract No. 28 for American wheat, the buyer was also deprived of the right to reject a tender of a higher grade of the same colour and description.[291] Unlike non-rejection clauses in some other commodity trades, the LCTA standard clause gave a discretion to arbitrators to permit rejection in specific contexts.

In 1930 one of the LCTA's most eminent members, Sir Herbert Robson,[292] raised his concern that buyers were acting opportunistically and rejecting grain

---

[286] 215 above. [287] *Szymanowski & Co v. Beck & Co* [1923] 1 KB 457, 467.
[288] [1921] 3 KB 435. It was a special case from an arbitration; the terms were likely from the General Produce Brokers' Association of London: Department of Commerce, Bureau of Foreign and Domestic Commerce, Market Methods and Trade Usages in London, *op cit*, 8.
[289] *Norrington v. Wright*, 115 US 188, 203 (1885).
[290] London Corn Trade Association, *Forms of Contract in Force*, London, LCTA, 1896. The only exception seems to have been the *East India Wheat Contract, Steamer Cargo, London Terms No.2*.
[291] e.g., LCTA *Canadian and United States of America Wheat Contract Parcels, tale quale*, No.28, 1938.
[292] Robson was director of Ross T Smyth & Co. and, inter alia, chair of the Baltic Exchange: H. Barty-King, The Baltic Exchange, *op cit*, 358.

owing to some small technical breach of the contract, which did not involve any, or only a small, breach.[293] He proposed that a clause be inserted in all grain contracts stipulating that buyers were not entitled to do this unless the goods shipped were of a distinctly different description, or unless there was *mala fides*. The association's Contract Committee decided against the idea.[294] Perhaps they anticipated unnecessary disputes in the interpretation of the proposed clause. Perhaps since arbitrations were conducted by members of the association they thought abuse could be limited. And perhaps they recognised the rash of claims as a product of the economic downturn and sympathised with the plight of buyers trying to avoid deals, at least without a reduction in price.

Default was a third area where standard form contracts in the commodities markets modified the common law. Default clauses applied where the seller refused or was unable to tender goods, or where the buyer refused or was unable to pay for the goods or the documents when payment was due. Default clauses might entitle the non-defaulting party to resell or repurchase as against the defaulter on giving notice that it was doing so. As Roche J put it in one case, 're-sale' and 'repurchase' might be an inelegant use of words in this context: the non-defaulting party had a right to buy and sell elsewhere in the market but the clause did not give a buyer, say, the right to re-sell or invoice back to their sellers.[295] Any loss on resale or repurchase was to be paid for by the defaulter. In this respect default clauses broadly tracked the common law. In explaining this to LCTA in 1920, the association's solicitor also opined that the wording recognised the common-law rule of anticipatory breach: when a party repudiated a contract and showed it did not intend to fulfil its side of the bargain, the other party might either immediately treat the other party as in default and claim damages with no further obligation to perform or, if more advantageous because of market conditions, wait until the time for performance and then claim damages.[296]

With time, default clauses moved away from the common law in various ways. First, some explicitly limited the non-defaulting buyer's right to claim in respect of a loss of profit on any sub-sales. Secondly, some default clauses provided for an invoicing back on default rather than for a resale or repurchase in the market. In a case involving the grain trade, the wording of the invoicing-back clause produced the result that a balance was due in favour of defaulting sellers. This followed because the price set in the contract at which invoicing back was to occur was, through a rapid fall in the market price, lower than the

---

[293] Judicial consideration of non-rejection clauses in international trade includes: *Meyer Ltd* v. *Osakeyhtio Carelia Timber Co Ltd* (1930) 37 Ll L Rep 212, 213; *Vigers Bros* v. *Sanderson Bros* [1901] 1 QB 608; *Robert A. Munro & Co.* v. *Meyer* [1930] 2 KB 312 (sale of cattle feed by London sellers CIF Hamburg); *White Sea Timber Ltd* v. *W W North Ltd.* (1932) 49 TLR 142.
[294] LMA, CLC/B/103/MS24174/008, Minutes, 2 January 1930.
[295] *Sven Hylander & Co* v. *Blake Dobbs & Co* (1925) 22 Ll L Rep 528 (sale of wheat on LCTA terms to Gothenburg firm).
[296] LMA, CLC/B/103/MS23174/004, Letter from Mr Tilleard, solicitor, 13 September 1910.

contract price.[297] The Court of Appeal rejected the argument that it was unreasonable to suppose buyers intended to pay for what was never received. Even if the court regarded the rule as unreasonable in a falling market the court could not relieve parties from obligations they had undertaken.[298] The same result was upheld in a sale of rubber on a standard contract of the General Produce Brokers' Association, the Lord Chief Justice adding that the clause had been 'acted upon for years between parties who thoroughly understood their business, and we are bound to apply it'.[299]

Thirdly, default was given an extended meaning in the clauses to include not just insolvency but suspending payment, committing an act of bankruptcy or acting in a way indicating insolvency. In these cases some contracts were closed out automatically at a price to be determined in accordance with its terms (e.g., the market price on the relevant day), while others gave the non-defaulting party the option to act on notifying the defaulter.[300] By the 1930s LCTA's Contracts No. 28 and 36 for North American wheat sales were of the latter type, giving the non-defaulting party a discretion in the case of a bankruptcy or insolvency. Under them, if exercised the option conferred to close out the contract, the terms of the default clause would entitle it to prove in the bankruptcy for any loss but could also mean it had to account for any profit occasioned if it had repurchased or resold.

In *Shipton, Anderson & Co (1927) Ltd (In liquidation) v. Micks, Lambert & Co*[301] the first sellers sold wheat to the now insolvent claimant, which in turn sold it to the respondents. All sales were on a similar LCTA standard contract. The respondents had in turn sold the wheat to other purchasers. Consequently, on the insolvency of their suppliers they (the respondents) purchased wheat of the contract description from the first sellers to meet their commitments. The respondents made a profit on the transaction and the liquidators of the insolvent claimant claimed it under the default clause. Branson J had no difficulty in denying the liquidators' claim since the respondents had been careful not to exercise their option to close out under the default clause. Instead, the parties were left with their common-law position. Under that, if with an anticipatory breach a party went into the market, made substitute purchases to fulfil its own commitments and ultimately made a profit, there was no obligation to account at common law to the liquidator. A specially constituted Default Clause Sub-Committee of the LCTA was appointed to consider the *Shipton, Anderson & Co* case. Unsurprisingly it concluded that since the judgment had made the position clear regarding the rights of the parties, no alteration to the clause was necessary.[302]

---

[297] *Lancaster v. J.F. Turner & Co Ltd* [1924] 2 KB 222 (sale on LCTA form for Chinese and Manchurian Cereals of 50 tons of Japanese green peas. Scrutton LJ dissented).
[298] at 230, per Bankes LJ.   [299] *Lang v. Crude Rubber Washing Co Ltd* [1939] 2 KB 173, 176.
[300] e.g., *Simmonds v. Millar & Co* (1898) 4 Com Cas 64 (one of LCTA's American grain contracts; right to repurchase).
[301] (1936) 55 Ll L Rep 384.   [302] LMA, CLC/B/103/MS 23274/010, 8 October 1936.

Generally speaking, then, the common law was facilitative and permissive in enabling trade associations to structure commodities transactions in the way they wished and to draft the standard forms they wanted. That did not mean that the courts were always approving. In *Bourgeois* v. *Wilson Holgate & Co Ltd*[303] Scrutton LJ said that a provision applying under contracts of the General Produce Broker' Association, which set a price for invoicing back on the seller's default, should be redrafted so that the courts would not be troubled again. He attributed the problem to what, he said, had long been known at the commercial bar and in courts with commercial work, namely that many in commerce expressed their contracts in language and ideas 'different from those of the Common Law of the country in which they live'.[304]

3 Delivery Orders: The Law Stands Firm

In exceptional cases the courts refused to countenance commercial practice. A striking example concerned delivery orders.[305] Here commercial practice was evident. Ships might arrive with a commodity before the bill of lading representing the goods. There was also the problem with a bulk cargo, where there was only one bill of lading, but which was sold on to several buyers. Once the cargo was divided the different buyers could not present a bill of lading to claim the portion of the cargo they had bought.[306] Moreover, goods might be stored in a warehouse on arrival or in anticipation of shipment, and there was no extant bill of lading covering the goods. To address the problem merchants early on used delivery orders. The owner of the cargo would give an order to the ship or its agent at the port of destination to deliver a commodity to a consignee, notwithstanding that the consignee did not have the bill of lading. Delivery orders could pass hand to hand as the goods were dealt with on the market. The difficulty was that the common law did not recognise the delivery order as a document of title, so its transfer could not transfer ownership rights to the commodity.[307] What the common law required was that the person in lawful possession of the commodity – such as the ship, its agent or a wharfinger – had

---

[303] (1920) 25 Comm Cas 260, (1920) 4 Ll L Rep 1 (sale of 3 ½ tons of Ceylonese essence of citronella CIF Marseilles).
[304] at 266–267. Despite Scrutton LJ's stricture the provision returned to the courts: see *JF Adair & Co Ltd (in Liquidation)* v. *Birnbaum* [1939] 2 KB 149, 161–162 (sale of 610 tons of Lampong black pepper for future delivery).
[305] The meaning of 'delivery order' depends on the context: see S. Thomas, 'Transfers of Documents of Title under English law and the Uniform Commercial Code' [2012] LMCLQ 573, 579n. Dock warrants were similar instruments, but with a different history: 399 below.
[306] At common law the bill of lading was a document of title, *Lickbarrow* v. *Mason* (1794) 5 TR 683, 101 ER 380. See L. Friedmann, 'Formative Elements in the Law of Sales: The Eighteenth Century' (1960) 44 *Minn LR* 411, 434–435; R. Aikens, M. Bools & R. Lord, *Bills of Lading*, London, Informa, 2006, Ch. 1.
[307] The Factors Acts 1889, s.1(4), made delivery orders documents of title (as did the Sale of Goods Act 1893, s. 62(1)) for the limited purpose of the nemo dat rule. See 150 above.

to 'attorn' to the buyer, in other words (as the Sale of Goods Act 1893 put it[308]) acknowledge to the buyer that he held the goods on his behalf.[309]

Despite the legal position, buyers paying against delivery orders might not in the ordinary run of cases experience any problem because the ship, the owner's agent or the warehouse would hand over the goods on presentation of the order. However, the unexpected case showed that reliance on delivery orders could expose a party to risks such as insolvency. *McEwan v. Smith*[310] was an illustration. There a vendor sold sugar in a warehouse in Greenock to a buyer, who in turn sold it on to a sub-buyer. When there were rumours about the buyer's solvency, the sub-buyer sought to take the sugar by presenting a delivery order the buyer had given him. However, the seller had already taken the sugar away. On appeal from the Court of Session in Edinburgh, the House of Lords held that even though the seller had handed over the delivery order, he was not deprived of his lien over the sugar for the price, since it was still in the warehouse and nothing further had been done – there had been no attornment.

Another illustration – this time in relation to a standard form contract issued by the Rubber Trade Association of London – is provided by *Heilbert, Symons & Co. Ltd. v. Harvey, Christie-Miller & Co.*[311] It involved a sale of faq sheet balata CIF London, where the buyers insisted on a bill of lading although the sellers contended that tender of a delivery order (called a 'ship's release') was sufficient. The terms of the Rubber Trade Association contemplated the splitting of parcels. The sellers also had evidence of what they said was a custom among rubber and balata brokers that when a cargo covered by one bill of lading was split, a delivery order would be given, safeguarded by a bank guarantee protecting the buyer against the consequences. Bailhache J held that even if this was good practice, the tender was inadequate because there was no bank guarantee. He went on to identify, *obiter*, the 'serious difficulty in law' in holding that the two documents – delivery order plus bank guarantee – could be good tender when, under the ordinary CIF contract, the purchaser was entitled to a bill of lading giving it a direct action against the shipowner or carrier.

Over a long period the issue of delivery orders vis-à-vis bills of lading stumped the LCTA's legal advisers. In 1907 a sub-committee was appointed 'regarding the reliability of a delivery order'. It decided not to re-open the 'Scotch case' – no doubt *McEwan v. Smith* – but to take counsel's opinion on delivery orders issued against a granary or a vessel.[312] That was obtained and was presumably unfavourable for nothing was done to LCTA's contracts.[313]

---

[308] s. 29(3).
[309] *Farina v. Home* (1846) 16 M & W 119, 153 ER 1124; *Dublin City Distillery (Great Brunswick Street, Dublin) Ltd v. Doherty* [1914] AC 823.
[310] (1849) 2 HLC 309, 9 ER 1109. [311] (1922) 12 Ll L Rep 455.
[312] LMA, CLC/B/103/MS23174/002, 30 July 1907.
[313] LMA, CLC/B/103/MS23172/004, 17 December 1907.

Delivery orders continued to be used, and two years later the association received a strong letter from the shipowners' interest protesting at the 'desire to set up a custom binding upon the shipowner to deliver against sub-delivery orders'. Shipowners, it said, were under no obligation to do this and could only be called on to deliver in parcels representing the total quantity of each bill of lading. If they did make the grain available against sub-delivery orders, they should state it was only 'as an act of grace under no obligation' and refuse to deliver parcels of less than 20 tons.[314]

Counsel was involved again two decades later over what the specially constituted LCTA Shipping Documents Delivery Orders sub-committee described as the 'vexed question' of delivery orders.[315] At the annual general meeting later that year the LCTA president held out some hope of progress, but he reported that it was futile to insert a clause in a contract relating to the matter which conflicted with the law of the land. So far it had not been possible to devise one which did, but the hope was for a clause which, although not giving a complete safeguard, might justify the authorities 'in refusing to override the intentions of the contracting parties solely because of the existing law'.[316] Subsequently, the association decided to issue a clause on adhesive slips to be attached to its contracts – 'Sellers have the option of tendering Delivery Orders . . . in which case Buyers have the option of payment on arrival of vessel' – until it was discovered that the clause might be subject to stamp duty.[317] The payment clause of LCTA forms continued to fudge the issue: the seller was obliged to 'provide documents entitling Buyer to obtain delivery of the grain' while for the buyer 'payment must be made in exchange for same'.

For bulk commodities some grain merchants would have a number of bills of lading, each covering a specific part of the cargo,[318] although this could only work if at the time of shipment, when the bills of lading were issued, it could be anticipated what size of lots buyers would want. As for the delivery order, the common law never recognised it as a document of title in the absence of custom and usage to that effect.[319] There was nothing the associations through contractual terms could do to change this.

4 Role of the Courts: Interpreting the Standard Form Contracts

Issues on the interpretation of standard form contracts of the commodity markets arrived in the courts mainly from arbitrators. As with interpreting

---

[314] Letter from UK Mutual Steam Ship Assurance Association Ltd., LMA, CLC/B/103/MS23174/003, 19 January 1911.
[315] LMA, CLC/B/103/MS23174/007, 24 February 1927.
[316] LMA, CLC/B/103/MS23172/008, 214.   [317] LMA, CLC/B/103/MS23172/008, 232, 235, 238.
[318] e.g., *T D Bailey, Son & Co* v. *Ross T Smyth & Co Ltd* (1940) 67 Ll L Rep147.
[319] *Merchant Banking Co of London* v. *Phoenix Bessemer Steel Co* (1877) 5 Ch D 205 was a case in the steel trade where such a custom was recognised. See also *Moore* v. *Campbell* (1854) 10 Ex 323, 156 ER 467; *Dublin City Distillery (Great Brunswick Street Dublin) Ltd* v. *Doherty* [1914] AC 823, 865.

contracts generally, for the English courts this was largely a matter of giving effect to their 'plain words'. Or at least that was the theory. That approach meant giving effect to the 'ordinary and grammatical meaning' of the words, their 'natural meaning', their 'plain natural sense and meaning', or their 'reasonable and literal sense'.

All these phrases appeared in the leading House of Lords decision of *Bowes* v. *Shand*.[320] As we have seen, the case concerned contracts made in London for the sale of 600 tons of Madras rice, to be shipped at Madras (Chennai), or coast, during the months of March and/or April 1874, *per Rajah of Cochin*. Almost all the rice was put on board during February and three bills of lading were issued for it, although the fourth bill of lading for the small quantity of rice remaining to be shipped was dated 3 March. At trial the evidence of the chairman of the Rice Brokers' Association was that March and/or April 1874 meant precisely that. The House of Lords agreed, holding that the buyer (colonial brokers in London) was entitled to reject the rice because it had not been shipped in March/April, the time of shipment being part of the description of the goods.[321] Overturning a unanimous and strong Court of Appeal – which did not seem to give their Lordships much pause as to how plain was the 'plain and ordinary meaning' of the time of shipment clause in the contract[322] – the House of Lords held that what had happened could not be a March and/or April shipment. There was no clear and consistent commercial custom and usage, it added, to suggest otherwise. Yet again the law preferred the bright-line rule, despite the potential for abuse by those seeking to renege on a deal.

Once the standard form contracts of trade associations became the norm in the commodities markets, there was, generally speaking, no reason for the courts to depart from what was ostensibly the plain meaning approach, tempered, of course, by basic rules of construction.[323] Under that approach there was no need to examine the purpose behind a clause or the sequence of events leading to its incorporation in the contract.[324] Nor would a court concern itself with any issue of an abuse of rights. Indeed, if a term of a contract applied, parties were perfectly entitled to invoke it to avoid a bad bargain or to take advantage of a falling or rising market.[325] Since mercantile

---

[320] (1877) LR 2 App Cas 455. See 309 above.
[321] A point essential to Lord Blackburn's judgment. Thus he was able to restore the conclusion which as Blackburn J he had reached in the Divisional Court ((1876) 1 QBD 470), and which the Court of Appeal had overturned!
[322] (1877) 2 QBD 112 ('shipped' was ambiguous; the Court of Appeal was also concerned that buyers would, without any real reason, obtain an excuse for rejecting contracts when prices had fallen: at 115).
[323] e.g., the expression 'force majeure' was construed in a limited way given the words which preceded it in the rules of the Liverpool Cotton Association: *Podar Trading Co, Bombay* v. *Francois Tagher, Barcelona* [1949] 2 KB 277.
[324] e.g., *Cia de Comercio Limitada Van Waveren* v. *Spillers Ltd* (1928) 32 Ll L Rep 31, 34 (the LCTA freight clause).
[325] e.g., *Bowes* v. *Shand*, at 465–466 per Lord Cairns LC.

practice was now codified in the contracts, it was difficult to argue for commercial custom and usage to the contrary.

There are many instances of the plain meaning approach in commercial cases concerning standard form contracts. Examples in the law reports of the plain meaning approach include the interpretation of clauses in an LCTA contract for the sale of parcels of rye and wheat on CIF terms to a firm in Gothenburg,[326] and a contract for the sale of tapioca on CIF terms from Java incorporating the conditions of sale of the Liverpool United General Produce Association.[327] The latter case illustrates how, without tempering, the plain or literal meaning approach could produce unusual results. The payment clause in that contract provided for cash 'against documents or delivery order'. Although it was labelled a CIF contract, Rowlatt J had held that it meant the alternatives 'quite plainly' were either 'documents' or a 'delivery order', and that it would 'be doing violence to the language' to interpret it to mean a delivery order *and* documents such as an insurance policy. Despite that, the Court of Appeal held that the words could not mean that all a seller had to produce was a delivery order since that would be unreasonable.

The capacity of the plain meaning approach to produce odd results sometimes led courts to break free with a more pragmatic approach. There was high authority that 'business sense will be given to business documents'[328] and there are echoes of this in the law reports. Considering a strike clause in an LCTA contract in the context of a shipment of maize meal from South Africa, Darling J said that taken literally the clause might mean what counsel had contended, but it was 'a business contract, and we have been asked to look at it as business men would look at it'.[329] To buttress his interpretation – after all, the arbitrators had stated a special case for the court, indicating that they as commercial parties were having difficulty interpreting the clause – Darling J invoked the well-known grammarian Lindley Murray. Murray was the author of *English Grammar* (1795), *Reader* (1799) and *Spelling Book* (1804), which in their many editions were hugely authoritative, but no doubt the bane of many a nineteenth-century schoolchild.

Moreover, commercial custom and practice was occasionally invoked to counteract the plain meaning of terms in standard form commodities contracts. This is yet another example of how English commercial courts generally avoided theory if it produced a commercially unacceptable result. A Court of Appeal decision in 1917 concerning a Rubber Trade Association of London standard form contract shows the point. The contract was for the sale in 1916 of twenty-five tons of plantation rubber, CIF, to be shipped from the Far East to New York direct or indirect, with liberty to call and ship at other ports.[330]

---

[326] *Sven Hylander & Co v. Blake, Dobbs & Co* (1925) 22 Ll L Rep 528, 529.
[327] *Denbigh, Cowan & Co v. R Atcherley & Co* (1920) 5 Ll L Rep 86, (1921) 6 Ll L Rep 383.
[328] *Glynn v. Margetson & Co* [1893] AC 351, 359, a bill of lading case.
[329] *Cox, McEuen & Co v. J J Cunningham Ltd* (1921) 7 Ll L Rep 50, 51.
[330] *Re An Arbitration between L Sutro & Co and Heilbut, Symons & Co* [1917] 2 KB 348.

Because of the First World War, a practice had grown up of shipping rubber from Singapore to New York via Seattle, then by rail across the United States. The arbitrators found that at the time the contract was made it could be said this was a business practice within the contemplation of the parties, and goods forwarded by this route would be regarded as good tender.

By majority the Court of Appeal rejected this. Even assuming this was custom and usage – in fact it was simply a business practice – it was inconsistent with the express terms of the contract. Not only did the shipment clause contemplate the rubber being carried from the Far East to New York – the port of discharge – by vessel or vessels, the payment clause provided the sellers could not demand cash against documents before arrival of the vessel or vessels at the port of discharge (New York). In other words, the express terms of the contract appeared inconsistent with long railway carriage.

Yet from the outset the decision was of doubtful import. Not only was there a strong dissent of Scrutton LJ, but the notion that commercial practice and usage could never be used to construe a contract was inconsistent with *Bowes* v. *Shand*, where Lord Cairns LC had expressly recognised that words may have a particular meaning by reason of the practice of the trade.[331] Branson J recognised this in the Commercial Court in 1939, but arguably bent the rules too far.[332] Parcels of copra were sold on London Copra Association Contract No. 2, shipment to be 'direct and/or indirect, with or without transhipment'. Shipment on the coastal steamer in the Philippines was within time, but transhipment to the vessel to carry the copra to Europe occurred after the contract date. The ocean bills of lading were ante-dated to accord with the date of coastal shipment. Although this was generally unacceptable, it was in accordance with local custom and usage and Branson J held that shipment was within the contractual period.

A more tempered approach to commercial custom and practice was adopted by the House of Lords the following year.[333] In a sale of 15,000 units of No 2 Yellow American corn under LCTA Contract No. 28, the House of Lords upheld a finding by LCTA's appeal committee as to the custom and practice of the trade in interpreting the clause, 'Separate documents for each 1000 units and each 1000 units to be considered a separate contract'. The clause was intended to address the situation where a cargo was split, so separate buyers or sub-buyers would each have a bill of lading and other shipping documents in relation their purchases. In this case the seller had given notice of appropriation of about 15,444 qrs. It sent a provisional invoice stating there were 15

---

[331] at 462.
[332] *NV Arnold Otto Meyer* v. *Andre Aune* (1939) 64 Ll L Rep 121. See also *EE & Brian Smith (1928) Ltd* v. *Wheatsheaf Mills Ltd* [1939] 2 KB 302 (custom supplemented LCTA arbitration rules). cf *Flatau Dick & Co* v. *Keeping* (1931) 39 Ll L Rep 232 (CA) (no custom in Baltic timber trade proved).
[333] *T D Bailey Son & Co* v. *Ross T Smyth & Co Ltd* (1940) 67 Ll L Rep147.

bills of lading, each for 1,000 units, and one bill of lading for 444 units. The market had fallen and the buyer rejected the provisional invoice with the excuse that the provisional invoice was not in accord with the clause. Its contention was that the extra 444 units should have been equally spread over the fifteen bills of lading. Lord Wright (with whom other members of the House of Lords agreed) said that the language of the clause was not sufficiently specific to justify a construction that the words 'each 1000 units' meant one-fifteenth of the actual quantity of 15,444 units declared by the sellers under their option. If he was wrong in that, the clause was a least ambiguous and opened the door to the arbitrators to cure the ambiguity 'by importing the custom and practice of the trade'.[334]

The pragmatic approach to construing standard contract terms of trade associations is also evident in other situations. One was where the parties had added another term to the standard printed terms. There was unlikely to be any difficulty if an association had issued this as a printed slip to be added to one of its contract forms.[335] The association would have already considered how the slip amendment meshed with other terms in a form. The problem arose when the parties put their own gloss on a standard printed form, which was not properly integrated.[336] An early case on the point involved the sale of timber FOB shipped at Wiborg (Vyborg, Russia) to Newcastle, *per Hiawatha*, where the payment clause provided that payment was to be on receipt of and in exchange for all the shipping documents, the 'all' being inserted in ink on the printed form by the buyer's agent in Newcastle.[337] Grove J warned against parties altering established printed forms, since they had been the subject of legal decisions and interpretations placed on their clauses. On the facts of the case, he held that the alteration had no effect. In a later case, also involving the shipment of timber, this time from a north Russian port, the court gave effect to typewritten clauses, not without difficulty given the effect of the printed clauses already in the contract.[338] Similarly, the court acted sympathetically where the parties had deleted a clause in a London Copra Association form, but not done the job properly and not made consequential amendments in other clauses.[339]

A related situation where the courts acted pragmatically was when parties botched the job of incorporating the terms of an association's standard form into their own contract. Incorporation always demanded care in the drafting, although the reality of commercial parties was, as Branson J put it in *Buckerfields Ltd. v. Smith*, that in 99 cases out of 100 they were more concerned

---

[334] at 158.
[335] e.g., *Louis Dreyfus & Co v. Produce Brokers' New Company (1924) Ltd* (1936) 54 Ll L Rep 60 (LCFTA Contract No. 6).
[336] *T.D. Bailey, Son & Co v. Ross T Smyth & Co Ltd* (1940) 67 Ll L Rep 147, 159, per Lord Wright.
[337] *Cederberg v. Borries, Craig & Co* (1885) 2 TLR 201.
[338] *Hollis Bros Co Ltd v. White Sea Timber Trust Ltd* (1936) 56 Ll L Rep 78.
[339] *Stephens, Paul & Co v. Goodlake & Nutter* (1921) 7 Ll LR 46.

with getting the business done than setting that out in precise detail.[340] In that case the first problem of construction arose because, as with other trade associations, the LCFTA, which was referred to in the bought note, had a number of standard form contracts, yet the incorporation term did not identify any one in particular. Branson J held that there were only two LCFTA contracts which could by any stretch of the imagination be held to apply to this type of transaction and both contained an identical clause, clause 15, relevant to the insurance money in the case.[341] Contrast a subsequent grain case, with a gummed on extension of shipment clause to LCTA Contract No. 54A, where the Danish buyers had signed the contract in ignorance of the addition.[342] Not only did the clause on its face not apply to Contract No. 54A – it was expressed to apply to other specified LCTA contracts – but it could not be presumed to apply because it was affixed by unilateral action of the seller.

5 'Remedying' Court Decisions

Compared with the large volume of arbitrations under these standard form contracts, there were relatively few instances where disputes found their way to court. When that occurred, whatever approach to interpretation the courts had adopted, they generally produced an outcome that the trade association responsible for the contract could live with. The relevant committee of the trade association such as the contracts committee might give some attention to these decisions, and consciously decide that since they were conformable to commercial purpose no action was necessary.[343] In their busy task of keeping the contracts up to date, and responding to the regular submissions for changes from individual merchants and other associations in the trade at home and abroad, what the courts occasionally said did not really feature in any more significant a way.

Occasionally, however, court decisions adopted an interpretation which impelled the sponsoring trade association of the relevant standard form contract to act. When in 1949 a court decided that, unless expressly authorised, arbitrators could not award interest,[344] standard form contracts in the commodity markets had to be amended if they did not already provide for this.[345] Similarly, there are instances where trade associations in different markets clubbed together to support a test case on a specific clause in a standard form

---

[340] (1936) 54 Ll L Rep 304, 306.
[341] The case also concerned the 'battle of the forms': only the bought note purported to incorporate LCFTA terms. Branson J's approach was simple: that the term had force as an added clause, not contradicted by anything contained in the seller's contract note: at 306.
[342] R. Simon & Co. Ltd v. Peder P. Hedegaard A/S [1955] 1 Ll R 299.
[343] e.g., the Standing Contracts Committee of the LCTA, minutes, 5 November 1936, LMA, CLC/B/MS/103/23174/010, discussing *Shipton, Anderson v. Micks Lambert* (1936) 55 Ll L Rep 384..
[344] *In re an Arbitration Between the Podar Trading Co Ltd Bombay and Francois Tagher, Barcelona* [1949] 2 KB 277. Followed *Chandris v. Isbrandtsen-Moller Co Inc* [1951] 1 KB 240.
[345] See LCTA, Standing Contracts Committee, Minutes, 8 March 1950, LMA, CLC/B/103/MS23174/011.

contract because of its more general ramifications. The support given by various trade associations for an appeal in *G H Renton & Co v. Palmyra Trading Corporation of Panama*,[346] concerning a strike clause in a standard form contract in the timber trade, offers an example.

A trade association would typically act to amend its standard form contracts to produce the result which they thought had always been intended when a court took a contrary view and the matter was significant.[347] The same applied if a court decision threw up an undesirable result which had never been contemplated. A flurry of decisions in the late 1920s about grain contracts, and the response of the London Corn Trade Association, is illustrative.[348] Uncharacteristically strong in 1929 was LCTA's reaction to the interpretation put on one of its freight clauses, its president going out of his way at the annual general meeting that year to comment that the High Court was 'interpreting certain clauses in some of our contracts in a totally different way from that in which they have been understood by us in the past'.[349]

The immediate concern was a decision of Roche J, a judge with an extensive background in admiralty and maritime matters when at the bar but whose later career marked him as one of a narrow and unimaginative spirit.[350] Roche J had held that a clause in Contract No. 32, that '[a]ny reduction of freight ... for ending a voyage at any particular port to be for buyer's benefit', meant precisely that, whereas the LCTA took the view of its appeal committee in the arbitration (which Roche J reversed) that, given the context, the clause related only to a situation where there was a reduction of freight outside not under the charterparty.[351] There was a strong feeling in the association that the court had got it wrong. In the result the Contracts Committee of the association consulted relevant parties, for example, the Centro de Cereales, the Australian Shippers' Association, and the East India Grain and Oilseeds Association. Ultimately the executive committee of the association directed an amendment of the freight clause to make clear that reductions of freight for the buyer's benefit were confined to reductions outside the charterparty.[352]

Amendments were made to contracts in less controversial circumstances following other judgments. In early 1928 the Court of Appeal had upheld a decision of Wright J, who in turn had confirmed an award of the LCTA appeal

---

[346] [1957] AC 149. The LCTA gave financial support for the litigation: LMA, CLC/B/103/MS23172/011, 387(3).
[347] Occasionally contracts were amended in the light of arbitration decisions, e.g., LMA, CLC/B/103/MS23174/004, LCTA, Executive Committee, minutes, 12 July 1910, 6 September 1910.
[348] Counsel was involved in redrafting the arbitration clause in 1955 'following certain adverse comments on the present wording by Judges in the High Court': CLC/B/103/MS23174/011, LCTA, Standing Contracts Committee, minutes, 20 July 1955.
[349] CLC/B/103/MS23172/008, 305, 313, 322, 348.
[350] R. Stevens, *Law and Politics The House of Lords as a Judicial Body 1800–1976*, London, Weidenfeld & Nicolson, 1979, 315–316.
[351] *Cia de Comercio Limitada Van Waveren v. Spillers Ltd, The Zamora* (1928) 32 Ll L Rep 31.
[352] CLC/B/103/MS23174/007, 1 November 1928.

committee in relation to the appropriation clause in the LCTA Black Sea and Danubian Grain Contract.[353] The clause provided that a notice of appropriation 'shall be given' within seven days from the date of the bill of lading. Wright J held that mere despatch of the notice within that period was insufficient. As Scrutton LJ put it in the Court of Appeal, 'the plain and the proper meaning' was that 'given' meant 'actually' given. Thus the seller had to ensure that its buyer received the notice within the seven days. Of course, there was nothing 'plain and proper' about this construction over the alternative, and at first instance Wright J had conceded that it might give rise to problems of compliance since sellers had to pass the appropriation notice down to buyers in any string of sub-sales.[354] The upshot was that the contract was amended to confirm that notices of appropriation had only to be despatched within the seven days. By the 1930s the clause had been amended to require notice to be given by cable or telegram if over a distance.[355]

Likewise, a House of Lords decision in the same year, 1928, led to LCTA contracts being amended to state expressly that as a general rule damages recoverable by the buyer for default by the seller would not include any loss of profit on sub-sales. In *R & H Hall Ltd* v. *W H Pim Jnr & Co Ltd*[356] Pim sold a cargo of Australian wheat CIF to Hall on LCTA Contract No. 12, and by notice of appropriation subsequently nominated the *Indianic* as the ship containing the cargo. Although it received the shipping documents it refused to tender them to Hall even though it knew that Hall had resold the cargo, on the same LCTA form. Instead, it delivered the grain under a different contract to another firm. Breach of contract was accepted; the issue was the measure of damages. The House of Lords reversed the Court of Appeal, which had confined damages to the difference between the price for which the cargo was bought and the price at which similar wheat could have been purchased in the market at the date of breach.[357] Instead the House of Lords upheld the decision of the trial judge (Rowlatt J), that Hall was entitled in addition to an indemnity for damages and costs which it would have to pay to its own sub-buyers. This followed because the very terms of the contract, such as the appropriation, arbitration and strike clauses, contemplated that there might be sub-sales. Accordingly, the second limb of *Hadley* v. *Baxendale*[358] applied, in that losses from a sub-sale could reasonably be supposed to have been in the contemplation of the parties at the time the contract was made and to be a probable result of the breach of it. In the course of his judgement, Lord Phillimore noted that if he and his fellow judges were adopting a construction not intended, to create heavy liabilities never planned, 'there will be an

---

[353] *Compagnie Continentale d'Importation* v. *Union der Sozialistischen Sovjet Republiken, Handelsvertretung in Deutschland* (1928) 30 Ll L Rep 140, (1928) 29 Ll L Rep 52.
[354] The arbitrators had taken this view, LCTA's appeal committee the other.
[355] cf. LCTA Black Sea and Danubian Grain Contract. Cargoes for Shipment, tale quale, No30, 1896, in London Corn Trade Association, *Forms of Contracts in Force*, London, LCTA, 1896.
[356] (1928) 30 Ll L Rep 159.   [357] (1927) 27 Ll L Rep 253.   [358] (1854) 9 Ex 341, 156 ER 145.

opportunity to revise the form contract'.[359] And this is precisely what happened. The contracts committee of the association set to work and decided to have counsel draft a clause for insertion in its contracts in light of the judgment. Contracts were amended to exclude loss of profits on sub-sales unless the arbitrators or appeal committee thought there were special circumstances.[360]

5.7 Disputes and Arbitration

In the first part of the nineteenth century commodity sales on the spot markets were by way of bought and sold notes, with no provision for arbitration. Even with contracts for sale at a distance there might not be an arbitration clause. That applied as well with sales of commodities to arrive.[361] However, the position was changing. A House of Lords Select Committee was informed in 1857 that one of the simplest broker's notes for the sale of tallow by a St Petersburg merchant contained an arbitration clause for disputes over quality, albeit of a rather inconclusive character (to be settled by arbitration 'in the usual manner').[362] There was also evidence that in Manchester sold notes made arbitration possible.[363]

The breakthrough for commodity arbitration came with the formation of trade associations from around the middle of the nineteenth century and their drafting of standard form contracts with compulsory arbitration included. Lawyers were typically excluded as arbitrators or representatives. The design of the arbitration was cheap, fast and, in the main, effective. That did not mean that disputes were typically arbitrated; textile mills, for example, compromised disputes by 'friendly allowances', rather than risk arbitration which could prove costly if the ruling was against them.[364]

1 Commodity Arbitration and the Trade Associations

> Oh, justice – what true justice there
> To weigh each question nice;
> Oh, what a fund of wisdom rare
> To give us sound advice.
> Or if – and arbitration held –

---

[359] at 165.
[360] I am grateful to Professor Victor Goldberg for information on the actual amendment. See also CLC/B/103/MS23174/007, 22 March 1928.
[361] e.g., *Simond v. Braddon* (1857) 2 CB(NS) 324, 140 ER 441; *Vernede v. Weber* (1856) 1 H&N 311, 156 ER 1222 (both sales of Burmese rice). See also *Jones v. Just* (1868) LR 3 QB 197.
[362] *Select Committee of House of Lords on the Mercantile Law Amendment Bill*, HL, No. 294, 1856, 20.
[363] Ibid., 27.
[364] J. Robins, 'A Common Brotherhood for Their Mutual Benefit: Sir Charles Macara and Internationalism in the Cotton Industry, 1904–1914' (2015) 16 *Enterprise & Soc* 844, 872.

> Injustice still you feel,
> Go the great committee men
> And lodge a last appeal.[365]

The lead with commodity arbitration came from the Liverpool brokers importing cotton from the American southern states. Arbitration seems to have existed before the 1840s if there was a dispute between them over a sale by a merchant, spinner or broker. The minutes of the Liverpool Cotton Brokers' Association for December 1842 read: '[T]he custom amongst cotton brokers of submitting disputes to arbitration, is one firmly established in the cotton trade.'[366] Since cotton as a commodity varied in quality, there were regular disputes. These were magnified with the disruption and speculation in cotton during the American Civil War.[367] The standard form contract of the association which resulted in 1863 contained an arbitration clause: 'In case of dispute arising out of this contract the matter to be referred to two respectable brokers for settlement, who shall decide as to quality and the allowance, if any, to be made.'[368] With time the system of arbitration for disputes over Liverpool cotton became more elaborate. Twenty years on, in 1886, a leading authority on the trade, Thomas Ellison, explained that 'several palpably incorrect decisions led to the establishment of the right of appeal'.[369] By that time the procedure was that each side would nominate a broker independent of the transaction, with the possibility of a third being brought in for cases where the two disagreed, the parties having a right of appeal to the association's committee.[370] In 1872 the committee adjudicated on 882 appeals, most of which were questions of the amount of variation in quality from a standard of cotton bought to arrive.[371] Not all sales of cotton from abroad were under the Liverpool association's conditions; in such cases, if there was to be arbitration, it had to be provided for in the relevant contract or agreed on an ad hoc basis.[372]

Other trade associations in Liverpool followed suit. The contract of the Liverpool Corn Trade Association provided that disputes were to be referred to arbitration in accordance with the printed rules of the association, and that no legal proceedings were to be taken until this had been done. Unsurprisingly the arbitration rule tracked that of the Liverpool Cotton Brokers' Association,

---

[365] Anon; quoted in F. Dolman, 'Where Merchants most do Congregate. The Liverpool Exchange' (1895) 9 *The Ludgate Illustrated Magazine* 599, 607.
[366] B, Simpson, 'Contracts for Cotton to Arrive: The Case of the Two Ships Peerless' (1989) 11 *Cardozo L R* 287, 304n.
[367] H. Arthurs, *'Without the Law': Administrative Justice and Legal Pluralism in Nineteenth-Century England*, Toronto, University of Toronto Press, 1985, 98–99.
[368] *The Times*, November 12, 1863, 6. See B. Simpson, *op cit*, 312; 300 above. But terms still provided for arbitration 'in the usual manner': see *Thorburn v. Barnes* (1867) LR 2 CP 384.
[369] T. Ellison, *The Cotton Trade of Great Britain*, London, E. Wilson, 1886, 274.
[370] see *Thorburn v. Barnes* (1867) LR 2 CP 384; *Fairlie v. Fenton* (1870) LR 5 Ex 169.
[371] *Judicature Commission, Third Report of the Commissioners*, C 957, 1874, Appendix, Evidence of the Liverpool Cotton Brokers' Association, 2. See also N. Hall, 'The Governance of the Liverpool Raw Cotton Market, c. 1840–1914' (2017) 53 *Northern History* 98.
[372] *Nickoll & Knight v. Ashton Edridge & Co* [1900] 2 QB 298, 302; on appeal [1901] 2 KB 126.

Figure 5.2 Arbitration by members of Liverpool Cotton Association, 1930s (A. Garside, Cotton goes to Market, 1935)

two arbitrators, to be members of the association, with no interest in the matter, one appointed by each side, a third being possible if these two deemed it necessary, with an appeal to the association's committee.[373] In evidence to the Royal Commission on the Judicature, the association commented that the provisions were very satisfactory, being expeditious 'a most important matter in fluctuating markets', cheap, and undertaken by those with practical knowledge of the trade.[374]

Matters seemed to move slower in London and, if arbitration clauses appeared, they were relatively open-textured. The contract which gave rise to *Bowes* v. *Shand*[375] for the sale of rice to be shipped at Madras (Chennai) contained a clause for 'arbitration by two sworn brokers in the usual manner', with the London Rice Brokers' Association being mentioned as the appellate body if either party was dissatisfied with the arbitrators' award.[376] *Reuter Hufeland & Co* v. *Sala & Co*[377] was a claim which arose when the buyer refused to accept tender of 20 tons only of the 25 tons (more or less) of Penang black

---

[373] The clause is at Judicature Commission, op cit, 3, Evidence of the Liverpool Corn Trade Association, 3. cf. ibid., 4, rules of the Liverpool General Brokers Association (no need for arbitrators to be members and no appeal mechanism).

[374] Ibid. For subsequent arbitration provisions of the Liverpool Corn Trade Association: J. Smith, Organised Produce Markets, *op cit*, 198–200.

[375] (1877) 2 App Cas 455.

[376] See LI, House of Lords Printed Cases, Judgments and appeal documents, 'Bowes v Shand', vol. 312, 1877, 805–810 (33–38).

[377] (1879) 4 CPD 239.

pepper, which the seller had contracted to supply. The contract of 1876 provided that any dispute arising out of it was to be settled as in *Bowes* v. *Shand* by arbitration 'in the usual manner'.[378]

This type of 'usual manner' clause did not give arbitrators *carte blanche*. They still had to act in accordance with the rules of natural justice. That lesson was brought home sharply in 1864 in a dispute over the quality of a cargo of Danish rapeseed, warranted to be at the time of shipment in sound, dry and merchantable condition.[379] The contract was contained in the bought and sold notes of the London brokers who negotiated the sale. There was provision there for arbitration 'in London in the usual way'. An umpire had been appointed when the arbitrators failed to agree. The umpire did not call the parties before him, but proceeded to make his award on the basis of the statements and documents the parties had submitted and, unknown to the other side, an inspection of samples at one of the arbitrator's premises, and communications with those by whom the cargo had been inspected and the samples taken. Despite evidence that this was in accordance with mercantile practice, and the wide berth the court said it would normally give to arbitrators, it held that there had been a breach of the fundamental principles of justice to hear both sides. Byles J emphasised that the ruling did not mean that arbitrators were bound by the strict rules of evidence.[380]

As for the marketing of foreign grain trade in London, disputes in the mid-nineteenth century seem rarely to have been settled by arbitration, except in the trade with South Russia and the Danube. At that point the trade was less than it was to become. Foreign exporters consisted of a limited number of well-established firms, selling directly or through their agents to importers, and thus able to resolve disputes amicably. With the increase in the amount of imported grain, importers advocated arbitration to avoid the cost and procedure of taking legal proceedings, especially in foreign courts. A system grew up of each side appointing an arbitrator, they in turn appointing an umpire in the event of a disagreement between them. There was resistance to arbitration from some exporters. At the time a complaint was made about poor quality, they would have been given, under the usual arrangements, a bill of exchange for payment in return for the shipping documents. A committee was formed in London in 1870 to advance the cause of arbitration in the grain trade, with an equal number of buyer and seller representatives. On application by the parties, that committee would appoint a sub-committee of three to report on

---

[378] at 240.
[379] *In the Matter of an Arbitration Between Thomas William Brook, F. & A. Delcomyn and F. & J. Badart, Freres* (1864) 16 CB (NS) 403, 143 ER 1184.
[380] at 418, 1190–1191, respectively. Erle CJ and Willes J to similar effect. Byles referred to the expertise and speed of arbitrators and cited the recently decided public law case, *Cooper* v. *The Wandsworth Board of Works* (1863)14 CB (NS) 180, 143 ER 414. As the author of a standard work on Bills of Exchange, still under that name, wits of the junior bar nicknamed Byles' horse 'Bills', giving an additional meaning to 'Byles on Bills': G. & V. Jones, 'Byles, Sir John Barnard (1801–1884)', *Oxford Dictionary of National Biography*.

how a dispute should be resolved. Although it had greater ambitions, the committee's work was confined in the main to the Baltic trade.[381]

2 LCTA's Scheme of Arbitration

> The Association [the LCTA], through its Committee, nominates as arbitrator some old and experienced member of the Exchange in whose ability and impartiality there is general confidence. Mr John Nesbit, Mr John Ross and Mr Keen are the gentlemen most frequently chosen for this office, and I am told that their fees as arbitrators amount during the year to a very considerable sum ... [T]he rapidity of the proceedings usually afford ... a remarkable contrast to those of a Court of Law. (*The Ludgate Illustrated Magazine*, February 1895)[382]

Matters in the London grain trade changed radically with LCTA's formation in 1878. Among its stated aims was to offer an authority to which members could refer for the settlement of disputes.[383] When it was incorporated in 1886 part of its objects was 'to encourage the settlement of disputes by arbitration'. Samples were to act as standards for the arbitrators. With time these were systematically collected and held by the association at the Baltic Exchange with which the grain in dispute could be compared.[384]

The obligation to arbitrate disputes and the way arbitration was to be conducted laid down in the association's first contract, American Grain Contract 1 of 1879, was that the buyer and seller agreed that, should any dispute arise, it would be settled in accordance with the tenth rule endorsed on the contract, the decision to be made a rule of the High Court of Justice on application of either party. Rule 10 provided that all disputes arising out of the contract were to be referred to two arbitrators, one chosen by each party. Should a party fail to appoint an arbitrator, should the two arbitrators fail to appoint a third in the case of disagreement or should any arbitrator fail to act, the executive committee of the association could make the necessary appointments.

Rule 10 also stated that the arbitrators had to be principals in the corn trade as merchants, factors or brokers, as well as members of the Corn Exchange or the Baltic Exchange. Coming from the trade, the arbitrators would have expertise in the commodity at issue. Those traders having an interest in the matter in dispute were incompetent to act.[385] Lawyers were, in the main,

---

[381] This paragraph is based on C. Chattaway, 'Arbitration in the Foreign Corn Trade in London' (1907) 17 *Econ J* 428, 428. Chattaway had spent some 50 years in the market when he wrote this.
[382] F. Dolman, 'Where Merchants most do Congregate. The Corn Exchange' (1895) 8 *The Ludgate Illustrated Magazine* 406, 413.
[383] A. Hooker, The International Grain Trade, *op cit*, 31.
[384] On the Baltic Exchange see 61–62, 315–316 above.
[385] The only copy of American Grain Contract 1 of 1879 I have located is in NBAC, N46/1080, Adelaide Steamship Co, Charter Book.

excluded.[386] Initially LCTA's contracts did not provide for an internal appeal from the arbitrators' award. A proposal at LCTA's second annual general meeting in 1880 by a prominent Greek trader, E. A. Mavrogordato, for an ability to appeal was resisted.[387] Soon after, his view won the day, and LCTA's contracts incorporated a right of appeal to an appeal committee constituted by five elected members of the association. An appeal was a rehearing of the case at which fresh evidence or new witnesses might be introduced.

Over time, the contracts and rules governing arbitration were further elaborated. In the 48 contracts in force in 1896, the contracts required not only that disputes arising out of them and questions of law should go to arbitration, but that the parties and those claiming under them should not bring any legal action until the matter had been arbitrated. The standard contracts also made an arbitration award a condition precedent to the right to sue on any claim arising out of the contract.[388] As evident in the extract from the February 1895 issue of the *Ludgate Illustrated Magazine*, quoted at the beginning of this section, there soon emerged a group of merchants who undertook arbitration on a regular basis. Under LCTA's early standard form contracts, arbitrators had to be principals engaged in the corn trade as merchants, millers, factors or brokers, and members of LCTA, the Corn Exchange or the Baltic Exchange and residing in the United Kingdom. In litigation in 1909 this provision came into sharp focus when it was discovered that arbitrations were frequently being conducted by persons who were not members of any of these bodies. On this basis the court upheld a challenge by a disgruntled party to an award concerning a cargo of Russian wheat under LCTA's Black Sea and Danubian Grain contract. Since the arbitrators were not qualified to act, it held, they had no jurisdiction and the award was null and void.[389] By the 1930s there was at least one full-time arbitrator, Sir Walter Roffey, who had been president of LCTA in the 1920s. He had a large clientele in the grain and animal feed trades and was a favourite with foreign parties.[390]

Awards were confidential and dissenting arbitrators were not able to express a differing view on an award. There was a lengthy debate at the LCTA annual meeting in 1928 about publishing the facts and decisions of technical arbitrations heard by the appeal committee.[391] Moving a motion to this effect, S. K.

---

[386] And continue to be: Y. Chernykh, 'The Last Citadel: The Restricted Role of Lawyers in Soft Commodity Arbitration', *Transnational Dispute Management*, vol. 14, no.2, May 2017.
[387] H. Barty-King, Food for Man and Beast, *op cit*, 24.
[388] London Corn Trade Association, Forms of Contracts in Force, *op cit*.
[389] *Jungheim, Hopkins & Co v. Foukelmann* [1909] 2 KB 948.
[390] Roffey was knighted in 1918 for services to the Ministry of Food during the First World War and service on the Royal Commission on Wheat Supplies. He was president of LCTA 1925–1926: 'Sir George Walter Roffey, Kt', *The Practical Psychologist*, vol. 1, no.2, February 1925, 10–11; H. Barty-King, Food for Man and Beast, *op cit*, 65–66.
[391] LMA, CLC/B/103/MS23172/008, Annual meeting 31 May 1928. Technical arbitrations concerned all matters other than quality, for example, failure to deliver or accept the grain, late delivery and payment.

Thorne saw two advantages of publication: first, the rulings would be available to later arbitrators as a guide and, secondly, and consequently, the need for changes in standard form contracts would be reduced because fewer errors would be made. There was opposition to the idea. Sir Herbert Robson said that each appeal differed and it would be necessary not only to publish the facts and the decision but the evidence of each case as well; Sir S. F. Mend stated that one of the first rules of any arbitrator was not to give reasons; and Mr H. Kahl suggested that while a decision might be correct, the reasons might be wrong (to which Thorpe retorted that publication would expose bad reasoning). At the end of the debate, only Thorpe and his seconder supported the motion.

LCTA's system of arbitration remained essentially the same during our period, and pressure for fundamental change was resisted, even in light of new legislation. That was evident when, as a result of the Arbitration Act 1934, arbitrators had to appoint an umpire immediately, whereas until then LCTA's standard forms provided that this had only to be done when there was a disagreement between the arbitrators.[392] Under the legislation parties could contract out of the provision. LCTA standard form contracts did just that.[393] Allowing the parties themselves to choose the arbitrators was a regular target of criticism. A suggestion in 1908 by LCTA's own solicitor that there be a rota of arbitrators was given short shrift with the association's policy of party autonomy in appointments.[394] In 1910 the British Chamber of Commerce in Smyrna (Izmir, Turkey) complained that the existing system was too pro-buyer and meant that 'the arbitrators practically became the advocates of the contesting parties'. Its proposal that the association itself appoint arbitrators from a panel randomly was peremptorily rejected as 'impractical'.[395] In resisting a panel system in the mid-1920s, the association acknowledged that there may be something in the criticisms by simultaneously reminding arbitrators that, although it was proper for them to submit the views of their principals to the other side, ultimately they must act in a judicial capacity, not as advocates.[396] The absence of a panel system was criticised at a meeting of the International Law Association in 1936, but nothing was done.[397] One reason LCTA might have resisted change was that allowing parties to choose their own arbitrator enhanced the acceptability of awards.[398]

---

[392] Arbitration Act 1934, s. 5(1); Arbitration Act 1889, s. 2, First Schedule.
[393] LMA, CLC/B/103/MS23172/009, 246 (Annual Report, 1934–1935).
[394] Ibid., 31 December 1908. The Liverpool Cotton Association had a rota system: S. Rosenbaum, *A Report on Commercial Arbitration in England*, Chicago, American Judicature Society, 1916, 25.
[395] LMA, CLC/B/103/MS23172/004, LCTA, Executive Committee, 18 October 1910.
[396] LMA, CLC/B/103/MS23174/007, LCTA, Arbitration Procedure Committee, 29 June 1926. On this occasion the idea was advanced by the Grain Trade Association of the San Francisco Chamber of Commerce.
[397] International Law Association, *Reports of the 39th Conference, 10–15 September 1936, Paris*, London, 1LA, 1937, 95.
[398] see A. Velkar, Markets and Measurements in Nineteenth Century Britain, *op cit*, 212.

The number of LCTA arbitrations varied. In 1902–1903 there were 2,142 arbitrations (69 appeals); in 1903–1904, 3,970 (70 appeals).[399] In the 1920s, the number varied from some 2,000 awards in 1923, to 4,000–5,000 in 1928.[400] On the eve of the First World War, LCTA's president attributed the decrease in the number of arbitrations at the time to the improvements in the drafting of its standard form contracts. He added that LCTA did not exist to promote arbitration, but to avoid it by well-considered amendments of its contracts.[401] Partly the number of arbitrations turned on events. The annual meeting of the association in 1928 was informed that there were less arbitrations in the past year 'no doubt owing to the excellent quality and condition of the Argentinian maize crop'.[402] By contrast the Mississippi floods and US embargo on exports in the early 1970s led to a spike in the number of arbitrations.[403]

Awards themselves were short and to the point and set out on LCTA standard forms. No reasoning was required, and all the arbitrators needed to do in filling in the standard form was to give the result (e.g., not shipped, quality inferior, failure to take up grain, sellers must pay a specified allowance, buyers refused to take up documents, deficiency on bill of lading weight).[404] LCTA arbitration was international in character. Taking a selection of arbitrations registered during the period 1915–1925, about 975 recorded a foreign port of destination compared with 250 having a United Kingdom port.[405] The ports of Hamburg, Antwerp, Genoa, Naples, Marseilles, Rotterdam, Bremen and Dunkirk appeared regularly. There was a steady flow of appeals to LCTA's appeal committee. In the first three full years, from 1886–1887 to 1888–1889, there were 60, 51 and 94 appeals, respectively, 205 in total. In 88 cases the first instance award was confirmed; in 94 cases it was varied.[406] The numbers for 1906–1907, 1907–1908 and 1908–1909 were 75, 102 and 63, respectively. Out of the total for those three years 130 awards were upheld and 129 varied.[407] Over the ten years period from 1919–1920 to 1928–1929, there were 775 appeals. The annual numbers were relatively

---

[399] LMA, CLC/B/103/MS23172/002, Annual reports for 1902–1903, 1903–1904. Annual reports from other years before World War I, if available, do not give the number of arbitrations, although some give appeal numbers.
[400] LMA, CLC/B/103/MS23172/008, Annual meeting 1928–1929, 322.
[401] LMA, CLC/B/103/MS23172/006, Annual meeting, 26 May 1914.
[402] LMA, CLC/B/103/MS23172/008, Annual meeting 1927–1928, 262.
[403] M. Bridge, 'The 1973 Mississippi Floods: Force Majeure and Export Prohibition' in E. McKendrick (ed.), *Force Majeure and Frustration of Contract*, London, Lloyd's of London Press, 1991; H. Barty-King, Food for Man and Beast, *op cit*, 88, 92.
[404] LMA, CLC/B/103/MS23198/001–014, Official arbitration awards. Over time the standard forms became lengthier, but not the reasoning.
[405] LMA, CLC/B/103/MS23197/001, Arbitration book, 1915–1925. The remainder did not record a port.
[406] LMA, CLC/B/103/MS23201/001, Appeal awards, September 1885-May 1889, 78–79, 125–126. The remaining cases were withdrawn or otherwise disposed of.
[407] LMA, CLC/B/103/MS23201/007, Appeal awards, 1 March 1906-31 December 1908. The discrepancies in the figures are in the records.

steady, the lowest in 1919–1920 (26), immediately after the war, the highest in 1925–1926 (120).[408]

In the great majority of cases parties complied with an award, because of a threat of social sanctions and, in extreme cases, exclusion from the relevant market (e.g., the Baltic Exchange) or the trade association.[409] However, there was a recurrent problem with the recalcitrant, particularly if abroad and not subject to these sanctions.[410] In the years prior to the First World War, the position with Russia caused LCTA special concern. Legal procedure for enforcing awards in Russia was 'tedious, costly and uncertain', the *Corn Trade News* noted in 1907.[411] One proposal LCTA made to the Russian government was that it would report defaulters to local grain bourses, which could then apply sanctions. As well, registration of firms with the bourses in Odessa and Nikolaeff – where non-compliance was a special concern – should be tightened.[412] The Russian problem dragged on to the eve of war in 1914. At one point LCTA contemplated keeping a 'black book', but was dissuaded from doing so when its solicitor advised that it would be responsible for its contents, including defamatory statements.[413] In 1930 LCTA considered amendments to its articles of association so that a failure to honour an arbitration award would be deemed to be conduct derogatory of a member's character.[414] The problem of non-compliance persisted. Twenty-five years later, in 1955, LCTA decided that in light of what the Incorporated Oil Seeds Association had done it would adopt a shaming clause, drafted by its solicitors, Thomas Cooper & Company, under which it could notify its members generally should a party fail to abide by an award.[415]

3 LCTA, Law and Lawyers

Within the rather wide boundaries set by law, commodity trade associations were in the driving seat when it came to arbitration policy and the drafting of

---

[408] LMA, CLC/B/103/MS23199/1, Register of appeals.
[409] J. Sgard, 'A Tale of Three Cities: The Construction of International Commercial Arbitration', *op cit*, 159.
[410] Other trade associations had the same problem: e.g., LMA, CLC/B/103/MS23224/002, London Copra Association 235, 266.
[411] *Corn Trade News*, 11 December 1907, 1715. The Arbitration (Foreign Awards) Act 1930 (based on the 1927 Geneva Convention) provided for foreign awards to be enforced in Britain.
[412] LMA, CLC/B/103/MS23174/002, LCTA, Sub-committee appointed to receive Mr M. U. Roulkowsky, Financial Agent of the Imperial Russian Government, 9 June 1909. The problem of enforcement in pre-Soviet Russia continued: LMA, CLC/B/103/MS23172/006, LCTA, Executive committee, 16 June 1914; letter from Russian government's commercial agent: 11 July 1914. See also M. Falkus, 'Russia and the International Wheat Trade, 1861–1914' (1966) 33 *Economica (NS)* 416, 420–421.
[413] LMA, CLC/B/103/MS23174/002, LCTA, Sub-committee on correspondence from Syndicat des Importateurs de Cereales Marseille, 29 September 1908.
[414] LMA, CLC/B/103/MS23174/008, LCTA, Sub-committee re Articles of Association, 23 January 1930.
[415] LMA, CLC/B/103/MS23174/011, LCTA Standing Contracts Committee, 6 July 1955; LMA, CLC/B/103/MS23172/011, LCTA, Executive committee, 20 January 1955, 298. An example of such notification is LMA, CLC/B/103/MS23174/012, LCTA Sub-committee minutes book.

the arbitration clauses in their standard form contracts. The English legal environment at the end of the nineteenth century when most of the trade associations were getting under way was favourable to arbitration. The Common Law Procedure Act 1854 empowered the court to stay legal proceedings brought by a party in breach of a submission to arbitration,[416] and submissions to arbitration were, except by leave, irrevocable.[417] The Arbitration Act 1889 gave added force to the parties' autonomy: written submissions to arbitration were as if they had been made an order of court (as well as being irrevocable);[418] terms were implied in the absence of written provision;[419] and awards were enforceable in the same manner as a judgment or an order of court.[420] By the time of the Act the judges were well-disposed to arbitration, if their attitude had ever been otherwise.[421] The courts were influenced, at least in part, by the favourable statutory environment.[422]

Through a requirement in their standard form contracts that disputes be arbitrated, the commodity associations could generally keep disputes away from court. There were limited exceptions. The court itself could interfere if there was an error of law on the face of the award, but this ground was narrowly construed.[423] Further, the court could grant a declaration that an award was void *ab initio* because, for example, the submission to arbitration was invalid.[424] Again that was unusual. Next, the court could act if the arbitrators were guilty of misconduct. In some instances this was given a wide interpretation, as where the arbitrators had refused to state a special case for the court.[425] With LCTA it was this ability of arbitrators to seek the assistance of the court by stating a special case which gave rise to the bulk of the relatively small number of court proceedings.[426] The consequence was that

---

[416] In English parlance a submission to arbitration was an agreement to arbitrate: see Arbitration Act 1889, s. 27.
[417] 17&18 Vict c.125, ss. 11, 17.
[418] s. 1. Under 9&10 Wm III, c.15 an application for contempt was possible as an enforcement tool.
[419] s. 2, First Schedule (e.g., two arbitrators could appoint an umpire: (b)).   [420] s. 12.
[421] S. Brekoulakis, 'The Historical Treatment of Arbitration under English Law and the Development of the Policy Favouring Arbitration' (2019) 39 *Oxford J Legal Stud* 124, 134–135. See also D. Roebuck, 'The Myth of Judicial Jealousy' (1994) *Arbitration Int'l* 395. cf. H. Arthurs, 'Without the Law': Administrative Justice and Legal Pluralism in Nineteenth-Century England, *op cit*, 78.
[422] *Kursell* v. *Timber Operators and Contractors Ltd* [1923] 2 KB 202, 211, per Salter J.
[423] *Champsey Bhara & Co* v. *Jivraj Balloo Spinning and Weaving Company Ltd* [1923] AC 480 (PC, Bombay High Court) (rules and regulations of the Bombay Cotton Trade Association).
[424] e.g., *Oil Products Trading Company Limited* v. *Societe Anonyme, Societe de Gestion D'Entreprises Coloniales* (1934) 150 LT 475 (palm oil; conditions No.21 of Liverpool United General Produce Association; alleged agent not authorised to make contract).
[425] *Re Arbitration between Lewis & Peat Ltd and Catz American Co (Inc) (No1)* (1926) 26 Ll L Rep 263.
[426] Arbitration Act 1889, s. 7 (b), 19; Arbitration Act 1934, s. 9(a), (b). cf. Common Law Procedure Act 1854, s. 5. See Q. Hogg, *The Law of Arbitration*, London, Butterworth & Co, 1936, 109–115.

arbitrators used this avenue to have what were tricky issues of law or contract interpretation authoritatively resolved.[427]

It was not possible for a commodity association like LCTA to curb the use of the special case procedure. LCTA learnt this early on at a time when its contracts contained a clause forbidding parties from applying to court for an order that an arbitrator state a case on a question of law. The court held that its jurisdiction could not be excluded by this type of clause and went on to direct that the arbitrators in those proceedings state a case.[428] The Refined Sugar Association did not learn the lesson, and in *Czarnikow* v. *Roth Schmidt & Company*[429] the Court of Appeal held invalid, as contrary to public policy, its Rule 19, that no one should require arbitrators to state a special case for the opinion of the court on a question of law arising in a reference. The association's rule produced Scrutton LJ's well-known rebuke, there must be 'no Alsatia in England where the King's writ does not run'.[430] Scrutton LJ had expressed similar sentiments, less colourfully, the previous year.[431] Errors of law apart, however, like other judges Scrutton LJ was not in favour of challenges to arbitration awards. In *Aronson* v. *Mologa Holzindustrie AG*[432] he expressed the wish that commercial parties 'when they put arbitration clauses in their contracts would be content with the arbitration they have chosen instead of trying to upset it as soon as the decision is against them'.[433]

LCTA appreciated that because the courts had a function in overseeing arbitration awards it needed to tread more carefully with its arbitration rules. By the 1930s the arbitration provisions in the 'Conditions and Rules' on the back of LCTA's standard form contracts were as long as all the other clauses combined. LCTA also involved its solicitors for advice on points of arbitration more frequently than on other matters. Arbitration policy was, however, jealously guarded. Shortly after its inception it constituted a sub-committee to consider the rules on arbitrations and appeals. The sub-committee discussed matters of policy such as the obligation of parties to an arbitration to disclose relevant

---

[427] e.g., *Re Arbitration between the Olympia Oil and Cake Company Ltd and the Produce Brokers Company Ltd* [1915] 1 KB 233 (whether valid tender of Far Eastern soya beans under contract of the Incorporated Oil Seed Association); *Re Lewis & Peat Ltd and Catz American Co (Inc)(No 2)* (1927) 28 Ll L Rep 51 (sale of Lampong pepper by Mincing Lane broker to US buyers on contract of London Produce Brokers' Association; was bill of lading proper tender?); *Meyer (Montague L) Ltd* v. *Osakeyhtio Carelia Timber Co Ltd* (1930) 36 Com Cas 17 (whether ready for shipment clause part of description of timber, not a mere warranty, so that buyer did not lose right to reject); *W. E. Marshall & Co* v. *Lewis & Peat (Rubber)* [1963] 1 Lloyd's Rep 562 (whether buyers forfeited right to arbitration under London Contract Form No 3 of Rubber Trade Association of London).
[428] *In an Arbitration between Reinhold & Co and Hansloh* (1895) 1 Com Cas 215.
[429] [1922] 2 KB 478.   [430] at 488.
[431] *Perez* v. *John Mercer* (1921) 7 Ll L Rep 1 (arbitration of the Manchester Chamber of Commerce on sale of cloth).
[432] (1927) 28 Ll L Rep 81.
[433] at 83. This account of Scrutton LJ's views is based on D. Foxton, *The Life of Thomas E. Scrutton*, Cambridge, Cambridge University Press, 2013, 252. See also Scutton LJ in *Re Olympia Oil & Cake Co and MacAndrew, Moreland & Co* [1918] 2 KB 771, 778.

matters to the arbitrator and the importance of arbitrators acting competently and impartially. It produced draft arbitration rules. Only then was LCTA's solicitor invited to make suggestions and drafting improvements.[434] (One legal question which the sub-committee canvassed was how the arbitration rules were to be binding on parties.[435]) Eventually the solicitor produced his recommended alterations to the rules. On that basis the sub-committee reported to LCTA's executive committee with its recommendations.[436] In later years the association's solicitors were consulted along similar, limited lines as they had been at the beginning. Mainly as a result of a specific arbitration or award, LCTA's committees would discuss an issue, advance a solution and, if needs be, formulate an amendment to the relevant clause. The solicitor's task was usually to advise whether there were legal impediments to a course of action and to suggest improvements in the expression of the committee's own draft. There are several examples. Was it necessary to add 'any rule of law or equity to the contrary notwithstanding' to a default clause, which conferred on the non-defaulting party the right to buy or sell in the market and to specified damages, some of which were in the discretion of the arbitrators?[437] Did specific provision have to be made in the arbitration rules so that claims not brought within six months of the time of shipment or final discharge of a cargo were void?[438] Was one notice of appeal sufficient when an award concerned several buyers and sellers?[439]

LCTA's solicitor was on tap, not on top. On various occasions LCTA's committees amended the solicitor's drafts and even ignored his advice when its adoption was not essential.[440] One example of the latter was the association's prolonged consideration of arbitration in relation to string contracts – where a cargo was sold and resold, possibly many times, before its discharge at a port.[441] In 1930 its solicitor supported what was the efficient solution, that if a dispute, say about quality, arose, the result of an arbitration between the last

---

[434] LCTA's solicitors were J. & A. A. Tilleard (see 309 above), then Thomas Cooper & Co. of 21 Leadenhall Street, City of London. Until near the end of our period, City solicitors were small, with only a handful of partners: D. Sugarman, 'Simple Images and Complex Realities: English Lawyers and Their Relationship to Business and Politics, 1750–1950' (1993) *Law & Hist Rev* 257, 265–266.

[435] LMA, CLC/B/103/MS23175, LCTA, Minutes of sub-committee appointed to examine the rules governing arbitrations and appeals, with report, 1884–1885, 30 September 1884, 3 March 1885. cf. LCFTA [London Cattle Feed Trade Association], CLC/B/103/MS23219, Minutes of executive committee and annual general meeting, 20 October 1922.

[436] Ibid., 12 August, 30 September, 14 October 1884, 21 March 1885.

[437] LMA, CLC/B/103/MS23174/004, LCTA, Sub-committee re revision of American contracts, 24, 30 March 1914. See also ibid., Sub-committee re China Manchurian Contract No. 4 revision, 5 February 1914.

[438] LMA, CLC/B/103/MS23174/007, LCTA, North America contracts committee, 12 December 1922, 23 January 1923.

[439] LMA, CLC/B/103/MS23174/008, LCTA, Contracts committee, 8, 16 November 1930, 19 February 1931.

[440] In 1937 a suggestion to brief counsel over a recent decision concerning arbitration was opposed 'as counsel's opinion was sometimes found to be in direct opposition to decisions in the High Court'!: LMA, CLC/B/103/MS23172/009, LCTA, Executive committee, 14 December 1937.

[441] 344 above.

buyer and first seller would be made to bind all those along the string. Concerned about the possible prejudice to intermediaries in the event of insolvency, the association decided against the change: there was a greater danger, it considered, in the cure than in the disease.[442] It was only in 1950 that LCTA made arbitration awards between the first seller and last buyer over quality and condition binding on all those along a string, long after that had been done by other trade associations.[443]

However, there were circumstances when LCTA's solicitor had a greater involvement in setting arbitration policy. The first was when the association undertook a general revision of its contracts. When that was done in 1908 the association's solicitor was more heavily engaged than usual with advice on arbitration issues and in drafting the relevant clauses.[444] A second occasion was with the disruption of war. An immediate issue on the declaration of war in 1914 concerned the implications of appointing arbitrators from German and Austrian firms.[445] Another was LCTA's decision to consider applications to appoint arbitrators on an ad hoc basis. That was despite the North American Export Grain Association in New York having urged LCTA not to approve any arbitrations until more normal conditions returned. It had argued that American exporters were facing many claims for arbitration, which it was impossible for them to defend properly, given the limited evidence they could obtain.[446] There were various other matters related to the war where the association's solicitor was called on to advise.[447]

5.8 Conclusion

In the early part of the nineteenth century dealings in commodities were typically spot trades, in other words for immediate rather than future delivery. The written record was terse, in the form of buy and sell notes. In 1857 Lord Campbell CJ contrasted what he conceived as a commercial desire for brevity with lawyers wanting certainty and matters spelt out in detail.[448] Yet the situation was changing with the advent of forward sales ('arrivals'). Within a

---

[442] LMA, CLC/B/103/MS23174/008, LCTA, Sub-committee re Arbitration Awards, 8 May, 23 March, 17 June, 10 July; December; LMA, CLC/B/103/MS23172/008, LCTA, Executive committee, 15 July 1930, 391.
[443] LMA, CLC/B/103/MS23172/011, LCTA, Executive committee, 14 March 1950, 53, Annual meeting, 72. The annual meeting recorded that arbitrators could also award interest.
[444] LMA, CLC/B/103/MS23174/002, LCTA, Sub-committee re Revision of Contract Forms, 18 March, 23 March, 10 December, 15 December 1908.
[445] LMA, CLC/B/103/MS23174/004, LCTA, Sub-committee [on] Arbitrators, 17, 24 September 1914.
[446] LMA, CLC/B/103/MS23172/006, LCTA Executive committee, 1 September 1914. A special sub-committee was appointed to consider the applications, assisted by the solicitor.
[447] LMA, CLC/B/103/MS23188/006, LCTA, Minutes of appeal committed and appeal court, 10 July 1914–17 March 1926, for example entries for 2 December 1914, 21 December 1914, 21 Aril 1915.
[448] *Humfrey* v. *Dale* (1857) 7 El & Bl 266, 278, 119 ER 1246, 1250.

relatively short period standard form contracts had become the norm in the international sale of important commodities. Standardisation of contracts and matters like a commodity's quality became especially important when futures trading emerged.

London- and Liverpool-based trade associations were responsible for drafting the most important of the standard form contracts. These were used internationally. The associations also represented the trade with other interests such as shipping and insurance. Contact with government was exceptional. At the heart of activity was drawing up and periodically revising their standard form contracts. Standardisation and organized markets combined to reduce transaction costs and to produce pricing efficiency. In their private law-making with standard form contracts, trade associations had as their goal certainty in expression. As to substance, the private law-making of the trade associations did not always involve decision-making in the neutral, disinterested manner sometimes portrayed. Changed conditions and specific events could be the trigger for considering an issue, and commercial realities entered in the choices made as to how these were to be addressed. Views might be sought from a range of different interests, including trade interests in exporting countries, and principles applied such as holding the balance between buyers and sellers and pursuing uniformity throughout an association's contracts. However, choices to favour particular interests were made, although the balance changed as economic power slipped away from Britain after 1914 and producer countries fostered commodity programmes, state marketing boards and international commodity agreements.[449]

Trade associations drew their standard form contracts within the framework of English common and statutory law. Contracts were deemed to be made and performed in England and were subject to English law. In many ways their efforts codified mercantile practice, whether in the quality standards set for a commodity, the manner it was to be shipped, insured or paid for, and how disputes were to be resolved. In providing for all this, their good fortune was that English common law was in the main permissive, facilitative and non-judgmental. It had a flexibility in its rules to ground the great majority of transactions which commercial practice demanded. If the trade associations wanted (and they often did), they could vary the common-law default rules, including the statutory rules in the Sale of Goods Act 1893, by appropriate drafting. Curbing rejection as a remedy for a defective cargo in favour of an allowance on price was a familiar step. Rejection was simply not the practical

---

[449] A. Magnan, *When Wheat was King*, Vancouver, University of British Columbia Press, 2016, 2, 13–15, 49–54; C. Gilbert, 'International Commodity Agreements: Design and Performance' (1987) 15 *World Development* 591; K. Khan, *The Law and Organisation of International Commodity Agreements*, The Hague, Martinus Nijhoff, 1982; D. McNicol, *Commodity Agreements and Price Stabilization: A Policy Analysis*, Lexington, Massachusetts, Lexington Books, 1978.

course when a seller would have to arrange for the cargo to be disposed of from abroad.

Drafting of the standard form contracts was an intensely practical exercise, undertaken by the members of a trade association with lawyers in the back seat. In the main, the association did the drafting, and if needs be its solicitor would then be called in to comment. Its solicitor's views might be rejected. With time, the greater complexity of issues, and the accretion of case law, meant a more regular dialogue between the trade associations and their lawyers as contractual terms were drafted and redrafted to achieve the association's commercial aims.

Notwithstanding the adoption of standard from contracts for the sale of commodities like grain, the auction remained the avenue for the sale of important commodities like tea and wool during our period. Auctions in London began in the first part of the nineteenth century and were international in character. Over time auctions were conducted closer to the places of production, India and Sri Lanka for tea and Australia and New Zealand for wool. Sales law was much modified by the terms and conditions adopted with the London auctions. Caveat emptor was very much the order of the day. Systems for inspection and testing were put in place so that buyers could assess the tea, wool and other products before committing themselves with a bid. Early on the courts facilitated commodity auctions. Their indulgence on terms and conditions extended to price manipulation through 'puffing' by sellers and buyers forming bidding rings. Control over these practices was through the terms and conditions which the trade itself promulgated, not down to the law.

When disputes about commodity sales arose, which the parties could not resolve, these were settled in the bulk of cases by the trade itself. Arbitration became a favoured avenue for dispute settlement, with members of the relevant trade association acting as arbitrators or sitting on any appeal body constituted under the rules. Lawyers were generally excluded, not only as arbitrators but as advocates. Only a very small proportion of these arbitrations ever ended in court, often because the arbitrators referred them. When this occurred, the judges generally decided the matter in a commercially friendly manner. By deft reasoning the exceptional statutory provision, contrary to commercial practice, could be avoided.[450] In any event the standard form contracts could always be amended in the light of a judgment to clarify the wording which a court had found wanting, or to produce the result the trade intended all along, as opposed to what the court had interpreted it to mean. Commercial practice first, law second.

---

[450] e.g., *C. E. B. Draper & Son Ltd* v. *Edward Turner & Son Ltd* [1965] 1 QB 424; 347 above.

6

Bank Finance for Trade and Industry

What is remarkable in this vast movement [the railways] is that the great leaders of the financial world took no part in it. The mighty loan-mongers, on whose fiat the fate of kings and empires sometimes depended, seemed like men who, witnessing some eccentricity of nature, watch it with mixed feelings of curiosity and alarm. Even Lombard Street, which never was more wanted, was inactive . . . . All seemed to come from the provinces, and from unknown people in the provinces. (Benjamin Disraeli, *Endymion*, 1880)[1]

6.1 Introduction

For well over a century there has been criticism of the British banks for their failure to provide longer-term finance to British industry. The comparison has regularly been made with what has been characterised as the supportive approach of the German banks to their industrial customers.[2] The difference has been described as one between the transactional banking of Britain and the relationship banking of Germany.[3] The criticism has extended beyond the banks: the City of London, the argument goes, turned its back on British industry to favour investments abroad and the safety of British, colonial and other government bonds.[4] Critics point to London Stock Exchange money going not into domestic industry but to companies conducting business elsewhere, initially in the United States (notably the railways) and later in places like the Far East and South America.[5] Criticism about the funding gap with British industry, and the banks' role in it, led to two high-profile inquiries during our period, both headed by

---

[1] London, Longmans, 1881. Leading banks were based on or near Lombard Street.
[2] e.g., H. Foxwell, 'The Financing of Industry and Trade' (1917) 27 *Economic J* 502.
[3] M. Baker & M. Collins, 'Methodological Approaches to the Study of British Banking History' (2007) 58 *Revue économique* 59, 66; M. Baker & M. Collins, 'English Commercial Banks and Organizational Inertia: The Financing of SMEs 1944–1960' (2010) 11 *Enterprise & Society* 65, 66.
[4] The literature is voluminous: see e.g., Y. Cassis & J. Van Helten (eds.), *Capitalism in a Mature Economy: Financial Institutions, Capital Exports and British Industry 1870–1939*, Aldershot, Edward Elgar, 1990 for both sides of the argument.
[5] See on overseas investment R. Michie, *The Global Securities Market: A History*, Oxford, Oxford University Press, 2006, 98–99, 144–145; D. Platt, *Britain's Investment Overseas on the Eve of the First World War*, Macmillan, Basingstoke, 1986, 90–91; D. Adler, *British Investment in American Railways 1834–1898*, Charlottesville, University of Virginia, 1970; chapter 3.6 above.

eminent judges, the Macmillan inquiry in 1931 and the Radcliffe inquiry in 1959.[6]

The picture is more complex than some of this criticism suggests. In the first part of the nineteenth century finance for early British industry was available from retained profits and from family, friends and other local business and professional associates. Often a local solicitor was a key figure in the transaction.[7] Short-term credit was available through the inland bill of exchange. Later in the nineteenth century there were important public issues on the provincial and the London stock exchanges for domestic industry.[8] When what became Imperial Chemical Industries (ICI) was floated in 1881, its shareholders were local business people in Lancashire and Cheshire, where it was based; it did not need the City of London.[9] Significant investment in shares in the textile areas of the north of England came from the firms' directors and their friends.[10] Smaller enterprises on incorporation might raise outside funds through the issue of debentures.[11] In some places like Sheffield banks were established by industrialists, partly as a source of finance, and a close banker-industrialist relationship continued throughout the century.[12]

Putting these larger issues to one side, what can be said is that the banks offered two essential source of finance: first, trade credit to finance the flow of imports and exports described in earlier chapters; and, second, working capital, which enabled industry to meet the wages of employees and the cost of raw materials in anticipation of the sale of finished products in home and export markets. These two aspects of bank finance – trade finance and advances of short-term capital to industry – are the focus of this chapter. During our period the law relating to both was well developed, pliable and generally facilitative of new types of commercial

---

[6] *Committee on Finance and* Industry, Report, Cmd. 3897, London, 1931; *Committee on the Working of the Monetary System. Report*, Cmnd. 827, London, 1959. Macmillan was a law lord 1930–1939, 1941–1952. Radcliffe was a law lord 1949–1964. See N. Duxbury, 'Lord Radcliffe out of Time' (2010) 69 *CLJ* 41, 46.

[7] P. Mathias, *The First Industrial Nation*, London, Methuen, 1969, 149–150; P. Hudson, *The Genesis of Industrial Capital: A Study of the West Riding Wool Textile Industry c.1750–1850*, Cambridge, Cambridge University Press, 1986, 124; P. Cottrell, *Industrial Finance 1830–1914*, London : Methuen, 1980, 22, 33, 35; M. Edwards, *The Growth of the British Cotton Trade 1780–1815*, Manchester, Manchester University Press, 1967, 32–33; B. Anderson, 'The Attorney and the Early Capital Market in Lancashire', in J. Harris (ed.), *Liverpool and Merseyside: Essays in Economic and Social History of the Port and its Hinterland*, London, Frank Cass, 1969.

[8] B. Cheffins, *Corporate Ownership and Control: British Business Transformed*, Oxford, Oxford University Press, 2008, 176, 181–184.

[9] W. Reader, *Imperial Chemical Industries A History*, London, Oxford University Press, 1970, vol. I, 55.

[10] F. Lavington, *The English Capital Market*, 2nd ed., London, Methuen, 1929, 208.

[11] J. Getzler, 'Role of Security over Future and Circulating Capital: Evidence from the British Economy circa 1850–1920', in J. Getzler & J. Payne (eds.), *Company Charges: Spectrum and Beyond*, Oxford, Oxford University Press, 2006, 236–240; D. Farnie, *The English Cotton Industry and The World Market 1815–1896*, Oxford, Clarendon Press, 1979, 242–243.

[12] L. Newton, 'Regional Bank-Industry Relations during the Mid-Nineteenth Century: Links between Bankers and Manufacturing in Sheffield, c.1850 to c.1885' (1996) 38 *Business Hist* 64.

transaction. Regulation was virtually non-existent, although the banks exercised self-regulation and complied with Bank of England and government requests to act in particular ways (sometimes with the advantage to them of less competition).[13] Underpinning the banks' performance in both areas were sophisticated institutional arrangements. These operated within a framework of supportive law.

The bedrock of trade finance was the bill of exchange. Banks would assist a customer importing goods by ensuring that the foreign exporter was paid as soon as the goods were shipped. In turn, these customers obtained credit until around the time the goods arrived and were or could be sold on to others. This was the acceptance business of the merchant banks, although from the late nineteenth century the joint stock banks also undertook acceptances. It all occurred within a well-established framework of what was later called 'negotiable instruments law'. The banks undertook to 'accept' a bill of exchange the exporter drew, thereby becoming primarily liable to pay it. Exporters could therefore obtain immediate payment by selling ('discounting') the bill of exchange in their own jurisdiction.

As we will see, the bill of exchange might have been drawn under a letter of credit issued by the importer's bank and payable by the bank's branch or its correspondent in the exporter's jurisdiction. Under the documentary letter of credit, which emerged in the 1840s, the exporter would hand over the shipping documents as a condition of being paid under the credit. The courts enthusiastically welcomed the documentary credit and nurtured its growth with favourable decisions. The most important of the shipping documents for the bank was the bill of lading, issued by the ship when the goods were on board ready for export. At common law it was a document of title to the goods, as well as evidencing the contract of carriage. It gave the bank control over the goods until it was reimbursed for the trade credit it had extended.

Once the goods arrived in the importer's jurisdiction, they might be stored for a period in a dock, warehouse or store. The dock owner might issue a dock warrant, acknowledging that the holder was entitled to the goods when it was presented. A bank might be prepared to make advances on the security of a dock warrant on the basis that it was a document of title to the goods, like the bill of lading. It had that character through statute, not the common law which was resistant to the idea. The dock warrant assisted an importer until it, in turn, sold the goods.

That in broad outline was the banks' role in financing trade. But the banks were also involved in providing short-term capital to industry. For these purposes the joint stock banks offered advances by means of an overdraft on the customer's account (who could draw up to that amount) or a loan (with the

---

[13] L. Arch, 'Disposed towards Self-Restraint: The London Clearing Banks, 1946–71', in K. Akrivou & A. Sison (eds.), *The Challenges of Capitalism for Virtue Ethics and the Common Good*, Cheltenham, Edward Elgar, 2016. The power to direct banks under the Bank of England Act 1946 s.4(3) was never used.

London banks). Both were repayable on demand, underlining their short-term character. The banks rarely refused industrial customers an advance, and then for largely understandable reasons, the advance sought was not for short-term purposes but for capital expenditure; the firm was new and a risk without a track record; the bank had little confidence in the management; and where security (collateral) was thought necessary to back the advance, what was available was thought to be inadequate.[14] The law supported the banks if they wanted to stand on their rights to cancel an overdraft or recall a loan. Accommodation (finance) bills of exchange were also used for the purpose of making advances to industry. There were no legal obstacles to this. Because of their association with financial crises, however, accommodation bills were frowned upon.

Where banks did provide an overdraft or a loan, security was often not required. If a bank did regard security as a precondition for an advance, it was often sufficient that the principals of the business provided a personal guarantee covering it. Otherwise collateral took the form of a deposit of title deeds to property, shares certificates or debentures. All of this was within a framework where lawyers were prominent in drafting and advising on the relevant documentation and acting when the security went wrong.[15] The floating charge over all the assets of a business emerged in the late nineteenth century, but it was only in the 1920s that the banks began using it, and then relatively infrequently compared with the other forms of security available. Although advances were as a matter of law short term (on demand), the reality was of banks providing longer-term funding to industry, with regular renewals of overdrafts and loans. As a leading economic historian pointed out some time ago, 'business not uncommonly got over a hump of a great decision to expand or survived a depression with bank capital'.[16]

Underpinning the banking system in its provision of trade finance and working capital for industry were institutional arrangements of the City of London. Marine insurance through the Lloyd's insurance market was one; the shipping market of the Baltic Exchange another.[17] There were also the City-based commodity markets, auctions and trade associations (which drew up the standard form contracts for trade and futures transactions) (Chapters 2, 5). Part 6.4 of this chapter explores two further examples. Both were largely untouched by law.

---

[14] F. Capie & M. Collins, 'Industrial Lending by English Commercial Banks, 1860s-1914: Why Did Banks Refuse Loans?' (1996) 38 *Bus Hist* 26.

[15] Lawyers advised on redrafting forms, including those for collateral, when banks reorganised and amalgamated: see e.g., RBS, WES/79, Westminster Bank, Correspondence between London and County Banking Co & its solicitors, 1896-1897, vol. 1.

[16] P. Mathias, *The First Industrial Nation*, op cit, 136. See also M. Collins & M. Baker, *Commercial Banks and Industrial Finance in England and Wales 1860-1913*, Oxford, Oxford University Press, 2003.

[17] H. Cockerell, *Lloyd's of London*, Cambridge, Woodhead-Faulkner, 1984, 12-20, 23, 26.

The first is the London money market. Its discount houses were separate institutions, unmatched in the world. They survived until the 1990s when the levers of monetary policy were transformed. Their role was as intermediaries between the Bank of England and the banks, and thus with the wider economy and its operations. They dealt in the bills of exchange used in financing trade, as well as other short-term instruments such as inland bills (an important component for part of the nineteenth century), accommodation paper and, most importantly in the twentieth century, the Treasury bills and other short-term government debt issued to fund the state.

Banks discounted bills of exchange with the discount houses (which in turn might rediscount them, including to the Bank of England) and deposited money with them on a short-term basis, often overnight.[18] The discount houses dealt on their own account in bills. They evolved from the bill brokers of the first part of the nineteenth century, whose work was stimulated by changes in country banking after the 1825 financial crisis.[19] Their relationship with the Bank of England in the nineteenth century was at times fraught but was essential because ultimately the Bank took bills from them in times of need as the lender of last resort.[20]

The other supporting act in the cast examined in this chapter is the Bankers Clearing House. (There were provincial counterparts.) In 1842 it was described as a '"poking place", in the corner of a court without a name, behind the Guardian Insurance office, in Lombard Street'.[21] Despite its inauspicious situation, it provided a model for clearing trades on the commodities exchanges (see Chapter 2.5), as well for other bodies such as the Railway Clearing House.[22] It was established before our period. It cleared payments by cheque and (to an extent) bills of exchange. The Bankers' Clearing House came into its own from the second quarter of the nineteenth century as an essential part of the payment system when the cheque began its rise to prominence as a popular method of commercial (and personal) payment.[23] Not all banks were admitted to the clearing house. For a while the private banks were able to exclude the new joint stock banks established from the 1820s. Even after the joint stock banks were eligible, not all were admitted. Nor were overseas or foreign banks members of the clearing house. Non-members had to enter agency and correspondent relationships with the clearing banks to

---

[18] R. Truptil, *British Banks and the London Money Market*, London, Jonathan Cape, 1936, 110–128.
[19] L. Pressnell, *Country Banking in the Industrial Revolution*, Oxford, Clarendon Press, 1956, 88, 99.
[20] 449 below.   [21] D. Hardcastle, *Banks and Bankers*, London, Whittaker & Co, 1842, 38.
[22] 245 above.
[23] L. Pressnell, Country Banking in the Industrial Revolution, *op cit*, 168; M. Poovey, *Genres of the Credit Economy: Mediating Value in Eighteenth- and Nineteenth-Century Britain*, Chicago, University of Chicago Press, 2008, 51–55, 426n, 462 n. See *Oxford History of the Laws of England, vol. 12, 1820–1914, Private Law*, Oxford, Oxford University Press, 2010, 730 (M. Lobban) on the importance of 1853 changes in stamp duty in the rise of the cheque.

6.2 Trade Finance

> The Red Ensign, we used to be advised, was upheld chiefly by a smallish steamer carrying coal from England and bringing back grain. There were of course other supporting factors. There were, very importantly, steel and cotton, our insular position, the battle and the breeze, the standard gold coin. (H. Tomlinson, *Under the Red Ensign*, 1926)

By the beginning of the twentieth century the so-called Bill on London – a bill of exchange, payable in London in pounds sterling – financed a large share of international trade. With some hyperbole it was said that the Bill on London was 'the same as gold', because it could always be discounted in London and the proceeds converted to gold when Britain was on the gold standard.[24] It allowed exporters or sellers of goods (either in Britain or abroad) to be paid at the point they shipped the goods, while at the same time enabling the importer or buyer to defer payment until the time the goods arrived, or even at the later point when the goods were sold. In other words, it was an instrument of both payment and credit.[25]

The Bill on London rested on three pillars. First, there were the first-class London banks which 'accepted' the bills – in other words, assumed primary liability that they would be paid. Second, there were the bill brokers and later the discount houses, whose existence meant that good bills could always be sold (discounted) in London. Third, there was the Bank of England, which once it accepted that it was the lender of last resort guaranteed that it would take eligible bills in times of financial stress. All this meant that London had an efficient and liquid money market.

Associated with the bill of exchange in financing international trade was the letter of credit. Banks opened these for customers so that their counterparty-exporters could obtain ready payment. Letters of credit divided into open credits and documentary credits. From the 1840s documentary credits became more common under the contracts between buyers and sellers. A bank would open a documentary credit in favour of the seller on the application of the buyer importing goods. The seller would be paid as soon as it presented the shipping documents to the bank (or possibly the bank's branch or correspondent in the exporter's country). Typically, payment under a letter of credit was by means of a bill of exchange. The shipping documents included the bill of lading, a certificate of insurance and the invoice for the goods.

The bill of lading was critical. It was the document which the ship issued to the exporter acknowledging the receipt of the goods for shipment. In

---

[24] Gillett Brothers Discount Co Ltd, *The Bill on London*, London, Chapman & Hall, 1952, 16.
[25] K. Llewellyn, 'Meet Negotiable Instruments' (1944) 44 *Colum LR* 299, 314.

Lickbarrow v. *Mason*[26] the Court of the King's Bench decided that the bill of lading was a document of title at common law, so that a consignee with the bill of lading, and without notice of other claims (such as the right in some circumstances of an owner of the cargo to stop delivery), could pass good title to a third party.[27] As Lord Hatherley LC later put it, it was 'the symbol of property, and which, for the purpose of conveying a right and interest in the property, is the property itself'.[28] As commercial justification for his legal analysis, he added that 'to shake any conclusion of that kind would be entirely to annihilate the course of mercantile procedure which has existed for a long period of time'.[29]

Bills of exchange and letters of credits were central to trade finance. But there were other elements associated with the financing of the import and export of goods.[30] In a world of fluctuating currencies there were the arrangements for foreign exchange, when buying and selling bills of exchange. Further, banks and their correspondents had to settle capital transfers between themselves, and for these purposes finance bills were drawn at 30, 60 or 90 days upon each other.[31] There was also the system of export credits, where between the wars governments began providing insurance to cover the risks faced by exporters.[32] For reasons of space these and other important aspects of trade finance during our period attract only passing attention. The topic examined in greater detail is the dock warrant, which was a document issued by the docks stating that the holder was entitled to goods they held. It could be used by the holder as security for an advance from a bank. The dock warrant fell by the wayside in commercial practice with containerisation.

1 The Bill of Exchange

> 'What do you want, man?' demanded Ralph sternly. 'Demnition [damnation] discount,' returned Mr. Mantalini, with a grin, and shaking his head waggishly . . . . 'I don't want to do business just now, in fact I would rather not; but as you are a friend – how many bills have you there?' 'Two,' returned

---

[26] (1794) 5 TR 683, 101 ER 380.
[27] Neatly summarised in verse: 'The Rule in Lickbarrow v Mason' (1922) 3 *Law Coach* 13.
[28] *Barber* v. *Meyerstein* (1870) LR 4 HL 317, 326.
[29] Ibid. Generally the ship would not deliver the goods to a person without the bill of lading. See *Glyn Mills Currie & Co* v. *East and West India Dock Co* (1882) 7 App Cas 591. On the bill of lading's history: R. Aikens, M. Bools & R. Lord, *Bills of Lading*, 2nd ed., London, Routledge, 2015, Ch 1; W. Bennett, *History and Present Position of the Bill of Lading*, Cambridge, Cambridge University Press, 1914.
[30] e.g., F. Dudeney, *The Exporter's Handbook and Glossary*, London, Pitman, 1916, pt II; *An Export Handbook*, London, Institute of Export, 1939, 33–38; W. Syrett, *Practice and Finance of Foreign Trade*, London, Macmillan, 1938.
[31] C. Goodhart, *The New York Money Market and the Finances of Trade 1900–1913*, Cambridge, Mass, Harvard University Press, 1969, 55; H. Greengrass, The Discount Market in London, *op cit*, 30–31.
[32] D. Aldcroft, 'The Early History and Development of Export Credit Insurance in Great Britain, 1919–1939' (1962) 30 *Manchester School* 69.

> Mr. Mantalini. 'What is the gross amount?' 'Demd trifling – five-and-seventy.' 'And the dates?' 'Two months, and four.' 'I'll do them for you – mind, for you; I wouldn't for many people – for five-and-twenty pounds,' said Ralph, deliberately . . . . 'Let me see the names,' replied Ralph, impatiently extending his hand for the bills. 'Well! They are not sure, but they are safe enough'. (Charles Dickens, *Nicholas Nickleby*, 1839)[33]

The bill of exchange was well known at the beginning of our period. In *Nicholas Nickleby* Charles Dickens writes of how Mantalini, who has taken two bills of exchange from his wife's millinery business, sells (discounts) them to Ralph Nickleby, Nicholas' uncle. The bills might have been drawn by Mrs Mantalini on customers who had bought some of her hats. She was providing credit and would be paid by presenting the bills for payment when they matured at 60 or 120 days hence. Ralph needed to know when exactly the bills were payable because that determined how long he would be out of his money and thus the discount rate he would apply. He also checked the names on the bills, in other words, which of Mrs Mantalini's customers had either accepted or indorsed them so they were liable to pay on them when they matured. There was always the risk that parties to a bill might default, and who they were and their reputation were other factors in what he was to pay Mantalini for them.

Mrs Mantalini's bills related to a domestic transaction. The same principles applied to bills of exchange utilised in international trade. They acted as an instrument of payment when, at a distance, it became impractical to pay with coin or bullion.[34] As with Mrs Mantalini's bills, they also acted as an instrument of credit. An exporter of goods would draw a bill (as drawer), directing the importer or the importer's bank (the drawee) to pay the price of goods sold to the exporter (the payee) 'or order' – in other words, any one the payee designated. The bill could be transferred to others by the exporter or further holder indorsing the back of it with their signature. If the importer or the importer's bank 'accepted' the bill, by signing it on its face, it had primary liability to any holder. A bill used for trade would typically be drawn so that payment was so many days after its date (e.g., 30, 60, 90 days) or possibly 'sight' (in other words, acceptance). Thus, the importer had credit for that period and could defer payment until the bill matured. The exporter might be paid immediately if able to sell (discount) the bill in the money market. The price would be at a discount because payment was being made earlier than the date of maturity of the bill. The discount represented the interest payable for that period (e.g., 30, 60, 90 days if they were discounted immediately).

---

[33] London, Macmillan, 1916 (reprint of 1st edition).
[34] G. Conder, 'Bills of Exchange' (1889) 10 *J Institute of Bankers* 415, 417. See also L. Neal, *The Rise of Financial Capitalism*, Cambridge, Cambridge University Press, 1991, 7

(i) The Law in Outline

All this could be done within a relatively stable if somewhat knotted framework of law. The bill of exchange can be traced back to ancient times and there was a case law in England early on.[35] At the beginning of our period the modern law of bills of exchange was in existence. There was an extensive jurisprudence and the range of treatises on the subject exceeded the writings on contract law.[36] Although bills of exchange law (later known as negotiable instruments law) was highly developed at the beginning of our period, there was still scope for disputes as there were always tricky issues to be litigated, for example, the authority of a person or company to draw, accept or indorse a bill,[37] whether a drawee could give a qualified acceptance to a bill,[38] and the effect of forgery by a party to a bill on the liability to pay.[39] There was also intermittent legislation clarifying and amending the law. As a matter of commercial practice the Summary Procedure on Bills of Exchange Act 1855 facilitated claims on unpaid bills of exchange by introducing an expedited procedure.[40] The summary procedure was continued under the Judicature Act of 1873.[41]

Then at the end of the nineteenth century, the law on bills of exchange was codified in the Bills of Exchange Act 1882. The codification was drafted by M. D. (later Judge) Chalmers.[42] He had given lectures to the Institute of Bankers about the need for codification and had prepared a digest of law on the subject. He later said that John Hollams – the prominent solicitor from the law firm which is now Clifford Chance – prompted the Associated Chambers of Commerce and the Institute of Bankers to fund his work. A view among bankers, Chalmers said, was that codification was necessary to overcome the confusion in the law, 'the chaotic state into which it has been thrown by the multiplication of statutes and legal decisions'. Chalmers himself denied that his draft bill was intended to promote the interests of bankers at the expense of others. He said that for his codification to work he had made inquiries among bankers and merchants, and that he had seen American authorities. The aim of his draft bill, he added, was to reproduce the existing law, although there were a limited number of provisions which consciously altered the law or affirmed

---

[35] B. Geva, *The Payment Order of Antiquity and the Middle Ages A Legal History*, Oxford, Hart Publishing, 2010.

[36] *Oxford History of the Laws of England, vol.12, 1820–1914, Private Law*, Oxford, Oxford University Press, 2010, 731 (M. Lobban); J. Holden, *History of Negotiable Instruments Law*, London, Athlone Press, 1955, 143–144, 203, 270.

[37] *Kreditbank Cassel GmbH* v. *Schenkers Ltd* [1927] 1 KB 826 (bills to import German toys).

[38] *Smith* v. *Vertue* (1860) 9 CBNS 214; 142 ER 84 ('Payable on giving up bill of lading for 76 bags of clover-seed per *Amazon* at the London and Westminster Bank, Borough Branch'.).

[39] J. Ames, 'The Doctrine of Price v Neal' (1891) 4 *Harv LR* 297 (forged signature of drawer ineffective).

[40] 18 & 19 Vic c.67.

[41] see also Supreme Court Rules, Order III, r.6 and Order XIV, r.1; *Walker* v. *Hicks* (1877) 3 QBD 8, 9, on the balance to be struck: speed versus giving a defendant the opportunity to pay.

[42] On Chalmers codifications: 5, 41, 203–204 above.

rules not always recognised in practice.[43] The encomium of a prominent commercial lawyer and judge of the interwar period, Sir Frank MacKinnon, was that the 1882 Act was 'the best drafted Act of Parliament ever passed'.[44] That was problematic.

Bills of exchange had advantages over other methods of providing trade credit. First, the claim embodied in a bill was transferrable by delivery of the bill (or by indorsement and delivery), and a holder of the bill could sue in its own name. Open account trading, where exporters simply sold on credit, was too risky. The goods might arrive, and on a falling market the importer might reject them for spurious reasons and not pay. International factoring of an exporter's receivables was inhibited. Although under English law contractual claims to payment (receivables) could be transferred by assignment, there were legal difficulties. For instance, the transferor might need to be joined when the transferee sued the debtor/obligor. The cross-border nature of claims in international trade compounded the problems.

By contrast, claims to payment under a bill of exchange were transferred by simple delivery of the instrument if payable to bearer or by indorsement and delivery if payable to order. This ease of transferability was the cornerstone of the market in bills; they could be freely bought and sold and a bank or discount house taking a bill could sue in its own name. The terms 'transferability' and 'negotiability' were often used interchangeably. In law negotiability meant something more: a person buying a bill – such as a bank or discount house discounting it in the money market – generally obtained a good title to it, even though the transferor had a defective title or no title at all. To obtain this benefit, the so-called holder in due course had to take the bill in good faith and for value. Negotiability was not an essential shield in the money market: the banks and discount houses were experts in handling bills, and simply refused to accept or discount the suspicious, or to take them as collateral.[45]

A second advantage of a claim to payment under a bill of exchange was that it was generally dissociated from any claims arising on the underlying or an associated transaction. Arguably this was the courts consciously moulding the law to commercial need by 'freeing the bill of the bickerings between drawer and drawee as a first step in a developing money economy'.[46] Admittedly after the Judicature Act 1873 an importer could more easily raise a counterclaim about the quality of goods when sued by the exporter on a bill drawn for payment. In practice, however, since a bill drawn in international trade was often discounted the holder of the bill would not be an immediate party to the

---

[43] M. Chalmers, *The Bills of Exchange Act 1882*, 3rd ed., London, Waterlow & Sons, 1882, iv-vi.
[44] *Bank Polski* v. *K. J. Mulder and Co* [1942] 1 KB 497, 500. MacKinnon was a pupil of Scrutton: see G. Rubin, 'MacKinnon, Sir Frank Douglas (1871–1946)', *Oxford Dictionary of National Biography*.
[45] see G. Pownall, *English Banking*, London, Blades, East & Blades, 1914, 29. see also J. Rogers, 'The Myth of Negotiability' (1990) 31 *Boston College LR* 265 on the earlier period.
[46] R. Steffen, *Cases on Commercial and Investment Paper*, 3rd edn, Brooklyn, Foundation Press, 1964, 25.

underlying transaction and thus have no responsibility for the quality of the goods. In that situation the importer would have to pursue its claim separately against its counterparty to the contract of sale. As to the importer raising related claims when sued on a bill, Jessel MR said in 1878 that he would hesitate allowing it.[47] For this reason it was later said that payment by means of a bill of exchange was to be treated as analogous to a payment in cash. That was the expression in *James Lamont & Co Ltd* v. *Hyland Ltd*,[48] an action on a bill of exchange drawn by the plaintiff and accepted by the defendants in respect of shipbuilding work on a vessel belonging to the latter. The rule was even more emphatically stated in *Brown Shipley & Co Ltd* v. *Alicia Hosiery Ltd*,[49] at the end of our period. There the bank was the indorsee of some bills which Alicia had accepted as the buyer of stockings. When it sued Alicia on the bills, the bank was met by a counterclaim that, on a separate transaction, it had given Alicia a delivery order in relation to hosiery in a warehouse over which it (the bank) had security, but which the warehouse refused to release until a number of invoices had been met. The Court of Appeal refused a stay of execution for the bank's claim on the bills.

(ii) Trade Bills and Bank Bills

By the twentieth century the books for bankers divided bills of exchange financing trade into three main categories, trade bills, bank bills and other bills.[50] So-called trade bills were drawn on an importer, making the importer primarily liable on the bill when it was accepted. The bank bill was where the importer had an arrangement with a bank to accept the bill, so the bank had primary liability on it when it accepted the bill. Acceptances of bills by first-class London banks commanded the finest rates of discount, since the risk of non-payment was minimal. These bills could be readily turned into cash in the money market. When drawn on a first-class London bank, and payable in pounds sterling in London, bills of exchange became known as the Bill on London. Among the third category of bills was the so-called agency bill, where the acceptor was an overseas bank or its London branch. Bills which these banks accepted were not readily saleable in London because the Bank of England would not take them. Nor would it take foreign domicile bills, those drawn and accepted by banks and businesses abroad.

Banks engaged in accepting bills of exchange were in what was described as the acceptance business. In the nineteenth century the acceptance business was the forte of the merchant banks, and because of this they were often known as acceptance houses. They were 'the commercial cadres of the age ... [t]heir principal instrument the bill of exchange ... fulfill[ing] all the functions necessary to make regular transactions possible between widely distant

---

[47] *Anglo-Italian Bank* v. *Wells* (1878) 38 LT 197, 199.   [48] [1950] 1 KB 585, 591.
[49] [1966] 1 Lloyd's Rep 668. See also [1970] 1 QB 195 on further aspects of the litigation.
[50] e.g., H. Greengrass, *The Discount Market in London*, London, Pitman, 1930, 26–27.

Figure 6.1 Bill of exchange drawn by The Bank of the United States to pay £750 to Stephen Whitney, accepted by Baring Brothers in London (The Syndics of Cambridge University Library, Jardine Matheson Archive)

places'.[51] The Barings and the Rothschilds were early in the field. In the 1830s Barings authorised the issuance of bills drawn on them, in advance of sales, against consignments from the United States of cotton, rice, tobacco and other commodities.[52] During the nineteenth century Barings had a larger acceptance business than the Rothschilds, although in the second half of the century firms like Kleinwort, Schroders and Brown Shipley & Co made a good deal of the running, with smaller firms like the Rathbones also very active.[53] Schroders' policy for a time was to manage risk by maintaining an acceptance business on a small scale with a large number of customers; other merchant banks serviced fewer but larger merchant firms.[54] Rathbones emulated the Barings system under which the bills had to state the shipment against which the bills were drawn to demonstrate that they were trade-related and not merely exchange transactions.[55] This became the standard practice for other banks.[56]

---

[51] D. Landes, 'The Old Bank and the New: The Financial Revolution in the Nineteenth Century', in F. Crouzet, W. Stern & W. Chaloner (eds.), *Essays in European Economic History 1789–1914*, London, Edward Arnold, 1969, 115.

[52] R. Hidy, *The House of Baring in American Trade and Finance. English Merchant Bankers at Work 1763–1861*, Cambridge, Mass, Harvard University Press, 1949, 131. See also P. Ziegler, *The Sixth Great Power Barings 1762–1929*, London, Collins, 1988, 134.

[53] S. Chapman, *The Rise of Merchant Banking*, London, Allen & Unwin, 1984, 17, 44–45, 116, 237; P. Ziegler, ibid., 189; N. Ferguson, *The World's Banker: The History of the House of Rothschild*, London, Weidenfeld & Nicolson, 1998, 292; J. Wake, *Kleinwort Benson*, Oxford, Oxford University Press, 1997, 116, 126; R. Roberts, *Schroders*, Basingstoke, Macmillan, 1992, 99 (Table 4.3).

[54] R. Roberts, ibid., 48.

[55] S. Marriner, *Rathbones of Liverpool 1845–73*, Liverpool, Liverpool University Press, 1961, 154–155.

[56] J. Tritton, 'Bills of Exchange and their Functions' (1902) 23 *J Institute of Bankers* 209, 214. *Guaranty Trust Company of New York* v. *Hannay & Co* [1918] 2 K.B. 623, 660 (expert evidence that of 23,000 bills in a period of five years, 93 per cent bore on their face words referring to the commercial transaction giving rise to the bill, per Scrutton LJ).

By the early twentieth century the large, amalgamated joint stock banks had entered the acceptance market and were soon keen rivals of the merchant banks.[57] The London acceptance business revived in importance after the First World War, but as a result of the Great Depression there was a drop off in trade in the early 1930s and thus of acceptances.[58] With the growth of international trade after the Second World War there was what one merchant banker described in the mid-1960s as a 'remarkable comeback' in bill finance for international trade.[59]

With a trade bill, the importer's prospective acceptance might not persuade a bank in the exporter's jurisdiction to discount it, and it might have to be held to maturity. *Naoroji* v. *Chartered Bank of India*[60] was an example. The plaintiff firm drew large numbers of bills upon merchants in Bombay (Mumbai), who were purchasing goods from Britain and perhaps elsewhere in Europe.[61] These it handed in batches to Hunter & Co, its agents in London, to be transmitted to Bombay and collected there. To do this Hunter & Co used the defendant bank in London, the Chartered Bank of India, which had a branch in Bombay.[62] The branch would arrange for the Bombay merchants to accept the bills, and to remit the proceeds to England when the bills were paid. The branch remitted payment by drafts drawn in the plaintiff's favour on City Bank.[63] (The Chartered Bank banked with City Bank.) On receipt of these drafts the Chartered Bank would hand them (under cover of a letter) to Hunter & Co, who in turn would deliver them to the plaintiff firm.[64]

A bill drawn on an importer might be discounted in the exporter's jurisdiction by attaching the shipping documents. In this way the trade bill slotted into a network of other documents – the shipping documents in this case, but in other cases a letter of credit or maybe a domestic bill. Brown Shipley & Co claimed to have been the first to use the so-called documentary bill in financing trade between the United States and Britain in the first part of the nineteenth century. To assure payment, the documentary bill involved appending the shipping documents to the bill of exchange drawn on a consignee of the

---

[57] 27 above.
[58] R. Truptil, *British Banks and the London Money Market*, London, Jonathan Cape, 1936, 261.
[59] G. Young, *Merchant Banking: Practice and Prospect*, London, Weidenfeld & Nicolson, 1966, 30. Young became a merchant banker after being deputy director of MI6: J. Lockhart, 'Young, George Kennedy (1911–1990)', *Oxford Dictionary of National Biography*.
[60] (1868) LR 3 CP 444 (Bovill CJ, Byles, Keating, Montague Smith JJ).
[61] Naoroji was a partner in Cama & Co and opened an English branch in 1855, the first Indian firm established in England: D. Lewis Jones, 'Naoroji, Dadabhai (1825–1917)', *Oxford Dictionary of National Biography*; R. Visram, *Ayahs, Lascars and Princes: Indians in Britain 1700–1947*, London, Pluto, 1986, 79. Naoroji's firm engaged Freshfields to conduct the litigation.
[62] Now part of Standard Chartered Bank.
[63] City Bank was London correspondent for 40 overseas banks providing bill finance for international trade, acquired in 1898 by Midland: A. Holmes & E. Green, *Midland: 150 Years of Banking Business*, London, B.T. Batsford, 1986, 96–97.
[64] In the litigation the plaintiff firm was seeking to collect on some of the bills sent to Bombay but the court held that the defendant bank could set off under the Bankrupt Act 1849 a larger sum which the plaintiff owed it.

goods.[65] That gave the bank or merchant discounting the bill (buying it) control over the goods, since the shipping documents included the bill of lading, a document of title to the goods. In 1847 the *Bankers' Magazine* gave the example of silk being exported from India, and the exporter being able to discount the bill in rupees in the Indian money market, attaching the bill of lading and the policy of insurance to the bill. The buyer of the bill thus had the security of the exporter's signature on the bill as well as the bill of lading. It would have its London agent arrange for the importer to accept the bill and thus undertake the obligation to pay. The agent could deal with the fabric on its arrival in Britain because it would have been sent the bill of lading in the mail.[66]

This was an example of exporting goods from India. *Jeffryes [Royal Bank of Liverpool] v. Agra and Masterman's Bank*[67] was the other way around, the export of goods to India. Louis Speltz was a merchant in Liverpool, purchasing cotton goods there for export to India, and drawing bills of exchange for the price upon the consignees to whom the goods were shipped. In general the bills were payable 90 days after sight. To get his money sooner, Speltz discounted the bills by indorsing and delivering them and the related bills of lading to Agra Bank. The Bank had the responsibility of forwarding them (and the shipping documents) to its operation in India, which presented the bills to the consignees upon whom they were drawn, first for acceptance and then at maturity for payment. Upon payment by the consignees in India Agra Bank gave them the bills of lading so that they could take delivery of the goods.

The *Agra case* illustrates how in the second half of the nineteenth century the documents representing the goods were in the possession of the holders of the bills of exchange until they were paid. By that means the payment of those bills at maturity was secured, since the consignees were not given the documents of title to the goods – essentially the bills of lading – until they paid on the bills of exchange they had accepted. The case also shows the many variations of how transactions were undertaken. Agra bank would discount Speltz's bills in the ordinary way, but it would not pay the full amount straight away. That was to cover any fall in the goods' value when they arrived at their destination. The difference they kept in a separate, so-called marginal account. In each case the bank would give Speltz a memorandum of receipt, in effect undertaking to pay Speltz the amount in the marginal account, plus interest, once the bills of exchange were paid.[68] The essential

---

[65] A. Ellis, *Heir of Adventure The Story of Brown, Shipley & Co Merchant Bankers 1810-1960*, London, Brown, Shipley & Co, 1960, 38.

[66] 'Banking Institutions of British India' (1847) 7 *Bankers' Magazine* 70, 71-72. *Latham v. Chartered Bank of India* (1874) LR 17 Eq 205 is an example.

[67] (1866) LR 2 Eq 674. Jeffreys was suing as the bank's public officer. The bank was India based: see S. Muirhead, *Crisis Banking in the East: The History of the Chartered Mercantile Bank of India, London and China 1853-93*, Aldershot, Scolar Press, 1996, 89-90, 95.

[68] The case arose when Speltz dishonestly indorsed by way of security to Royal Bank of Liverpool the Agra bank receipts and then failed.

point was that the bill of exchange worked in tandem with the shipping documents.[69]

In practice the picture drawn of a division between trade bills on the one hand and bank bills on the other was not as straightforward as the books on banking practice suggested. Bills might be drawn on an importer, but with a bank as payee, so that if indorsing the bill the bank accepted liability on it, but not the primary liability it would have if it had accepted it.[70] Bills might be drawn not on the importer but on a trading house, whose reputation was such that they could be discounted in the exporter's jurisdiction.[71]

The Bill on London, as we have seen, involved a bill of exchange payable in pounds sterling in London, which was accepted by a first-class London bank. Such bills were universally acknowledged and 'readily convertible in the money market of London'.[72] If it were known that a bill of exchange was drawn under a credit issued by a first-class London bank covering, say, exports from India, so that it was bound eventually to be accepted by the bank, it should be readily discountable in the Indian money market. As a precaution, however, a bank might require that a Bill on London be drawn so as not to exceed a specified amount to prevent the bank's overexposure to a specific trader.

Part of the network of documents of which a trade bill was part, in addition to the shipping documents, might be a domestic bill of exchange relating to further dealings in the goods once they had arrived from abroad. A simple example is provided by *Greenhalgh and Sons* v. *Union Bank of Manchester*.[73] There cotton brokers in Liverpool, Greenhalgh and Sons, sold bales of cotton being shipped from Alexandria, Egypt, to Winson & Co, who were cotton merchants in Manchester. That was no doubt under trade bills. Winson & Co. sold the cotton to textile spinners, the Tulketh Mill and the Ocean Spinning Company, who paid under domestic bills of exchange. Greenhalgh had refused payment by cash when Winson insisted on a cash discount, and so payment by Winson & Co was by it accepting bills drawn on it by Greenhalgh at three months after the date of the bill of lading. In the litigation, the issue (not relevant for us) was whether the bills drawn and accepted by the spinning mills were specifically appropriated to meet Greenhalgh's bills when paid in to one of Winson's accounts.

As already foreshadowed, a further part of the documentary network in which the bill of exchange operated in financing international trade was the letter of credit. To that we now turn.

---

[69] See Scrutton LJ's clear account in *Guaranty Trust Company of New York* v. *Hannay & Co* [1918] 2 KB 623, 659–660.
[70] cf. *Brown Shipley, & Co* v. *Kough* (1885) 29 Ch D 848.
[71] *Phelps, Stokes & Co* v. *Comber* (1885) 29 Ch D 813 (bills drawn on Liverpool firm and discounted in New York).
[72] W. Willis, *The Law of Negotiable Securities*, London, Stevens & Haynes, 1869, 63.
[73] [1924] 2 KB 153. See S. Beckert, *Empire of Cotton*, London, Penguin Random House, 2014, 207ff on the network of brokers getting the cotton from Liverpool to the mills.

2 Letters of Credit

> Her father, instead of giving her an unlimited order on his banker, or even putting an hundred pounds bank bill into her hands, gave her only ten guineas, and promised her more when she wanted it. (Jane Austin, *Northanger Abbey*, 1803)[74]

The letter of credit, which Catherine in Jane Austen's novel had hoped her father might have his bank furnish her for her travels, was what was called an 'open credit'. It would have been addressed to the bank's agents or correspondent banks elsewhere, requesting them to pay Catherine up to the sum mentioned in it. The open letter of credit had a long pedigree and in the twentieth century became the travellers' cheque.[75] It was used by Italian merchants in the fourteenth century.[76] Certainly by the late eighteenth century several decisions of Lord Mansfield demonstrate that it was available in England for business purposes.[77] In the nineteenth century open letters of credit continued to be used for private travellers like Catherine, as well as for commercial purposes.[78] Thus, the Charing Cross branch of the National Bank in *Conflans Stone Quarry Co Ltd v. Parker, Public Officer of the National Bank*[79] prepared credits for the quarry company, which was working certain stone quarries in France, to remit moneys to its agent there.

(i) Open and Documentary Letters of Credit

As with other commercial developments, the precise history of open and documentary letters of credit for international trade is somewhat unclear. In the first part of the nineteenth century Americans trading out of Boston were granted open letters of credit by some English banks to assemble cargos of silks, spices and teas in the Far East.[80] Open letters of credit were issued by some of the merchant banks like Brown Shipley and Company, with its heavy North American trade in goods such as cotton. These were undertakings to pay over a certain period, but there was no requirement for the exporter to prove

---

[74] Completed 1808, published 1818.
[75] *Martin* v. *Boure* (1601) Cro Jac 6; 79 ER 6 is said to be the first reported English case. See J. Smith & G. Dowdeswell, *A Compendium of Mercantile Law*, London, Stevens, 1859, 9.
[76] B. Kozolchyk, 'The Legal Nature of the Irrevocable Commercial Letter of Credit' (1965) 14 *American J Comp L* 395, 395–396.
[77] *Mason* v. *Hunt* (1779) 1 Doug 297, 99 ER 192. See also *Pillans* v. *Van Mierop* (1765) 3 Burr 1663, 97 ER 1035; *Russel* v. *Langstaffe* (1780) 2 Doug 514, 99 ER 328. See G. McMeel, 'Pillans v Van Mierop (1765)', in C. Mitchell & P. Mitchell (eds.), *Landmark Cases in the Law of Contract*, Oxford, Hart Publishing, 2008. See also R. Trimble, 'The Law Merchant and the Letter of Credit' (1948) 61 *Harv LR* 981, 989–992.
[78] 'On the Law of Letters of Credit and Bankers' Drafts' (1850) 10 *Bankers' Magazine* 487. For standard forms for open credit see J. Gilbart, *A Practical Treatise on Banking*, 4th ed., London, Longman et al, 1836,112.
[79] (1867) LR 3 CP 1.
[80] G. Gilmore, 'Formalism and the Law of Negotiable Instruments' (1979) 13 *Creighton LR* 441, 447.

that the cotton had been shipped.[81] That may have been because shipping was organised through Brown Shipley's American associate, Brown Brothers, so it knew what was going on. Alternatively, a bank might have been prepared to take the risk of paying on an open credit because of competitive pressures.[82] In other cases open letters of credit were available because of the trust built up between the bank and its customers. This seems to have been the position with the Anglo-Australian and Australian banks as regards the export of wool to Europe.[83]

By mid-century, however, there were instances where a bank's undertaking to pay was conditional on the presentation of shipping documents.[84] In 1868 in *Maitland* v. *Chartered Mercantile Bank of India, London and China*[85] the bank gave evidence that marginal letters of credit[86] could be open or documentary: with documentary credits the importer would have 'a well-known house (not necessarily a bank) give an undertaking to the exporter that against the presentation of conforming shipping documents the bank would pay or accept a bill of exchange drawn by the exporter for the price of the goods'.[87] Disputes about documentary credits began featuring in the courts. The collapse of Agra Bank led to at least two cases. In *Re Barber & Co ex parte Agra Bank*[88] the bank opened a letter of credit in favour of Sylhet and Cachar Tea Co Ltd of Calcutta. Under it the company could draw bills of exchange at six months' sight, to the value of the tea shipped during the season. The bills were to be accompanied by the bills of lading, a policy of insurance, and an invoice for the tea shipped. The bills would then be accepted by the purchaser, Barber & Co, and forwarded to the bank, to be applied to what it had paid to the tea company under the credit. In *Re Agra Bank ex parte Tondeur*[89] there was a similar letter of credit. This time it was issued at the request of Tondeur & Co of Melbourne by Agra &

---

[81] E. Perkins, *Financing Anglo-American Trade: The House of Brown 1800–1880*, Cambridge, Mass, Harvard University Press, 1975, 25, 115, 121, 131; J. Brown, *A Hundred Years of Merchant Banking. A History of Brown Brothers and Company, Brown, Shipley & Company and the Allied Firms*, New York, Brown Brothers & Co, 1909, 32.

[82] R. Hidy, The House of Baring in American Trade and Finance. English Merchant Bankers at Work 1763–1861, *op cit*, 353.

[83] A. Barnard, *The Australian Wool Market 1840–1890*, Melbourne, Melbourne University Press, 1958, 99, 102.

[84] E.P. Ellinger, *Documentary Letters of Credit-A Comparative Study*, Singapore, University of Singapore Press, 1970, 29–30. See also G. Xiang & R. Buckley, 'The Unique Jurisprudence of Letters of Credit: Its Origins and Sources' (2003) 4 *San Diego Int'l LJ* 91, 105; P. Ellinger & D. Neo, *Law and Practice of Documentary Letters of Credit*, Oxford, Hart, 2010, 3–4. .

[85] (1868) 38 LJ Ch 363. See also (1865) 2 Hem & M 440, 71 ER 534.

[86] So called because the person named in the margin to the bill of exchange undertook that another would pay or have the recipient's bills accepted: H. Macleod, *Theory and Practice of Banking*, 3rd ed., London, Longmans, 1879, vol. II, 510.

[87] at 367.   [88] (1870) LR 9 Eq 725.

[89] (1867) LR 5 Eq 160. The failure of the Bank of Liverpool gave rise to *Prehn* v. *The Royal Bank of Liverpool* (1870) LR 5 Ex 92 (documentary credit in favour of grain merchants at Alexandria, Egypt). See N. Miller, 'Problems and Patterns of the Letter of Credit' [1959] *U Illinois LF* 162, 164.

Masterman's branch in that city in favour of A. Seurin & Co of Mauritius, who was selling a cargo of sugar.

In the first part of the 1870s both Lord Hatherley LC and Lord Cairns LC remarked that the court was very familiar with documentary credits.[90] There may have been an element of boasting in this; it certainly conveyed an enthusiasm for such a convenient device. From the exporter's point of view, letters of credits offered definite advantages over a bill of exchange in making sure of payment, even where the bill was accompanied by the shipping documents. By the time a bill of exchange drawn by the exporter was with the importer or its bank, the importer's situation may have deteriorated, and it might not pay on or accept the bill. The exporter would almost invariably incur expense in retrieving the situation.[91] By contrast, with a letter of credit the exporter obtained the undertaking of a bank that it would pay on presentation of complying documents. Typically, this was the time of shipment, in other words, once the exporter obtained the bill of lading evidencing that the goods had been shipped and could present it to the bank. The bill of lading as the document of title to the goods was the key document for the bank (or its branch or agent) to receive before it paid out, along with the invoice, an insurance policy, and possibly also (as required by the contract of sale) a certificate of quality, inspection or origin.[92] In the years prior to the First World War most US cotton was exported to Europe under documentary credits.[93]

(ii) The Role of the Banks

We have, therefore, in our Documentary Credit Department an organisation which specialises in facilitating these transactions. As the vast numbers of commercial firms all over the world render it almost impossible for each firm to have an accurate knowledge of the status of all the other firms with whom it may be asked to do business, the Bank is ready to lend the support of its name and reputation and to act as an intermediary, helping both sides of commercial operations. (Hambros Bank, 1939)[94]

Documentary credits were largely the preserve of the merchant banks until the First World War.[95] By the early twentieth century Kleinworts,

---

[90] *Re Barned's Banking Co* (1871) LR 5 HL 157, 166 (transactions giving rise to letter of credit 'of a very ordinary character'); *Morgan* v. *Larivière* (1875) LR 7 HL 423, 432 (court 'perfectly familiar' with documentary credits).
[91] A. Davis, *Law relating to Commercial Letters of Credit*, London, Pitman, 1939, 13–14.
[92] e.g., *Equitable Trust Co of New York* v. *Dawson Partners Ltd* (1927) 27 Ll L Rep 49 (HL) (quality certificate from experts and signed by Chamber of Commerce for Batavia (Indonesia)).
[93] J. Arnold, 'Financing of Cotton' (September 1911) 38 *Annals Amer Acad Pol & Soc Sc* 285–286 (a good explanation of the practicalities). See also J. Killick, 'The Transformation of Cotton Marketing in the Late Nineteenth Century: Alexander Sprunt and Son of Wilmington, N. C. 1884–1956' (1981) 55 *Business Hist Rev* 143, 159.
[94] *Hambros Bank Ltd 1839–1939*, London, Hambros Bank, 1939, 34.
[95] M. Ackrill & L. Hannah, *Barclays: The Business of Banking 1690–1996*, Cambridge, Cambridge University Press, 2000, 100, presumably refers to travellers' letters of credit.

for instance, had built up a large letter of credit business with the assistance of Goldman Sachs.[96] Banks were paid a commission on the documentary credits issued. The joint stock banks did not issue them in a significant way until after the First World War.[97] At that point the uncertainty in trade conditions greatly extended their use, and the bulk of imports and exports were financed this way.[98] Lord Sumner, a judge with his ear to the commercial ground, thought that this was because, in difficult times for trade like the 1920s, there was a breakdown in trust on the part of exporters in relying on a buyer's credit. Exporters were increasingly stipulating in sales contracts that payment must be under a documentary credit, preferably by a bank in the country of export.[99] There was also a desire to protect against sharp fluctuations in exchange rates.[100]

The London-based merchant banks issued letters of credit in favour of exporters around the world. As the system developed, banks employed correspondent banks in exporters' jurisdictions to notify and in some cases confirm the credit (in other words, accept liability itself, receiving an indemnity from the issuing bank for doing so). For a substantial time there was an overlap in terminology between confirmed and irrevocable credits.[101] After the Second World War the confirmed credit came to mean that the correspondent bank undertook an independent obligation to pay, provided compliant documents were presented.[102] The banks had arrangements among themselves to indemnify and pay their correspondents in these circumstances.

(iii) The Bank-friendly Common Law and the Rise of the UCP

Documentary credits were untrammelled by legislation. The law was judge-made and accommodated commercial practice. This applied to doctrine but also to fact finding, which was 'to be measured in the light of commercial considerations and the commercial purpose of the contract'.[103]

---

[96] S. Diaper, *History of Kleinwort, Sons & Co. in Merchant Banking 1858–1966*, PhD thesis, University of Nottingham, 1983, 261; C. Ellis, *The Partnership. The Making of Goldman Sachs*, London, Allen Lane, 2008, 6–7.

[97] e.g., C. Collins, *History Law and Practice of Banking*, London, James Cornish, 1882, 240. cf. T. Moxon, *English Practical Banking*, 15th ed., Manchester, John Heywood, 1910, 46. Moxon was a banker with the Lancashire and Yorkshire Bank, which in 1928 was acquired by the Bank of Liverpool and Martins Ltd and is now part of Barclays.

[98] L. Minty, *English Banking Methods*, London, Pitman, 1930, 493. Minty was a former banker.

[99] e.g., *Urquhart Lindsay and Co Ltd v. Eastern Bank Ltd* [1922] 1 KB 318.

[100] *The Kronprinsessan Margareta* [1921] 1 AC 486, 510. See also A. Davis, Law relating to Commercial Letters of Credit, *op cit*, 10.

[101] H. Hart, *Law of Banking*, 4th ed., London, Stevens, 1931, vol. II, 645–650; *Halsbury's Laws of England*, 2nd ed., London, Butterworth, 1931, vol. I, 845.

[102] *Pavia & Co S.P.A. v. Thurmann-Nielsen* [1952] 2 QB 84, 88 per Lord Denning.

[103] *Sinason-Teicher Inter-American Grain Corporation v. Oilcakes and Oilseeds Trading Co Ltd* [1954] 1 WLR 935, 941, per Devlin J (case from LCTA appeal committee; issue of reasonable time; bank guarantee, but treated as letter of credit case). Affirmed [1954] 1 WLR 1394.

As to doctrine, three examples make the point. The first was the principle which emerged that the bank's undertaking on the documentary credit was separate from the underlying contract. Consequently, it was not subject to any claim or defence which the importer might have on the sales contract. This rule was underlined in a series of challenges in the decade after the Second World War, when British Imex Industries Ltd sold a large quantity of reinforced steel to a Jordanian firm, trading as Hamzeh Malas & Sons, for delivery in two instalments. Payment was to be made by means of two confirmed letters of credit opened by the Arab Bank Ltd, and confirmed by the Midland Bank in London, one in respect of each instalment. The goods were shipped in late November 1957. On the morning of 10 December 1967 Donovan J refused to continue an overnight injunction whereby Hamzeh Malas & Sons sought to prevent the British firm from realising the second letter of credit on the ground that the first instalment of steel rods was defective. On appeal the same day the Court of Appeal held that Donovan J was correct: the opening of a confirmed letter of credit constituted a bargain between the bank and the seller of the goods, which imposed upon the bank an absolute obligation to pay, irrespective of any dispute between the parties as to whether the goods were up to standard. Jenkins LJ reasoned that the law should follow commercial practice.[104]

A further example of how the English courts fell in with commercial practice was when a bank was faced with shipping documents which did not comply with the terms of the letter of credit. Banks, the courts held, were entitled to refuse payment unless the exporter tendered documents which complied strictly with its terms. Lord Sumner famously enunciated the doctrine of strict compliance in *Equitable Trust Company of New York* v. *Dawson Partners Ltd*, justifying it in terms of the bank's interests: 'There is no room for documents which are almost the same, or which will do just as well .... The bank's branch abroad, which knows nothing officially of the details of the transaction thus financed, cannot take upon itself to decide what will do well enough and what will not.'[105]

A corollary of the rule about strict compliance was that a bank could reject documents where the goods were described differently from the credit, even if it was understood in a trade that the descriptions were interchangeable. Bankers were not obliged, the courts held, to know the practices of the trades they financed. The leading case was *J. H. Rayner and Co Ltd* v. *Hambro's Bank Ltd*.[106] In accordance with instructions from a Danish correspondent bank, Hambros opened a confirmed credit in favour of Rayner covering a cargo of

---

[104] Hamzeh Malas & Sons v British Imex Industries Ltd [1958] 2 QB 127, at 129. On 11 December the British firm presented the bank with the shipping documents. The bank refused to pay. On 20 December Salmon J held that the bank was wrong to refuse, noting 'the speed and convenience with which the commercial community can have its disputes determined' in the Commercial Court: *British Imex Industries Ltd* v. *Midland Bank Ltd* [1958] 1 QB 542, 549.
[105] (1927) 27 Lloyd's L Rep 49, 52. See also *English Scottish & Australian Bank Ltd* v. *Bank of South Africa* (1922) 13 Ll L Rep 21.
[106] [1943] 1 KB 37.

'Coromandel groundnuts' from Madras (Chennai). Rayner presented bills of lading for 'machine-shelled groundnut kernels', accompanied by an invoice for 'Coromandel groundnuts'. Hambros refused to pay. Rayner sued. The judge accepted evidence from Mincing Lane that the term 'machine-shelled groundnut kernels' was universally understood in the trade to be identical with 'Coromandel groundnuts' and entered judgment in Rayner's favour. The Court of Appeal allowed the appeal: it would be quite impossible for banking business if banks had to know the way all their customers carried on their business.[107]

As regards the standard to which customers could hold a bank in examining documents, again the English courts adopted a bank-friendly approach. In *National Bank of Egypt* v. *Hannevig's Bank Ltd*[108] Hannevig's Bank was interested on joint account with a Manchester merchant importing onions from Egypt. It requested its correspondent, the National Bank of Egypt, to have the latter's Alexandria branch open a confirmed sight credit in favour of the exporter there. Payment was against the delivery of bills of lading, a marine and war risk insurance certificate and an invoice, and the Egyptian bank paid on receiving them. Hannevig's Bank (in effect, the Egyptian bank's customer) refused to reimburse it. Its objection was that the bills of lading in question had words stating that some of the bags in which the onions were packed were dirty or torn or that the contents had been spilt. In the end the Court of Appeal decided the case based on correspondence between the banks (reading it 'from a business point of view', per Bankes LJ). In the course of his judgment, however, Scrutton LJ referred to the small reward banks earned in issuing a letter of credit and remarked that they could not be expected to comb through the documents finding problems.[109]

Under the standard of strict compliance, a bank could refuse to pay when exporters presented it with non-compliant documents. It could also avoid liability to its customers if it had paid out under a credit when discrepancies were later discovered in the documents, provided it had exercised reasonable judgment in handling them. The need for the bank to act expeditiously in taking up documents, coupled with the fact that it might not know the details of a customer's trade, were behind these doctrinal developments. A further development along the same lines was the finding that a bank was not in default when acting upon a reasonable interpretation of a customer's ambiguous expression in its application to the bank for the credit, or when accepting a document which fell fairly within the wide description the customer had provided.[110]

---

[107] at 41. See generally H. Finkelstein, 'Performance of Conditions under a Letter of Credit' (1925) 25 *Columbia LR* 724, 733.
[108] (1919) 3 *Legal Decisions Affecting Bankers* 213.
[109] at 214. The passage is not reproduced in [1919] Lloyd's List LR 69. Approved by Salmon J in *British Imex Industries* v. *Midland Bank Ltd* [1958] 1 QB 542.
[110] *Midland Bank, Ltd* v. *Seymour* [1955] 2 Lloyd's Rep 147, 151–152; *Commercial Banking Co of Sydney* v. *Jalsard Pty Ltd* [1973] AC 279, 286 (PC).

English doctrinal law regarding documentary credits developed rapidly, mainly from the 1920s. There was an increase in litigation in those turbulent times and as more banks like the joint stock banks entered the market.[111] The common law of documentary credits developed in a typically incremental manner, commercially sensitive and pragmatic. These qualities were most evident with the fundamental question of how in law the bank's undertaking to pay vis-à-vis the beneficiary of the credit (the exporter) could be binding as soon as it was issued. How could this be reconciled with the conventional demands of English contract law that consideration must flow from the promisee (the beneficiary) for the undertaking to have contractual force? Without consideration the undertaking would simply be an offer by the bank until some later point, perhaps when the documents were furnished. Without a doctrine of consideration, other legal systems did not have this difficulty.[112]

The issue gave rise to some legal anguish. When in 1932 Professor Harold Gutteridge QC published the first English book on documentary credits law, he canvassed various theories as to how the bank's undertaking could be legally binding *ab initio*, including that it was acting as a guarantor of the importer, that it was representing that it held funds for the exporter, so that it was estopped from denying its liabilty, and that it was acting as the buyer's agent.[113] Four years later the Law Revision Committee, of which Gutteridge was a member, considered the issue in a report about the doctrine of consideration.[114] The committee concluded that since commercial credits 'are now playing a leading part in the business world, especially where foreign trade is concerned ... it is highly desirable that no legal doubt should be cast on their validity'.[115] Given the problems with the doctrine of consideration, the committee recommended conferring a statutory right on third parties such as the exporter with a documentary credit to enforce its claim to payment.[116] With the arrival of the Second World War nothing was done.

When the matter came before the courts it was addressed in a typically English fashion. Before the Court of Appeal in 1957, the doctrinal problems were simply ignored. It was plain enough, said Jenkins LJ, that the opening of a confirmed letter of credit constituted a bargain between the bank and the exporter imposing 'an absolute obligation to pay', irrespective of underlying

---

[111] E. Sykes, *Banking and Currency*, 4th ed., London, Butterworth, 1918, 257–258.

[112] See B. Kozolchyk, 'Letters of Credit', *International Encyclopedia for Comparative Law*, ix, Ch. 5, 135–143.

[113] H. Gutteridge, *The Law of Bankers' Commercial Credits*, London, Sweet & Maxwell, 1932, 17–27. On Gutteridge, Lord McNair, 'Gutteridge, Harold Cooke (1876–1953)', *Oxford Dictionary of National Biography*; R. Cranston, 'Praising the Professors: Commercial Law and the LSE', in R. Rawlings (ed.), *Law, Society and Economy*, Oxford, Clarendon, 1997, 114–115, 119–121.

[114] *Sixth Interim Report (Statute of Frauds and the Doctrine of Consideration)*, Cmd 5449, London, HMSO, 1937.

[115] Ibid., 28.   [116] Ibid., 31–32. cf. A. Finlay, 'Confirmed Credits' (1938) 85 *LJ* 4.

disputes between the parties as to whether the goods met the contractual standard.[117] The justification was simple. An elaborate commercial system had been built up on the footing of bankers' confirmed credits, Jenkins LJ said, and it would be wrong to interfere with it.[118] By means of judicial fiat, the problem was solved. The binding nature of a bank's undertaking to pay on compliant documents had become the common law, subject of course to a later adverse ruling.[119] As in other areas, the English courts took a pragmatic view and upheld the commercial understanding of documentary credits (which extended to similar abstract payment obligations), regardless of what might be the conceptual difficulties.[120]

The development of documentary credits law followed a more systematic path elsewhere. There was a considerable body of case law in the United States in the nineteenth century; the subject was 'more considered in America than in this country'.[121] In the first part of the twentieth century the American law schools took more than a passing interest.[122] In 1921 the American Acceptance Council assumed the work of the Commercial Credit Conference of US bankers in unifying the practice of the commercial letter of credit by drawing up standard forms for use in such transactions.[123] There were comparable moves to draft rules for documentary credits by banks in continental jurisdictions.

The first attempt at international uniformity was at a conference of the International Chamber of Commerce in 1929. That failed, but the next attempt in Vienna in 1933 was more successful. The first Uniform Customs and Practices for Documentary Credits (UCP) was adopted and used in various European countries and by individual American banks. However, British and Commonwealth banks kept aloof.[124] They did so as well from the 1951 revision, disagreeing with the UCP's approach on a number of points.[125] Given the UCP's widespread adoption elsewhere, however, it was difficult to ignore, even if only to compare the different solutions the UCP had adopted,

---

[117] *Hamzeh Malas & Sons v. British Imex Industries Ltd* [1958] 2 QB 127, 129. Sellers and Pearce LJJ agreed.

[118] at 129.

[119] Law Commission, *Privity of Contract: Contracts for the Benefit of Third Parties*, Law Com no 242, Cm 3329, London, HMSO, 1996, 54n.

[120] See R. Goode, 'Abstract Payment Undertakings', in P. Cane and J. Stapleton (eds.), *Essays for Patrick Atiyah*, Oxford, Clarendon, 1991.

[121] J. Walker, *A Treatise on Banking Law*, London, Stevens, 1885, 105.

[122] e.g., P. Thayer, 'Irrevocable Credits in International Commerce: Their Legal Effects' (1936) 36 Columbia LR 1031 (Pt 1), (1937) 37 Columbia LR 1326 (Pt 2).

[123] *Standard Forms Commercial Letters of Credit*, New York, American Acceptance Council, 1938.

[124] See forms: W. Syrett, *Practice and Finance of Foreign Trade*, London, Macmillan, 1938, 120–112 (Syrett was a well-known teacher of trainee bankers) and S. Thomas, *Banking and Exchange*, London, Gregg Publishing, 1930, 458–459. See also *An Export Handbook*, London, Institute of Export, 1939, 34–35; C. Schmitthoff, *The Export Trade*, London, Stevens, 1948, 145ff.

[125] The areas of disagreement are summarised in P. Ellinger, 'The Uniform Customs—Their Nature and the 1983 Revision' [1984] *LMCLQ* 578, 579.

compared with the common law.[126] It was only with the 1962 revision that British banks began to come on board and to incorporate the UCP by reference into their standard forms.[127] It was a sharp turn-around, and by the end of our period documentary credits issued by British banks were typically governed by the UCP. Once the UCP became incorporated into a letter of credit by reference, its rules were binding between the parties as a matter of contract law.

Despite the rise of the documentary credit, other methods for financing international trade were in evidence. One was barter. Another was trading on open account. An estimate at the end of our period was that some 60 per cent of trade between Britain and what was then the European Economic Community (of which Britain was not yet a member) was on this basis.[128] Trust between the parties was such that payment against shipping documents or under a letter of credit was thought unnecessary. Where in other parts of the world such trust did not exist, letters of credit remained the norm.

3 Dock Warrants and Bank Finance

What an incalculable mass of figures must be collected in those commercial heads! What legions of £.s.d! What a chaos of cash debtor, contra creditor, bills payable, and bills receivable; waste-books, day-books, cash-books and journals; insurance policies, brokerage, agio, tare and tret, dock warrants and commercial bedevilment! They file off to their several avocations, to spin money for others. (George Sala, 1859)[129]

In describing the arrival of the thousands of clerks in the morning rush hour outside the Bank of England in the early 1860s, Sala recognised the role of the dock warrant as one, perhaps a small, element in the financial life of the City. These warrants were issued by the docks, wharves and warehouses where imported goods were being stored. They acknowledged the holder of the warrant as having the right to take delivery of the goods they represented. There are examples of banks advancing money on the security of dock warrants in the first half of the nineteenth century.[130] Certainly from the 1870s the London banks were doing this regularly.[131] Despite banking practice, dock warrants never

---

[126] e.g., M. Megrah, 'Commercial Letters of Credit' (1952) 102 *LJ* 410.
[127] H. Gutteridge & M. Megrah, *The Law of Bankers' Commercial Credits*, 7th ed., London, Europa, 1984, 6. See also 'Documentary Credits: Study submitted to the United Nations by the International Chamber of Commerce' in United Nations, General Assembly, A/CN.9/15, 6 January 1969, Annex 1, 6.
[128] P. Lunn & B. Wheble, *British Banks and International Trade*, London, Institute of Bankers, 1972, 5–7; B. Kozolchyk, 'Letters of Credit', in J. Ziegel, (ed.), *International Encyclopedia of Comparative Law*, Tubingen, Mohr, 1979, vol. IX, Ch. 5, 4n.
[129] G. Sala, *Twice Round the Clock*, London, Houlston & Wright, 1859.
[130] *Phillips* v. *Huth* (1840) 6 M & W 572, 151 ER 540. F. Huth & Co were merchant bankers: C. Jones, 'Huth, (John) Frederick Andrew (1777–1864)', *Oxford Dictionary of National Biography*.
[131] e.g., J. Dun, British Banking Statistics, *op cit*, 86.

achieved the status of being a document of title at common law. That status was reserved for the bill of lading, although as Lord Wright acknowledged in the *Mercantile Bank of India case* in 1938[132] some Private Acts of Parliament had conferred the privilege of being a document of title on some dock warrants.

In light of the common-law position, the doyen of banking practice in the first part of the nineteenth century James Gilbart opined that advances on the security of dock warrants 'must be considered as beyond the rules which prudent bankers lay down for their own government'.[133] By the 1880s banking opinion was more robust. A fellow of the Institute of Bankers wrote that dock warrants were good collateral in the hands of a banker and, when endorsed, property passed without further assignment.[134] In lectures given to the Institute of Bankers in 1901, it was said that the difference between the bill of lading and the dock warrant was 'no longer so important as it once was, especially to bankers, because in the large majority of cases when advances are made on the security of such documents, the transaction comes ... within the provisions of the Factors Act'.[135]

There was no attempt in these remarks to differentiate between dock warrants given statutory backing in a Private Act of Parliament as a document of title and others. The argument that the Factors Acts treated dock warrants as documents of title did little to advance the argument, for it had a limited ambit.[136] The legislation meant that the banks could take a pledge of goods in a dock or warehouse under the *nemo dat* rule as an innocent third party as long as the prerequisites of the Acts were satisfied. However, this had little practical effect since banks generally kept a watchful eye on their customers and were careful in the type of collateral they took. The key point for our purposes is that the common law remained unchanged despite commercial practice treating dock warrants as documents of title, without it seems distinguishing between one type and another. [137]

(i) Early History

Dock warrants emerged with the building of well-organised docks and warehouses in the early nineteenth century in both London and Liverpool. Thus the St Katharine Dock Company issued dock warrants from its beginning in

---

[132] *Official Assignee of Madras v. Mercantile Bank of India Ltd* [1935] AC 53, 60 (PC, India).
[133] J. Gilbart, *A Practical Treatise on Banking*, 5th ed., London, Longman, Brown, Green & Longmans, 1849, vol. I, 47. Gilbart was the general manager and later a director of the London and Westminster Bank until his retirement in 1860. He was made an FRS in 1846.
[134] C. Collins, History, Law and Practice of Banking, *op cit*, 1882, 248.
[135] A. Butterworth, *Bankers' Advances on Mercantile Securities*, London, Sweet & Maxwell, 1902, 37–38.
[136] 152, 351 above; 405 below.
[137] What follows is a modified version of part of 'Commercial Lore and Commercial Law', in J. Lowry & L. Mistelis (eds.), *Commercial Law: Perspectives and Practice*, London, Butterworth, 2006, 83–89.

1828.[138] Its *Code of Instructions, Bye Laws etc* of 1828 is an exemplar of nineteenth-century business administration. It provided that consignees in the ship's manifest could obtain delivery of their goods by warrant or order. If by warrant, the authority for delivery had to be indorsed on it; if by order the order had to be signed by the consignee, and the name of the party to whom delivery was to take place had to be inserted on the order and indorsed by the consignee.[139] Goods would not be delivered to other than those whose names appeared as consignees on the ship's manifest until they proved that they were duly authorised to receive them.[140] Warrants were to be issued to importers – to indorsees of bills of lading – or to proprietors by transfer.[141] Different warrants could be given for different parts of a consignee's goods when the bulk was divided.[142]

Dock warrants were administratively convenient. Procedures needed to be standardised. The 1828 St Katharine Dock Company's Code noted in particular that when goods went into one of the docks' warehouses, orders for the delivery or transfer of goods should be exchanged for warrants, 'it being desirable, with a view to security, uniformity of practice, and general convenience, that the taking out of the latter documents, should be encouraged'.[143] In addition to the administrative benefit to the docks was the advantage for merchants. As the Code put it, 'A Warrant will be the only document issued by the Dock-Company entitled to be considered a legal symbol of goods in their custody'.[144] Transfer was by indorsement, unless the warrants were to bearer or specially indorsed (so that they were not further transferable).

So for the docks the transfer of a warrant meant the transfer of the goods – they regarded it as in the nature of a document of title. Warrants could be subdivided for transfer to different parties. If only part of the goods were sold, a warrant could be issued to the owner of the remainder. As the St Katharine Dock Company's Code said: 'For the convenience of Merchants, they will be allowed to lodge their warrants ... and to give sub-orders, in virtue thereof, for the delivery of the whole, or any part of the goods therein specified.'[145] Warrants could be used by merchants for trading on the increasingly sophisticated commodities markets which, as we have seen, developed in London in the nineteenth century.[146]

Early on important City of London opinion agreed that dock warrants were like documents of title. That view was clearly expressed at a meeting of merchants and others which occurred at the Baltic Coffee House on

---

[138] St Katharine Docks displaced over 11,000 inhabitants and the hospital of St Katharine. With an astonishing lack of foresight they were located so far up the Thames that they were unable to accommodate the advent of larger steamships: P. Stone, *The History of the Port of London*, Barnsley, Pen & Sword Books, 2017, 116–122; J. Pudney, *London's Docks*, London, Thames & Hudson, 1975, 62–64.

[139] MLD, PRA, St Katharine Dock Company, *Code of Instructions, Bye Laws etc.*, 1828, 34.
[140] Ibid. [141] Ibid., 37. [142] Ibid., 38. [143] Ibid., 36. [144] Ibid.
[145] Ibid., 39. See also 163. [146] Chapter 2 above.

11 November 1823 under the chairmanship of Benjamin Hawes.[147] The occasion of the meeting was a decision of the London Dock Company to refuse to honour a transfer certificate for tallow on the basis that the title of the purchaser – Hawes' firm – was defective by reason of a failure to weigh what had been sold.[148] The importers were claiming a right of stoppage *in transitu* despite what were subsequent sales of the transfer certificate. The meeting passed a unanimous resolution. It began by observing that the use of London Dock Company transfer certificates had 'hitherto been productive of great facility in mercantile operations'. It noted that according to the usage of merchants transfers made of them had always been considered and acted upon as actual transfers of them, and that 'the fullest Credit has been given to them by Merchants either by their paying for the Goods particularized in the Transfer Notes or by their making advances upon the Goods transferred'. The resolution characterised the failure of the London Dock Company to deliver the goods in line with the transfer certificate as a breach of good faith and potentially 'utterly subversive' of the usage, 'highly injurious to the interests of commerce and production of the most ruinous consequences to individuals'. A deputation was formed, including Thomas Tooke, instrumental in the formation of the Baltic Committee and a prominent free trader and economist, to take up the matter with the London Dock Company and also Watson's Wharf, which had adopted the same approach.[149]

The London Dock Company called in the lawyers, two of the most eminent commercial barristers of the day. The first was J.B. Bosanquet, by then a serjeant and later a judge in the Court of Common Pleas. He had numerous family connections in the banking and mercantile world, and at the bar had general retainers from the East India Company and the Bank of England.[150] The second was Frederick Pollock, already a FRS and FGS, later to be Attorney-General and a judge, who founded a dynasty prominent in the law, army and church.[151] The brief to counsel set out the apparent implications of the Baltic Coffee House Resolutions, that the dock company should deliver to anyone having a transfer certificate, notwithstanding a defect in that person's title. It then posited that this could not be the result if the dock company was given notice of a forgery or of a gross fraud in the progress of the certificate

---

[147] Earlier that year a Baltic Committee had been formed: D. Kynaston, *The City of London*, London, Pimlco, 1994, vol. I, 52–53; H. Barty-King, *The Baltic Exchange*, London, Hutchinson Benham, 1977, 62–66. It became the Baltic Exchange, the market for chartering ships as well as for dealings in tallow and grain. See 6–7, 61–62 above.

[148] This and the following two paragraphs are drawn from MLD, PRA, BA 645, London Dock Company, *Legal Matters and Disputes 1802–1861*, 231ff. On tallow and the Baltic 6, 66, 108, 111, 119 above.

[149] Tooke's younger brother, William, a solicitor, took a prominent part in the formation of the St Katharine Dock Company.

[150] A. Simpson, *Biographical Dictionary of the Common Law*, London, Butterworths, 1984, 67–68 (J. Anderson).

[151] Pollock having had 24 children, Professor Brian Simpson recalled the piscatorial reference to 'shoals of Pollocks', ibid., 423–424.

through different hands. What of the position where the dock company did not know the contract between vendor and purchaser but the order presented to it was to 'weigh and deliver transfer or release'? Must it weigh, and if it must and had not done so, must it refuse to deliver to a subsequent holder of the transfer certificate if the importer for this reason challenged its title to the goods?

Counsel's opinion on 4 December 1823 was brief. Given the wording of the order, delivery was not complete and weighing was necessary. The dock company was not bound 'to deliver Goods to the Holder of a Transfer Certificate on his order where circumstances have subsequently been disclosed affecting his Title to the Goods'.[152] As regards whether a warrant was a document of title, counsel were cagey, adopting the time-honoured practice of hedging on an issue not essential to answering the question they had been posed. Perhaps this refusal to commit themselves was not surprising since the case law was giving mixed messages about the status of these instruments.

(ii) The Early Jurisprudence

In *Spears* v. *Travers*[153] the defendants had bought sugar from the importers and there had then been several sales ending with the plaintiff. The sugar had remained at the West India Docks, each purchaser taking the dock warrant. The defendants, however, took the sugar by fraudulently representing to the docks that the original dock warrant was lost. Gibbs CJ at Nisi Prius said that the plaintiff, to whom the warrant was transferred for valuable considerable, was entitled to recover in trover. The special jury in the case observed 'that in practice the indorsed warrants and certificates are handed from seller to buyer as a complete transfer of the goods'.

Yet in *Zwinger* v. *Samuda*[154] and *Lucas* v. *Dorrien*[155] West India dock warrants for coffee and sugar respectively had been pledged as security for loans. In *Zwinger*, Serjeant Best (later a judge of the King's Bench and Common Pleas) argued that there could be no mercantile custom as to dock warrants since, unlike bills of lading, they were only of a few years' standing. In *Lucas* he contended that the mere pledge of personal property, without delivery, was void, and that the jury in *Spears* v. *Travers* had merely opined on mercantile practice, making no finding about custom. Although their decisions did not turn on it, it is evident that Dallas and Park JJ rejected Best's arguments and were clear that property in goods would pass by delivery and indorsement of West India dock warrants. In both cases, however, Burrough J explicitly rejected the notion of a mercantile usage to this effect; all the evidence showed

---

[152] For earlier opinions by counsel on transfer certificates, not inconsistent with this: see MLD, PRA, London Dock Co., *op.cit.*, 136–139, 147–148, 163–165, 213–229.
[153] (1815) 4 Camp 251; 171 ER 80.   [154] (1817) 7 Taunt 265; 129 ER 106.
[155] (1817) 7 Taunt 278; 129 ER 112.

was a practice that showed that 'no inconvenience results from the use of these warrants'.[156]

While the docks were seeking the best legal advice, the merchants had turned to the courts. Hawes & Sons brought a test case before the Court of the King's Bench at the Guildhall against Watson's Wharf, which as we have seen was following the practice of the London Dock Company.[157] The tallow in that case had been imported by Raikes & Co, who sold it to Moberly & Bell, who in turn on-sold it to Hawes & Sons. The warrant passed down the line. Moberly & Bell then failed financially and Raikes, not having been paid, gave notice to the wharf not to deliver the tallow on the basis that what remained in the latter's warehouse had not been weighed. Weighing, it was argued, was necessary to ascertain the price. Consequently, property in this tallow had not passed. The result was the importer as unpaid seller could exercise its right of stoppage in transit.

At the hearing on 22 December 1823 the Lord Chief Justice expressed the view that the wharf could not resist delivery in accordance with the transfer certificate, since it had acknowledged that it held the tallow in Hawes' name. Thus the situation differed from that when certificates passed without the wharf knowing and acknowledging that it held on behalf of anyone in particular. In the light of the decision, the London Dock Company asked Bosanquet and Pollock the same day whether the judgment affected their opinion. With the Christmas vacation imminent, in an even shorter opinion the following day, 23 December, counsel opined that it did not, reasserted the need to weigh, and added that 'the safest course for the company to adopt is to file a Bill of Interpleader should the Goods be claimed both by the Vendors and the Vendees'.

So the position with dock warrants was not plain sailing. First was the situation raised in the London Dock Company Opinion and *Hawes v. Watsons Wharf*: was the right of a vendor, such as an importer, to stoppage *in transitu* valid against its immediate purchaser also exercisable against subsequent indorsees of the warrant? In *Hawes v. Watsons Wharf* the Lord Chief Justice thought not, but that was not the settled position. The other issue raised there was whether the goods needed to be weighted for the warrant to be effective. The Bosanquet/Pollock opinion said that weighting was necessary, a matter specifically addressed in the St Katharine Dock Company *Code of Instructions, Bye Laws etc.* (1828): '[A]ll tally, tareing, weighing and gauging, must take place before warrants can be issued.'

---

[156] *Zwinger* at 270; 108. In *Lucas* he said: 'I will not call it a custom' (at 293; 118). See also 'Mercantile Law. The Contract of Sale' (1831) 5 *Law Magazine* 149, 167.

[157] *Hawes v Watson* (1823) Ry & Mood 6, 171 ER 923. Affirmed at (1824) 2 B & C 540, 107 ER 484. Watson's Wharf was a relatively small wharf between the Hermitage and Wapping entrances to the London Docks: C. Ellmers & A. Werner, *London's Riverscape*, London, London's Found Riverscape Partnership, 2000, 15–16.

As ever in a commercial market, there was sometimes a danger of commercial fraud. As far as the docks themselves were concerned, they attempted to protect themselves from rival claims to goods by a rule that they would not deliver them, even to an importer, if the warrants were out, because they could be in other hands.[158] The Factors Acts gave some protection. If an owner entrusted the warrants for goods to a mercantile agent, he could pass good title to a third person such as a bank advancing money on a pledge of the documents. For this exception to the *nemo dat* rule to operate, the warrant needed to be entrusted to the mercantile agent for the purpose of selling the goods, or raising money on them, the disposition would have to have been made in the ordinary course of its business, and the buyer would have to have taken it in good faith and the belief that the mercantile agent was entitled to act.[159] Conversely, a purchaser from an importer could also be a victim of fraud if it permitted the importer to remain in possession of the dock warrant, and the importer acted fraudulently by selling again to a second person.[160]

(iii) Mercantile Opinion and the Law

Mercantile opinion seemed clear: dock warrants should be treated as akin to documents of title. Banks advanced money on them.[161] But the common law did not follow. The position was not helped by *The Contract of Sale*, published in 1845 by Colin Blackburn, later one of the great common-law judges of the second half of the nineteenth century, but at this point of only seven years' call to the bar.[162] Instead of taking a bold approach, Blackburn justified dock warrants not been treated as documents of title. First, they differed from bills of lading in that, when goods were at sea, the purchaser could not take possession. By contrast, where goods were in the docks there was no physical obstacle to the holder of a dock warrant presenting it to the docks, and taking actual or constructive delivery.[163] Second, Blackburn contended, bills of lading were ancient documents, whereas dock warrants were of recent invention, for which no custom of merchants had been established. As to the authorities, Blackburn added, these amounted 'to no more than expressions of opinion at Nisi Prius by two learned Judges, Park J and Dallas J, which are too little to establish a custom'.[164]

Blackburn J's view was expressly endorsed in Court of Exchequer in *Farina v. Home*,[165] a case where a warrant issued by a wharfinger for imported *eau de cologne* had been indorsed to the defendant. Not until the wharfinger had attorned to the defendant as consignee – in other words, acknowledged that

---

[158] MLD, Box 116, Letter, Dock Superintendent to Eastwood & Holt, 12 January 1914.
[159] Factors Act 1825, s.2. Section 1 of the 1825 Act included dock warrants among documents of title like the bill of lading, but that was for the purposes of the Act only. See 400 above.
[160] *Johnson v. Credit Lyonnais Co* (1877) 3 CPD 32.
[161] W. King, *History of the London Discount Market*, London, Routledge, 1936, 189–190.
[162] C. Fifoot, *Judge and Jurist in the reign of Victoria*, London, Stevens, 1959, 16–17.
[163] C. Blackburn, *The Contract of Sale*, London, Benning & Co, 1845, 297–298. [164] Ibid., 301.
[165] (1846) 16 M & W 119; 153 ER 1124.

the cologne was held for him – was there constructive delivery. In the meantime, added Lord Parke, 'the warrant, and the indorsement of the warrant, is nothing more than an offer to hold the goods as the warehouseman of the assignee'.[166] The same approach was taken in *Kingsford* v. *Merry*, where delivery orders for tartaric acid held at the Custom-quay were made out to a fraudster who purported to buy it as the agent of a merchant. On the strength of having the delivery orders the fraudster obtained dock warrants for the goods and pledged them for an advance to the defendant, Thomas Merry & Son, produce brokers in the City of London. Pollock CB's judgment for the Court of Exchequer was in favour of the innocent defendant: property in the acid had passed by delivery of the warrants.[167] That decision was reversed by the Exchequer Chamber in favour of the plaintiffs, the manufacturers of the acid, on the grounds that there was never a contract of sale to the fraudster.[168]

Kingsford v. *Merry*, wrote *The Saturday Review*, turned the City 'into a state of unwonted perturbation', 'much as is a shell had fallen'.[169] Later Benjamin rather haughtily ascribed the excitement to a failure of City merchants to understand that the protection of the Factors Acts only applied where a warrant was 'entrusted' to a mercantile agent, not where the mercantile agent had obtained it fraudulently.[170] Following the judgment, Thomas Merry & Son had circulated merchants about the case and called for legislation. Reporting on the circular, *The Times* observed that the case 'appears to afford one of the strongest illustrations ever presented of the unsound state of our commercial law'. It added that the issue was also of great practical importance to bankers and others making advances on warrants, 'since it demonstrates that these documents, hitherto looked upon only as second to bank-notes in point of security, can no longer be regarded with confidence'.[171]

A meeting of City merchants followed, chaired by Lord Rothschild, although it seemed that the speakers there were not unanimous either about what the law required and what it should be. *The Saturday Review* thought that their uncertainty about what their legal rights were demonstrated that in the great operations of commerce, reliance was placed on a well-understood code of honour and usage rather than on the positive law. Observing that merchants were constantly passing property to an immense amount by dock warrants and the like, and were in the habit of raising money on them, it went on to support

---

[166] at 123, 1126.
[167] (1856) 11 Ex 577; 156 ER 960. The fraudster was convicted and transported. Tartaric acid was used, inter alia, in food manufacture.
[168] (1856) 1 Hurl & N 503; 156 ER 1299.
[169] 'Commerce v Law', (1857) 3 *The Saturday Review* 99, 99.
[170] J, Benjamin, *Sale of Personal Property*, London, Henry Sweet, 1868, 617. See also *Fuentes* v. *Montis* (1868) LR 4 CP 93; (1868) LR 3 CP 268 (money advanced on dock warrants).
[171] 'Money-Market and City Intelligence', *The Times*, 24 December 1856, 5. See also M. Lobban, 'The Politics of English Law in the Nineteenth Century', in P. Brand & J. Getzler (eds.), *Judges and Judging in the History of the Common Law and Civil Law*, Cambridge, Cambridge University Press, 121.

the passage of legislation to address the issue, given that the common law 'has lost some of the facility with which it used to adapt itself to the requirements of commercial business'.[172]

So the courts were not prepared to treat the dock warrant as a document of title.[173] They could have done this through the recognition of custom and usage, given what seemed to be the near universal view in the commercial community that they had that character. Their recent origin should have been no bar.[174] Nor were the categories of document of title closed. *Merchant Banking Co of London* v. *Phoenix Bessemer Steel Co*[175] held that an iron warrant was a document of title by custom. There steel rails manufactured by the defendant iron works in Sheffield were under the relevant contract of sale deliverable FOB vessels in Liverpool. Warrants covering the rails issued by the steel works were used by the buyer to raise an advance from the bank. The buyer failed. Evidence was given that warrants in the form signed by the steel works had been known since 1846, had been in general use in the trade since 1866, and that the form had then been settled by counsel. Jessel MR held that by the usage of the iron trade, as well as by the intention of the parties, the bank was holder for value of the warrants and entitled to the goods free from any vendor's lien.[176]

Dock owners and merchants turned to Parliament. Private Acts were passed authorising specific docks and wharves to issue dock warrants having the status of documents of title. Thus under the London and St Katharine Dock Act 1864 those docks could issue warrants which were documents of title, transferable by indorsement, and giving the holder property in the goods specified.[177] With the creation of the Port of London Authority in 1908, all its London docks were covered by the rule.[178] Legislation of this nature was also passed for docks outside London.[179] But legislation by way of private Acts could only reach so far. A Dock Warrants Bill 1877, which would have applied more gener-

---

[172] 'Commerce v Law' (1857) 3 *The Saturday Review* 99, 99.
[173] *Gunn* v. *Bolckow Vaughan & Co* (1875) LR 10 Ch App 491 (wharfinger's certificates for iron rails not documents of title by custom). cf. *Farmeloe* v. *Bain* (1876) 1 CPD 445 (delivery order for zinc issued by Golden Heart Wharf, London – point conceded). Pulling asserted that dock warrants were negotiable, but that was wrong: A. Pulling, *Laws, Customs, Usages and Regulations of the City and Port of London*, 2nd ed. London, Stevens, 1844, 377, 467. See also J. Grant, *The Law relating to Bankers and Banking*, London, Butterworth, 1856, 190 (dock warrants, duly endorsed, are a good security).
[174] See the bold approach in *Goodwin* v. *Robarts* (1875) LR 10 Ex 337, affd (1876) 1 App Cas 476. See 50–51 above.
[175] (1877) 5 Ch D 205. See also RBS, NAT/1112/1, National Provincial Bank, Advice of Mr Watson, 1877, p.61.
[176] at 215–217.   [177] s.108.
[178] e.g., Port of London (Consolidation) Act 1920, s. 168. See H. Le Mesurier, *The Law relating to the Port of London Authority*, London, Butterworth, 1934, 93–95.
[179] e.g., Mersey Dock Acts Consolidation Act 1858. See H. Purchase, *The Law Relating to Documents of Title to Goods*, London, Sweet & Maxwell, 1931, 65.

ally, got nowhere and was not even printed.[180] Without legislation the view taken by lawyers was that without attornment by the dock or wharf to the holder of a dock warrant, it could not by itself be used to pledge goods.[181]

Despite the legal difficulties, banks regarded dock warrants as sufficiently secure that they could advance money on them, without on the surface distinguishing between which dock had issued them. By the early twentieth century standard form agreements had emerged for taking security over dock warrants. The form used in 1907 by Robarts, Lubbock & Co, a private bank in London, provided that, in consideration of a loan, the customer deposited with the bank warrants for named goods (in that case 113 bales of tobacco with specified ship marks) 'as collateral security for the due payment' of an advance with interest. The agreement provided that the bank was authorised to sell the goods, or any other goods for which the warrants or delivery orders might be substituted. There was a provision for margin: the customer stated the market price of the goods, and engaged to keep it up, in the event of a decrease, either by depositing other approved collateral or by paying off such parts of the loan as the bank required. Under the agreement, the security also extended to any sums in which the customer might be indebted to the bank while any goods or warrants remained in its possession, either on joint or separate account.[182]

A century later the scheme set out in the St Katharine Dock's 1828 Code was still in operation. The scale was much greater, since these docks had been enveloped in the Port of London Authority. The standard forms were also more elaborate. The merchant would submit a standard form requesting a dock warrant. This would specify the goods (mark, number, description), set out the details of the ship on which they had arrived (name, master, origin, arrival details), and identify any bill of lading and by whom dock charges would he paid.[183] Outstanding claims by the shipowner for freight were noted: under the early statutes through to the Merchant Shipping Act 1894[184] the docks, if notified, were obliged to preserve such claims. A stop procedure for warrants had evolved in instances where documents of title such as the bill of lading had not been lodged or the payment of charges or freight was pending. The stop was lifted when these issues were settled. (There were special

---

[180] House of Commons, A Bill to declare and amend the Law with reference to Dock Warrants, Bill No 94, 1877 (not printed). I am grateful to the Parliamentary Library of the House of Commons for this information.

[181] RBS, NAT/1112/1, National Provincial Bank, Advice of Mr Manistry. See also A. Carter, 'Of Dock Warrants, Warehouse-Keepers' Certificates, etc' (1892) 8 *LQR* 301, 303–304.

[182] Coutts Archives, Robarts Lubbock & Co, Agreement dated 31 December 1907, loan of £660 with warrants covering 113 bales of tobacco with specified ship marks and numbers. Robarts, Lubbock & Co was a private bank which merged with Coutts & Co in 1914. See E. Healey, *Coutts & Co 1692–1992: The Portrait of a Private Bank*, London, Hodder & Stoughton, 1992, 403–408.

[183] MLD, PRA, Port of London Authority (Dock and Traffic Manager's Office), *Tenth Report of Research Committee* 1934, vol. 2, Exhibit Nos. 156–170 [hereafter Tenth Report].

[184] s.494.

arrangements in force in connection with sugar warrants for ED & F Mann, a City of London commodities broker, which in modern times moved into commodities futures and options dealing.[185]) The dock warrants were sent to those entitled to them, by hand if they were in the City of London or in the immediate vicinity of the docks, or by post.[186] Several forms of receipt for warrants were in use.

In the interwar period, dock warrants had become standard.[187] Bankers treated them as something akin to a document of title, without paying much (if any) attention to the legal difficulties if they were not issued under the protection of one of the private Acts referred to earlier.[188] As one authority put it in 1930, comparing dock warrants with the financing of imported goods in transit where bills of lading were available: 'A bank is more often called upon, however, to lend money against goods that are warehoused in this country. In this case the document the bank requires is the Dock Warrant.'[189] Another described how it was quite common to make advances against produce, cotton and other commodities imported and awaiting sale by way of pledge of warrants covering them. 'When goods are taken off ship the dock company usually issues a "prime warrant" .... When the landing charges are paid the "prime warrant" may be exchanged for dock warrants.'[190] Towards the end of our period containerisation – which meant that the large-scale warehousing of imported goods was no longer needed at the ports – put paid to the device of the dock warrant.

6.3 Financing Business

> It is by making huge advance to a few firms, and in one form or another renewing these huge loans, that ruin overtakes banking companies. Such advances are not proper banking. (R. Patterson, *Blackwood's Magazine*, 1879)[191]

The conventional wisdom of English banking was that the banks should not lend to industry for capital needs. Rather, they should limit themselves to providing short-term finance through bills of exchange or by way of an overdraft or short-term loan, all of which might need to be secured by the customer providing collateral. The rationale for limiting advances to the short term became that the banks obtained their funds from deposits, which were

---

[185] See A. Jenkins, *The House of Man*, London, E. D. & F. Man, 1985. See 319 above.
[186] Tenth Report, vol. I, 96–101.
[187] *In Re Automatic Bottle Makers Ltd* [1926] Ch 412, 425, per Sargant LJ.
[188] J. Dunnage, *The Importer's Handbook*, London, Pitman, 1932, 198–200. See also F. Staveacre, *Tea and Tea Dealing*, London, Pitman, 1929, 66–67. cf. the lawyer's view: H. Purchase, *Documents of Title to Goods*, op cit, 67–68; H. Gutteridge, 'The Law of England and America Relating to Warehouse Receipts' (1921) 3 *J Comp Legislation & Int'l L* 5, 12.
[189] H. Easton, *The Work of a Bank*, 5th ed. by H. Hodder, London, Effingham Wilson, 1930, 208. The book was first published in 1898. See also T. Moxon, *English Practical Banking*, Manchester, John Heywood, 15th ed., 1910, 104.
[190] L. Minty, *English Banking Methods*, 4th ed., London, Pitman, 1930, 364–365.
[191] R. Patterson, 'Bank Failures and their Remedies' (1879) 125 *Blackwood's Magazine* 753, 764.

subject to withdrawal at short notice. Liquidity was essential to reduce risks. Balances needed to be held in cash or in investments which could be quickly disposed of in evil days.[192] If an advance were to be made, it had to be repayable on demand. Bank crises, it was said, underlined this truth, since failed banks typically had large and long-outstanding advances, usually concentrated in a few borrowers.[193] When in 1959 the Radcliffe Committee canvassed the historic roots of the banks' preference for short-term lending in the mid-twentieth century, it accepted that it lay in the awareness of the risks to which a small bank exposed itself if it could not turn its assets quickly into cash to meet sudden demands from its depositors. It added that the preference 'still has some sound basis in that it limits the range of judgment required in the lending banker'.[194]

The books on good banking practice retailed the conventional wisdom. The oracle of nineteenth-century banking practice James William Gilbart, general manager of London & Westminster Bank from the 1833 for almost three decades, warned against granting advances beyond two to three months because of the danger of their becoming what he termed 'dead' loans.[195] That caution against long-term finance was repeated by another acknowledged authority on good banking practice, George Rae, author of *The Country Banker*, published in 1885, but first available under the pseudonym Thomas Bullion as *The Internal Management of a Country Bank* in 1850.[196] One of Rae's canons was that, as regards advances, the banker should always give the bank the benefit of the doubt, another, that calling up an overdraft was distinct from having it repaid if it had become an addition to the business customer's fixed capital.[197] These canons were carried over into later editions[198] and endorsed by others.[199] In this view of the world, the task of financing the longer-term needs of British industry was for others.[200]

---

[192] e.g., F. Stead, *Bankers' Advances*, 3rd ed. by C. Cookson, London, Pitman, 1930, 4–5.

[193] The nineteenth-century literature is reviewed in M. Collins & M, Baker, *Commercial Banks and Industrial Finance in England and Wales 1860–1913*, Oxford, Oxford University Press, 2003, ch.7.

[194] *Committee on the Working of the Monetary System*, Report, Cmnd, 827, London, HMSO, 1959 (Radcliffe committee), para. 136. See also E. Nevin & E. David, *The London Clearing Banks*, London, Elek, 1970, 186.

[195] e.g., J. Gilbart, *A Practical Treatise on Banking*, London, Bell & Daldy, 1865, vol. I, 35.

[196] *The Country Banker*, London, J. Murray, 1885; *The Internal Management of a Country Bank in a Series of Letters on the Functions and Duties of a Branch Manager*, London, R. Groombridge & Sons, 1850. The letters had appeared over the previous three years in the *Bankers' Magazine*: p. iv. Rae became manager of the North and South Wales Bank Ltd, which was based in Liverpool and was acquired by Midland Bank Ltd in 1908 (now HSBC Bank plc).

[197] *The Country Banker*, ibid., 3, 43.

[198] *The Country Banker*, 7th ed. by E. Sykes, London, John Murray, 1930, 3, 7, 12, 18, 30–31, 60–61.

[199] e.g., T. Moxon, *English Practical Banking*, 15th ed., Manchester, Heywood, 1910, 76; E. Sykes, *Banking and Currency*, 4th ed., London, Butterworth, 1918, 175 (Sykes was secretary of the Institute of Bankers); H. Easton, *The Work of a Bank*, London, E. Wilson, 1930,183.

[200] R. Sayers, *Modern Banking*, 3rd ed., Oxford, Oxford University Press, 1953, 239.

The reality was somewhat different from this orthodoxy. Banks did provide finance to industry for what were effectively capital works. There are some notable examples. The Barclays and their Quaker circle were involved in funding the pioneering Stockton to Darlington railway and other infrastructure projects like the Regent's Canal.[201] In 1836 St Katharine Dock in London received a substantial loan of £180,000 from the Royal Bank of Scotland to buy warehouses belonging to the East India Company; the loan was advanced on the security of the rates and profits of the dock and warehouses.[202] In 1838 the London and Westminster Bank advanced £25,000 to the Eastern Counties Railway 'to enable it to pursue its works with vigour', and in 1841 it made advances to the Blackwall Railway, although it pressed the railway to reduce its overdraft.[203]

These were not aberrations of the first part of the century. In the 1880s the jute manufacturer Thomas Duff & Co was rapidly expanding and took out bank loans against the personal guarantees of the directors.[204] Glyn, Mills & Co provided overdraft finance to Powell Duffryn & Co (a large Welsh coal producer) in 1877 covered by short bills, and in 1881 it provided an overdraft and a loan to John Brown & Co (operator of the Atlas steel works in Sheffield) against the deposit of the company's debentures.[205] In 1921 the car manufacturer Morris Motors had an overdraft of almost £85,000 with its bankers, Gillett & Co, but it was paid off in two years as a result of Morris' strategy of a significant price reduction on his vehicles, coupled with persuading suppliers to offer extended credit (e.g., Dunlop Rubber Company on its tyres).[206] Ferranti had a substantial overdraft with the Westminster Bank in the 1920s, but when it reached £97,000 in 1929 the company instructed its solicitors to prepare a scheme to increase the company's capital through an issue of ordinary and cumulative preference shares.[207]

Moreover, banks might also provide indirect support to industry. In 1905 the National Provincial Bank gave what might now be described as a performance guarantee (or demand guarantee) when Corrie Brothers and Co Limited and the Glamorgan Coal Company Limited tendered to supply 80,000 tons of coal to the Italian Government. The parties had deposited £8,000 in support of the tender. The bank guaranteed that the deposit would

---

[201] M. Ackrill & L. Hannah, Barclays: the Business of Banking 1690–1996, op cit, 37–38.
[202] D. Souden, *The Bank and the Sea*, Edinburgh, Royal Bank of Scotland, 2003, 94. Another bank to advance money for the dock, £150,000, was Glyn's: R. Fulford, *Glyn's, 1753–1953: Six Generations in Lombard Street*, London, Macmillan, 1953, 119.
[203] T. Gregory, *The Westminster Bank*, London, Oxford University Press, 1936, vol. I, 267. In 1879 its shareholders were told it made no advances to factories, mines or ships.
[204] A. Wearmouth, *Thomas Duff & Co and the Jute Industry in Calcutta 1870–1921*, PhD thesis, University of Dundee, 2015, 104.
[205] RBS, GM/201/1, Glyn, Mills, Currie & Co, Terms with Customers, 2, 9. In 1872 the bank agreed to consider favourably a request from the engineering firm Vickers & Sons Co Ltd for £20,000: ibid., 17. On John Brown & Co, 427 below.
[206] M. Adeney, *Nuffield A Biography*, London, Hale, 1993, 75–76.
[207] J Wilson, *Ferranti and the British Electrical Industry 1864–1930*, Manchester, Manchester University Press, 1988, 144. On Ferranti: 226, 279, 290 above.

be paid should the companies not proceed if it were to be awarded the tender. In turn Corrie had given an indemnity that the bank would be paid should the deposit be called upon. Mr Churchward of counsel gave advice approving the indemnity when the bank's solicitor, Wilde Sapte, raised doubts about it.[208]

Further light on what happened in practice comes from a study of some 3,010 accounts held during the years 1880–1914 by industrial businesses with some 20 English banks (spread over 268 provincial branches).[209] The data showed a marked rise in the size of advances during the period. Partly that reflected the increased scale of operations of the sample businesses as a result of the incorporation boom of the second half of the nineteenth century; partly, the enhanced capacity of the banks to lend as a result of the extensive bank amalgamations which were occurring at this time.[210]

Advances to industry in the study were overwhelmingly for trading or working capital – for example, to purchase materials, finance stocks or cover working expenses – although the proportion for these purposes declined from three-quarters between 1880 and 1884 to near two-thirds between 1910 and 1914. Cash flow difficulties accounted for another 11–13 per cent of the sample. Advances for capital investment were never high.[211] As to the duration of advances, more than 95 per cent were for 12 months or less, and although overdrafts were routinely renewed, they averaged no more than 19 months. There were some exceptional cases where overdrafts were of a longer duration.[212]

For the period 1920–1968 a parallel study of advances by the London clearing banks (resulting from 4,267 loan applications) found that about a half were by means of overdraft. Loans were a much lower proportion and declined in relative importance over time (18.8 per cent in the interwar years, 14 per cent in the 1940s, some 5 per cent in the later post-war decades).[213] Loans were often repayable on demand, although the banks rarely took advantage of this. About 90 per cent of the advances were made to public companies. About a half of the advances were made to the manufacturing sector, within this 'metal goods and mechanical engineering' and 'textiles, leather and clothes' comprising the two largest categories.[214] The advances were overwhelmingly short term, 50 per cent formally agreed for no longer than six months and 99 per cent for no more

---

[208] RBS, NAT/1112/1, National Provincial Bank, Law Book 1870–1913, 19.
[209] F. Capie & M. Collins, 'Banks, Industry and Finance 1880–1914' (1999) *Business Hist* 37; M. Collins & M, Baker, Commercial Banks and Industrial Finance in England and Wales 1860–1913, op cit, Ch. 9. Lloyds Bank and the Midland Bank were overrepresented in the sample.
[210] Ibid., 40. See also 26 above. [211] Ibid., 50–51. [212] Ibid., 54–57.
[213] M. Collins & M. Baker, 'English Bank Business Loans,1920–1968: Transaction Bank Characteristics and Small Firm Discrimination' (2005) 12 *Fin Hist R* 135, 144. In addition to overdrafts and loans, advances were also by means of bill discounts and 'credits'.
[214] Ibid., 138, 168. The sample was based on 4,267 loan applications to Barclays, Lloyds, Martins, the Midland, the National Provincial and the Westminster banks.

than 12 months.[215] Some two-thirds to four-fifths of advances were for trade credit and to finance trade and other working capital needs. Fixed capital expenditure for the purchase or improvement of plant and machinery accounted for 3.4 to 6.8 per cent of the sample, with the proportion falling over the longer term. Very few advances were for the development of new products or new processes.[216]

1 Short-term Finance: Overdrafts and On-demand Loans

As he returned Wolley waylaid him and drew him into a corner. A conference took place, the banker turning the money in his fob as he listened, his face grave. Presently the clothier entered on a second explanation. In the end Ovington nodded. He called Rodd from the counter and gave an order .... When he re-entered the parlour ... Arthur, who was bending over his papers looked up. 'Wolley wanted his notes renewed, I suppose?' he said .... The banker nodded. 'And three hundred more on his standing loan.' Arthur whistled. 'I wonder you go on carrying him, sir.' 'If I cut him loose now ....' 'There would be a loss, of course.' 'Yes, but that is not all, lad. Where would the Railroad scheme be? Gone. And that's not all, either. His fall would deal a blow to credit. ' (S. Weyman, *Ovington's Bank*, 1922)[217]

In the first part of the nineteenth century many local banks advanced short-term funds to industry by buying (discounting) bills of exchange drawn in a customer's favour. The bank might retain the bill until it matured (e.g., after 60, 90 days), or might rediscount the bill to obtain immediate funds.[218] Instructions to its branches by the National Provincial Bank in the mid-nineteenth century required that a bill have two good signatures, that an unaccepted bill should not be discounted without referring it to London, and that generally there should be no cash advanced against a foreign bill, nor should it be discounted, until advice of payment had been received.[219] Finance by way of discounting bills of exchange fell away during the nineteenth century and banks advanced finance to business by way of overdrafts and loans, either secured or unsecured.[220]

Writing in 1836 Gilbart told of loans being advanced through a loan account, and twenty years later he wrote: 'In London advances are generally made by

---

[215] Ibid., 140 Table 1   [216] Ibid., 142–143.
[217] S. Weyman, *Ovington's Bank*, London, John Murray, 1922.
[218] e.g., S. Shapiro, *Capital and the Cotton Industry*, Ithaca, Cornell University Press, 1967, 79–81; T. Ashton, 'The Bill of Exchange and Private Banks in Lancashire 1790–1830', in T. Ashton & R. Sayers, *Papers in English Monetary History*, Oxford, Oxford University Press, 1954. See also L. Pressnell, Country Banking in the Industrial Revolution, *op cit*, 292–293.
[219] RBS, NAT/1175, *Instruction book for local directors and staff of branches of National Provincial Bank of England*, c1840, with amendments (1850s) and pasted in instructions (1856–1858), 29–31.
[220] S. Nishimura, *The Decline of Inland Bills of Exchange in the London Money Market 1855–1913*, Cambridge, Cambridge University Press, 1971.

loans; in the country, by overdraft.'[221] The sixth edition of Gilbart's book stated that in London loans from banks were generally short, two to three months. If there was no time specified for repayment these were, in his words, 'dead' loans, and if bankers did not exercise caution ordinary loans could become dead loans. Where a bank was to advance money, Gilbart added, it needed to know the purpose of the borrowing.[222] The difference between the London banks (loans), and the county or provincial banks (overdrafts) still existed at the end of the nineteenth century.[223] The amalgamated joint stock banks and increased competition in the early twentieth century changed this. Procedures were standardised and tightened across their branches. More centralised control could affect the length of advances and the extent to which security might be required.[224]

The orthodoxy about short-term advances was a central tenet of twentieth-century banking. The secretary of the Institute of Bankers explained in 1918 that there might not be too much difference between an overdraft and a loan in terms of the interest payable. The key was that loans, as with overdrafts, must be made repayable on demand. By far the larger proportion of bank failures which had occurred, he continued, was attributable to a bank's assets being locked up in large loans to a few borrowers, loans which had gradually acquired a permanent character, and ended becoming bad debts. 'The province of a banker', he added, 'is to tide over temporary lack of ready money, not to provide capital on which the customer carries on his business'.[225]

The reality, as we have seen, might be somewhat removed from this. For an industrial customer in difficulty, banks might nurse its account by rolling over advances, sometimes for a considerable period, as long as there were prospects that eventually they would be repaid.[226] Rolling over short-term advances meant, of course, that a company could use the moneys for capital expenditure. There might be additional reasons for a bank's leniency. In the passage from *Ovington's Bank* quoted at the head of this section, we see that the bank is prepared to extend the advances to the textile manufacturer Wolley because otherwise his business might fail, adversely affecting economic confidence, and also because Ovington wanted him to back a railway scheme it was promoting in the area. At the end of the day, however, the bank had the threat, backed by law, that it could immediately recall any on-demand advance.

---

[221] J. Gilbart, *A Practical Treatise on Banking*, London, Longman, 4th ed., 1836, 6th ed., 1856, vol. I, 34. See also A. Crump, *A Practical Treatise on Banking, Currency and the Exchanges*, London, Longmans, Green & Co, 1866, 76; J. Dun, *British Banking Statistics*, London, E. Stanford, 1876, 85. Crump was a bank manager and formerly with the Bank of England; Dun was general manager of Parr's Bank, based in Warrington, which post-WWI became part of Westminster Bank.
[222] The whole passage was reproduced 1901 ed., op cit, vol. I, 249–252.
[223] C. Goodhart, *The Business of Banking 1891–1914*, London, Weidenfeld & Nicolson, 1972, 153.
[224] F. Lavington, *The English Capital Market*, 3rd ed., London, Methuen, 1934, 127–128, 136, 180.
[225] E. Sykes, Banking and Currency, *op cit*, 175.
[226] P. Cottrell, 'Domestic Finance, 1860–1914', in R. Floud & P. Johnson (eds.), *The Cambridge Economic History of Modern Britain*, Cambridge, Cambridge University Press, 2004, 263; M. Ackrill & L. Hannah, Barclays: the Business of Banking 1690–1996, *op cit*, 94–95.

(i) The Bank Overdraft

Overdrafts became the most common avenue for short-term lending, as we saw from the empirical work on bank accounts during the period 1880–1968.[227] With an overdraft, customers were permitted to overdraw on their current account up to a specified limit and for a specified time. During our period the understanding among bankers, or 'customary right' as one bank manager called it, was that, particularly if unsecured, the overdraft could be recalled or cancelled in their discretion at any time. Overdrafts, bankers were told, should only be granted to account holders of acknowledged position and undoubted responsibility. The application for an overdraft had to state, according to the tenets of orthodox banking, the purpose for which it was required, the source from which it would be repaid, and the date it would be discharged.[228] The reality with many banks, certainly in the late nineteenth and early twentieth centuries, was that overdrafts were almost synonymous with having a bank account. They were granted to almost every business which applied for them and the facility, albeit subject to regular review, could run for years, often decades.[229] In the twentieth century the overdraft was associated with the ability to take an account into debit by writing cheques up to the limit in the overdraft agreement.[230]

When the character of overdrafts was subject to judicial consideration, the bankers' understanding was endorsed: overdraft financing was repayable on demand. As Pollock CB put it in 1864, using the language of estates in real property, 'there is no tenancy of a man's credit which requires any time to put an end to it'.[231] Thus at common law there was no obligation on the bank to act reasonably in making demand, to give reasonable notice of the demand or to allow a grace period. English law had a bright-line rule. Banks did not have to consider whether the customer if given time would be able to raise funds elsewhere to repay the overdraft, indeed, whether the customer's business would survive cancellation of the facility. The legal position if the bank granted an overdraft was that it was lending the amount to customers, inverting (as Grant explained) the ordinary position of the bank where, as accountable for moneys which customers had deposited, it was their debtor.[232] As a loan to customers, the overdraft meant they were the bank's

---

[227] 412 above.
[228] J. Hutchison, *The Practice of Banking*, London, E. Wilson, 1881, vol. I, 51 (Hutchison was a bank manager); T. Moxon, *English Practical Banking*, Manchester, John Heywood, 15th ed., 1910, 77; C. Collins, Law and Practice of Banking, *op cit*, 177. There are some standard forms at 26–27, 52 of Hutchinson.
[229] M. Collins & M. Baker, Commercial Banks and Industrial Finance in England and Wales 1860–1913, *op cit*, 196. But cf. 195: bankers did not regard frequent renewals as equivalent to long-term loans, since they were repayable on demand.
[230] R. Sayers, *Modern Banking*, London, Oxford University Press, 1938, 12, 232.
[231] Cumming v Shand [Royal Bank of Liverpool] (1860) 5 Hurl & N 95, 98, 157 ER 1114, 1116.
[232] J. Grant, The Law relating to Bankers and Banking, *op cit*, 1856, 1. See also *Cuthbert* v. *Robarts Lubbock & Co* [1909] 2 Ch 226.

debtor.[233] Interest was payable on an overdraft, to the extent that it was used. The customer might need to provide security to obtain the bank's agreement for an overdraft. As regards the position of customers overdrawing the account (e.g., exceeding their overdraft), the law was that a bank had no obligation to the customer to allow this, for example, by paying a cheque which would take the customer over the limit.[234] If the bank refused to pay, it would return the cheque through the clearing system as unpaid.

There were few limits imposed by law on the unbridled power of the banks to cancel overdraft financing. One was the narrow rule, which Lord Herschell LC pointed to in 1894 in the House of Lords, that a bank could not refuse to honour cheques or bills, within the limits of the overdraft, which had been drawn and put in circulation before notice of cancellation.[235] Perhaps reflecting on his own overdraft, he added that, whatever the law might provide, business realities could confine a bank's course of action, in that 'it is obvious that neither party would have it in contemplation that when the bank had granted an overdraft it would immediately, without notice, proceed to sue for the money'.[236]

The courts also recognised that a course of dealing with the bank might mean that a customer could not have an overdraft facility cancelled immediately, but only after the bank gave reasonable notice. In *Cumming* v. *Shand, Registered Public Officer of the Royal Bank of Liverpool*[237] the customer was an importer in Liverpool of products from the West Indies. Exporters there would draw bills of exchange on his account in the ordinary way for acceptance. Under an arrangement with the bank he handed them the bills of exchange, with the bills of lading annexed, and the bank paid the bills, debiting his account with the amount. The bank would give the bills of lading to his broker, on receiving the latter's undertaking to pay the amount out of the proceeds of the goods when they were sold. Notwithstanding the balance was against the customer until the broker reimbursed the bank, he was allowed to draw on his current account as if the amount advanced on the bills had not been debited. For this accommodation the bank charged a commission. Then the bank changed tack. The usual procedure had been followed with the importation of twenty puncheons of rum from Trinidad. The bank paid out £1,900 on the relevant bills and debited the customer. His account was overdrawn, although if this item was excluded there was a balance in his favour of £200. The market price of rum had declined. Without notice to the customer, the bank refused to pay

---

[233] cf. *In re Cefn Cilcen Mining Company* (1868) LR 7 Eq 88, a case of doubtful authority. See J. Walker, *A Treatise on Banking Law*, 2nd ed., London, Stevens, 1885, 63–64; H. Hart, *The Law of Banking and Stock Exchange Transactions*, 4th ed., London, Stevens, 1931, vol. II, 746–773.

[234] *Cunliffe Brooks & Co.* v. *Blackburn and District Benefit Building Society* (1884) 9 App Cas 857, 864, per Lord Blackburn.

[235] *Rouse* v. *Bradford Banking Co Ltd* [1894] AC 586, 596. See also *Fleming* v. *Bank of New Zealand* [1900] AC 577 (Privy Council, New Zealand).

[236] Ibid.

[237] (1860) 5 Hurl & N 95; 157 ER 1114. On the Royal Bank of Liverpool see G. Chandler, *Four Centuries of Banking*, London, Batsford, 1964, vol. I.

a cheque he had drawn for £199. The customer sued the bank. At the Liverpool Assizes Willes J left it to the jury whether the course of dealing was that the sums guaranteed by the brokers were not to be brought into account against him, or whether the bank was merely in the habit of indulging him and could immediately put a stop to it. If they concluded that there was a course of business, Willes J asked the jury secondly, whether the bank was bound to give him reasonable notice that they were ending it. The jury, found for the customer on both points, and on appeal the Court of Exchequer upheld its decision.[238]

There were cases where a bank exercised its right to make immediate demand for repayment of an overdraft. One example is associated with the takeover in 1931 of Lanchester Motor Company by BSA, the manufacturer (amongst other things) of Daimler cars. The rationale of the takeover was for Daimler to increase its market share with more popular and less expensive motor cars, although it quickly became apparent that it was a bad investment.[239] The deal was rushed through in a fortnight after Lanchester's bankers demanded repayment of a £38,000 overdraft and the company faced amalgamation or insolvency. One historian speculates that there 'must be a suspicion that the extensive influence of BSA directors was behind the bank's arbitrary decision to re-call the loan and trigger the Lanchester cash crisis which forced them into BSA's clutches'.[240]

(ii) Loan Accounts and Loan Agreements

From the beginning of our period loan finance was typically provided through an entry in a loan register or a separate loan account. The bank would credit the current account with the amount, the debit being noted in the ledger or on the loan account.[241] The current account could be drawn upon when needed. However, interest would be charged on the full amount of the loan, irrespective of the balance on the current account. By contrast interest on an overdraft was confined to what was overdrawn. In practice there was generally no financial advantage to the customer in having an advance by way of overdraft since there would be a charge for granting an overdraft and a lower interest rate on a loan.[242]

The courts held, to the banks' advantage, that a loan account was distinct from a current account. In the leading case, a bank had agreed in 1894 to grant a Yorkshire textile mill a fixed loan of £3,600, and to allow an overdraft of £2,500, on the company depositing debentures as security, as well as two of its

---

[238] (1860) 5 Hurl & N 95, 98; 157 ER 1114, 1116.
[239] R. Lloyd-Jones, M. Lewis, M. Matthews and & J. Maltby, 'Control, Conflict and Concession: Corporate Governance, Accounting and Accountability at Birmingham Small Arms 1906–1933' (2005) 32 *Accounting Hist J* 149, 166.
[240] R. Davenport-Hines, *Dudley Docker: The Life and Times of a Trade Warrior*, Cambridge, Cambridge University Press, 1984, 226.
[241] e.g., *Waterlow* v. *Sharp* (1869) L.R. 8 Eq 501 (bank permitted customer, a railway company, to draw cheques against a sum entered in the books of the bank under the title 'Loan Account'). See also J. Gilbart, *A Practical Treatise on Banking*, London, Longman, 6th ed., 1856, vol. I, 34.
[242] see E. Sykes, Banking and Currency, *op cit*, 173–174.

directors giving a personal guarantee.[243] The Court of Appeal held that what was paid into the current account could not discharge any outstanding balance on the loan account.[244] The justification was that if it were otherwise a business would be hampered because it could never safely draw on its current account so long as the credit balance did not exceed the amount due on the loan account.[245] In fact, the rule meant that however large the payments customers might make into their current account, they would not by that alone discharge their liability on the loan account.[246]

Throughout most of our period, agreements for banks loan were relatively simple. The provisions with respect to any security given in support of the loan might be more detailed, in particular if they conferred a power on the bank to sell any collateral should the customer default. In an 1836 case merchants in India, Palmer & Co, borrowed a large sum from the Bank of Bengal. In the written terms of the agreement, the firm promised in short order to repay three months after its date, with interest at the rate of 5 per cent per annum; acknowledged that it had deposited East India Company bonds as collateral security; and authorised the bank, in default of repayment, 'to sell the Company's paper for the reimbursement of the Bank, rendering to Palmer and Co. any surplus'.[247] That pattern of simplicity continued. Even in the 1930s little was required.[248] In the application form for a loan the customer would need to state the purpose of the loan.[249] This was one part of the vetting stage seeking to reduce, indeed eliminate, the risk of default. The agreement would then spell out its terms succinctly, focusing on the interest rate and how that was to be calculated. The agreement would also need to state whether the loan was repayable on demand or at a future date.

In the 1930s it was said that for advances on a loan account 'the banker will rarely agree to make the loan for a definitely *fixed* period, but will usually stipulate that he may at any time claim repayment on demand'.[250] Where loans were for fixed periods, these would be short (say 6 months) to control for risk.

---

[243] *Bradford Old Bank Ltd* v. *Sutcliffe* [1918] 2 KB 833. Bradford Old Bank became part of Barclays in 1916, having merged with the United Counties Bank Ltd in 1907.

[244] The courts had held that banks were able to combine a credit in one current account with a debit in another held, for example, at a different branch: *Garnett* v. *M'Kewan* [public officer, London and County Banking Company] (1872) LR 8 Ex 10. Otherwise 'there would be a real hardship on bankers and a difficulty in their conducting business', per Bramwell B at 15. cf. *WP Greenhalgh & Sons* v. *Union Bank of Manchester* [1924] 2 KB 153 (bank agreed with cotton merchants that bills accepted by mills to which cotton sold would be paid into specific account to pay its own selling brokers). See also *Mutton* v. *Peat* [1900] 2 Ch 79.

[245] op cit, at 839, per Pickford LJ (later Lord Sterndale MR). See also Scrutton LJ at 847.

[246] cf. *In re European Bank* (1872) LR 8 Ch App 41 (balance of the loan account satisfied; bank retained lien on securities deposited for customer's current account).

[247] *Young* v. *Bank of Bengal* (1836) 1 Moore 87, 89, 18 ER 34, 35 (Privy Council, India).

[248] See form in L. Minty, *English Banking Methods*, 4th ed., London, Pitman, 1930, 319–320.

[249] J. Gilbart, *A Practical Treatise on Banking*, London, Longman, 6th ed., 1856, vol. I, 33–37. The passage is reproduced J. Gilbart, ed. A. Michie, *The History, Principles and Practice of Banking*, London, George Bell & Sons, 1901, vol. I, 249–252.

[250] S. Thomas, *Banker and Customer*, 4th ed., London, Gregg Publishing, 1936, 491.

Short-term business loans granted by Lloyds Bank and the Midland Bank on industrial accounts in the 1930s were frequently renewed. In many cases an absence of collateral or unsatisfactory trading results meant that this was not a formality and there might be protracted negotiations and closer bank supervision of the account for the future.[251] Short-term lending continued to be the practice in the 1950s. Advances might relate to capital projects, but for only an interim period, for example, before the issue of debentures or shares to cover the expenditure. Advances were typically repayable on demand. The bank needed to have that right in reserve, bankers believed, although their experience was that unless there was a real jeopardy to their interests, they 'tend to regard themselves as bound by a gentleman's agreement and are content not to enforce their strict legal rights'.[252]

It was only towards the end of our period that the clearing banks engaged, and then in a desultory manner, in offering longer-term loan finance. In 1959 the Radcliffe committee had recommended that 'the banks should be ready to offer term loan facilities within reasonable limits, having due regard to their liquidity requirements, as an alternative to a running overdraft for creditworthy industrial and commercial customers'.[253] As a result of the Radcliffe committee's recommendations some banks introduced term loans, although their main response to the committee's concern was to boost the availability of instalment credit for commercial purposes through their asset finance subsidiaries.[254] The term loans they offered had capital and interest repayable on a monthly basis, and usually did not require security. Term lending over five years was concentrated on exporters and ship-building and was provided under a government guarantee.[255] Medium-term international bank lending came at the end of our period, with the growth of the Euromarkets.[256] New York practices were carried across with this lending since before the 1960s New York banks had been undertaking some medium-term international lending. Until then, as we have seen, loan agreements drafted in London tended to be short. Further, although there were standard clauses in London loan agreements, there was a lack of uniformity in the banks' agreements. The New York approach was different, longer and more uniform agreements. It was said that many bankers felt that American-drafted loan agreements were 'too long, sometimes out of touch with market practice and

---

[251] D. Ross, 'The Clearing Banks and Industrialisation – New Perspectives on the Interwar Years', in Y. Cassis & J. Van Helten (ed.), *Capitalism in a Mature Economy: Financial Institutions, Capital Exports and British Industry 1870–1939*, Aldershot, Edward Elgar, 1990, 60.

[252] J. Clemens, *Bank Lending*, London, Europa Publications, 1963, 36. (The author spent his career as a banker.)

[253] *Committee on the Working of the Monetary System, Report*, Cmnd 827, 1959, para. 942.

[254] *Committee to Review the Functioning of Financial Institutions*, Report, Cmnd.7937, London, HMSO, 1980, 222, para. 799 (the Wilson committee). See also M. Baker & M. Collins, 'English Commercial Banks and Organizational Inertia: The Financing of SMEs, 1944–1960' (2010) 11 *Enterprise & Society* 65, 82–83.

[255] E. Nevin & E. David, The London Clearing Banks, *op cit*, 238–239.   [256] 25 above.

less clearly drafted' and that there was a 'growing resistance from customers and bankers to this length and obscurity'.[257]

Bank loans, even on-demand loans, had more law encrusted onto them than overdrafts. First, if a bank committed itself to provide a loan, it was in ordinary circumstances obliged to provide it. But that rule did not have much purchase, since if sued by a prospective borrower for a failure to make funds available, damages would be nominal. That was because the court assumed that the prospective borrower could obtain the funds elsewhere. In special circumstances, however, the damages might be greater. In *Manchester and Oldham Bank Ltd* v. *W A Cook & Co*[258] the bank was to lend some £8,300 to the firm for the purchase of a colliery, which would then be mortgaged to the bank as security for repayment. The bank's solicitor drew up the relevant documents, which its manager had agreed, but the funds were never provided. At one point the customer signed a document that it would pay bank charges whether the transaction went through or not. The court awarded damages of £3,000 to the putative borrower. Both Day and Smith JJ reasoned that the bank knew the purpose for which the funds were needed.

Second, there were the awkward rules about interest. As in so many areas of English law, however, the contract could be drafted in such a manner as to overcome them and, as in this case, to promote one side's interests (the bank's). The rule in English law was that interest was not payable on money borrowed unless agreed, but in the case of a bank's advances the obligation to pay interest was implied as a matter of custom and usage.[259] There was a long-standing rule that if the payment of interest was in arrears, it would constitute an unlawful penalty for the bank to charge a higher rate of interest retrospectively on the outstanding amount. The justification was that the amount of default interest would not necessarily be related to the bank's loss from the default, depending on when the default occurred in the life of the loan.[260] But there were ways for overcoming this. Thus it became accepted that a lender could set interest at say 5 per cent, but reduce that to 4 per cent if the borrower paid on time.[261] As was said on one occasion in the House of Lords, this was an 'extremely fine and nice distinction', but it not an unlawful penalty for late payment.[262] Another possibility was to compound interest, in other words, the bank could add the amounts of unpaid interest to the principal and charge interest on the

---

[257] T. Donaldson, *International Lending by Commercial Banks*, London, Macmillan, 1979, 108. (The author was in the London branch of Morgan Guaranty Trust – now J.P. Morgan – for many years.)

[258] (1883) 49 LT 674. The bank went into liquidation around March 1885: *Re Winterbottom, ex p Winterbottom*, (1886) 18 QBD 446, 446.

[259] J. Grant, The Law relating to Bankers and Banking, 1856, *op cit*, 3n. The rule otherwise was that money lent did not carry interest: *Page* v. *Newman* (1829) 9 B & C 378, 109 ER 140; *London, Chatham and Dover Railway Co* v. *South Eastern Railway Co* [1893] AC 429.

[260] see Halsbury's Laws of England, 2nd ed., London, Butterworth, 1936, vol. 23, 278.

[261] *Seton* v. *Slade* (1809) 2 Ves Jr 32; 34 ER 984.

[262] *Wallingford* v. *Mutual Society* (1880) 5 App Cas 685, 702, per Lord Hatherley.

combined sum (interest on interest). Although generally frowned upon, it was said that compound interest was possible in English law 'as to mercantile accounts current for mutual transactions'.[263] If compound interest was to be imposed, it needed to be clearly expressed in the loan agreement.[264]

It was also possible for the bank to charge a higher interest rate prospectively on the amount outstanding from the date of default. The principle had long been recognised in mortgage cases.[265] The issue came before the courts in 1883 in a case where railway contractors borrowed £4000,000 for construction work on the Buenos Ayres and Campana Railway Company.[266] The sum was to be advanced in tranches, and to be repaid at specified dates by instalments. Interest floated with the market rate. It was 6 per cent per annum, but if the bank rate exceeded 4 per cent it would be the 6 per cent plus the excess. The agreement provided that if any instalment was not repaid by the contractors when due, in addition to interest there was to be paid 'a commission of 1 percent for every month or part of a month that may elapse between the due date and the date of the payment of such instalment, upon the whole amount of such instalment'. The court had no difficulty in upholding this additional payment: it was not a penalty but 'a distinct, separate, substantive contract to pay something in case the borrower makes default'.[267]

A third area of law concerned the procedure the bank needed to follow in the event of non-payment on a loan agreement. As with bank overdrafts, customers were bound to repay on-demand loans without the benefit of any notice or grace period. As Blackburn J put it in 1862, 'a debtor who is required to pay money on demand, or at a stated time, must have it ready, and is not entitled to further time in order to look for it'.[268] Where loans were for a fixed period, an acceleration clause might be inserted in the agreement. Under it, the whole amount of the loan and the outstanding interest could become immediately repayable on the customer's default. When the enforceability of acceleration clauses came before the House of Lords, it had no difficulty in upholding them under the principle of freedom of contract. In the leading case in 1880, a clause in a 20-year mortgage rendered the total sum due repayable by the borrower on any default in payment. The argument of his behalf was that the clause was in

---

[263] *Ferguson* v. *Fyffe* (1841) 8 Cl & F 121, 140; 8 ER 49, 56. See also *Caliot* v. *Walker* (1794) 2 Anst 495, 145 ER 946.
[264] *London Chartered Bank of Australia* v. *White* (1879) 4 App Cas 413, 424 (Privy Council, Victoria).
[265] *Burton* v. *Slattery* (1725) 5 Bro PC 233, 2 ER 648. See also *Herbert* v. *Salisbury and Yeovil Railway Co* (1866) LR 2 Eq 221.
[266] *General Credit and Discount Company* v. *Glegg* (1883) 22 Ch D 549. The General Credit and Discount became part of Union Discount Company: see W. King, *History of the London Discount Market*, London, Routledge, 1936, 257–258, 261; 450 below. On the railway, its establishment as a UK company and its funding, see C. Lewis, *British Railways in Argentina 1857–1914*, London, Athlone, 1983, 33.
[267] at 553.
[268] *Brighty* v. *Norton* (1862) 3 B & S 305, 312, 122 ER 116, 118. See also *Moore* v. *Shelley* (1883) 8 App Cas 285, 293 (Privy Council, New South Wales).

breach of the English rule against penalties.[269] That was rejected.[270] Lord Blackburn put the freedom of contract justification most clearly: 'That being the contract between the parties that is not the case of a penal sum.'[271] The case law suggests that at this point it was the building and insurance societies, not the banks, which utilised acceleration clauses. That is not surprising when it was these institutions which offered long-term mortgage loans for buildings. During our period, the banks preferred on-demand rather than fixed-term advances for short-term capital needs.

2 Security for Bank Advances

> We were really much disgusted with the Law of Guarantee, which is so studiously technical. It, however, shews that the advice given in the Book of Proverbs is a good working maxim and that is not to become surety for anybody. (Parker Rhodes & Co, solicitors, Rotherham, 1919)[272]

Industrial customers desiring a bank overdraft or loan might be required to provide collateral as security for the advance. George Rae's advice to bankers in 1885 was that 'no one is as safe without security as with it'.[273] Without security, he added, a banker was dependent on 'the unerring accuracy of your own judgment as to the means and character of the borrower'.[274] Summing up his advice, he said: 'The only rule, therefore, which insures safety in every case is never to make any advance without security.'[275] Rae gave as a reason that the greater competition in banking at the time he was writing accentuated the need for security, since competition was attenuating the return on profit.[276] Despite Rae's strictures, the existence of unsecured advances was acknowledged in some of the literature for trainee bankers, albeit that it was attributed to the very reason Rae gave for requiring security, 'the intense competition between the banks'.[277]

This latter view reflected the widespread practice on the ground. An examination of some 3,000 accounts held at 20 English banks over the period 1880–1914 found that about two-thirds of bank advances in the provinces at the beginning of the period, and some one half towards the end, did not involve the formal deposit of securities. Rather, they were either unsecured

---

[269] 261n, 276 above.
[270] *Wallingford v. Mutual Society* (1880) 5 App Cas 685. cf. *Keene v. Biscoe* (1878) 8 Ch D 201. See also *Protector Endowment Loan and Annuity Company v. Grice* (1880) 5 QBD 592.
[271] at 705. See also Lord Selborne LC at 696. Even if there was no specified period for repayment of a loan, the course of dealing between the customer and bank might be such that reasonable notice to close a loan account was necessary: *Buckingham & Co v. London and Midland Bank Ltd* (1895) 12 TLR 70, 72 (jury decision).
[272] SCA, X308/2/2/1, John Brown & Co Ltd, letter, Parker Rhodes & Co, Rotherham to C. E. Ellis, Atlas Works, 29 June 1919.
[273] The Country Banker, *op cit*, 34.   [274] Ibid., 35.   [275] Ibid., 36.
[276] See also 246; H. Macleod, *Elements of Banking*, London, Longmans, Green & Co, 1894, 246.
[277] H. Easton, *The Work of a Bank*, 5th ed. by H. Hodder, London, Effingham Wilson, 1930, 171.

or backed by personal guarantees.[278] With unsecured lending, a bank would take a view about the standing and assets of the customer to assess whether an advance would be repaid. In effect, the study found, overdrafts were available to every respectable business with a bank account, provided it could demonstrate that it was in possession of assets commensurate with the amount to be borrowed.[279] In part the decline in the provision of unsecured advances after 1880 matched the changing structure of British industrial firms, with the incorporation of many sole traders and partnerships.[280] The upshot was that in the absence of other security the banks began to ask for personal guarantees from a company's directors. Without at least a personal guarantee from them, a bank could not rely as with an unincorporated business on the unlimited liability of those behind it.

The 1880–1914 study revealed that over that period the three most frequent forms of security given in support of industrial lending were (in order) the personal guarantee; charges over debentures, shares and other market securities; and various claims against a borrower's property, especially charges over factories, premises and other real estate.[281] With the proportion of unsecured lending contracting during the period, the debenture was the category of security expanding to fill the gap, from an insignificant number in 1880 to 15 per cent of the total in 1914.[282] That was partly because debentures were more available with the boom in incorporation, albeit that the boom was heavily populated by private, frequently family-based companies which issued debentures to raise capital.[283]

That was the situation in one of law's landmark cases, *Salomon v. Salomon & Co Ltd*, where Aron Salomon had incorporated his boot manufacturing business.[284] There were also instances where a company wishing to delay the issue of debentures to the general public – for instance, because market conditions were unfavourable – obtained a bank loan, secured by debentures, as an interim source of funding. Given the illiquidity of security over property this, the third most popular type of security, was a fifth or less of the collateral given to banks during this period.

A comparable study for the period 1920–1968 of loan applications to the London clearing banks found that there was a rising proportion of unsecured

---

[278] F. Capie & M. Collins, 'Banks, Industry and Finance 1880–1914', *op cit*, 43–44.
[279] Ibid., 43.
[280] See *Oxford History of the Laws of England, vol.12, 1820–1914, Private Law*, Oxford, Oxford University Press, 2010, 667–670 (M. Lobban).
[281] F. Capie & M. Collins, 'Banks, Industry and Finance 1880–1914', *op cit*, 45–48. Life policies, promissory notes and uncalled capital were provided as other forms of security.
[282] Unfortunately the figures are not subdivided between debentures in other companies given as security and debenture(s) over the company's own assets.
[283] F. Capie & M. Collins, 'Banks, Industry and Finance 1880–1914', *op cit*, 47. See P. Cottrell, 'Finance in the Age of the Corporate Economy', in P. Cottrell, A. Teichova & T. Yuzawa (eds.), *Finance in the Age of the Corporate Economy*, Aldershot, Ashgate, 1996, 7–9.
[284] [1897] AC 22. See G. Rubin, 'Aron Salomon and his Circle', in J. Adams (ed.), *Essays for Clive Schmitthoff*, Abingdon, Professional Books, 1983; E. Lim, 'Of "Landmark" or "Leading" Cases: Salomon's Challenge' (2014) 41 *J Law & Soc* 523.

loans. About 16 per cent of the sample business loans were unsecured in the interwar years, nearly a third during the 1940s, and over 45 per cent in the 1950s and 1960s.[285] Banks were confident that the short duration of a loan, past activity on the account, a regular perusal of a firm's financial statements and an adequate 'break-up value' of the assets made it safe to lend without security.[286] A much higher proportion of loans to public companies, compared with private companies, were granted without security. This discrepancy rose in the post-1950 years to three times as much (37.3 per cent compared to 12.1 per cent). In part that was because more information was available about public companies; in part, because private companies tended to be more recent creations (thus lacking a track record), and to have fewer assets.[287]

If security was taken during the 1920–1968 period, property was the most important, accounting for 46 per cent of secured loans between the wars, 35 per cent in the 1940s, and 38 per cent in the 1950s and 1960s. The deposit of market securities was also common. Over the period debentures accounted for 11 to over 20 per cent of security, shares 6 to 13 per cent. The relative importance of debentures increased as that of shares fell.[288] Personal guarantees continued to be important, notably those given by the directors of borrowing companies. There were some inter-company guarantees where the borrower was in a corporate group or had commercial links with other companies.[289]

The security side of bank lending was encrusted with law and drew in the lawyers, first to draft standard form documents and, if necessary, register them; second, to spell out for banking practice the implications of recent court decisions and legislation; third, to advise whether a bank's existing security was sound; and fourth, to recommend what ought to be done in light of events such as the default or insolvency of a customer. How lawyers contributed is illustrated by some of the advice recorded by the National Provincial Bank in its 'Law Books' during the years 1870–1949. Subjects included the liability of the bank as contributory having taken an equitable charge over shares, 1870 (A. J. Watson of counsel); the implications of *Colonial Bank* v. *Whinney*[290] for security (Wilde Sapte, solicitors); the effect of dock warrants in the absence of attornment, 1885 (Mr Manisty of counsel); security over produce, 1900 (Horace Avory of counsel); the nature of a charge over company shares, 1910 (Wilde Sapte); whether a bank might make advances against debentures deposited as security, despite receiving notice of subsequent debentures being issued, 1922 (F. Luxmore KC); the effect of a general charge over warehouse warrants representing cloth in a business's own strong room, 1923 (Wilde Sapte); the release of a joint guarantor, 1922 (Wilde Sapte); the impact of the Law of Property Act 1925 on a memorandum of deposit

---

[285] M. Collins & M Baker, 'English Bank Business Loans, 1920–1968: Transaction Bank Characteristics and Small Firm Discrimination', *op cit*, 146–147.
[286] Ibid., 148–149. See S. Thomas, *Banker and Customer*, 4th ed., London, Gregg Publishing, 1936, 497–505 on steps bankers were to take with unsecured lending in the interwar years.
[287] Ibid., 165.   [288] Ibid., 148.   [289] Ibid., 148, 166.   [290] (1886) 11 App Cas 426.

of title deeds, 1926 (F. McMullan of Lincoln's Inn); an all moneys charge, 1949 (Mr Sykes of counsel); and the implications of a floating charge over Scottish assets, 1956.[291]

Earlier we saw how security could be taken over documents of title like bills of lading and dock warrants.[292] Security over the goods stored in warehouses (godowns) was particularly popular in Asia and the US.[293] The most common forms of security when English banks advanced moneys to industry during our period were, as we have seen, first, the personal guarantee; second, charges over shares and debentures; and, third, mortgages and other charges over land, factories and the other property of a business. Let us examine in greater detail these three bank favourites.

(i) Personal Guarantees

In practice, as we have seen, banks often made advances to a business conditional on its principals giving a personal guarantee, sometime called personal security. Although widely used, the personal guarantee was not regarded as ideal. As George Rae wrote, it offered 'a less stable form of cover to a bank than the collateral security of shares or other property, because the position of a surety [guarantor] may change for the worse without your knowledge'.[294] In some cases, as another adviser to bankers put it, it was difficult to judge the nature and character of a potential guarantor. The banker might obtain a bank reference about them, but other bankers 'are naturally prone to take the most favourable view of their own customer's position'.[295] After opining that a guarantee 'in fact, is hardly a security at all', an Associate of the Institute of Bankers and bank manager advised in the 1920s that it was desirable that a guarantor should back the personal undertaking with security.[296] With time that became standard practice: the guarantor's undertaking to pay was not sufficient in itself but had to be backed by the guarantor providing collateral.

Apart from the practical objections to a personal guarantee, there were legal drawbacks facing a bank in taking one. The law relating to guarantee (surety)

---

[291] RBS, NAT/1112/1, National Provincial Bank, Law Book 1870–1913, 1, 3, 61, 66–67; RBS, NAT/1112/2, National Provincial Bank, Law Book 1916–1949, 17, 19, 28–29, 31, 46, 47, 49, 74, 124; RBS, NAT/1112/3, Provincial Bank, Law Book 1949–1954, 378, 381–382, 387–388. Other advice received is referred to elsewhere in the chapter. Note the description 'Wilde Sapte' even though this firm of solicitors had other names, e.g., Wilde, Berger & Co, Wilde Berger & Moore, and Wilde Moore & Wigston.

[292] see 399, 408 above. For views of the banking mentors on this type of security: J. Gilbart, Practical Treatise on Banking, *op cit*, 1856, v.1, 37–38. See also the 1901 edition, vol. 1, 253–254; A. Butterworth, *Banker's Advances on Mercantile Securities*, London, Sweet & Maxwell, 1902, 10–25, 51–54, 91(based on lectures to Institute of Bankers in 1901); E. Sykes, Banking and Currency, 4th ed., 1918, *op cit*, 183–185.

[293] e.g., *Hong Kong & Shanghai Bank* v. *Glover & Co*, Supreme Court & Consular Gazette, vol. 5, 17 July 1869, 35; *Von Dreitche* v. *Hong Kong & Shanghai Bank* [1887] ColConC 36.

[294] G Rae, The Country Banker, *op cit*, 91–92. See also T. Moxon, English Practical Banking, 10th ed., *op cit*, 86–87.

[295] E. Sykes, *Banking and Currency*, 4th ed., London, Butterworth, 1918, 181.

[296] L. Fogg, *Bankers' Securities against Advances*, London, Pitman, 1922, 12.

had a long history,[297] and various protections had grown up for guarantors. The *Law Magazine* spelt out the reason in 1829, that advantage might be taken 'of promises hastily and incautiously made by persons, whose only interest in the transaction was, perhaps, a wish to do a friendly office'.[298] Statute introduced a number of safeguards which banks needed to surmount, for example, a guarantee had to be in writing and signed by the surety, and with an unincorporated business (not uncommon for a substantial part of our period) a continuing guarantee covering its borrowing was revoked as to future transactions by any change in its constitution.[299]

Apart from statute, the banks faced difficulties in the common law. Just one example was the warning bankers received about 'giving time' to their customers when payment on an advance, guaranteed by a third party, was due. Giving time meant 'giving indulgence more than the law and the custom of bankers prescribes, and such undue indulgence, in the absence of an express stipulation, or of the consent of the Guarantor, will discharge him'.[300] Discharge of a guarantor would occur not only if there was an extension of time for payment of an advance, but with other variations in its terms which the guarantor had not approved. The rationale for the common law rule was that if a guarantor had agreed to a potential liability, the bank could not unilaterally extend or amend it by agreeing, for instance, to an increase in the customer's indebtedness or to a longer period for repayment.[301] Banks might overcome some of these problems, but not all, in the drafting of the guarantee.[302] Once the Institute of Bankers' examination became formalised in the first part of the twentieth century, the trainee banker was expected to have a relatively sophisticated understanding of the legal issues surrounding the taking of personal guarantees.[303]

There were also difficult issues as well for potential guarantors. The view expressed about personal guarantees by the solicitors Parker Rhodes & Co, contained in the quotation at the beginning of this section, reflected the frustration of their client C. E. Ellis about the legal implications of giving

---

[297] Professor Carey, 'A Course of Lectures on the Law of Contract: Lecture VI' (1845) 6 *Law Times* 12; J. Smith, *Compendium of Mercantile Law*, 6th ed. by G. Dowdeswell, London, Stevens & Norton, 1859, Ch. 11; W. Lloyd, 'The Surety' (1917) *U Penn LR* 40; W. Morgan, 'The History and Economics of Suretyship' (1927) 12 *Cornell LQ* 153 (Pt 1); T. Hewitson, *Suretyship: Its Origin and History in Outline*, Sydney, Law Book Co, 1927.

[298] 'Mercantile Law' (1829) 1 *Law Magazine* 243, 252.

[299] Statute of Frauds Amendment Act 1828, 9 Geo 4, c.14, s. 6.; Mercantile Law Amendment Act 1856,19 & 20 Vic c.97, s.4; Partnership Act 1890, s.18. See *Halsbury's Laws of England*, 2nd ed., London, Butterworths, 1935, vol. 16, 31, 78.

[300] C. Collins, *Law and Practice of Banking*, London, James Cornish & Sons, 1882, 244. See e.g., *Rouse v. Bradford Banking Co Ltd* [1894] AC 586; *Ward v. National Bank of New Zealand Ltd* (1883) 8 App Cas 755.

[301] *Holme v. Brunskill* (1878) 3 QBD 495, 505, per Cotton LJ; *Bolton v. Salmon* [1891] 2 Ch 48.

[302] e.g., *Union Bank of Manchester Ltd v. Beech* (1865) 3 Hurl & C 672, 159 ER 695.

[303] L. Minty, *Practice and Law of Banking*, London, 'Bank Officer' Ltd, 1924 (answers to questions set at the examinations of the Institute of Bankers), 79–82.

a personal guarantee, and the hurdles in the way of extricating oneself from a guarantee once given. As his father before him, Ellis had become the managing director of the large steel manufacturer and shipbuilder, John Brown & Co Ltd of Sheffield.[304] (John Brown had established his famous Atlas works in the city in the 1850s, and at end of the century the company had expanded into shipbuilding with the acquisition of the Clydebank Shipbuilding and Engineering Co near Glasgow.[305]) Ellis' brother was a director of a separate business, a Bradford ironworks, Thwaites Brothers Ltd. Perhaps as the *Law Magazine* had described it 'a wish to do a friendly office' for his brother, in 1906 Ellis had guaranteed a special loan account which Thwaites had with the London City and Midland Bank.

In early 1913 C. E. Ellis received the opinion of Holman (later Sir Holman) Gregory KC as to how to obtain his release from the guarantee against the background, it seems, of the bank's threatened claim against Thwaites on the special loan account.[306] Following that advice Ellis wrote to Thwaites offering to pay off the bank and to make arrangements with it regarding repayment of the moneys.[307] Thwaites refused. After Ellis issued a statement of claim against Thwaites in September 2013, the company agreed to negotiate with the bank for Ellis' release from the guarantee.[308] It was the bank's turn to refuse to budge: it took the view that the proposal from Thwaites that the Ellis guarantee be replaced by guarantees from two of Thwaites' directors was unacceptable. After further negotiations (no doubt interrupted by the war), the matter was eventually resolved in 1919.[309] Ellis was none too impressed with the law, a sentiment his solicitors also expressed, perhaps to mollify him.

Apart from legal technicalities, another reason that personal guarantees were unpopular with some businesses was that their directors had thought that through incorporation they had limited their liability. Giving a personal guarantee put paid to that. The banks contended that if directors wanted an overdraft or loan and were confident in their company's prospects, why should

---

[304] Ellis (later Sir Charles) was called as a barrister in 1878 and during the First World War was Director-General of Ordnance Supply: C. Corker, 'Continuity and Change in the Sheffield Armaments Industry 1919–1930' (2018) 24 *J Management Hist* 174, 182.

[305] R. Lloyd-Jones & M. Lewis, 'Personal Capitalism and British Industrial Decline: The Personally Managed Firm and Business Strategy in Sheffield 1880–1920' (1994) 68 *Bus Hist Rev* 364, 371–372; I. Johnston, *Ships for a Nation John Brown & Company Clydebank*, Glasgow, West Dunbartonshire Libraries & Museum, 2000; A. Grant, *Steel and Ships The History of John Brown's*, Michael Joseph, London, 1950; *100 Years in Steel*, Firth & John Brown Ltd, Sheffield, 1937; *John Brown and Company Limited: Atlas Works, Sheffield, Shipyard and Engineering Works, Clydebank*, London, John Brown & Company, 1903.

[306] SCA, X308/2/2/1, John Brown & Co Ltd, Opinion of Holman Gregory KC to Parker Rhodes & Co, Rotherham, 7 January 1913. The opinion referred, inter alia, to S. Rowlatt, *Law of Principal and Surety*, London, Sweet & Maxwell, 1898, 181.

[307] Ibid., letter, C. E. Ellis to Thwaites, 28 February 2013.

[308] Ibid., Statement of Claim, 25 September 1913; Mumford Johnson & Co, Bradford (Thwaites' solicitors), letter, 8 August 1913.

[309] Ibid., letters, 22 October 1913; 10 November 1913. The file reveals Ellis' despair about his brother's financial travails.

they not incur a risk when they were asking the bank to do precisely that?[310] *Bradford Old Bank Ltd* v. *Sutcliffe*[311] provides an example. Samuel Sutcliffe & Son Ltd was a textile mill incorporated in 1890.[312] In 1894 two of directors of Sutcliffes gave a guarantee to cover losses on debentures the company gave as security for a loan to the company of £3,600 and an overdraft of £2,500.[313] The company continued with the bank after it amalgamated with the Birmingham District and Counties Banking Company in 1907. In 1912 the new bank demanded payment under the guarantee. The Court of Appeal saw no obstacle to holding that the guarantors were not discharged by the bank's amalgamation, and that its claim for the amount outstanding on the loan account was not barred by the Statute of Limitations which only ran from the demand in 1912.[314]

(ii) Security over Shares and Debentures

The principle that marketable securities like bonds, shares and debentures could constitute good collateral for bank advances was established early with government and similar paper. In law security was by way of pledge if the instruments were payable to bearer. In *Wookey* v. *Pole*[315] an Exchequer bill in blank was placed for sale in the hands of brokers. Instead, they deposited it with their bankers as security for an advance to the amount of its value. The Court of the King's Bench held that property in the bill had passed to the bankers as would bank notes and bills of exchange indorsed in blank. If this type of collateral was taken, a bank was complying with the tenet that it must hold liquid assets since government and similar paper was readily saleable as a matter of fact and law. There was no issue in the Privy Council in 1836 as to the bank's right under its agreement with a firm of merchants to sell on default of payment the East India Company paper deposited with it as collateral security.[316]

Then from the 1840s, as George Rae later put it, shares in the railway companies emerged as the 'champion example of banking cover'[317] albeit that taking these as collateral was not without its hiccups. In its instructions to its bank officers in the 1840s, the National Provincial Bank had advised that only if nothing else was available should security be taken over railway shares – 'being

---

[310] M. Collins & M. Baker, Commercial Banks and Industrial Finance in England and Wales 1860–1913, *op cit*, 187.

[311] [1918] 2 KB 833; 417 above.   [312] *The Textile Mercury*, 29 March 1890, 230–231.

[313] see 834 for the guarantees' terms; liability was limited to £6100 plus interest.

[314] Statutes of Limitation dated back to 21 Jac 1, c.16: see *Halsbury's Laws of England*, 2nd ed., London, Butterworth, 1936, vol. 20, 595n.

[315] (1820) 4 B & Ald 1, 106 ER 839.

[316] *Young* v. *Bank of Bengal* (1836) 1 Moore 87, 18 ER 34 (PC, India). See also *Bank of Bengal* v. *Macleod* (1849) 5 Moo Ind App 1, 18 ER 795 (East India Company promissory notes as security for advances); *Russian Commercial and Industrial Bank* v. *Comptoir d'Escompte de Mulhouse* [1925] AC 112 (Brazilian and Chinese government bonds given by Russian bank as security for opening a letter of credit by French bank in the Russian bank's favour).

[317] The Country Banker, *op cit*, 101.

of an objectionable character' – and then they had to be transferred into the name of the bank and the railway company notified of this.[318]

The issue became whether a bank had to take all these steps. In 1865, Parr's Bank took the advice of James Bacon QC of Lincoln's Inn about the strength of its security over railway shares in the event of a customer's insolvency.[319] Did the deposit of the railway share certificates, with a memorandum giving the bank the right to sell them on default of repayment, constitute good security without giving notice to the railway company? The bank's solicitors were concerned with the opinion expressed in the second edition of Grant's treatise on banking law that no notice was necessary to perfect the bank's security interest.[320] Citing *Watts v. Porter*[321] and *Dunster v. Glengall*[322] Bacon advised that to protect the bank in the event of the customer's bankruptcy, the shares had to be transferred to the bank and the railway company had to be notified of the transfer.[323] Bacon's view was confirmed when in 1886 the bank raised the issue again, on this occasion with Joseph Walton, then a leading junior in commercial and shipping work in Liverpool, but later a well-respected judge in the Commercial Court.[324] Transfers in blank had been given to the bank, but had not been completed. Unless that had been done and notice given to the railway company of the transfer of the shares, Walton advised, the customer's trustee in bankruptcy would take them free of what was only an equitable mortgage which the bank had over them.[325]

With the popularity of incorporation in the second part of the nineteenth century, banks took shares and debentures as collateral in many companies other than the railways. By 1876, John Dun could list 'good railway or other stock transferred to bank' as suitable security for banks, along with guarantees; mortgages, foreign and colonial government and other first-class bonds payable to bearer; and, for London banks, dock warrants and other vouchers for goods and produce.[326] With fully paid up shares the Companies Act 1867 empowered companies to issue bearer shares transferable by delivery.[327] With

---

[318] RBS, NAT/1175, Instruction book for local directors and staff of branches of National Provincial Bank of England, *op cit*, 25.
[319] Bacon was a clever cartoonist, appointed chief judge under the Bankruptcy Act 1869, who eventually retired from the bench aged 88: J. Rigg, revised H. Mooney, 'Bacon, Sir James (1798–1895)', *Oxford Dictionary of National Biography*.
[320] J. Grant, *The Law relating to Bankers and Banking*, 2nd ed. by R. Fisher, London, Butterworths, 1865. That was the view in the first edition: J. Grant, The Law relating to Bankers and Banking, 1856, *op cit*, 169, 188–190.
[321] (1854) 3 El & Bl 743, 118 ER 1319.   [322] 3 Irish Ch Rep 47.
[323] RBS, PAB/148, Counsel's opinion for Parr's Banking Co Ltd relating to deposit of share certificate, Opinion James Bacon, 14 December 1865.
[324] N. Jones, 'Walton, Sir Joseph (1845–1910)', *Oxford Dictionary of National Biography*.
[325] RBS, PAB/148, Counsel's opinion for Parr's Banking Co Ltd relating to deposit of share certificate, Opinion Joseph Walton, 27 June 1886. cf. *Societe Generale de Paris* v. *Walker* (1885) 11 App Cas 20 (shares in Tramways Union Co Ltd); *Thornton* v. *Union Discount Co of London* (1891) 7 TLR 322 (Mexican railway bonds).
[326] J. Dun, British Banking Statistics, *op cit*, 86.   [327] 30& 31 Vict, c.131, ss.27, 28.

bearer shares, the security banks took was by way of pledge, a well-recognised technique of giving collateral. That did not exclude legal arguments seeking to undermine a bank's security, although these were generally unsuccessful.[328]

But most shares were not payable to bearer. For convenience the practice grew up with them (as we saw with Parr's Bank) that the customer would deposit their share certificates with the bank, accompanied by a memorandum giving the bank the right to sell on the customer's default. Early on it was recognised that the practice created in the bank's favour an equitable mortgage of the shares. *Ex parte Moss*[329] in 1849 went further. There shareholders (now bankrupt) in a public company deposited their shares with bankers as security for advances without a written memorandum. The Vice Chancellor held that the bankers could sell the shares on evidence of a custom that there did not need to be a written memorandum.[330] In a series of cases the courts put paid to other challenges to this type of security. The contention in *Ex parte Robert Stewart*[331] was that section 19 of the Joint Stock Companies Act 1856 prevented it. That section provided that the company was not bound by any trust, and that no notice of a trust should have any effect against it. The argument was that the section precluded an equitable mortgage of a company's shares, and a bank giving notice to a company of the deposit of its shares and its interest in them. 'That argument', Lord Westbury said succinctly in rejecting it, 'goes to destroy the power of a shareholder to make any effectual equitable mortgage'.[332]

By the early 1870s, the practice was established that a charge over shares for an advance was effected by the deposit of the share certificates, the notification to the company (to protect against the company claiming a lien over them if the shares were not fully paid), and the execution of share transfers (in accordance with the company's articles) in blank, which the bank could complete in its favour if necessary. In 1874 Sir George Jessel MR held that in these circumstances the lender had an implied power to fill in the blanks. He also rejected an argument that since the articles of the company required that the transfer of its shares should be by 'instrument in writing', that meant by deed, even if the invariable practice of the company might have been to require a deed when shares were being charged.[333] The very convenience of depositing blank transfers along with the shares overcame qualms that a fraudster might somehow purloin the blanks, fill them in and thus dispose of the shares to a bona fide purchaser without notice. In several decisions in the 1880s the House of Lords

---

[328] e. g., *Bentinck v. London Joint Stock Bank* [1893] 2 Ch 120 (New York, Pennsylvania, and Ohio Railroad Company bonds).
[329] (1849) 3 De G & S 599, 64 ER 623.
[330] cf. *Carter v. Wake* (1877) 4 Ch D 605 (no memorandum accompanying the deposit of bonds of the Canada Southern Railway Company).
[331] (1864) 4 De G J & S 543, 46 ER 1029 (shares in Victoria Silver, Lead and Zinc Company Ltd deposited with Stourbridge and Kidderminster Banking Company for advance.)
[332] at 547, 1031.
[333] *In re Tahiti Company Company* (1874) LR 17 Eq. 273 (the lender in this case was a stockbroker, not a bank).

upheld the system of depositing share certificates with blank transfers against claims by other creditors in the customer's insolvency or by those subsequently taking from fraudsters.[334] That did not mean that challenges went away. In the years up to the First World War they occurred with regularity, for example, in cases where coal merchants deposited the shares they held in their supplier with their bank as security for an advance;[335] where a bank had taken an equitable charge over shares owned by a business partnership in a manufacturing company to secure the business's account;[336] and where the London County and Westminster Bank took debentures in a private company as security for that company's overdraft.[337]

The use of debentures as security for bank advances was a corollary of their more frequent issue by companies as a means of raising capital in the last part of the nineteenth century. Advertisements in *The Times* over three decades from 1880 show a dramatic increase in the years 1887 to 1897 of floating charges as a proportion of all debenture advertisements.[338] The practice by the early twentieth century was that a company would issue debentures, secured by a charge over the present and future property and assets of the undertaking. This was the floating charge.[339] The charge might be held for the debenture holders by trustees appointed under a deed between the company and them. The company might undertake that, without the authority of the debenture holders or their trustee, it would not create any further charge over its assets ranking pari passu with, or in priority to the charge created by the debentures. On default the debenture holders would be empowered to appoint a receiver to collect and distribute the company's assets.[340] Backed by a charge, the debenture holders would have priority over unsecured creditors in the distribution. Shareholders were last in the queue. What was seen as the unfair advantage which debenture holders had when a company failed led to the provision in the

---

[334] *Colonial Bank* v. *Whinney* (1886) 11 App Cas 426; *Société Générale* v. *Walker* (1885) 11 App Cas 20.
[335] *Bradford Banking Co Ltd* v. *Henry Briggs Son & Co* (1886) 12 App Cas 29.
[336] e.g., *London and Midland Bank* v. *Mitchell* [1899] 2 Ch 161. The shares were in Joseph Rodgers & Co Ltd, it seems cutlers and silver and electro-plate manufacturers in Sheffield.
[337] *Coleman* v *London County and Westminster Bank Ltd* [1916] 2 Ch 353.
[338] J. Amour, 'Should we Redistribute in Insolvency?', in J. Getzler & J. Payne, *Company Charges: Spectrum and Beyond*, Oxford, Oxford University Press, 2006, 196–197.
[339] Lord Macnaghten's well-known definition was that the floating charge was ambulatory, shifting and hovering until crystallised: *Illingworth* v. *Houldsworth* [1904] AC 355, 358. On the history of the floating charge: *Oxford History of the Laws of England*, vol.12, *1820–1914, Private Law*, Oxford, Oxford University Press, 2010, 663–668 (M. Lobban); J. Amour, 'The Chequered History of the Floating Charge' (2014) 13 *Griffith LR* 25; R. Nolan, 'Property in a Fund' (2004) 120 *LQR* 108, 117–130; R. Gregory & P. Walton, 'Fixed and Floating Charges—A Revelation' [2001] *LMCLQ* 123; R. Pennington, (1960) 'The Genesis of the Floating Charge' (1960) 23 *MLR* 25.
[340] Examples of debentures: see *Encyclopaedia of the Laws of England with Forms and Precedents*, 1st ed., London, Butterworths, 1904, vol. 5, 77–87; F. Gore-Browne, *Concise Precedents under the Companies Acts*, 2nd ed., London, Jordan & Sons, 1900, 498–500; J. Reeder, *The Development of the Law relating to Debentures with special reference to the Floating Charge*, University of Birmingham, PhD thesis, 1976, 215–223.

Companies Act 1900 that company charges had to be registered with the Companies Registrar; potentially, at least, unsecured creditors had notice of the commercial reality.[341]

Once companies began to issue debentures, the books directed at bankers added debentures to shares and bonds as suitable instruments for them to take as security for an advance.[342] That was matched in practice. By the early twentieth century, some banks were advancing very large sums on the security of the borrower's own debentures. At the international level, in 1904 Brown Shipley & Co established a credit of £150,000 in favour of the Russian Petroleum and Liquid Fuel Company Ltd on it depositing as security some £100,000 of its debentures.[343] (At the time Russia was the dominant producer of petroleum and the company was part of a significant British investment in the industry.[344]) In the sample of 3,000 accounts of industrial customers mentioned earlier, whereas in the 1880s the incidence of debentures as security was insignificant, by 1914 it occurred with up to 15 per cent of advances. These figures covered the debentures of other companies which the borrower might hold as an investment, as well as debentures which the borrower itself had issued.[345]

In the first part of the twentieth century the most common form of security for banks, at least those in London, was the deposit of securities listed on the Stock Exchange. 'Government stock, good debentures and other "gilt-edged" securities', the secretary of the Institute of Bankers advised, 'form excellent cover for a banker against advances'.[346] However, he added, mining shares and certain classes of industrial shares were to be avoided by the prudent banker. Not only were they speculative, but they were also seldom fully paid so that the company's liquidator would make claims from shareholders on its insolvency. Apparently practice varied among bankers, but in his view it was certainly wiser in the majority of cases to have the shares transferred and registered.[347] In fact commercial convenience meant that the deposit of the share certificates, together with blank transfers, continued to be the dominant practice. In a typical form of agreement the customer would vouch that the value of the securities deposited exceeded by a specified percent the amount of the loan, and that if that value fell the customer would provide

---

[341] s. 14. See J. Getzler, 'Role of Security over Future and Circulating Capital: Evidence from the British Economy circa 1850–1920', in J. Getzler & J. Payne, Company Charges: Spectrum and Beyond, *op cit*, 2006, 231–232; W. Cornish, S. Banks, C. Mitchell, P. Mitchell & R. Probert, *Law and Society in England 1750-1950*, 2nd ed., Oxford, Hart, 2019 254; L. Gullifer, 'Piecemeal Reform: Is It the Answer?', in F. Dahan (ed.), *Research Handbook on Secured Financing in Commercial Transactions*, Cheltenham, Edward Elgar Publishing, 2015, 422–423.

[342] e.g., T. Moxon, *English Practical Banking*, 10th ed., Manchester, John Heywood, 1899, 93.

[343] *London Investment Trust Ltd* v. *Russian Petroleum and Liquid Fuel Co Ltd* [1907] 2 Ch 540. On the Russian company: G. Jones, *The State and the Emergence of the British Oil Industry*, London, Macmillan, 1981, 55–57.

[344] R. Tolf, *The Russian Rockefellers*, Stanford, California, Hoover Institution Press, 1976, 119–120.

[345] 422–423 above. [346] E. Sykes, Banking and Currency, *op cit*, 1. [347] Ibid., 178.

additional collateral to the bank's satisfaction, or pay off so much of the loan as to restore the margin. If the customer failed to do this, or if it failed to repay the advance, the agreement authorised the bank to realise the securities as it deemed fit, with the customer obliged to pay any difference between the net proceeds of sale and the amount due, plus interest and the cost of realisation.[348]

(iii) Land, Factories and Other Property of the Business

The legal mortgage of property was the safest form of security. Early on English law recognised that the deposit of title deeds to land, factories and other real property constituted an equitable mortgage. Neither a legal nor equitable mortgage of such property was especially popular as security for banks when an industrial or commercial enterprise sought an overdraft or loan. Since it would take time to realise if it came to that, it was contrary to the tenet that the bank should have only liquid assets. Shortly after the London and Westminster Bank opened its doors in 1834, it told prospective customers in the provinces that it did not consider it expedient to advance money 'upon Mortgage or similar dead securities'.[349] In 1845 it declined a request for an advance of £20,000 on the mortgage of two collieries as collateral security, the bank being 'indisposed to advance money on inconvertible security'.[350] The Bank's general manager, Gilbart, advised that in London advances must never be made on the security of property deeds alone, and if they were taken a solicitor's view of the property's value was essential, which should be much higher than the advance.[351] He added 'that the most dangerous of all loans are those which are made against unmarketable securities, such as mills, iron-works, coal-mines, landed property, etc., and which from their nature are not likely to be repaid at maturity, but are likely to be asked to be renewed and attain for an indefinite period'.[352]

George Rae made the same point: there could be six months' delay in realising a legal mortgage, and an equitable mortgage by way of the deposit of the title deeds alone brought the possibility of loss though the existence of a previous encumbrance or by legal difficulties in realising the security.[353] As to mortgages over industrial property, Dun's warning was even starker: 'If advances are exceptionally made against the [property] deeds of works of other manufacturing premises, these should not be relied upon beyond their

---

[348] see the form at A. Butterworth, Bankers' Advances on Mercantile Securities, *op cit*, 92. See also the forms in RBS, GM/445/1, Glyn, Halifax, Mills & Co, Letters of hypothecation 1850–1913.
[349] T. Gregory, *The Westminster Bank*, London, Oxford University Press, 1936, vol. I, 266–268.
[350] Ibid., 243.
[351] J. Gilbart, Practical Treatise on Banking, *op cit*, 1856, vol. 1, 37–38. See also the 1901 edition, vol. 1, 253–254. Gilbart thought the system more justified with country bankers since they knew their customers better.
[352] J. Gilbart, Practical Treatise on Banking, ibid.
[353] The Internal Management of a Country Bank in a Series of Letters on the Functions and Duties of a Branch Manager, *op cit*, 87. Rae added the need for a solicitor to be involved: 79.

undoubted value under the adverse circumstances of a forced sale, and denuded of trade fittings and machinery.'[354] This had some foundation in reality: the merchant bank Bensons had experience when cotton mills had closed and on sale fetched only a fraction of their value as going concerns.[355] By the end of the nineteenth century the proportion of industrial property taken as security for bank advances had declined.[356]

None of this meant that mortgages were not taken as bank security over an industrial enterprise's property.[357] The secretary of the Institute of Bankers advised in 1918 that taking the title deeds to property was a very general and 'very fair' form of security, although he added that it suffered from the disadvantage that it was not readily marketable and that a forced sale might result in a price below the market value.[358] If banks were to take this form of security, he recommended that they should never take a legal mortgage but rather an equitable mortgage by way of a deposit of title deeds, which they should tightly guard; that they must have a solicitor prepare an immediate report on the genuineness and correctness of the security; that they should undertake regular valuations of the property; and that they should avoid second mortgages at all costs.[359]

Inevitably disputes arose and some were litigated. One such issue concerned the bank's position when the property it took was subject to a prior charge of debenture holders. Thus in *Roper* v. *Castell & Brown Ltd*[360] the company had issued debentures in 1885 secured on all its present and future property by a floating charge. That prohibited it from creating any mortgage or charge upon its freehold or leasehold property in priority to the debentures. The company secured its overdraft with the Union Bank of London[361] in 1895 by depositing the title deeds of some of its property by way of a memorandum of charge under seal. The bank had no notice of the existence of the debentures and made no inquiries. The debenture holders claimed that their rights under the floating charge had priority over the bank's equitable charge. Romer J held that the bank's equity was stronger, since the debenture holders had allowed the title deeds to remain with the company.

---

[354] J. Dun, British Banking Statistics, *op cit*, 86.   [355] J. Wake, Kleinwort Benson, *op cit*, 100.
[356] see M. Collins and M. Baker, Commercial Banks and Industrial Finance in England and Wales 1860–1914, *op cit*, 184. With small firms, mortgages were taken over the domestic property of the principals: e.g., RBS/WES/88, Security forms and contract notes of W. Pinnock, customer of London & County Banking Co Ltd. Pinnock was a commodity broker in Mark Lane, London.
[357] *Deeley* v. *Lloyds Bank Ltd* [1912] AC 756 (Brockmoor Steel and Iron Works; Lloyds Bank overdraft). See also *Irvine* v. *Union Bank of Australia* (1877) 2 App Cas 366 (rice mill in Rangoon (Yangon) charged to bank for advance of some £15,000); *Small* v. *National Provincial Bank of England* [1894] 1 Ch 686 (factory mortgaged to bank for overdraft). See 423 above.
[358] E. Sykes, Banking and Currency, 4th ed., *op cit*, 179–180.   [359] Ibid., 179–180.
[360] [1898] 1 Ch 315. See also *In Re Connolly Brothers Ltd (No 2)* [1912] 2 Ch 25 (a non-bank lender purchase money security case).
[361] It amalgamated in 1918 with National Provincial Bank of England to form National Provincial & Union Bank of England, eventually part of National Westminster Bank.

Prior to the First World War it does not seem that it was usual for banks to use the floating charge as a form of security themselves. As we have seen banks came across floating charges in the context of taking the debentures of companies as security, but these were not floating charges which they themselves had taken. The books directed at bankers did not contemplate the floating charge as bank security, concentrating their treatment on the forms of security already mentioned.[362] Apart from the banks not wanting to go through the registration process for floating charges, another reason might have been a resistance from customers who objected to the publicity associated with the registration of a floating charge in favour of their bank. This seems to have been the position of the Morgan Crucible Company Ltd in 1908, when it sought £25,000 from the bankers Glyn Mills & Co, now part of Royal Bank of Scotland.[363] The company refused to give a letter of hypothecation, on the basis that it would have to be registered under section 10 of the Companies Act 1907.[364] The parties agreed a compromise: the bank would rank *pari passu* with other creditors, but the company would produce annual balance sheets so the bank could better monitor its financial health.[365]

However, in the 1920s we see from the case law that the banks began taking floating charges as security themselves.[366] They remained unpopular with customers. The in-house solicitor at the National Provincial Bank, one of the large clearing banks, noted in 1923 that there were advantages to the bank in having security over all the assets of a corporate borrower, over 'its body and soul ... without limit'. Although it was popular with the Realisation Department of the bank, he added, 'it is such a stringent security that I do not believe a company south of the Midlands would be likely to give you such a security'.[367] The company in *National Provincial and Union Bank of England v. Charnley*[368] was north of the Midlands, a food processor in west

---

[362] e.g., E. Sykes, Banking and Currency, 4th ed., 1918, *op cit*, 176–186; Institute of Bankers, *Questions on Banking Practice*, 7th ed., London, Blades, 1921, 376–415; *Grant on the Law relating to Bankers and Banking Companies*, 7th ed. by H. Jacobs, London, Butterworth, 1924, 592–606.

[363] There is a brief history of the company: Monopolies and Mergers Commission, *The Morgan Crucible Company plc and Manville Corporation. A Report on the Merger Situation*, Cm 1551, London, TSO, 1991, 3–4.

[364] An amended version of s. 14 of the Companies Act 1900.

[365] RBS, GM/445/1, Glyn, Halifax, Mills & Co, Letters of hypothecation 1850–1913, 11 June, 1908. The bank noted that the 'general question to be raised with Birchams [solicitors] [was] whether such loans really come within the section'.

[366] e.g., *A. L. Underwood, Limited v. Bank of Liverpool and Martins* [1924] 1 KB 775 (Henry King & Co, from 1923 part of Lloyds Bank); *In Re Automatic Bottle Makers Ltd* [1926] Ch 412 (William Deacon's Bank; part of Royal Bank of Scotland from 1930); *In Re Lewis Merthyr Consolidated Collieries Ltd* [1929] 1 Ch 498 (Lloyds Bank). See also L. Fogg, *Bankers' Securities against Advances*, London, Pitman, 1922, 99; M. Emanuel, *Banking Law, Theory and Practice*, London, Virtue & Co, 1926, 192–195.

[367] RBS, NAT/1112/2, National Provincial Bank, Law Book 1916–1949, January 1923, 32. Further comment on his note was that a debenture might encourage other third parties to lend to companies.

[368] [1924] 1 KB 431. See RBS, NAT/1112/2, National Provincial Bank, Law Book 1916–1949, 93.

Lancashire.[369] To secure its overdraft with the bank it 'demise[d] unto the bank the hereditaments and premises described in the schedule hereto together with all and singular the fixed and movable plant machinery and fixtures implements and utensils now or hereafter fixed to or placed upon or used in or about the said hereditaments and premises'. The litigation arose when the motor vans the company owned were seized by the sheriff for debts owed to another creditor. Despite a misdescription in the charge registered at Companies House, the Court of Appeal upheld the bank's claim to the vans as well as other company property.

By the 1930s a bank taking security by way of a floating charge for advances was no longer novel, and there are examples at that time of Lloyds Bank and the Midland Bank taking them with industrial customers.[370] However, it was by no means common practice when a bank made an advance. Bankers were warned that the floating charge was not a panacea. A Gilbart lecturer for the Institute of Bankers in the 1930s explained to his banking audience the 'undesirability' of taking a floating charge by itself, 'for the company is at perfect liberty to sell its stock, call in its book debts, pay off its unsecured creditors, and leave you high and dry with a charge that has nothing to fix on when the time arrives to deal with your security'.[371] He went on to caution that a charge taken within six months of insolvency would fail in the absence of new money lent.[372] Other books directed at bankers reinforced the message about the care needed in registering a floating charge.[373] The warnings of bank educators were not always heeded and as a result of mishaps a bank's expectations of security sometimes fell flat.[374] Nonetheless, the floating charge had arrived as a form of bank security and was utilised to the end of our period (and beyond).

3 Accommodation (Finance) Bills

> Practically, an accommodation bill is a forgery .... [F]orgery, properly understood, equally includes the production of documents that are morally false. It matters not whether the delusion is effected by imitating the forms of the letters and figures, as in a forged Bank-note, or by imitating the form of expression, as in an accommodation bill. (*Westminster Review*, 1859)[375]

---

[369] The business in another case, *National Provincial Bank of England Ltd* v. *United Electric Theatres Ltd* [1916] 1 Ch 132, was in Walsall in the Midlands.

[370] D. Ross, 'The Clearing Banks and Industrialisation – New Perspectives on the Interwar Years', in Y. Cassis & J. Van Helten (ed.), Capitalism in a Mature Economy: Financial Institutions, Capital Exports and British Industry 1870–1939, *op cit*, 61, 64.

[371] R. Jones, *Studies in Practical Banking*, London, Pitman, 1935, 73. The passage was repeated in the last, the 5th ed., edited by J. Holden, 1960, 71. Jones was with the Westminster Bank.

[372] Ibid. see Companies Act 1929, s. 266.

[373] L. Minty, English Banking Methods, 4th ed., 1930, *op cit*, 334–335; J. Milnes Holden, *Securities for Banker' Advances*, London, Pitman, 1954 (5th and last ed., 1971).

[374] *In Re Introductions Ltd* [1969] Ch 199 (National Provincial Bank's debenture for overdraft void since it knew money was for *ultra vires* purpose).

[375] 'The Morals of Trade' (1859) 15 *Westminster Review* 357, 377–378. See also 'Accommodation Bill Swindling' (1845) 3 *Banker's Magazine* 1.

(i) Accommodation paper stunted

As we have seen, banks funded trade by accepting or discounting bills of exchange. As a result exporters were paid when the goods were shipped, and importers obtained credit until the maturity of the bills, which might be a time around when the goods had arrived and were being sold. The bill of exchange slotted into a mesh of arrangements including the shipping documents (importantly, a bill of lading, a document of title to the goods) and a letter of credit. The system of trade finance offered through bills of exchange was sophisticated and efficient, underpinned institutionally by the banks and the discount houses, and built on a firm foundation of law and practice governing bills of exchange and, in time, documentary credits.

As with trade-related bills, banks could have accepted, indorsed or discounted bills drawn by a customer needing working capital for its business, to be discounted in the ordinary way in the money market. There was nothing in bills of exchange law preventing this type of accommodation bill. But during most of our period the utilisation of the accommodation bill as a reputable instrument of business financing was spoilt for two reasons. First, they were associated with individuals short of funds scamming the system – having a friend, for no immediate return (but possibly returning the favour), lend their name to a bill of exchange they drew to make it presentable for discount in the market. The law reports told the story: banks and others, into whose hands such bills fell, losing out when those who had drawn or accepted them, and in some cases misrepresented them, failed to pay.[376]

Second, and more importantly, accommodation bills used for raising business finance were mixed up, as we will see, in nineteenth-century financial crises. The upshot was that respectable opinion took the line (as in the extract quoted at the outset from a mid-nineteenth issue of the *Westminster Review*) that accommodation bills were poison: bills of exchange must be associated with a genuine trade, so that they were self-liquidating when the buyer sold the goods whose purchase they had financed. Only towards the end of our period did the accommodation bill redeem itself, and then disguised as a 'finance bill', issued under an 'acceptance credit'.

Although under a cloud, cases surfaced in the courts where industry had in fact raised finance by the issue of bills, which were then discounted by banks and bill brokers to provide working capital.[377] One sector where accommodation paper featured was the financing of railway construction after the 'mania' for stock exchange investment of the 1840s waned. By the 1850s there were low

---

[376] e. g., *Churchill* v. *Siggers* (1854) 3 El & Bl 929, 118 E.R. 1389; *Jewell* v. *Parr* (1853) 13 CB 909, 138 ER 1460 (1853); *Graham* v. *Johnson* (1869) LR 8 Eq 36; *In Re Solomons* [1904] 1KB 106; *Barclays Bank* v. *Tom* [1923] 1 KB 221.

[377] *In the Matter of Bulmer* (1853) 3 De G M & G 218, 43 ER 86 (ship-owner; Kensignton & Co, bankers, London); *Re Baillie & Harrison, Ex p Harrison* (1866) LR 2 Ch App 195 (fertiliser manufacturer); *Re Barned's Banking Co Ex p Stephens* (1868) LR 3 Ch App 753 (ship building; London bank); *Jones* v. *Gordon* (1877) 2 App Cas 616 (Yorkshire woollen manufacturer and London agent; bill broker); *Yorkshire Banking Company* v. *Beatson and Mycock* (1880) 5 CPD 109, 112–113 (chemical manufacturer, Rotherham).

(or nil) returns on ordinary railway shares and share issues in other sectors of the economy were more attractive. What was the solution? Rather than paying the contractors and locomotive builders cash, the railway companies issued them shares and debentures.[378] At one point the London Chatham and Dover Railway was paying its contractors half in cash and half in shares.[379] Obviously, until a line was working and generating income, these shares and debentures were of no benefit to the contractors in meeting the construction costs unless they could be sold, but probably at a discount.

Railway contractors turned to the finance houses, such as the London Financial Association and the International Financial Society.[380] They accepted the accommodation bills which the contractors drew, and the bills could then be discounted in the market. The finance houses would be repaid by instalments, with interest, and would also charge commission. They took as security for repayment by the contractors on the accommodation bills the shares and debentures the railway companies had paid them.[381] This method of financing railway construction included railways abroad.[382] Thus the large discount house Overend Gurney & Co discounted bills for up to periods of 12 months drawn for the benefit of the Atlantic and Great Western Railway Company, which had been accepted by the Oriental Financial Corporation.[383] Then in the mid-1860s things turned sour. In light of the increasing reluctance of the Bank of England to discount bills, and a growing lack of market confidence, the finance houses became unable to provide funds in this way. The 1866 crisis had begun. Railway contractors began to fail and their bills could not be met. That affected other institutions which held worthless railway paper from lines not completed. Pressure was also placed on the discount houses, since they had discounted these accommodation bills, some of which were now in their portfolios.[384] The result was, as Bramwell B pointed out, financial institutions and others held bills which were nothing more than advances (or renewals of advances) and which, he could have added, were poorly secured or completely unsecured.[385] As we will see later, this type

---

[378] H. Pollins, 'Railway Contractors and the Finance of Railway Development in Britain' (1957) 3 J *Transport Hist* 41, 103.

[379] K. Lampard, 'The Promotion and Performance of the London Chatham & Dover Railway' (1985) 6 J *Transport Hist* 48, 57, 60.

[380] See 'International Financial Society' *Herapath's Railway (and Commercial) J*, 19 August 1876, 906.

[381] P. Cottrell, 'Railway Finance and the Crisis of 1866: Contractors' Bills of Exchange, and the Finance Companies' (1975) 3 J *Transport Hist* 20, 28–29, 35.

[382] Ibid., 28, 29–30. See also D. Adler, *British Investment in American Railways 1834–1898*, Charlottesville, University Press of Virginia, 1970, 40–41; *In re Peruvian Railways Company* (1867) LR 2 Ch App 617.

[383] e.g., *Oriental Financial Corporation v. Overend, Gurney, & Co* (1871) LR 7 Ch App. 142 (unnecessary to decide whether bills were accommodation bills).

[384] W. King, *History of the London Discount Market*, London, Routledge, 1936, 135–136.

[385] *City Discount Company Ltd v. McLean* (1874) LR 9 CP 692, 699.

of accommodation paper had a significant role in the collapse in May 1866 of the largest of the discount houses, Overend Gurney & Co.[386]

The joint stock banks were not major players in accepting accommodation paper because of the conventional wisdom against it. But raising finance through accommodation paper certainly occurred and in some cases the joint stock banks were active participants in discounting it.[387] In *Ex parte Thomas George White*[388] Turner LJ observed that 'in many cases joint stock banks, by giving accommodation without sufficient inquiry, are themselves the cause of the injury of which they complain'.[389] Those remarks underlined that banks might hold accommodation paper in their portfolios without knowing it.[390] This might occur when a bank bought a parcel of bills in the market – in practice in the London market different bills of exchange were parcelled together for discount – and accommodation paper was amongst them. It was only when an instrument in those parcels went unpaid that the reality dawned. Thus on the insolvency of the Aberdare Iron Company in the 1870s, the London and Westminster Bank discovered that it had accommodation paper in its vaults which Aberdare had issued (and had been accepted by E. Corry, a metal merchant).[391] It is a little ironic that the leading figure associated with that bank, James William Gilbart, had deprecated a bank's involvement with such paper.[392]

(ii) Regulating Accommodation Paper?

In 1871 one suggestion was that the law should prevent accommodation bills carrying the phrase 'for value received', since 'no value was ever, in any shape or form whatever, so "received"'.[393] The author went further: the law should refuse to allow accommodation paper without an underlying value.[394] Nothing was done. One potential check on accommodation bills came *ex post facto*. On bankruptcy, the courts could take into account factors which justified a longer period before a bankrupt's discharge, and an involvement with accommodation paper was one. The early nineteenth-century sentiment of the courts – 'accommodation bills have ruined great numbers of men', said the Lord Chancellor with distaste in 1820[395] – was still being expressed in the bankruptcy courts mid-century. However, by then the higher courts were more indulgent. Absent

---

[386] W. King, History of the London Discount Market, *op cit*, 247–250; W. Scammell, *The London Discount Market*, London, Elek Books, 1968, 184. See 446 below.

[387] e.g., *In Re Firth* (1879) 12 Ch D 337, 338. The case involved the London and Yorkshire Bank, a joint stock bank established in London in 1872, later acquired by the Union of London & Smiths Bank and thus to be part of the National Provincial Bank of England.

[388] (1853) 3 De G & J 75, 44 ER 1197.   [389] Ibid., at 79. 1199.

[390] e.g., *In re Fothergill* (1876) 3 Ch D 445.

[391] *Re Fox, Walker, & Co* (1880) 15 Ch D 400, 401. See also *In re Oriental Commercial Bank* (1871) LR 7 Ch App 99; *Re Fothergill, ex p Turquand* (1876) 3 Ch D 445, 448.

[392] 440 below.

[393] A Bank Manager, *Papers on Banking and Finance*, London, Bemrose & Sons, 1871, 41.

[394] Ibid., 41–42.   [395] *Rowe* v. *Young* (1820) II Bligh 391, 4 ER 372.

dishonesty, or a misrepresentation that the bills were not accommodation bills, their view was that the issue of accommodation bills was not a basis for penalising bankrupts by extending the time for their discharge.[396]

For a considerable period the reputation of accommodation bills sealed their fate in polite circles as an acceptable instrument for financing business. The mere fact that the drawer had resorted to this device was presumably because it was without funds, one banking authority explained, and 'no Banker', he concluded, 'will therefore discount a Bill that he knows to be an Accommodation Bill'.[397] Gilbart's injunction against the banker handling accommodation bills was reiterated when his book was disinterred for the twentieth century.[398] The losses suffered following a massive fraud in 1875 in accommodation bills were still in the collective memory of bankers to justify this. The fraud was perpetrated by Alexander Collie. It began with the collapse of Aberdare Iron Co and the Plymouth Iron Co,[399] led to the collapse of Sanderson & Co, one of the larger discounters, involved losses to four of the joint stock banks, and brought about mercantile failures thought to have involved defaults of up to £20million.[400]

Chalmers' Bills of Exchange Act 1882 acknowledged the existence of accommodation bills and did not attempt to regulate their use. Accommodation parties were defined along the lines of a guarantor: those who sign a bill as drawer, acceptor or indorser without receiving value, but for the purpose of lending their name to another person.[401] The Act went on to provide that accommodation parties were liable on the bill to a holder for value, and it was immaterial whether the holder knew the party to be an accommodation party when they took the bill.[402] There were further provisions in relation to the presentation for payment, notice of dishonour and discharge of accommodation paper.[403] The agnosticism of the 1882 Act did nothing to ignite legal enthusiasm for accommodation bills when they had been so recently discredited.[404] In the following years there was occasional litigation involving them, but in the main the facts were unusual or

---

[396] *Ex parte Samuel Hammond* (1855) 6 De GM & G 699, 710; 43 ER 1405, 1409. See also *In re Baillie & Harrison* (1866) LR 2 Ch App 195.

[397] C. Collins, *History, Law and Practice of Banking*, London, James Cornish & Sons, 1882, 188.

[398] e.g., A. Michie (ed), J. Gilbart, *History, Principles and Practice Of Banking*, London, G. Bell, 1904, v.1, 163–166.

[399] *Re Fox, Walker, & Co* (1880) 15 Ch D 400. See 450 below.

[400] *In re Collie ex parte Manchester and County Bank* (1876) 3 Ch D 481. See also *In re Collie* (1878) 8 Ch D 807; *In re Collie* (1881) 17 Ch D 334. Alexander Collie & Co had run the blockade to import cotton during the US Civil War from southern states. Its extensive fraud with bills of exchange in the 1870s ran up debts of £3 million with banks. Westminster Bank took a big hit along with others: see T. Gregory, *The Westminster Bank*, London, Oxford University Press, 1936, vol. I, 295; W. King, *History of the London Discount Market*, London, Routledge, 1936, 289. See also R. Saville, *Bank of Scotland A History 1695-1995*, Edinburgh, Edinburgh University Press, 1996, 504–505; *Young v. United States*, 97 US 39 (1877).

[401] s. 28(1). [402] s. 28(2). [403] ss. 46(2)(d), 50(2)(d), 59(3).

[404] There was no mention of accommodation bills in the 1st edition of what became the standard text: J. Paget, *Law of Banking*, London, Butterworth & Co, 1904.

exceptional,[405] or their use was marked by fraud and so did nothing to enhance their reputation.[406] But the position began to change with changed economic realities.

(iii) The Post-First World War Revival

Accommodation paper never really went away as a device for raising business finance, although it failed to gain a firm foothold. Immediately after the First World War it featured in the House of Lords as a means to assist a buyer purchasing nearly 20,000 cases of Australian tinned soup being disposed of by the government as surplus to requirements.[407] For a while the disappearance of smaller financial institutions, and the central control operating in the large joint stock banks, meant that dealing in accommodation bills was limited.[408] But in 1928, under the name 'finance bills', the Bank of England gave accommodation paper limited approval to support finance houses offering hire purchase.[409] Finance bills in other areas surged in the boom of the late 1920s.[410] But this was short-lived, and in 1929 the Bank of England reaffirmed its traditional rule against the general discounting of accommodation bills; bills of exchange had to be 'commercial' bills, in other words trade-related bills, to be discountable at its discount office.[411]

Hard times as a result of the Great Depression in the 1930s offered some scope for accommodation paper. The prominent discount house Gilletts promoted it as a way to finance shipbuilding and, of course, generate an income for themselves when discounting business had diminished.[412] As the Bank of England struggled to revive the economy, accommodation bills financing hire purchase were again ruled acceptable, if in limited amounts, although those to fund shipbuilding and the film industry were beyond the pale.[413] In 1933 the confectionery company Rowntree needed finance. It obtained an acceptance credit facility from Erlangers, a merchant bank, under which the bank agreed to accept and then discount sight bills of £5,000, payable at six months and up to a credit limit of £400,000.[414] In 1937 the Bank of England reiterated its general warning to accepting houses against accommodation bills.

---

[405] *In Re Pinto Leite and Nephews* [1929] 1 Ch 221 (small merchant bank in London; Portugese company); *In Re Russo-Asiatic Bank* [1934] Ch 720 (accommodation bills to rehabilitate Russian credit in London in 1915: at 731).

[406] *Premier Industrial Bank, Limited* v. *Carlton Manufacturing Co Ltd* [1909] 1 KB 106.

[407] *Gerald McDonald & Co* v. *Nash & Co* [1924] AC 625, 644 per Lord Sumner.

[408] J. Sykes, *English Banking Administration*, London, Pitman, 1925, 47–48.

[409] R. Sayers, *The Bank of England 1891–1944*, Cambridge, Cambridge University Press, 1976, 278.

[410] N. Macrae, *The London Capital Market*, London, Staples Press, 1955, 133–134.

[411] S. Bowden & M. Collins, 'The Bank of England, Industrial Regeneration, and Hire Purchase between the Wars' (1992) 45 *Econ Hist R* 120, 128.

[412] R. Sayers, *Gilletts in the London Money Market 1867–1967*, Oxford, Clarendon, 1968, 96, 99.

[413] R. Sayers, The Bank of England 1891–1944, *op cit*, 538; H. Greengrass, The Discount Market in London, *op cit*, 33.

[414] *Inland Revenue Commissioners* v. *Rowntree & Co Ltd* [1948] 1 All ER 482.

Then in the 1950s and 1960s accommodation (finance) paper under a so-called acceptance credit had its day in the sun. Gilletts again promoted it to industry and had a certain success in the Midlands, especially with companies which had found bank finance tight.[415] For a time the Bank tolerated manufacturing and trading companies issuing finance bills, generally for amounts of not less than £25,000 and designed to provide short-term working finance.[416] With some large acceptance credits syndicates of banks might be involved.[417] Finance houses offering hire purchase continued to raise money via accommodation paper.[418] In 1965, for monetary policy reasons the Bank of England imposed restrictions on the extensive use of accommodation bills for hire purchase.[419] However, these restrictions were later relaxed, and by the early 1970s a number of companies were issuing bills which they immediately discounted to obtain funds, which in some cases they on-lent to others.[420]

It was about this time that the use of bills of exchange as a finance, rather than a trade-related, instrument emerged in a significant way elsewhere in the Commonwealth. For example, in Australia banks established so-called bill line facilities, for a fee, whereby for the period of the agreement customers could draw bills of exchange on the bank, of at least 180 days' duration, which the bank would accept and discount or return for the customer to discount in the market.[421] Alternatively, the bank might agree to indorse bills drawn on some other person, making them more acceptable for discount in the market. The advantage to banks of a bill line facility was that it was a means of accommodating businesses whose limited liquidity ruled out overdraft or loan finance.

6.4 Institutional Underpinning

The doors of the offices were now all closed, and no lights were showing. The black brick precipices, where the firms huddled together by day like cave dwellers were empty, and their piled-up populations had departed. Julius

---

[415] R. Sayers, Gilletts in the London Money Market 1867–1967, *op cit*, 138–139. See also The Bill on London, *op cit*, 85ff.

[416] cf. the financing in *Brown Shipley & Co v. Alicia Hosiery* [1966] 1 Lloyd's Rep 668; *Alicia Hosiery v. Brown Shipley & Co* [1970] 1 QB 195.

[417] G. Fletcher, *The Discount Houses in London*, London, Macmillan, 1976, 142–144.

[418] V. Fox-Smith, *Hire-purchase Credit and Finance*, London, Stevens, 1962 185. See *Lombard Banking Ltd v. Central Garage and Engineering Co Ltd* [1963] 1 QB 220 (bills used for 'stocking loan' by finance house to finance car dealer). See also R. Goode, *Hire-purchase Law and Practice*, 2nd ed., London, Butterworth, 190, 671–674.

[419] Ibid.

[420] J. Grady & M. Weale, *British Banking 1960–85*, Basingstoke, Macmillan, 1986, 136.

[421] G. Walker, 'The Australian Revival of the Bill of Exchange' (1978) 52 *Aust. L.R.* 244; C. Craigie, 'Legal Aspects of Establishing a Bill Line Facility' (1980) 12 *Commercial Law Association [of Australia] Bulletin* 87. See also G. Robertson, 'Commercial Bills of Exchange used for Finance Purposes in New Zealand' (1976) 3 *Auckland LR* 1; P. Ellinger, 'Securitibank's Collapse and the Commercial Bills Market of New Zealand' (1978) 20 *Mal LR* 84; P. Bevans, 'Canadian Bankers' Acceptances', in R. Miner, *Current Issues in Canadian Business Law*, Toronto, Carswell, 1986.

F. Greenbaum (Stock and Share Brokers), F. Macreagh (Stirling) Fuel Engineers, Wigginson, Wigginson & Cheap, Solicitors and Commissioners for Oaths. (Norman Collins, *London Belongs to Me*, 1945)[422]

The City of London throughout our period was a vast collection of markets, commercial businesses and financial institutions. In his walk home to Kennington from Battlebury & Sons on his final day in the office, Mr Josser passed just a few of these in the opening pages of Norman Collins' novel. Mr Josser was a clerk in a firm of 'power specialists' and it would be no disrespect to him to suggest that he was unlikely to know much of the institutional underpinnings of the area of London he worked. As we saw in part 6.2 of the chapter, the Bill on London was one such support, playing a central role in financing international trade throughout our period. In a textbook case, exporters around the world would draw a bill of exchange, payable in pounds sterling in London, which a London bank would agree to accept, so assuming primary liability to pay it on maturity. That meant the bill could be readily discounted.

Underpinning the use of bills in this way was the money market, populated by the bill brokers and the discount houses, where bills were discounted and rediscounted, in ordinary parlance bought and sold. Behind the bill brokers and the discount houses was the Bank of England. The Bank had repurchase arrangements for Consols, and Indian and other government debt, but if it chose to enter the money market for monetary policy or regulatory reasons, trade-related bills had an attraction because of their availability and marketability.[423] After some equivocation, the Bank finally accepted the responsibility to act as lender of last resort by taking bills from the discount houses and others at times when money was tight. That mitigated the extent to which the joint stock banks might need to curb the credit available to their customers by increasing interest rates, reducing overdraft limits and calling in loans.

After examining the role of the discount houses and Bank of England in the workings of the money market, the chapter turns to the role of the London Bankers' Clearing House in processing the collection of cheques and, to an extent, bills of exchange on their maturity. In non-transferable form cheques can be traced back to the first century, in transferable form, to early post-medieval Amsterdam.[424] In Britain they came into vogue as a major instrument of commercial payment in the nineteenth century. Banks began issuing books of cheques to their customers for use in making payment.[425] For a period cheques were also used, to a limited

---

[422] N. Collins, *London Belongs to Me*, London, Collins, 1945.
[423] A. Coleby, 'Bills of Exchange: Current Issues in a Historical Perspective', *Bank of England Quarterly Bulletin*, December 1982, 514.
[424] B. Geva, *The Payment Order of Antiquity and the Middle Ages A Legal History*, op cit, 471.
[425] 380 above.

extent, as a means of international payment.[426] The widespread use of cheques in the community generated a considerable volume of case law.[427] It was largely through the Bankers' Clearing House that banks could swiftly and efficiently collect payment on the cheques their customers paid in.

1 Discount Houses and the Money Market

> The Landlord ... wrote me the enclosed letter some time ago. Yesterday he called, but was not, of course, admitted, since I was allegedly absent. The devil of it is that, because of the Overend Affair, this fellow lives on his house rents; in addition, he will not accept bills of exchange. (Karl Marx to Frederick Engels, 18 November 1868)[428]

Marx's landlord, and many others, suffered from the collapse of the large discount house Overend Gurney in 1866. The ramifications were unsurprising given that the firm, as the editor of the *Economist* Walter Bagehot described it, 'stood next to the Bank of England' in importance.[429] Following the 1866 crisis, discount houses became an important institutional prop to Britain's financial prominence. The discount houses bought bills of exchange at a discount to their face value (hence the term discount house), taking surplus funds as short-term deposits from the commercial banks (with whom they did not compete for deposits from the public), and rediscounting the bills on their own account to the banks and the Bank of England.

(i) From Bill Brokers to Discount House

A stylised history is of a journey from the bill brokers of the late eighteenth century, through the specialised discount houses of the nineteenth and twentieth centuries and the sophisticated money market in which they operated, to their demise in the last decade of the twentieth century with more banks involving themselves in the sterling money market, and the Bank of England rearranging the way it conducted monetary policy operations.[430]

Initially the bill brokers acted as intermediaries with so-called inland bills, the bills of exchange used in domestic financing. They came into their own after the 1825 financial crisis when banks could not obtain liquidity, with many

---

[426] H. Harfield, 'Checks in International Trade' (1960) 15 *Bus Lawyer* 638, 638. See also *Importers Company Ltd v. Westminster Bank Ltd* [1927] 1 KB 869.

[427] Professor Gutteridge claimed that litigation arising out of the drawing or cashing of cheques formed the great bulk of case law on negotiable instruments 1884–1934: 'Contract and Commercial Law' (1935) 51 *LQR* 91, 124.

[428] K. Marx & F. Engels, *Collected Works*, London, Lawrence & Wishart, 1988, vol. 43, 161.

[429] *Lombard Street A Description of the Money Market London*, H. S. King, 1873, 17. See J. Grant, *Bagehot*, New York, Norton, 2019.

[430] W. King, *History of the London Discount Market*, London, Routledge, 1936; W. Scammell, *The London Discount Market*, London, Elek Books, 1968, 118–247; G. Fletcher, The Discount Houses in London, *op cit*, 3–71.

failing. Banks surviving the crisis no longer wanted to hold their funds in bills, offering an opportunity to the bill brokers to act as principals. After 1830 there was the benefit that bill brokers could open accounts with the Bank of England, which might buy eligible bills which the discount houses offered.[431] By mid-century trade-related bills were the stock in trade of the discount houses. As we have seen these financed the expansion of international trade as merchant banks and later joint stock banks undertook liability by accepting or indorsing them. By the 1840s the largest discount house was Overend, Gurney & Co, followed by Alexander & Co. In the 1847 banking crisis smaller discount houses Sanderson & Co and Bruce, Buxton & Co suspended payment, and there were failures in the 1857 banking crisis a decade later.[432] In that crisis Overend Gurney and some other discounters survived with the help of the Bank of England, which provided liquidity through bill purchases. Following the 1857 crisis the Bank of England limited the extent to which it would take bills from the discount houses, to encourage them to increase their reserves, rather than relying on the liquidity it provided. For this and other reasons there was bad blood between the Bank of England and Overend Gurney.

Overend Gurney and other discount houses moved significantly into longer-term, illiquid, and speculative investments, especially in railways.[433] What also came out in the wash with the 1866 crisis were the slack and risky practices in the quality of bills the discount houses had been taking.[434] Despite profits on the bill broking side, from late 1860 Overend Gurney was making losses on accommodation bills and its speculative investments. In an attempt to shore up the firm and raise capital, it became a limited liability company. It was able to do this following the Companies Act 1862.[435] The prospectus for its launch was brief and fraudulent, concealing a deficit of over £3 million.[436] For a while the position stabilised. However, it was a time of political and financial uncertainty, a falling stock market and company failures.

---

[431] D. Kynaston, *Till Time's Last Sand A History of the Bank of England 1694–2013*, London, Bloomsbury Publishing, 2017, 144.

[432] W. King, 'The Extent of the London Discount Market in the Middle of the Nineteenth Century' (1935) 2 *Economica*, New Series, 321.

[433] P. Cottrell, 'Railway Finance and the Crisis of 1866: Contractors' Bills of Exchange and the Finance Companies' (1975) 3 *J Transport Hist*, 20; W. King, History of the London Discount Market, *op cit*, 246–250. For Overend Gurney and London shipbuilding, including the Millwall Ironworks see A. Arnold, 'Charles Mare, London Ironmaster and Shipbuilder' (2011) 36 *London Journal* 23, 30–33.

[434] e.g., *Oriental Financial Corporation* v. *Overend, Gurney, & Co* (1874) LR 7 H.L 348 (the Atlantic and Great Western Railway Company); *Re Fox, Walker, & Co* (1880) 15 Ch D 400 (Sanderson & Co and the Aberdare Iron Company).

[435] 25 & 26 Vict c. 89.

[436] *Oakes* v. *Turquand* (1867) LR 2 HL 325, 341–343; *Peek* v. *Gurney* (1873) LR 6 HL 377, 387–91; P. Johnson, *Making the Market Victorian Origins of Corporate Capitalism*, Cambridge, Cambridge University Press, 2010, 210–211.

(ii) The Overend Gurney Crisis and Aftermath

What triggered the immediate crisis was a judgment on 8 May 1866.[437] That held that Overend Gurney and other plaintiffs could not sue the acceptor of bills of exchange which they held. The bills were drawn by John Watson & Co, a railway contractor in what, as we have seen, had become a popular method of funding railway construction.[438] The bills were accepted by the Mid-Wales Railway Company, payable at the Agra and Masterman's Bank. At the trial earlier that year Erle CJ had held in the plaintiffs' favour, but gave leave to the railway company to move for a nonsuit. The Court of Common Pleas then held that the statute under which the railway company was constituted did not give it power to draw, accept or indorse bills of exchange or promissory notes. The reasoning was that it was not a trading company but had only limited powers to borrow to build and to run the railway. Underlying at least some of the judgments was the fear that were the court to take the contrary view, the market would be inundated with accommodation paper.[439] Following the judgment there was a run on Overend Gurney's deposits. The amount of the Mid-Wales Railway Company's bills was not especially large, but the market was aware that Overend Gurney had taken similar bills from other businesses.[440]

On 9 May Overend Gurney applied to the Bank of England for assistance, but after inspecting its books the Bank of England refused to provide liquidity on the ground that the firm was insolvent. Despite its prominence and standing, it was not too big to fail. Mid-afternoon on 10 May 1866, Overend Gurney suspended payment. Panic ensued. The Bank of England used its reserves to support the banks and the other discount houses with liquidity through bill purchases and repurchase agreements for government debt. The banks and discount houses could thus meet the demands of depositors including, in the case of the discount houses, commercial bank depositors. Alongside this was the decision of the Chancellor of Exchequer that, should it be necessary (which it was not), the government would pass legislation to enable the Bank of England to issue notes beyond the limit set by the 1844 law.[441] The Bank increased the interest rate on discounts and advances to 10 per cent.

---

[437] Bateman, *National Discount Company (Limited), Overend, Gurney, & Co (Limited)* v. *Mid-Wales Railway Company* (1866) LR 1 CP 499.

[438] See *In re Contract Corporation* v. *Claim of Ebbw Vale Company* (1869) LR 8 Eq 14.

[439] See especially at p. 510, Byles J, author of the standard work on Bills of Exchange, then in its 8th edition.

[440] R. Sowerbutts and M. Schneebalg, 'The Demise of Overend Gurney', *Bank of England Quarterly Bulletin*, 2016 Q2, 94, 99; R. Aliber & C. Kindleberger, *Manias, Panics and Crashes A History of Financial Crises*, 7th ed., Basingstoke, Palgrave Macmillan, 2015, 169; M. Duckenfield, S. Altorfer & B. Koehler, *History of Financial Disasters 1763–1995*, London, Pickering & Chatto, 2006, vol. II, 65ff.

[441] Section 2 of the Bank Charter Act 1844, 7 & 8 Vict c. 32, limited the note issue: see 26–27 above. See I. Frame, 'Between the "Bank Screw" and "affording assistance to the mercantile world": Rules, Standards and the Bank Charter Act of 1844' (2019) 83 *MLR* 64.

Confidence was restored although in the aftermath of the crisis seven banks and many commercial enterprises failed.[442] Many investors, including Marx's landlord, suffered as a result.[443] Since the shareholders in Overend Gurney had paid part only of the value of their shares, they were now called on to contribute the rest in its insolvency. Attempts to avoid liability for the unpaid calls were unsuccessful when they came to court.[444] So these shareholders not only lost their investment but also had to pay an additional amount on the firm's demise. As the *Law Times* put it, 'the shares were not merely worthless, and the purchase money thrown away, but ... were, in truth, *damnosa hereditas* – a negative quality'.[445] But it was not only the creditors and shareholders of Overend Gurney and the other banks and companies which failed who were affected but also their employees. For example, one of the immediate victims of the crisis was the Millwall Ironworks and Shipbuilding Co, in which the firm had invested. Its collapse was a factor in the unemployment and hardship which followed in the East End of London, with the area becoming a byword for poverty.[446]

The collapse of Overend Gurney led to criminal prosecutions of six of its directors in relation to the incorporation of the company in 1865. It was a private prosecution brought by a disgruntled shareholder, Dr Adam Thom.[447] Under the system which lasted well into the twentieth century, there was initially a committal hearing, which decided whether there was a case to answer before a matter went to trial. The prosecution surmounted this hurdle and the trial was held at the Guildhall before the Lord Chief Justice of the Queen's Bench, Sir Alexander Cockburn, and a jury.[448] The charges included making, circulating and publishing false statements with intent to deceive a member of the company under section 84 of the Larceny Act 1861; conspiracy to publish a prospectus with intent to deceive; and obtaining money by false pretences. The jury were directed that whilst there might have been misrepresentations supporting a civil action, before they could convict they had to be satisfied that there was a deliberate intention and design to cheat and defraud the

---

[442] W. King, History of the London Discount Market, *op cit*, 244.
[443] J. Juxon, *Lewis & Lewis*, London, Collins, 1983, 83–87. (George Lewis of this firm of solicitors was retained by some of the firm's shareholders.)
[444] *Oakes v. Turquand* (1867) LR 2 HL 325; *Re Overend Gurney & Co (Barrow's Case)* (1868) LR 3 Ch App 784; see R. Grossman & M. Imai, 'Contingent Capital and Bank Risk-Taking among British Banks before the First World War 1' (2013) 66 *Econ Hist Rev* 132, 138.
[445] 'Misrepresentation in the Prospectus of a Company' (1873) 55 *Law Times* 268, 268.
[446] A. Arnold, *Iron Shipbuilding on the Thames 1832–1915*, Aldershot, Ashgate, 2000, 77–79.
[447] see A. Thom, *Overend and Gurney Prosecution, in its Relation to the Public and the Court of Queens' Bench*, London, Wilson, 1869. Thom had been the first judge of Rupert's Land (Canada).
[448] Cockburn liked the limelight of controversial cases: see M. Lobban, 'Cockburn, Sir Alexander James Edmund, twelfth baronet (1802–1880)', *Oxford Dictionary of National Biography*.

Figure 6.2 Overend Gurney trial, December 1869 (Alamy Ltd)

public.[449] Cockburn CJ also told the jury that the prosecution had not shown that any misunderstanding about the prospectus was due to its wording rather than a popular delusion as to the prosperity of the previous firm. Perhaps unsurprisingly in light of this direction the jury returned a not guilty verdict within ten minutes, to loud cheers. When order was restored Cockburn CJ commented that he had never seen a prosecution less warranted; the terms of his summing up, which had ensured the acquittals, is something which would not be countenanced today.

There was a good deal in the way of civil proceedings in the wake of Overend Gurney's collapse. There were the immediate issues around liability on bills and otherwise arising in its liquidation.[450] Towards the other end of the spectrum were the cases involving other institutions hit by the crisis. Agra and Masterman's Bank, with a large Indian business, had stopped payment in early June 1866. It was one of the lucky ones, being rather exceptionally resuscitated some six months after its stoppage under a scheme of arrangement approved by the Vice Chancellor.[451] John Morris, from the firm Ashurst

---

[449] *The Queen* v. *Gurney and Others*, Times, 23 December 1869. See also G. Elliott, *The Mystery of Overend & Gurney*, London, Methuen, 2006, 197–221.

[450] *Overend Gurney & Co Ltd (Liquidators)* v. *Oriental Financial Corp Ltd (Liquidators)* (1874) LR 7 HL 348; *Re Land Credit Co of Ireland ex parte Overend Gurney & Co* (1869) LR 4 Ch App 460.

[451] *In Re Agra and Masterman's Bank* (1871) LR 12 Eq 509 (Note).

Morris Crisp, was the successful solicitor in the case. He said later that what assisted him considerably in that, and other cases following the crisis, was 'the support I received from the Judges who considered the ordinary machinery of the Court not equal to dealing with such exceptional cases'.[452] Along the spectrum were the civil proceedings against some Overend Gurney directors alleging misrepresentation in the prospectus. Sir William Peek, for instance, claimed that he had been induced to purchase shares because the prospectus concealed the firm's insolvency and that, as a result, he had lost money when it collapsed.[453] Peek was a Conservative MP and was immortalised in the law reports when his later investment, in the Plymouth, Devonport and District Tramway Ltd, also went wrong.[454] In *Peek* v. *Gurney*[455] while accepting that the directors had concealed material facts, the House of Lords held that Peek's claims failed compared with those of the original allottees from whom he had bought the shares on the secondary market, since they had a closer connection with the misrepresentations.[456]

More significantly, what came out of the Overend Gurney crisis was the publication in 1873 by Walter Bagehot of his famous *Lombard Street; A Description of the Money Market*[457] and its case that the Bank of England should act as the lender of last resort.[458] There is no need to enter the debate as to when exactly the Bank of England assumed that role. There is a good case that it had done so before the crisis, although as a privately owned entity it did not unambiguously accept the responsibility at the time.[459] The important point is that the book advanced the case that, to stem systemic failures in similar panics, the Bank of England should act in this way. Acting as lender of last resort has become a fundamental tenet of central banking.[460]

---

[452] LMA/4537/F/10/005, Ashurst Morris Crisp and Company, Report of proceedings at John Morris's 80th birthday celebration, 11–12. See 30, 32 above.

[453] see also *Overend Gurney & Company* v. *Gibb* (1872) LR 5 HL 480.

[454] *Derry* v. *Peek* (1889) 14 App Cas 337. See M. Lobban, 'Nineteenth Century Frauds in Company Formation: Derry v Peek in Context' (1996) 112 *LQR* 287, 321–323; C. Reed, 'Derry v. Peek and Negligence' (1987) 8 *J Leg Hist* 64.

[455] (1873) LR 6 HL 377.

[456] C. Gerner-Beuerle, 'Law and Finance in Emerging Economies: Germany and Britain 1800–1913' (2017) 80 *MLR* 263, 284–286.

[457] London, H. S. King, 1873, 17.

[458] V. Bignon, M. Flandreau & S. Ugolini 'Bagehot for Beginners: The Making of Lender-of-last-resort Operations in the Mid-Nineteenth Century' (2012) 65 *Econ Hist Rev* 580; V. Bignon, M. Flandreau & S. Ugolini, 'Where It All Began: Lending of Last Resort and the Bank of England during the Overend-Gurney Panic of 1866', in M. Bordo and W. Roberts, eds., *The Origins, History, and Future of the Federal Reserve*, New York, Cambridge University Press, 2013.

[459] M. Collins, 'The Bank of England as Lender of Last Resort, 1857–1878' (1992) 45 *Econ Hist Rev* 145, 145.

[460] R. Lastra, 'Lender of Last Resort an International Perspective' (1999) 48 *ICLQ* 340; F. Capie & G. Wood (ed.), *The Lender of Last Resort*, London, Routledge, 2007.

(iii) The Money Market Post Crisis

Following the 1866 crisis the discount houses became specialists in the money market: they bought and sold bills, took short-term deposits from banks with surplus cash and enjoyed privileged access at the Bank of England when they needed discounting facilities or advances. As regards discounting, they dealt mainly in trade-related bills, rather than accommodation bills, although there were still instances when a discount house was tempted into railway investments.[461] As a result the money market was largely segregated from the capital market.[462] The Bank of England developed a close relationship with the discount houses, even more so after the Treasury Bills Act 1877, which authorised the issue of short-term government paper of no more than 12 months' duration.[463] The discount houses became the specialists in distributing Treasury bills to the market. Between 1870 and 1914 the scale, liquidity and international character of the London money market were unmatched. The arrangements between the Bank of England, the banks and the discount houses showed their strength at times like the Barings crisis in 1890, when the Bank of England led the rescue efforts.[464]

Bills of exchange law facilitated the workings of the discount houses and the money market. If a bill was paid on maturity, that was the end of the matter. If a bill was returned unpaid from the acceptor – who was primarily liable on a bill – the holder would turn to the other intermediaries, including those discounting it. Care was therefore needed in choosing the bills to be discounted. As well as the financial viability of those liable on a bill, their legal capacity to accept or indorse the bill had also to be checked. The discount houses became experts in vetting bills. Apart from this general legal framework, the workings of the discount houses and the money market were outside the reach of formal law. Instead, the Bank of England exercised informal control, by monitoring the bills discount houses were taking through occasional purchases of parcels of bills from them. As well the Bank had the ultimate threat of denying rediscounting facilities to deviant institutions.[465]

The practices of the London money market emerged unscathed, indeed enhanced, as a result of their very occasional encounter with the civil law. *Re Fox, Walker, & Co*[466] arose when one of the discounters, Sanderson & Co, failed.[467] It had discounted accommodation bills from Aberdare Iron Co, which was insolvent. These had been accepted by Fox, Walker, & Co, a locomotive builder

---

[461] G, & P. Cleaver, *The Union Discount*, London, Union Discount Co of London, 1985, 22.
[462] C. Sissoko, 'How to Stabilize the Banking System: Lessons from the pre-1914 London Money Market' (2016) 23 *Fin Hist Rev* 1, 2–3.
[463] Treasury Bills Act 1877, s.4.
[464] See e.g., J. Körnert, 'The Barings Crises of 1890 and 1995: Causes, Courses, Consequences and the Danger of Domino Effects' (2003) 13 *J Int' Fin Markets Inst & Money* 187.
[465] M. Flandreau & S. Ugolini, 'The Crisis of 1866', in N. Dimsdale & A. Hotson (ed.), *British Financial Crises since 1825*, Oxford, Oxford University Press, 2014, 86–89.
[466] (1880) 15 Ch D 400.   [467] See 440, 445 above.

of Bristol, also insolvent. The court held that, although it was not formal party to these bills, Sanderson & Co could sue the acceptor's estate for what it had paid out to those, including the London and Westminster Bank, to whom it had rediscounted the bills. At the hearing a sub-manager of that bank had given evidence that the almost invariable practice of bill brokers in the London market was not to indorse the bills they rediscounted, but to give a general guarantee to the purchasers of bills from them in relation to their soundness.[468] That was clearly a practice of convenience, since the discounters would handle many bills and parcels of bills every day and it would take great effort to indorse them all formally. The Court of Appeal treated the practice as trade usage: Sanderson & Co had paid the bank under the guarantee and should now be able to sue the acceptor of the bills on an implied authority to make itself liable under its guarantee.[469]

In the years prior to the First World War the London money market was well established. The Bank of England performed the central role of discounting eligible bills for the discount houses or lending them funds on the security of bills. Its discounting facility was concentrated on the discount houses. They did not compete with the commercial banks in overdraft and other lending business and so did not provide the same threat of abuse of the Bank's discount window in times when credit was being squeezed. With the First World War and the decline in international trade, the supply of bills for discount dried up. The discount houses dealt in government debt on a much larger scale as Treasury bills were issued to fund the war.

After the war trade resumed, but the bill of exchange never resumed its dominant position in the business of the discount houses, given the vastly increased use of short-term government paper to fund the war and government after that. To the discount houses, dealing in Treasury bills was conceived of as largely mechanical, not requiring the same skills needed to assess the quality of bills offered for discount.[470] The Bank of England still discounted bills and retained an informal control over the process. One way it did this was that in the interwar and post–Second World War its special buyer in the bill market, Seccombe, Marshall and Campion, purchased sample bills to assess the quality of those on the market.[471] Another was that the Governor of the Bank held regular meetings with the discount houses, where he could exercise moral suasion.

Apart from the Bank of England's oversight, the money market was governed by a network of agreements between the discount houses and the banks. For example, from the 1890s the discount houses had short, formal agreements with a number of banks as to what was called privilege money. That was money

---

[468] at 401.
[469] at 418, per Thesiger LJ. See also See also *Misa* v. *Raikes Currie, G. Grenfell Glyn* (1876) 1 App Cas 554 (custom of bill brokers as to dates for paying for foreign bills).
[470] W. King, The Changing Discount Market, (1947) 31 *The Banker* 171, 172.
[471] J. Orbell & A. Turton, *British Banking: A Guide to Historical Records*, Aldershot, Ashgate, 2001, 469; G. Fletcher, 'Seccombe, Lawrence Henry (1877–1954)', *Oxford Dictionary of National Biography*

that a discount house could call on late in the day if it had misjudged the market and was unable to balance the books, thus avoiding the embarrassment of having to approach the Bank of England.[472] By a 'jealously guarded tradition', it was said, the day-to-day dealings between the discount houses and the banks – about the bills of exchange and Treasury bills to be bought and sold, the money to be lent and the rates for these transactions – were all done by word of mouth between the representatives of the discount houses on their rounds to the banks. There was no written confirmation, although in practice representatives of the discount house would make a discreet note once outside the bank, and these would then be entered in the firm's money book. Disputes were compromised.[473]

2 The Bankers' Clearing House and the Payment System

The Clearing House is a large room fitted with drawers: each banker, using the house, has one of these, marked with his name or firm. In the morning, and at half-past three o'clock in the afternoon of each week day, a clerk from each banker, using the house, attends, bringing with him the cheques on other banks that have been paid into his bank since last clearing; these he deposits in the drawers of the respective banks on which they are drawn; he then credits their accounts separately, with the different amounts of the cheques they have placed in his drawer, as against his bank. Balances are then struck from all the accounts, and the claims between the various banks transferred from one to another, until they are so wound up and mutually cancelled, that each clerk has only to settle, in cash, with two or three others, and thus, by means of comparatively small sums in money, the balances are immediately paid. (James Grant, 1856)[474]

The bankers' clearing house enabled banks promptly to collect payment on the cheques their customers had been given in payment. The clearing house had the obvious advantage to banks of reducing the amount of cash they needed to maintain to meet the presentation of cheques. If both the drawer and payee of a cheque were customers of the same bank, payment could be made internally by adjustments to their accounts. The clearing house came into its own with the growth of the cheque system.

About the clearing house was a network of relationships. There were those between the clearing banks themselves. Understandings about access to the clearing house was one aspect, in other words, who could be a clearing bank.

---

[472] R. Sayers, *Gilletts in the London Money Market 1867–1967, op cit*, 53–55.
[473] *This is Bill-Broking*, London, Allen, Harvey & Ross, 1966, 6; G. Fletcher, The Discount Houses in London, *op cit*, 89
[474] J. Grant, *The Law Relating to Bankers and Banking*, London, Butterworths, 1856, *op cit*, 57–58. See a detailed contemporary account: J. Gilbert, *A Practical Treatise on Banking*, 6th ed., London, Bell & Daldy, 1856, vol. II, 388–398, 455–456. There is a description of the operations as found by a jury by way of special verdict in *Warwick v. Rogers* (1843) 5 Man & G 340, 348–349; 134 ER 595, 598–599.

Then there were the rules governing its operation, although these were crisp and mechanical. There were also supplementary agreements. A simple example was that banks gave guarantees to other banks in the clearing house to cover mutilated, improperly indorsed or unsigned instruments.[475] Apart from the implicit and explicit agreements between the clearing banks, there were agency arrangements between the clearing banks and other banks who wanted access to the clearing house's facilities.

A bank clearing system had been inaugurated in London in the 1770s on a semi-formal basis, although earlier in the eighteenth century the Scottish banks had established clearing mechanisms to deal with the bank notes they issued.[476] In London, bank messengers (the walk clerks) would meet after lunch each day in a room rented in a public house in Dove Court, Lombard Street, to exchange cheques and settle the balances with Bank of England notes and coins. In 1777 there were thirty-three private banks in the clearing house, although it was not until the middle of the nineteenth century that the joint stock banks and the Bank of England became members. Bank of England membership facilitated the settlement of balances by movements on the accounts which banks had with it, rather than by direct payments between the banks.

Although a committee to oversee the clearing was in existence before then, a meeting of bankers resolved in February 1821 to appoint a 'permanent committee' to adopt rules for the organisation and protection of the clearing house. That committee resolved the following month that payments could be made before a general balance was struck – the previous rule – and that in future each clerk would report to the inspector as soon as he was prepared to pay or receive net amounts. If the balance upon his sheet was found to agree (or nearly agree) with the statement furnished by the bank, the inspector would then direct the creditor first ready to receive its balance to be paid by the debtor first prepared to pay.[477] Two inspectors were appointed. From 1833 the clearing house was at premises built at 10 Lombard Street and remained there for 150 years.[478]

The clearing house circumvented the need for banks to send clerks to other banks to collect moneys owed – they could present bills and cheques centrally at the clearing house – and reduced the amount of cash a bank needed as a result of the netting between the banks. The consequent reduction in the number of inter-bank payments and the amount of currency needed in the economy featured in the debates about monetary policy in the first part of the

---

[475] RBS, GM/236/1 & GM/236/2, Guarantee books of Glyn, Mills, Currie & Co, p.1.
[476] e.g., P. Matthews, *The Bankers' Clearing House*, London, 1921, 5–6 (Matthews was chief inspector at the Clearing House for some 30 years from 1891); T. Jones, *Clearings and Collections; Foreign and Domestic*, New York, Columbia University, 1931, 21–22; J. Holden, *The History of Negotiable Instruments in English Law*, London, Athlone Press, 1955, 214–215.
[477] P. Matthews, *op cit*, 11, who sets out the rule.
[478] Cheque and Credit Clearing Company, *The Great British Cheque Report*, London, Cheque and Credit Clearing Company Ltd, 2009, 8.

nineteenth century.[479] Initially netting was bilateral, but in 1841 it became multilateral, as Grant explained in the quotation above.[480] Net amounts owing were paid by a bank giving an order to the Bank of England to debit its account in favour of the account of the clearing house.[481] After a long struggle, in 1854 the joint stock banks were allowed to be members of the clearing house. Country banks could join from 1858.

The courts quickly became familiar with the operation of the clearing house.[482] As early as 1811 Lord Ellenborough held that a bank fulfilled its obligation to its customer by presenting bills through the clearing house rather than directly at the bank indicated as the place they would be paid in the acceptance written on them.[483] *Warwick v. Rogers*[484] was another case where the courts used the clearing house rules as the template for the legal standard. It concerned what we have seen was a typical means of payment on a foreign transaction. A merchant in Smyrna had drawn a bill for £300 in favour of Alexander Bargigli on Richard Jellicoe, a merchant in London, who accepted the bill, payable at his bankers, Rogers, Olding and Co, the defendants. Bargigli discounted the bill and it ended up in the hands of the plaintiff, who presented it for payment at the clearing house through his bank, Barclay & Co. In accordance with the practice of the clearing house, just described, Jellicoe's account with the defendant bank being in credit, it cancelled the acceptance by drawing lines across his name on the bill. It then entered the bill in its 'paid-clearing-book', which contained the amount paid to the clearing house in the course of the day. Later that day Jellicoe found that he was insolvent and ordered the defendants not to pay. They wrote on the bill: '[C]ancelled by mistake – orders not to pay' and returned it to Barclays before the time when matters were settled for the day. In giving the court's judgment Tindal CJ found in favour of the defendant bank, essentially because it had acted in accordance with clearing house practice.

Payment through the clearing house, in accordance with its practices, as the reasonable course for bankers to take, was underlined in other decisions.[485] As we saw (p. 49 above) Willes J opined, during argument, that '[a] man who employs a banker is bound by the usage of bankers', a suggestion that customers would be bound as well by rules of the clearing house. The courts recognized that no obligation was cast on a bank simply by accepting items at the clearing house; its officers were entitled to consider the matter back at the bank and to return the items through the clearing according to the rules where, for

---

[479] *Select Committee on Banks of Issue*, HC No 602, 7 August 1840, 198–199, 343, 366.
[480] J. Grant, The Law of Bankers and Banking, 1856, *op cit*, 57–58.
[481] See forms at W. Howarth, *Our Clearing System and Clearing Houses*, London, Effingham Wilson, 1884, 62–63. Howarth provides a detailed account of the working of the clearing, statistics and bank membership (with branches).
[482] There are references in e.g. *Robson v. Bennett* (1810) 2 Taunt 388, 127 ER 1128; *Boddington v. Schlenker* (1833) 4 B & Ad 752, 110 ER 639; *Robarts v. Tucker* (1851) 16 QB 560, 117 ER 994.
[483] *Reynolds v. Chettle* (1811) 2 Camp 596, 170 ER 1263.   [484] (1843) 5 M & G 340, 134 ER 595.
[485] Banks in Newcastle settled through the branch of the Bank of England there: *Pollard v. The Bank of England* (1871) LR 6 QB 623.

example, its customer countermanded payment.[486] To the courts, the clearing house became the accepted way that banks collected bills and cheques.[487] That did not make it mandatory.[488] By the end of the nineteenth century the courts were giving direct effect to the rules of the clearing house and pinned liability on a bank failing to comply with them.[489]

In October 1895 the clearing house had been incorporated as a private company, the Bankers' Clearing House Ltd, with the member banks holding an equal number of shares.[490] The only potential defect in the clearing system identified by the prominent economic commentator Ernest Seyd was if one of the banks collapsed: he thought this unlikely, since there was careful vetting of banks before they could become members. In any event, he added, should this occur the understanding was that all its payments in the clearing would be unwound. 'Our Law Courts would uphold this understanding as a "Banking law" established by custom', he confidently asserted.[491] The comment exhibited a touching faith in the courts to reach a pragmatic and commercially acceptable result.

If the bank clearing system was on a firm legal foundation, its structure was frugal. Seyd described it as a 'mere mechanical operation', 'not an official establishment', and 'simply like a private club'.[492] There were rules which continued virtually unchanged well into the twentieth century. A hallmark of the rules was their brevity.[493] In addition to the rules, the clearing house sometimes issued circulars with which members were expected to comply. For example, in 1927 the clearing house issued a circular that if a drawee bank marked a cheque as good for payment at the request of a collecting bank, that was equivalent to payment and the collecting bank would be paid if it presented the cheque within the day.[494] Almost half the clearing house rules were devoted to timing, the opening times of the different clearings (town, country) and, most importantly, the times by which bills of exchange, cheques, bankers' payments and so on had to be received. Under the rules the total amount of what was delivered had to be agreed by each clearing bank before their

---

[486] e.g., *Warwick* v. *Rogers* (1843) 5 M & G 340; 134 ER 595.
[487] *Matthiessen* v. *London and County Bank* (1879) LR 5 CPD 7, 17, per Lindley J.
[488] *Auchteroni & Co* v. *Midland Bank Ltd* [1928] 2 KB 294 (fraudster presenting bill over counter to acceptor/buyer's bank; unusual but not such as to raise suspicion).
[489] *Parr's Bank Ltd* v. *Thomas Ashby & Co* (1898) 14 TLR 563.
[490] The memorandum and articles are at LMA, CLC/B/029/MS32028X, Bankers' Clearing House.
[491] E. Seyd, *The London Banking and Bankers' Clearing House System*, London, Cassell, Petter and Galpin, 1872, 58–59.
[492] Ibid., 41–42.
[493] 'The Rules and Regulations to be Observed at the Clearing House', in J. Gilbart (revd ed. by A. Michie), *The History, Principles and Practice of Banking*, George Bell, London, 1899, vol. II, 317–319. For the virtually identical rules in the 1920s, except that they reflected its division in 1907 into three clearings, each with a definite geographical area: town, metropolitan and country: P. Matthews, *op.cit.*, 43–45.
[494] E. Lomnicka, R. Hooley & C. Hare, *Ellinger's Modern Banking Law*, 5th ed., Oxford, Oxford University Press, 2011, 411.

representatives left the clearing house. The rules conferred on the inspectors power to preserve order in the clearing house.

Several rules dealt with 'returns', in other words, items which had been returned into the clearing unpaid through a lack of funds, an irregularity of endorsement, and so on. Those returns received by the time appointed for final delivery 'must be received by the Clearers and credited the same day'.[495] Banks which accepted and paid an item returned to it in error 'may require repayment through the clearing the following day'.[496] However, clearers could not debit the clearing house with a return until the owner could be found (a problem with drafts not crossed or bills not receipted). Moreover, no return could be received without an answer, in writing on it, as to why payment was refused. If that were done, clearers were obliged to give credit.[497]

In the 1840s, the well-known authority on banking J.W. Gilbart had called for statutory regulation of the clearing house because for all practical purposes it had become a public institution, interwoven with London's finance and trade.[498] That was at a time when the clearing house was controlled by the private banks and all joint stock banks, including his own, the London and Westminster Bank, were excluded. Gilbart obviously saw legislation as a way of remedying the injustice. The argument seemed to be strengthened as a result of the Railway Clearing Act 1850, whereby the railway clearing house was underpinned by statute. That clearing house settled claims for payment when goods and passengers crossed from one railway to another. The Act provided for the membership and management of the clearing house, entrusted the secretary with power to settle conclusively the balances owing between the various railway companies, and enabled the clearing house to sue a recalcitrant company for any outstanding balance even if no longer a member.[499] At one point Gilbart drew up rules for a separate clearing house. Eventually, his bank was admitted in 1854; later other joint stock banks were admitted as members of the clearing house.[500] Nothing more was heard from Gilbart about legislation.

From 1821 the operation of the clearing house was supervised by a committee of the banks using it, later called the Committee of London Clearing Bankers. As late as the 1950s the committee never possessed

---

[495] Clearing House, Rules and Regulations, Town Clearing, in P. Matthews, *The Bankers' Clearing House, op cit*, 44.
[496] Ibid. [497] Ibid.
[498] T. Gregory, *The Westminster Bank*, London, Oxford University Press, 1936, vol. I, 175.
[499] 13 & 14 Vict, c.33, ss.2–10, 12, 14. See P. Bagwell, *The Railway Clearing House in the British Economy 1842–1922*, London, Allen & Unwin, 1968; R. Edwards, '"Keeping unbroken ways": the Role of the Railway Clearing House Secretariat in British Freight Transportation c.1923–c.1947' (2013) 55 *Business History* 479.
[500] B. Geva, *The Payment Order of Antiquity and the Middle Ages A Legal History, op cit*, 495.

a formal constitution or any formal rules.[501] It was through the committee that the Bank of England dealt with the banks.[502] The committee's focus was mainly on the larger issues affecting the banks. The law only very occasionally intruded: the committee might lobby about legislation the government proposed and might consider whether to support litigation regarding the banks' interests.[503] The committee sometimes sought legal advice about payment and other issues. For example, in 1865 it resolved that papers about the revocability of a bank's payment slip should be submitted to Freshfields, who were instructed to brief Mr Bovill and Mr Lush.[504] Counsel in that case advised that in accordance with the usage of bankers the payment slip once signed became binding.[505] In 1890 the committee took the opinion of Mr Rigby QC and Mr H.H. Cozens-Hardy regarding the liability of a bank in the case of a forged transfer of stock.[506] In 1896 the committee itself litigated (unsuccessfully) regarding whether stamp duty was due on the payment orders banks gave their customers to have goods released from customs.[507]

As for the clearing house it worked smoothly. The committee needed to intervene only intermittently. That might involve decisions on relatively perfunctory matters, such as timings within the clearing house and how it was to be operated. There was the occasional serious issue such as how to deal with mistaken payments and certified cheques.[508] If necessary, the committee would resolve a dispute between members over payment in the clearing. Thus in 1884 the committee resolved that the London and Westminster Bank should refund £10 to the London & South Western Bank after the former had presented a cheque to them through the clearing which had been previously crossed by Glyn Mills & Co.[509] Unusually, the committee might decide that the rules of the clearing house should be changed. Thus in 1871 it resolved that the rules should provide that differences of more than £1,000 accidentally

---

[501] J. Reveley & J. Singleton, 'Clearing the Cupboard: The Role of Public Relations in London Clearing Banks' Collective Legitimacy-Seeking, 1950–1980', (2014) 15 *Enterprise & Society* 472, 473–474, 478.

[502] R. Sayers, *The Bank of England 1891–1944*, Cambridge, Cambridge University Press, 1976, 552.

[503] LMA, CLC/B/029/MS32006/002, Committee of London Clearing Bankers, Minute book, 1852–1906, 2 August 1876 (lobbying on Crossed Cheques Bill); 22 February 1882 (support for Bills of Exchange Bill); 8 June 1871 (declined to support Bank of England in litigation against it); 7 December 1905 (re *Lyons* v. *Tramways Syndicate Ltd* [1906] 2 Ch 216 – debentures as security for loans).

[504] Ibid., 24 April 1865. Bovill became Chief Justice of the Common Pleas; Lush became a member of the Court of Appeal.

[505] Ibid., 18 September 1865.   [506] Ibid., 21 November 1890. Both were later judges.

[507] *Committee of London Clearing Bankers* v. *Inland Revenue Commissioners* [1896] QB 542. See ibid., 3 October 1894, 23 January 1896.

[508] Ibid., 18 September 1865 (time for marking cheques); 22 December 1868 (return of foreign bills cancelled in error); 7 November 1871 (bank must give answer on whether it will pay cheque by return of post); 25 July 1898 (attention to be given to differences in out-side payments in preference to those in-side); 7 December 1905 (certified cheques at request of customer to be replaced by bank cheques).

[509] Ibid., 1 April 1884.

passed over were to be settled by transfer at Bank of England first thing the following morning.[510]

The committee detested legal intervention into the workings of the clearing house. It sought to have disputes between the banks resolved internally. Parr's Bank earned a sharp rebuke when it sued Thomas Ashby & Co over a disputed payment in the clearing.[511] A cheque drawn on Ashby had been paid into Parr's, who sent it to the clearing house, whereupon it was sent to Ashby for collection. Instead of deciding then and there whether to pay the cheque, Ashby prevaricated. Under the rules if it did not intend to pay a cheque, it had 'to return it direct'. The following day, Ashby finally telegrammed that it would not pay. Meanwhile, Parr's had honoured an acceptance of the customer, which it would not have done if the cheque had been returned unpaid. Parr's was successful in its claim for the amount of the acceptance, but the committee resolved to 'strongly deprecate any resort to the law in such cases. They consider that all disputes arising between parties enjoying the privileges of the Clearing House should be submitted to the Committee.'[512]

Despite Gilbart's early campaign, the bankers' clearing house continued into the twentieth century untouched, in large part, by an arm of the state.[513] The general framework of legislation as regards the instruments cleared such as the Crossed Cheques Act 1876 and the Bills of Exchange Act 1882 did not impinge on its operation. The Bank of England had joined the clearing house in 1864 and offered general oversight.[514] The system worked efficiently. It was described by the economist Jevons as bringing the paper system of commerce 'nearly to perfection'.[515] It was the model for other clearing houses in England, and was conceded to be the genesis of bankers' clearing houses in the United States and elsewhere.[516] It contributed to the role of the Bank of England as a central bank able to exercise informal control of the payment system.[517]

That did not mean that the Bankers Clearing House in Lombard Street was the only way payments were settled in London. There were other methods, within the banks themselves when the payer and payee had accounts at the

---

[510] Ibid., 26 July 1876.
[511] *Parr's Bank Ltd* v. *Thomas Ashby & Co* (1898) 14 TLR 563. Parr's became part of RBS, Ashby, part of Barclays: J. Orbell & A. Turton, *British Banking A Guide to Historical Records*, Aldershot, Ashgate, 2001, 57–58, 429–430.
[512] LMA, CLC/B/029/MS32006/002, Committee of London Clearing Bankers, Minute book, 1852–1906, 22 November 1898.
[513] A Bankers' Clearing House Ltd was formed in 1895 to hold property; all members had equal shares.
[514] D. Kynaston. *Till Time's Last Sand A History of the Bank of England 1694–2013*, London, Bloomsbury Publishing, 2017, 188; C. Hadjiemmanuil, *Banking Regulation and the Bank of England*, London, LLP, 1996, 308–321.
[515] W. Jevons, *Money and the Mechanism of Exchange*, London, Henry King & Co, 1875, 263.
[516] F. Andrews, 'The Operation of the City Clearing House' 51 *Yale LJ* 582, 584, 600.
[517] B. Norman, R. Shaw & G Speight, *The History of Interbank Settlement Arrangements: Exploring Central Banks' Role*, Bank of England Working Paper, No 412, 2011.

same bank, and through arrangements such as the so-called 'walks clearing'.[518] Parallel systems developed, such as the London dollar clearing with the advent of the Euromarkets in the 1960s.[519] Nor did it mean that when very occasionally an issue reached the courts the judges always accepted the practices of the clearing house as constituting universal banking custom.[520] But in the main the clearing house remained unaffected by law. Its rules were largely operational and avoided defining the rights and duties of the parties.[521] Internally, when the rules had to be interpreted, there was an aversion to a legalistic approach and to intervention by the courts.[522] Disputes between its members were settled informally.

6.5 Conclusion

Practical matters engage, as a rule, the attention of bankers very closely, and to the exclusion of the consideration of the legal powers under which they carry on their business. They are most careful, as a body, to avoid overstepping the law in any way, but they do this perhaps more by the observance of habitual prudence . . . . The legal points which they have to consider usually refer to such matters as the correctness of cheques, the endorsements on them, their own position with respect to any security. (Bankers' Magazine, 1885).[523]

The banks offered trade finance within a well-polished, if sometimes uneven, framework of bills of exchange law and practice. Statutory intervention was supportive, most importantly the law's codification in the Bills of Exchange Act 1882. The 1882 Act was not intended to break new ground but to present the common law straightforwardly and shorn of its rigidities.[524] Bills of exchange made possible the high-volume traffic across oceans of commodities and manufactured goods. Exporters could obtain the purchase price on shipping the goods by discounting the bill of exchange drawn to pay for them; the importer obtained credit until the bill matured. Banks provided these payment and credit services for a price, in part the discount in the amount paid on the face value of the bill.

As a condition of payment banks might require that the exporter hand over the shipping documents, including the bill of lading. That was the document of title to the goods given by the ship at the time they were dispatched. This system of ensuring that the bank had control over the

---

[518] R. Truptil, *British Banks and the London Money Market*, London, Jonathan Cape, 1936,189.
[519] *Libyan Arab Foreign Bank* v. *Bankers Trust Co* [1989] Q.B. 728, 753–754.
[520] *Bank of Baroda Ltd* v. *Punjab National Bank* [1944] AC 176, 183; *Barclays Bank plc* v. *Bank of England* [1985] 1 All ER 385, 394.
[521] W. Howarth, Our Clearing System and Clearing Houses, *op cit*, 120ff.
[522] *Payment Clearing Systems*, London, Association of Payment Clearing Services, 1986, Appendix 3 (Child Report).
[523] 'The Banking Law of England at the Present Time', *Bankers' Magazine*, vol. 45, November 1885, 75.
[524] M. Chalmers, 'An Experiment in Codification' (1886) 16 *LQR* 125, 126.

goods was formalised with the documentary letter of credit: a buyer-seller contract obliged the buyer-importer to arrange a letter of credit through a bank under which the seller-exporter as beneficiary was paid on presentation of the shipping documents. Unlike bills of exchange law with its ancient lineage, the law of documentary credits emerged around the middle of the nineteenth century once the device arrived on the scene. There was an enthusiasm among the senior judges for the new device, and they did much to cultivate it. The common law followed commercial practice.

When doctrine cast a shadow over the enforcement of the bank's undertaking to pay the beneficiary of a credit – on the basis that there was no consideration to support it – the judges, as Grant Gilmore put it in another context, 'put away their learning and went along with the expressed needs of commerce'.[525] There was no hint of legislation for documentary letters of credit. Nor, despite the efforts of the International Chamber of Commerce (ICC) and others, did foreign influences gain a foothold. It was only at the end of our period, and well after a century of the common law, that the ICC's Uniform Customs and Practices for Documentary Credits (UCP) held sway.

It was not always plain sailing for commercial practice in the waters of the common law. The bill of lading was recognised as the document of title par excellence. When the dock warrant arrived on the scene, also acknowledging the holder's right to goods, it was very much treated as an upstart. Its commercial purpose was exemplary, to enable owners of goods stored at a dock or in its warehouses to deal with them, or to raise finance on the back of them, by simple transfer of the document. In the eyes of the common law, however, the dock warrant was not the equal of its beloved bill of lading. Individual dock companies had to call on Parliament to confer that privilege on their warrants in the private Acts constituting them.

In providing non-trade-related finance to business the banks had the full backing of the law. The distilled wisdom of leading bankers was that advances should be short term. With both overdrafts and on-demand loans the courts enabled the banks to enforce that policy. The law provided that they could act, even precipitously, if they wished to reduce or withdraw an overdraft. In practice the banks extended overdrafts to almost every business which applied for one, and, if their monitoring of the account did not uncover anything untoward, it could run for years. Short-term loans were favoured by the London banks. The contracts were spartan. The courts would give effect, if necessary, to a clause enabling it to be recalled on demand. There were some legal wrinkles with the provisions in loan agreements governing interest, but nothing clever drafting could not work around. Given the huge number of

---

[525] G. Grant & A. Allan, 'Chattel Security: I' (1948) *57 Yale LJ* 517, 543.

advances overall, disputes between customers and their banks inevitably arose over advances and other matters, some demanding the involvement of solicitors and counsel if triggered, say, by insolvency or fraud.[526]

Often banks would lend unsecured. But when banks required security as the condition of an advance, law and lawyers made their mark. If security was thought necessary, a personal guarantee might suffice. Historically the law had been protective of guarantors but drafting of the agreement could give a bank considerable comfort. Legal input might be necessary to draft standard forms, and even to advise on particular security transactions. Where security was taken over bonds payable to bearer, and documents of title such as bills of lading and dock warrants, the old-fashioned pledge worked well and was relatively straightforward. With the 'new property' of the nineteenth century such as shares and debentures, the position was more complex. The courts had an important facilitative role in recognising that the bank with whom these instruments were deposited gained an equitable interest. The safest course was for the bank to become the legal – not just the equitable – owner, and that is what lawyers advised. However, convenience dictated the second-best course of the customer completing blank transfers, accompanying the deposit, which could be registered with the company *in extremis*. Although the floating charge over a company's assets emerged in the late nineteenth century to secure debenture holders, it was only in the 1920s that the banks began using it as a security device themselves, and then not extensively.

Regulatory law had little if any part to play in the institutional underpinning of most aspects of bank finance. This should not be surprising when during our period the banks themselves were unregulated except, in the case of the joint stock banks, by general company law. The Bank of England was largely passive, although there was a certain amount of informal supervision. In its sampling of bill portfolios for discount by discount houses and the banks, the Bank might drop 'unmistakable hints from time to time if their composition seemed to be stretching the notion of a bill of exchange too far'.[527] Apart from these indirect forms of control, contract was the prime regulator of financial institutions. As a member of the Bankers' Clearing House, a bank assumed obligations to the other members and to the clearing house itself. Otherwise law and lawyers stopped at the entrance: the clearing house was governed by a skeletal system of operational rules and disputes were settled informally. As for the money market, it too was governed by a network of formal and informal agreements between the Bank of England, the discount houses and the banks. Daily transactions were done by word of

---

[526] RBS, WES/1501/1-2, London and County Banking Co, Register of branch matters in solicitors' hands.
[527] G. Young, *Merchant Banking*, London, Weidenfeld & Nicolson, 1966, 18.

mouth and disputes were resolved informally. Although extreme examples, these symbolise law's role in the commercial and banking worlds of our period. It provided a framework in which parties could make deals to their own design; state law rarely, if ever, intervened; and if it did, it did so, in the main, in facilitative, rather than curtailing, mode.

Index

Abbott CJ (Lord Tenterden), 118, 119, 131, 151, 214
Aberdare Iron Co, 439, 440, 450–451
Abinger, Lord (Sir James Scarlett), 151, 209
Acceleration clauses, 421–422
Acceptance business, 24, 386–388
Accommodation bills
   evolution of, 437–439
   financial crises, connection with, 437–439
   fraud and, 437, 440
   joint stock banks and, 439
   overview, 379
   railways and, 437–439
   regulation of, 439–441
   revival of, 441–442
Accommodation of commercial practices
   commercial sensitivity, 56–57
   contractual interpretation, 55–56
   determinative, practice as, 52–54
   ejusdem generis and, 55–56
   overview, 31, 48
   spectrum of, 52
   standard form contracts, 53, 56
   supporting authority, practice as, 54–55
Adelaide Chamber of Commerce, 336
Advances
   accommodation bills (*See* Accommodation bills)
   agency houses and, 16
   on dock warrants, 408
   joint stock banks and, 27
   loans (*See* Loans)
   overdrafts (*See* Overdrafts)
   overview, 377–378, 411–413
   purposes of, 412
   reluctance of banks, 409–410
   security for (*See* Security for advances)
   short-term finance, 413–414
   statistics, 412–413
   unsecured lending, 422–424
Agency bills, 386
Agency houses
   advances and, 16
   buying agents, 17
   emergence of, 16
   home commission agents, 17
   indents, 17
   managing agents (*See* Managing agents)
Agency law
   agents (*See* Agents)
   brokers and, 76–78
   in commercial context, 129
   distribution of goods and, 275–276
   as equitable principle, 47
   evolution of, 130–131
   foreign principal doctrine, 155–157
   fraud, liability of principal for, 137–139
   liability of agents as principals, 153–154, 198
   managing agents and, 187
   overview, 128
   power-conferring aspect of, 130
   principal–agent distinction, 133–134
   reasonable compliance with principal's instructions, 128, 143, 148–150, 197–198
   undisclosed principal doctrine (*See* Undisclosed principal doctrine)
Agents. *See also* Agency law
   agent abuse, 131–132
   apparent authority, 144–145, 197
   arbitration and, 176–177
   authority of, 143–145
   brokers compared, 167–168
   buying agents, 17
   'chameleon' character, brokers and agents, 171–173
   coffee, 15–16

Agents (cont.)
   commercial convenience and, 197–198
   commercial realities, impact on legal
      doctrine, 156–157
   commission agents, 128, 154–155
   companies and, 129
   compradors, 140, 141–142
   confirming agents (*See* Confirming agents)
   consignment, trend away from, 14–15
   contract, liability based on, 154
   cotton, 13–14
   custom and usage, liability based on, 153–154
   del credere agents (*See* Del credere agents)
   distribution of goods by, 20
   emergence of, 13–16
   estoppel and, 145
   evolution of, 127–128
   Factors Acts and, 143, 150–153, 198
   fiduciary duties of, 132
   foreign principal doctrine, 155–157
   fraud committed by, 137–139
   functions of, 196–197
   'holding out', 143
   home commission agents, 17
   law, role of, 142–143
   liability as principals, 153–154, 198
   litigation and, 177–178
   local agents, 140–142
   managing agents (*See* Managing agents)
   misuse of term, 134–136
   multifunctional agents, 165, 173–178
   nemo dat and, 150
   ostensible authority, 144–145, 197
   overview, 2, 13, 128–129, 196–197
   petrol, 135
   principals distinguished, 133–134
   reasonable compliance with principal's instructions, 128, 143, 148–150, 197–198
   retailers incorrectly termed 'agents', 134–136
   rubber, 171–173
   sale of goods by, 21
   standard form contracts and, 143–144
   statute, liability based on, 154
   stock and station agents, 165
   textiles, 14–15
   tyres, 136
   undisclosed principal doctrine (*See* Undisclosed principal doctrine)
   usual authority, 144–145
   wheat, 15

Agra Bank, 389–390, 392–393, 446, 448
A. J. Dew & Co, 276
Alexander & Co, 445
Alexandra Brickworks Ltd, 186
Alliance Insurance, 175–176
Ambler, Eric, 127
American Acceptance Council, 398
American Bar Association, 204
American Metal Co, 166
American Viscose Corp, 20
Andrew Yule & Co, 179, 181
Anglo-American Oil Co Ltd, 277
Anglo-Persian Oil Co Ltd, 189
Antony Gibbs & Sons, 24
Apparent authority, 144–145, 197
Appropriation, 308–309, 345–346
Arab Bank Ltd, 395
Arbitration
   agents and, 176–177
   appeals, 366, 368–369
   arbitrators, 365–366, 367
   awards, 368
   confidentiality of, 366–367
   corn, 362–363, 365–369
   cotton, 362
   criticism of, 367
   grain, 364
   judicial intervention in, 370–371
   LCTA and, 365–369, 370–371
   in Liverpool, 362–363
   in London, 363–365
   noncompliance with awards, 369
   overview, 375
   publication of awards, 366–367
   resistance to, 364–365
   standard form contracts and, 330–331
   statistics, 368
   trade associations and, 362–365
   'usual manner' clauses, 363–364
Arbitration Act 1889, 370
Arbitration Act 1934, 367
Arbuthnot Latham (bank), 90
Argentine North Eastern Railway Co Ltd, 251
Arrivals contracts, 83–86
A. Seurin & Co, 392–393
Ashurst J, 32
Ashurst Morris Crisp (solicitors), 448–449
Aske, Robert, 52–53
Asquith, H. H., 118
Associated Chambers of Commerce, 384
Associated Enterprises Ltd, 239–240

Index

Assurance Co Act 1909, 54
Astbury J, 54
Atkin, Lord, 32, 42, 43, 45, 47, 54, 56–57, 122, 215, 239, 268–269, 272, 289, 329
Atlantic and Great Western Railway Co, 438
Attenborough, L. G., 181
Auctioneers Act 1845, 323
Auctions
   caveat emptor and, 324–325
   contractual conditions, 323–324
   decline of, 320–321
   disputes, 323, 324
   freedom of contract in, 322–323
   highest bidders, 323–324
   implied terms, 324–325
   in London, 318–322
   manipulation of, 327
   mistake, effect of, 325–326
   overview, 317–318, 375
   'puffery' and, 327–328
   rigged bidding, 329–330
   'ring' agreements, 328–329
   rubber, 319–320
   tea, 319, 321–322
   wool, 318–319, 320, 321–322
Auctions (Bidding Agreements) Act 1927, 329, 330
Austen, Jane, 391
Austin Motor Co, 28–29, 202, 274–275
Australia
   accommodation bills in, 442
   auctions in, 320
   Australian Royal Commission (Wheat), 315
   stock and station agents in, 165
   Tasmanian Transport Commission, 235, 236, 237
Australian Shippers' Association, 359
Autonomy of parties, 31

Bacon, James, 255, 256, 429
Bagehot, Walter, 444, 449
Bailhache J, 268–269, 352
Baldwin Locomotive Works, 229, 231
Balfour, Guthrie & Co Ltd, 15
Balfour Williamson & Co, 44–45
Baltic Co Ltd, 66
Baltic Committee, 402
Baltic Exchange
   arbitration and, 365, 366
   bank finance and, 29, 379
   bought and sold notes and, 298
   brokers and, 77, 78–80, 168
   commodity markets and, 62, 64
   cornering markets and, 111
   emergence of, 6–7
   futures markets and, 82–83
   membership in, 66–68
   speculation in, 78–80, 108
   standard form contracts and, 302, 314
Baltimore Chamber of Commerce, 339
Bank bills, 386, 390
Bank Charter Act 1833, 26
Bank Charter Act 1844, 26, 27
Bankers' Clearing House
   Bank of England and, 30, 38, 453, 454, 457–458, 461–462
   circulars, 455
   clearing and settlement and, 89
   Committee of London Clearing Bankers, 456–458
   historical background, 453–454
   joint stock banks and, 26
   jurisprudence regarding, 454–455
   lack of judicial intervention in, 458–459
   operation of, 456–458
   overview, 9, 23, 38, 380–381, 443–444, 452–453, 461–462
   regulation, calls for, 456
   returns, 456
   rules of, 455–456
Bankes LJ, 329
Bank finance. *See also specific bank*
   accommodation bills (*See* Accommodation bills)
   advances (*See* Advances)
   Bankers' Clearing House (*See* Bankers' Clearing House)
   bill brokers, 380, 443, 444–445
   bills of exchange (*See* Bills of exchange)
   clearing and settlement (*See* Clearing and settlement)
   criticism of, 376–377
   custom and usage in, 50
   discount houses, 380, 443, 445
   dock warrants (*See* Dock warrants)
   emergence of, 4, 22–23
   finance houses (*See* Finance houses)
   historical background, 22–23, 377
   institutional underpinnings, 379
   joint stock banks (*See* Joint stock banks)
   legislative framework, 37
   letters of credit (*See* Letters of credit)

Bank finance (cont.)
  loans (*See* Loans)
  merchant banks (*See* Merchant banks)
  money market, 23, 380, 443, 450–452
  Overdrafts (*See* Overdrafts)
  overview, 2, 23
  private law-making and, 38
  security for advances (*See* Security for advances)
Bank of Bengal, 418
Bank of England
  accommodation bills and, 441–442
  agency bills and, 386
  Bankers' Clearing House and, 30, 38, 453, 454, 457–458, 461–462
  bank finance and, 378
  bill brokers and, 443, 444–445
  Bill on London and, 381
  cornering markets and, 115–116
  discount houses and, 443, 445
  dock warrants and, 399, 402
  money market and, 450–452
  Overend Gurney crisis and, 446, 449
  overview, 29–30
  private law-making and, 37, 38, 59
Bank of the United States of Pennsylvania, 110–111
Barber & Co, 392–393
Barclays (bank), 26, 411, 454
Bargigli, Alexander, 454
Baring, Alexander, 119
Barings Brothers & Co, 22, 23, 24–25, 29, 90, 387
Barnard's Act, 113
Battye and Pilgrim, 150–151
B. Davis Ltd, 281–282, 283–284, 285–286
Beale, Phipson, 255
Bearer shares as security, 429–430
Becos Traders Ltd, 270
Beetroot Sugar Association, 10, 93
Bengal Nagpur Railway, 231
Benjamin, Judah Philip, 33, 78, 79, 119, 210, 213, 345–346, 406
Bennett, Arnold, 89, 244–245
Benson J, 187
Bensons (bank), 434
Berlin Chamber of Commerce, 336
Berlin Produce Exchange, 336
Berry, Barclay & Co, 310
Best CJ, 143, 209, 327–328, 403–404
Beyer Peacock & Co, 229–230, 232–233

Bhashyam Ayyangar J, 187
Biddle, Nicholas, 110–111
Bilateral settlement, 95–97
Bill brokers, 380, 443, 444–445
Bill on London, 24, 381, 386, 390, 443
Bills of exchange
  acceptance business and, 386–388
  accommodation bills (*See* Accommodation bills)
  advantages of, 385–386
  agency bills, 386
  bank bills, 386, 390
  dissociation from underlying claims, 385–386
  historical background, 384
  law governing, 384–386
  merchant banks and, 24
  negotiability of, 385
  open account trading versus, 385
  overview, 378, 381, 383, 443, 459
  time for payment, 383
  trade bills, 386, 388–390
  transferability of, 385
Bills of Exchange Act 1882,
  accommodation bills and, 440–441
  Bankers' Clearing House and, 458
  bank finance and, 459
  bills of exchange and, 384–385
  certainty in law and, 41
  codification of, 33, 35
  custom and usage and, 53
  overview, 203
Bills of lading
  delivery orders and, 351–353
  dock warrants and, 400, 405–406
  international commodity sales and, 310–311
  letters of credit and, 395–396
  overview, 381–382, 459, 460
  trade bills and, 389–390
Bills of Sale Act 1882, 255
Bills of Sale Acts, 37, 254–256, 259
Binny's (managing agents), 179
Birkenhead, Lord (F. E. Smith), 42
Birmingham Wagon Co, 28, 246, 247–249, 251
Bishirgian, Garabed, 115–117
Bishirgian & Co, 115
Black, William, 73
Blackburn, Colin (Lord), 56, 79, 86, 138, 147, 149, 154–155, 156, 157, 212, 216–217, 222, 289, 405–406, 421, 422
Blacker Main Coal Co, 254–256

Blackwall Railway, 411
Blank transfers as security, 430–431
Blixen, Karen, 294
Block discounting, 262
Blyth Greene Jourdain & Co Ltd, 169–170
Blyth Shipbuilding and Dry Docks Co, 216
Board of Trade, 40–41, 161, 273
Boileau, Hugh, 261–262
Bombay Burmah Trading Co Ltd, 182–183, 192–193, 195–196
Bombay Chamber of Commerce, 195
Booth, William, 263
Borneo Co Ltd, 172–173, 179, 185–186
Borsig (locomotive manufacturer), 229
Bosanquet, J. B., 402, 404
Bought and sold notes, 296–299
Boulton, Matthew, 220–221, 242
Bovill & Sons, 102
Bovill CJ, 79
Bowen LJ (Lord), 113, 136–137
Bramwell, Lord, 121, 125, 156, 289
Branson J, 54, 356, 357–358
Braudel, Fernand, 61–62
Bray J (Reginald), 32, 157, 160, 255
Bremen Cotton Association (Verein der Bremer Baumwollhändler), 69
Brett LJ. *See* Esher, Lord
Brewster, Charles, 260
Bridges, W. S., 176
British Cycle and Motor Cycle Manufacturers and Traders Union Ltd, 269
British Dyestuffs Corp, 220
British Imex Industries Ltd, 395
British India Steam Navigation Co Ltd (BIN), 184
British Rail, 229
British Wagon Co, 28, 247, 250–251
Brittains Ltd, 268
Brokers
  agency law and, 76–78
  agents compared, 167–168
  'chameleon' character, brokers and agents, 171–173
  commercial practice versus legal theory, 72–73
  contracts in own name, 74–75
  custom and usage and, 73
  customers, rights and liabilities regarding, 76–80
  emergence of, 71–72
  fiduciary duties of, 78–80
  mercantile characteristics of, 167–168
  other brokers, rights and liabilities regarding, 73
  overview, 63, 71
  rules regarding, 74, 76
  transaction costs and, 75
Broomhall, George, 63–64
Brown Brothers, 391–392
Browne, J. Balfour, 48
Brown Shipley & Co, 387, 388, 391–392, 432
Bruce, Buxton & Co, 445
Brunner, Roscoe, 241–242
Brunner Mond and Co Ltd, 220, 237–242, 291. *See also* Imperial Chemical Industries (ICI)
Bruseh Tin and Rubber Estates Ltd, 186
BSA (motor vehicle manufacturer), 417
Buckley J, 279
Buenos Ayres and Campana Railway Co, 421
Building and land societies, hire purchase and, 250
Bullion, Thomas, 410
Bunge (grain traders), 7
Burney B, 328
'Business against Chancery', 43
Business financing. *See* Advances
Buying agents, 17

Cahill, Gordon, Reindel & Ohl (solicitors), 288
Cairns, Lord, 48–49, 356, 393
Caledonian Railway Co, 221
Callenders Cable & Construction Co Ltd, 270
Cammell Laird and Co Ltd, 202, 223–224, 291
Campbell, Lord, 54, 298, 373
Canada
  Board of Grain Commissioners, 308
  Canada Grain Act 1912, 308
  Canadian Grain Commission, 308
  commodity markets in, 64
  grain quality, ensuring, 308
  Manitoba Grain Act 1900, 308
Capital. *See* Advances
Cardozo, Benjamin (US Supreme Court Justice), 267
Carey & Browne, 89–90, 325
Cargill (grain traders), 7
Caveat emptor, 209, 210, 212, 324–325
Central Electricity Board (CEB), 219, 226–228, 290

Centro de Cereales, 359
Certainty of law
    'Business against Chancery', 43
    equitable principles and, 43–47
    merits versus, 41–43
    necessity of, 41
    overview, 31
    predictability, lack of, 32–34
    standard form contracts and, 335–336, 374
Chalmers, Mackenzie D., 35, 41, 203–205, 208, 290, 328, 384–385, 440–441
Chamberlain's Wharf, 69
Chamber of Shipping, 53, 336
'Chameleon' character, brokers and agents, 171–173
Champdany Jute Co, 190–192
Chartered Bank of India, 388
Chelmsford, Lord (F. Thesiger), 79, 149
Chicago Board of Trade, 64, 80, 81, 98–99, 101
China
    compradors, 140, 141–142
    grain quality, ensuring, 308
    local agents in, 140, 141–142
China Merchants Steam Navigation Co, 178
Chorley, Lord, 51, 160, 257
Churchill & Sim, 160
Circle clauses, 343–344
City Bank, 388
Clavell, James, 153, 173
Clearing and settlement
    Bankers' Clearing House (*See* Bankers' Clearing House)
    bilateral settlement, 95–97
    closing out rules, 102–103
    coffee, 96–97
    commodity clearing houses, 89–94
    compensation upon default, 104–105
    cotton, 91–92
    default, risk of, 102–103
    filières, 93–94
    grain, 92–93
    guarantees of contracts, 106
    insurance funds, 106–107
    in Liverpool, 91–92
    in London, 92–93
    margins, 95
    metals, 97–98
    novation, 95, 98–101
    overview, 63, 89
    prevention of settlement risk, 103–104
    registration, 94–95
    ring settlement, 97–98
    rules, 38
    settlement risk generally, 101
    strings, 94–95
    sugar, 93–94, 103
    tea, 93
    'walks clearing', 458–459
    war, risk of, 103
Cleasby B, 75
Clifford Chance (solicitors), 89–90, 297, 384
Closing out rules, 102–103
Clydebank Shipbuilding and Engineering Co, 427
Coal Drops, xv, xvi
Cockburn CJ (Alexander), 50, 51, 144, 447–448
Cocoa Trade Association, 304
Coffee Trade Association of London, 8
Cohen, Alroy, 284
Collie, Alexander, 440
Collins, Norman, 442–443
Colonial Sugar Refinery Ltd (CSR), 168–171
Commercial context of commercial law, 1–2, 3–5, 58–59. *See also specific topic*
Commercial Court, 59–60
Commercial Credit Conference, 398
Commercial Sale Rooms, London (Mincing Lane), 7–8, 68, 325
Commission agents, 128, 154–155
Commissioner of Customs and Excise, 323
Committee of London Clearing Bankers, 456–458
Committee of the Linseed Association, 303
Commodity arbitration. *See* Arbitration
Commodity auctions. *See* Auctions
Commodity markets. *See also specific market*
    auctions (*See* Auctions)
    brokers (*See* Brokers)
    coffee, 6, 7
    disciplinary action, 70
    emergence of, 4
    futures markets (*See* Futures markets)
    grain, 6–7, 62
    hedging and, 121
    historical background, 6–8, 61–62
    informal nature of, 64
    law, role of, 124–126
    market integrity (*See* Market integrity)
    membership in, 62–63
    non-interference by courts, 69–70
    organisation of, 62–63, 65–66
    other countries compared, 64

overview, 2, 5–6
prerequisites for, 123–124
private law-making and, 38, 125–126
rubber, 7
spices, 7
standard form contracts and, 126
sugar, 7
suspension or expulsion from, 66–68
tea, 7, 8–9
wagering and, 121–123
wool, 8
Common Law Procedure Act 1854, 370
Companies
agents and, 129
managing agents and, 191
Companies Act 1862, 89, 125–126, 445
Companies Act 1867, 429
Companies Act 1900, 431–432
Companies Act 1907, 435
Competition law, impact on distribution agreements, 273–275
Compradors, 140, 141–142
Comptroller of Corn Returns, 109
Confirming agents
as buyers of goods, 163–164
del credere agents distinguished, 158
evolution of, 162–163
independent contractual assumption of liability by, 164
legal force of undertakings, 163–164
letters of credit compared, 162, 163
overview, 128, 198
standard form contracts and, 163
Consignment, trend away from, 14–15
Constructive notice, 45–46
Consumer Credit Act 1974, 264–265
Continental (grain traders), 7
Continental Guaranty Corp, 28–29
Contra proferentem, 217, 218
Cooke & Sons, 75
Cooperative Wholesale Society (CWS), 241–242
Cornering markets
common law and, 113–114
cotton, 111–112
'great pepper corner', 115–117, 125–126
law, role of, 125–126
overview, 110–111
reform proposals, 112–113
self-regulation, 113–114

Corn Exchange (Mark Lane, London), 62, 365, 366
Corn Laws, 6, 109
Cornwall Minerals Railway Co, 253
Corporate bonds, 24–25
Corrie, MacColl & Co, 330–331
Cory Brothers & Co, 411–412
Cosulich Line, 216
Cotton LJ, 113, 121, 131
Cox & King (Agents) Ltd, 270
Cozens-Hardy, H. H. (Lord), 457
Craandyk, H., 313, 314, 344, 345
Craig & Co Ltd, 308
Cranworth, Lord, 132
Crawford & Bayley, 195
Criagie Lynch (solicitors), 192
Cripps, Sir Stafford, 285–286
Crossed Cheques Act 1876, 458
Crowther Committee, 264
Current accounts, 417–418
Curzon, George Nathaniel, 110–111
Custom and usage
agent's liability based on, 153–154
annexing incidents to contract, 48–49
in bank finance, 50
brokers and, 73
contractual interpretation, 48–49
criticism of, 50–51
decline of, 51–52
dock warrants and, 403–404
in hire, 50
in hire purchase, 50
interpretation of standard form contracts and, 355–357
overview, 47, 48
ports, use of, 49–50
in sale of goods, 50
standard form contracts and, 50, 51, 355–357
Czarnikow, Caesar, 124, 168, 169–170
Czarnikow & Co, 103, 128, 167, 168–171

Daimler, 417
Dalgety & Co, 165
Dallas J, 403–404, 405
Dana, Richard Henry Jr., 139–140
Darling, Lord, 329, 355
David Sassoon & Co Ltd, 141–142, 308
Davidson J, 285
Davis, Herbert (Boydie), 281–284, 285–286
Day J, 420

Deacon & Hastings, 175
Debentures and shares as security
  bearer shares, 429–430
  blank transfers, 430–431
  equitable mortgages created, 430
  evolution of, 428–433
  floating charges, 431–432, 434–436, 461
  overview, 423, 424, 425
  railway shares, 428–429
  securities, 432–433
Declaration (court order), 308–309, 345–346
Deferred hire. See Hire purchase
Del credere agents
  commodities involved with, 159
  confirming agents distinguished, 158
  corn, 158–159
  decline of, 159–160
  defined, 157–158
  guarantees of contracts by, 157–158
  overview, 128, 198
  timber, 160–161
Delivery orders, 351–353
Deloitte, Plender, Griffiths and Co (accountants), 237
Denning, Lord, 53–54, 55
Description, compliance with, 207–209, 289–290
Devlin, Lord, 52
Dick & Stevenson, 219, 221–222
Dickens, Charles, 382–383
Diplock J (Lord), 46
Discount houses, 380, 443, 445
Disraeli, Benjamin, 376
Distillers Ltd, 281, 283
Distribution of goods
  agency law and, 275–276
  by agents, 20
  'best endeavours', 265, 281–286, 287–289
  competition law, impact of, 273–275
  contracts, 265, 270–271
  controlling distributors generally, 271
  distribution networks, 40–41
  docks and, 19
  electrical equipment, 265, 270–271
  exclusivity, 277–278
  forms of distributors, 266–268
  hire (See Hire)
  hire purchase (See Hire purchase)
  informality in agreements, 265, 268–269
  infrastructure, 18–19
  by manufacturers, 19–20
  merchant agent basis, 270
  motor vehicles, 265, 271–275, 287–289
  overview, 2, 18–19, 21, 202, 264–265, 292–293
  petrol, 265, 277–281
  pricing, 270–271
  railways and, 19
  resale price maintenance and, 21, 265 (See also Resale price maintenance)
  restraint of trade and, 279
  sale of goods (See Sale of goods)
  solus agreements, 277–281
  subsidiaries, by, 20
  termination of contracts, 265, 287–289
  tying, 278
  tyres, 265, 275–276
  warehouses and, 19
  whisky, 265, 281–286
Docker, Dudley, 247
Docks, 19
Dock warrants
  advances on, 408
  bills of lading and, 400, 405–406
  custom and usage and, 403–404
  as documents of title, 401–403, 405–409
  Factors Acts and, 400, 405, 406
  fraud and, 405
  historical background, 400–403
  mercantile opinion regarding, 405–409
  overview, 378, 382, 399–400, 460
  pledged as security, 403–404
  transferability, 401
  trover, recovery in, 403
  weighing and, 404
Dock Warrants Bill 1877 (proposed), 407–408
Documentary letters of credit, 392–393. See also Letters of credit
Dodwells & Co, 138–139
Dojima Rice Exchange, 80
Donovan J (Lord), 395
Dowdeswell, G. M., 252
Drew & Napier, 173
Duff, Lyman, 286
Dun, John, 430, 433–434
Dunlop Pneumatic Tyre Co, 275–276
Dunlop Rubber Co, 202, 291, 411
Dunstan & Co, 175–176

East-Asiatic Co Ltd, 308
Eastern Counties Railway, 411
East India Co, 319, 323, 402, 411, 428

East India Grain and Oilseeds Association, 359
E. John & Co, 139
Ejusdem generis, 55-56
Elder Smith & Co, 165
Electricity (Supply) Act 1926, 226
Ellenborough, Lord, 212, 454
Ellis, C. E., 426-427
Ellison, Thomas, 96, 362
Engels, Frederick, 130
Equitable assignment, 44-45
Equitable principles, 43-47
  agency law, 47
  constructive notice, 45-46
  equitable assignment, 44-45
Erlangers (bank), 441
Erle CJ, 446
Esher, Lord, 55, 114, 121, 138, 167-168, 259
Esso Petroleum, 202, 277, 279, 280
Estoppel, agents and, 145
Euromarkets, 25, 420, 459
European Economic Community, 399
Eve J, 69
Exchange business, 24
Exclusion of implied terms of sale, 217-218
Exporters Association of Shanghai, 335
Exports Credits Guarantee Department, 161
Express warranties, 205-206

Factors Act 1823, 151
Factors Act 1825, 151
Factors Act 1842, 151-152, 172
Factors Act 1877, 152
Factors Act 1889, 152, 259, 260
Factors Acts
  agents and, 36, 143, 150-153, 198
  constructive notice and, 46
  dock warrants and, 400, 405, 406
Farwell LJ, 213
Fergus Motors Inc., 287-289
de Ferranti, Sebastian, 226
de Ferranti, Vincent, 226, 227-228
Ferranti International plc, 201-202, 219, 226-228, 265, 270-271, 290, 411
Fertilisers and Feeding Stuffs Act 1926, 347
Fiduciary duties
  of agents, 132
  of brokers, 78-80
Filières, 93-94
Finance bills. *See* Accommodation bills
Finance houses
  emergence of, 27-29
  overview, 23
  wagon companies, 27-28
Finance leases, 244
Financial advice, 25
Financial Services Act 1986, 108, 118
Finlay, Lord, 88, 136
Finlay Clerk & Co, 190
Finlay Muir & Co, 190
Fitness for purpose, 209-211, 223-226, 289-290
Floating charges as security, 431-432, 434-436, 461
Food Council, 327
Food Research Institute, 81
Force majeure clauses, 335-336
Ford Motor Co, 272
Foreign principal doctrine, 155-157
Fowler & Co, 137-138
Fox, Walker, & Co, 450-451
Foy Morgan & Co, 161
France, commodity clearing houses in, 90
Francis Hollins & Co, 137-138
Franklin, Miles, 318
Fraud
  accommodation bills and, 437, 440
  agents, committed by, 137-139
  dock warrants and, 405
  heavy manufactured goods and, 220
  innocent misrepresentation, 206
  sale of goods and, 206-207, 237-242
  speculation contrasted, 109-110
Frederic, Harold, 110
Freedom of contract, 30-31, 34-35, 322-323
Freshfield, J. W., 297-298
Fuhrmeister & Co, 308
Futures markets
  arrivals contracts and, 83-86
  commodities, 81-83
  emergence of, 80-81
  grain, 81-83
  hedging and, 87
  law, role of, 87-89
  in Liverpool, 81-82
  in London, 82-83
  metals, 82
  overview, 62, 63
  speculation and, 78-80, 84-86, 87
  spot markets contrasted, 83
  standard form contracts and, 86-87, 334-335

Futures markets (cont.)
  wagering and, 118–121
  wheat, 81–83

Galsworthy, John, 330
Gaming. *See* Wagering
Gaming Act 1845, 118, 119–121, 122, 124, 125
de Ganahl, Charles, 225
Gannow Engineering Co Ltd, 269
Garnac (grain traders), 7
Garraway's Coffee House, 7
General Motors, 25
General Petroleum Co Ltd, 135
General Produce Brokers' Association, 115–116, 330, 350, 351
George Peabody & Co, 23–24
Germany
  commodity clearing houses in, 90
  commodity markets in, 64
  novation in, 100–101
Gibbs CJ, 87–88, 403
Gilbart, James William, 400, 410, 413–414, 433, 439, 440, 456, 458
Gilletts (discount house), 411, 441, 442
Gilmore, Grant, 460
Gissing, George, 117–118
Glamorgan Coal Co Ltd, 411–412
Gloucester Wagon Co, 246–247, 248–249, 250, 252, 253
Glyn, Mills & Co, 25, 411, 435, 457
Goldman Sachs, 393–394
Goldsbrough Mort & Co, 165
Gore-Brown, Francis, 70, 92
Gorman, William, 227–228
Gossages & Co, 239–240, 241–242
Government bonds, 24–25
Grain and Feed Trade Association (Gafta), 12, 295, 317
Grain Futures Association, 82
Grant, James, 429, 452
Gray Mackenzie & Co, 196
Great Cobar Ltd, 166
Great Indian Peninsula Railway Co, 246–247
'Great pepper corner', 115–117, 125–126
Great Western Railway (GWR), 249, 252
Greene, Graham, 127
Greene, William, 285–286
Greenhalgh and Sons, 390
Grossmith, George, 256
Grossmith, Weedon, 256
Grove J, 357

Guarantees of contracts
  in clearing and settlement, 106
  by del credere agents, 157–158
Guthrie, Edwin, 113
Guthries (agency house), 140–141, 179
Gutteridge, Harold, 397

Hague Rules, 311
Haldane, Richard (Lord), 139, 193
Halhed, William, 112
Halliday Bulloch & Co, 154–155
Halliday Fox & Co, 154–155
Halsbury, Lord, 46, 55, 56
Halse Rogers J, 284, 286
Hambro's Bank Ltd, 90, 393, 395–396
Hamilton, J. A. *See* Sumner, Lord (J. A. Hamilton)
Hamzeh Malas & Sons, 395
Hannay, Maxwell, 191
Hanworth, Lord. *See* Pollock, Sir Ernest (Lord Hanworth)
Hartley, L. P., 242
Hatherley, Lord, 114, 382, 393
Hawes, Benjamin, 401–402
Hawes & Sons, 404
Hawkins J, 118
Hay, John, 179
Heavy manufactured goods. *See also specific company*
  contract conditions, 235–236
  excavators, 221–222
  express contract terms, 219, 220–222
  fraud and, 220
  goods manufactured to specification, 222–224
  inspections, 219, 231–232, 235–236
  locomotives, 228–237 (*See also* Locomotives)
  monitoring, 219, 232
  oil refineries, 224–226
  on-site assessment, 219, 232–233
  overview, 201–202, 290–291
  safeguarding clauses, 234
  shipbuilding, 223–224
  specifications, 231, 234–235
  transformers, 226–228
Hedging
  commodity markets and, 121
  futures markets and, 87
Helby, Charles, 259–260
Helps & Sons (solicitors), 249

Index

Henry R. Merton & Co Ltd, 166
Herschell, Farrer (Lord), 46, 196, 197, 204, 260, 416
Hewart, Lord, 117
Hibery J, 122
Hire
  custom and usage in, 50
  historical background, 242–243
  overview, 2, 18, 21, 202
  railway wagons and, 248–249
Hire purchase
  block discounting and, 262
  building and land societies and, 250
  criticism of, 263
  custom and usage in, 50
  furniture, 259
  historical background, 242, 243–244
  legal status of, 259–261
  motor vehicles, 291
  option to purchase, 250–251
  overview, 2, 18, 21, 202, 291–292
  pianos, 257–258, 259–260
  promissory notes and, 262
  railway wagons and, 247–251
  regulation of, 263–264
  rise of, 256–258
  sewing machines, 257
  standard form contracts and, 251
  techniques of, 261–262
Hire Purchase Act 1938, 263–264, 292
Hire Purchase Trade Association, 258
Hire Traders' Protection Association, 258, 259–260, 263, 291
H. K. Bayley & Co, 137–138
H. Neumann (importer), 336
Hodson, Lord, 280
Hollams, John, 57–58, 60, 297–298, 323–324, 384
Hollams, Son & Coward (solicitors), 89–90. *See also* Clifford Chance (solicitors)
Holmes, Oliver Wendell (US Supreme Court Justice), 96
Holmes, Valentine, 285–286
Holmes Wilson & Co, 133
Home commission agents, 17
Hong Kong, managing agents in, 179, 180–181
Hong Kong and Shanghai Bank (HSBC), 22–23, 115–116, 139, 141
Hoo Mei Pin, 141–142
Howard, John, 174

Howeson, John, 115–117
Hunter & Co, 388

Ilustre, Vicente, 175
Imperial Chemical Industries (ICI), 19, 202, 220, 377. *See also* Brunner Mond and Co Ltd
Implied terms of sale
  compliance with description, 207–209, 289–290
  exclusion of, 217–218
  fitness for purpose, 209–211, 223–226, 289–290
  merchantability, 211–213, 289–290, 346–347
  overview, 207
  sale by sample, 213–215, 289–290
Incorporated Oil Seed Association, 303, 313, 369
India
  Companies Act 1956, 195, 196
  foreign principal doctrine in, 157
  Indian Companies Act 1882, 183
  Indian Companies Act 1913, 182
  Indian Companies Act VII 1913, 194
  Indian Companies Act XIX 1857, 183
  Indian Contract Act 1872, 157, 187
  local agents in, 140, 142
  managing agents in, 178, 179, 180–181, 193–196
Indo-China Steam Navigation Co Ltd, 184–185
Industrial Discount Co, 262
Innocent misrepresentation, 206
Instalment sales. *See* Hire purchase
Institute of Bankers
  bank finance and, 414
  bills of exchange and, 384
  dock warrants and, 400
  overview, xvi
  security for advances and, 425, 426, 432, 434, 436
Institute of Export, xvi, 162, 269
Institute of London Underwriters, 334
Institution of Electrical Engineers for the United Kingdom, 226–227
Insurance funds, 106–107
Interest on loans, 420–421
International Chamber of Commerce (ICC), 398, 460
International Commodities Clearing House, 89

International commodity sales
  appropriation, 308–309, 345–346
  auctions (*See* Auctions)
  basic contract terms, 304–305
  bills of lading and, 310–311
  bought and sold notes, 296–299
  cocoa, 304
  corn, 301–302
  cotton, 300–301
  declaration, 308–309, 345–346
  early reluctance regarding contracts, 296–299
  fair average quality (faq) samples, 306–307
  globalisation of standard form contracts, 313–317
  grain, 315
  linseed, 6, 66, 68, 207, 298, 302, 302–303
  Liverpool trade associations and, 300–302
  London trade associations and, 302–304
  overview, 2, 294–295
  private law-making and, 295
  pro rata clauses, 309–310
  quality of grain, ensuring, 306–308
  rubber, 315
  standard form contracts and, 295, 312–313
  standardisation of contract terms, 304–306
  tallow, 303–304
  trade associations and, 299
International Convention for the Unification of Certain Rules of Law Relating to Bills of Lading (Hague Rules), 311
International Cotton Association, 12, 295
International Financial Society, 438
International Law Association, 313, 367
Interpretation of standard form contracts, 353–358
  alteration of contracts, 357–358
  custom and usage and, 355–357
  plain meaning, 353–355
Ipoh Tin Dredging Ltd, 181
Isaac Pitman & Sons, xvi

James and Shakespeare Ltd, 115–116
James Finlay & Co, 179, 190–192
J. & O. Ryder & Co, 147
Japan Cereals Export Association, 332–333
Jardine Matheson & Co, 128, 143–144, 165, 173–178, 179, 184–185, 266
Jardine Skinner & Co, 173–174, 179
Jellicoe, Richard, 454
Jenkins LJ, 395, 397–398

Jessel, Sir George, 407, 430
J. Henry Schröder & Co, 24, 89–90, 312, 387
J. H. Friedland (importers), 336
J. H. Rayner and Co Ltd, 395–396
John Brown & Co Ltd, 411, 427
Johnson Jeeks & Colclough (solicitors), 161
John Watson & Co, 446
Joint stock banks
  accommodation bills and, 439
  advances and, 27
  emergence of, 25–26
  overview, 23
Joint Stock Companies Act 1856, 66, 185, 430
Joseph Crosfield & Sons, 238–242
Jowitt, William, 285–286
J. P. Morgan & Co, 23–24
J. R. Crompton and Brothers Ltd, 268–269
Judicature Act 1873, 43, 384, 385
Judicature Acts, 252

Kahl, H., 367
Kaltenbach and Fisher & Co, 171–172
Karri and Jarrah Co Ltd, 160
Kay J, 253
Kern, William, 68
Keynes, John Maynard, 63–64, 80, 81, 92, 121
Kleinwort Sons & Co, 24, 90, 387, 393–394
Kuwait, managing agents in, 196
Kyslant, Lord, 116

Lanchester Motor Co, 417
Larceny Act 1861, 36, 116, 447
Lavie, Germain, 132
Lawrence, A. T., 326
Law Revision Committee, 397
LCH Group, 9
Leeman's Act, 112, 113
Legal context of commercial law
  accommodation of commercial practices (*See* Accommodation of commercial practices)
  certainty of law (*See* Certainty of law)
  custom and usage (*See* Custom and usage)
  overview, 2, 3, 30–34, 59–60
  private law-making (*See* Private law-making)
Legislative framework, 35–37
Leiter, Joseph, 110–111
Letters of credit
  banks, role of, 393–394
  confirming agents compared, 162, 163

dissociation from underlying contracts, 395
documentary letters of credit, 392–393
emergence of, 391
evolution of law, 397–398
open letters of credit, 391–392
overview, 378, 381, 391, 459–460
rejection of, 395–396
strict compliance, 395–396
Uniform Customs and Practices for Documentary Credits (UCP), 398–399
Lever, William H. (Lord Leverhulme), 34, 238, 240, 241–242
Lever Brothers Ltd, 220, 237–242, 291
Lewis, Robert, 171
Lewis & Peat, 128, 171–173
Lewis Lazarus & Sons, 270
Limited Liability Act 1855, 185, 246
Lindley, Lord, 45–46, 120, 193
Liverpool Corn Exchange, 10, 11
Liverpool Corn Trade Association (LvCTA)
  arbitration and, 362–363
  clearing and settlement and, 91–92
  commodity markets and, 65–66, 70
  compensation upon default and, 105
  emergence of, 11
  futures markets and, 81
  prevention of settlement risk and, 104
  pro rata clauses and, 309
  standard form contracts and, 86, 301–302
Liverpool Cotton Association Ltd
  bi-lateral settlement and, 96
  Bylaws & Rules, 12
  emergence of, 10
  expulsion of members, 69
  international commodity sales and, 295, 300–301
  periodic settlement and, 103–104
  standard form contracts and, 300–301
Liverpool Cotton Brokers' Association
  arbitration and, 362–363
  arrival contracts and, 84, 86
  clearing and settlement and, 105
  emergence of, 10–11
  expulsion of members, 67, 68
  members, 71–72
  standard form contracts and, 313, 345–346
Liverpool Cotton Exchange
  brokers and, 72
  cornering markets and, 111
  emergence of, 10
  futures markets and, 80, 81–82

joint stock banks and, 27
speculation and, 122
undisclosed principal doctrine and, 146
Liverpool Grain Contract Insurance Co Ltd, 106–107
Liverpool Union Bank, 27
Liverpool United General Produce Association, 355
Liversay & Co, 75
Llewellyn, Karl, 200, 201
Lloyds Bank, 26, 419, 436
Lloyd Scott & Co Ltd, 189
Lloyd's of London, 29, 302, 334, 338–339, 342, 379
Loans
  acceleration clauses, 421–422
  current accounts versus, 417–418
  failure of banks to provide, 420
  interest on, 420–421
  loan accounts, 417–418
  loan agreements, 418
  overdrafts distinguished, 413–414, 417
  overview, 378–379, 460–461
  short-term lending, 418–419
  standard form contracts, 420
  statistics, 412
  term loans, 419–420
Local agents, 140–142
Locomotive Manufacturers' Association (LMA), 229, 234
Locomotives, 228–237
  contract conditions, 235–236
  engine manufacturers, 229–231
  inspections, 231–232, 235–236
  monitoring, 232
  on-site visits, 232–233
  overview, 228–229
  safeguarding clauses, 234
  specifications, 231, 234–235
  Tasmanian tender, 233–237
Lombard Bank, 28
Lombard North Central, 28
London & South Western Bank, 457
London and St Katharine Docks Act 1864, 407
London and Westminster Bank, 22, 29, 410, 411, 431, 433, 439, 451, 456, 457
London Cattle Food Trade Association (LCFTA), 9–10, 347, 357–358
London Chatham and Dover Railway, 438
London City and Midland Bank, 22–23, 427
London Clearing House, 89

London Copra Association
  arbitration and, 330–331
  emergence of, 9–10
  interpretation of standard form contracts, 356, 357
  standard form contracts and, 313, 316, 343–344
London Corn Trade Association (LCTA)
  American and Australian Grain Committee, 306–307
  arbitration and, 365–369, 370–371 (*See also* Arbitration)
  bills of lading and, 310–311
  Black Sea Grain Committee, 305–306
  China, grain from, 308
  China and Manchurian Feeding Stuffs Committee, 308
  clearing and settlement and, 91, 92–93, 125
  closing out rules and, 102
  Contracts Committee, 309, 317, 332, 333, 334, 335, 343, 349, 359
  default and, 349–350
  Default Clause Sub-Committee, 350
  delivery orders and, 352–353
  emergence of, 9
  exclusion of merchantability, 346–347
  Executive Committee, 305
  fair average quality (faq) samples, 306–307
  foreign members of, 316–317
  futures markets and, 82–83
  international character of, 315–317
  international commodity sales and, 312–313
  interpretation of standard form contracts, 353–355, 356–357, 358
  judicial decisions, amendment of standard form contracts in response to, 359–360
  lawyers, role of, 341–344
  legacy of, 12
  merchantability and, 213
  North American Contracts Committee, 309, 311, 342–343
  pro rata clauses and, 309
  rejection as remedy and, 348–349
  sale by sample and, 214–215
  Shipping Documents Delivery Orders Sub-Committee, 353
  solicitors, 371–373
  standard form contracts and (*See* Standard form contracts)
  Sub Committee re Revision of Contracts, 343
  Sub Committee re Sampling Rules, 307
  United States, grain from, 307
London Dock Co, 401–403, 404
London Financial Association, 438
London General Produce Brokers' Association, 8
London Metal Exchange
  agents and, 166
  cornering markets and, 111, 114
  emergence of, 11
  futures markets and, 82
  ring settlement and, 97–98
  speculation and, 122
London Oil and Tallow Trades Association, 9–10, 299, 303–304, 312, 333, 338
London Pepper Sales Control Committee, 116
London Produce Broker's Association, 313
London Produce Clearing House (LPCH)
  auctions and, 320–321
  bilateral settlement and, 96–97
  brokers and, 74, 76
  clearing and settlement and, 38
  closing out rules and, 102–103
  commodities cleared, 90–91
  compensation upon default and, 104
  Continental influence on, 90
  cornering markets and, 113, 117
  emergence of, 9, 89–90
  futures markets and, 82
  guarantees of contracts and, 106
  novation and, 99–100, 101
  organisation of, 65
  rules of, 91
London Rice Brokers' Association, 303, 354, 363–364
London Rubber Trade Association, 9–10, 313, 315, 320, 352, 355–356
London School of Economics, 52
London Stock Exchange, 29, 70, 103, 319–320, 376, 432
London Tin Corp, 115
Loreburn, Lord, 56
Loss, liability for, 32
Louis Dreyfus & Co Ltd, 7, 310, 332, 336
Low, Lord, 191, 192
Lynch, C. B., 192

Macaulay, R. H., 192–193
MacEwen & Co, 185
Mackinnon Frew & Co, 14
Mackinnon LJ (Frank), 51, 385

Mackinnon Mackenzie & Co, 14, 179, 184
Macmillan Inquiry, 376–377
Macnaghten, Edward (Lord), 145, 214, 255, 260
Malaysia, managing agents in, 196
Managing agents
  abuses by, 178, 193–196
  agency law and, 187
  as agents, 187–189
  commissions, 188, 189–190
  company law and, 191
  conflicts of interest, 188, 189–190
  constitutions, control under, 182–183
  contracts, control under, 183–186
  control of companies by, 181–186
  defined, 182
  fees, 188
  functions of, 179–181
  legal structure of, 181–186
  multiple companies, 181
  overview, 17–18, 128–129, 178–181, 198–199
  regulation of, 193–196
  shareholders versus, 189–193
  shipping services, 184–185
  single companies, 181
  termination of, 189
Manganese Bronze, 223–224, 291
Mansfield, Lord, 41–42, 54, 327–328, 391
Margarine Unie, 220
Marine Insurance Act 1906, 203
Market control. *See* Distribution of goods
Market integrity
  cornering markets (*See* Cornering markets)
  overview, 63
  speculation and, 107–108
  wagering (*See* Wagering)
Marx, Karl, 444
Matheson & Co, 173–174
Maugham, W. Somerset, 165
Maule B, 119
Mavrogordato, E. A., 366
Maximos, N. C., 75
McCardie J, 54, 122, 348
McNair J, 164
Medway Oil and Storage Co, 224–226
Mellish LJ, 157–158
Mellor J, 212
Mend, S. F., 367
Mercantile Law Commission, 297
Merchandise Marks Act 1862, 36, 292

Merchandise Marks Act 1887, 36, 292
Merchantability, 211–213, 289–290, 346–347
Merchant banks
  acceptance business, 24
  bills of exchange and, 24
  corporate bonds and, 24–25
  emergence of, 23–24
  exchange business, 24
  financial advice and, 25
  government bonds and, 24–25
  overview, 23
  securities and, 24–25
Merchant Shipping Act 1894, 408
Mersey Steel and Iron Co, 206–207
Metallgesellschaft AG, 166
Metropolitan, Carriage, Wagon and Finance Co, 247
Meyer, Charles, 171–172
Michelin, 136
Midland Bank, 22, 26, 115–116, 395, 419, 436
Midland Railway Co, 249
Mid-Wales Railway Co, 446
Mill Owners' Association, 195
Millwall Ironworks and Shipbuilding Co, 447
Mincing Lane, 7–8. *See also specific establishment*
Minneapolis Chamber of Commerce, 101
Misrepresentation. *See* Fraud
Misrepresentation Act 1967, 206
Moberly & Bell, 404
Mocatta J, 279
Mollett & Co, 78–80
Moneylenders Acts, 256–257
Money market, 23, 380, 443, 450–452
Monkswell, Lord, 141–142
Monopolies and Restrictive Practices (Inquiry and Control) Act 1948, 273
Monopolies and Restrictive Practices Commission, 327
Monopolies Commission, 273, 276, 280–281, 293
Morgan Crucible Co Ltd, 435
Morgan Grenfell, 25
Morris, John, 30, 32–33, 448–449
Morris Motors, 28–29, 411
Mortgages as security, 433–434
Motor Agents Association, 279
Motor Trade Association, 271–272, 276, 277, 292
Moulton, Lord, 206
Muir, John, 190–192

Multifunctional agents, 165, 173–178
Murphy, Thomas F. (US Judge), 288–289
Murray, Lindley, 355

National Association of British and Irish
    Millers, 336
National Bank, 391
National Provincial Bank, 22, 26, 411–412, 413,
    424–425, 428–429, 435–436
National Westminster Bank, 26, 28, 411
Negotiable instruments. See Bills of exchange
Nemo dat, 150
Nettlefold & Chamberlain, 266
Newton, Lucy, 22
New York Cotton Exchange, 64, 101
New York Produce Exchange, 117, 307, 340
New Zealand, foreign principal doctrine
    in, 157
Nicholls & Co, 187
Nicolopulo & Co, 214
Nigerian Railways, 233
N. M. Rothschild & Sons, 22, 23, 24–25, 90, 387
Nobel Explosives, 220
Normative force of law. See Accommodation of
    commercial practices; Custom and usage
North American Export Grain Association,
    311, 316, 333, 334, 340–341, 373
North British Locomotive Co Ltd, 229, 233
North Central Wagon and Finance Co Ltd, 28,
    247, 254–256
Northcliffe, Lord, 238
Novation, 95, 98–101
Noyes Brothers, 270

Ocean Spinning Co, 390
Oliverson, Lavie and Peachey (solicitors), 132
Open account trading, 385, 399
Oriental Financial Corp, 438
Orr Dignam & Co, 183–184
Ostensible authority, 144–145, 197
Overdrafts
    cancellation of, 416–417
    demand for immediate repayment, 417
    emergence of, 415
    loans distinguished, 413–414, 417
    overview, 378–379, 460–461
    repayable on demand, 415–416
    statistics, 412
Overend Gurney & Co, 438, 439, 444,
    445–449
Owen, F. A., 192

Page J, 133
Paget, John, 46
Pahang Consolidated Co Ltd, 186
Paley, William, 130
Palmer & Co, 418
Parke, Baron, 49, 119, 209, 329, 406
Parker Rhodes & Co, 422, 426–427
Park J, 403–404, 405
Parr's Bank, 429, 458
Parry & Co, 179
Party substitution, novation by, 98–101
Patterson, R., 409
Payment clauses, 339–341, 342–343
Payne & Routh, 336
Peacock CJ, 142
Pearce, Lord, 164, 280
Peat, William, 171
Peek, William, 449
Penzance, Lord, 56
Pepys, Samuel, 317
Pereira J, 139
Personal guarantees
    at common law, 426
    guarantors, drawbacks for, 426–427
    legal drawbacks of, 425–426
    limited liability, effect on, 427–428
    overview, 423, 424, 425
Petrofina, 279, 280
Phillimore, Lord, 134, 135, 276, 360–361
Plantation House, 8
Platt Bros & Co Ltd, 266
Plymouth, Devonport and District Tramway
    Ltd, 449
Plymouth Iron Co, 440
Pollock, Sir Ernest (Lord Hanworth), 122,
    123, 262
Pollock, Sir Frederick, 45, 98, 148, 197, 402, 404
Pollock CB, 207, 217, 406, 415
Port of London Authority, 407, 408
Pothier, Robert Joseph, 204
Powell Duffryn Steam Coal Co Ltd, 250, 411
Praschauer & Co, 336
Preece Cardew & Rider, 236–237
Price fixing. See Resale price maintenance
Price's Patent Candle Co Ltd, 239
Priestley, J. B., 3–4
Principals. See Agency law; Agents
Private law-making
    bank finance and, 38
    characteristics of, 38–40
    commodity markets and, 38, 125–126

delivery orders, 351–353
dispute settlement generally, 361
distribution networks, 40–41
international commodity sales and, 295
markets and institutions, 37–40
overview, xvii–xviii
standard form contracts (*See* Standard form contracts)
Promissory notes, 262
Property as security, 423, 424, 425, 433–434
Pro rata clauses, 309–310
Public sales. *See* Auctions
'Puffery', 327–328
Pulling, Alexander, 74–75

Quiller-Couch, Thomas, 132–133

Radcliffe Committee, 376–377, 410, 419
Rae, George, 410, 422, 425, 428–429, 433
Raikes & Co, 404
Railway Clauses Consolidation Act 1845, 245
Railway Clearing Act 1850, 456
Railway Clearing House, 245, 380
Railways
  accommodation bills and, 437–439
  distribution of goods and, 19
  railway shares as security, 428–429
Railways Clauses Consolidation Act 1845, 255
Railway wagons
  default and, 251–253
  hire and, 248–249
  hire purchase and, 247–251
  historical background, 245–246
  manufacturers, 246–247
  sale and leaseback and, 253–256
  sale of, 247
  wrongful disposal of, 253
Ralli Brothers, 140, 170
Ranger, Maurice, 111–112
Rathbones (bank), 387
Reasonable compliance with principal's instructions, 128, 143, 148–150, 197–198
Reece, W. H., 246
Refined Sugar Association, 10, 371
Regent (oil company), 277
Regent's Canal, 411
Registrar of Restrictive Trading Agreements, 273–274, 275
Reid, Lord, 280
Resale price maintenance
  motor vehicles, 265, 271–275
  overview, 21, 265, 292
  petrol, 265, 277–281
  tyres, 265, 275–276
Resale Prices Act 1964, 274
Resch's Ltd, 282
Restrictive Practices Act 1956, 273–274, 275, 276
Restrictive Practices Court, 273–274, 275
Rew & Freeman, 137
Rigby, John, 193, 255, 457
'Ring' agreements, 328–329
Ring settlement, 97–98
Robarts, Lubbock & Co, 408
Robert Stephenson and Hawthorns Ltd, 202, 229, 230, 231–232, 233, 237
Robson, Herbert, 348–349, 367
Roche, Lord, 208, 223–224, 262, 284, 286, 349, 359
Roffey, Walter, 366
Rogers, Olding and Co, 454
Romer, LJ, 53, 216, 217, 434
Roosevelt, Theodore, 307
Rose and Frank Co, 268–269
Roskill, E. W. (Lord), 342
Rothschild, Lord, 406
Rowlatt J, 225, 239, 355
Rowntree (confectionery), 441
Royal Bank of Scotland, 411, 435
Royal Commission on the Judicature, 363
Royal Exchange, 6, 24, 118, 119
Royal Mail Steam Packet Co, 116
Rubber Exchange, 319–320
Rucker & Bencraft, 89–90
Russell, Lord, 279, 286
Russia, noncompliance with arbitration awards, 369
Russian Petroleum and Liquid Fuel Co Ltd, 432

Safeguarding clauses, 234
St Katharine Dock Co, 152, 400–401, 404, 408, 411
Sala, George, 399
Sale and leaseback, 244, 253–256, 291
Sale by sample, 213–215
Sale of Food (Weights and Measures) Act 1926, 36
Sale of goods
  acceptance, 215
  by agents, 21
  alkali, 237–242

Sale of goods (cont.)
  breach of quality standards, 215–216
  caveat emptor and, 209, 210, 212
  commercial necessity and, 200–201
  compliance with description, 207–209, 289–290
  contra proferentem and, 217, 218
  custom and usage in, 50
  exclusion of implied terms, 217–218
  express warranties, 205–206
  finance leases, 244
  fitness for purpose, 209–211, 223–226, 289–290
  fraud and, 206–207, 237–242
  heavy manufactured goods (*See* Heavy manufactured goods)
  hire (*See* Hire)
  hire purchase (*See* Hire purchase)
  historical background, 200–201, 203–205
  implied terms generally, 207
  Industrial Revolution and, 220–221
  innocent misrepresentation and, 206
  legislative framework, 36–37
  merchantability, 211–213, 289–290, 346–347
  overview, 2, 18, 289
  rejection for breach of quality standards, 215–216
  rescission, 206
  sale and leaseback, 244, 253–256, 291
  sale by sample, 213–215, 289–290
  'work and materials' distinguished, 216–217
Sale of Goods Act 1893,
  agency law and, 134
  auctions and, 324, 328
  certainty of law and, 41
  commercial necessity and, 201
  compliance with description, 208
  distribution of goods and, 264, 271
  drafting of, 203–205
  exclusion of implied terms, 217
  exclusion of merchantability, 346–347
  express contract terms and, 222
  Factors Acts and, 152
  fitness for purpose, 210–211, 225
  freedom of contract and, 346
  heavy manufactured goods, 219
  hire purchase and, 263–264
  implied terms, 207
  merchantability, 211, 212
  overview, 33, 35, 290

rejection for breach of quality standards, 215–216, 347–348, 374–375
sale by sample, 214–215
'work and materials' distinguished, 216
Salisbury, Lord, 175
Salmon, Lord, 149
Salmond J, 157
Salomon, Aron, 423
Sample, sale by, 213–215, 289–290
Samuel Courtauld & Co, 20
Samuel McGregor & Co Ltd, 308
Samuel Montagu & Co, 24
Sanderson & Co, 440, 445, 450–451
San Francisco Produce Exchange, 307
Sayers, Dorothy L., 127
Scarlett, James. *See* Abinger, Lord
Schwarz Gaumer & Co, 308
Scott & Co, 214
Scott LJ (Leslie), 283–284, 285–286, 342
Scrutton LJ, 31, 32, 57, 123, 135, 151, 157, 225, 289, 329, 348, 351, 356, 360, 371, 396
Seccombe, Marshall and Campion, 451
Second Bank of the United States, 23
Secretain, Pierre, 111
Securities
  merchant banks and, 24–25
  as security, 432–433
Security for advances
  debentures and shares as (*See* Debentures and shares as security)
  dock warrants as, 408
  floating charges as, 431–432, 434–436, 461
  importance of, 422
  mortgages as, 433–434
  overview, 379, 461
  personal guarantees (*See* Personal guarantees)
  property as, 423, 424, 425, 433–434
  standard form contracts and, 424
  unsecured lending, 422–424
Seddon, Thomas, 137
Selborne, Lord, 98
Selfridges (department store), 202, 275–276, 291
Sellers J, 347
Settlement. *See* Clearing and settlement
Settlement Association, 103–104
Seyd, Ernest, 455
Shareholders, managing agents versus, 189–193

Shares as security. *See* Debentures and shares as security
Shaw J, 139
Shaw Wallace & Co, 179
Sheard Stubbs & Co, 100
Shearman J, 329
Shell Oil, 277, 281
Shipton, Anderson & Co, 104, 107
Shroff, Dorabji Cursetji, 192–193
Silica Gel Corp, 224–226
Simon, John (Lord Simon LC), 239, 240
Simonds, Gavin (Lord Simonds LC), 256, 285–286, 292
Singapore
  agents in, 172–173
  local agents in, 140–141
    managing agents in, 179, 196
    rubber exports from, 320
Singapore Chamber of Commerce Rubber Association, 173
Singer Sewing Machine Co, 257, 267
Skelton & Co, 227
Skoda Works, 270–271
Slater, Isaac, 248
Smith, Adam, 107, 108
Smith, Charles W., 76, 108
Smith, J. G., 123–124
Smith, Montague, 174
Smith J, 420
Snowden & Hopkins, 205
Society of Motor Manufacturers and Traders, 271–272
Society of Sugar Refiners of London, 65
Solvay & Cie, 238
Somervell, LJ (Lord Somervell), 53
Sonnett, John F., 288
Sources for study, xvi–xvii, 3
Specification, goods manufactured to, 222–224
Speculation
  cotton, 84–86, 108
  fraud contrasted, 109–110
  futures markets and, 78–80, 84–86, 87
  market integrity and, 107–108
  tallow, 78–80, 84, 108, 119
Speltz, Louis, 389–390
Spillers Ltd, 100, 310, 336
Spot markets, 83
Sri Lanka, managing agents in, 196
Standard form contracts
  accommodation of commercial practices, 53, 56

  agents and, 143–144
  alteration of, 357–358
  arbitration and, 330–331 (*See also* Arbitration)
  balancing of interests, 336–337
  certainty of law and, 335–336, 374
  changed circumstances, impact of, 332–335
  circle clauses, 343–344
  commodity markets and, 126
  common law, modifying, 345–346, 374–375
  competing interests and, 331–332
  complexity in drafting, 331–332
  confirming agents and, 163
  conflicting interests, 337
  custom and usage and, 50, 51, 355–357
  default and, 349–350
  drafting of, 375
  emergence of, 302, 373–374
  empire, impact on globalisation of, 315
  English law governing, 344, 374
  exclusion of merchantability, 346–347
  force majeure clauses, 335–336
  futures markets and, 86–87, 334–335
  globalisation of, 313–317
  hire purchase and, 251
  importers versus exporters, 337–338
  international commodity sales and, 295, 312–313
  interpretation of, 353–358
  judicial decisions, amendment in response to, 358–361
  labour movement, impact of, 333
  lawyers, role of, 341–344
  Liverpool trade associations and, 300–302
  Lloyds conditions, 338–339
  loans, 420
  London trade associations and, 302–304
  merchantability and, 213
  payment clauses, 339–341, 342–343
  plain meaning of, 353–355
  rejection for breach of quality standards and, 347–349, 374–375
  representing trade as whole, 336–337
  security for advances and, 424
  simplicity in drafting, 330–331
  statutes, incorporating, 346
  strike clauses, 341, 342
  technological innovation, impact of, 333
  trade associations and, 9–10, 11, 374
  underlying principles, 335–337
  uniformity in, 337

Standard form contracts (cont.)
  variety in, 305–306
  war, impact of, 314–315, 334
Standard Motor Co Ltd, 202, 287, 293
Standard Oil Co, 277. *See also* Esso Petroleum
Standard-Triumph International, 202, 287–289
Stanford University, 81
Statute of Frauds 1677, 298, 323
Steam engines, 220–221
Steel Co of Australia, 233
Stephen J, 285
Stock and station agents, 165
Stockton and Darlington Railway Co, 231–232
Stokes & Co, 147
Story, Joseph (US Supreme Court Justice), 72, 79, 130–131, 149
Strick Scott & Co Ltd, 189
Strike clauses, 341, 342
Sugar Association of London, 10, 93, 103
Summary Procedure on Bills of Exchange Act 1855, 384
Sumner, Lord (J. A. Hamilton), 31, 45, 88–89, 226, 289, 394, 395
Surrey Commercial Docks, 145, 321
Swedish Match Co, 186
Swinfen Eady, J (Lord), 46
S. Wolberg (exporter), 336
Sylhet and Cachar Tea Co Ltd, 392–393

Talbot J, 284
Tasmanian Railways, 233
Tea Brokers' Association of London, 8
Tea Buying Brokers' Association, 8
Tea Clearing House, 69, 93
Tenterden, Lord. *See* Abbott CJ (Lord Tenterden)
Term loans, 419–420
Thom, Adam, 447
Thomas Ashby & Co, 458
Thomas Cooper & Co, 369
Thomas Duff & Co, 179, 411
Thomas Merry & Son, 406
Thomson, Bonnar and Co, 132, 298
Thorne, S. K., 366–367
Thwaites Brothers Ltd, 427
Tindal CJ, 209–210, 454
Tomlinson, H., 381
Tondeur & Co, 392–393
Tooke, Thomas, 108, 402
Tooth & Co Ltd, 282–286

Tozer Kemsley & Milbourne, 270
Trade associations. *See also specific association*
  arbitration and, 362–365 (*See also* Arbitration)
  corn, 9
  cotton, 10–11
  effect of, 11–12
  emergence of, 4
  grain, 9, 11
  historical background, 9–12
  international commodity sales and, 299
  legacy of, 12
  in Liverpool, 10–11
  in London, 9–10, 11
  metals, 11
  private law-making by (*See* Private law-making)
  rubber, 9–10
  standard form contracts and, 9–10, 11, 374 (*See also* Standard form contracts)
  sugar, 10
Trade bills, 386, 388–390
Trade finance
  Bill on London, 24, 381, 386, 390, 443
  bills of exchange (*See* Bills of exchange)
  bills of lading and, 381–382, 389–390, 395–396
  dock warrants (*See* Dock warrants)
  letters of credit (*See* Letters of credit)
  overview, 377–378, 381–382
Trade usage. *See* Custom and usage
Trading nation, Britain as, 4, 5
Treasury Bills Act 1877, 450
Trollope, Anthony, 107
Tudor, H. E., 259
Tulketh Mill, 390
Turner LJ, 439
Tyre Manufacturers' Conference, 276

Undisclosed principal doctrine
  commercial convenience and, 146–147, 197
  criticism of, 148
  double payment, risk of, 147–148
  emergence of, 146
  overview, 128, 143
Unfair Contract Terms Act 1977, 264–265
Uniform Customs and Practices for Documentary Credits (UCP), 398–399, 460
Unilever, 19, 202, 220
Union Bank of London, 434

Union Insurance Co, 176
United Alkali Co, 220
United Dominions Trust (UDT), 28–29, 55, 244
United Molasses Co Ltd, 223
United States
  Bureau of Foreign & Domestic Commerce, 273
  Commodity Exchange Act of 1936, 64
  commodity markets in, 64, 70–71
  cornering markets in, 110–111, 117
  Department of Agriculture, 307
  Grain Futures Act of 1922, 64
  grain quality, ensuring, 307
  Grain Standards Act, 307
  Harter Act, 346
  letters of credit in, 398
  novation in, 98–99, 101
  speculation in, 121–122
United States Steel Products Co, 133
Unsecured lending, 422–424
Upjohn J (Lord Upjohn), 275
Usage. *See* Custom and usage
Usual authority, 144–145

Vauxhall Motors, 25
Verne, Jules, 219, 246–247
Victoria Docks, 49–50
Virginia and Baltick, 6
Virginia and Maryland, 6
Volkart Brothers, 140
Volkswagen, 272
Vulcan Foundry Ltd, 230, 233, 234, 237

Wagering
  commodity markets and, 121–123
  futures markets and, 118–121
  overview, 118
Wagon Owners' Association, 246, 255
'Walks clearing', 458–459
Wallace, George, 182–183
Wallace, Lewis, 182–183
Wallace, William, 182–183
Wallace & Co, 182–183, 192–193, 195–196. *See also* Wallace Brothers
Wallace Brothers, 160–161. *See also* Wallace & Co
Walton, Joseph, 429
Wang Gan-Ying, 141–142
Warehouses, 19
Warner, Burnett and Dowling, 249
Warrington LJ, 122
Watson, Lord, 146, 260
Watson, Thomas, 283–284, 285
Watson's Wharf, 402, 404
Watt, James, 220–221, 242
Weber, Max, xvii
Weguelin, T. M., 132, 298
Westbury, Lord, 430
Weyman, S., 413
W. H. Pim, Junr & Co, 310
Wilberforce, Lord, 123
Wilde, Serjeant, 327–328
Wilde Sapte (solicitors), 411–412
Willes J, 49, 78, 138, 205, 417, 454
William Brandt and Sons, 89–90
William Henry & Co, 115, 116
Willliams, R. H., 138–139
Winnipeg Grain and Produce Exchange, 64
Winn LJ, 55
Winson & Co, 390
Wm Mackinnon & Co, 14
Wong Yat Sun, 174–175
Wood, William Page, 114
Wool Exchange, 8, 319, 322
'Work and materials', sale of goods distinguished, 216–217
Working capital. *See* Advances
Wormald, John, 18
W. R. Arbuthnot & Co, 68
Wright, Johnstone, 227–228
Wright, Lord, 55, 213, 216, 289, 310, 347, 357, 359–360, 400
W. R. Paterson & Co, 142